Arbitration in Malaysia

Arbitration in Malaysia

A Commentary on the Malaysian Arbitration Act

Thayananthan Baskaran

Published by:
Kluwer Law International B.V.
PO Box 316
2400 AH Alphen aan den Rijn
The Netherlands
E-mail: international-sales@wolterskluwer.com
Website: lrus.wolterskluwer.com

Sold and distributed in North, Central and South America by:
Wolters Kluwer Legal & Regulatory U.S.
7201 McKinney Circle
Frederick, MD 21704
United States of America
Email: customer.service@wolterskluwer.com

Sold and distributed in all other countries by:
Air Business Subscriptions
Rockwood House
Haywards Heath
West Sussex
RH16 3DH
United Kingdom
Email: international-customerservice@wolterskluwer.com

Printed on acid-free paper.

ISBN 978-90-411-8665-2

e-Book: ISBN 978-90-411-8673-7
web-PDF: ISBN 978-90-411-8674-4

© 2019 Thayananthan Baskaran

All rights reserved. No part of this publication may be reproduced, stored in a retrieval system, or transmitted in any form or by any means, electronic, mechanical, photocopying, recording, or otherwise, without written permission from the publisher.

Permission to use this content must be obtained from the copyright owner. More information can be found at: lrus.wolterskluwer.com/policies/permissions-reprints-and-licensing

Printed in the United Kingdom.

To my father, M R Baskaran

Table of Contents

Foreword		xix
Preface		xxi
Preliminary		1
1.	Short Title and Commencement	1
§1.01	Commentary	1
2.	Interpretation	3
§2.01	Introduction	4
§2.02	Award	4
§2.03	High Court	4
§2.04	Minister	6
§2.05	State	6
§2.06	Presiding Arbitrator	6
§2.07	Arbitration Agreement	6
§2.08	Party	7
§2.09	Seat of Arbitration	7
§2.10	International Arbitration and Domestic Arbitration	7
§2.11	Arbitral Tribunal	10
§2.12	Arbitration	11
§2.13	Third Party	12
§2.14	Arbitration Rules	13
§2.15	Claim and Counterclaim	13
3.	Application to Arbitrations and Awards in Malaysia	14
§3.01	Introduction	14
§3.02	Domestic and International Arbitration	14
§3.03	Commercial	15
§3.04	Seat of Arbitration in Malaysia	15
§3.05	Opt-In or Opt-Out	17
3A.	Representation	19

Table of Contents

§3A.01	Introduction	19
§3A.02	Purpose	19
4.	Arbitrability of Subject Matter	21
§4.01	Introduction	21
§4.02	Contrary to Public Policy	22
§4.03	Not Capable of Settlement by Arbitration	22
5.	Government to Be Bound	23
§5.01	Commentary	23

CHAPTER 1
General Provisions 25

6.	Receipt of Written Communications	25
§6.01	Introduction	25
§6.02	Autonomy	26
§6.03	Broad Interpretation of Written Communication	26
§6.04	Court Proceedings	27
7.	Waiver of Right to Object	28
§7.01	Introduction	28
§7.02	Requirements	28
	[A] Derogable Provision	28
	[B] Knowledge of Non-compliance	30
	[C] Failure to State Objection	30
	[D] Proceeding with the Arbitration	31
§7.03	Effect of Waiver	31
8.	Extent of Court Intervention	32
§8.01	Introduction	32
§8.02	Intervention	32
§8.03	Express and Implied Provision	33
	[A] Section 10	35
	[B] Section 11	35
	[C] Section 12	38
	[D] Section 14	38
	[E] Section 18	38
	[F] Section 37	38
	[G] Section 39	42
	[H] Section 42	43
	[I] Section 44	44

CHAPTER 2
Arbitration Agreement 45

9.	Definition and Form of Arbitration Agreement	45
§9.01	Introduction	46
§9.02	The Substance of an Arbitration Agreement	46
	[A] Existing and Future Disputes	47
	[B] Defined Legal Relationship	47

	[C]	Capable of Settlement by Arbitration	50
§9.03		The Form of an Arbitration Agreement	50
	[A]	Recorded in Any Form	51
	[B]	Exchange of Pleadings	52
	[C]	Reference in an Agreement	52
10.		Arbitration Agreement and Substantive Claim Before Court	57
§10.01		Introduction	57
§10.02		General Scheme	59
§10.03		Specific Provisions	60
	[A]	'A Court ...'	60
	[B]	'... Before Which Proceedings Are Brought ...'	61
	[C]	'... In Respect of a Matter Which is the Subject of an Arbitration Agreement ...'	62
		[1] Arbitration and Exclusive Jurisdiction Clauses	63
		[2] Linking Words in an Arbitration Clause	65
		[3] Jurisdictional Issues	65
	[D]	'... Shall ...'	66
	[E]	'... Where a Party Makes an Application Before Taking Any Other Steps in the Proceedings ...'	67
		[1] Appearance	68
		[2] Qualified Position	69
		[3] Resisting Injunction	71
		[4] Discovery	71
		[5] Resisting Winding-Up	72
		[6] Defence	73
		[7] Before	73
	[F]	'... Stay Those Proceedings and Refer the Parties to Arbitration ...'	73
	[G]	'... Unless It Finds That the Agreement Is Null and Void, Inoperative or Incapable of Being Performed.'	76
		[1] Lean Towards Arbitration	76
		[2] Section 29 of the Contracts Act 1950	77
		[3] Fraud and Mistake	78
		[4] Multiplicity	78
		[5] Incomplete Agreement	79
		[6] Absence of Disputes	79
	[H]	'... That There Is In Fact No Dispute Between the Parties with Regard to the Matters to Be Referred.'	80
	[I]	'The Court, in Granting a Stay of Proceedings Pursuant to Subsection (1), May Impose Any Conditions as It Deems Fit.'	83
	[J]	'This Section Shall Also Apply in Respect of an International Arbitration, Where the Seat of Arbitration Is Not in Malaysia.'	83
§10.04		Effect of a Stay	84
11.		Arbitration Agreement and Interim Measures by High Court	86
§11.01		Introduction	86

ix

Table of Contents

§11.02	General Principles		88
	[A]	Cause of Action	89
	[B]	Arbitration Agreement	89
	[C]	Interim in Nature	89
	[D]	Aid the Arbitration	90
	[E]	Arbitral Proceedings to Be Commenced Within Reasonable Time	93
§11.03	Merits		93
§11.04	Before or During Arbitral Proceedings		94
§11.05	Specific Principles		94
	[A]	Maintain the Status Quo	94
	[B]	Prevent Harm to the Arbitral Process	96
	[C]	Preserve Assets	96
	[D]	Preserve Evidence	97
	[E]	Security for Costs	98
§11.06	Application to International Arbitration with a Seat Outside Malaysia		98

CHAPTER 3

Composition of Arbitrators		101
12.	Number of Arbitrators	101
§12.01	Introduction	101
§12.02	Two-Level System	102
§12.03	Party Autonomy	102
§12.04	Three Arbitrators or a Single Arbitrator	103
13.	Appointment of Arbitrators	104
§13.01	Introduction	105
§13.02	No Restriction on Nationality	106
§13.03	Party Autonomy	106
§13.04	Default Procedure	107
§13.05	Assistance with Agreed Procedure	108
§13.06	Director's Failure to Act	109
§13.07	Guidelines for Appointment	109
§13.08	No Appeal	110
14.	Grounds for Challenge	111
§14.01	Introduction	111
§14.02	Disclosure	111
§14.03	Grounds	112
§14.04	Estoppel	114
15.	Challenge Procedure	116
§15.01	Introduction	116
§15.02	Default Procedure	117
§15.03	Application to High Court	117
§15.04	Preventing Dilatory Tactics	117
16.	Failure or Impossibility to Act	119
§16.01	Introduction	119

x

Table of Contents

§16.02	Inability and Delay	119
§16.03	Application to High Court	120
§16.04	Withdrawal Does Not Imply Acceptance	120
§16.05	Mandatory or Non-mandatory	121
17.	Appointment of Substitute Arbitrator	122
§17.01	Introduction	122
§17.02	Additional Grounds for Termination	123
§17.03	Substitution	124
§17.04	Effect of Substitution	124

CHAPTER 4
Jurisdiction of the Arbitral Tribunal 127

18.	Competence of Arbitral Tribunal to Rule on its Jurisdiction	127
§18.01	Introduction	128
§18.02	Kompetenz-Kompetenz and Separability	128
	[A] The Two Principles	128
	[B] Lean Towards Arbitration	129
	[C] Reform and Wide Powers	131
	[D] Potential Limits to These Wide Powers	132
§18.03	Time Limits	135
§18.04	Rulings and Appeals	137
19.	Power of Arbitral Tribunal to Order Interim Measures	140
19A.	Conditions for Granting Interim Measures	140
19B.	Application for Preliminary Orders and Conditions for Granting Preliminary Orders	141
19C.	Specific Regime for Preliminary Orders	141
19D.	Modification, Suspension or Termination	142
19E.	Provision of Security	142
19F.	Disclosure	142
19G.	Costs and Damages	142
19H.	Recognition and Enforcement	142
19I.	Grounds for Refusing Recognition or Enforcement	143
19J.	Court-ordered Interim Measures	143
§19.01	Introduction	144
§19.02	Definition of Interim Measures	146
§19.03	Two Preconditions for Interim Measures	146
§19.04	Five Types of Interim Measures	147
§19.05	Three Conditions for Interim Measures	148
	[A] Harm Not Adequately Reparable by an Award of Damages	148
	[B] Such Harm Substantially Outweighs the Harm Likely to Result to the Respondent	149
	[C] Reasonable Possibility That the Applicant Will Succeed on the Merits	149
§19.06	Application of the Three Conditions	150
§19.07	Definition of Preliminary Orders	150

Table of Contents

§19.08	Two Preconditions for Preliminary Orders	151
§19.09	Additional Conditions for Preliminary Orders	151
§19.10	Five Safeguards for Preliminary Orders	152
§19.11	Modification, Suspension or Termination	153
§19.12	Security	153
§19.13	Disclosure	154
§19.14	Costs and Damages	154
§19.15	Recognition and Enforcement of Interim Measures	154
§19.16	Refusal of Recognition and Enforcement of Interim Measures	156
§19.17	Court-Ordered Interim Measures	157

CHAPTER 5
Conduct of Arbitral Proceedings 159

20.	Equal Treatment of Parties	159
§20.01	Introduction	159
§20.02	Fundamental Principle	160
§20.03	Setting Aside	161
§20.04	Comprehensive	166
21.	Determination of Rules of Procedure	167
§21.01	Introduction	167
§21.02	Party Autonomy	167
§21.03	Arbitral Tribunal's Discretion	169
§21.04	Examples of the Arbitral Tribunal's Power	170
22.	Seat of Arbitration	171
§22.01	Introduction	171
§22.02	Party Autonomy	172
§22.03	Arbitral Tribunal's Discretion	173
§22.04	Abstraction	173
23.	Commencement of Arbitral Proceedings	174
§23.01	Introduction	174
§23.02	Party Autonomy	176
§23.03	Default	176
§23.04	Limitation	177
24.	Language	181
§24.01	Introduction	181
§24.02	Party Autonomy	181
§24.03	Default	182
§24.04	Statements, Hearing and Award	183
§24.05	Documents	183
25.	Statements of Claim and Defence	184
§25.01	Introduction	184
§25.02	Party Autonomy	187
§25.03	Writing	187
§25.04	Documents	188
§25.05	Amendments	188

26.	Hearings	189
§26.01	Introduction	189
§26.02	Autonomy and the Importance of an Oral Hearing	191
	[A] Where the Parties Have Agreed on an Oral Hearing	191
	[B] Where the Parties Have Agreed That No Hearing Will Be Held	191
	[C] Where the Parties Have Not Agreed on Whether an Oral Hearing Is to Be Held	192
§26.03	Notice	193
§26.04	Communication	193
27.	Default of a Party	194
§27.01	Introduction	194
§27.02	Party Autonomy	194
§27.03	Default	195
	[A] Where the Claimant Fails to Deliver the Statement of Claim	195
	[B] Where the Respondent Fails to Deliver His Statement of Defence	195
	[C] Where Any Party Fails to Attend the Hearing or Provide Documentary Evidence	196
	[D] Where the Claimant Fails to Proceed with the Claim	196
§27.04	Safeguards	196
28.	Expert Appointed by Arbitral Tribunal	198
§28.01	Introduction	198
§28.02	Party Autonomy	198
§28.03	Cooperation	199
§28.04	Right to be Heard	199
§28.05	Impartiality and Independence	199
29.	Court Assistance in Taking Evidence	200
§29.01	Introduction	200
§29.02	Application	201
§29.03	Orders	201

CHAPTER 6
Making of Award and Termination of Proceedings 203

30.	Law Applicable to Substance of Dispute	203
§30.01	Introduction	203
§30.02	Party Autonomy	206
§30.03	Determination by the Arbitral Tribunal	207
§30.04	Equity and Conscience	208
§30.05	Agreement and Trade Usage	208
§30.06	Third-Party Determination	209
§30.07	Setting Aside	209
31.	Decision Making by Panel of Arbitrators	210
§31.01	Introduction	210
§31.02	Party Autonomy	211
§31.03	Default	211

Table of Contents

32.	Settlement	213
§32.01	Introduction	213
§32.02	Termination	213
§32.03	Award on Agreed Terms	213
§32.04	Form and Effect	214
33.	Form and Contents of Award	215
§33.01.	Introduction	215
§33.02	Award Must Be in Writing	218
§33.03	Award Must Be Signed	218
§33.04	The Award Must Contain Reasons	219
§33.05	The Award Must State Its Date	220
§33.06	The Award Must State Its Seat	221
§33.07	The Award Must Be Delivered	221
§33.08	Additional Requirements Agreed by the Parties	222
§33.09	Interest	222
	[A] Party Autonomy	222
	[B] Default Powers	222
	[1] Post-award Interest	223
	[2] Pre-award Interest	223
34.	Termination of Proceedings	225
§34.01	Introduction	225
§34.02	Final Award	226
§34.03	Withdrawal	226
§34.04	Agreement	227
§34.05	Unnecessary or Impossible	227
§34.06	Death	229
35.	Correction and Interpretation of Award or Additional Award	230
§35.01	Introduction	230
	[A] Strictly Construed	232
	[B] Time	232
	[C] Form	232
§35.02	Correction	232
§35.03	Interpretation	233
§35.04	Additional Award	233
36.	An Award is Final and Binding	235
§36.01	Introduction	235
§36.02	Final and Binding	235
§36.03	Agreement to Exclude Recourse	237
§36.04	Res Judicata	239

CHAPTER 7
Recourse Against Award 241

37.	Application for Setting Aside	241
§37.01	Introduction	242
§37.02	An Award May Be Set Aside by the High Court Only If …	243

			Table of Contents
	[A]	Award	243
	[B]	May	244
	[C]	Set Aside	245
	[D]	High Court	247
	[E]	Only If	247
§37.03	The Party Making the Application Provides Proof		248
	[A]	Incapacity of a Party	249
	[B]	Validity of the Arbitration Agreement	251
	[C]	Lack of Notice or Inability to Present Case	252
	[D]	Excess of Jurisdiction	252
		[1] General	252
		[2] The Test	253
		[3] The Application of the Test	254
		[4] Waiver	255
		[5] Not Bound by the Arbitral Tribunal's Award	256
	[E]	Composition and Procedure	256
§37.04	The High Court Finds That ...		256
	[A]	Not Capable of Settlement by Arbitration	257
	[B]	Public Policy	257
		[1] Fraud or Corruption	261
		[2] Natural Justice	262
§37.05	Time Limit		264
§37.06	Remission		265
§37.07	Security		266

CHAPTER 8
Recognition and Enforcement of Awards — 267

38.	Recognition and Enforcement		267
§38.01	Introduction		267
§38.02	The Need for an Application		269
§38.03	High Court		269
§38.04	Reciprocity		270
§38.05	Enforced as a Judgment		271
§38.06	Conditions and Procedure		272
	[A]	Procedure	272
	[B]	The Two-Stage Test	274
		[1] Stage 1	274
		[2] Stage 2	277
39.	Grounds for Refusing Recognition or Enforcement		281
§39.01	Introduction		281
§39.02	'Recognition and Enforcement of an Award, Irrespective of the State in Which It Was Made ...'		283
§39.03	'... May Be Refused ...'		283
§39.04	'... Only ...'		283
§39.05	'... At the Request of the Party Against Whom It is Invoked ...'		286

xv

Table of Contents

§39.06	Grounds for Refusing Recognition and Enforcement		287
	[A]	Incapacity of Party	289
	[B]	Invalidity of Arbitration Agreement	289
	[C]	Notice and Inability to Present Case	291
	[D]	Jurisdiction	291
	[E]	Composition and Procedure	292
	[F]	Not Binding, Suspended or Set Aside	294
		[1] Not Binding	294
		[2] Set Aside or Suspended	295
		[3] Application to Set Aside or Suspend	296
	[G]	Arbitrability	297
	[H]	Public Policy	297

CHAPTER 9
Additional Provisions Relating to Arbitration — 301
40. Consolidation of Proceedings and Concurrent Hearings — 301
§40.01 Introduction — 301
§40.02 Autonomy — 302
    [A] PAM Contract 2018 — 302
    [B] AIAC Arbitration Rules 2018 — 303
41. Determination of Preliminary Point of Law by Court — 305
§41.01 Introduction — 305
§41.02 Question of Law — 306
§41.03 Consent — 306
§41.04 Course of the Arbitration — 307
§41.05 Criteria — 307
§41.06 Formal Requirements — 307
§41.07 Arbitration May Proceed — 307
41A. Disclosure of Information Relating to Arbitral Proceedings and Awards Prohibited — 309
§41A.01 Introduction — 309
§41A.02 The Need for an Express Provision on Confidentiality — 309
§41A.03 The Confidentiality of Arbitral Proceedings and the Award — 311
§41A.04 The Three Exceptions to Confidentiality — 311
    [A] Legal Right or Interest and Enforce or Challenge the Award — 311
    [B] The Authorities — 312
    [C] The Adviser — 312
41B. Proceedings to Be Heard Otherwise Than in Open Court — 314
§41B.01 Introduction — 314
§41B.02 Enhancement of Existing Provisions on Privacy of Court Proceedings — 314
§41B.03 The Privacy of Court Proceedings under the Arbitration Act 2005 — 315
§41B.04 Order for Open Court Proceedings — 315
42. Reference on Questions of Law — 316
§42.01 Introduction — 316
§42.02 Threshold Requirements — 318

	[A]	Question of Law		320
		[1]	Facts and Evidence	322
		[2]	Law	323
		[3]	Construction	324
		[4]	Mixed Fact and Law	325
		[5]	Damages	327
		[6]	Interest	327
		[7]	Costs	327
	[B]	Arising Out of an Award		328
	[C]	Not the Same Question		329
	[D]	Substantially Affects the Rights of One or More of the Parties		331
	[E]	Mandatory Time Period		332
	[F]	Identify the Question of Law		332
	[G]	Grounds on Which the Reference Is Sought		333
	[H]	Particulars of Each Ground		333
	[I]	Service of the Application		334
§42.03	Determination Stage			334
	[A]	The Correct Approach		334
	[B]	Not an Appeal		335
	[C]	Minimal Intervention		336
	[D]	Relationship with an Application to Set Aside		338
§42.04	Relief Stage			339
§42.05	Order to State Reasons			339
§42.06	Order for Security			340
43.	Appeal			341
§43.01	Introduction			341
44.	Costs and Expense of an Arbitration			342
§44.01	Introduction			342
§44.02	Determination of Costs			343
	[A]	Agreement on How Costs Will Be Determined		344
	[B]	Arbitral Tribunal Determines Costs		346
	[C]	Where the Arbitral Tribunal Determines Who Pays Costs and the High Court Taxes the Amount of Costs		347
	[D]	Where Costs Are Not Determined		347
§44.03	Offer to Settle			348
§44.04	Order for Delivery			348
§44.05	Review			348
45.	Extension of Time for Commencing Arbitration Proceedings			350
§45.01	Introduction			350
§45.02	Undue Hardship			350
§45.03	Restraint of Legal Proceedings			351
§45.04	Unambiguous			352
46.	Extension of Time for Making Award			354
§46.01	Introduction			354
§46.02	Party Autonomy			354

xvii

Table of Contents

§46.03	Procedure	355
§46.04	Discretion and Preconditions	355
	[A] Tribunal Processes Exhausted	355
	[B] Substantial Injustice	356

CHAPTER 10
Miscellaneous 357

47.	Liability of Arbitrator	357
§47.01	Introduction	357
§47.02	Purpose of Immunity	358
§47.03	Limits of Immunity	358
	[A] Bad Faith	358
	[B] Not in Discharge of Functions	359
§47.04	Non-derogable	359
48.	Immunity of Arbitral Institution	360
§48.01	Introduction	360
§48.02	Purpose of the Immunity	360
§48.03	Limits of Immunity	360
	[A] Bad Faith	361
	[B] Discharge of the Function	361
§48.04	Non-derogable	361
49.	Bankruptcy	362
§49.01	Introduction	362
§49.02	Adoption of the Arbitration Agreement	362
§49.03	Non-adoption of the Arbitration Agreement	362
50.	Mode of Application	364
§50.01	Introduction	364
§50.02	Scope	364
§50.03	High Court	365
§50.04	Relationship Between Arbitration Act 2005 and Rules of Court 2012	366
51.	Repeal and Savings	367
§51.01	Introduction	367
§51.02	Repeal	367
§51.03	Arbitral Proceedings	368
§51.04	Court Proceedings	369

Appendix	371
Glossary	399
Index	401

Foreword

The paradox of arbitration lies in its confidentiality and freedom of choice; yet it would be hard to find another area of law that calls, nay, demands, for uniformity, consistency, predictability and control than arbitration. This is where the United Nations Commission on International Trade Laws (UNCITRAL) Model Law on International Commercial Arbitration plays its quintessential role. In its march towards providing that workable platform for commerce and business, legal practitioners and judicial systems, many jurisdictions have found it the preferred if not the right choice. Malaysia was no exception.

When, after over fifty years of applying and enforcing the Arbitration Act of 1952, left over from the pre-Independence days, where the reception of that Act, on the ground, was frequently short and wanting, it was felt that Malaysia needed to do more. Amendment of the 1952 Act was not enough; an entirely new piece of legislation seemed the only credible response.

And, so the Arbitration Act 2005 [Act 646] was enacted. The Act provides for both domestic and international arbitration, as defined in the Act, and it adopts substantially the UNCITRAL Model Law in respect of both types of arbitrations. Consonant with the inscribed principle of party autonomy, the extent of the application of the Act, in either case, is subject to parties' choice. Since the Arbitration Act came into force on 15 March 2006, it would not be wrong to say that the Act has certainly changed the law and the landscape of arbitration in Malaysia.

The courts of Malaysia have interpreted the Act in the last decade and more, with a rigour that has seen the Act taken back to Parliament for no less than three separate sets of amendments. The most recent exercise was in 2018, driven principally by the Federal Court's decision in *Far East Holdings Bhd & Anor v. Majlis Ugama Islam dan Adat Resam Melayu Pahang and other appeals* [2018] 1 MLJ 1 on the scope and application of section 42 of the Arbitration Act 2005. Section 42 was the mechanism under which an arbitrating party may refer questions of law arising out of an award in a domestic arbitration to the courts. The Federal Court in *Far East Holdings* gave what is generally regarded as a tad too 'wide' an interpretation to the scope of section 42. In

Foreword

response, Parliament amended the Act in early 2018 to delete section 42. A party may no longer refer questions of law arising out of an award to the courts.

This book is an extensive commentary on the Arbitration Act 2005, drawing primarily on the courts' interpretation of the Act. It is timely and a much-needed book, for the same reasons why the Act was enacted in the first place. The writing and the publication of this book is a reflection of the maturity now reached by the arbitral community of Malaysia. Practitioners and business need to know where Malaysia stands in the law of arbitration. This book meets that need: tracing the origin of the provisions of the Act to the Model Law and other legislation on which the Act is based, keeping track of the developments since enactment and filling the gaps as to how the developments and the decisions of our courts have kept pace or otherwise with other Model Law and non-Model jurisdictions.

It is a painstaking and diligent piece of work that can only be properly discharged by someone both familiar and competent in this field. Thayananthan Baskaran must be commended and congratulated for having undertaken this exercise, so well. I am confident that his superb work will not only provide guidance on the history of the Arbitration Act 2005 and its development since the Act came into force; it will be a useful and resourceful compendium to anyone associated, in any measure or degree, with arbitration.

Dato' Mary Lim Thiam Suan
Judge of the Court of Appeal of Malaysia
June 2019

Preface

Arbitration in Malaysia has been governed by laws since the Arbitration Ordinance XIII of 1809 enacted two hundred and ten years ago. The Ordinance applied in the Straits Settlement, which comprises the present-day states of Malacca and Penang, in Malaysia, and Singapore. The laws that governed arbitration in Malaysia up to the Arbitration Act 1952[1] were based on the laws of England.

The Arbitration Act 2005 came into force on 15 March 2006, the Ides of March. The Act introduced the UNCITRAL Model Law on International Commercial Arbitration to Malaysia and significantly changed the law of arbitration in Malaysia.

This book is a commentary on the Arbitration Act 2005. The commentary follows the Act section by section. In sequential order, it provides the text of a section of the Act, followed by an explanation of the purpose of the section. The commentary then traces the origin of each section of the Act to the Model Law or the statute it is based on, as well as the history of the Model Law or statute. This is followed by an explanation of provisions of each section in terms of their application and effect.

The commentary is primarily based on the interpretation of the Arbitration Act 2005 by the courts of Malaysia in the decade since it has been in force.

Insofar as particular provisions of the Arbitration Act 2005 have yet to be the subject of a judgment, reliance is placed on the Analytical Commentary. This report[2] provides a summary of why a certain provision of the 1985 Model Law was adopted and what it is intended to cover, as well as an explanation and interpretation of particular words. The report, however, does not give a full account of the *travaux preparatoires*.

---

1. British North Borneo, as Sabah, a State now in Malaysia was then known, and Sarawak adopted the English Arbitration Act of 1952 as their respective Ordinance in 1952. In 1963, North Borneo and Sarawak joined the Federation of Malaysia. On 1 Nov. 1972, Malaysia adopted the arbitration laws prevailing in Sabah and Sarawak and it became known as the Arbitration Act 1952, which is based on the English Arbitration Act 1950.
2. *See* Analytical Commentary, Introduction, para. 5.

Preface

Apart from this report, reliance is also placed on the rules of statutory interpretation in interpreting provisions of the Arbitration Act 2005 that have yet to be interpreted by the courts.

I would like to thank Roveena Tara, my wife, who encouraged me to write this book and then endured me writing this book over the last four years late into the early hours. Parama Kausala Devi Baskaran, my mother, who edited the initial drafts of the book. Kevin Richard Nathan and Tan Zu Hao, my colleagues at the Malaysian Bar, who assisted me with the research for this book. Lee Yong Lie and Elizabeth Florence Lee, who typed this book from the original illegible manuscript, which now fills thirty notebooks. Thank you.

Thayananthan Baskaran
Damansara Heights and the Temple
Monday, 6 May 2019

Preliminary

An Act to reform the law relating to domestic arbitration, provide for international arbitration, the recognition and enforcement of awards and for related matters.

ENACTED by the Parliament of Malaysia as follows:

PRELIMINARY

1. Short Title and Commencement

    (1) This Act may be cited as the Arbitration Act 2005.
    (2) This Act comes into operation on a date to be appointed by the Minister by notification in the Gazette.

§1.01 COMMENTARY

The Arbitration Act 2005 came into operation on 15 March 2006. As the long title of the Act states, the Act was intended to reform the law of arbitration in Malaysia. This was to be achieved principally by incorporating the 1985 Model Law into the laws of Malaysia with certain amendments.

As the Arbitration Act 2005 was intended to reform the law on arbitration by incorporating the 1985 Model Law one must be cautious when relying on authorities based on the Arbitration Act 1952.

In this context, the Federal Court, in *Far East Holdings Berhad & Ors v. Majlis Ugama Islam dan Adat Resam Melayu Pahang* [2017] 8 AMR 313 at paragraphs 93, 100, 108 and 109, after reviewing the history of arbitration legislation in Malaysia, held that the Arbitration Act 2005 should be interpreted independently.[1] Judgments under the

---

1. See also *Albilt Resources Sdn Bhd v. Casaria Construction Sdn Bhd* [2010] 3 MLJ 656 at paras 63-64, 67-69, CA.

Arbitration Act 1952 were no longer relevant, as the Arbitration Act 2005 had radically changed the law on arbitration in Malaysia, by adopting the 1985 Model Law.

2. *Interpretation*

(1) In this Act, unless the context otherwise requires –

'award' means a decision of the arbitral tribunal on the substance of the dispute and includes any final, interim or partial award and any award on costs or interest but does not include interlocutory orders;

'High Court' means the High Court in Malaya and the High Court in Sabah and Sarawak or either of them, as the case may require;

'Minister' means the Minister charged with the responsibility for arbitration;

'State' means a sovereign State and not a component state of Malaysia, unless otherwise specified;

'presiding arbitrator' means the arbitrator designated in the arbitration agreement as the presiding arbitrator or chairman of the arbitral tribunal, a single arbitrator or the third arbitrator appointed under subsection 13(3);

'arbitration agreement' means an arbitration agreement as defined in section 9;

'party' means a party to an arbitration agreement or, in any case where an arbitration does not involve all the parties to the arbitration agreement, means a party to the arbitration;

'seat of arbitration' means the place where the arbitration is based as determined in accordance with section 22;

'international arbitration' means an arbitration where –

(a) one of the parties to an arbitration agreement, at the time of the conclusion of that agreement, has its place of business in any State other than Malaysia;

(b) one of the following is situated in any State other than Malaysia in which the parties have their places of business:
   (i) the seat of arbitration if determined in, or pursuant to, the arbitration agreement;
   (ii) any place where a substantial part of the obligations of any commercial or other relationship is to be performed or the place with which the subject-matter of the dispute is most closely connected; or

(c) the parties have expressly agreed that the subject matter of the arbitration agreement relates to more than one State;

'domestic arbitration' means any arbitration which is not an international arbitration;

'arbitral tribunal' means an emergency arbitrator, a sole arbitrator or a panel of arbitrators.

(2) For the purposes of this Act –

(a) in the definition of 'international arbitration' –
   (i) where a party has more than one place of business, reference to the place of business is that which has the closest relationship to the arbitration agreement; or
   (ii) where a party does not have a place of business, reference to the place of business is that party's habitual residence;

(b) *where a provision of this Act, except section 3, leaves the parties free to determine a certain issue, such freedom shall include the right of the parties to authorize a third party, including an institution, to determine that issue;*

(c) *where a provision of this Act refers to the fact that the parties have agreed or that they may agree or in any other way refers to an agreement of the parties, that agreement shall include any arbitration rules referred to in that agreement;*

(d) *where a provision of this Act refers to a claim, other than in paragraphs 27(a) and 34(2)(a), it shall also apply to a counterclaim, and where it refers to a defence, it shall also apply to a defence to that counterclaim.*

§2.01 INTRODUCTION

Section 2 of the Arbitration Act 2005 defines various terms used in the Act and also provides rules for the interpretation of the Act. Section 2 is based in part on Articles 1 and 2 of the 1985 Model Law. We will consider each individual provision of this section below.

§2.02 AWARD

The definition of 'award' is broad and covers every type of award that may be made by an arbitral tribunal save for interlocutory orders.

§2.03 HIGH COURT

The definition of 'High Court' in the Arbitration Act 2005 differs from Article 2(c) of the 1985 Model Law, which defines 'court' as 'a body or organ of the judicial system of a state'.

The definition in the Act is more specific than the 1985 Model Law. This may be because the intention behind both provisions differs.

The definition in the 1985 Model Law, according to the Analytical Commentary,[2] appears self-evident and accordingly superfluous. However, the definition of 'court' and 'arbitral tribunal' was included to distinguish the two. This is because, in certain languages, common words are used for both entities. Furthermore, certain arbitral institutions include the word 'court' in their name, for example the International Chamber of Commerce International Court of Arbitration and the London Court of International Arbitration.

The intention behind the definition of 'High Court' in the Arbitration Act 2005 appears to be to designate a court to perform various functions under the Act. In this

---

2. *See* Analytical Commentary, Article 2, commentary 1.

regard, its purpose is more akin to Article 6 of the 1985 Model Law rather than Article 2(a).

The definition of 'High Court' effectively means that the following applications have to be made to this court under the Act:

(1) an application for interim measures under section 11(1);
(2) an application for a decision on an unsuccessful challenge against an arbitrator for lack of impartiality, independence or qualifications under section 15(3);
(3) an application for a decision on the termination of an arbitrator's mandate due to inability to perform the functions of that office under section 16(2);
(4) an appeal against a ruling on a preliminary question by an arbitral tribunal that it has jurisdiction under section 18(8);
(5) an application for assistance in taking evidence under section 29(1);
(6) an application to set aside an award under section 37(1);
(7) an application for the recognition and enforcement of an award under section 38(1);
(8) an application for the determination of a question of law arising in the course of the arbitration under section 41(1);
(9) an application for costs to be taxed, where the arbitral tribunal has ordered that costs and expenses be paid but has failed to specify the amount under section 44(1)(b);
(10) an application for an arbitral tribunal to deliver an award, where the arbitral tribunal refuses to deliver the award before the payment of its fees and expense, under section 44(4);
(11) an application for extension of time for commencement of the arbitration proceedings under section 45; and
(12) an application for extension of time for the making of an award under section 46(1).

It should also be noted that sections 15(5) and 18(10) of the Arbitration Act 2005 provide that no appeal shall lie against a decision of the High Court made under these sections. This is to prevent delay and provide finality.

Although the words 'High Court' are defined, section 10(1) of the Arbitration Act 2005 refers to 'a court' rather than the High Court. This would suggest that an application for stay of proceedings pending arbitration may be made in any court in which the proceedings were commenced and not necessarily in the High Court.

This interpretation of the definition of High Court and section 10 were confirmed by the High Court, in *UBA Urus Bina Asia Sdn Bhd v. Quirk & Associates Sdn Bhd & Anor* [2016] 4 CLJ 468 at paragraph 37, where it was, *inter alia*, held:

> Unlike ss. 11, 15, 18, 29, 37, 38, 39, 41, 42, 43, 44, 45, 46 and 50 of the Arbitration Act 2005, where the word 'court' is specifically identified as the 'High Court', the words used in s. 10 is 'a court'. Arguably, this will include the Magistrates and Sessions courts as the term 'court' is not defined in s. 2 of the Arbitration Act 2005; but the term 'High Court' is. With the amendments to the financial limits of the

subordinate courts, applications for orders under s. 10 can properly come within the jurisdiction of the subordinate courts.

§2.04 MINISTER

The 'Minister' is defined as the minister charged with the responsibility for arbitration, who is presently the Minister in the Prime Minister's Department in charge of Legal Affairs.

§2.05 STATE

The definition of 'State' seeks to distinguish between sovereign nations and the thirteen component states of Malaysia.

The High Court, in *Twin Advance (M) Sdn Bhd v. Polar Electro Europe BV* [2013] 3 CLJ 294 at paragraph 27, decided, based on the words 'an award from a foreign State' in section 38 and 'an award, irrespective of the State in which it was made' in section 39, that an award made in any State may be enforced in Malaysia under these sections, which provide for the recognition and enforcement of awards. The High Court also held that, unlike sections 38 and 39, section 37 that provides for the setting aside of awards does not refer to a foreign 'State'. Therefore, an application to set aside an award may only be made in the foreign state in which the award was made and not in Malaysia.

§2.06 PRESIDING ARBITRATOR

The definition of 'Presiding Arbitrator' envisages three distinct scenarios:

(1) an arbitrator designated as the presiding arbitrator or chairman of the arbitral tribunal in the arbitration agreement;
(2) a single arbitrator; or
(3) the third arbitrator appointed by the two party-appointed arbitrators, where the parties have failed to agree on the procedure for the appointment of the arbitral tribunal under section 13(3) of the Arbitration Act 2005.

The High Court, in *Pendaftar Pertubuhan Malaysia v. Establishmen Tribunal Timbangtara Malaysia & Ors* [2011] 6 CLJ 684 at paragraph 26, emphasized that there must be an arbitration agreement between the parties before there could be a presiding arbitrator under this definition. In the absence of such an agreement, the presiding arbitrator would not have jurisdiction.

§2.07 ARBITRATION AGREEMENT

The definition of 'arbitration agreement' simply cross refers to the definition in section 9 of the Arbitration Act 2005. This important definition is considered in §9.03 *infra*.

§2.08 PARTY

The definition of 'Party', which appears self-evident, encompasses two scenarios:

(1) a party to an arbitration agreement; and
(2) a party to an arbitration, where the arbitration does not involve all the parties to the agreement.

The second scenario appears to be intended to deal with arbitrations that only include the two parties in dispute but arise from a multiparty arbitration agreement.

Although the definition of 'party' appears self-evident, it has surprisingly generated a fair amount of controversy.

Quite uncontroversially, the High Court, in *Pendaftar Pertubuhan supra* at paragraph 26, emphasized that there could be no 'party' within this definition in the absence of an arbitration agreement. Perhaps, more controversially, the High Court, in *Sundra Rajoo v. Mohamed Abd Majed & Anor* [2011] 6 CLJ 923, included an arbitrator within this definition of a 'party' on the basis that an arbitration agreement is a trilateral agreement between the parties and the arbitrator.

In this context, the High Court, in *Sundra Rajoo supra* at paragraph 10(f), *inter alia*, held:

> The learned counsel for the applicant say that (i) the applicant should be regarded as a party to the arbitration within the meaning of s. 2 of AA 2005 and assert that a contract exists between the parties and the arbitrators; the aforementioned contract is bi-lateral and creates rights and obligations for both the arbitrators and parties. (ii) However, where arbitration is administered by an arbitral institution, the contractual relationship becomes triangular.
>
> There is much merit in the applicant's submission.

§2.09 SEAT OF ARBITRATION

The definition of 'seat of arbitration' simply cross refers to section 22 of the Arbitration Act 2005 and will be considered in §22.01 to §22.04 *infra*.

§2.10 INTERNATIONAL ARBITRATION AND DOMESTIC ARBITRATION

The definition of 'international arbitration' in sections 2(1) and 2(2) of the Arbitration Act 2005 reflects Articles 1(3) and (4) of the 1985 Model Law.

The definition of 'international arbitration' in the Arbitration Act 2005 slightly modifies the definition in the 1985 Model Law. The words 'different States' in Article 1(3)(a) and 'outside the State' in Article 1(3)(b) of the 1985 Model Law are substituted with the words 'State other than Malaysia'. The geographically neutral definition used in the 1985 Model Law appears preferable as an arbitration is international if it involves two different States regardless of whether one of them is Malaysia.

Other than this change, the words 'place of arbitration' in Article 1(3)(b)(i) of the 1985 Model Law is substituted with the words 'seat of arbitration' in the Arbitration Act 2005. This is simply a stylistic change, as the term seat of arbitration is used consistently in the Arbitration Act 2005 instead of the place of arbitration.

The definition of 'international arbitration' is of significance as it determines which Parts of the Arbitration Act 2005 apply to the arbitration under section 3.

Due to this significance, and the need for certainty, a precise definition of international arbitration was sought.[3] However, too precise a definition may remove many arbitrations, which are truly international. As such, Article 1(3) of the 1985 Model Law has defined international arbitration with varying degrees of precision.

Article 1(3)(a) of the 1985 Model Law sets the basic criterion that the parties have their place of business in different States. This definition is adopted from Article 1(1) of the 1980 United Nations Convention on Contracts for the International Sale of Goods. The key determining factor here is the place of business of a party. Other characteristics of a party, such as nationality or place of registration or incorporation, are accordingly not relevant.[4]

The criterion used in Article 1(3)(a) of the 1985 Model Law is that the parties have their places of business 'in different States'. Therefore, it is irrelevant[5] whether either party has its place of business in the State enacting the 1985 Model Law. Therefore, assuming[6] State X has enacted the 1985 Model Law, an arbitration would be an international arbitration if it was between State Y and State Z or between State Y and State X.

Unfortunately, this does not appear to have been recognized in the Arbitration Act 2005, which substitutes the words 'in different States' with the words 'States other than Malaysia'. The definition, therefore, may restrict international arbitration to a scenario where one party has its place of business in Malaysia and the other party has its place of business outside Malaysia, without clearly capturing the scenario where both parties have their place of business in different States outside Malaysia.

The Federal Court, in *Tan Sri Dato' Seri Vincent Tan Chee Yioun & Anor v. Jan De Nul (M) Sdn Bhd & Anor and another appeal* [2018] MLJU 1545 at paragraphs 41, 43, 45 and 48, held that the definition of the words 'international arbitration' in section 2 of the Arbitration Act 2005 was exhaustive. Therefore, these words could not mean anything other than what was expressly provided in section 2.

The Federal Court also held that the express words used in section 2(1)(a) of the Arbitration Act 2005 to define international arbitration were clear, unambiguous and plain. The requirements for an international arbitration under section 2(1)(a) was that there must be:

(1) a party;
(2) to an arbitration agreement; and

---

3. *See* Analytical Commentary, Article 1, commentary 23.
4. *See* Analytical Commentary, Article 1, commentary 24.
5. *See* Analytical Commentary, Article 1, commentary 25.
6. *See* Analytical Commentary, Article 1, commentary 25.

(3) such a party must have its place of business in any State other than Malaysia.

The Federal Court emphasized the need to refer to the specific arbitration agreement between the parties to ascertain if there was an international arbitration, as such an agreement was one of the requirements under section 2(1)(a).

The Federal Court also emphasized that section 2(1)(a) required a 'party' to be from a State other than Malaysia, but there was no requirement for such a party to be a substantive party. The extent of such a party's involvement in the arbitral proceedings was immaterial in determining if the arbitration was international or otherwise.

Article 1(3)(b) of the 1985 Model Law defines international arbitration by reference to place. Where the (a) place of arbitration, (b) place where a substantial part of the commercial relationship is to be performed or (c) the place with which the subject matter of the dispute is most closely connected differs from the State in which the parties have their place of business, then the arbitration is international. Again, it is not relevant[7] to the test of internationality whether any of these places is the State that enacted the 1985 Model Law.

Unfortunately, this was not recognized in the Arbitration Act 2005, which substitutes the words 'outside the State' with the words 'any State other than Malaysia'. This may confine the definition of international arbitration to a scenario where the parties have their place of business in Malaysia but the places of arbitration, substantial performance or closest connection is outside Malaysia.

The three relevant places referred to in Article 1(3)(b) are the places of arbitration, substantial performance and closest connection. Of these three, only the place of arbitration is an arbitration-related criterion. Therefore, an international link may not be established by any other arbitration-related criterion such as a foreign arbitrator or choice of foreign law.[8]

The place of arbitration is relevant where 'determined in, or pursuant to, the arbitration agreement' under Article 1(3)(b)(i). Where the place of arbitration is specified in the arbitration agreement, this criterion for internationality may easily be determined at the outset. However, where the place of arbitration is to be determined subsequently pursuant to the arbitration agreement, there could be a long period of uncertainty as to whether the arbitration is international or otherwise. The Analytical Commentary[9] takes the position that this criterion will not be met by a stipulation authorizing the arbitral tribunal to determine the place of arbitration.

The second place referred to is the place of substantial performance. This scenario[10] would arise where two parties agree to a sole distributorship in a foreign market or an employer and a contractor agree to perform works overseas.

---

7. *See* Analytical Commentary, Article 1, commentary 26.
8. *See* Analytical Commentary, Article 1, commentary 27.
9. *See* Analytical Commentary, Article 1, commentary 28.
10. *See* Analytical Commentary, Article 1, commentary 29.

The third place is the place that has the closest connection with the dispute. This is likely to be very exceptional[11] and may be intended to cater to scenarios where the international character cannot be ascertained until the dispute has arisen.

The final criterion is set out in Article 1(3)(c) of the 1985 Model Law and provides for a situation where the parties have agreed that the subject matter of the arbitration agreement relates to more than one country. The word 'country' is substituted with the word 'State' in the Arbitration Act 2005 and is consistent with the definition and use of this term in the Act. This provision covers the situation where parties have expressly agreed, to avoid any uncertainty, that an arbitration is international. The parties' right to agree to this further strengthens the principle of party autonomy.

Article 1(4) of the 1985 Model Law, which is reflected in section 2(2)(a) of the Arbitration Act 2005, sets out the test for determining the place of business. Where a party has more than one place of business, regard will be given to the place of business that has the closest relationship to the arbitration agreement. In this context, the Analytical Commentary[12] provides the example of a contract, including the arbitration clause, being fully negotiated at a branch office separate from the principal office, which would make the branch the most closely connected with the arbitration agreement.

The other scenario provided for by Article 1(4)(b), which is reflected in section 2(2)(a)(ii), is where a party does not have a place of business, in which case reference is to be made to his habitual residence.

The definition of 'domestic arbitration' in section 2(1) of the Arbitration Act 2005 is not taken from the 1985 Model Law, which does not define this term, as the 1985 Model Law is concerned with international commercial arbitration. The definition of a domestic arbitration is, in any event, simply the opposite of an international arbitration.

§2.11 ARBITRAL TRIBUNAL

Section 2 of the Arbitration Act 2005 defines an 'arbitral tribunal' as an emergency arbitrator, a sole arbitrator or a panel of arbitrators. The words 'an emergency arbitrator' were inserted by the Arbitration (Amendment) (No 2) Act 2018.

Apart from this recent insertion, the definition of 'arbitral tribunal' in section 2 of the Arbitration Act 2005 reflects the definition in Article 2(b) of the 1985 Model Law. This definition of an 'arbitral tribunal' does not require an arbitrator to have any particular qualifications or experience and adheres to the principle of party autonomy. This has been somewhat colourfully described by the Court of Appeal in *Garden Bay Sdn Bhd v. Sime Darby Property Berhad* [2017] AMEJ 1599 at paragraph 9:

> In essence, the Convention allows an arbitration award made in one Convention country to be enforceable in another country. The Convention supports party autonomy. Parties to an arbitration agreement can even agree to appoint a tribal

---

11. *See* Analytical Commentary, Article 1, commentary 30.
12. *See* Analytical Commentary, Article 1, commentary 32.

chief of a remote part of Malaysia as an arbitrator and agree to be bound by his award. That award can be enforceable in any Convention countries.

There was a concern that the original definition of an 'arbitral tribunal' in section 2 of the Arbitration Act 2005 may not allow for an emergency arbitrator. This may have rendered any order by an emergency arbitrator unenforceable. These concerns became pressing with the widespread adoption of emergency arbitration provisions in the rules of arbitration institutions. For example, Schedule 3 of the 2018 Asian International Arbitration Centre (AIAC) Arbitration Rules provide for the appointment of an emergency arbitrator. To overcome these concerns, the definition of 'arbitral tribunal' was amended by the Arbitration (Amendment) (No 2) Act 2018 to expressly include an 'emergency arbitrator'.

§2.12 ARBITRATION

The Arbitration Act 2005 does not define 'arbitration'. However, the courts have defined arbitration in several judgments after the Arbitration Act 2005 came into force.

These judgments start with *Majlis Amanah Rakyat v. Kausar Corp Sdn Bhd* [2009] MLJU 1697 at page 12, where arbitration was defined as follows:

> In this connection, counsel for the Defendant also submitted for my consideration the useful passage by Lord Mustill sitting in the Judicial Committee in the case of *Pupuke Service Station Ltd v Caltex Oil (NZ) Ltd* (which was included as an appendix in the *Gold & Resource Development* decision), which is very pertinent to note for purposes of this application. The passage reads:
>> Arbitration is a contractual method of resolving disputes. By their contract parties agreed to entrust the differences between them to the decision of an Arbitrator or panel of Arbitrators, to the exclusion of the courts, and they bind themselves to accept that decision, once made, whether or not they think it right. In prospect, this method often seems attractive. In retrospect, this is not always so. Having agreed at the outset to take his disputes away from the court the losing party may afterwards be tempted to think better of it, and ask the court to interfere because the Arbitrator has misunderstood the issues, believed unconvincing witness, decided against the weight of evidence, or otherwise arrived at a wrong conclusion. All developed systems of arbitration law have in principle set their face against accommodating such a change of mind. The parties have made the choice, and must abide by it. This general principle is, however, applied in different ways under different systems, according to the nature of the complaint.

This definition of arbitration has subsequently been adopted in *Xavier Francis & Anor v. Quality Property Development Sdn Bhd* [2013] 1 LNS 764 at paragraph 15 and *Sanlaiman Sdn Bhd v. Kerajaan Malaysia* [2013] 3 MLJ 755 at paragraph 48.

The High Court, in *Cyber Business Solutions Sdn Bhd v. Elsag Datamat SPA* [2012] 1 CLJ 115 at paragraph 15, defined arbitration slightly differently in the following terms:

> Arbitration is a process of resolving a dispute or a grievance outside a court system by presenting it for decision to an impartial third party. Both sides in the dispute

must agree in advance to the choice of arbitrator and certify that they will abide by the arbitrator's decision. Hence, the forum for arbitration derived its jurisdiction from the agreement by both parties and no other … .

The Federal Court, in *Thai-Lao Lignite Co Ltd & Anor v. Government of the Lao People's Democratic Republic* [2017] 6 AMR 219 at paragraph 149, defined arbitration by reference to the two core principles, that is a contract and dispute resolution, as follows:

'There is no universal definition of arbitration … Each jurisdiction may apply its own 'spin' in deciding what may and what may not be arbitrated, and how the arbitral process is to be conducted … Different commentators have defined arbitration differently. However there are core principles that can be found in all the definitions. The core principles include: the need for an arbitral agreement; a dispute, a reference to a third party for its determination; and an award by the third party' (*Arbitration of Commercial Disputes* by Andrew Tweeddale and Keren Tweeddale at 2.01 and 2.02).

Apart from these judgments, Rene David, in *Arbitration in International Trade* (Springer 1985), defines arbitration as follows:

Arbitration is a device whereby the settlement of a question, which is of interest for two or more persons, is entrusted to one or more persons – the arbitrator or arbitrators – who derive their powers from a private agreement, not from the authorities of the State, and who are to proceed and decide the case on the basis of such an agreement.

Based on these definitions, there are two constituent elements of arbitration:

(1) first, the arbitrator's task is to resolve a dispute; and
(2) second, the source of this judicial role is contract.

There is therefore both[13] a judicial and a contractual element.

§2.13 THIRD PARTY

Section 2(2)(b) of the Arbitration Act 2005 reflects Article 2(d) of the 1985 Model Law. This section is intended to prevent too strict an interpretation of the provisions of the Act which leave the parties free to agree on matters. The broad interpretation allowed by this section enables the parties to authorize a third party to determine these issues. In practice, this will include terms in an arbitration agreement that allow an arbitral institution to determine the number of arbitrators, the place of arbitration and other procedural matters.[14]

---

13. *See* Emmanuel Gaillard and John Savage, *Fouchard, Gaillard, Goldman on International Commercial Arbitration* (Kluwer Law International 1999) at para. 11.
14. *See* Analytical Commentary, Article 2, commentary 3.

§2.14 ARBITRATION RULES

Section 2(2)(c) of the Arbitration Act 2005 reflects Article 2(e) of the 1985 Model Law. Like section 2(2)(b), this section is also intended to prevent too strict an interpretation of the provisions of the Act that allow the parties the freedom to agree on various matters. This section makes clear that such freedom includes the freedom to agree on a set of arbitration rules, which will determine various matters.

The High Court, in *AV Asia Sdn Bhd v. Pengarah Kuala Lumpur Regional Centre for Arbitration & Anor* [2013] 10 CLJ 115, considered section 2(2)(c) in the context of an arbitration agreement that referred to the KLRCA Arbitration Rules. In particular, the issue was whether the number of arbitrators ought to be determined in accordance with the 2012 KLRCA Arbitration Rules, Part II, Article 7(1), which provides for three arbitrators to be appointed where the parties are unable to agree on the number of arbitrators, or section 12(2)(b) of the Arbitration Act 2005, which provides for a single arbitrator to be appointed in the case of domestic arbitration, where the parties have failed to agree. Although the High Court declined jurisdiction on the basis of sections 8 and 18 of the Arbitration Act 2005, it is submitted that, based on section 2(2)(c), Article 7(1) of Part II of the 2012 KLRCA Arbitration Rules would have prevailed, as the parties had not entirely failed to determine the number of arbitrators under section 12(2). Instead, the parties had determined this to the extent of agreeing on the KLRCA Arbitration Rules, as allowed by section 2(2)(c). And, in accordance with Article 7(1) of Part II of these Rules, the number of arbitrators should be three.

§2.15 CLAIM AND COUNTERCLAIM

Section 2(2)(d) of the Arbitration Act 2005 reflects Article 2(f) of the 1985 Model Law. Essentially, this section equates the application of the Act on claims to counterclaims and on defences to defences to counterclaims. There are two exceptions, which both relate to the termination of the proceedings where a claim is not communicated or is withdrawn. Naturally, if a counterclaim is not communicated or withdrawn, the proceedings would not similarly terminate but would instead continue.

3. *Application to Arbitrations and Awards in Malaysia*

(1) This Act shall apply throughout Malaysia.
(2) In respect of a domestic arbitration, where the seat of arbitration is in Malaysia –
   (a) Parts I, II and IV of this Act shall apply; and
   (b) Part III of this Act shall apply unless the parties agree otherwise in writing.
(3) In respect of an international arbitration, where the seat of arbitration is in Malaysia –
   (a) Parts I, II and IV of this Act shall apply; and
   (b) Part III of this Act shall not apply unless the parties agree otherwise in writing.
(4) For the purposes of paragraphs (2)(b) and (3)(b), the parties to a domestic arbitration may agree to exclude the application of Part III of this Act and the parties to an international arbitration may agree to apply Part III of this Act, in whole or in part.

§3.01 INTRODUCTION

Section 3 of the Arbitration Act 2005 provides for the application of the Act in Malaysia. Section 3 differs materially from Articles 1(1) and (2), which are the equivalent provisions of the 1985 Model Law.

§3.02 DOMESTIC AND INTERNATIONAL ARBITRATION

Unlike the 1985 Model Law, section 3 does not expressly limit the application of the Act to international commercial arbitration.

Instead of the Act being limited to international arbitration, it applies to both domestic and international arbitration in the manner provided in section 3. Although the 1985 Model Law was designed to establish a special regime for international arbitration, States were free[15] to take the 1985 Model Law as a basis for legislation on domestic arbitration, so as to avoid a dichotomy within a State's arbitration law.

As of 2010,[16] thirty-seven of the eighty countries that have adopted the 1985 Model Law have also chosen to enact the Model Law as their domestic arbitration legislation.

Although Malaysia has a unitary system for domestic and international arbitration, the definition of international arbitration remains significant, as different parts of the Arbitration Act 2005 apply to domestic and international arbitration as set out in section 3.

---

15. *See* Analytical Commentary, Article 1, commentary 22.
16. *See* Dr Peter Binder, *International Commercial Arbitration and Conciliation in Model Law Jurisdictions* (3rd edn, Sweet & Maxwell 2010) at para. 1-029.

§3.03 COMMERCIAL

Unlike Article 1(1) of the 1985 Model Law, the Arbitration Act 2005 is not limited to 'commercial' arbitration. The word 'commercial' is not expressly defined in the 1985 Model Law. Instead, there is a footnote to Article 1(1) of the 1985 Model Law, which provides:

> The term 'commercial' should be given a wide interpretation so as to cover matters arising from all relationships of a commercial nature, whether contractual or not. Relationships of a commercial nature include, but are not limited to, the following transactions: any trade transaction for the supply or exchange of goods or services; distribution agreement; commercial representation or agency; factoring; leasing; construction of works; consulting; engineering; licensing; investment; financing; banking; insurance; exploitation agreement or concession; joint venture and other forms of industrial or business cooperation; carriage of goods or passengers by air, sea, rail or road.

The Arbitration Act 2005 is not limited to 'commercial' arbitration in this sense. This wider application of the Arbitration Act 2005 and its significance will be considered further under §4.01 *infra* in the context of arbitrability of the subject matter of arbitration.

§3.04 SEAT OF ARBITRATION IN MALAYSIA

Section 3(2) and (3) of the Arbitration Act 2005 limit the application of the Act to domestic and international arbitration with a seat in Malaysia and do not expressly provide for international arbitrations with a seat outside Malaysia. When the Act was initially enacted there was no exception to this unlike Article 1(2) of the 1985 Model Law, which provides that 'The provisions of this Law, except Articles 8, 9, 35 and 36, apply only if the place of arbitration is in the territory of this State.'

The 1985 Model Law accordingly only applies if the place of arbitration is the State in which it is enacted with four exceptions for stay of proceedings, interim measures and the recognition and enforcement of an award.

The initial absence of these exceptions in the Arbitration Act 2005 gave rise to some degree of uncertainty.

For example, in *Innotec Asia Pacific Sdn Bhd v. Innotec GmbH* [2007] 8 CLJ 304, the High Court took the position that although section 3 only expressly applied to domestic and international arbitration with a seat in Malaysia, it did not expressly exclude the application of the Act to international arbitrations with a seat outside Malaysia. As such, the High Court was of the view that it retained the power under section 10 to stay proceedings pending an international arbitration outside Malaysia.

In this regard, the High Court, in *Innotec Asia supra* at paragraph 46, *inter alia*, held:

> Section 3 of the Arbitration Act 2005 merely dictates the application of certain Parts in the Act to both domestic and international arbitrations, where the seat of arbitration is in Malaysia. The language of the section is clear to this effect.

However, s. 3 of the Act does not expressly exclude the power of the court to stay proceeding for the purpose of referring the dispute to international arbitration. It is therefore incorrect and erroneous on the part of the plaintiff to suggest that the Arbitration Act 2005, following s. 3, only applies to arbitration (domestic or otherwise) where the seat is in Malaysia and excludes international arbitration. The language of the section does not lend support to such interpretation.

However, subsequently, the High Court, in *Aras Jalinan Sdn Bhd v. Tipco Asphalt Public Company Ltd & 2 Ors* [2008] 4 AMR 59, declined to follow the reasoning in *Innotec Asia supra*.

The High Court, in *Aras Jalinan supra*, instead held that since section 3 did not expressly confer jurisdiction with respect to international arbitration with a seat outside Malaysia, the High Court did not have such jurisdiction. The High Court accordingly refused to grant an interim injunction under section 11 of the Arbitration Act 2005.

In this context, the High Court, in *Aras Jalinan supra* at paragraphs 20 and 25, *inter alia*, held:

> [20] The abovementioned provisions refers specifically to two broad categories of arbitrations and awards to which the Act applies: By virtue of 3(2), in respect of a domestic arbitration where the seat of arbitration is in Malaysia and in 3(3), in respect of an international arbitration where the seat of arbitration is in Malaysia. In short the Act applies to domestic and international arbitrations where the seat of arbitration is in Malaysia. The Act is silent on a third category, viz. in respect of an international arbitration where the seat of arbitration is outside Malaysia. The specific reference to the abovementioned categories of arbitrations to which the Act applies suggests that the Act does not apply in any other circumstance.
>
> ...
>
> [25] The repeal of the Arbitration Act 1952 and the enactment of the current Act clearly indicate a deliberate intention to move away from the English model to Model Law. Had Parliament intended, it would have incorporated Article 1(2) of Model Law or the equivalent s 7 of the Arbitration Act of New Zealand 1996. The New Zealand Act provides which sections, if any are applicable to foreign arbitrations. New Zealand is one example of a jurisdiction that has adopted Model Law and the relevant Article to confer express jurisdiction to courts where the seat of arbitration is foreign. As Parliament has chosen to adopt the arbitral regime of Model Law but not adopted Article 1(2) of Model Law, the inescapable conclusion is that there is no intention of Parliament to confer such jurisdiction.

This judgment was affirmed by the Court of Appeal.

Some of this uncertainty has been removed by the Arbitration (Amendment) Act 2011, which came into force on 1 July 2011.

The Arbitration (Amendment) Act 2011 has amended sections 10 and 11 to expressly provide that these sections will apply to an international arbitration with a seat outside Malaysia. These amendments bring the Arbitration Act 2005 closer to the 1985 Model Law, which has similar provisions in Article 1(2).

Unfortunately, the Arbitration (Amendment) Act 2011 did not similarly amend sections 38 and 39, which provide for recognition and enforcement of awards, to reflect the further exceptions in Article 1(2) of the 1985 Model Law.

As a result, there remains some degree of uncertainty with respect to sections 38 and 39. This issue was considered by the High Court, in *Twin Advance (M) Sdn Bhd v. Polar Electro Europe BV* [2013] 3 CLJ 294 at paragraphs 23, 27. The High Court was of the view that although section 3 only provided for the application of the Act to domestic and international arbitration with a seat in Malaysia, sections 38 and 39 specifically allowed for the recognition and enforcement of awards arising from an international arbitration with a seat outside Malaysia.

Therefore, in the light of sections 10(4), 11(3), 38 and 39, it now appears that the Arbitration Act 2005, like the 1985 Model Law intended, will only apply to domestic and international arbitration with a seat in Malaysia save for exceptions with regard to stay, interim measures and recognition and enforcement of awards.

§3.05 OPT-IN OR OPT-OUT

Sections 3(2)-(4) of the Arbitration Act 2005 are drafted to the effect that Parts I, II and IV apply to domestic and international arbitration with a seat in Malaysia. Part III applies to domestic arbitration unless the parties specifically agree to exclude this Part, which is referred to in practice in short as 'the opt-out'. On the other hand, Part III does not apply to international arbitration unless the parties agree to include it, which is known as 'the opt-in'.

This has been recognized by the High Court, in *AV Asia Sdn Bhd v. Pengarah Kuala Lumpur Regional Centre for Arbitration & Anor* [2013] 10 CLJ 115 at paragraph 12, where it was, *inter alia*, held:

> Actually, from as early as s. 3(4), the parties to arbitration are given a choice as to the application of Part III of the Act; and that choice extends even to whether that application is in whole or in part. Part III concerns 'additional provisions relating to arbitration' and it relates to matters such as consolidation of proceedings and concurrent hearings; determination of preliminary point of law by court; reference of questions of law; appeal; costs and expenses of an arbitration; extensions of time for commencing arbitration proceedings and award.

Similarly, the High Court, in *MMC Engineering Group Bhd & Anor v. Wayss & Freytay (M) Sdn Bhd* [2015] 10 MLJ 689 at paragraph 16, *inter alia*, held:

> Section 42 of the Arbitration Act 2005 is peculiar to the Malaysian arbitration scene. This recourse to the courts is available in all domestic arbitrations unless the parties have specifically opted out of its operation; and unavailable to international arbitrations unless the parties have specifically opted in to its application. This is clear from the provisions of s 3. Section 42 was amended in 2011 to introduce sub-s 42(1A).

This was confirmed by the Federal Court, in *Tan Sri Dato' Seri Vincent Tan supra* at paragraphs 52 and 54, where it was, *inter alia*, held:

> [52] Undeniably, in the present case all the parties agreed that the Submission Agreement shall be governed by and construed in accordance with the laws of Malaysia. This must of necessity mean that the Act applies. Nonetheless, it must also be understood that the applicability or otherwise of Part III thereof must be a

matter of the particular provisions of the Act, which excludes the applicability of Part III (which section 42 is found), to international arbitrations as defined in the Act unless the parties to an arbitration agreement agree otherwise in writing.

...

[54] Based on the clear and unambiguous language of sections 2 and 3 of the Act, it is plain for us to see that Part III (including section 42) is expressly excluded for international arbitration (with no exceptions) unless the parties otherwise agree in writing ... .

The courts explained the 'opt-in' and 'opt-out' principles in *MMC Engineering* and *Tan Sri Dato' Seri Vincent Tan supra* by reference to section 42 of the Arbitration Act 2005. These principles continue to apply based on section 3. However, section 42 has been deleted by the Arbitration (Amendment) (No 2) Act 2018.

3A. Representation

Unless otherwise agreed by the parties, a party to arbitral proceedings may be represented in the proceedings by any representative appointed by the party.

§3A.01 Introduction

Section 3A of the Arbitration Act 2005 allows a party to be represented by any person of their choice regardless of such persons' qualifications or admission to practise in Malaysia as an advocate and solicitor. Section 3A of the Arbitration Act 2005 has no equivalent in the 1985 Model Law. Section 3A was introduced by the Arbitration (Amendment) (No 2) Act 2018.

§3A.02 Purpose

Prior to the introduction of section 3A of the Arbitration Act 2005, the position on party representation differed between Malaya, on the one hand, and Sabah and Sarawak on the other. This difference arose from there being separate Bars for Malaya, Sabah and Sarawak. Each of these Bars is in turn regulated by a different statute. The Bar in Malaya is governed by the Legal Profession Act 1976, while the Bar in Sabah is governed by the Advocates Ordinance 1953 and Sarawak by a distinct Advocates Ordinance 1953.

Insofar as Malaya is concerned, the position has always been that a party may be represented by a person who is not admitted as an advocate and solicitor in Malaysia. This was confirmed by the High Court, in *Zublin Muhibbah Joint Venture v. Government of Malaysia* [1990] 3 CLJ Rep 371 at pages 373 and 374, where it was, *inter alia*, held:

> An advocate and solicitor who is a qualified person under s 36(1) is given exclusive right by the law to appear and plead in all Courts of Justice in Malaysia. This s 36(1) does not give exclusive right to him, nor prohibit him from appearing in other tribunals which are not Courts of Justice in this country. An unauthorised person is prohibited under pain of penalty from performing any of the acts mentioned in s 37 of the Act. However, s 37 of the Act is specified in the sense that those acts to be performed must be done in the Courts in Malaysia, or relating to any proceedings in any Court in Malaysia.
>
> An arbitral forum is not a Court of Justice in Malaysia as envisaged by the Legal Profession Act 1976. It is a private tribunal. Subject to s 12 of the Arbitration Act 1952, the arbitrator is appointed by the parties to an arbitration agreement to adjudicate on certain specific facts before him, and ultimately to settle the disputes between the contracting parties arising out of their contract. The parties who may appear before the arbitrator are those provided for by the arbitration agreement, or if the agreement does not so provide, then the provisions of s 13 of the Arbitration Act shall apply. Any person who assists a party in presenting his case may also attend, e.g., a shorthand writer, an assessor, an engineer, an architect, and such parties should not be excluded without good ground when their presence are desired by a party or the award of the arbitrator may be set aside.

This was later given statutory force in Malaya by the Legal Profession (Amendment) Act 2013, which introduced section 37A. Section 37A expressly provides that provisions prohibiting a person other than an advocate and solicitor from practising in Malaya in sections 36 and 37 of the Legal Profession Act 1976 shall not apply to arbitral proceedings:

> 37A Sections 36 and 37 not to apply to arbitral proceedings
> (1) Sections 36 and 37 shall not apply to-
>   (a) any arbitrator lawfully acting in any arbitral proceedings;
>   (b) any person representing any party in arbitral proceedings; or
>   (c) any person giving advice, preparing documents and rendering any other assistance in relation to or arising out of arbitral proceedings except for court proceedings arising out of arbitral proceedings.
> (2) In this section, 'arbitral proceedings' means proceedings in an arbitration which is governed by the Arbitration Act 2005 [Act 646] or would have been governed by such Act had the seat of arbitration been Malaysia.

However, the position in Sabah was different. Only an advocate admitted to practise in Sabah was entitled to represent a party in arbitral proceedings based on sections 2(1) and 8(1) of the Advocates Ordinance 1953. This was confirmed by the Federal Court, in *Samsuri Baharuddin & Ors v. Mohamed Azahari Matiasin & Another Appeal* [2017] 3 CLJ 287 at paragraph 35, where it was, *inter alia*, held:

> In our view, by virtue of the first limb of s 8(1) of the Ordinance, the Sabah advocates have exclusive right to represent a party in arbitration proceedings in Sabah. This statutory right given to the Sabah advocates cannot be taken away by relying merely on the fact that barristers and solicitors in England have non-exclusive right to appear for parties in arbitration proceedings, which should form part of the functions included in the expression phrase 'to practise in Sabah'. We therefore agreed with the conclusion of the High Court Judge that foreign lawyers who are not advocates within the meaning of the Ordinance are prohibited by the same from representing parties to arbitration proceedings in Sabah.

Based on *Samsuri Baharuddin supra*, a similar position would have applied in Sarawak, as sections 2(1) and 8(1) of the Sarawak Advocates Ordinance 1953 are *in pari materia* to sections 2(1) and 8(1) of the Sabah Advocates Ordinance 1953.

The differing positions between Malaya and Sabah and Sarawak have now been overcome by section 3A of the Arbitration Act 2005. Section 3A expressly allows a party to be represented by any person of their choice regardless of whether they have been admitted as an advocate and solicitor in Malaya, Sabah or Sarawak.

4. *Arbitrability of Subject Matter*

   (1) *Any dispute which the parties have agreed to submit to arbitration under an arbitration agreement may be determined by arbitration unless the arbitration agreement is contrary to public policy or the subject matter of the dispute is not capable of settlement by arbitration under the laws of Malaysia.*
   (2) *The fact that any written law confers jurisdiction in respect of any matter on any court of law but does not refer to the determination of that matter by arbitration shall not, by itself, indicate that a dispute about that matter is not capable of determination by arbitration.*

§4.01 INTRODUCTION

Section 4 of the Arbitration Act 2005 provides for the arbitrability of the subject matter of an arbitration agreement. Essentially, all matters are arbitrable unless they are contrary to public policy. Furthermore, merely because any other statute provides for a dispute to be resolved by the courts, this does not necessarily mean that such a dispute cannot be resolved by arbitration.

Section 4(1) was amended by the Arbitration (Amendment) (No 2) Act 2018 to include the words 'or the subject matter of the dispute is not capable of settlement by arbitration under the laws of Malaysia'. Section 4(1) was amended because there was some ambiguity previously as to whether a dispute may not be submitted to arbitration only when the arbitration agreement, as opposed to the subject matter of the dispute, was contrary to public policy. The amendment seeks to remove this ambiguity by expressly providing that a dispute may not be referred to arbitration where the agreement is contrary to public policy or the subject matter of the dispute is incapable of settlement by arbitration.

Section 4(2) corresponds to Article 1(5) of the 1985 Model Law, but the two provisions are quite different. Article 1(5) provides that 'This Law shall not affect any other law of this State by virtue of which certain disputes may not be submitted to arbitration or may be submitted to arbitration only according to provisions other than those of this Law.'

Article 1(5) and section 4(2) take a different approach. While Article 1(5) provides that any other Law of the State which prevents disputes from being submitted to arbitration will not be affected by the 1985 Model Law, section 4(2) provides that any other statute that refers to the resolution of disputes by the courts will not prevent the resolution of such disputes by arbitration.

Generally, the Arbitration Act 2005 appears to take a broader perspective on the arbitrability of the subject matter of the dispute, as compared to the 1985 Model Law. There is no requirement under the Arbitration Act 2005 for the arbitration to be commercial in nature. This in itself increases the scope of the arbitrability of the subject matter under the Act considerably.

§4.02 CONTRARY TO PUBLIC POLICY

One of the two express restrictions is an arbitration agreement that is contrary to public policy. The Federal Court, in *Arch Reinsurance Ltd v. Akay Holdings Sdn Bhd* [2018] MLJU 2117 at paragraphs 63-67, held that there was no universally accepted test as to what 'public policy' was. However, there were recognized categories of disputes that could not be resolved by arbitration. For example, a dispute will not be arbitrable if:

(1) the dispute involves an issue of public policy;
(2) the dispute involves an issue of public rights;
(3) the dispute involves the interests of third parties; or
(4) the dispute is covered by a statute which provides for access to the courts.

In particular, the Federal Court, in *Arch Reinsurance supra*, held that any dispute arising from a chargee's statutory demand on a chargor under a registered charge would not be arbitrable, as an arbitration agreement could not take away the right of a registered chargee to apply to the courts for an order for sale of the charged land under the National Land Code 1965, in the event the chargor failed to comply with the chargee's statutory demand.

The Federal Court, in *Arch Reinsurance supra*, emphasized that the National Land Code 1965 was a complete and comprehensive code governing the tenure of land in Malaysia. In particular, the provisions of the National Land Code 1965 setting out the rights and remedies of parties under a statutory charge over land are exhaustive and exclusive, and any attempt at contracting out of these rights would be void as being contrary to public policy.

§4.03 NOT CAPABLE OF SETTLEMENT BY ARBITRATION

The second restriction is against disputes, the subject matter of which is not capable of settlement by arbitration under the laws of Malaysia. This would apply to disputes that cannot be resolved by arbitration in Malaysia, for example criminal matters.

5. *Government to Be Bound*

This Act shall apply to any arbitration to which the Federal Government or the Government of any component state of Malaysia is a party.

§5.01 COMMENTARY

Section 5 of the Arbitration Act 2005 simply provides that the Act will apply to an arbitration to which the Federal or State Governments are party, which appears self-evident. There does not appear to be any corresponding provision to this section in the 1985 Model Law.

In cases involving Government departments or state Governments, the High Court has referred to this section to confirm the application of the Arbitration Act 2005 to arbitrations to which the Government is a party. In this context, reference may be made to the judgments of the High Court, in *Pendaftar Pertubuhan Malaysia v. Establishmen Tribunal Timbangtara Malaysia & Ors* [2011] 6 CLJ 684 at paragraph 20 and *David Liew Kong Ming (practicing as D Liew Architect) v. Government of the State of Sabah* (HC, 24 December 2010).

CHAPTER 1
General Provisions

6.   Receipt of Written Communications

   (1) Unless otherwise agreed by the parties –
      (a) a written communication is deemed to have been received if it is delivered to the addressee personally or if it is delivered at his place of business, habitual residence or mailing address; and
      (b) where the places referred to in paragraph (a) cannot be found after making a reasonable inquiry, a written communication is deemed to have been received if it is sent to the addressee's last known place of business, habitual residence or mailing address by registered post or any other means which provides a record of the attempt to deliver it.
   (2) Unless otherwise agreed by the parties, a written communication sent electronically is deemed to have been received if it is sent to the electronic mailing address of the addressee.
   (3) The communication is deemed to have been received on the day it is so delivered.
   (4) This section shall not apply to any communications in respect of court proceedings.

§6.01   INTRODUCTION

Section 6 of the Arbitration Act 2005 provides for the means of service of documents. Section 6 mirrors Article 3 of the 1985 Model Law save for section 6(2), which is an addition.

§6.02 AUTONOMY

Section 6 of the Arbitration Act 2005 is a non-mandatory provision, as it begins with the words 'unless otherwise agreed by the parties'. In practice, the parties would have often agreed otherwise, in this context, by adopting a set of arbitration rules, which usually provide for means of service.

In this regard, Article 2 of the 2013 UNCITRAL Arbitration Rules, which form part of the 2018 AIAC Arbitration Rules, provides for means of service in similar terms:

> Notice and Calculation of Periods of Time
> 1. A notice, including a notification, communication or proposal, may be transmitted by any means of communication that provides or allows for a record of its transmission.
> 2. If an address has been designated by a party specifically for this purpose or authorised by the arbitral tribunal, any notice shall be delivered to that party at that address, and if so delivered shall be deemed to have been received. Delivery by electronic means such as facsimile or email may only be made to an address so designated or authorised.
> 3. In the absence of such designation or authorisation, a notice is:
>   (a) Received if it is physically delivered to the addressee; or
>   (b) Deemed to have been received if it is delivered at the place of business, habitual residence or mailing address of the addressee.
> 4. If, after reasonable efforts, delivery cannot be effected in accordance with paragraphs 2 or 3, a notice is deemed to have been received if it is sent to the addressee's last known place of business, habitual residence or mailing address by registered letter or any other means that provides a record of delivery or of attempted delivery
> 5. A notice shall be deemed to have been received on the day it is delivered in accordance with paragraphs 2, 3 or 4, or attempted to be delivered in accordance with paragraph 4. A notice transmitted by electronic means is deemed to have been received on the day it is sent, except that a notice of arbitration so transmitted is only deemed to have been received on the day when it reaches the addressee's electronic address.
> 6. For the purpose of calculating a period of time under these Rules, such period shall begin to run on the day following the day when a notice is received. If the last day of such period is an official holiday or a non-business day at the residence or place of business of the addressee, the period is extended until the first business day which follows. Official holidays or non business days occurring during the running of the period of time are included in calculating the period.

§6.03 BROAD INTERPRETATION OF WRITTEN COMMUNICATION

Article 3 of the 1985 Model Law does not define the words 'written communication'. However, reference to personal service, 'mailing address' and 'registered letter' suggested that the type of written communication envisaged is the traditional letter.

To avoid this limited interpretation of written communication, section 6(2) of the Arbitration Act 2005 expressly allows for electronic means of communication. This is particularly important in the context of international arbitration, where most, if not all, communication is done electronically for the speed and cost advantages.

§6.04 COURT PROCEEDINGS

Section 6(4) of the Arbitration Act 2005 provides that section 6 shall not apply to court proceedings. This is because court proceedings have their own rules for communication as set out in the Rules of Court 2012.

7. Waiver of Right to Object

A party who knows –

> *(a) of any provision of this Act from which the parties may derogate; or*
> *(b) that any requirement under the arbitration agreement has not been complied with,*
> *and yet proceeds with the arbitration without stating its objection to such non-compliance without undue delay or, if a time limit is provided for stating that objection, within that period of time, shall be deemed to have waived its right to object.*

§7.01 INTRODUCTION

Section 7 of the Arbitration Act 2005 gives statutory force to the doctrine of waiver or estoppel in the context of the derogable provisions of the Act and the arbitration agreement. Section 7 is identical to Article 4 of the 1985 Model Law.

Section 7 of the Arbitration Act 2005 is similar to Article 32 of the 2013 UNCITRAL Arbitration Rules, which form part of the 2018 AIAC Arbitration Rules. Article 32 of the 2013 UNCITRAL Arbitration Rules, however, allows for the waiver of any provision of the Rules and the arbitration agreement. This is understandable, in the context of arbitration rules, any provision of which may be altered.

§7.02 REQUIREMENTS

The Analytical Commentary sets out four requirements for the application of Article 4 of the 1985 Model Law, which are equally applicable to section 7 of the Arbitration Act 2005.

[A] Derogable Provision

First,[1] the waiver can only apply to a derogable provision of the Arbitration Act 2005 and not to a non-derogable provision of the Act. In this regard, the non-derogable provisions of the Act include:

(1) section 20, which requires the parties to be treated with equality;
(2) section 25(1), which provides for exchange of statements of claim and defence;
(3) sections 26(3)-(5), which provide for notice of hearings and communication of documents;
(4) section 29, which provides for court assistance in taking evidence;

---

1. *See* Analytical Commentary, Article 4, commentary 2.

(5) section 32, which provides for settlement;
(6) sections 33(1), (2), (4) and (5), which provide that the award must be in writing, signed, dated and state the seat;
(7) section 34, which provides for termination of the arbitral proceedings; and
(8) sections 35(1)-(3), which provide for correction of the award.

And, the derogable provisions of the Act include:

(1) section 6, which provides for modes of receipt of written communication;
(2) section 12, which provides that the parties are free to determine the number of arbitrators;
(3) section 13(1), which provides that the parties may agree on the nationality of the arbitrator;
(4) section 13(2), which provides for the procedure for the appointment of arbitrators;
(5) section 15, which provides for the procedure to challenge an arbitrator;
(6) section 17(2), which provides for the procedure for the appointment of substitute arbitrators;
(7) section 17(3), which provides for the effect of an order or ruling by an arbitrator made prior to the appointment of a replacement;
(8) section 19, which provides for the power of an arbitrator to order interim measures;
(9) section 21, which provides that the parties are free to agree on the procedure to be followed by the arbitrator subject to the other provisions of the Act;
(10) section 22, which provides for the place of arbitration;
(11) section 23, which provides for the commencement of arbitration;
(12) section 24, which provides for the language of arbitration;
(13) section 25(3), which provides for amendments or supplements to the claim or defence;
(14) section 26(1), which provides for an oral hearing or documents-only arbitration;
(15) section 27, which provides for defaults by the parties;
(16) section 28, which provides for tribunal-appointed experts;
(17) section 30, which provides for the law applicable to the substance of the dispute;
(18) section 31(1), which provides for the making of an award by majority;
(19) section 35(4), which provides for an additional award;
(20) section 44, which provides for the costs and expenses of arbitration; and
(21) section 46, which provides for an extension of time for the making of an award.

The Federal Court, in *Thai-Lao Lignite Co Ltd & Anor v. Government of the Lao People's Democratic Republic* [2017] 6 AMR 219 at paragraph 215, emphasized that a party's failure to object to the other party's non-compliance with a prescribed time period under the Arbitration Act 2005 would result in the party losing the right to object:

> *The Arbitration Act 2005* by Sundra Rajoo and WSW Davidson at 171 proposed that whether a jurisdictional issue could be later raised would depend on the nature of the jurisdictional issue; see also *A Guide to the UNCITRAL Model Law on International Commercial Arbitration* by Howard M. Holtzmann & Joseph E. Neuhaus at 482-483]. Equally, if a party raises an out of time challenge but the other party does not object to the lateness of the challenge, and the tribunal rules on the plea, the other party cannot rely on the delay to prevent the High Court from deciding the matter under art 16(3) [the equivalent of section 18(8) of AA 2005]' (*Williams & Kawharu supra* at 7.4.6). On the facts, even if the plea under section 18(3) or (5) of AA 2005 were made out of time, the Appellants could not rely on delay, which was not an issue during the arbitral proceedings, to prevent the High Court from deciding the matter under Section 37 of AA 2005. On the facts, where there was no objection to lateness, the Appellants could not raise the 'out of time' argument. As such, we reject the 'out of time' argument.

With regards to the arbitration agreement,[2] a waiver will only apply to provisions of the agreement that correspond to derogable provisions of the Arbitration Act 2005 and not to the non-derogable provisions.

[B]   Knowledge of Non-compliance

Second, a party must know of the non-compliance. The draft Model Law in the Analytical Commentary was broader and allowed for a situation where 'a party who knows or ought to have known'. However, there were objections to the extension of the waiver doctrine to constructive knowledge through the use of the words 'ought to have known'. These words were accordingly not included in the 1985 Model Law and are not found in section 7 of the Arbitration Act 2005. It is important to keep this in mind when considering the second condition of section 7 that what is required is knowledge of the non-compliance and not merely constructive knowledge.[3]

[C]   Failure to State Objection

Third, the party must have failed to state his objection without undue delay or within any period provided for. Where a period is provided[4] for in the Arbitration Act 2005 or the arbitration agreement, this should take precedence over the more general words 'without undue delay'.

---

2. *See* Analytical Commentary, Article 4, commentary 2.
3. *See* Dr Peter Binder, *International Commercial Arbitration and Conciliation in UNCITRAL Model Law Jurisdictions* (3rd edn, Sweet & Maxwell 2010) at paras 1-093-1-094.
4. *See* Analytical Commentary, Article 4, commentary 4.

[D] Proceeding with the Arbitration

Fourth, a party only loses his right to object when, without stating his objections, he proceeds. The Analytical Commentary suggests[5] that the following would amount to proceeding with the arbitration: (a) appearance at the hearing or (b) communication with the arbitral tribunal or the other party. Mere inaction due to circumstance beyond a party's control is unlikely to amount to proceeding, for example if a party fails to communicate due to a postal strike.

§7.03 EFFECT OF WAIVER

Where these four conditions are satisfied, and a party has waived his right to object, he will not be allowed to raise this ground of objection in the subsequent arbitration proceedings. Perhaps, more importantly, he will also not be entitled to raise such a ground in attempting to set aside any subsequent award. Furthermore, where the award is sought to be enforced in another jurisdiction that has also adopted the Model Law or a provision similar to Article 4 thereof, a party will not be entitled to raise such a ground in objecting to the recognition and enforcement of the award.[6]

---

5. *See* Analytical Commentary, Article 4, commentary 5.
6. *See* Analytical Commentary, Article 4, commentary 6.

8. Extent of Court Intervention

No court shall intervene in matters governed by this Act, except where so provided in this Act.

§8.01 INTRODUCTION

The present section 8 of the Arbitration Act 2005 was inserted by the Arbitration (Amendment) Act 2011. Prior to the amendment, section 8 read as follows 'Unless otherwise provided, no court shall intervene in any of the matters governed by this Act.'

The present section 8 closely reflects Article 5 of the 1985 Model Law, which provides 'In matters governed by this Law, no court shall intervene except where so provided in this Law.'

§8.02 INTERVENTION

The Analytical Commentary states[7] that Article 5 requires that any instance of court involvement be listed out in the statute. This is intended to remove any residual powers of the court, which are not listed, and thereby provides certainty.

The Federal Court, in *Thai-Lao Lignite Co Ltd & Anor v. Government of the Lao People's Democratic Republic* [2017] 6 AMR 219, confirmed that in accordance with section 8, a court should only intervene in accordance with the Arbitration Act 2005. However, the Federal Court emphasized that there was no question of the 1985 Model Law promoting more or less court intervention. The Federal Court, in *Thai-Lao supra* at paragraph 240, *inter alia*, held:

> But that is not to say that the court has a free hand to intervene. Section 8 of AA 2005 provides that 'No court shall intervene in matters governed by this Act, except where so provided in this Act'. Unless so provided by AA 2005, the court shall not intervene in the arbitral process or in arbitral awards. Whether the UNCITRAL Model law promotes more or less curial interference does not arise.

Subsequently, the Court of Appeal, in *La Kaffa International Co Ltd v. Loob Holding Sdn Bhd and another appeal* [2018] MLJU 703, appeared to go further, when the court held that section 8 did not remove the inherent jurisdiction of the courts. However, the Court of Appeal recognized that this inherent jurisdiction is limited, in matters governed by the Arbitration Act 2005. In such matters, the courts in exercising their right to intervene, as expressly provided by the Act, should do so in accordance with their inherent jurisdiction but would be slow to go outside such express provisions. On the other hand, where the matter was not governed by the Act, the courts retained their inherent jurisdiction. In this context, the Court of Appeal, in *La Kaffa International supra* at paragraphs 21, 24 and 29, held:

---

7. *See* Analytical Commentary, Article 5, commentary 2.

[21] It will not be a correct statement of law to say that the court has lost its inherent jurisdiction to act on matters related to arbitration. The relevant section which attempts to restrict the inherent jurisdiction of the court in matters related to arbitration is section 8 of AA 2005 ... .

...

[24] Section 8 is similar to Article 5 of the UNCITRAL Model Law. It is now trite that section 8 advocates a minimum intervention and not no intervention at all in matters specifically not governed by AA 2005. Support for the proposition is also found in UNCITRAL Secretarial note 25-03-1985 which say:
4. Another important consideration in judging the impact in article 5 is that the above necessity to list all instances of court involvement in the Model Law applies only to the 'matters governed by this Law.' The scope of article 5 is, thus, narrower than the substantive scope of application of the Model Law, i.e. 'international commercial arbitration' (article 1), in that it is limited to those issues which are in fact regulated, whether expressly or impliedly, in the Model Law.
5. Article 5 would, therefore, not exclude court intervention in any matter not regulated in the model law.

...

[29] In our view, the court under AA 2005 is not ousted of its inherent jurisdiction or the powers to order interim measures order though by virtue of section 8, the court will be slow to provide a relief if it is not clearly spelt out in AA 2005 itself ... .

§8.03 EXPRESS AND IMPLIED PROVISION

However, there is a degree of uncertainty attached to the words 'matters governed by this Act' in section 8 of the Arbitration Act 2005. This is because, on the one hand, section 8 is not intended to cover the whole scope of arbitration but is limited to matters governed by the Act. On the other hand, what is governed by the Arbitration Act 2005 covers both what is 'in fact regulated, whether expressly or impliedly'.[8]

The Federal Court, in *Far East Holdings Bhd & Anor v. Majlis Ugama Islam dan Adat Resam Melayu Pahang* [2017] 8 AMR 313, considered this issue and decided that section 8 would not prevent court intervention in matters not regulated by the Arbitration Act 2005. The Federal Court, in *Far East supra* at paragraph 114, *inter alia*, held:

> The AA 2005 is devoid of a provision in the words of s 81(2) of the UK Arbitration Act 1996. But the AA 2005 is nonetheless clear that 'No court shall intervene in matters governed by this Act, except where so provided in this Act'. Pertinent to 'where so provided in this Act', the AA 2005 provides for court intervention in the matters stated in ss 10, 11, 13(7), 15(3), 18(8), 29, 37, 41, 42, 44(1), 44(4), 45, and 46 of the AA 2005. 'Where a party seeks intervention is one of those situations, the court is permitted to intervene only in the manner prescribed by the model law, and in the absence of any express provision the court must not intervene at all. By contrast, where the situation is not of a type to which the model law is addressed,

---

8. *See* Analytical Commentary, Article 5, commentary 4.

the court may intervene or decline to intervene in accordance with the provisions of the relevant domestic arbitration law' (*A Guide to the UNCITRAL Model Law on International Commercial Arbitration: Legislative History and Commentary* by Howard M Holtzmann and Joseph E Neuhaus, published in 1994 at p 224). Accordingly, s 8 would ... not exclude court intervention in any matter not regulated by (the AA 2005)' (*The Arbitration Act 2005* at p 8.17); matters which are not governed by the Model Law include the following areas: the inherent jurisdiction in the court to grant an injunction to stay arbitral proceedings; and the whole topic of confidentiality of arbitral proceedings (for a non-exhaustive list of matters not governed by the Model Law, see *A Guide to the UNCITRAL Model Law on International Commercial Arbitration* at p 218).

At the end of the day, much will depend on the particular provision of the Act when deciding whether a matter is implicitly provided for or not provided for at all. This issue is also perhaps theoretical to an extent, as it has rarely arisen in practice, where the courts have generally decided that matters are expressly governed by the Act and they must act accordingly.

In this context, the provisions of the Arbitration Act 2005 that expressly allow for court intervention include:

(1) section 10(1) – application for stay;
(2) section 11(1) – application for interim measures;
(3) section 13(7) – application for the appointment of an arbitrator, where the Director of the AIAC fails to act;
(4) section 15(3) – application for a decision on an unsuccessful challenge against an arbitrator;
(5) section 16(2) – application for a decision on termination of the mandate of an arbitrator;
(6) section 18(8) – appeal against ruling that an arbitral tribunal has jurisdiction;
(7) section 29(1) – application for assistance in taking evidence;
(8) section 37(1) – application for setting aside;
(9) section 38(1) – application for recognition and enforcement;
(10) section 39(1) – grounds for refusing recognition or enforcement;
(11) section 41(1) – application for determination of the preliminary point of law;
(12) section 42(1) – reference on questions of law arising out of an award, which provision has been deleted;
(13) section 44(1)(b) – application for taxation of costs, where arbitral tribunal does not specify the amount of such costs;
(14) section 44(4) – application for delivery of the award, where the arbitral tribunal refuses to deliver its award before payment of its fees and expense;
(15) section 45 – application for extension of time to commence arbitration proceedings; and
(16) section 46(2) – application for extension of time for the making of an award.

Chapter 1: General Provisions §8.03[B]

We will now consider how the courts have applied section 8 in the context of these express provisions of the Arbitration Act 2005.

[A] Section 10

The High Court, in *Sunway Damansara Sdn Bhd v. Malaysia National Insurance Bhd & Anor* [2008] 3 MLJ 872 decided that, in the light of section 8, a stay must be granted under section 10 unless one of the exceptions applied and there was no room for discretion. The High Court, in *Sunway Damansara supra* at paragraphs 21 and 22, held that:

> [21] In his final submissions counsel for the plaintiff referred to s 8 of the new Act and submits that the said provision does not exclude the court from intervening ... However counsel for the second defendant submits that the said provision clearly shows that the court shall not interfere. On this issue I am of the opinion that the extent of the court's power to intervene is limited to what is expressed in the said provision, which is, unless the Act provides otherwise the court cannot intervene, in the present case I find no ground to intervene.
>
> [22] In conclusion I agree with what has been said by Ramly Ali J in *Innotec's* case that s 10(1) imposes upon the court an obligation to stay proceedings unless the plaintiffs case falls within the words of the exception. I find that none of the grounds put forward by the plaintiff come within the exceptions. That being the case this is not a matter in respect of which the court has a discretion. I therefore allowed the second defendant's application as prayed.

The High Court, in *CLLS Power System Sdn Bhd v. Sara-Timur Sdn Bhd* [2015] 1 LNS 149 at paragraph 31, held that the provisions of section 10 must be strictly complied with, in the light of the amended section 8.

The High Court, in *MMIP Services Sdn Bhd v. Overseas Assurance Corporation (Malaysia) Bhd* [2016] 5 CLJ 637, decided that section 8 did not apply in relation to the effect of an order made by the courts. Section 10 would also not apply to issues relating to an order of the courts, which could not be covered by an arbitration agreement. In this context, the High Court, in *MMIP Services supra* at paragraph 54, held:

> TIMB has relied on ss. 8 and 10 of the AA ... Section 8 of the AA does not apply in this case as this case does not concern AA. Section 10(1) of the AA only applies if the arbitration agreement applies to the four questions. As explained above, the arbitration agreement cannot apply to the question on effect of High Court's confirmation order. Consequently, s. 10(1) of the AA has no relevance to the third party notice. Even if the arbitration agreement applies to the four questions, TIMB can only apply to stay the third party proceedings under s. 10(1) of the AA and not to strike out the third party notice.

[B] Section 11

The High Court, in *Cobrain Holdings Sdn Bhd v. GDP Special Projects Sdn Bhd* (HC, 29 October 2010), appears to emphasize that an application for an interim measure should properly be made under section 11, in the light of section 8, rather than Order 29 of the Rules of the High Court 1980, which was applicable at the time, or the inherent jurisdiction of the courts. In this context, the High Court, in *Cobrain Holdings supra* at pages 5 and 6, held that:

> At the outset, it has to be said that the reliance on Order 29 and the inherent jurisdiction of this court was an alternative basis, and the Plaintiff did not actively pursue its case on this basis, but more on Section 11 of the Arbitration Act, 2005. Such an approach is consistent with Section 8 of the Act ... This preliminary position has to be emphasised since it encapsulates the principles of party autonomy and minimalist intervention by the courts of law. From this basic principal, a number of subsidiary principles arise which have a direct bearing on the outcome of these cases.
>
> As has been emphasised in numerous cases, when parties have contractually resorted to arbitration as a forum of choice, the court of law should be slow to interfere in the arbitration proceedings, and should do so only where the governing statutory framework grants it the jurisdiction. Any necessary application should first be made to the arbitral tribunal, unless of course the particular jurisdiction happens not to be conferred on the arbitral tribunal within the statutory framework. These principles are stated and emphasised in the leading House of Lords decision in *Channel Tunnel Group Ltd v. Balfour Beatty Construction* [1993] A.C. 334 ... .

The High Court, in *Metrod (Singapore) Pte Ltd v. GEP II Beteiligungs GmbH & Anor* [2013] 5 AMR 186, decided that it does have the power to grant interim measures under section 11, and in accordance with section 8, after the commencement of arbitration proceedings. In this context, the High Court, in *Metrod supra* at paragraph 19, held:

> It is observed that the orders sought here are not confined to the contracting parties. This application may then be made to court without having first being made to the arbitral tribunal. This was remarked in *Cobrain Holdings Sdn Bhd v. GDP Special Projects Sdn Bhd* (KL High Court Originating Summons No. 24NCC-71-2010 & Anor) citing with approval the Singapore decision of *NCC International AB v Alliance Concrete Singapore Pte Ltd* [2008] 2 SLR (R) 565. Bearing in mind the intention of Parliament as reflected in s 8 of Act 646, it must be that the court has jurisdiction to hear and grant interim measures even where arbitration has already commenced elsewhere. The simple existence of arbitration cannot be a bar to this application given the terms upon which this power is predicated.

The High Court, in *Jayapadu Oil & Gas Sdn Bhd v. Chersonese Oil Sdn Bhd* [2014] 5 AMR 716, decided that although it was entitled to grant interim measures under section 11, this power must be exercised in a manner supportive of the arbitration, bearing in mind the minimalist intervention envisaged by section 8. In this context, the High Court, in *Jayapadu Oil supra* at paragraph 18, held that:

> Section 11 of Act 646 in itself does not state the test to be applied when considering the particular application at hand. Be that as it may, it is imperative that one is reminded of the autonomous nature of arbitration and the application of s 8; the latter being a statutory pronouncement of the minimalistic intervention of and by

the court. Another factor to bear in mind is that the object behind s 11 is to provide for some relief or measure during the interim period from the initiation or invocation of arbitration to the rendering of the award. In other words, the court's role here is more supportive; to aid and facilitate the arbitration which is the mode chosen by the parties to resolve their dispute. That must include the element of ensuring that that mode is not jeopardised, compromised or frustrated. That will also extend to any award that may be rendered by the arbitral tribunal appointed or to be appointed under the agreed arrangements; as may be gathered from the reliefs or measures that may be sought from the High Court at this stage. At s 11(1)(g), the interim measure may include orders that ensured that any award which is eventually rendered by the arbitral tribunal is not rendered 'ineffectual by the dissipation of assets by a party'. Therefore, the remedies sought are intended to support and even protect those intentions of the parties.

Similarly, the High Court, in *Bumi Armada Navigation Sdn Bhd v. Mirza Marine Sdn Bhd* [2015] 5 CLJ 652 at paragraphs 46, 90, held that:

[46] I am mindful of s. 8 AA which embodies a 'minimalist' approach by our courts as explained by David Wong JCA in the Court of Appeal case of *Capping Corporation Limited & Ors v. Aquawalk Sdn Bhd & Ors* [2013] 1 LNS 574; [2013] 6 MLJ 579, at 588 and 589 ... In my opinion, s. 11(1) AA expressly allows judicial 'intervention' in a very limited form – the court may grant interim (and not permanent) relief pending the disposal of arbitration. The court's power to grant interim relief, does not:

(a) deprive parties of their freedom to contract and to agree to resolve disputes by way of arbitration; and

(b) usurp the role and function of an 'arbitral tribunal' (defined in s. 2(1) AA as 'a sole arbitrator or a panel of arbitrators') to decide the merits of the dispute in question.

...

[90] To ensure that the arbitral tribunal has unfettered power to decide this dispute as intended by the parties in the arbitration clause and in conformity with the 'minimalist' approach embodied in s. 8 AA, this court states the following:

(a) no finding of fact and/or law has been made by this court in court encl. no. 5 and OS as regards the merits of this dispute. The arbitral tribunal is free and is indeed duty bound to decide solely the merits of this dispute. The arbitral tribunal should not be influenced in any manner by this judgment ... .

(b) pending the disposal of arbitration, the parties may apply to the arbitral tribunal to vary this order as expressly allowed by this order. Both parties are, of course, entitled to apply to this court to vary or discharge this order; and

(c) if the arbitral tribunal dismisses the plaintiff's claim at the end of the arbitral proceedings, the arbitral tribunal is empowered to enforce the plaintiff's undertaking and assess all loss and damage suffered by the defendant as a result of the Mareva injunction granted in this order.

The Court of Appeal, in *La Kaffa International supra* at paragraph 29, held that section 8 did not remove the court's inherent jurisdiction to grant interim measures, but the courts would be slow to provide relief not expressly provided for in section 11.

[C] Section 12

The High Court, in *AV Asia Sdn Bhd v. Pengarah Kuala Lumpur Regional Centre for Arbitration & Anor* [2013] 10 CLJ 115 at paragraph 17, suggests that because section 12 does not allow the courts to determine the number of arbitrators, the courts do not have the power to do so in accordance with section 8.

[D] Section 14

The High Court, in *Sundra Rajoo v. Mohamed Abd Majed & Anor* [2011] 6 CLJ 923 at paragraph 10(e), suggests that although section 14 only provides for a party to challenge an arbitrator and not for a co-arbitrator to challenge another co-arbitrator, the court still had the inherent jurisdiction to allow such a co-arbitrator's challenge. This judgment was prior to the Arbitration (Amendment) Act 2011 came into force on 1 July 2011 and materially altered section 8. This judgment should accordingly now be read with caution.

[E] Section 18

The High Court, in *AV Asia supra* at paragraph 17, suggests that the question of the number of arbitrators goes to the jurisdiction of the arbitral tribunal and should accordingly be determined by the arbitral tribunal under section 18 without any intervention by the courts in accordance with section 8.

[F] Section 37

The High Court, in *Taman Bandar Baru Masai Sdn Bhd v. Dindings Corporations Sdn Bhd* [2010] 5 CLJ 83, decided that the courts would not ordinarily interfere with awards under section 37 of the Arbitration Act 2005, in the light of section 8. The High Court also cautioned against the reliance on judgments based on the Arbitration Act 1952 in this respect. The High Court, in *Taman Bandar Baru supra* at paragraphs 19 and 20, held:

> [19] ... The court's jurisdiction to intervene is almost prohibited. The AA 2005 must be seen to be a new chapter to the law, practice, and intervention of court etc in arbitration proceedings. The jurisdiction to ensure that courts do not intervene and meddle with arbitration proceedings is clearly set out in various provisions of the Act. Pre-2005 cases which provide room for interference with arbitrator's decision must now be treated as otiose, as AA 2005 has been shrewdly worded to ensure that courts ordinarily do not interfere with arbitration awards.
>
> [20] I will say that draftsmen of provisions such as ss. 8, 9, 37 and 42 have with great ingenuity asserted that court should not interfere with arbitrator's award without out rightly saying so. If they have said so out rightly, it will stand to be unconstitutional. Thus, it will appear that it is going to be difficult to frame any question of law pursuant to AA 2005 when the subject matter of complaint is one which is restricted by ss. 9, 37, or 42 etc. It is now for the courts themselves to

restrain from interference unless it is a case of patent injustice which the law permit the court in clear terms to intervene. It is trite that AA 2005 is meant to promote one-stop adjudication ... .

The High Court, in *PT Permata Hijau Sawit & 2 Ors v. Pacifik Inter-Link Sdn Bhd* [2011] 6 AMR 343 at paragraphs 32 and 34, decided that as section 8 allowed for intervention under a specific provision of the Act, the courts were entitled to consider an issue when it was raised under such a provision, like section 37. This is in accordance with the intention behind section 8. However, the High Court went on to suggest that when considering such an issue, the courts had 'the inherent jurisdiction to do justice and examine the finding of facts by the tribunal to see that the findings of facts are well supported by the evidence presented to the tribunal'. This may perhaps be going a little beyond the boundaries set by sections 8 and 37, especially as section 8 is intended to remove any residual power or inherent jurisdiction of the courts on matters governed by the Act. Perhaps, in this regard, this judgment can best be explained as having been made under section 8 prior to its amendment, when it was unclear whether the inherent jurisdiction of the courts had been removed. The position after the amendment to section 8 is clearly that such inherent jurisdiction on matters governed by the Act is removed.

The High Court, in *Kelana Erat Sdn Bhd v. Niche Properties Sdn Bhd & Another Case* [2013] 4 CLJ 1172, decided that, in the light of section 8, the courts would only intervene on matters specifically set out in section 37. This is a concise and precise statement of the law on the interplay between sections 8 and 37. The High Court, in *Kelana Erat supra* at paragraph 16, held:

> When read together with the prior provision of s. 8 which states that 'Unless otherwise provided, no court shall intervene in any of the matters governed by this Act' it would appear that there is a palpable paradigm shift and a discernible difference where Arbitration under the 2005 Act is concerned compared to the Arbitration Act 1952 in that the court would tend to take a hands-off approach and would only intervene on matters specifically set out in s. 37 where setting aside an award is concerned.

The High Court, in *Twin Advance (M) Sdn Bhd v. Polar Electro Europe BV* [2013] 3 CLJ 294, decided that, in the light of section 8, an award made in a foreign state could not be set aside in Malaysia. This decision is in accordance with established principles in international arbitration, reflected in section 37, that an award will only be set aside at the seat of arbitration. The High Court, in *Twin Advance supra* at paragraph 39, held:

> ... I am of the view that our s. 8 AA 2005 which is akin to Article 5 of the Model Law as adopted by the AA 2005 should similarly be interpreted in line with the Model Law that the court should exclude its general or residual powers or its inherent jurisdiction to indirectly vary the substantive provisions of AA 2005 which does not categorically provide or intend so. The parties in the said contract had chosen Singapore as the seat of arbitration and must be taken to have chosen Singapore as the jurisdiction for any subsequent proceedings of challenge to the award. They cannot resile to depart from this entrenched principle accepted internationally relating to the seat of arbitration. Any challenge or any application to set aside such a foreign award made in a foreign state must be in the foreign state.

The Court of Appeal, in *Kerajaan Malaysia v. Perwira Bintang Holdings Sdn Bhd* [2015] 1 CLJ 617, decided that an application to set aside an award must be viewed against the background of minimal intervention prescribed by section 8. In this context, the Court of Appeal, in *Perwira Bintang supra* at paragraph 10, held:

> ... The policy to be adopted by our courts is that of minimal intervention consistent with the policy underlying the UNCITRAL Model Law, which Malaysia has incorporated with suitable amendments. Section 37 mirrors the Model Law (Article 34). However, s. 42 has no direct equivalent provision in the Model Law. Nevertheless, this court has to carefully consider whether we should strictly construe and adhere to the principles of party autonomy, finality of arbitration awards and minimal court intervention rigidly on the facts of this appeal, even though in the context of a domestic arbitration. We have kept these issues uppermost in mind, since the grounds advanced by *Perwira Bintang* and addressed by the learned judge in the High Court, have brought these issues to the fore.

The High Court, in *Kluang Health Care Sdn Bhd v. Lee Yong Beng & Another Case* [2016] 1 CLJ 281, similarly held that a minimalist approach, as provided for in section 8, would be taken in applications to set aside. In this regard, the High Court, in *Kluang Heath Care supra* at paragraph 31, held:

> Section 8 of the Arbitration Act 2005 therefore clearly reminds the court of a minimalistic approach when it comes to arbitration and arbitral awards; and the courts have been extremely mindful of this caution. The parties have made their choice for dispute resolution loud and clear; and the court is merely giving effect to that choice. The court does not sit in appellate capacity over these arbitral awards; hence the applicant's complaints are a non-starter.

The Federal Court, in *Far East supra* at paragraph 115, held that, in the light of section 8, an award would not be set aside for an error of law on the face of the award, as there was no such ground in section 37:

> ... Since the setting aside of an award is a matter governed by the AA 2005, the court is permitted to set aside an award only in manner prescribed by the AA 2005. The court is not permitted to set aside an award in manner not prescribed by the AA 2005. 'Error of fact or law on the face of the award' is not prescribed as a ground for court intervention. Hence, under the AA 2005, there is no jurisdiction to set aside an award on the ground of 'error of fact or law on the face of the award'... .

Apart from a minimalist approach being taken when considering the grounds for setting aside an award under section 37(1), the High Court has also relied on section 8 to hold that the period for applying to set aside an award under section 37(4) is mandatory. The High Court has held that such a period is mandatory, despite the use of the word 'may' in section 37(4), which is usually interpreted to mean a statutory requirement is merely directory and not mandatory. The High Court also relied on the express exceptions in section 37(5) to interpret the period in section 37(4) as being mandatory, as such express exceptions would not be required unless the period was mandatory.

In this context, the High Court, in *JHW Reels Sdn Bhd v. Syarikat Borcos Shipping Sdn Bhd* [2013] 7 CLJ 249 at paragraph 19, held:

> Having considered the submissions and the provisions in our Arbitration Act, I tend to be of the view that on a proper reading of s. 37(4) the time limit imposed is mandatory. This view accords with the generally accepted view that under the Model Law, the time limit is strict and express power must be given under the law itself before the court can extend time. This view also accords with the principle of minimal intervention by the courts of law as strongly underlined in our s. 8 of the Act. Support for this strict reading can be found within the four corners of s. 37 itself. Unlike art. 34 of the Model Law which provides no exceptions, our s. 37(5) provides two exceptions ... .

The High Court, in *Kembang Serantau Sdn Bhd v. JEKS Engineering Sdn Bhd* [2016] 2 CLJ 427 at paragraphs 29 and 30, held:

> [29] ... Sometimes, as it is the case here, the sentence construction simply does not permit the use of the word 'shall'; and the word 'may' is then used. This usage does not detract from the basic object or intention of the provision which is to require mandatory or strict compliance. More important is to revert to the jurisprudence referred to in *Government of the Lao People's Democratic Republic v. Thai-Lao Lignite Co Ltd & Anor*, that the court adopts a minimalistic approach when dealing with arbitration and arbitration related matters. Such an approach does not spell a lack or want of jurisdiction of the court; but rather that the court declines jurisdiction in such matters; giving effect to and enforcing contractual obligations of the parties; the bedrock of the concept of party autonomy.
>
> [30] The significance of s. 8 cannot be overstated; that the court's intervention is only where it is so provided. The matters that may be referred to arbitration, matters concerning procedure and the conduct of arbitrations, the role of the arbitrators and the involvement of the court are all matters governed by the Act. Where the provisions do not provide for the intervention of the court, the court ought to decline intervention even if the court would treat the matter differently if it was a non-arbitration matter. I am aware that this is quite a liberal interpretation of s. 8 but given one of the basic principles of arbitration is party autonomy especially in international commercial arbitration, I am comfortable with that understanding. These matters are recognised as part of the bargain entered into out of the parties' own free will. Parliament has seen fit to treat this lot of cases in a different manner. Absent fraud and the complaints of corruption, I see no reason why such an approach is wrong or that the jurisprudence and approach of other like-minded Model Law jurisdictions are not persuasive.

These two judgments of the High Court are despite the earlier judgment of the Court of Appeal, in *Government of The Lao People's Democratic Republic v. Thai-Lao Liqnite Co Ltd & Anor* [2011] 1 LNS 1903 at paragraphs 14 and 16, where it was, *inter alia*, held that the courts had an unfettered discretion to extend time based on the use of the word 'may' in section 37(4) of the Arbitration Act 2005, and item 8 of the Schedule to the Courts of Judicature Act 1964, as well as Order 3 Rule 5(1) and (2) of the then Rules of the High Court 1980, which has been deleted in the Rules of Court 2012:

> [14] On the issue of jurisdiction, this court is in agreement with the learned High Court judge, that the High Court has the jurisdiction to grant an extension of time

to set aside an arbitral award, based on the wording of section 37(4) of the Arbitration Act 2005. The court has an unfettered discretion to grant an extension of time. The court may extend such period of time although the application is only made after the expiration of the said period. This is supported by item 8 of the schedule to Courts of Judicature Act 1964 which empowers the court to enlarge or abridge the time prescribed by any written law for doing any act or taking any proceeding, although any application therefore is not made until after the expiration of the time prescribed. Order 3 Rule 5(1) and (2) of the Rules of the High Court 1980, also provides for the same power to the court.

...

[16] In an application for extension of time of this nature, the court needs to consider the following factors:

(a) the length of the delay;
(b) the reason for the delay;
(c) the prospect of success; and
(d) the degree of prejudice to the Respondents if the applications is granted.

The High Court, in *Dato' Dr Muhammad Ridzuan Mohd Salleh & Anor v. Syarikat Air Terengganu Sdn Bhd* [2012] 6 CLJ 156 at paragraph 20, had similarly held that the courts retained a discretion to extend the time to apply to set aside an award:

It was submitted by the plaintiffs that this court has the discretion to extend time for the application to set aside an award beyond the 90 days period as the word used is 'may' and not 'shall'. I agree that there is a discernible difference between a peremptory 'shall' and a permissive 'may'. The former is mandatory whereas the latter is not. The former takes away any discretion for extension of time for instance whereas the latter leaves some room for the exercise of discretion to extend time in the context of a time frame to do a particular act. Parliament could have used the word 'shall' if they had wanted to as 'shall' is used in the context of a time frame to make an application in s. 42(2) of the Act ... .

However, the Court of Appeal allowed an appeal against this judgment, in *Syarikat Air Terengganu Sdn Bhd v. Dato Dr Muhammad Ridzuan Mohd Salleh & Anor* [2013] 1 LNS (0) 1. The grounds of the judgment of the Court of Appeal are not available.

It is submitted that the better view is that the courts do not have the inherent jurisdiction to extend the time for an application to set aside an award. Section 8 removes any such inherent jurisdiction. The judgment in *Thai-Lao Lignite supra* can perhaps best be explained as being prior to the amendment to section 8 and hence is unlikely to be still applicable.

[G]   Section 39

The High Court, in *Murray & Roberts Australia Pty Ltd v. Earth Support Company (SEA) Sdn Bhd* [2015] 6 CLJ 649 at paragraph 62, decided that, in the light of the minimalist approach provided for in section 8, a party could only rely on a ground set out in sections 39(1)(a) and (b) in resisting the enforcement of an award.

[H] Section 42

Section 42 of the Arbitration Act 2005 has been deleted by section 12 of the Arbitration (Amendment) (No 2) Act 2018. This section explains how the courts interpreted section 42 when it was in force, in the light of section 8.

As stated above, in the context of section 37, the High Court, in *Taman Bandar Baru supra* at paragraphs 19 and 20, decided that the courts would not ordinarily interfere with awards, in the light of section 8. This applies equally to section 42, which was also addressed in *Taman Bandar Baru supra*.

The Court of Appeal, in *SDA Architects v. Metro Millenium Sdn Bhd* [2014] 3 CLJ 632 at paragraph 47(a), affirmed the position taken in *Taman Bandar Baru supra* that section 8 almost prohibited intervention in relation to an award unless specifically allowed by section 42.

The High Court, in *Telekom Malaysia Berhad v. Eastcoast Technique (M) Sdn Bhd & Another Case* [2014] 6 CLJ 1067, similarly decided that, in the light of section 8, the courts would be reluctant and would rarely intervene under section 42. The High Court, in *Telekom Malaysia supra* at paragraph 40(iv), held:

> It must be said that the High Court is very slow, and indeed reluctant to intervene in arbitration awards. The cases in which the court exercises its powers of intervention are expressly restricted as provided by s. 8 of the Act. As such it is only in rare cases that the court will intervene in an arbitration award. But as set out in the test in relation to s. 42 above, a clear error of law or misapplication of the law to the fact, as in the instant case warrants a rectification of the law. This is also a case where the rights of one of the parties, ie, Telekom has been substantially affected. But of utmost importance is the need to ensure that the law in relation to undue influence remains intact and is correctly applied.

This is also reflected in the judgment of the High Court, in *Tune Insurance Malaysia Bhd & Anor v. Messrs K Sila Dass & Partners* [2015] 9 CLJ 93 at paragraph 63.

As stated above, the Court of Appeal, in *Perwira Bintang supra* at paragraph 10, decided that the minimalist approach prescribed by section 8 would be kept in mind when considering applications under section 37. This also applies to section 42. Perhaps, even more strongly, because section 42 is not found in the 1985 Model Law, as pointed out by the Court of Appeal.

However, the foregoing authorities should be read in the light of the judgment of the Federal Court, in *Far East supra* at paragraph 66, which emphasizes that section 42 should be applied as it stands without restrictions:

> The proper test is 'substantially affects the rights of one or more of the parties'. The test of illegality stated in *Cairns Energy*, of patent injustice stated in *Ajwa Food Industries* and of manifestly unlawful and or unconscionable or perverse in *Kerajaan Malaysia v. Perwira Bintang*, do not conform to s 42 which should be read as it stands. The language of a statute should not be substituted with other words ... .

[I] Section 44

The High Court, in *Magnificient Diagraph Sdn Bhd v. JWC Ariatektura Sdn Bhd* [2009] 1 LNS 622, decided that, in the light of section 8, the courts would not interfere with the determination of costs, which was within the jurisdiction of the arbitral tribunal under section 44. The High Court, in *Magnificient Diagraph supra* at paragraph 4(b), held:

> From the reading of the said section, it is clear that the jurisdiction to determine costs vests with the arbitrator. Courts will not ordinarily interfere with the jurisdiction of the arbitrator. In addition, in contrast to the Arbitration Act 1952, the AA 2005 restricts undue interference of the court in the arbitral process. This is reflected in section 8 of AA 2005 ... .

CHAPTER 2
Arbitration Agreement

9. *Definition and Form of Arbitration Agreement*

    (1) In this Act, 'arbitration agreement' means an agreement by the parties to submit to arbitration all or certain disputes which have arisen or which may arise between them in respect of a defined legal relationship, whether contractual or not.
    (2) An arbitration agreement may be in the form of an arbitration clause in an agreement or in the form of a separate agreement.
    (3) An arbitration agreement shall be in writing.
    (4) An arbitration agreement is in writing -
        (a) if its content is recorded in any form, whether or not the arbitration agreement or contract has been concluded orally, by conduct, or by other means; or
        (b) if it is contained in an exchange of statement of claim and defence in which the existence of an agreement is alleged by one party and not denied by the other.
    (4A) The requirement that an arbitration agreement be in writing is met by any electronic communication that the parties make by means of data message if the information contained therein is accessible so as to be useable for subsequent reference.
    (5) A reference in an agreement to a document containing an arbitration clause shall constitute an arbitration agreement, provided that the agreement is in writing and the reference is such as to make that clause part of the agreement.
    (6) For the purpose of this section, 'data message' means information generated, sent, received or stored by electronic, magnetic, optical or similar means, including, but not limited to, electronic data interchange, electronic mail, telegram, telex or telecopy.

§9.01 INTRODUCTION

Section 9 of the Arbitration Act 2005 defines an arbitration agreement, which is the premise of any arbitration, and the source of the arbitral tribunal's jurisdiction. Section 9(1) provides for the substance of an arbitration agreement, while sections 9(2)-(5) deal with matters of form.

Section 9 of the Arbitration Act 2005 reflects Option I Article 7 of the 2006 Model Law save for minor differences in drafting.

Option I Article 7 of the 2006 Model Law in turn reflects Article II(1) and (2) of the 1958 New York Convention, which provides:

1. Each Contracting State shall recognize an agreement in writing under which the parties undertake to submit to arbitration all or any differences which have arisen or which may arise between them in respect of a defined legal relationship, whether contractual or not, concerning a subject matter capable of settlement by arbitration.
2. The term 'agreement in writing' shall include an arbitral clause in a contract or an arbitration agreement, signed by the parties or contained in an exchange of letters or telegrams.

Option I Article 7 of 2006 Model Law is based on Articles II(1) and (2) of 1958 New York Convention because, by adopting the definition of an arbitration agreement in the Convention, there is an implied guarantee of recognition of such an arbitration agreement in the more than 150 countries that are party to the Convention.[1]

Section 9 of the Arbitration Act 2005 was amended by the Arbitration (Amendment) (No 2) Act 2018. The amendments were to substitute section 9(4) and insert the new sections 9(4A) and (6). These amendments were to bring the Arbitration Act 2005 in line with the 2006 Model Law. The amendments are primarily to allow for arbitration agreements that are recorded by way of electronic communication.

Prior to these amendments, section 9(4) read as follows:

An arbitration agreement is in writing where it is contained in –

(a) a document signed by the parties;
(b) an exchange of letters, telex, facsimile or other means of communication which provide a record of the agreement; or
(c) an exchange of statement of claim and defence in which the existence of an agreement is alleged by one party and not denied by the other.

§9.02 THE SUBSTANCE OF AN ARBITRATION AGREEMENT

Section 9(1) of the Arbitration Act 2005, which reflects Article 7(1) of Option I of the 2006 Model Law and Article II(1) of the 1958 New York Convention, deals with the substance of the arbitration agreement.

---

1. *See* Analytical Commentary, Article 7, commentary 1.

There are two elements to this definition of an arbitration agreement, which are that the arbitration agreement may cover all or certain dispute:

(1) which have arisen or may arise; and
(2) in respect of a defined legal relationship, whether contractual or not.

We will consider these two elements below.

[A] Existing and Future Disputes

The first element of the definition is intended to cover an arbitration agreement with respect to existing disputes (i.e., a *compromis*) as well as disputes that may arise in the future (i.e., a *clause compromissoire*). The second type of arbitration agreement is the one more frequently encountered in practice. Its inclusion in the definition in Article 7(1) of Option I of the 2006 Model Law is because at the time certain national laws did not recognize an arbitration agreement to refer future disputes to arbitration.[2] This type of arbitration agreement has, however, always been recognized in Malaysia.

[B] Defined Legal Relationship

The second element is that an arbitration agreement may cover a dispute arising from a defined legal relationship, whether contractual or not. This wide definition of an arbitration agreement in section 9(1), coupled with the absence of any restriction to commercial arbitration in section 3 and the broad concept or arbitrability in section 4, gives the Arbitration Act 2005 a particularly large scope.

An arbitration agreement may, therefore, cover disputes that arise from certain relations resembling those of contract under Part VI of the Contracts Act 1950, in particular with regards to disputes on claims for unjust enrichment and quantum meruit under section 71 of the Contracts Act 1950. Furthermore, an arbitration agreement may cover disputes arising from a claim in tort.

More widely still, the Analytical Commentary takes the position that 'defined legal relationship' should be given a wide interpretation so as to include all non-contractual commercial cases occurring in practice, as for example a third party interfering with contractual relations, an infringement of trademark or other unfair competition.[3] This would be even wider under the Arbitration Act 2005, as it is not restricted to commercial cases.

This wide definition of an arbitration agreement under section 9 of the Arbitration Act 2005 has been recognized by the courts. For example, the High Court, in *Taman Bandar Baru Masai Sdn Bhd v. Dindings Corporation Sdn Bhd* [2010] 5 CLJ 83 at paragraph 19, *inter alia*, held:

---

2. *See* Analytical Commentary, Article 7, commentary 2.
3. *See* Analytical Commentary, Article 7, commentary 4.

This section gives a wider meaning to the definition and form of arbitration agreement unlike the previous Act. For example, the inclusion of the phrase, 'whether contractual or not', in s. 9 gives wider jurisdiction to the arbitrator to even cover a dispute arising out of tort. In essence, this section gives or attempts to give wider jurisdiction to the arbitrator to deal with all issues relating to the parties which arises in consequence of the arbitration agreement. Thus, parties to the arbitration cannot complain that the arbitrator has exceeded his jurisdiction by simply relying on Pre-AA 2005 cases … .

Similarly, the High Court, in *Kelana Erat Sdn Bhd v. Niche Properties Sdn Bhd & Another Case* [2013] 4 CLJ 1172 at paragraphs 36 and 37, *inter alia*, held:

[36] The more expansive and extensive definition of an 'arbitration agreement' under the 2005 Act justifies such a practical approach in promoting arbitration as a one-stop centre to resolve any and every dispute arising out of or under an Agreement … .

[37] As can be seen the solutions to be provided by an arbitration under the 2005 Act are intended to be comprehensive and conclusive, full and final. The rather more restrictive definition of an 'arbitration agreement' under the 1952 Act in s. 2 thereof 'means a written agreement to submit present or future differences to arbitration, whether the arbitrator is named therein or not'.

The High Court has also given a broad meaning to linking words such as 'in relation to', 'in connection with' or 'arising under', which are frequently found in arbitration agreements. The High Court has decided that these words should be broadly interpreted to allow all disputes between the parties, including disputes as to the validity and enforceability of the contract, to be resolved by the arbitral tribunal.

In this context, the High Court, in *KNM Process Systems Sdn Bhd v. Mission Biofuels Sdn Bhd* [2012] MLJU 839 at paragraph 26, *inter alia*, held:

… I am of the considered view that the approach in *Fiona Trust* should be followed. Quite apart from the broad reading to be given to 'linking words' such as 'in relation to' or 'in connection with' or 'arising under', the principle that it is to be presumed that rational businessmen would intend to have the same forum decide disputes between themselves in respect of the same broad subject matter, unless they have expressed otherwise by clear language, has much to commend it both in terms of legal principle, logic, commercial sense and policy … .

This was followed by the High Court in *RUSD Investment Bank Inc & 2 Ors v. Qatar Islamic Bank & 2 Ors* [2015] 1 LNS 231 at paragraphs 13-13.1.

Similarly, the Court of Appeal, in *Protasco Bhd v. Tey Por Yee & Another Appeal* [2018] 5 CLJ 299 at paragraph 59, held that an arbitration agreement should be interpreted widely to include all disputes between the parties, including disputes involving conspiracy, fraud and a trust, as the parties, as rational business people, would have wanted all their disputes decided together:

The position is even clearer in Malaysia by reason of s 10 which grants a mandatory stay of court proceedings so as to give effect to the arbitration agreement. Applying *Fiona Trusts*, it follows that Protasco and PT ASU as rational business people would have wanted the entirety of their dispute determined by an arbitral tribunal and not just that part relating to the dispute arising out of the contract. In other words, both the conspiracy to injure/defraud and the imposition of a constructive trust dispute would be dealt with in any putative arbitration.

However, the High Court has also recognized that even the broad scope of an arbitration agreement has its boundaries. In this regard, the High Court has decided that an arbitration agreement would not be wide enough to cover disputes arising from an order made by the courts, in *MMIP Services Sdn Bhd v. Overseas Assurance Corporation (Malaysia) Bhd* [2016] 5 CLJ 637 at paragraph 53:

> ... the arbitration agreement applies solely in respect of 'all disputes, controversies or differences which may arise out of, in relation to or in connection with' the BPTA. The four questions concerned, among others, whether the defendant had assumed TIMB's liability under the High Court's confirmation order (question on effect of High Court's confirmation order).
>
> The question on effect of High Court's confirmation order, in my view, cannot come within the scope of the arbitration agreement. I refer to s. 9(1) of the AA ...
>
> It is clear that under s. 9(1) of the AA, the arbitration agreement concerns 'all or certain disputes which have arisen or which may arise between' the defendant and TIMB regarding the BPTA. The arbitration agreement cannot include the question on effect of High Court's confirmation order which involves a question of law in respect of the construction of the relevant provisions of the IA.

The Federal Court, in *Thai-Lao Lignite Co Ltd & Anor v. Government of the Lao People's Democratic Republic* [2017] 6 AMR 219 at paragraphs 188 and 194, also emphasized that an arbitration agreement was limited to disputes arising under the contract it referred to and that the powers of an arbitral tribunal are limited by the arbitration agreement:

> [188] The arbitration agreement provided 'In the event that a dispute arises out of this Agreement including any matter relating to the interpretation of this Agreement ... either party may submit the dispute to arbitration conducted in Malaysia at the Kuala Lumpur Regional Centre for Arbitration in accordance with the UNCITRAL Rules ... '. Article 1 of the PDA defined 'agreement' as 'this agreement'. The Appellants submitted 'the dispute [which arose] out of this Agreement' to arbitration. Ordinary contract law principles would read 'a dispute [which] arises out of this Agreement' as 'a dispute which arises out of the PDA'. US law should also read 'arises out of this contract' as arises 'out of the instant contract' and not some other contract ... Following the plain text, only a dispute that arose out of the PDA could be arbitrable under Article 14.1 of the PDA.
>
> ...
>
> [194] Article 14.1 of the PDA determined the jurisdiction that the parties gave to the Arbitral Tribunal ... .

[C] Capable of Settlement by Arbitration

Neither section 9(1) of the Arbitration Act 2005 nor Article 7(1) of Option I of the 2006 Model Law which it reflects includes the requirement for a 'subject matter capable of settlement by arbitration' in Article II(1) of the 1958 New York Convention.

The Arbitration Act 2005 deals with this issue separately under section 4 in the context of the arbitrability of the subject matter of arbitration, and reference should be made to §4.01-§4.03 *supra* with regard to this.

The 2006 Model Law does not address this expressly, as it was felt that if the subject matter was incapable of settlement by arbitration, the arbitration agreement would in any event be null and void under the applicable national law. Furthermore, it was felt that the provisions on setting aside and enforcement of an award in the 2006 Model Law adequately dealt with this issue.[4]

§9.03 THE FORM OF AN ARBITRATION AGREEMENT

Sections 9(2)-(6) of the Arbitration Act 2005, which reflect the last sentence of Article 7(1) and the whole of Articles 7(2) to (6) of Option I of the 2006 Model Law and Article II(2) of the 1958 New York Convention, provide for the form of the arbitration agreement.

Section 9(2) recognizes that an arbitration agreement may be in the form of either an arbitration clause or a separate agreement. In practice, an arbitration agreement that deals with future disputes would usually be in the form of a clause, while an arbitration agreement that deals with existing disputes will normally be in the form of a separate agreement.[5]

Sections 9(3)-(6) of the Arbitration Act 2005 essentially provide that an arbitration agreement must be in writing and then illustrates how this requirement might be achieved.

The requirement that the arbitration agreement be an 'agreement in writing' in Article II(2) of the 1958 New York Convention is preserved in Article 7(2) of Option I of the 2006 Model Law and section 9(3) of the Arbitration Act 2005.

The reason for this as stated above is to ensure the arbitration agreement and any subsequent award are recognized by parties to the 1958 New York Convention. If the requirements for an arbitration agreement were less stringent than the 1958 New York Convention in a particular state, there is a risk that an award made in that state may not be enforceable in another state that is party to the 1958 New York Convention.

For example, if State X recognized an oral arbitration agreement and State Y did not have any national law for the enforcement of an award other than the 1958 New York Convention, an award made in State X may not be enforceable in State Y.

This is the reason why the definition of an arbitration agreement in the 1985 Model Law cleaves closely to the 1958 New York Convention.

---

4. *See* Analytical Commentary, Article 7, commentary 5.
5. *See* Analytical Commentary, Article 7, commentary 3.

However, while following the 1958 New York Convention closely, the 2006 Model Law has also reduced the stringent requirement of the Convention to some extent by what may be termed as illustrations of agreements in writing. The three significant illustrations that relax the stringent requirement of an agreement in writing appear to be:

(1) a recording in any form;
(2) an exchange of pleadings where the existence of an arbitration agreement is not denied; and
(3) a reference in an agreement to a document containing an arbitration clause.

We will consider these three illustrations in §9.03[A], §9.03[B] and §9.03[C] *infra*.

[A] Recorded in Any Form

Section 9(4)(a) of the Arbitration Act 2005 provides for a broadest possible interpretation of the words an 'agreement in writing'. An agreement in writing is said to include an agreement eventually recorded in any form, regardless of whether the arbitration agreement or the contract in which it is contained was reached orally, by conduct or other means. In adopting such a broad interpretation, section 9(4)(a) of the Arbitration Act 2005 reflects Article 7(3) of Option I of the 2006 Model Law.

Section 9(4)(a) of the Arbitration Act 2005 and Article 7(3) of Option I of the 2006 Model Law expand on the definition in Article II(2) of the 1958 New York Convention quite considerably in this regard. The 1958 New York Convention only provides for an exchange of letters and telegrams.

The expansion in section 9(4)(a) of the Arbitration Act 2005 and Article 7(3) of Option I of the 2006 Model Law, in particular the use of the words 'recorded in any form', is intended to cover modern and future means of communication.[6]

The impetus for the use of these words came from the 1975 Montreal Protocol No 4 to the 1929 Warsaw Convention. Article 5(III) of the 1975 Montreal Protocol No 4 provides:

> Any other means which would preserve a record of the carriage to be performed may, with the consent of the consignor, be substituted for a delivery of an air way bill.

The 1975 Montreal Protocol No 4 had electronic communications in mind, as the aviation industry was one of the first to use this means of communication.

The Secretariat's Report at paragraph 21 confirms that the exchange need not be signed.

The High Court, in *Usahasama SPNB-LTAT Sdn Bhd v. Borneo Synergy (M) Sdn Bhd* [2009] 7 CLJ 779 at paragraphs 11-19, 25, 41, recognized that an arbitration

---

6. *See* Analytical Commentary, Article 7, commentary 7.

agreement could be contained in an exchange of letters under section 9(4)(b) of the Arbitration Act 2005, prior to the amendments by the Arbitration (Amendment) (No 2) Act 2018.

Somewhat unusually, in *Usahasama SPNB-LTAT supra*, the exchange of letters appears to have novated the underlying contract, including the arbitration agreement, to a third party. The High Court also appeared to decide that an assignment of money due under a contract to a third party would also include the assignment of the benefits of the arbitration clause in that contract. Further, the High Court appears to have decided that the conduct of the parties could be considered to determine whether a contract, including the arbitration clause it contained, had been novated.

[B] Exchange of Pleadings

Section 9(4)(b) of the Arbitration Act 2005 provides that an arbitration agreement is in writing, where it is not denied in an exchange of pleadings.

This reflects Article 7(5) of Option I of the 2006 Model Law. This also represents a significant expansion of the definition of an agreement in writing in Article II(2) of the 1958 New York Convention. There is no concept similar to this in the 1958 New York Convention.

Indeed, it is possible that section 9(4)(b) goes beyond an 'agreement in writing' envisaged by the 1958 New York Convention. This is because even an oral arbitration agreement may not be denied in an exchange of pleading and will therefore be recognized under the Arbitration Act 2005. But, such an oral agreement is unlikely to be recognized under the 1958 New York Convention. There may accordingly be difficulty in enforcing an award pursuant to such an oral agreement in States that do not have a national law that goes beyond the 1958 New York Convention.

[C] Reference in an Agreement

Section 9(5) of the Arbitration Act 2005 provides for a situation commonly encountered in practice, where an agreement refers to another document which includes an arbitration clause. The section provides that such a reference will amount to an arbitration agreement provided that:

(1) the agreement is in writing; and
(2) the reference is such as to make that clause a part of the agreement.

Section 9(5) of the Arbitration Act 2005 reflects Article 7(6) of Option I of the 2006 Model Law. There is no equivalent provision in the 1958 New York Convention. The 2006 Model Law included this provision to clarify the 1958 New York Convention, as divergent approaches were taken by national courts on this matter.[7]

---

7. *See* Analytical Commentary, Article 7, commentary 8.

It is important to bear in mind that, based on the words 'reference ... to a document containing an arbitration clause' in section 9(5) of the Arbitration Act 2005, which reflects Article 7(6) of Option I of the 2006 Model Law, the reference in the agreement needs only to be to the document, and no explicit reference to the arbitration clause in the document is required.[8]

The requirements for an arbitration agreement under section 9(5) of the Arbitration Act 2005 were lucidly explained by the High Court, in *Y & Y Property Development Sdn Bhd v. City-Lite Letrik Sdn Bhd* [2014] 1 LNS 1480 at paragraphs 21-23:

> [21] In order for an incorporation by reference to be effective under Section 9(5), the following conditions must be met:
>
> (a) There must be a reference in the subject agreement to another document that contains an arbitration clause;
>
> (b) That subject agreement must be in writing; and
>
> (c) The reference in the subject agreement must have the effect of making the arbitration clause part of the subject agreement.
>
> [22] It is not sufficient for an agreement to simply refer to another document that contains an arbitration clause. That reference must be of a nature that makes the arbitration clause part of the subject agreement – in other words, incorporating it by reference ... .
>
> [23] Note that there is no need for there to be a specific or express reference to the arbitration clause. It suffices if, for example, the subject agreement provides that the terms of another agreement will apply to the subject agreement, thereby incorporating by reference all the terms of that other agreement, including its arbitration clause.

The reference in an agreement to a document containing an arbitration clause occurs frequently in practice. We will consider below judgments that have determined whether such a reference is sufficient to meet the requirements of section 9(5) of the Arbitration Act 2005 set out above.

The High Court, in *Total Safe Sdn Bhd v. Tenaga Nasional Berhad & Anor* [2009] 1 LNS 420 at paragraph 8, dealt with a common situation in the construction industry, where a letter of acceptance refers to a tender, which in turn incorporates the invitation to tender. The High Court decided that the letter of acceptance did not incorporate the arbitration clause in the invitation to tender, as the letter of acceptance only referred to the tender and not the invitation to tender. Furthermore, the tender was not produced in evidence and the invitation to tender, which was produced, was incomplete and did not name the party that had issued the invitation to tender.

The High Court, in *Mersing Construction & Engineering Sdn Bhd v. Kejuruteraan Bintai Kindenko Sdn Bhd & 3 Ors* [2010] 1 LNS 793 at pages 7-9, dealt with a subcontract that incorporated the terms of the main contract. The main contract included the International Federation of Consulting Engineers (FIDIC, its acronym in French) General Conditions of Contract Edition 1999. The High Court decided that the subcontract did not incorporate the arbitration clause in the FIDIC General Conditions,

---

8. *See* Analytical Commentary, Article 7, commentary 8.

as only the appendix to the main contract was produced in evidence. This appendix only referred to a dispute adjudication board and not to arbitration.

The Court of Appeal, in *AGIBS Engineering & Construction Sdn Bhd v. Paragon Advance Solutions Sdn Bhd* [2011] 1 LNS 1019, decided that a letter of award for subcontract works in the construction industry, which provided that the subcontract shall be governed by the terms and conditions of the main contract, incorporated the arbitration clause in the main contract into the subcontract. The main contract appears to have been on the terms of the Public Works Department (PWD) form of contract. The Court of Appeal also decided that there was no requirement for the agreement to be signed. The Court of Appeal held, in *AGIBS Engineering supra* at paragraph 9, *inter alia*:

> In *Bina Puri Sdn Bhd v. EP Engineering Sdn Bhd & Anor* [2008] 3 CLJ 741; [2008] 3 MLJ 564, it was held by the Court of Appeal that it is trite law that an agreement to arbitrate must be in writing; but it is not a law that an agreement to arbitrate by itself must be signed. Suffice that there is such an agreement. Depending on the facts and circumstances of each case, an agreement to arbitrate in one contract may be incorporated in another contract. There may be express incorporation or incorporation by conduct. In the present case, the letter of award dated 13 November 2006 at p. 81 of the appeal records incorporates the terms and conditions of the main contract which provides for arbitration clause under cl. 54. The respondent is estopped from denying that it has no knowledge of the arbitration clause which is specifically stated in the main contract the terms and conditions of which have been expressly agreed to be bound with.

The Court of Appeal, in *Duta Wajar Sdn Bhd v. Pasukhas Construction Sdn Bhd & Anor* [2012] 4 CLJ 844 at paragraph 31, decided that an invitation to quote issued to a subcontractor in the construction industry, which referred to the main contract, did not incorporate the arbitration clause in the main contract, as there was no evidence of the terms of the main contract.

The Federal Court, in *Ajwa for Food Industries Co (MIGOP) Egypt v. Pacific Inter-Link Sdn Bhd* [2013] 7 CLJ 18, decided that unsigned contracts for the sale and purchase of palm oil products, which referred to the seller's standard terms and conditions that included an arbitration clause, incorporated an arbitration agreement by reference. The Federal Court held that the contracts for sale need not be signed as it could be inferred from the conduct of the parties that they had agreed to the terms of such contracts. This satisfied the requirement that there was an agreement in writing. The Federal Court also held that there was no need for the contracts for sale to specifically refer to the arbitration clause in the standard terms and conditions so long as the standard terms were incorporated. Further, the Federal Court held that there was no need for the standard terms referred to to be signed. The Federal Court, in *Ajwa for Food supra* at paragraphs 22, 25-27, *inter alia*, held:

> [22] On the question of whether the Sales Contracts are binding without the signature, we agree with the submission of the respondent that the Sales Contracts are not subject to any condition that they be signed before coming into effect. It is common knowledge that international agreements between parties doing business from different parts of the world ranging especially in international sales of goods

Chapter 2: Arbitration Agreement §9.03[C]

and charter parties are concluded and performed without the need for signatures, so long as parties have agreed on the terms. Likewise, the Sales Contracts setting out the agreed terms, despite the lack of signature as in the present case are valid and enforceable contracts ... .

...

[25] We are of the view that an arbitration agreement need not be signed ... [26] Section 9(5) of the Act therefore clarifies that the applicable contract law remains available to determine the level of consent necessary for a party to become bound by an arbitration made 'by reference'. Section 9(5) of the Act in our view addresses the situation where the parties, instead of including an arbitration clause in their agreement, include a reference to a document containing an arbitration agreement or clause. It also confirms that an arbitration agreement may be formed in that manner provided, firstly, that the agreement in which the reference is found meets the writing requirement and secondly, that the reference is such as to make that clause part of the agreement. The document referred to need not to be signed by the parties to the contract. See the case of *Astel-Peiniger Joint Venture v. Amos Engineering & Heavy Industries Co Ltd* [1994] 3 HKC 3281. We are of the view that the mere fact the arbitration clause is not referred to in the contract and that there is a mere reference to standard conditions which was neither accepted nor signed, is not sufficient to exclude the existence of the valid arbitration clause. There is no requirement that the arbitration agreement contained in the document must be explicitly referred to in the reference. The reference need only be to the document and no explicit reference to the arbitration clause contained therein is required.

[27] On the contention of the appellant that the Courts below had been swayed in coming to their conclusion and decision in favour of the respondent that there was an agreement to refer their disputes to arbitration based on past conduct and transactions of the parties, we are of the view the Courts below were not in error. Such previous conducts and transactions of the parties were merely considered for the purpose of imputing knowledge of the appellant of the provisions of the STC and the arbitration agreement ... .

The High Court, in *Y & Y Property supra* at paragraphs 28 and 29, decided that a subcontract for the performance of construction works, which refers to the main contract in its recitals, does not thereby incorporate the terms of the main contract including the arbitration clause therein.

The High Court, in *CLLS Power System Sdn Bhd v. Sara-Timur Sdn Bhd* [2015] 1 LNS 149 at paragraphs 23 and 24, decided that a letter of award issued by a main contractor to a subcontractor for the performance of construction works, which expressly referred to the Malaysian Institute of Architects (PAM, its acronym in Malay) form of contract did not incorporate the arbitration clause in the PAM form because the letter of award provided that the letter and the tender would form a binding contract until the formal contract documents were executed.

The Court of Appeal, in *Best Re (L) Limited v. Ace Jerneh Insurance Bhd* [2015] MLJU 0256, decided that the reference in an agreement to a document containing an arbitration clause need only be a reference to the document and need not be a reference to the arbitration clause in the document. The Court of Appeal, in *Best Re supra* at paragraph 43, *inter alia*, held:

On our part, whilst we are appreciative of the fact that the English s 6(2) and our s 9(5) of the Act are similarly worded, we must also consider the intention of the legislature when it decided to adopt the UNCITRAL Model Law in drafting s 9(5). As we have seen above, when the Model Law was proposed the working group on the Model Law made it very clear (and this is supported by the numerous comments by textbook writers and commentators on the Model Law) that it was not the intention of Article 7(2) of the Model Law to make it a necessary requirement to make specific reference to an arbitration clause or agreement in one document before it can be incorporated in another agreement. The working group on the Model Law made it very clear that a general reference would suffice to give effect to the incorporation. In our opinion the principle that the Court should attempt to give business efficacy in interpreting and construing a commercial document or contract, must be applied liberally to save the commercial transactions entered into between the parties and not to disrupt them. This does not, however, mean that the Court must disregard all established principles of construction of documents and contracts. What it means is that within the perimeter of these principles, the Court ought to be courageous enough to apply the principle in most beneficial way that would contribute to the efficacy of doing business and to ensure that the law stays abreast with the real commercial world. This is particularly important because the business community and the commercial people are normally innovative and creative. The ways of doing businesses keep changing and the law has to keep up with it lest it becomes obsolete and could hamper and stifle trade and commerce.

The High Court, in *NR Rubber Industries Sdn Bhd v. Sritong Rubber Latex Company Limited* [2017] 1 LNS 916 at paragraphs 43, 46-48, decided that a contract for the sale and purchase of latex, which referred to the standard form TRA/MRE Preserved NR Latex Contract (TRA is an acronym for the Thai Rubber Association, and MRE is an acronym for the Malaysian Rubber Exchange), did not incorporate the arbitration clause in the standard form, as the arbitration clause was not specifically incorporated. Furthermore, the arbitration clause in the standard form required the parties to the contract to elect between the arbitration rules of the Thai Rubber Arbitration Committee or the MRE and for this election to be stated in the contract for sale, which was not done.

The Federal Court, in *Arch Reinsurance Ltd v. Akay Holdings Sdn Bhd* [2018] MLJU 2117 at paragraphs 48 and 49, considered a subscription agreement, which included an arbitration clause, and referred to a charge to be issued as security. The Federal Court held that the subscription agreement and the charge were separate and distinct contracts. As such, the arbitration clause in the subscription agreement was not incorporated in the charge. The Federal Court relied on the entire agreement clause in the subscription agreement to hold that the arbitration clause in the subscription agreement was not intended to apply to the charge. The Federal Court also emphasized that it was not uncommon in commercial transactions to split multifaceted transactions into different agreements containing different dispute resolution provisions.

Chapter 2: Arbitration Agreement §10.01

10. *Arbitration Agreement and Substantive Claim Before Court*

(1) A court before which proceedings are brought in respect of a matter which is the subject of an arbitration agreement shall, where a party makes an application before taking any other steps in the proceedings, stay those proceedings and refer the parties to arbitration unless it finds that the agreement is null and void, inoperative or incapable of being performed.

(2) The court, in granting a stay of proceedings pursuant to subsection (1), may impose any conditions as it deems fit.

(2A) Where admiralty proceedings are stayed pursuant to subsection (1), the court granting the stay may, if in those proceedings property has been arrested or bail or other security has been given to prevent or obtain release from arrest—

(a) order that the property arrested be retained as security for the satisfaction of any award given in the arbitration in respect of that dispute; or

(b) order that the stay of those proceedings be conditional on the provision of equivalent security for the satisfaction of any such award.

(2B) Subject to any rules of court and to any necessary modifications, the same law and practice shall apply in relation to property retained in pursuance of an order under subsection (2A) as would apply if it were held for the purpose of proceedings in the court making the order.

(2C) For the purpose of this section, admiralty proceedings refer to admiralty proceedings under Order 70 of the Rules of the High Court 1980 [P.U. (A) 50/1980] and proceedings commenced pursuant to paragraph 24(b) of the Courts of Judicature Act 1964.

(3) Where the proceedings referred to in subsection (1) have been brought, arbitral proceedings may be commenced or continued, and an award may be made, while the issue is pending before the court.

(4) This section shall also apply in respect of an international arbitration, where the seat of arbitration is not in Malaysia.

§10.01 INTRODUCTION

Section 10 of the Arbitration Act 2005 provides for an important negative effect of an arbitration agreement, which is, that a court will not hear and determine a matter that is the subject of an arbitration agreement. Instead, the courts will stay the proceeding and refer the parties to arbitration.[9]

Section 10 of the Arbitration Act 2005 is similar to Article 8 of the 1985 Model Law, which provides:

Article 8. Arbitration agreement and substantive claim before court

---

9. *See* Analytical Commentary, Article 8, commentary 1.

(1) A court before which an action is brought in a matter which is the subject of an arbitration agreement shall, if a party so requests not later than when submitting his first statement on the substance of the dispute, refer the parties to arbitration unless it finds that the agreement is null and void, inoperative or incapable of being performed.
(2) Where an action referred to in paragraph (1) of this article has been brought, arbitral proceedings may nevertheless be commenced or continued, and an award may be made, while the issue is pending before the court.

In particular section 10(1) reflects Article 8(1) save that:

(1) the word 'action' has been substituted with 'proceeding', the latter being broader;
(2) the words 'in a matter' have been substituted with 'in respect of a matter', the latter again appearing broader;
(3) the word 'request' has been substituted with the word 'application', in conformity with Malaysian civil procedure rules in the Rules of Court 2012;
(4) the words 'not later than when submitting his first statement on the substance of the dispute' have been substituted with 'before taking any other steps in the proceedings'. The words used in the 1985 Model Law provide greater certainty. There remains considerable debate on the meaning of the words 'other steps' used in the Arbitration Act 2005;
(5) the words 'stay those proceedings and' have been inserted in the Arbitration Act 2005 before the words 'refer the parties to arbitration'. Again, this is due to Malaysian civil procedure rules, where the courts would stay the proceedings in court and refer the parties to arbitration; and
(6) previously, section 10(1)(b) of the Arbitration Act 2005 provided:

'that there is in fact no dispute between the parties with regard to the matters to be referred.'
This subsection is not found in Article 8(1) of the 1985 Model Law and was deleted by the Arbitration (Amendment) Act 2011.

Section 10(2) of the Arbitration Act 2005 is not found in the 1985 Model Law. This section allows the courts to impose conditions when granting a stay.

Sections 10(2A)-(2C) were introduced by the Arbitration (Amendment) Act 2011 to address concerns of the admiralty bar. These new provisions allow the courts to order the detention of property or provision of security pending the determination of disputes in admiralty proceedings. There are no equivalent provisions in the 1985 Model Law.

Section 10(3) of the Arbitration Act 2005 closely resembles Article 8(2) of the 1985 Model Law. This provision confirms that irrespective of proceedings commenced in court, arbitral proceedings may be commenced, continued and concluded. This is to reduce the risk of dilatory tactics of a party breaching his agreement to arbitrate.[10]

---

10. *See* Analytical Commentary, Article 5, commentary 5.

Section 10(4) was introduced by the Arbitration (Amendment) Act 2011. This provision clarifies that a court may stay proceedings in favour of a foreign arbitration with a seat outside Malaysia. This new provision serves a similar purpose as Article 1(2) of 1985 Model Law, which makes an exception for Article 8. This new provision clarified the law, as it had previously been argued that section 10 did not apply to foreign arbitrations with a seat outside Malaysia.[11]

While sections 10(1) and (3) of the Arbitration Act 2005 resemble Article 8(1) and (2) of the 1985 Model Law, the provisions of the 1985 Model Law, in turn, reflect Article II(3) of the 1958 New York Convention.

Article II(3) of the 1958 New York Convention provides:

> The court of a Contracting State, when seized of an action in a matter in respect of which the parties have made an agreement within the meaning of this article, shall, at the request of one of the parties, refer the parties to arbitration, unless it finds that the said agreement is null and void, inoperative or incapable of being performed.

Article 8 of the 1985 Model Law, which was closely modelled on Article II(3) of the 1958 New York Convention, made two significant additions to the Convention.

First, the 1985 Model Law included a time element to the request by a party to have the matter referred to arbitration. The time element included in Article 8(1) of the 1985 Model Law is that such a request must be made by a party no later than when submitting his first statement on the substance of the dispute. There is a similar provision in section 10(1) of the Arbitration Act 2005, which requires an application to be made before a party takes any other step in the proceedings. The failure by a party to make such a request or application would result in the party being unable to invoke the arbitration agreement at a later phase of the proceedings.[12]

Second, the 1985 Model Law introduced Article 8(2), which is not found in the 1958 New York Convention. Section 10(3) of the Arbitration Act 2005 reflects Article 8(2) of the 1985 Model Law. As stated above, these provisions allow the arbitral proceedings to continue, despite pending proceedings in court.

§10.02 GENERAL SCHEME

The general scheme of section 10(1) of the Arbitration Act 2005 is that:

(1) the applicant must show:
 (a) the existence of an arbitration agreement; and
 (b) that the proceedings in court are in respect of a matter that is subject to such an arbitration agreement.
(2) the court must then stay such proceedings, unless;
(3) the respondent shows that:
 (a) the applicant has taken a step in such proceedings;

---

11. *See Innotec Asia Pacific Sdn Bhd v. Innotec GmbH* [2008] 8 CLJ 304.
12. *See* Analytical Commentary, Article 8, commentaries 3 and 4.

(b) the arbitration agreement is null and void, inoperative or incapable of being performed.

The general scheme of section 10(1) was explained by the Court of Appeal, in *Lembaga Pelabuhan Kelang v. Kuala Dimensi Sdn Bhd & Anor Appeal* [2010] 9 CLJ 532 at paragraph 20:

> In considering the respective burden of proof under s. 6 (Singapore) in *Tjong Very Sumito supra*, VK Rajah JA opined as follows:
> In order to obtain a stay of proceedings in favour of arbitration under s. 6, the party applying for a stay (the applicant) must first show that he is party to an arbitration agreement, and that the proceedings instituted involve a matter which is the subject of the [arbitration] agreement. In other words, the applicant has to show that the proceedings instituted fall within the terms of the arbitration agreement. If the applicant can show that there is an applicable arbitration agreement, then the court must grant a stay of proceedings unless the party resisting the stay can show that one of the statutory grounds for refusing a stay exists, ie, that the arbitration agreement is 'null and void, inoperative or incapable of being performed'.

§10.03 SPECIFIC PROVISIONS

Due to the significance of section 10, we will now consider the specific provisions of this section.

[A] 'A Court ...'

It is important to note that, unlike the other provisions of the Arbitration Act 2005 that refer specifically to the High Court, section 10(1) refers more generally to 'court'.

The word 'court' is broad enough to include any court, which would include the Magistrates Court and the Sessions Court, apart from the High Court, in which the proceedings may have been commenced. A party may accordingly apply for a stay in any court in which the proceedings were commenced.

This was recognized by the High Court, in *Uba Urus Asia Sdn Bhd v. Quirk & Associates Sdn Bhd & Anor* [2016] 4 CLJ 468 at paragraph 37, where it was held:

> Unlike ss. 11, 15, 18, 29, 37, 38, 39, 41, 42, 43, 44, 45, 46 and 50 of the Arbitration Act 2005, where the word 'court' is specifically identified as the 'High Court', the words used in s. 10 is 'a court'. Arguably, this will include the Magistrates and Sessions courts as the term 'court' is not defined in s. 2 of the Arbitration Act 2005; but the term 'High Court' is. With the amendments to the financial limits of the subordinate courts, applications for orders under s. 10 can properly come within the jurisdiction of the subordinate courts.

[B] '... Before Which Proceedings Are Brought ...'

Again, the word 'proceedings' used in section 10(1) is general. Proceedings would include any claim, action or suit, as well as originating summons. Essentially, every means of commencing proceedings in the courts is covered.

This was recognized by the High Court, in *ZAQ Construction Sdn Bhd & Anor v. Putrajaya Holdings Sdn Bhd* [2014] 4 CLJ 895 at paragraph 37, where it was held:

> It is also observed that the term 'proceedings' is used in sub-s. 10(1) as opposed to 'claim, action or suit'. This term may be said to include any claim, action or suit as well as any originating summons filed whether under the Rules of Court 2012 or under s. 50 of Act 646.

There is a continuing debate as to whether the word 'proceedings' may be broad enough to include a winding-up petition. The High Court, in *NFC Labuan Shipleasing I Ltd v. Semua Chemical Shipping Sdn Bhd* [2017] 1 LNS 943 at paragraphs 34 and 35, held that a winding-up petition was sui generis and did not amount to a substantive claim before the court within the meaning of section 10. As such, an application to stay such a petition pending arbitration would not be allowed:

> [34] It bears repetition that the petition is sui generis as winding-up proceedings feature a distinct characteristic of a wider legal process. Even though it may be initiated by a single petitioning creditor, upon the granting of the order for winding-up, the process which enables what may be regarded as the collective enforcement of proven debts of the company will be activated, for the benefit of not just the petitioner but instead the general body of unsecured creditors, all on pari passu basis. It must be recognized that a winding-up petition is not a claim for payment. It is, instead, what may be regarded as a class action in the public interest which brings into operation the statutory regime for realising and distributing the assets of a company for the benefit of its creditors. This is manifestly not the objective of having the alleged dispute referred to arbitration. The reliefs are certainly not the same and the end results, of a successful civil dispute subject to arbitration and a winding-up petition, if granted, could not be more different and are miles apart.

> [35] A stay application of a winding-up petition pending arbitration could thus be viewed to be of doubtful relevance and validity. A winding-up petition is not in the nature of a substantive claim before the Court that is contemplated by Section 10 of the AA. Section 10 talks about a matter in a substantive claim, as stated in its heading. But a winding-up process is essentially a proceeding to wind up for the inability to pay debt, as was alleged in this instant case. The respondent, in response, need only to show the debt to be disputed and to rebut presumption of insolvency. The affidavit in opposition is designed to help a debtor to achieve this.

However, the High Court, in *Goh Nguang Chian v. Dynapack Eoss Packaging Sdn Bhd* [2018] MLJU 885 at paragraphs 46 and 48, held that it was not unusual for a winding-up petition to be stayed under section 10 of the Arbitration Act 2005. The High Court emphasized that a dispute remains arbitrable, although winding-up is not available as a remedy before an arbitrator:

[46] The staying of petitions presented under Section 466 of the CA 2016 (then Section 218 of the Companies Act 1965) on the basis of an arbitration agreement is not unusual:

...

[48] The disputes underlying a petition to wind up a company are arbitrable. The fact that a remedy may not be available to an arbitrator is not a ground to render a dispute non-arbitrable. As such, it is clear that the Substantive Dispute is arbitrable in Malaysia.

The High Court, in *Goh supra* did not refer to the earlier judgment of the High Court, in *NFC Labuan supra*. Subsequently, the High Court, in *Awangsa Bina Sdn Bhd v. Mayland Avenue Sdn Bhd* (HC, 2 May 2019) at paragraphs 12, 25 and 28, considered the conflicting judgments in *NFC Labuan* and *Goh supra*, and followed *NFC Labuan supra*. The High Court held that section 10 of the Arbitration Act 2005 did not apply to a winding-up petition. However, the High Court emphasized that the courts retained a discretion to dismiss a winding-up petition, where there was an arbitration agreement between the parties provided that there was a prima facie dispute between the parties. The High Court held that a prima facie dispute arises when a claim is denied:

[12] I am inclined to agree with the decision in NFC Labuan that Section 10 of the Arbitration Act does not apply to winding up petitions ... .

...

[25] Applying the decisions in *Salford Estates*, *Bdg v Bdh* and the *Lasmos* case, I should ascertain whether there is a prima facie dispute of the debt claimed by the Petitioner ... .

...

[28] However, applying the lower threshold of merely showing a prima facie dispute, since the debt here is the subject matter of an arbitration clause, I am of the view that the Respondent has discharged the burden of showing a prima facie dispute, bearing in mind that a denial of the indebtedness constitutes a dispute. The merits or otherwise of the dispute are matters to be decided by the arbitrator and not by this Court and the Respondent had given notice of arbitration to the Petitioner. Accordingly, I would not stay the winding up petition pending arbitration under section 10 of the Arbitration Act 2005 but, in the exercise of my discretion under section 465 of the Companies Act 2016, I would dismiss the winding up petition on the ground that the Respondent has shown the existence of a prima facie dispute which ought to be referred to arbitration.

[C] '... In Respect of a Matter Which is the Subject of an Arbitration Agreement ...'

The key term here is 'arbitration agreement'. The meaning of these words is set out in section 9 of the Arbitration Act 2005, which has been considered in §9.01, §9.02 and §9.03 *supra*. In the absence of an arbitration agreement, the courts will not grant a stay under section 10.

For example, the High Court, in *Mersing Construction & Engineering Sdn Bhd v. Kejuruteraan Bintai Kindenko* [2010] 1 LNS 793 at page 10, after finding that an

Chapter 2: Arbitration Agreement §10.03[C]

arbitration agreement had not been incorporated in a building subcontract between the parties went on to hold that:

> Section 10(1) of the abovementioned Act clearly provides that the matter must be the subject of an arbitration agreement before the Court can consider an application for a stay of proceedings. Under the said Act arbitration agreement means '… an agreement by the parties to submit to arbitration all or certain disputes which have arisen or which may arise between them in respect of a defined legal relationship, whether contractual or not.' The arbitration agreement may be in the form of an arbitration clause in an agreement or in the form of a separate agreement. In the instant case the Appendix to the Main Contract only makes reference to a Dispute Adjudication Board for settlement of dispute. There is no specific or express provision that the dispute will be referred to arbitration.

[1] Arbitration and Exclusive Jurisdiction Clauses

An issue that has frequently been considered by the courts is the apparent contradiction between an exclusive jurisdiction clause and an arbitration clause.

In this context, the Court of Appeal, in *Lembaga Pelabuhan Kelang v. Kuala Dimensi Sdn Bhd & Another Appeal* [2010] 9 CLJ 532, declined to grant a stay, after finding that an arbitration clause in a principal development agreement had been superseded by a clause giving exclusive jurisdiction to the courts in a subsequent supplemental agreement. Furthermore, the court decided that the use of the word 'may' in the arbitration clause meant that the parties might opt for civil proceedings. The Court of Appeal, in *Lembaga Pelabuhan Kelang supra* at paragraph 30, *inter alia*, held:

> … unlike the peremptory word 'shall', the permissive word 'may' used in the arbitration clause ie, cl. 11.1 of DA1 is capable of readily abandoning the discretion to refer to arbitration, and opting for litigation instead, as expressed and contractually agreed by the parties in the supplemental agreements DA2 and DA3 via 'the submission to court jurisdiction clauses' that 'the parties hereto hereby submit to the jurisdiction of the courts of Malaysia in all matters connected with the obligation and liabilities of the parties under this supplemental agreement.' This construction is further strengthened when the parties have contractually agreed that the principal agreement DA1 including the word 'may' in the arbitration clause shall be read subject to 'the submission to court jurisdiction clauses' in the supplemental agreements which shall prevail. The irresistible conclusion is that while it is true the parties had originally intended to have the discretion to refer their disputes to arbitration, that discretion has been subsequently displaced, compromised or abandoned when they have expressly submitted to the jurisdiction of the court ie, to litigate all matters connected with the obligation and liabilities of the parties under DA2 and DA3 to which DA1 is subject. The High Court actions are therefore within the jurisdiction of our High Court.

Similarly, the High Court, in *Sime Engineering Sdn Bhd v. Ahmad Zaki Resources Berhad* [2011] MLJU 370 at page 11, considered a joint venture agreement that included an arbitration clause, which provided that disputes may be referred to arbitration. The joint venture agreement also provided that the parties would submit to the non-exclusive jurisdiction of the Malaysian courts. The High Court, followed *Lembaga Pelabuhan Kelang supra*, and declined to grant a stay on the grounds that the arbitration clause and the court jurisdiction clause were contradictory and, in any event, the arbitration clause was permissive.

However, the High Court, in *Majlis Perbandanan Alor Gajah v. Sunrise Teamtrade Sdn Bhd* [2013] 7 CLJ 872 at paragraphs 14 and 15, also considered a joint venture agreement that had an arbitration clause that provided that disputes may be referred to arbitration after termination. In addition, the joint venture agreement provided for the exclusive jurisdiction of the courts and for disputes that could not be amicably resolved to be referred to the courts during the progress of the agreement. The High Court held that these provisions were complimentary. The exclusive jurisdiction given to the courts was for the purpose of supervising the arbitration, with the courts having a role to play in relation to arbitration under the Arbitration Act 2005. The provisions in the joint venture agreement that allowed for reference of disputes to the courts and to arbitration were not contradictory, as the former was for disputes that arose during the progress of the agreement while the latter was for disputes arising from termination. The High Court also held that the use of the word 'may' in the arbitration clause meant that once one of the parties had opted for arbitration, arbitration was mandatory. In this regard, the High Court distinguished *Lembaga Pelabuhan Kelang supra* on the grounds that in that case the supplemental agreement clearly superseded the principal agreement. The High Court accordingly granted a stay.

Similarly, the High Court, in *Hamidah Fazilah Sdn Bhd v. Universiti Tun Hussein Onn Malaysia (UTHM)* [2017] 7 MLJ 274 at paragraph 54, held that there was no contradiction between an exclusive jurisdiction clause and an arbitration clause in the PWD standard form of building contract, as parties to an arbitration required the courts for assistance:

> As we are all aware, when it comes to certain reliefs in aid of arbitration and more so when it comes to setting aside and enforcement of an arbitral award, the parties seeking such reliefs would still have to come to the relevant court for assistance. To avoid bickering over what law to apply and which court to apply for such reliefs, parties have addressed this issue at the outset in governing law clause. As both the parties are incorporated in Malaysia and carrying out their business here and as the project is here, it makes every sense for the laws of Malaysia to apply. Parties have agreed to submit to the exclusive jurisdiction of the courts of Malaysia where there is a need to come to the Malaysian courts to apply for interim measures such as an injunction for instance under s 11 of the Arbitration Act 2005 or for setting aside the award under s 37 or to refer a question of law under s 42 or under s 38 for enforcement of the arbitral award.

Subsequently, the High Court, in *Thien Seng Chan Sdn Bhd v. Teguh Wiramas Sdn Bhd & Anor* [2017] MLJU 1117 at paragraph 59 and *Maya Maju (M) Sdn Bhd v. Putrajaya Homes Sdn Bhd* [2018] MLJU at paragraphs 54 and 56, followed *Hamidah Fazilah supra*. It is submitted that the better approach is that an exclusive jurisdiction clause and an arbitration clause are complimentary. The exclusive jurisdiction clause is meant to fix the court that has supervisory jurisdiction over the arbitration for

Chapter 2: Arbitration Agreement §10.03[C]

purposes of interim measures, setting aside, etc. and is not meant to negate or contradict the arbitration clause.

[2] Linking Words in an Arbitration Clause

Apart from this issue, the courts have also considered how broad an arbitration agreement is. In this context, the High Court, in *KNM Process Systems Sdn Bhd v. Mission Biofuels Sdn Bhd* [2013] 1 CLJ 993 at paragraph 26, followed the judgment of the House of Lords, in *Fiona Trust & Holding Corporation and Others v. Privalov and Others* [2007] 4 All ER 951, and it held that 'linking words' such as 'in relation to', 'in connection with' or 'arising under' commonly found in an arbitration clause should be given a broad reading, allowing all disputes to be resolved by a single tribunal in accordance with the presumption that a rational businessman would desire this. In the light of this broad reading of the arbitration clause, the stay was allowed by the High Court.

However, the boundaries of an arbitration agreement are recognized as the High Court, in *MMIP Services Sdn Bhd v. Overseas Assurance Corporation (Malaysian) Bhd* [2016] 5 CLJ 637 at paragraph 54, held that section 10 of the Arbitration Act 2005 would apply to questions on the effect of a court order, which were not covered by the arbitration agreement.

Similarly, the Federal Court, in *Thai-Lao Lignite Co Ltd & Anor v. Government of the Lao People's Democratic Republic* [2017] 6 AMR 219 at paragraph 188, interpreted the words 'arise out of this agreement' in an arbitration agreement as meaning that only disputes arising from the subject contract may be referred to arbitration.

[3] Jurisdictional Issues

The courts have leaned in favour of arbitration by holding that any dispute as to jurisdiction should be determined by the arbitral tribunal under section 18 rather than by the courts under section 10.

The Federal Court, in *Press Metal Sarawak Sdn Bhd v. Etiqa Takaful Bhd* [2016] 5 MLJ 417 at paragraph 38, recognized the competency of an arbitral tribunal to rule on its own jurisdiction:

> The court must acknowledge the competency of an arbitral tribunal to decide on its own jurisdiction without interference. The intention of Parliament is clear. Reading ss 8, 10 and 18 together would indicate that Parliament has given the arbitral tribunal much wider jurisdiction and powers; and such powers extend to cases where even its own jurisdiction or competence or the scope of its authority, or the existence or validity of the arbitration agreement or clause, is challenged. To comply with the requirements of s 10(1) the court should restrict its enquiry only to the issue of whether there is in existence a binding arbitration agreement or clause between the parties and whether the arbitration agreement or clause is null and void, inoperative or incapable of being performed. If the court is satisfied that the arbitration agreement or clause does not fall into any of these exceptions, it must order a stay of proceedings and refer the matter to arbitration.

[D]   '... Shall ...'

It is now settled that the use of the imperative 'shall' in section 10(1) of the Arbitration Act 2005 means that it is mandatory for the courts to grant a stay once the requirements of the section are met. The courts do not have the discretion as to whether to grant a stay and, instead, must do so once these requirements are met.

There are several authorities for this proposition; the appellate authorities are considered below.

The Federal Court, in *Press Metal supra* at paragraph 32, confirmed that:

> The clear effect of the present s 10(1) of the 2005 Act is to render a stay mandatory if the court finds that all the relevant requirements have been fulfilled; while under s 6 of the repealed 1952 Act, the court had a discretion whether to order a stay or otherwise.

Similarly, the Federal Court, in *Far East Holdings Bhd & Anor v. Majlis Ugama Islam dan Adat Resam Melayu Pahang and other appeals* [2018] 1 MLJ 1 at paragraph 108 and *Arch Reinsurance Ltd v. Akay Holdings Sdn Bhd* [2018] MLJU 2117 at paragraph 54, reaffirmed the position taken in *Press Metal supra*.

The Court of Appeal, in *Renault SA v. Inokom Corporation Sdn Bhd & Anor and Other Applications* [2010] 5 CLJ 32 at paragraph 22, *inter alia*, held:

> The provision on stay of court proceedings pending arbitration is found in s. 10 of the 2005 Act. The requirement to stay is mandatory ... .

Similarly, the Court of Appeal, in *Albilt Resources Sdn Bhd v. Casaria Construction Sdn Bhd* [2010] 7 CLJ 785 at paragraph 43, held:

> ... Suffice for me to say that s. 10 of the same Act imposes a mandatory obligation to stay the proceedings and refer the parties to arbitration. The word 'shall' that appears in s. 10 of the same Act must necessarily mean 'directory' or 'mandatory' ... .

The Court of Appeal, in *Lembaga Pelabuhan Kelang v. Kuala Dimensi Sdn Bhd & Another Appeal* [2010] 9 CLJ 532 at paragraphs 18 and 19, confirmed that a stay must be granted mandatorily but listed out exceptions that are not exhaustive in the following terms:

> [18] In my view, the general rule under s. 10(1) is that where proceedings are brought in respect of a matter which is the subject of an arbitration agreement, the peremptory word 'shall' makes it mandatory for the court to grant a stay of those proceedings and refer the parties to arbitration ... .
>
> [19] In exceptional circumstances (the categories of which are not closed), stay may be refused. Illustrations include:
> (1) Under s. 10(1)(a), where the court (be it noted, not the arbitral tribunal) finds that the agreement is null and void, inoperative or incapable of being performed ... .
> (2) '[W]here the party applying for a stay has waived or may be estopped from asserting his rights to insist on arbitration, such as where the parties have agreed subsequently that disputes may be resolved by litigation. The facts of

such a case would fall to be decided in accordance with the usual contractual analysis of estoppel and or waiver on the basis that the arbitration agreement is "inoperative," see s. 6(2) of the IAA. There are no impediments, under the IAA, preventing the parties to an arbitration agreement from agreeing to resolve the matter in any manner that they may find more convenient. In such a case, the agreement to arbitrate will be treated as having been waived as the parties are free to modify their agreement at any time': per VK Rajah JA in *Tjong Very Sumito, supra*, in para [54].
(3) (a) If one of the parties named in the legal proceedings is not a party to the arbitration agreement;
  (b) If the alleged dispute does not come within the terms of the arbitration agreement; or
  (c) If the application is out of time ... .
(4) Where a party has taken any other steps in the court proceedings, as stated in s. 10(1).

The Court of Appeal, in *Kenneth Chung Kuo Ting & Anor v. John Tsang Shing Chi & Anor* [2015] 1 CLJ 346 at paragraph 27, similarly held that a stay was mandatory in the following terms:

Section 10 of the Arbitration Act 2005, makes it mandatory for the court to stay proceedings and to refer the parties to arbitration for determination of a dispute if all the requirements thereunder are satisfied ... .

Therefore, it is well established that it is mandatory for the courts to grant a stay under section 10(1) once the requirements of this section are met and provided none of the exceptions apply.

[E] '... Where a Party Makes an Application Before Taking Any Other Steps in the Proceedings ...'

The key words here are 'steps in the proceedings'. A party must apply for a stay before taking any such steps.

There remains some degree of uncertainty as to what precisely amounts to such steps. This uncertainty is unfortunate and could perhaps have been avoided if the Arbitration Act 2005 had adopted the words used in the 1985 Model Law, i.e. 'first statement on the substance of the dispute', which appear clearer and less ambiguous than 'other steps'.

The test as to what amounts to such a step is perhaps best explained by the Court of Appeal, in *Comos Industry Solution GmbH v. Jacob & Toralt Consulting Letrikon Sdn Bhd & Ors* [2011] 1 LNS 1770 at paragraph 14:

Our s.10 is differently worded. But the principles are the same. Whether an action amounts to a step in the proceedings is determined by the nature of the action and whether it indicates an unequivocal intention to proceed with the suit and to abandon the right to refer the dispute to arbitration. An application is not a step in the proceedings, if it does not express the willingness of the defendant to go along with the determination of the courts instead of arbitration. A defendant who has specifically stated in the application or supporting affidavit that he intends to seek a stay is not estopped from asserting his right to invoke arbitration. An application, which is made in the event that the specific application for a stay is unsuccessful, is not a step in the proceedings.

Essentially, the question is whether a party has shown an unequivocal intention to proceed with the suit and abandon the right to refer the dispute to arbitration. This question will in turn depend on the action taken by the party.

We will consider below various actions taken by parties and whether these have amounted to steps in the proceedings.

[1]   Appearance

The question of whether the filing of an unconditional appearance amounted to a step in the proceedings under section 6 of the Arbitration Act 1952, which is the precursor to section 10 of the Arbitration Act 2005, was finally settled, after much uncertainty, by the Federal Court, in *Sanwell Corp v. Trans Resources Corp Sdn Bhd & Anor* [2002] 3 CLJ 213. The Federal Court decided that the filing of an unconditional appearance did not amount to a step in proceedings, as it was a mandatory step required by the Rules of the High Court 1980, the civil procedure rules applicable at the time.

Unfortunately, the question of whether the filing of an unconditional appearance amounts to a step in the proceedings has been reopened since the coming into force of the Arbitration Act 2005 on the grounds that section 10 differs from its precursor, section 6 of the Arbitration Act 1952.

In this regard, the High Court, in *Winsin Enterprise Sdn Bhd v. Oxford Talent (M) Sdn Bhd* [2010] 3 CLJ 634 at paragraph 17, appeared to suggest:

> ... that because of the language deployed in s 10(1) where stay is now mandatory ... applicants who seek to rely on an arbitration agreement must make the application for stay promptly, even before the filing of an appearance.

However, the High Court, in *Busuk Jamilah bte Salim & 70 Ors v. Siti Rahfizah Binti Mihaldin & Anor* [2009] LNS 1358 at pages 6 and 7, held that the filing of an unconditional appearance did not amount to a step in the proceedings. In this regard, the High Court followed *Sanwell Corp supra*.

Similarly, the High Court, in *Life Plaza Sdn Bhd v. Pasukhas Construction Sdn Bhd* [2012] 5 CLJ 120 at paragraph 23, held based on *Sanwell Corp supra* that the filing of an unconditional appearance does not amount to a step in the proceedings.

The Rules of Court 2012 came into force on 1 August 2012. These new rules have abolished the provisions on conditional appearance in Order 12 Rule 6. Further, the new rules provide, by Order 12 Rule 9 and Rule 10(2):

> Appearance not to constitute a waiver (O. 12 r. 9)
>
> 9. The appearance by a defendant in an action shall not be treated as a waiver by him of any irregularity in the writ or service thereof or in any order giving leave to serve the writ out of the jurisdiction or extending the validity of the writ for the purpose of service.
>
> ...

Chapter 2: Arbitration Agreement §10.03[E]

Dispute as to jurisdiction (O. 12 r. 10)

...

(2) A defendant who wishes to contend that the Court should not assume jurisdiction over the action on the ground that Malaysia is not the proper forum for the dispute shall enter an appearance and, within the time limited for serving a defence, apply to the Court for an order to stay the proceedings.

Therefore, it appears that the filing of an appearance under the Rules of Court 2012 will not amount to a step in the proceedings. This was confirmed by the High Court, in *Thien Seng supra* at paragraphs 20 and 21, where it was, *inter alia*, held:

> [20] At the outset, let it be recorded that it is not in dispute that D1 had not taken any other steps in the litigation proceedings other than entering its appearance. That is acceptable for without it the Plaintiff may take a judgment in default of appearance. The Federal Court in *Sanwell Corp v. Trans Resources Corp Sdn Bhd & Anor* [2002] 2 MLJ 625 observed as follows at p 638:
>> We reaffirm that *Sime Axa Assurance* correctly decided that an entry of an unconditional appearance does not constitute a step in the proceedings within the meaning of s 6 of the Act. It is obvious that a conditional appearance entered with a view of making an application to set aside the writ or service of the writ under O 12 r 7 of the RHC would not amount to a step in the proceedings either. In short, an entry of appearance under O 12 of the RHC would not amount to a step in the proceedings within the meaning of s 6 of the Act ... .
>
> [21] Though decided under the old section 6 of the Arbitration Act 1952 the same principle would apply and more so when there is now no O. 12 r. 6 ROC on the entry of conditional appearance and with that O.12 r.7 has been deleted too with respect to an application to set aside writ arising from the entry of a conditional appearance.

[2] Qualified Position

It is settled that, even if a party takes a step in the proceedings, if the party qualifies his position by stating that the step is taken without prejudice to his right to apply for a stay, then this will not amount to an unequivocal step whereby he abandons his right to arbitration.

In this regard, the High Court, in *Nam Fatt Corporation Bhd & Anor v. Petrodar Operating Co Ltd & Anor* [2010] 9 CLJ 732 at paragraph 75, held:

> I am fortified in my view that the 1st defendant has not taken any further step in the proceeding as they have applied promptly for a stay of the proceeding and they have made it abundantly clear that their application to set aside the ad-interim injunction is done without prejudice to and subject to their application to set aside the service of the writ out of jurisdiction and to stay the proceeding in this court. As was stated in *Seloga Jaya Sdn Bhd (supra)*, resisting an application for an interlocutory injunction by putting in evidence in affidavit form and through counsel, appearing in court to argue against the injunction cannot amount to 'taking any other steps in the proceeding'. Otherwise the 1st defendant would be in a Catch-22 situation. If he objects to the injunction he is damned because that could be construed as taking a further step in the proceeding by way of filing an

> affidavit to set aside the injunction. If he does nothing to set aside the injunction the injunction will continue to be in force by default if not by design of the plaintiffs. It is a case of head I win and tail you lose! That cannot be the position of the law. Indeed there is a palpable paradigm shift in the Arbitration Act 2005 towards affirming parties agreement to go for arbitration and the court will only refuse the parties intention if the defendant can be shown to have so irreversibly and irrevocably taken positive further steps in the proceeding that one can affirmatively, assuredly and avowedly say that the defendant has abandoned its intention to arbitrate altogether.

This judgment was affirmed on other grounds by the Federal Court, in *Petrodar Operating Co Ltd v. Nam Fatt Corp Bhd (in liquidation) & Anor* [2014] 6 MLJ 189.

Similarly, the Court of Appeal, in *Comos Industry Solution GmbH v. Jacob & Toralt Consulting Letrikon Sdn Bhd* [2011] 1 LNS 1770 at paragraph 15, held:

> The action of the appellant only gave away the following intention. Prayer (a) of encl. 41, for an order to set aside the writ on the ground that German and not local courts had jurisdiction, clearly evinced that the appellant was not prepared to proceed with the suit. Prayer (b) of encl. 41, for an order 'that the first defendant be permitted 21 days from the date of an order herein to file the defence in the event this Honourable Court dismisses the application herein subject to the first defendant having the liberty to apply to this Honourable Court for such orders as it considers appropriate and or necessary', applied for time to file a statement of defence. But that was not a prayer simpliciter, for time to file a statement of defence, without qualification. That prayer was made on the stated basis that it was only made if prayer (a) were dismissed and if the appellant had the liberty to apply for such orders as it deemed 'appropriate and or necessary'. Prayer (b) itself did not state what orders that the appellant would consider 'appropriate and or necessary'. But that should not be a mystery. In the affidavit filed in support of encl. 41, the appellant openly reserved the right to refer the dispute to arbitration. Indeed, in all papers filed, the appellant unceasingly challenged the jurisdiction of the court below and reserved the right to refer the dispute to arbitration. The appellant indicated only that it was against the dispute being tried by the court below. Given the qualifications under which it was made, the prayer for time to file a statement of defence was only a precautionary step to obviate the risk of a judgment in default of pleadings, should prayer (a) be refused ... .

The High Court, in *Life Plaza Sdn Bhd v. Pasukhas Construction Sdn Bhd* [2012] 5 CLJ 120 at paragraph 30, appeared to extend this concept further by deciding that a defence filed under protest would not amount to a step in the proceedings:

> With the benefit of hindsight, the court finds that since the defendant's application for stay had been filed before it had taken any positive steps in the proceedings; the court should have allowed encl. 4 to be heard before directing the defendant to file its defence which could be considered as taking a positive step in the proceedings. In the circumstances of this case and the court's own role in directing that the defence be filed, the court is of the considered view that this act of filing the defence should be viewed in the context of 'other action' as set out in *Sanwell Corporation (supra)*. In light of para. 7 of the defence and the many protestations from learned counsel that there had been no abandonment of its rights to refer the dispute to arbitration, the court finds that the filing of the defence on the express instructions of the court was not indicative of an unequivocal intention to proceed with the suit and to abandon its right to have the dispute disposed off by

arbitration. As such, the court finds that the filing of the defence in the circumstances of this case does not amount to the defendant having taken a positive step in the proceedings.

The Court of Appeal, in *Borneo Samadana Sdn Bhd v. Siti Rahtizah Mihaldin & Ors* [2008] 5 CLJ 435 at paragraphs 7 and 8, considered a slightly different position, where a party applied for stay and, in the event this was dismissed, applied for security for costs in the alternative. The Court of Appeal held that the alternative prayer would not amount to a step, as the primary prayer was for a stay.

[3] Resisting Injunction

The position is clear that merely resisting an application for an interlocutory injunction does not amount to a step in the proceedings.

The High Court, in *Nam Fatt Corporation supra* at paragraph 75, as considered in §10.03[E][2] *supra*, held that merely resisting an application for an interlocutory injunction by filing affidavits and counsel submitting on the issues would not amount to a step in the proceedings.

Similarly, the Court of Appeal, in *AGIBS Engineering & Construction Sdn Bhd v. Paragon Advance Solutions Sdn Bhd* [2011] 1 LNS 1019 at paragraph 12, held:

> The said application was made by the appellant at the beginning of the proceedings before the appellant takes any other steps in the proceedings. The respondent has raised the issue that the appellant has taken steps in the proceedings when the appellant defended the respondents injunction application. The court cannot agree with the respondent on this point. In defending the respondent's injunction application against the appellant, the appellant cannot be said to have abandoned its right to a stay application under s. 10 ... .

The High Court, in *Inai Kiara Sdn Bhd v. East Coast Economic Region Development Council* [2018] MLJU 1448 at paragraph 16(iii), also confirmed that a party opposing an application for an interim injunction has not thereby taken a step in the proceedings, as such a party has no choice but to oppose the application.

[4] Discovery

The courts have taken different views on whether a notice to produce documents, which is the first step in the process of discovery, amounts to a step in the proceedings.

The High Court, in *Life Plaza supra* at paragraphs 25 and 26, held that such a notice did not amount to a step in the proceedings on the following grounds:

> [25] In this case the defendant had also served on the plaintiff a notice to produce documents mentioned in the pleadings as well as a letter asking for further and better particulars. The court notes the arguments of learned counsel for the defendant that these were steps taken to determine what the exact claim against the defendant was. The court is of the considered view that this step taken by the defendant would fall within the category of 'other action' as stated by the Federal Court in *Sanwell Corporation*. And to determine if the serving of the said notice and

letter amounts to its having taken a positive step, the court would have to consider whether such action indicates an unequivocal intention to proceed with the suit and to abandon its right to refer to arbitration.

[26] In this regard, the court is in agreement with learned counsel for the defendant that the serving of the notice and letter on the plaintiff does not amount to the defendant having taken positive steps. The court is unable to see how asking for particulars or for inspection of documents could be seen as amounting to an unequivocal intention to proceed with the suit. As such, on this score, the court finds that such action by the defendant does not amount to it having taken any positive steps in the proceedings.

However, the High Court, in *CLLS Power System Sdn Bhd v. Sara-Timur Sdn Bhd* [2015] 1 LNS 149 at paragraph 33, held that such a notice amounted to a step in the proceedings:

> In this case, the step taken by the Defendant, that is the issue and service of a 'Notice To Produce Documents Referred to in Pleadings dated 4.12.2014 Pursuant to Order 24 Rule 10 of the Rules of Court 2012' even before the filing of this application on 12.12.2014, deprives the Defendant of this order for a mandatory stay. Such a Notice issued under Order 24 Rule 10 serves as part of the discovery process available for claims filed in Court. There are serious ramifications and consequences upon the issue and service of such a Notice. A party who is served with such a Notice must respond within 4 days to the Notice. Where a party fails to comply with such a Notice, the other party may apply to Court for an order of discovery.

In this regard, much will depend on the nature of the documents being sought by the notice. If the documents sought are to ascertain the nature of the claim and allow the party seeking the documents to decide once the nature of the claim is ascertained whether an application for stay would be justified, the notice should not amount to a step.

[5] *Resisting Winding-Up*

The High Court, in *NFC Labuan supra* at paragraph 31, held that an affidavit filed to oppose a winding-up petition would amount to a step in the proceedings:

> Accordingly, the pursuit of the respondent's resistance to the winding-up petition by the filing and service of the affidavit in opposition, more so when compounded with arguably the swift action taken by the respondent to file and serve the said affidavit vis-à-vis its filing of this instant application for stay late in the day, as well as its non-objection to the petitioner's application for extension of time to further challenge the respondent's own affidavit, would all render the same to amount to the taking of steps in the proceedings of the winding-up petition that would thus prevent the proceedings to be stayed for reference to arbitration under Section 10 of the AA. As such, this stay application is unmeritorious and thus must fail.

[6] Defence

The High Court, in *Tactical Force Sdn Bhd v. Nice Network Diversified Sdn Bhd* [2011] 1 LNS 140 at paragraphs 92-94, effectively held that the filing of a defence would amount to a step in the proceedings.

This would appear obvious. There are, however, various other factual permutations in relation to the filing of a defence that have been considered by the courts.

In this context, the High Court has adopted a strict position, and held, in *Winsin Enterprise supra* at paragraph 15, that seeking an extension to file a defence would amount to a step in the proceedings. The same position was taken by the High Court, in *Mun Seng Fook v. AIG Malaysia Insurance Bhd* [2018] MLJU 310 at paragraph 21.

On the other hand, the High Court, in *Life Plaza supra* at paragraph 30, decided that the filing of a defence under protest would not amount to a step in the proceedings.

The question really is whether the step taken is unequivocal or otherwise. Where an extension is sought, or even a defence is filed, under protest or without prejudice to a party's right to apply for a stay, this should not amount to a step in the proceedings.

[7] Before

The Court of Appeal, in *PLB-KH Bina Sdn Bhd v. Hunza Trading Sdn Bhd* [2014] MLJU 1427, clarified that an application for stay should be made before taking any step in the proceeding. After the application is made it appears that other steps may be taken.

In this regard, the Court of Appeal, in *PLB-KH Bina supra* at paragraph 47, held:

> It was clear from that provision that for a stay to be considered by the court, the party applying had to file for the same before taking any other step in the subject proceedings itself. The application for stay here by PLB-KH Bina had been filed first in time and the application to strike out was a subsequent application. In our view therefore PLB-KH Bina's was therefore not disentitled of their right to seek a stay or to pursue with this appeal against the dismissal of the prior application for stay before the court. We could not agree with Counsel for Hunza Trading, therefore, that PLB-KH Bina had abandoned their application for stay under s 10(1) AA 2005 or that this appeal had been rendered academic now.

[F]   '… Stay Those Proceedings and Refer the Parties to Arbitration …'

The key word here is 'parties'. The High Court, in *AV Asia Sdn Bhd v. Measat Broadcast Network Systems Sdn Bhd* [2010] 1 LNS 1601 at pages 9 and 10, confirmed, in accordance with section 2 of the Arbitration Act 2005, that the word 'parties' used in section 10(1) means parties to the arbitration agreement. This judgment was later affirmed by Federal Court, although this issue did not arise, in *AV Asia Sdn Bhd v. Measat Broadcast Network Systems Sdn Bhd* [2014] 3 MLJ 61.

Similarly, the Federal Court, in *Jaya Sudhir a/l Jayaram v. Nautical Supreme Sdn Bhd & 2 Ors* (FC, 1 July 2019) at paragraphs 32, 38, 40 and 91, held that section 10 of the Arbitration Act 2005 only applied to a 'party' as defined in section 2, meaning a party to the arbitration agreement. Conversely, section 10 did not apply to a person who is not a party to the arbitration agreement. The question that arises is what happens when there is a party to the proceeding in court who is not a party to the arbitration agreement. Traditionally, the courts held that the presence of a party in the civil proceedings other than the party to the arbitration agreement would not prevent a stay being granted. The proceedings involving the party who is not a party to the arbitration agreement will also be stayed pending the outcome of the arbitration.

In this regard, the Court of Appeal, in *Renault SA v. Inokom Corporation Sdn Bhd & Anor and other Applications* [2010] 5 CLJ 32 at paragraphs 16-18, held:

> [16] The fact that Tan Chong and TC Euro have been named as alleged co-conspirators does not change the fact that a mechanism for resolving disputes between Renault, Inokom and Quasar has been agreed upon. Therefore, mechanism should be rightly invoked and the disputes resolved by arbitration and not by litigation in court. The parties should honour art. 11 and give it life and meaning, to resolve disputes amicably. A devious attempt to circumvent art. 11, by instituting an action against Renault jointly with parties not subject to the arbitration clause, should not be encouraged.
>
> [17] The action as between Inokom, Quasar and the alleged co-conspirators (Tan Chong & TC Euro, who were not parties to the arbitration clause) can be stayed pending the outcome of the arbitration.
>
> [18] We are not persuaded by counsel for Inokom and Quasar that the disputes are inseparable and unsuitable for determination by an arbitral proceeding, as it involves third parties to the master agreement who are not subject to the arbitration clause. We are not persuaded that any award made by the arbitral tribunal against Renault would not be binding and enforceable against Tan Chong and TC Euro, to warrant the refusal of stay under s. 6 of the 1952 Act. We are further not persuaded that it is undesirable to have two proceedings before two different tribunals, who might reach inconsistent findings, to warrant the refusal of stay under s. 6 of the 1952 Act. In any event, Tan Chong and TC Euro have applied to have the claim as against them struck off summarily and if they succeed, multiplicity of proceedings is a non issue.

The judgment in *Renault supra* was followed[13] by the High Court, in *AV Asia supra* at pages 9 and 10:

> ... I think the following principle of law is well settled by the decision of the Court of Appeal in *Renault SA v. Inokom Corporation Sdn Bhd & Anor and other appeals (supra)*: the inclusion of third parties in an Action which are not subject to an arbitration agreement will not be a ground to refuse stay of proceedings. There is no scope for the court to refuse a stay of proceedings on the ground that third parties are involved. The court will uphold the right to arbitration notwithstanding the fact that there is a claim against a third party (see: *Russell on Arbitration*, 23rd Edition paragraph 7-048).

---

13. *See* the judgments prior to *Renault supra*, in *Standard Chartered Bank Malaysia Bhd v. City Properties Sdn Bhd & Anor* [2008] 1 CLJ 496 at para. 23, HC; *Sunway Damansara Sdn Bhd v. Malaysia National Insurance Bhd & Anor* [2008] 3 MLJ 872 at para. 18, which take the same position. See also the judgment that follow *Renault supra*, in *Thien Seng supra* at paras 53 and 54, HC.

Subsequently, the courts have taken a more nuanced approach in dealing with civil proceedings that include persons who are a party to an arbitration agreement, as well as, persons who are not a party to such an arbitration agreement. The courts, in such situations, now recognize that they have four options:

(1) to stay the whole civil proceedings, including those against the persons who are not party to the arbitration agreement. Here, the arbitral proceedings will proceed first followed by the civil proceedings;
(2) to stay the civil proceedings between the persons who are party to the arbitration agreement on condition that the arbitral proceedings between these persons only proceed after the civil proceedings. Here, the civil proceedings will proceed first followed by the arbitral proceedings;
(3) to stay the civil proceedings between the persons who are party to the arbitration agreement and allow the civil proceedings between the persons who are not party to the arbitration agreement and the arbitral proceedings to proceed. Here, the arbitral proceedings and the civil proceedings will proceed concurrently; and
(4) to stay the civil proceedings on certain issues and allow other issues to proceed in the arbitral proceedings and civil proceedings concurrently.

In deciding which of these four options to select, the courts will consider the overlap between the arbitral proceedings and the civil proceedings in terms of:

(1) the parties;
(2) the issues;
(3) the factual matrix giving rise to the cause of action;
(4) the principal witnesses; and
(5) the relief and remedy sought.

The courts, in adopting this more nuanced approach, have been influenced by the judgment of the Court of Appeal of Singapore, in *Tomolugen Holdings Ltd and another appeal v. Silica Investors Ltd; and other appeals* [2015] SGCA 57. This can be seen from the judgment of the Court of Appeal, in *Protasco Bhd v. Tey Por Yee & Another Appeal* [2018] 5 CLJ 299 at paragraphs 50 and 51.

The Federal Court, in *Jaya Sudhir supra* at paragraphs 60-62, 66-69, 81 and 98, held that, when a person who is not a party to an arbitration agreement applies to restrain arbitral proceedings, the courts would consider the factors usually considered when an application is made for an interim injunction. These factors include whether there are serious issues to be tried and where the balance of convenience lies.

The primary consideration is what would be the fairest approach to all parties. This depended, when there were parallel civil and arbitral proceedings, on:

(1) whether there would be a multiplicity or duplicity of proceedings;
(2) whether there was a risk of inconsistent findings; and

(3) whether the interests of the person who was not a party to the arbitral proceedings would be affected.

The Federal Court, in *Jaya Sudhir supra* at paragraph 91, recognized that 'party autonomy and self-restraint by courts when intervening in arbitral process' was the policy and object of the Arbitration Act 2005. However, such policy considerations did not apply to a person who was not a party to an arbitration agreement, as the Arbitration Act 2005 would not apply to such a person.

[G] '... Unless It Finds That the Agreement Is Null and Void, Inoperative or Incapable of Being Performed.'

[1] Lean Towards Arbitration

This part of section 10(1) of the Arbitration Act 2005 should be read together with section 18(1), which provides:

> 18. Competence of arbitral tribunal to rule on its jurisdiction.
> (1) The arbitral tribunal may rule on its own jurisdiction, including any objections with respect to the existence or validity of the arbitration agreement.

Based on sections 10(1) and 18(1), both the courts and the arbitral tribunal have jurisdiction to determine the existence and validity of an arbitration agreement. The courts have leaned towards allowing the arbitral tribunal to determine these issues in accordance with section 18(1).

In this regard, the High Court, in *CMS Energy Sdn Bhd v. Poscon Corporation* [2008] 1 LNS 543 at pages 8 and 9, held:

> In my view the language used in that section [ie section 18] confers on the arbitration a broad and wide powers to decide on issues raised before it – not only the substantive issues but also on the point of preliminary objections as to its jurisdiction. That section also allows any party to the arbitration who is not happy with the preliminary rulings by the arbitrator to appeal to the High Court against such rulings within 30 days of its receipt.
>
> ...
>
> In my view if section 10 and section 18 of the Act are read together there is no unmistakable intention of the legislature that the Court should lean towards arbitration proceedings. Under section 10(1) of the Act, the Court shall stay all proceedings before it in respect of a matter which is the subject of an arbitration agreement, and refer the parties to arbitration unless the Court is satisfied as to any of the condition in paragraph (a) or (b) of the section as shown above. And in this case none of the condition is applicable.

[2] Section 29 of the Contracts Act 1950

The Court of Appeal, in *Borneo Samudera Sdn Bhd v. Siti Rahfizah Mihaldin & Ors* [2008] 5 CLJ 435 at paragraph 9, also clarified that an arbitration agreement itself cannot be void under section 29 of the Contracts Act 1950 in the following terms:

> To summarise, we are not in agreement with the learned judge that the arbitration agreement is void. Exceptions 1 and 2 to s. 29 of the Contracts Act 1950 make that absolutely clear. These exceptions house the ratio in *Scott v. Avery* [1856] 10 ER 1121, namely that an agreement to arbitrate does not oust the jurisdiction of the ordinary courts and is therefore not illegal and void. Were it otherwise, no arbitration clause would ever survive. We may add that we are also satisfied, having regard to the facts of this case, the opposition to the stay does not fall within s. 10(1)(a) or (b) of the Arbitration Act 2005.

In this regard, section 29 of the Contracts Act 1950 provides:

> 29. Agreements in restraint of legal proceedings void
>
> Every agreement, by which any party thereto is restricted absolutely from enforcing his rights under or in respect of any contract, by the usual legal proceedings in the ordinary tribunals, or which limits the time within which he may thus enforce his rights, is void to that extent.
>
> Exception 1
>
> Saving of contract to refer to arbitration dispute that may arise.
>
> This section shall not render illegal a contract by which two or more persons agree that any dispute which may arise between them in respect of any subject or class of subjects shall be referred to arbitration, and that only the amount awarded in the arbitration shall be recoverable in respect of the dispute so referred.
>
> Exception 2
>
> Saving of contract to refer questions that have already arisen.
>
> Nor shall this section render illegal any contract in writing, by which two or more persons agree to refer to arbitration any question between them which has already arisen, or affect any law as to references to arbitration.
>
> Exception 3
>
> Nor shall this section render illegal any contract in writing between the Government and any person with respect to an award of a scholarship by the Government wherein it is provided that the discretion exercised by the Government under that contract shall be final and conclusive and shall not be questioned by any court.
>
> In this exception, the expression 'scholarship' includes any bursary to be awarded or tuition or examination fees to be defrayed by the Government and the expression 'Government' includes the Government of a State.

In the light of Exception 1 and 2 to section 29 of the Contracts Act 1950, this issue should not have arisen, as it is clear that an arbitration agreement is not void under section 29.

[3] Fraud and Mistake

The courts have consistently held that an arbitration agreement will generally be wide enough to cover disputes involving allegations of fraud or mistake.

In this regard, the High Court, in *Winsin Enterprise Sdn Bhd v. Oxford Talent (M) Sdn Bhd* [2010] 3 CLJ 634 at paragraphs 10 and 11, held that a widely drafted arbitration clause would cover disputes involving allegations of mistake:

> [10] On the facts, the plaintiff's submission is that the current proceedings are not in respect of a matter which is the subject of an arbitration agreement. According to learned counsel a claim for repayment of monies paid either mistakenly or erroneously in excess falls outside the scope of cl. 34 of the contract. This claim also does not relate to the works under the contract. Learned counsel for the defendant on the other hand submitted that the claim for repayment is challenged primarily on grounds of accuracies of calculation. It is related to the works under the contract.
>
> [11] Having considered the language in cl. 34 of the contract it is clear that the parties intended that the scope or type of matters that shall be compulsorily referred to arbitration is very wide. Clause 34(1)(i) provides that 'In the event that any dispute or difference arises between the employer ... and the contractor, either during the progress or after completion or abandonment of the Works regarding any matter or thing of whatsoever nature arising thereunder ... then such disputes or differences shall be referred to arbitration'. This includes a dispute concerning overpayment in the manner described in the statement of claim. Therefore the first condition in s. 10(1) is satisfied.

The High Court, in *Busuk Jamilah Bte Salim & 70 Ors v. Siti Rahfizah Binti Mihaldin & Anor* [2009] 1 LNS 1358 at page 7, held that allegations of fraud may be determined under a widely drafted arbitration agreement:

> ... It is clear to me that the question as to whether the Sale and Purchase Agreements are null and void and of no legal effect due to the alleged fraudulent or reckless misrepresentation by the defendants is a question that comes within the scope of clause 17 of the Sale and Purchase Agreements, namely 'any dispute or difference between the parties arising out of or in relation to this Agreement'.

Similarly, the Court of Appeal, in *Protasco Bhd v. Tey Por Yee & Another Appeal* [2018] 5 CLJ 299 at paragraph 59, held that an arbitration agreement should be interpreted widely to include all disputes between the parties, including disputes involving conspiracy and fraud.

[4] Multiplicity

This issue has been considered in §10.03 [F] *supra* in the context of the use of the word 'parties' in section 10(1) of the Arbitration Act 2005. The argument has also been made that, where there are parties to the civil proceedings, who are not parties to the arbitration agreement, the arbitration agreement is 'incapable of being performed', as all the parties to the civil proceedings will not be party to the arbitration and there is accordingly a risk of multiplicity of proceedings and conflicting decisions. However, these arguments have been rejected by the courts, who have held that multiplicity of proceedings is not a ground for declining a stay.[14] This is now subject to the more nuanced approach adopted by the courts that allows for the four options considered in §10.03 [F] *supra.*

[5] Incomplete Agreement

The High Court, in *Inai Kiara Sdn Bhd v. East Coast Regional Development Council* [2018] MLJU 1448 at paragraphs 16(viii)-(x), held that in a multi-tier dispute resolution clause, where a claimant was required to refer a dispute to an officer named in the appendix to the contract prior to referring the dispute to arbitration, the failure of the parties to specify the officer named in the appendix to the contract resulted in the arbitration agreement being inoperative and incapable of being performed.

However, where such an officer is named in the appendix to the contract, the claimant must refer the dispute to the officer before referring the dispute to arbitration. The claimant cannot attempt to circumvent the multi-tier dispute resolution clause by not referring the dispute to the officer and then contending that the arbitration agreement is inoperative and incapable of being performed. This was confirmed by the High Court, in *Maya Maju (M) Sdn Bhd v. Putrajaya Homes Sdn Bhd* [2018] MLJU 1629 at paragraphs 23-27 and 77.[15]

These judgments are of significance, as these multi-tier dispute resolution clauses which require a reference to an officer named in the appendix prior to arbitration are found in the PWD standard forms of building contract.

[6] Absence of Disputes

Section 10(1)(b) of the Arbitration Act 2005 used to provide that a stay shall be granted unless there is, in fact, no dispute between the parties. This subsection was deleted by the Arbitration (Amendment) Act 2011.

After the amendment, an ingenuous argument was raised to revive section 10(1)(b). The argument was that, in the absence of a dispute, the arbitration agreement became 'inoperative or incapable of being performed', as there was no dispute to be referred to arbitration.

However, this argument was rejected by the High Court, in *Zaq Construction Sdn Bhd & Anor v. Putrajaya Holdings Sdn Bhd* [2014] 4 CLJ 895 at paragraphs 63-65, where it was held:

> [63] Moving on to the statutory constraints or grounds for refusing a stay under sub-s. 10(1). The plaintiffs argued that the arbitration agreement is inoperative or incapable of being performed because of the position of the statement of final

---

14. See *Standard Chartered supra, Sunway Damansara supra, Renault supra, AV Asia supra.*
15. See *Usahasama SPNB-LTAT Sdn Bhd v. Abi Construction Sdn Bhd* [2016] MLJU 1596 at paras 17 to 21, HC, where it was held that a claimant must comply with conditions precedent to a reference to arbitration, including referring the dispute to an officer named in the appendix.

accounts. With this statement and what it represents, there is no dispute or difference to refer to arbitration in which case, the arbitration agreement is said to be inoperative and incapable of being performed.

[64] With respect, I disagree. The statutory constraints in sub-s. 10(1) refer to those elements, where if present, will render the arbitration agreement invalid or unenforceable by reason, say of illegality or frustration. For the arbitration agreement to be inoperative or incapable of being performed, those constraints must relate to the arbitration agreement itself.

[65] These terms also refer to situations or circumstances where it is legally or practically impossible to make a valid reference to arbitration pursuant to the arbitration clause or arbitration agreement. For instance, the arbitration agreement provides for a non-existent venue; or the time limited for its invocation has lapsed
...

[H] '... That There Is In Fact No Dispute Between the Parties with Regard to the Matters to Be Referred.'

As stated above, section 10(1)(b) of the Arbitration Act 2005 used to provide that a stay should not be granted when there was in fact no dispute between the parties. This subsection was deleted by the Arbitration (Amendment) Act 2011 to prevent the courts from having to assess whether a dispute in fact existed and thereby encroach into the jurisdiction of the arbitral tribunal.

We consider below the position both prior and subsequent to the amendment. The position prior to the amendment is considered largely for historic and academic purposes. Some of the positions taken prior to the amendments have also informed the current position.

Prior to the amendments, the courts were reluctant to hold that there was no dispute between the parties. Any dispute was viewed as being sufficient unless the matter was plain and obvious and the court could determine that defence was frivolous and vexatious without a meticulous examination of the merits. Furthermore, it was sufficient for a dispute to exist if an assertion to this effect was made even if such an assertion could easily be demonstrated to be wrong.

In this context, the High Court, in *Bina Par Development Sdn Bhd v. Manoharan Paranjothy* [2009] 1 LNS 415 at page 7, held that the penultimate certificate issued under a building contract could be disputed.

Similarly, the High Court, in *Gadang Engineering (M) Sdn Bhd v. Bluwater Developments Bhd* [2010] 6 CLJ 277 at paragraph 8, held that final accounts issued under a building contract could be disputed, where the final accounts had not been issued in accordance with the mechanism of the building contract and there was a dispute as to whether the person who signed these accounts had the authority to do so.

The High Court, in *FSBM Holdings v. Technitium Sdn Bhd* [2010] MLJU 1103 at page 2, held that a claim for goods sold and delivered could be disputed and explained the principles behind section 10(1)(b) in the following terms:

> As regards requirement (b), the learned commentators are of the view that Malaysian courts should adopt the 'bona fide dispute' test, instead of the 'arguable

grounds for disputing liability' test. It must be said however that even under the previous section 6, the Federal court in *Tan Kok Cheng & Sons Realty Co v Lim Ah Pat (t/a Juta Bena)* [1995] 3 MLJ 273, held there was no requirement for the dispute to be bona fide for the court to exercise its discretion to order a stay. Any dispute difference will suffice, as a court is not required to critically examine the merits of the claim. The court may be justified in refusing stay only in plain and obvious cases, where a reasonable tribunal, without undertaking a meticulous examination the merits, is bound to hold that the issues raised by a Defendant is frivolous or vexatious. The court's discretion to refuse a stay is therefore limited to cases involving fraud, or where there is no dispute that falls within the Arbitration Clause. Since the court is not required to critically examine the merits of the claim, evidently the approach to the court's exercise of discretion under section 10 cannot be equated with the approach the court takes when considering a summary judgment application. This means to say the existence of a bona fide dispute should be taken as meaning nothing more than the existence of some dispute which can be referable to the Arbitration Agreement, and if it exists, the action should be stayed pending arbitration … .

The High Court, in *MCM Bulk shipping (M) Sdn Bhd v. Raz Intan Industries Sdn Bhd* [2012] MLJU 401 at page 2, clarified that a dispute could exist even where there was no reply to the notice of arbitration.

After the amendments, the courts have held that it is no longer necessary for a party to identify the dispute, or for the courts to delve into the facts, as this would amount to an encroachment into the role to be played by the arbitral tribunal.

In this context, the Court of Appeal, in *TNB Fuel Services Sdn Bhd v. China National Coal Group Corp* [2013] 1 LNS 288 at paragraph 24, held:

> The present form of Section 10 of the Arbitration Act 2005 is the result of the amendment to that section which came into force on 1st July 2011 (Act A1395). It is generally accepted that the effect of the amendment is to render a stay mandatory unless the agreement is null and void or impossible of performance. The Court is no longer required to delve into the facts of the dispute when considering an application for stay … .

Subsequently, the High Court, in *Zaq Construction Sdn Bhd & Anor v. Putrajaya Holdings Sdn Bhd* [2014] 4 CLJ 895 at paragraph 28, held:

> Save for this amendment to sub-s. 10(1), the intention in sub-s. 10(1) has always been the same. In my view, from the time of its first enactment in 2005, the provisions on stay have always been in mandatory terms. What this amendment has done is to remove what may be said to be a somewhat cumbersome and sometimes difficult to grapple with exception found in para. (b). There was frequently concern that in determining whether or not there was in fact a dispute between the parties, the court was embarking on an unnecessary journey and intervening on what was understood as autonomous party choices.

The Federal Court, in *Press Metal supra* at paragraph 33, confirmed that:

> What the court needs to consider in determining whether to grant a stay order under the present section 10(1) (after the 2011 Amendment) is whether there is in existence a binding arbitration agreement or clause between the parties, which agreement is not null and void, inoperative or incapable of being performed. The

court is no longer required to delve into the details of the dispute or difference. (see *TNB Fuel Services Sdn Bhd (supra)*). In fact the question as to whether there is a dispute in existence or not is no longer a requirement to be considered in granting a stay under section 10(1). It is an issue to be decided by the arbitral tribunal.

The High Court, in *Rightmove Sdn Bhd v. YWP Construction Sdn Bhd & Anor* [2015] 7 MLJ 687 at paragraph 16, also held:

> For our purposes, learned counsel for the plaintiffs in his submission said that in 3.3 'However, the 1st defendant has failed to identify what are the disputes which necessitate or should be referred to arbitration.' Surely such assertion could only stand in the old s 10(1) (see para (10) hereinabove) we are here dealing with the amended s 10(1) (see para (14) hereinabove). From the short history of the case the first defendant had fulfilled the following pre-condition: (i) the proceedings have been brought before the court; (ii) there was an agreement between the parties which contains an arbitration clause and (iii) the applicant has not taken any other steps in the proceedings. The plaintiffs can only challenged the defendant's application for a stay if he could establish the agreement between the parties is null and void, inoperative or incapable of being performed. There is nothing of that sort here. I do not see this being raised in the plaintiff's affidavit. I shall not delve into this as it is not the plaintiff's case that the agreement was null and void, inoperative or incapable of being performed. But I need only say even if the agreement has been terminated a stay of proceeding would still be allowed under s 10 (see *Agibs Engineering & Construction Sdn Bhd v Paragon Advance Solutions Sdn Bhd* [2011] 1 LNS 1019).

Similarly, the High Court, in *Juang Setia Sdn Bhd v. Tindak Murni Sdn Bhd* [2018] MLJU 229 at paragraphs 20 and 25, held that:

> [20] The question as to whether there is a dispute in existence or not is no longer a requirement to be considered in granting the stay. A stay of proceedings is a stay of proceedings which have already been filed in court. Thus, an application for a stay of proceedings can only be filed by the defendant after the plaintiff had commenced proceedings in court, but before the defendant takes any other steps in the proceedings.
>
> ...
>
> [25] The arbitrator has jurisdiction to deal with all the matters and issues brought up by the parties. This court is no longer required to delve into the details of the dispute or difference. The court should lean more towards granting a stay pending arbitration under s. 10(1) of the 2005 Act, even in cases where the court is in some doubt about the validity of the arbitration clause or where it is arguable whether the subject matter of the claim falls within or outside the ambit of the arbitration clause. In fact the question as to whether there is a dispute in existence or not is no longer a requirement to be considered in granting a stay under Section 10(1) Arbitration Act 2005. See *TNB Fuel Services Sdn Bhd v. China National Coal Group Corp* [2013] 1 LNS 288 CA.

[I] 'The Court, in Granting a Stay of Proceedings Pursuant to Subsection (1), May Impose Any Conditions as It Deems Fit.'

The courts are entitled under section 10(2) of the Arbitration Act 2005 to 'impose any conditions' when granting a stay. The courts have availed themselves of this provision to impose conditions when granting a stay.

For example, in *Majlis Ugama Islam Dan Adat Resam Melayu Pahang v. Far East Holdings Bhd & Anor* [2007] 10 CLJ 318 at paragraph 22, the High Court affirmed an order made by the Session Court, which granted a stay and, as a condition, referred the matter to the Director of the Kuala Lumpur Regional Centre for Arbitration to appoint an arbitrator under section 13(5) of the Arbitration Act 2005.

The High Court, in *Gadang Engineering (M) Sdn Bhd v. Bluwater Developments Bhd* [2010] 6 CLJ 277 at paragraph 11, granted an application for stay on condition that the arbitral proceedings be completed within one year, failing which, the party who had applied for summary judgment be entitled to proceed with that application.

The High Court, in *FAMG Idaman Resources v. Jasmada Sdn Bhd* [2018] MLJU 1081 at paragraphs 33, 36, 45-52 and 64 and 65, recognized that when a stay is granted under section 10, it is the plaintiff in the civil proceedings that is compelled to commence arbitral proceedings if the plaintiff wishes to pursue their claims. Despite recognizing this, the High Court granted the stay on condition that the defendant in the civil proceedings commence arbitral proceedings within thirty days. The grounds for this unusual condition appear to be that the defendant did not dispute the plaintiff's claim but had a counterclaim in excess of such a claim. Furthermore, the plaintiff was in financial difficulty.

As can be seen from the foregoing, section 10(2) of the Arbitration Act 2005 allows for a diverse range of conditions to be imposed by the courts when granting the stay.

[J] 'This Section Shall Also Apply in Respect of an International Arbitration, Where the Seat of Arbitration Is Not in Malaysia.'

Section 10(4) of the Arbitration Act 2005 was introduced by the Arbitration (Amendment) Act 2001.

Section 10(4) was introduced to clarify that a stay may be granted for an international arbitration seated outside Malaysia.

This clarification was necessary, as it had been argued, albeit unsuccessfully, in *Innotec Asia Pacific Sdn Bhd v. Innotec GmbH* [2008] 8 CLJ 304, that in the light of section 3, the Arbitration Act 2005 only applied to domestic and international arbitration with a seat in Malaysia.

It is now clear that a stay may be granted with respect to an international arbitration with a seat outside Malaysia. This is consistent with Article 1(2) of the 1985 Model Law.

§10.04 EFFECT OF A STAY

The courts have also considered the effect of granting a stay on subsequent proceedings in court.

The Court of Appeal, in *Kenneth Chung Kuo Ting & Anor v. John Tsang Shing Chi & Anor* [2015] 1 CLJ 346, considered a situation where the High Court had given a judgment based on admissions after granting a stay. The Court of Appeal held that the High Court had no jurisdiction to give such a judgment after granting a stay. The Court of Appeal, in *Kenneth Chung supra* at paragraph 21, held:

> The effect of the order is very clear ie, all further proceedings in the action in question be stayed and the parties be referred to arbitration. The stay order was still in force at the time when the learned Judicial Commissioner made the order under O. 27 r. 3 of the RHC 1980 on 14 June 2010 against the appellants. There was no appeal against the said order. Therefore any further proceedings instituted by the plaintiffs (including their application under O. 27 r. 3 of the RHC 1980) must be stayed pending determination of the dispute by the arbitrator or until the arbitration process completed. The learned Judicial Commissioner has no jurisdiction to make a further order in relation to the action, unless the earlier stay order has been set aside.

The High Court, in *UBA Urus Bina Asia Sdn Bhd v. Quirk & Associates Sdn Bhd & Anor* [2016] 4 CLJ 468, considered a situation where the Sessions Court after granting a stay directed a party to commence arbitration within seven days or forego its right to arbitration. The High Court held that once the stay had been granted, the Sessions Court was *functus officio* and should not have imposed any such conditions. If the Sessions Court was minded to impose such conditions, the Sessions Court should have done so when granting the stay pursuant to section 10(2) of the Arbitration Act 2005 and not subsequently. The High Court, in *UBA Urus supra* at paragraphs 22, 26 and 27, held:

> [22] When an order for stay is granted under s. 10, it is not to say that the court has no jurisdiction to hear the dispute in the first place for the court has that jurisdiction. It, however, declines to do so only because it has chosen to give effect to the parties' agreement to arbitrate their disputes. Hence, the words 'refer the parties to arbitration'. By that agreement to arbitrate, or the arbitration agreement, the parties have made their choice of forum resolution of dispute and that is the basic concept behind party autonomy. In short, there is an agreement to arbitrate rather than agreement to litigate. When the court grants an order of stay, the order is not dependent on arbitration or arbitration proceedings being afoot, proposed or brought; it is dependent on the very existence of an agreement to arbitrate.
>
> ...
>
> [26] Here, there was no appeal following the decision of the learned Sessions Court Judge. More important and of relevance for our present purpose is that at the material time of the making of the order, the court did not deem it fit impose any terms or conditions to the order of stay that was granted. If the court was of the view that conditions or terms ought to be imposed under sub-s. 10(2), such terms or conditions then ought to have been imposed at the time the order of stay was granted. Once that order of stay under sub-s. 10(1) has been made, and the order has been sealed or perfected; there is nothing left before the court. The court is

clearly *functus officio*. The court does not concern itself nor does it need to concern itself with the mechanism or details of the procedure behind that reference to arbitration. That is left entirely to the parties.

[27] In this case, the order of the Sessions Court dated 30 September 2015 was a complete order granted with no other terms except an order as to costs. Hence, the directions and decisions of the court given subsequent to that date, especially on 5 November 2015, whether under sub-s. 10(2) or otherwise, are clearly wrong and invalid. These orders made after 30 September 2015 are certainly not orders or decisions that are appealable given that they do not form part of that order of 30 September 2015.

Therefore, it is clear that once a stay is granted without conditions, the courts have no jurisdiction over the matter and are *functus officio*. This is, of course, subject to any application being made to the courts subsequently, for example for interim measure or for enforcement.

11. *Arbitration Agreement and Interim Measures by High Court*

   (1) *A party may, before or during arbitral proceedings, apply to a High Court for any interim measure and the High Court may make the following orders for the party to –*
       (a) *maintain or restore the status quo pending the determination of the dispute;*
       (b) *take action that would prevent or refrain from taking action that is likely to cause current or imminent harm or prejudice to the arbitral process;*
       (c) *provide a means of preserving assets out of which a subsequent award may be satisfied, whether by way of arrest of property or bail or other security pursuant to the admiralty jurisdiction of the High Court;*
       (d) *preserve evidence that may be relevant and material to the resolution of the dispute; or*
       (e) *provide security for the costs of the dispute.*
   (2) *Where a party applies to the High Court for any interim measure and an arbitral tribunal has already ruled on any matter which is relevant to the application, the High Court shall treat any findings of fact made in the course of such ruling by the arbitral tribunal as conclusive for the purposes of the application.*
   (3) *This section shall also apply in respect of an international arbitration, where the seat of arbitration is not in Malaysia.*

§11.01 INTRODUCTION

Section 11 of the Arbitration Act 2005 allows the High Court to grant various forms of interim measures in aid of arbitral proceedings. Section 11 like section 10 of the Arbitration Act 2005 gives effect to the arbitration agreement but in another context. While section 10 excludes the jurisdiction of the courts over proceedings that are the subject matter of an arbitration agreement, section 11 allows for the courts to grant interim measures. This is because such interim measures by the courts may be necessary to aid the arbitral proceedings.[16]

Section 11 of the Arbitration Act 2005 is based on Article 9 of the 1985 Model Law. Article 9 of the 1985 Model Law provides as follows:

> Article 9. Arbitration agreement and interim measures by court
>
> It is not incompatible with an arbitration agreement for a party to request, before or during arbitral proceedings, from a court an interim measure of protection and for a court to grant such measure.

---

16. *See* Analytical Commentary, Article 9, commentary 1.

Chapter 2: Arbitration Agreement §11.01

Section 11 of the Arbitration Act 2005 differs from Article 9 of the 1985 Model Law insofar as it is not expressly provided that 'it is not incompatible with an arbitration agreement' for a party to apply for an interim measure. These words in Article 9 make it clear that an application to the courts for interim measures is not prohibited by an arbitration agreement and also does not amount to a waiver of the arbitration agreement.[17]

As these words usefully clarify that such applications are not a waiver, it is unclear why they were not included in section 11 of the Arbitration Act 2005.

Apart from this, section 11 of the Arbitration Act 2005 differs from Article 9 of the 1985 Model Law in that the various types of interim measures that can be granted by the High Court are listed under section 11(1). This list of interim measures was substituted by the Arbitration (Amendment) (No 2) Act 2018. The amendment was to ensure that the type of interim measures that may be granted by the High Court under section 11(1) was the same as the measures that may be granted by the arbitral tribunal under section 19(2), which in turn reflects Article 17(2) of the 2006 Model Law. The interim measures under section 11(1) are now identical with the measures under Article 17(2) save that:

(1) the words 'whether by way of arrest of property or bail or other security pursuant to the admiralty jurisdiction of the High Court' in section 11(1)(c) are not found in Article 17(2)(c); and
(2) section 11(1)(e) is not found in Article 17(2).

Prior to the amendment in 2018, section 11(1) provided for the following interim measures:
(a) security for costs;
(b) discovery of documents and interrogatories;
(c) giving of evidence by affidavit;
(d) appointment of a receiver;
(e) securing the amount in dispute, whether by way of arrest of property or bail or other security pursuant to the admiralty jurisdiction of the High Court;
(f) the preservation, interim custody or sale of any property which is the subject matter of the dispute;
(g) ensuring that any award which may be made in the arbitral proceedings is not rendered ineffectual by the dissipation of assets by a party; and
(h) an interim injunction or any other interim measure.

The interim measures in section 11(1) though similar to the measures available prior to the amendment in 2018 are not identical. Generally:

---

17. *See* Analytical Commentary, Article 9, commentary 2.

(1) the current section 11(1)(a) corresponds with the former section 11(1)(h), with the former section 11(1)(f) as a particular type of interim injunction;
(2) the current section 11(1)(b) does not directly correspond with any provision of the former section 11(1);
(3) the current section 11(1)(c) corresponds with the former section 11(1)(e);
(4) the current section 11(1)(d) is a particular form of the former section 11(1)(h), which was general;
(5) the current section 11(1)(e) corresponds with the former section 11(1)(a); and
(6) the current section 11(1) does not expressly provide for the interim measures listed under sections 11(1)(b), (c) and (d).

Section 11(2) of the Arbitration Act 2005 is not found in the 1985 Model Law. Section 11(2) attempts to grapple with the issue of a potential conflict between the findings of the arbitral tribunal and the High Court by providing that any findings of fact by the arbitral tribunal will be binding on the High Court. The 1985 Model Law does not attempt to deal with this issue or the narrower issue of a potential conflict between interim measures ordered by the courts and the arbitral tribunal under Articles 9 and 17 of the 1985 Model Law, respectively.[18]

Section 11(3) of the Arbitration Act 2005 allows the High Court to grant interim measures in aid of an international arbitration with a seat outside Malaysia. This reflects Article 1(2) of the 1985 Model Law, which makes an exception for Article 9.

While section 11 of the Arbitration Act 2005 is based on Article 9 of the 1985 Model Law, Article 9 is in turn based on Article 26(3) of the 1976 UNCITRAL Arbitration Rules, which provides:

> A request for interim measures addressed by any party to a judicial authority shall not be deemed incompatible with the agreement to arbitrate, or as a waiver of that agreement.

This is now reflected in Article 26(9) of the 2013 UNCITRAL Arbitration Rules, which forms part of the 2018 AIAC Arbitration Rules.

§11.02 GENERAL PRINCIPLES

General principles applicable to section 11(1) of the Arbitration Act 2005 have been developed by the courts. These principles were comprehensively summarized by the High Court, in *Bumi Armada Navigation Sdn Bhd v. Mirza Marine Sdn Bhd* [2015] 5 CLJ 652. These principles are considered below in the sequence they were set out in *Bumi Armada supra*. The judgment of the High Court, in *Bumi Armada supra*, was affirmed by the Court of Appeal.

---

18. *See* Analytical Commentary, Article 9, commentary 5.

[A] Cause of Action

The applicant must have a cause of action against the respondent. In this context, the High Court, in *Bumi Armada supra* at paragraph 47(a), held:

> the applicant must have a cause of action against the party whom interim relief is sought. In this regard, I rely on a case concerning an application for an interlocutory restraining injunction decided by the Supreme Court in *Khoo Soo Teong v. Khoo Siew Ghim & Anor* [1991] 3 CLJ 2063; [1991] 1 CLJ (Rep) 212; [1991] 3 MLJ 158, at 159.

[B] Arbitration Agreement

There must be an arbitration agreement as defined under section 9 of the Arbitration Act 2005, which is considered in §9.01, §9.02 and §9.03 *supra*.[19]

[C] Interim in Nature

The measures applied for must be interim in nature and should not be permanent in effect. In this context, the High Court, in *Metrod (Singapore) Pte Ltd v. GEP II Beteiligungs GmbH & Anor* [2013] 1 LNS 324 at paragraph 16, held:

> ... An application for such interim reliefs in the nature as set out at (a) to (h) of section 11(1) is intended to be of an interim nature; and not permanent. It is also intended to support, assist, as well as facilitate the arbitration proceedings ... .

This was followed by High Court, in *Bumi Armada supra* at paragraph 47(c), which further emphasized, in practical terms, that measures of an 'interim' nature should be subject to variation or discharge by a subsequent order of the courts or the arbitral tribunal:

> ... if the court grants any interim relief under s. 11(1) AA, such relief should only have interim effect and may be subject to the following circumstances:
>
> (i) the court has the subsequent power to vary and/or discharge the interim relief in question; and/or
> (ii) the arbitral tribunal in question should be empowered by the court granting the interim relief, to vary the interim relief if there are subsequent facts or circumstances to necessitate such a variation. If the court granting the interim relief, grants power to the arbitral tribunal to vary the interim relief pending the disposal of arbitration, there is no necessity for parties to 'return' to court for any variation of the interim relief. This will save precious judicial time and effort in hearing any application to vary any interim measure previously granted by the court under s. 11(1) AA ... .

---

19. See *Bumi Armada supra* at para 47(b).

[D]   Aid the Arbitration

The interim measures should aid and not impede the arbitral proceedings. This principle has been repeatedly emphasized by the courts. For example, the High Court, in *Merino-Odd Sdn Bhd v. PECD Construction Sdn Bhd* [2009] 1 LNS 718 at paragraph 4(e), held:

> Notwithstanding the above case laws, court is given wide powers as interim measures to ensure a successful outcome of the arbitration proceedings. This is clearly spelt out in section 11 of AA 2005 which the plaintiff is in essence relying on. However, court must be very cautious in granting orders which may delay or impede arbitration proceedings.

Similarly, the High Court, in *Jiwa Harmoni Offshore Sdn Bhd v. Ishi Paower Sdn Bhd* [2009] 1 LNS 849 at paragraph 2(a), held:

> The powers granted to court pursuant to section 11 are powers which are not meant to be oppressively invoked by a party to arbitration proceedings. It must be exercised with utmost care and circumspection to ensure and support the arbitration mechanism and not do any act which will stifle the arbitral process. In addition, when such powers are also vested with the arbitrator, the application must first be made before the arbitrator ...

The High Court, in *Cobrain Holdings Sdn Bhd v. GDP Special Projects Sdn Bhd* [2010] 1 LNS 1834 at pages 9, 18 and 19, held:

> Thus there is a clear overlap between section 11(1)(a), (b), (c) and (f) with section 19(1)(a), (b), (c) and (d). Going by the basic principles as stated earlier, where there is a concurrent jurisdiction, a party should first apply before the arbitral tribunal, unless there are countervailing factors, since the role of the High Court is to 'support arbitration' ... .
>
> ...
>
> In this connection I find the principle stated in *NCC International AB v. Alliance Concrete Singapore Pte Ltd, supra*, especially persuasive and useful. The Singapore Court of Appeal has, as indicated earlier, clearly specified some instances where the court of law may intervene, namely where third parties over whom the arbitral tribunal has no jurisdiction are involved, where matters are very urgent or where the court's coercive powers of enforcement are required. And these powers should be seen as powers to support the arbitral process. These principles fit well within the general corpus of arbitration cases dealing with interim measures, and in particular cases where applications are made to secure an award sum. Even where a sum has been awarded after an arbitration, the law does not confer an automatic right to have it secured by a court order unless the applicant provides some justification to the satisfaction of the court ... the stress is on the court's jurisdiction to achieve justice between the parties and a balancing of benefit and prejudice between them. The effect of an interim measure granted should additionally not be oppressive to the Defendant.

The High Court, in *Metrod supra* at paragraph 16 made similar observations and went on to hold at paragraph 18 that:

It is observed that the orders sought here are not confined to the contracting parties. This application may then be made to Court without having first being made to the arbitral tribunal ... the Court has jurisdiction to hear and grant interim measures even where arbitration has already commenced elsewhere. The simple existence of arbitration cannot be a bar to this application given the terms upon which this power is predicated.

The High Court, in *Interactive Brokers LLC v. Neo Kim Hock & Ors* [2014] 8 CLJ 747 at paragraph 59, held:

> The submission by the defendants that the injunction should not be allowed as this can be requested and given in the arbitration itself cannot with respect hold water as the provision of s. 11 of the AA as narrated earlier do allow for parties to resort to the High Court for the injunction pending arbitration.

The High Court, in *Bumi Armada supra* at paragraphs 47(d) and 52, followed *Metrod supra* and held that:

> [47] (d) the interim relief must support, assist, aid and/or facilitate the proposed arbitral proceedings – *Metrod (Singapore) Pte Ltd*. If arbitral proceedings are not subsequently commenced or if the interim relief in question does not support, assist, aid and/or facilitate the proposed arbitral proceedings:
>
> (i) the application for and the granting of interim relief may constitute an abuse of court process ... .
> (ii) the interim relief granted may oppress the party who is the subject matter of the interim relief.
>
> I must point out that s. 11(1) AA does not provide that the court's power to grant relief is 'for the purposes of and in relation to arbitral proceedings' as provided in s. 44(1) of the 1996 Act. It is hoped that the legislature may clarify this matter as the court's power to grant any interim measure under s. 11(1) AA should be 'for the purposes of and in relation to arbitral proceedings'; and
>
> ...
>
> [52] In view of the above reasons, especially the court's wide power under s. 11(1) AA to grant interim measures even before the commencement of arbitral proceedings, I reject the defendant's contention that instead of filing the OS, the plaintiff should have applied to the arbitral tribunal for interim relief under s. 19(1)(d) AA ... .
>
> If I have acceded to the above submission by the defendant, this will render s. 11(1) AA ineffective and a party to an 'arbitration agreement' will not be able to obtain any interim relief in the interest of justice ... .

The High Court, in *IJM Construction Sdn Bhd v. Lingkaran Luar Butterworth (Penang) Sdn Bhd* [2018] 7 MLJ 341 at paragraphs 12 and 13, held:

> [12] There is nothing in AA which stipulates that the arbitrator's exercise of powers under s 19 shall be to the exclusion of the court's exercise of powers under s 11, nor any statutory provision to the effect that the arbitrator's decision under s 19 is final and binding upon the court. Section 11(2) by specifically limiting the conclusiveness to the arbitrator's findings of fact, would imply that the part of the arbitrator's ruling or decision on interim measure other than the findings of fact are

open to reconsideration and fresh decision by the High Court under a s 11(1) application.

[13] It follows this court has the power to hear the application under s 11 and res judicata cannot be applied to the extent of nullifying or defeating the express statutory provisions of ss 11 and 19.

The Court of Appeal, in *Obnet Sdn Bhd v. Telekom Malaysia Berhad* [2018] MLJU 1400 at paragraphs 23 and 26, *inter alia*, held:

> [23] In this respect, we are constrained to observe that although the learned Judge accepted that he was bound by the findings of fact relevant to the discovery application, he nevertheless, in our respectful view, treated the discovery application as if it was an appeal. With respect, the learned Judge was bound by the learned Arbitrator's finding that the disclosure of the Settlement Agreement ought not to be allowed as such disclosure would be prejudicial to the State Government. Whatever the merits of such a finding, the High Court had no jurisdiction to interfere.
>
> ...
>
> [26] It must then follow that in principle s. 11 of AA 2005 is designed to support and facilitate the arbitral process and not to displace it. The approach, in the context of s. 11, must be not to encroach on the procedural powers of the arbitrators but to reinforce them ... As stated by s. 11 itself, the relief sought must be of an interim nature and, by implication, not permanent. It is plain that the interim measures are not intended to displace the powers of the arbitrator. They are certainly not there for the High Court to exert some supervisory function over the arbitral process. In the circumstances, the learned Judge ought to have declined to order discovery.

Therefore, interim measures should only be granted by the High Court, where such measures will aid, facilitate or support the arbitral proceedings and not where they will impede such proceedings.

Within this broad principle, the question arises as to what the applicant should do when both the High Court and the arbitral tribunal are empowered to grant the same type of interim measures under sections 11 and 19 of the Arbitration Act 2005.

Initially, the courts took the position that where the High Court and the arbitral tribunal's power to grant interim measures overlapped, a party should first apply to the arbitral tribunal for such interim measures as can be seen from *Jiwa Harmoni supra*.

Subsequently, the High Court, in *Cobrain Holdings supra*, while recognizing that an application for interim measures should first be made to the arbitral tribunal, where there was an overlap between the powers of the High Court and the arbitral tribunal, allowed for circumstances where an application may be made directly to the High Court. This would include circumstances where third parties over whom the arbitral tribunal had no jurisdiction were involved, where matters were very urgent or where the court's coercive powers were required.

The first of these circumstances, where a third party was involved, arose in *Metrod supra*, and the High Court followed *Cobrain Holdings supra* and allowed the application to be made directly to the High Court.

Thereafter, the High Court, in *Interactive Brokers supra* and *Bumi Armada supra*, appears to have taken a broader position and allowed an application to be made to the High Court for interim measures, even where the powers of the High Court and arbitral tribunal overlapped, without apparently considering the circumstances outlined in *Cobrain Holdings supra*.

The position should be that where there is an overlap between the powers of the High Court and the arbitral tribunal under sections 11 and 19, an application for interim measures should be made to the arbitral tribunal first. However, where there is a third party involved, an emergency or a need for coercive powers, an application may be made to the High Court immediately.

Apart from this, as emphasized in *IJM Construction supra*, the High Court may reconsider an application for interim relief after an order by an arbitral tribunal. However, based on *Obnet supra*, the High Court's reconsideration of any decision by the arbitral tribunal will be limited, as the High Court will be bound by the findings of fact made by the arbitral tribunal.

[E]   Arbitral Proceedings to Be Commenced Within Reasonable Time

The arbitral proceedings should be commenced within a reasonable time and without delay.

In this context, the High Court, in *Bumi Armada supra* at paragraph 47(e), held:

> arbitral proceedings should be commenced within a reasonable time. Any unreasonable delay in the commencement and/or conduct of arbitral proceedings may:
>
> (i) constitute an abuse of court process; and/or
> (ii) oppress the party who is the subject matter of the interim relief.
>
> The applicant for interim relief from court, should adduce affidavit evidence to show reasons:
> (1) why arbitral proceedings cannot be commenced within a reasonable time and hence, the need to apply to court for interim relief under s. 11(1) AA; or
> (2) if arbitral proceedings have already been instituted, why the applicant is not able to apply for interim relief from the arbitral tribunal and needs to apply to court for such relief.

§11.03   MERITS

Apart from these general principles, it is important to note that the courts will not decide the merits of the dispute between the parties pursuant to an application for interim measures under section 11(1) of the Arbitration Act 2005.

In this regard, the High Court, in *Bumi Armada supra* at paragraph 49, held:

> ... the court should not decide on the merits of the dispute which should be decided solely by the arbitral tribunal as agreed by the parties in question ... .

§11.04 BEFORE OR DURING ARBITRAL PROCEEDINGS

Section 11(1) of the Arbitration Act 2005 expressly provides that an application for interim measures may be made to the High Court 'before or during arbitral proceedings'.

Based on these express words, the High Court, in *I-Expo Sdn Bhd v. TNB Engineering Corporation Sdn Bhd* [2007] 1 LNS 304 at page 4, *Bumi Armada supra* at paragraph 39 and *Fadzly Enterprise Sdn Bhd v. Small Medium Enterprise Development Bank Malaysia Berhad* [2017] 1 LNS 1305 at paragraph 22, has confirmed that an application for interim measure may be made before the arbitral proceedings are commenced.

The High Court, in *Itramas Technology Sdn Bhd v. AmBank (M) Berhad* [2009] 1 LNS 923 at paragraph 4 and *Metrod supra* at paragraph 18, also confirmed, based on these express words of section 11(1), that an application to the High Court for interim measures may be made after the arbitration proceedings have commenced, that is during the arbitral proceedings.

§11.05 SPECIFIC PRINCIPLES

Apart from the general principles outlined above, specific principles will apply depending on the type of interim measures sought under section 11(1). The Court of Appeal, in *La Kaffa International Co Ltd v. Loob Holding Sdn Bhd* [2018] MLJU 703 at paragraph 29, held that section 8 did not remove the inherent jurisdiction of the courts to grant interim measures, although the courts would be slow to provide relief not expressly provided for in the Act.

The courts have adopted the usual principles that apply to each particular type of interim measure sought. Each particular type of interim measure sought that has been considered by the courts and the principles applied are outlined below.

[A] Maintain the Status Quo

The High Court, in *Bungy Malaysia Sdn Bhd v. Menara Kuala Lumpur Sdn Bhd* [2011] 3 CLJ 906 at paragraph 6.1.18, applied the general principles applicable in court for the grant of an interim injunction, as set out by the Court of Appeal, in *Keet Gerald Francis Noel John v. Mohd Noor @ Harun Abdullah & Ors* [1995] 1 MLJ 193 at pages 206 and 207, to an application for an interim injunction under the former section 11(1)(h).

These principles are that a court hearing an application for an interim injunction should consider:

(1) whether there are bona fide serious issues to be tried;
(2) where the justice of the case lies. The court should consider the harm that would be caused if the injunction is granted against the harm that would be caused if it is refused. The court should also consider the applicant's financial position to meet his undertaking as to damages in this context; and

(3) that the remedy is discretionary. As such, the court is entitled to take into account all discretionary considerations, such as:
  (a) any delay in making the application;
  (b) any adequate alternative remedy, such as an award of monetary compensation; and
  (c) any question going to the public interest.

The Court of Appeal, in *La Kaffa International supra* at paragraphs 32, 35 and 36, applied the general principles applicable to mandatory injunctions to section 11. These principles are that:

(1) the applicant usually has an unusually strong and clear case against the respondent;
(2) damages will not be an adequate remedy to the applicant;
(3) the cost to the respondent to do work to prevent or lessen the likelihood of a future apprehended wrong must be considered and balanced against the likely damage to the applicant:
  (a) where the respondent has acted unreasonably, the order may be granted even if the cost incurred by the respondent as a result is greater than the damage likely to be suffered by the applicant; and
  (b) where the respondent has acted reasonably, but wrongfully, the cost likely to be incurred by the respondent is important because:
    (i) no legal wrong has accrued as yet; and
    (ii) if heavy damages do occur, the applicant has his remedies in law.
(4) if an order is granted, the respondent must know exactly what he must do.

These principles are likely to continue to be applicable under the current section 11(1)(a).

The former section 11(1)(f) provided for a particular type of interim measure for the preservation, interim custody or sale of any property which is the subject matter of the dispute. The High Court, in *Ikatan Innovasi Sdn Bhd v. KACC Construction Sdn Bhd* [2008] 3 CLJ 48, strictly construed the former section 11(1)(f) of the Arbitration Act 2005 and held that it would only apply to property, which is the subject matter of the arbitration. In this regard, the High Court, in *Ikatan Innovasi supra* at paragraph 14, held:

> Reading s. 11(1)(f) and (g) of the Arbitration Act 2005 quoted above, there is no doubt that the High Court has the power to grant interim relief or measures to a party partaking in an arbitration proceedings before or during the proceedings. However para. (f) of the section seems to be restricted to preservation of the property which is the subject matter of the dispute before the arbitration proceedings. In this respect, the plaintiff's disputes with the defendant which the plaintiff is referring to the arbitration in this case do not involve any property. The disputes are only related to liquidated sum in the form of payment for works done under a contract. Thus para. (f) of s. 11(1) of the Arbitration Act may not be applicable in this instant.

This strict construction of the former section 11(1)(f) is unlikely to limit the scope of the current section 11(1)(a), as the present provision is broadly drafted and is not limited to 'property which is the subject matter of the dispute'.

[B] Prevent Harm to the Arbitral Process

This provision makes it clear that the High Court may grant interim measures not only to protect the parties but also to protect the arbitral process itself. The provision is not limited to situations where harm would be caused to such process but includes situations where harm is likely to be caused. This is because, at the time such interim measures are sought, it may be difficult to prove the harm would actually be caused.[20] In practice, an application may be made under this provision to restrain other arbitral or civil proceedings that are likely to harm the arbitral process.[21]

[C] Preserve Assets

The High Court, in *Bauer (Malaysia) Sdn Bhd v. Embassy Court Sdn Bhd* [2009] 1 LNS 848 at paragraphs 3(c) and (d), further explained the principles applicable to the former section 11(1)(e):

> (c) When dealing with Section 11(e) of AA 2005 courts need to look at the justice of the case and the competing interest. Section 11(e) AA 2005 in my view is not a provision which is enacted to give priority to a prospective creditor in arbitration. It must be construed to be a restrictive provision to ensure that the respondent is not disabled from conducting its day to day affairs in the ordinary course of business. The learned author OP Malhotra in his book '*The Law and Practice of Arbitration and Conciliation 2006*' dealt with the related provision in the Indian Act and says at page 395 as follows:-
>
>> This power, therefore, can be exercised only where an identified fund is in dispute-as for example, it is alleged that the respondent is trustee for the claimant in respect of a specific sum of money ie, where the right of a party to a specific fund is in dispute in a reference, the court has power to order the fund to be paid into court or otherwise secured. But this power has to be exercised with discretion. For instance, in *Global Co v. National Fertilizer Ltd* a single judge of the New Delhi High Court declined to order the National Fertilizers Ltd, a Government of India undertaking to furnish security claimed by the petitioner on the vague ground of his financial interest.
>
> (d) In addition, I will say the power of the court to secure the amount in dispute is a drastic power and that power as a general rule will only be used where there is an identified fund in dispute and is not available to a party seeking to recover damages in advance of the hearing before the arbitrator (see Mustill & Boyd, *The Law and Practice of Commercial Arbitration in England* 2nd edition, page 332; Ng

---

20. *See* United Nations, General Assembly, Report of the Working Group on Arbitration on the work of its 39th Session, 8 Dec. 2003, A/CN.9/545 at para 25.
21. *See* David D. Caron and Lee M Caplan, *The UNCITRAL Arbitration Rules, A Commentary* (2nd edn, Oxford University Press 2013) at pp 518-519.

Seng Kiok dan lain-lain v. Chooi Mun Sou dan lain-lain [1993] 2 CLJ 431; [1993] MLJU 279; *Richo Ltd v. International Ford Co* [1989] 1 ALL ER 613).

This was subsequently followed by the High Court, in *Jiwa Harmoni supra* at paragraph 2(d).

The need for an identified fund under the former section 11(1)(e) is unlikely to apply to the current section 11(1)(c), which uses the broader words 'preserving assets' rather than 'securing the amount in dispute'.

Apart from this, the High Court, in *Bumi Armada supra* at paragraph 58, held that the same principles would apply to the former section 11(1)(g) of the Arbitration Act 2005, as to an application for a Mareva injunction pending disposal of a suit and summarized these principles as follows:

> In deciding whether to grant a Mareva injunction under s. 11(1)(f), (g) and (h) AA before or after during arbitral proceedings, I adopt the same following tests as applied by cases in respect of Mareva injunctions pending disposal of suits:
>
> (a) the plaintiff should have a 'good arguable case';
> (b) the defendant has assets within this jurisdiction;
> (c) there is a risk of dissipation of the defendant's assets; and
> (d) the balance of convenience should be in favour of granting the Mareva injunction.

These principles were also applied by the High Court, in *Ikatan Innovasi supra* and *Interactive Brokers supra*.

In addition, the High Court, in *Ikatan Innovasi supra* at paragraph 15, explained that the former section 11(1)(g) covers both movable and immovable properties.

> But para. (g) of the same section of the Act, in my opinion, is wider in scope. The language of that paragraph suggests that the High Court may make such order as the court thinks just and appropriate in the circumstances in order to ensure the award that the applicant or plaintiff may obtain in the arbitration proceedings is not just a hollow piece of paper and of no value, because there is no assets that can be realized from the defendant in order to satisfy the award. The paragraph also does not confine the order that can be made to either movable or immovable assets. Thus, both types of asset may be restrained by the High Court order.

These principles, which are well established, are likely to continue to apply to an application for a Mareva injunction under the current section 11(1)(c).

[D] Preserve Evidence

This provision makes it clear that the High Court has the jurisdiction to grant an order preserving evidence in relation to arbitral proceedings. This provision was considered important by the Working Group on the 2006 Model Law, as the 'preservation of evidence was not necessarily dealt with to a sufficient extent by all domestic rules of civil procedure'.[22] These principles are, however, well settled in Malaysia. The general principles for the grant of such an application are that:[23]

(1) there must be an extremely strong prima facie case;
(2) the damage, potential or actual, must be very serious to the applicant;
(3) there must be clear evidence that the respondent has in their possession incriminating documents or things; and
(4) there is a real possibility that the respondent may destroy such material.

[E] Security for Costs

The High Court, in *Jiwa Harmoni supra*, confirmed that the same principles that apply in court in relation to applications for security for costs will apply in relation to the former section 11(1)(a) of the Arbitration Act 2005. The High Court, in *Jiwa Harmoni supra* at paragraph 2(c), held:

> The case laws relating to grounds when the court will order for security for costs are well settled and will apply to any application for security for costs before the arbitrator. As a general rule, a plaintiff ordinarily resident in Malaysia, cannot be subject to an application for security for costs purely on the grounds of impecuniosities. However, when the plaintiff is a corporate entity, section 351 of CA 1965 will apply. That does not mean security for costs will be granted as of right. It is only a discretionary relief. Such discretion will not be ordinarily exercised in favour of the applicant unless the justice of the case demands so ... .

These principles will continue to apply to the current section 11(1)(e), which allows for security for costs to be granted in the same way as the former section 11(1)(a).

§11.06 APPLICATION TO INTERNATIONAL ARBITRATION WITH A SEAT OUTSIDE MALAYSIA

Section 11(3) of the Arbitration Act 2005 was introduced by the Arbitration (Amendment) Act 2011 to allow the High Court to grant interim measures in aid of international arbitrations with a seat outside Malaysia.

This amendment reversed the effect of the judgment of the High Court, in *Aras Jalinan Sdn Bhd v. Tipco Asphalt Public Company Ltd & Ors* [2008] 5 CLJ 654, which was affirmed by the Court of Appeal. This judgment was to the effect that an interim injunction could not be granted in aid of an international arbitration with a seat in Malaysia.

The change in the law brought about by section 11(3) was recognized by the High Court, in *Bumi Armada supra* at paragraph 47(a), where it was held:

---

22. *See* Report of the Working Group on Arbitration A/CN.9/545 *supra* at para 27.
23. *See generally Arthur Anderson & Co v. Interfood Sdn Bhd* [2005] 6 MLJ 239, CA.

... Section 11(3) AA allows Malaysian courts to grant interim relief for 'international arbitration, where the seat of arbitration is not in Malaysia' (please see ss. 2(1) and 2(2)(a) AA for the meaning of 'international arbitration'). Section 11(3) AA has been introduced by the 2011 Amendment Act and empowers Malaysian courts to give interim relief for a cause of action which arises outside Malaysia ... .

CHAPTER 3
Composition of Arbitrators

12. *Number of Arbitrators*

(1) The parties are free to determine the number of arbitrators.
(2) Where the parties fail to determine the number of arbitrators, the arbitral tribunal shall –
   (a) in the case of an international arbitration, consist of three arbitrators; and
   (b) in the case of a domestic arbitration, consist of a single arbitrator.

§12.01 INTRODUCTION

Section 12 of the Arbitration Act 2005 provides for the number of arbitrators in situations both where parties agree to the number and where they do not.

Section 12 of the Arbitration Act 2005 reflects Article 10 of the 1985 Model Law save that section 12 provides for a single arbitrator in the case of domestic arbitration.

This difference is because the Arbitration Act 2005 provides for both domestic and international arbitration under section 3, while the 1985 Model Law only provides for international arbitration under Article 1(1).

Article 10 of the 1985 Model Law is in turn based on Article 5 of the 1976 UNCITRAL Arbitration Rules, which provides:

> Article 5 – Number of arbitrators
>
> If the parties have not previously agreed on the number of arbitrators (ie one or three), and if within fifteen days after the receipt by the respondent of the notice of arbitration the parties have not agreed that there shall be only one arbitrator, three arbitrators shall be appointed.

The current 2013 UNCITRAL Arbitration Rules provide for more flexibility in Article 7. This article provides for three arbitrators by default, unless a party has not objected to a proposal by the other party that there be only a sole arbitrator and the appointing authority determines this is appropriate. Article 7 of the 2010 UNCITRAL Arbitration Rules provides:

> Article 7 – Number of Arbitrators
> 1. If the parties have not previously agreed on the number of arbitrators, and if within 30 days after the receipt by the respondent of the notice of arbitration the parties have not agreed that there shall be only one arbitrator, three arbitrators shall be appointed.
> 2. Notwithstanding paragraph 1, if no other parties have responded to a party's proposal to appoint a sole arbitrator within the time limit provided for in paragraph 1 and the party or parties concerned have failed to appoint a second arbitrator in accordance with articles 9 or 10, the appointing authority may, at the request of a party, appoint a sole arbitrator pursuant to the procedure provided for in article 8, paragraph 2 if it determines that, in view of the circumstances of the case, this is more appropriate.

The 2013 UNCITRAL Arbitration Rules form part of the 2018 AIAC Arbitration Rules.

§12.02 TWO-LEVEL SYSTEM

Section 12 of the Arbitration Act 2005 and Article 10 of the 1985 Model Law illustrate the 'two-level system', which is typical of the Arbitration Act 2005 and the 1985 Model Law that it reflects.[1]

The 'two-level system' allows the parties to first agree on any issue and, second, in the absence of an agreement, provides for a set of default provisions. These types of provisions are found throughout the Arbitration Act 2005 and are usually prefaced by the words 'unless otherwise agreed'.

§12.03 PARTY AUTONOMY

Section 12(1) of the Arbitration Act 2005 recognizes the parties' right to agree on the number of arbitrators. This freedom is given primacy and any number agreed upon between the parties will be given effect to. This includes situations where parties have agreed to an even number of arbitrators, which is not prohibited by the Arbitration Act 2005. However, it would be prudent to agree on an uneven number of arbitrators to avoid a deadlock.[2]

It is also important to bear in mind that the parties' freedom to agree on the number of arbitrators under section 12(1) includes the freedom to allow a third party or a set of arbitration rules to determine the number of arbitrators under sections 2(2)(b) and (c) of the Arbitration Act 2005.

This issue arose in *AV Asia Sdn Bhd v. Pengarah Kuala Lumpur Regional Centre for Arbitration & Anor* [2013] 10 CLJ 115, where it was argued that a single arbitrator

---

1. *See* Analytical Commentary, Article 10, commentary 1.
2. *See* Analytical Commentary, Article 10, commentary 2.

should be appointed, as it was a domestic arbitration under section 12(2) of the Arbitration Act 2005, although the parties had agreed to the 2012 KLRCA Arbitration Rules under section 12(1) that provided for three arbitrators. However, the High Court declined to determine this issue on the grounds that it had no power to intervene under section 12 and left the issue to be determined by the arbitral tribunal under section 18 of the Arbitration Act 2005.

§12.04 THREE ARBITRATORS OR A SINGLE ARBITRATOR

In the absence of agreement, section 12(2) of the Arbitration Act 2005 provides that three arbitrators shall be appointed for an international arbitration and a single arbitrator for domestic arbitration.

The terms 'international arbitration' and 'domestic arbitration' are defined in section 2(1) of the Arbitration Act 2005 and reference should be made to §2.10 *supra* in this regard.

The provision on international arbitration in section 12(2)(a) of the Arbitration Act 2005 reflects Article 10(2) of the 1985 Model Law. Three arbitrators were chosen as the default by the 1985 Model Law, as it is the most common number in international arbitration. Single arbitrators are also common for less complex matters to save time and costs. However, it was felt that if the parties wanted a single arbitrator for these reasons, they would have expressly provided for this, with the default provision serving as an added inducement.[3]

A single arbitrator is provided for in the case of domestic arbitration, probably because this is again the most accepted number for domestic arbitration in Malaysia.

For example, the standard forms of building contracts published by the PWD and the Malaysian Institute of Architects both provide for a single arbitrator.

---

3. *See* Analytical Commentary, Article 10, commentary 3.

13. Appointment of Arbitrators

   (1) Unless otherwise agreed by the parties, no person shall be precluded by reason of nationality from acting as an arbitrator.
   (2) The parties are free to agree on a procedure for appointing the arbitrator or the presiding arbitrator.
   (3) Where the parties fail to agree on the procedure referred to in subsection (2), and the arbitration consists of three arbitrators, each party shall appoint one arbitrator, and the two appointed arbitrators shall appoint the third arbitrator as the presiding arbitrator.
   (4) Where subsection (3) applies and –
      (a) a party fails to appoint an arbitrator within thirty days of receipt of a request in writing to do so from the other party; or
      (b) the two arbitrators fail to agree on the third arbitrator within thirty days of their appointment or such extended period as the parties may agree,
      either party may apply to the Director of the Asian International Arbitration Centre (Malaysia) for such appointment.
   (5) Where in an arbitration with a single arbitrator –
      (a) the parties fail to agree on the procedure referred to in subsection (2); and
      (b) the parties fail to agree on the arbitrator,
      either party may apply to the Director of the Asian International Arbitration Centre (Malaysia) for the appointment of an arbitrator.
   (6) Where, the parties have agreed on the procedure for appointment of the arbitrator –
      (a) a party fails to act as required under such procedure;
      (b) the parties, or two arbitrators, are unable to reach an agreement under such procedure; or
      (c) a third party, including an institution, fails to perform any function entrusted to it under such procedure,
      any party may request the Director of the Asian International Arbitration Centre (Malaysia) to take the necessary measures, unless the agreement on the appointment procedure provides other means for securing the appointment.
   (7) Where the Director of the Asian International Arbitration Centre (Malaysia) is unable to act or fails to act under subsections (4), (5) and (6) within thirty days from the request, any party may apply to the High Court for such appointment.
   (8) In appointing an arbitrator the Director of the Asian International Arbitration Centre (Malaysia) or the High Court, as the case may be, shall have due regard to –
      (a) any qualifications required of the arbitrator by the agreement of the parties;
      (b) other considerations that are likely to secure the appointment of an independent and impartial arbitrator; and
      (c) in the case of an international arbitration, the advisability of appointing an arbitrator of a nationality other than those of the parties.

(9) No appeal shall lie against any decision of the Director of the Asian International Arbitration Centre (Malaysia) or the High Court under this section.

§13.01 INTRODUCTION

Section 13 of the Arbitration Act 2005 provides for the appointment of the arbitral tribunal, either in the manner agreed upon by the parties or, in the absence of an agreement, in accordance with the provisions of the Act. In this way, section 13 continues the 'two-level system' found in section 12, where the parties are given the freedom to agree, but if there is no agreement, the provisions of the Arbitration Act 2005 apply.

Section 13 of the Arbitration Act 2005 largely reflects Article 11 of the 1985 Model Law save for some alterations in drafting and three significant changes:

(1) the words 'subject to the provisions of paragraphs (4) and (5) of this article' found in Article 11(2) of the 1985 Model Law were not included in section 13(2) of the Arbitration Act 2005. These words in Article 11(2) are intended to show that Articles 11(4) and (5) of the 1985 Model Law are mandatory.[4]

Sections 13(6), (8) and (9) of the Arbitration Act 2005 are the equivalent of Articles 11(4) and (5) of the 1985 Model Law. It is submitted that section 13(6), and its equivalent Article 11(4), despite Article 11(2), is not mandatory. This is because both section 13(6) and Article 11(4) provide that 'unless the agreement on the appointment procedure provides other means of securing the appointment' and to that extent is not mandatory and is still subject to agreement between the parties.

Sections 13(8) and (9) like Article 11(5) provide for matters to be considered by the appointing authority and that the decision of the appointing authority may not be appealed against. These provisions, save for section 13(8)(c), would appear to be mandatory even in the absence of words to this effect in section 13(2);

(2) 'the court or other authority' referred to in Article 11 of the 1985 Model Law is specified as the Director of the AIAC in section 13 of the Arbitration Act 2005. Section 13(7) of the Arbitration Act 2005 provides that, if the Director of the AIAC does not act within thirty days, any party may apply to the High Court. There is no equivalent provision to section 13(7) in the 1985 Model Law. This additional provision is necessary in the Arbitration Act 2005 as the appointing authority is the head of an arbitral institution rather than the courts; and

---

4. *See* Analytical Commentary, Article 11, commentary 2.

(3) section 13(8)(c) of the Arbitration Act 2005 omits the words 'in the case of a sole or third arbitrator' found in Article 11(5) of the 1985 Model Law. It is submitted that these words should not have been omitted, as the need for an arbitrator of a nationality other than the parties in international arbitration only arises in the context of a sole or presiding arbitrator. The two party-appointed arbitrators are not required to be of a nationality other than the party appointing them, and, in practice, frequently a party-appointed arbitrator will be of the same nationality as the party who appointed him.

§13.02 NO RESTRICTION ON NATIONALITY

Section 13(1) of the Arbitration Act 2005, like Article 11(1) of the 1985 Model Law, prohibits any person being prevented from acting as an arbitrator on the grounds of nationality. This provision was included in the 1985 Model Law because some national laws precluded foreigners from acting as arbitrators even in international cases.[5]

There are no provisions under the laws of Malaysia that preclude foreigners from acting as arbitrators. Therefore, section 13(1) of the Arbitration Act 2005 gives statutory force to the existing position.

However, it must be borne in mind that section 13(1) of the Arbitration Act 2005, like Article 11(1) of the 1985 Model Law, is a derogable provision, meaning that the parties may agree otherwise. In this context, parties do agree in international matters that a single arbitrator or the presiding arbitrator, in the case of an arbitral tribunal comprising three arbitrators, will be of a nationality other than the nationality of the two parties.

§13.03 PARTY AUTONOMY

Section 13(2) of the Arbitration Act 2005, like Article 11(2) of the 1985 Model Law, recognizes the parties' freedom to agree on the procedure for the appointment of an arbitral tribunal. This freedom should be interpreted broadly as including the right to agree that these matters be decided by a third party or in accordance with arbitration rules pursuant to sections 2(2)(b) and (c) of the Arbitration Act 2005.[6]

Although the words 'subject to the provisions of paragraphs (4) and (5) of this article' found in Article 11(2) are not found in section 13, as submitted in §13.01 *supra*, the effect of section 13 as a whole is the same. To that extent, the freedom granted to the parties under section 13(2) is to some extent limited by sections 13(6), (8) and (9).

Section 13(2) is the first step in the 'two-level system' mentioned earlier. If the parties have failed to agree on a procedure for the appointment of arbitrators, then the procedure in sections 13(3)-(5) will apply.

---

5. *See* Analytical Commentary, Article 11, commentary 1.
6. *See* Analytical Commentary, Article 11, commentary 2.

§13.04 DEFAULT PROCEDURE

Sections 13(3)-(5) of the Arbitration Act 2005, which reflect Article 11(3) of the 1985 Model Law, are the second step in the 'two-level system' and provide for the default provisions that apply when the parties have not agreed on the procedure for the appointment of arbitrators.

Sections 13(3) and (4) provide for a situation where an arbitral tribunal of three arbitrators is to be appointed. Section 13(3) provides that each party will appoint an arbitrator and the two arbitrators will then appoint a third arbitrator. Section 13(4) further provides that where the procedure set out in section 13(3) breaks down due to a party not appointing an arbitrator within thirty days of being requested to do so by the other party or the two arbitrators not appointing a presiding arbitrator within thirty days, then either party may apply to the Director of the AIAC to appoint an arbitrator.

Section 13(5) provides for a situation where a sole arbitrator is to be appointed. Here, either party may apply to the Director of the AIAC to appoint an arbitrator if the parties are unable to agree on an arbitrator. Unlike section 13(4), a time limit of thirty days is not given for the parties to agree on the appointment of a sole arbitrator. The absence of a time limit was acceptable in this case since the persons expected to agree are the parties and their inability to agree would become apparent from the application to the Director of the AIAC for the appointment of an arbitrator.[7]

Sections 13(3)-(5) of the Arbitration Act 2005, like Article 11(3) of the 1985 Model Law, only provide the default procedure for the appointment of a sole arbitrator and an arbitral tribunal of three arbitrators, as these numbers are the most common in international commercial arbitration.[8]

The Arbitration Act 2005 does not provide a default procedure for the appointment of an arbitral tribunal comprised of two, four or more arbitrators, as it was thought to be undesirable to list out the default procedure for an unlimited number of arbitrators.[9]

The Court of Appeal, in *Sebiro Holdings Sdn Bhd v. Bhag Singh & Anor* [2015] 4 CLJ 209 at paragraph 13, recognized the importance of sections 13(3)-(5) in breaking any deadlock between the parties and ensuring the arbitral tribunal was constituted:

> It bears reiterating that though arbitration is intended for a voluntary process, once a dispute has arisen, even parties acting bona fide find it difficult to agree, ex post facto. Parties may attempt to obstruct the appointment to delay the arbitration. This can frustrate the agreement. In our view, sub-ss. 13(3) and (5) of Act 646 are a means of breaking deadlock that render the agreement inoperable … .

The High Court, in *Pendaftar Pertubuhan Malaysia v. Establishmen Tribunal Timbangtara Malaysia & Ors* [2011] 6 CLJ 684 at paragraph 26, emphasized that before these default provisions could operate there must first be an arbitration agreement between the parties.

---

7. *See* Analytical Commentary, Article 11, commentary 6.
8. *See* Analytical Commentary, Article 11, commentary 5.
9. *See* Dr Peter Binder, *International Commercial Arbitration and Conciliation in UNCITRAL Model Law Jurisdictions* (3rd edn, Sweet & Maxwell 2010) at para 3.031.

The High Court, in *Majlis Ugama Islam dan Adat Resam Melayu Pahang v. Far East Holdings Bhd & Anor* [2007] 10 CLJ 318 at paragraph 22, decided that, when a court granted a stay, the court may also refer the dispute to the Director of the KLRCA for the appointment of an arbitrator under these default provisions:

> The parties in this case cannot agree on a common arbitrator. Section 13 is thus invoked and the court by its power under s. 10(2) made an order referring the dispute to the D-KLRCA for an appointment of an arbitrator as provided for under s. 13(5) of the 2005 Act. Though s. 13(5) states that parties may apply to the D-KLRCA for the appointment of an arbitrator, this court feels that the fact this court itself makes the order to refer to D-KLRCA, is in itself within its power under s. 10(2) to make such consequential order or condition as it deems fit and to reflect and give spirit to the intention of s. 13 of the Act.

§13.05 ASSISTANCE WITH AGREED PROCEDURE

Section 13(6) of the Arbitration Act 2005, which resembles Article 11(4) of the 1985 Model Law, provides for assistance where the agreed procedure between the parties for the appointment of an arbitral tribunal has broken down. Section 13(6) envisages three situations where the agreed procedure may break down; all these situations deal with circumstances where a person has failed to act as he should under the agreed procedure. The first scenario is where a party has failed to act, the second is where the parties or two arbitrators have failed to agree and the third is where a third party, usually the arbitral institution, has failed to act.

In all three situations, a party may apply to the Director of the AIAC to take the necessary measures unless the agreement on procedure provides for such a scenario.

Section 13(6) does not expressly provide for the type of measures to be taken by the Director of the AIAC. It is unclear whether the Director should take the step which the person had failed to take under one of the three scenarios in section 13(6) or should directly appoint an arbitrator even if there is some preliminary step that has yet to be taken by a person.

For example, an arbitration agreement provides that Party A shall nominate three arbitrators, from which, Party B may select two arbitrators from the three nominated, and Party A may then appoint one of these two arbitrators as the sole arbitrator. If Party B does not select two arbitrators from the three nominated by Party A, it is unclear whether the Director of the AIAC should select two arbitrators from the three proposed by Party B or directly appoint a sole arbitrator. This question is of significance, as it may amount to grounds for setting aside an award under section 37(1)(a)(vi) of the Arbitration Act 2005.

The purpose of section 13(6) of the Arbitration Act 2005 is to prevent undue delay or a deadlock by means of assistance from the Director of the AIAC. Given the purpose of this provision, it is submitted that the Director should directly proceed to appoint the arbitral tribunal in the event of a breakdown in the procedure.

Section 13(6) allows for assistance by the Director of the AIAC unless the agreement on procedure provides other means. The reference to an agreement on procedure should be given a liberal meaning to include any agreement for the deadlock to be resolved by a third party or arbitration rules pursuant to sections 2(2)(b) and (c) of the Arbitration Act 2005. There is, of course, the scenario where the third party, who is usually the arbitral institution, itself fails to act, in which case a party may also seek assistance from the Director of the AIAC.

§13.06 DIRECTOR'S FAILURE TO ACT

Section 13(7) provides that if the Director does not act within thirty days, a party may apply to the High Court for the appointment of an arbitrator. Section 13(7) of the Arbitration Act 2005 does not have an equivalent provision in the 1985 Model Law.

Section 13(7) is included in the Arbitration Act 2005 because an arbitral institution rather than the courts is designated as the default appointing authority. While this carries with it the advantage of speed, convenience and reduced costs, there is a risk that the arbitral institution itself may not act. As such, there is a need for a default provision allowing parties to apply to the High Court in the event the Director of the AIAC does not act.

§13.07 GUIDELINES FOR APPOINTMENT

Section 13(8) of the Arbitration Act 2005, which reflects Article 11(5) of the 1985 Model Law, provides guidelines for the appointment of arbitrators to the Director of the AIAC and the High Court.

It is submitted that the first two guidelines are binding as they flow from the arbitration agreement or the need for an independent and impartial arbitrator under section 12 of the Arbitration Act 2005.[10]

The third guideline in section 13(8)(c) should be viewed in the light of section 13(1) of the Arbitration Act 2005. While there is a prohibition against restricting persons on the grounds of nationality from acting as arbitrators, it is recognized that in international arbitration it may be advisable to have an arbitrator of a nationality other than the parties. As mentioned in §13.01 *supra*, it is unfortunate that the words 'in the case of a sole or third arbitrator' in Article 11(5) of the 1985 Model Law were omitted from section 13(8)(c) of the Arbitration Act 2005, as the need for an arbitrator of a nationality other than that of the parties only arises in the context of a sole or third arbitrator in international arbitration.

It is submitted that the third guideline is discretionary and not mandatory, as is implicit from the use of the word 'advisability'. As such, the parties may stipulate otherwise in their agreement with respect to the nationality of the arbitrators.

The Court of Appeal, in *Sebiro Holdings Sdn Bhd v. Bhag Singh & Anor* [2015] 4 CLJ 209, clarified that the Director of the AIAC's powers under section 13(8) of the Arbitration Act 2005 are administrative powers and not judicial. The Director is accordingly not required to allow the parties a chance to be heard or to consider any

---

10. *See* Analytical Commentary, Article 11, commentary 8.

jurisdictional issue. The Court of Appeal, in *Sebiro Holdings supra* at paragraph 17, held:

> It should be noted that the power exercised by the Director of the KLRCA under sub-ss. 13(4) and (5) of Act 646 is an administrative power. The Director of the KLCRA is not required to determine the question of the validity of the arbitration agreement, the maintainability and arbitrability of the claim and other jurisdictional matters. The subsections merely provide for the Director of the KLRCA to appoint arbitrator(s) in the event the parties fail to agree on the arbitration. The director's function is not a judicial function where he has to afford the right to be heard to the parties before an arbitrator(s) is appointed.

§13.08 NO APPEAL

Section 13(9) of the Arbitration Act 2005, which reflects Article 11(5) of the 1985 Model Law, provides that no appeal shall lie against any decision by the Director of the AIAC or the High Court on the appointment of an arbitrator.

This provision is appropriate for two reasons. First, as explained in *Sebiro Holdings supra*, the decision on the appointment of an arbitrator is an administrative matter. Second, there is the need for the arbitral tribunal to be constituted as soon as possible without delays caused by appeals.[11]

---

11. *See* Analytical Commentary, Article 11, commentary 7.

14. *Grounds for Challenge*

(1) A person who is approached in connection with that person's possible appointment as an arbitrator shall disclose any circumstances likely to give rise to justifiable doubts as to that person's impartiality or independence.
(2) An arbitrator shall, without delay, from the time of appointment and throughout the arbitral proceedings, disclose any circumstances referred to in subsection (1) to the parties unless the parties have already been informed of such circumstances by the arbitrator.
(3) An arbitrator may be challenged only if –
 (a) the circumstances give rise to justifiable doubts as to that arbitrator's impartiality or independence; or
 (b) that arbitrator does not possess qualifications agreed to by the parties.
(4) A party may challenge an arbitrator appointed by that party, or in whose appointment that party has participated, only for reasons which that party becomes aware of after the appointment has been made.

§14.01 INTRODUCTION

Section 14 of the Arbitration Act 2005 sets out the grounds for challenging an arbitrator. There are three grounds, which are lack of impartiality, independence or qualifications.

Section 14 of the Arbitration Act 2005 reflects Article 12 of the 1985 Model Law. In particular, sections 14(1) and (2) reflect Article 12(1) and sections 14(3) and (4) reflect Article 12(3) and (4).

Article 12 of the 1985 Model Law in turn reflects Articles 9 and 10 of the 1976 UNCITRAL Arbitration Rules. Article 12(1) of the 1985 Model Law reflects Article 9 of the 1976 UNCITRAL Arbitration Rules, while Article 12(2) of the 1985 Model Law reflects Article 10 of the 1976 UNCITRAL Arbitration Rules.

§14.02 DISCLOSURE

Unlike a judge, most arbitrators continue to practise in their chosen professions. This can give rise to conflicts of interest. Sections 14(1) and (2) of the Arbitration Act 2005 provide for this by requiring an arbitrator to disclose any circumstances likely to give rise to justifiable doubts as to his impartiality or independence. This obligation to disclose is broader than may be assumed on two counts.

First, the obligation to disclose is not limited to the parties. The arbitrator is also obliged to make disclosure to the arbitral institution that approaches him for an appointment.[12] Furthermore, an arbitrator is also required to make disclosure to his co-arbitrators in the case of an arbitral tribunal comprising two or more arbitrators.[13]

---
12. *See* Analytical Commentary, Article 12, commentary 2.
13. *See Sundra Rajoo v. Mohamed Abd Majed & Anor* [2011] 6 CLJ 923, HC.

Second, the obligation to disclose is not limited to the time of appointment. Instead, as expressly provided under section 14(2) of the Arbitration Act 2005, this is a continuing duty.

This continuing obligation is important because circumstances change. Therefore, an arbitrator who was not initially conflicted may later become potentially conflicted, due to, for example, a new business affiliation or acquisition of shares.[14]

The obligation to disclose covers not only the present and the future but also the past. This was emphasized by the High Court in *Sundra Rajoo supra*, where the party-appointed arbitrator was required to disclose prior appointments by the same party. However, as decided by the High Court, in *MMC Engineering Group Bhd & Anor v. Wayss & Freytag (M) Sdn Bhd & Anor* [2015] MLJU 477, this obligation may not extend to making disclosure of allegations, even of a criminal nature, made against an arbitrator in a prior unrelated arbitration.

§14.03 GROUNDS

Section 14(3) of the Arbitration Act 2005 provides that the only grounds for challenging an arbitrator are a lack of impartiality, independence or qualifications. It is important to note that these are the 'only' grounds for challenge provided by the Arbitration Act 2005. The use of the word 'only' indicates that these grounds are exhaustive.[15]

Instead of listing out specific grounds for challenge, the Arbitration Act 2005 has adopted a broad test in section 14(3)(a). The words 'impartiality' and 'independence' have distinct but overlapping meanings.

'Impartiality' is the autonym of bias. And, bias is a predisposition to decide in favour of one party without proper regard to the merits of the dispute.[16] The test is a 'real danger of bias' and only a possibility needs to be shown, not a probability.[17] 'Independence' is the absence of any relationship between the parties, a party or the dispute.[18]

The High Court, in *Sundra Rajoo supra* at paragraph 10(b), has emphasized that a party-appointed arbitrator in an arbitral tribunal comprised of three arbitrators is required to be impartial and independent:

> It must be noted that: (i) the requirement of impartiality is a principle of natural justice; (ii) it is a fundamental principle that an arbitrator must remain independent and impartial; (iii) where an arbitral tribunal contains party-nominated arbitrators, the presumption remains that, even if nominated by one of the parties, the arbitrator will be independent and impartial; (iv) a party-nominated arbitrator is usually appointed in international arbitrations by reason of culture or background, to be broadly sympathetic with the case to be put forward, but who will be

---

14. *See* Analytical Commentary, Article 12, commentary 3.
15. *See* Analytical Commentary, Article 12, commentary 4.
16. *See MMC Engineering supra* at para. 171, HC; *Sabah Medical Centre Sdn Bhd v. Syarikat Neptune Enterprise Sdn Bhd & Anor* [2012] 10 CLJ 767 at para. 2, HC.
17. *See Sabah Medical Centre supra* at para. 3, HC.
18. *See MMC Engineering supra* at para. 171.

strictly impartial when it comes to assessing the facts and evaluating the arguments on fact and law; (v) a party may nominate an arbitrator who is generally predisposed towards it personally, or as regards to its position in the dispute, provided that the person concerned is at the same time capable of impartial and judicial application to the evidence and arguments submitted by both parties.

A variety of situations have been considered by the courts in determining whether an arbitrator lacks impartiality or independence.

As stated above, the High Court, in *Sundra Rajoo supra*, emphasized that a party-nominated arbitrator must be impartial and independent. In this regard, the High Court, in *Sundra Rajoo supra* at paragraph 10(h), specifically held that if an arbitrator did not disclose all his other appointments by the party who appointed him within a given period of time, the arbitrator would be removed.

This reflects the general perception that the frequent appointment of an arbitrator by a party may give rise to partiality towards that party. However, in a commodities arbitration, like the palm oil arbitration in *Sundra Rajoo supra*, it is not uncommon for a party to repeatedly appoint the same arbitrator due to the small specialized pool of arbitrators.[19]

The High Court, in *Tan Sri Dato' Professor Dr Lim Kok Wing v. Thurai Das a/l Thuraisingham & Anor* [2011] 1 LNS 717, considered a situation where the same arbitrator had been appointed in two arbitrations arising from a building project. The first arbitration was between the contractor and the employer, while the second arbitration was between the architect and the employer. The employer challenged the arbitrator in the first arbitration on the grounds that the arbitrator would be influenced by events in the second arbitration. The High Court, in *Tan Sri Dato' Professor Dr Lim Kok Wing supra* at page 17, decided that it was 'most improbable' that the arbitrator would be so influenced and dismissed the challenge.

The High Court, in *Sabah Medical Centre supra*, decided that statements made by an arbitrator in an interim award that appeared to determine issues that had yet to be heard did give rise to justifiable doubts as to his impartiality. In this regard, the High Court, in *Sabah Medical Centre supra* at paragraph 13, held:

> In his interim award the arbitrator assures that he has not made up his mind on issues relating to the set-off claims. This is cold comfort to SMC because by having those negative thoughts at the back of his mind, there is a real possibility that the arbitrator has prefixed his conclusions on the bona fides of SMC's claims. Such negative predisposition will be difficult to displace and SMC should not be put through a hearing which appears to be predetermined. It strikes at the very heart of the rule that no person shall be condemned unless given the opportunity of being heard: *Ridge v. Baldwin* [1964] AC 40. In *Metramac, supra*, the Federal Court held that language by a judge suggesting that careful consideration has been given does not preclude scrutiny of the judgment for bias.

The High Court, in *MMC Engineering supra*, considered a situation where a party-appointed arbitrator in an arbitral tribunal of three arbitrators had been charged

---

19. *See* 2014 IBA Guidelines on Conflict of Interest in International Arbitration, Orange List, para 3.1.3 and footnote 5.

with bribery in relation to an earlier unrelated arbitration. There were pending civil and criminal proceedings arising from these allegations of bribery. Apart from this, it was also alleged that the arbitrator had used submissions, delivered by a party in the present arbitration, to prepare submissions for use in the earlier arbitration to assist the party who bribed him. The High Court, in *MMC Engineering supra* at paragraph 172, held that these allegations did not give rise to justifiable doubts as to impartiality as there was a failure to establish a causal link between the earlier arbitration and the present arbitration:

> As was the case with the character ground, matters concerning the arbitrator's impartiality and independence must be determined by reference to the parties and issues in or to a particular arbitration. It is not enough if not unsafe, to accuse an arbitrator of bias, that he lacks impartiality or independence in one arbitration proceeding as a basis for alleging bias and the like against that arbitrator in another arbitration proceeding. This is regardless the seriousness of the allegation in the first arbitration proceeding. I would venture to say that to accept such an allegation is extremely far-reaching; not to mention that it violates the basic tenets of fairness and justice to the arbitrator accused of such lapses to find against him by way of setting aside the seeds of his work; without more.

Based on these authorities, there is an emphasis placed on the facts directly related to the arbitration. Where the challenge arises from facts directly related to the arbitration, like the arbitrator's failure to disclose prior appointments by a party in *Sundra Rajoo supra* and the intemperate interim award in *Sabah Medical Centre supra*, the courts are more likely to uphold the challenge. However, where the facts are not directly related to the arbitration, like the other arbitrations in *Tan Sri Dato' Dr Lim Kok Wing supra* and *MMC Engineering supra*, it appears that the courts are reluctant to allow the challenge.

Apart from impartiality and independence, an arbitrator may also be challenged if he does not have 'qualifications agreed to by the parties'. It is essential that these qualifications have been agreed upon by the parties, usually in the arbitration agreement. If the parties have agreed that an arbitrator should have certain qualifications, either party may challenge the arbitrator if he does not possess such qualifications. However, where there is no such agreement, a party cannot later insist on particular qualifications and challenge an arbitrator for lacking such qualifications. This was recognized by the Court of Appeal, in *Sebiro Holdings Sdn Bhd v. Bhag Singh & Anor* [2015] 4 CLJ 209 at paragraphs 18-21.

§14.04 ESTOPPEL

Section 14(4) of the Arbitration Act 2005 gives statutory force to the rules of estoppel in the context of the appointment of an arbitrator. A party is estopped from challenging an arbitrator, who he appointed or participated in appointing, on the grounds the party already knew of before the appointment.

In this regard, the word 'participated' used in section 14(4) should be construed broadly to include situations where the party has been involved in the process of appointment of the arbitrator, for example, the list-procedure under Article 6(3) of the 1976 UNCITRAL Arbitration Rules.[20]

---

20. *See* Analytical Commentary, Article 12, commentary 6.

15. *Challenge Procedure*

> *(1) Unless otherwise agreed by the parties, any party who intends to challenge an arbitrator shall, within fifteen days after becoming aware of the constitution of the arbitral tribunal or of any reasons referred to in subsection 14(3), send a written statement of the reasons for the challenge to the arbitral tribunal.*
>
> *(2) Unless the challenged arbitrator withdraws from office or the other party agrees to the challenge, the arbitral tribunal shall make a decision on the challenge.*
>
> *(3) Where a challenge is not successful, the challenging party may, within thirty days after having received notice of the decision rejecting the challenge, apply to the High Court to make a decision on the challenge.*
>
> *(4) While such an application is pending, the arbitral tribunal, including the challenged arbitrator, may continue the arbitral proceedings and make an award.*
>
> *(5) No appeal shall lie against the decision of the High Court under subsection (3).*

§15.01 INTRODUCTION

Section 15 of the Arbitration Act 2005 provides the procedure for challenging an arbitrator, where the parties have not agreed on such a procedure. Sections 15(1) and (2) of the Arbitration Act 2005 reflect Article 13(2) of the 1985 Model Law, while sections 15(3)-(5) reflect Article 13(3). Section 15 of the Arbitration Act 2005 and Article 13 of the 1985 Model Law differ in the following aspects:

(1) Article 13(1) of the 1985 Model Law is not included in the Arbitration Act 2005. Article 13(1) provides:

> The parties are free to agree on procedure for challenging an arbitrator, subject to the provisions of paragraph (3) of this article.

(2) the opening words of Article 13(3) of the 1985 Model Law, i.e. 'if challenge under any procedure agreed upon by the parties or under the procedure of paragraph (2) of this article ...', are not included in the corresponding section 15(3) of the Arbitration Act 2005.

These provisions in Article 13 of the 1985 Model Law that have been omitted from section 15 of the Arbitration Act 2005 make it clear that the parties are free to agree on the procedure for challenge to an arbitrator subject to the ultimate decision on a challenge being made by the court.

By omitting these provisions from section 15 of the Arbitration Act 2005, it is less clear whether this position applies in Malaysia. From the opening words of section 15(1) of the Arbitration Act 2005, it appears clear that the parties are free to agree on the procedure. However, it is unclear whether sections 15(3)-(5) are mandatory.

§15.02 DEFAULT PROCEDURE

Sections 15(1) and (2) of the Arbitration Act 2005 follow the usual 'two-level system'. The parties are free to agree on the procedure for challenge, failing which the default procedure applies.

Under the default procedure, a party must submit a written statement of the grounds of challenge within fifteen days of the constitution of the arbitral tribunal or of the party becoming aware of the grounds.

Thereafter, the arbitral tribunal must make a decision on the challenge, unless the challenged arbitrator withdraws or the other party agrees with the challenge.

Where the arbitral tribunal comprises three arbitrators, they would all need to make a decision on the challenge. A challenge is not a question of procedure that can be decided by the presiding arbitrator alone under section 31(2) of the Arbitration Act 2005.[21]

In the case of a sole arbitrator, it is unclear whether a formal decision is required, as requiring such a decision would be of little 'practical relevance'.[22]

It has been suggested that in the case of a sole arbitrator, the decision not to withdraw itself amounts to a decision on the challenge, allowing a party to apply to the High Court under section 15(3).[23]

§15.03 APPLICATION TO HIGH COURT

Section 15(3) of the Arbitration Act 2005 allows a challenging party that was unsuccessful to apply to the High Court for a decision.

The High Court, in *Tan Sri Dato' Professor Dr Lim Kok Wing v. Thurai Das a/l Thuraisingham & Anor* [2011] 1 LNS 717 at pages 13 and 14, emphasized that the procedure set out in sections 15(1) and (2) must first be complied with before any application may be made to the High Court under section 15(3).

This approach of the High Court is consistent with section 8 of the Arbitration Act 2005 and the policy of minimalist intervention envisaged by that section. In accordance with this policy, the arbitral tribunal must be allowed to decide matters first before they are raised before the courts.

§15.04 PREVENTING DILATORY TACTICS

As stated above, sections 15(3)-(5) of the Arbitration Act 2005 reflect Article 13(3) of the 1985 Model Law. Article 13(3) was a compromise between two divergent views. One of the views was that no appeal should lie against the arbitral tribunal's decision on the challenge, with any dissatisfaction being taken up later in an application to set aside the final award. This was to prevent dilatory tactics but would have had the

---

21. *See* Analytical Commentary, Article 13, commentary 4.
22. *See* Analytical Commentary, Article 13, commentary 4.
23. *See* Dr Peter Binder, *International Commercial Arbitration and Conciliation in UNCITRAL Model Law Jurisdictions* (3rd edn, Sweet & Maxwell 2010) at para 3-074.

unfortunate result of leaving a challenged arbitrator on the tribunal until the final award. The other view was that an appeal against any decision of the arbitral tribunal on a challenge could be made immediately with the proceedings suspended pending a decision by the courts on the challenge. This would however result in deliberate dilatory tactics.[24]

As a compromise, section 15(3) allows for an immediate appeal to the High Court but puts in place these safeguards against dilatory tactics:[25]

(1) first, an application to the High Court must be made within thirty days under section 15(3);
(2) second, the arbitral tribunal may continue the proceedings and even make an award, despite an application in the High Court pending under section 15(4); and
(3) third, no appeal lies against any decision of the High Court in this regard under section 15(5).

---

24. *See* Analytical Commentary, Article 13, commentary 5.
25. *See* Analytical Commentary, Article 13, commentary 6.

16. *Failure or Impossibility to Act*

(1) *Where an arbitrator becomes in law or in fact unable to perform the functions of that office, or for other reasons fails to act without undue delay, that arbitrator's mandate terminates on withdrawal from office or if the parties agree on the termination.*

(2) *Where any party disagrees on the termination of the mandate of the arbitrator, any party may apply to the High Court to decide on such termination and no appeal shall lie against the decision of the High Court.*

(3) *Where, under this section or subsection 15(2), an arbitrator withdraws from office or a party agrees to the termination of the mandate of an arbitrator, it shall not imply acceptance of the validity of any ground referred to in this section or subsection 14(3).*

§16.01 INTRODUCTION

Section 16 of the Arbitration Act 2005 deals with an arbitrator's inability to perform his function and the steps that can be taken as a result of such a disability.

Section 16 of the Arbitration Act 2005 reflects Article 14 of the 1985 Model Law with minor differences in drafting. Sections 16(1) and (2) of the Arbitration Act 2005 are based on Article 14(1) of the 1985 Model Law, and section 16(3) is based on Article 14(2).

Article 14 of the 1985 Model Law is in turn based on Article 13(2) of the 1976 UNCITRAL Arbitration Rules, which provides:

> In the event that an arbitrator fails to act or in the event of the de jure or de facto impossibility of his performing his functions, the procedure in respect of the challenge and replacement of an arbitrator as provided in the preceding articles shall apply.

A similar provision is found in Article 12(3) of the 2013 UNCITRAL Arbitration Rules, which forms part of the 2018 AIAC Arbitration Rules.

§16.02 INABILITY AND DELAY

Section 16(1) of the Arbitration Act 2005 provides three situations, where an arbitrator's mandate may terminate by either his withdrawal or the parties' agreement:

(1) where the arbitrator becomes in law unable to perform the functions of his office;
(2) where the arbitrator becomes in fact unable to perform the functions of his office; or
(3) where the arbitrator for other reasons fails to act without undue delay.

We will consider each of these three situations below.

First, an arbitrator will be unable to perform his function in law if he is declared bankrupt or convicted of crime. Second, an arbitrator will be unable to perform his functions in fact due to death or disability. In practice, little controversy is likely to arise from these two situations, when either the arbitrator will withdraw or the parties will agree to the termination of his mandate.

Controversy may, however, arise in the context of the third situation. Here, the question will be whether the arbitrator for other reasons has failed to act with undue delay. In this context, the Analytical Commentary suggests[26] that the following considerations would be relevant:

> It is submitted that in judging whether an arbitrator failed to act the following considerations may be relevant: Which action was expected or required of him in the light of the arbitration agreement and the specific procedural situation? If he has not done anything in this regard, has the delay been so inordinate as to be unacceptable in the light of the circumstances, including technical difficulties and the complexity of the case? If he has done something and acted in a certain way, did his conduct fall clearly below the standard of what may reasonably be expected from an arbitrator? Amongst the factors influencing the level of expectations are the ability to function efficiently and expeditiously and any special competence or other qualifications required of the arbitrator by agreement of the parties.

It should be noted that these considerations are based on the words 'for other reasons fails to act' in the draft Model Law, which did not include the succeeding words 'without undue delay' found in the 1985 Model Law and the Arbitration Act 2005. However, it is submitted that these considerations are equally applicable to the Arbitration Act 2005.

§16.03 APPLICATION TO HIGH COURT

Section 16(2) of the Arbitration Act 2005 allows a party to apply to the High Court for a decision on the termination of the mandate of an arbitrator, where the other party disagrees. As stated above, this is most likely to arise where the ground for the termination is the arbitrator's failure to act without undue delay. To prevent dilatory tactics, section 16(2) provides that no appeal shall lie against the decision of the High Court in this regard.

§16.04 WITHDRAWAL DOES NOT IMPLY ACCEPTANCE

Section 16(3) of the Arbitration Act 2005 provides that an arbitrator's withdrawal or a parties' agreement on termination due to inability or delay will not amount to an acceptance of the validity of these grounds. This is intended to facilitate a withdrawal and prevent lengthy controversies.[27] However, this provision will not discharge an

---

26. *See* Analytical Commentary, Article 14, commentary 4.
27. *See* Analytical Commentary, Article 14 bis, commentary 1.

arbitrator where he can be shown to have acted in bad faith under section 47 of the Arbitration Act 2005.

§16.05 MANDATORY OR NON-MANDATORY

Unlike other provisions of the Arbitration Act 2005 that follow the 'two-level system' allowing parties to agree first failing which the provisions of the Act apply, section 16 does not expressly allow for the first step enabling parties to agree first but instead skips directly to the second stage.

This gives rise to concern as parties may well have agreed by way of arbitration rules on the rules for dealing with an arbitrator who is unable to act or who delays the proceeding.

For example, Article 15 of the 2017 ICC Rules of Arbitration provides:

> Replacement of Arbitrators
> 1. An arbitrator shall be replaced upon death, upon acceptance by the Court of the arbitrator's resignation, upon acceptance by the Court of a challenge, or upon acceptance by the Court of a request of all the parties.
> 2. An arbitrator shall also be replaced on the Court's own initiative when it decides that the arbitrator is prevented de jure or de facto from fulfilling the arbitrator's functions, or that the arbitrator is not fulfilling those functions in accordance with the Rules or within the prescribed time limits.
> 3. When, on the basis of information that has come to its attention, the Court considers applying Article 15(2), it shall decide on the matter after the arbitrator concerned, the parties and any other members of the arbitral tribunal have had an opportunity to comment in writing within a suitable period of time. Such comments shall be communicated to the parties and to the arbitrators.
> 4. When an arbitrator is to be replaced, the Court has discretion to decide whether or not to follow the original nominating process. Once reconstituted, and after having invited the parties to comment, the arbitral tribunal shall determine if and to what extent prior proceedings shall be repeated before the reconstituted arbitral tribunal.
> 5. Subsequent to the closing of the proceedings, instead of replacing an arbitrator who has died or been removed by the Court pursuant to Articles 15(1) or 15(2), the Court may decide, when it considers it appropriate, that the remaining arbitrators shall continue the arbitration. In making such determination, the Court shall take into account the views of the remaining arbitrators and of the parties and such other matters that it considers appropriate in the circumstances.

Although not expressly provided in section 16, it appears implicit from section 16(1), which allows the parties to agree on the termination of the mandate of the arbitrator, that the parties should also be free to agree on the procedure for such a termination.[28]

---

28. *See* Dr Peter Binder, *International Commercial Arbitration and Conciliation in UNCITRAL Model Law Jurisdictions* (3rd edn, Sweet & Maxwell 2010) at para 3.098.

17. *Appointment of Substitute Arbitrator*

(1) A substitute arbitrator shall be appointed in accordance with the provisions of this Act where –
  (a) the mandate of an arbitrator terminates under section 15 or 16;
  (b) an arbitrator withdraws from office for any other reason;
  (c) the mandate of the arbitrator is revoked by agreement of the parties; or
  (d) in any other case of termination of mandate.
(2) Unless otherwise agreed by the parties –
  (a) where a single or the presiding arbitrator is replaced, any hearings previously held shall be repeated before the substitute arbitrator; or
  (b) where an arbitrator other than a single or the presiding arbitrator is replaced, any hearings previously held may be repeated at the discretion of the arbitral tribunal.
(3) Unless otherwise agreed by the parties, any order or ruling of the arbitral tribunal made prior to the replacement of an arbitrator under this section shall not be invalid solely on the ground there has been a change in the composition of the arbitral tribunal.

§17.01 INTRODUCTION

Section 17 of the Arbitration Act 2005 expressly provides for the procedure for appointment of a substitute arbitrator. Section 17 also provides, although this may be missed at first glance, for additional grounds for the termination of the mandate of the arbitrator.

Section 17(1) of the Arbitration Act 2005 reflects Article 15 of the 1985 Model Law. Sections 17(2) and (3) of the Arbitration Act 2005 do not have equivalent provisions in the 1985 Model Law. The 1985 Model Law does not expressly provide for the effect of substitution of an arbitrator. This is perhaps because this was considered a matter of procedure that could be determined by the new arbitrator under Article 19(1) of the 1985 Model Law.

Section 17(2) of the Arbitration Act 2005 appears to be based on Article 14 of the 1976 UNCITRAL Arbitration Rules, which provides:

> Article 14
>
> If under articles 11 to 13 the sole or presiding arbitrator is replaced, any hearings held previously shall be repeated; if any other arbitrator is replaced, such prior hearings may be repeated at the discretion of the arbitral tribunal.

This provision of the 1976 UNCITRAL Arbitration Rules has been amended to read as follows in Article 15 of the 2013 UNCITRAL Arbitration Rules, which forms part of the 2018 AIAC Arbitration Rules:

Article 15

If an arbitrator is replaced, the proceedings shall resume at the stage where the arbitrator who was replaced ceased to perform his or her functions, unless the arbitral tribunal decides otherwise.

§17.02 ADDITIONAL GROUNDS FOR TERMINATION

Section 17(1) of the Arbitration Act 2005 provides three additional grounds for the termination of the mandate of the arbitrator.

There are therefore nine grounds for the termination of a mandate of an arbitrator:

(1) lack of impartiality under section 14(3)(a);
(2) lack of independence under section 14(3)(a);
(3) lack of agreed upon qualifications under section 14(3)(b);
(4) inability in law under section 16(1);
(5) inability in fact under section 16(1);
(6) failure to act without undue delay under section 16(1);
(7) an arbitrator's withdrawal from office under section 17(1)(b);
(8) the parties agree to the revocation of the mandate of the arbitrator under section 17(1)(c); and
(9) any other case of termination of mandate under section 17(1)(d).

The last three of the grounds set out above are the additional grounds for termination of the mandate of an arbitrator included in section 17 of the Arbitration Act 2005.

The grounds for termination of mandate by withdrawal of the arbitrator or by agreement of the parties appear to have been included in section 17 as these are consensual grounds for termination that would not require any determination by the courts, unlike the grounds under sections 14 and 15 of the Arbitration Act 2005.

At first glance, it does not seem justified that an arbitrator should simply be entitled to withdraw under section 17(1)(b) of the Arbitration Act 2005. However, it would be difficult to compel an arbitrator to perform where he no longer wishes to do so. It would also be impractical to insist on a just cause for withdrawal or to list out all such possible causes.[29] Although an arbitrator is entitled to withdraw under section 17(1)(b) of the Arbitration Act 2005, he may be liable if he has done so in bad faith under section 47 of the Arbitration Act 2005.

The second new ground provided by section 17(1)(c) is where the parties agree to revoke the mandate of the arbitrator. Given the essentially consensual nature of arbitration, this ground appears justified.[30]

---

29. *See* Analytical Commentary, Article 15, commentary 3.
30. *See* Analytical Commentary, Article 15, commentary 2.

The third new ground provided by section 17(1)(d) provides for any other reason for termination of the mandate of the arbitrator and is intended as a general catch-all provision to cover the myriad reasons that could arise in practice for the termination.

§17.03 SUBSTITUTION

Apart from the additional grounds for termination, section 17(1) expressly provides that a 'substitute arbitrator shall be appointed in accordance with the provisions of this Act'.

The use of the imperative 'shall', and the absence of the usual words 'unless otherwise agreed' that reinforces the 'two-level system', would appear to suggest that this provision on the substitution of an arbitrator is mandatory. However, the words 'provisions of the Act' used in section 17(1) would also include section 13 of the Arbitration Act 2005 that leaves the parties free to agree on the procedure for the appointment of an arbitrator. These provisions would equally apply when a substitute arbitrator is being appointed. Therefore, although section 17(1) appears mandatory at first glance, it does allow the parties the freedom to decide on the procedure for the appointment of a substitute arbitrator.[31]

The Arbitration Act 2005, like the 1985 Model Law, does not attempt to deal with a situation where the process of repeated withdrawal and substitution of a party-appointed arbitrator may be used to disrupt the proceedings. The Analytical Commentary suggests[32] that this may be overcome by adopting a provision similar to Article 56(3) of the 1965 Washington Convention, which provides:

> If a conciliator or arbitrator appointed by a party shall have resigned without the consent of the Commission or Tribunal of which he was a member, the Chairman shall appoint a person from the appropriate Panel to fill the resulting vacancy.

§17.04 EFFECT OF SUBSTITUTION

As stated above, sections 17(2) and (3) of the Arbitration Act 2005 provide for the effect of substitution. Section 17(2) appears to be based on Article 14 of the 1976 UNCITRAL Arbitration Rules. Sections 17(2) and (3) follow the usual 'two-level system' which allows the parties to agree on the effect of substitution, failing which the default provisions in these sections will apply.

Essentially, sections 17(2) and (3) appear to lean towards preserving as much as possible from the arbitral proceedings prior to the substitution by only requiring a rehearing if a single or presiding arbitrator is replaced but otherwise leaving it to the discretion of the arbitral tribunal. These provisions also preserve the validity of rulings

---

31. *See* Dr Peter Binder, *International Commercial Arbitration and Conciliation in UNCITRAL Model Law Jurisdictions* (3rd edn, Sweet & Maxwell 2010) at para 3.114.
32. *See* Analytical Commentary, Article 15, commentary 5, footnote 51.

and orders made by the arbitral tribunal prior to the substitutions. The intention of these provisions is to minimize the disruption caused by the substitution.

In the context of section 17(3), it is important to note that although the substitution in itself will not affect the validity of any prior ruling or order, other grounds might. For example, if an arbitrator has been substituted due to the initial arbitrator's lack of impartiality, although the substitution in itself is unlikely to affect the prior orders he made, the lack of impartiality is likely to have this effect.

CHAPTER 4
Jurisdiction of the Arbitral Tribunal

18. Competence of Arbitral Tribunal to Rule on its Jurisdiction

(1) The arbitral tribunal may rule on its own jurisdiction, including any objections with respect to the existence or validity of the arbitration agreement.
(2) For the purposes of subsection (1)—
   (a) an arbitration clause which forms part of an agreement shall be treated as an agreement independent of the other terms of the agreement; and
   (b) a decision by the arbitral tribunal that the agreement is null and void shall not ipso jure entail the invalidity of the arbitration clause.
(3) A plea that the arbitral tribunal does not have jurisdiction shall be raised not later than the submission of the statement of defence.
(4) A party is not precluded from raising a plea under subsection (3) by reason of that party having appointed or participated in the appointment of the arbitrator.
(5) A plea that the arbitral tribunal is exceeding the scope of its authority shall be raised as soon as the matter alleged to be beyond the scope of its authority is raised during the arbitral proceedings.
(6) Notwithstanding subsections (3) and (5), the arbitral tribunal may admit such plea if it considers the delay justified.
(7) The arbitral tribunal may rule on a plea referred to in subsection (3) or (5), either as a preliminary question or in an award on the merits.
(8) Where the arbitral tribunal rules on such a plea as a preliminary question that it has jurisdiction, any party may, within thirty days after having received notice of that ruling appeal to the High Court to decide the matter.
(9) While an appeal is pending, the arbitral tribunal may continue the arbitral proceedings and make an award.

(10) No appeal shall lie against the decision of the High Court under subsection (8).

§18.01 INTRODUCTION

Section 18 of the Arbitration Act 2005 allows the arbitral tribunal to rule on its own jurisdiction. For this purpose, section 18 provides that an arbitration clause in a contract shall be treated as an independent agreement. Section 18 also provides for the timelines and procedure for challenging an arbitral tribunal's jurisdiction, as well as appeals from rulings made by the arbitral tribunal on its jurisdiction.

Section 18 of the Arbitration Act 2005 reflects Article 16 of the 1985 Model Law. In particular, sections 18(1) and (2) reflect Article 16(1), and sections 18(3)-(6) reflect Article 16(2), while sections 18(7)-(10) reflect Article 16(3).

The only significant difference between section 18 of the Arbitration Act 2005 and Article 16 of the 1985 Model Law is the use of the word 'appeal' in section 18(8) as compared to the word 'request' in Article 16(3). The significance of the use of the word 'appeal' is considered in §18.04 *infra* in the context of section 18(8).

§18.02 KOMPETENZ-KOMPETENZ AND SEPARABILITY

[A] The Two Principles

Sections 18(1) and (2) of the Arbitration Act 2005 provide for two important and complementary principles in modern international commercial arbitration.

First, section 18(1) provides for the principle of *Kompetenz-Kompetenz*, meaning that the arbitral tribunal has the power, or the competence, to rule on its own jurisdiction or competency. This principle implicitly recognizes that the arbitral tribunal should be the first to rule on its own jurisdiction with ultimate control by the courts.[1]

Second, section 18(2) provides for the separability of the arbitration clause, meaning that even if the contract in which the clause is found is determined to be null and void, the arbitration clause survives as an independent agreement. This complements the principle of *Kompetenz-Kompetenz*, as the arbitral tribunal has the power under the notionally separate arbitration clause to determine if the contract is null and void.[2]

These two important principles have been recognized by the Court of Appeal, in *Capping Corp Ltd & Ors v. Aquawalk Sdn Bhd & Ors* [2013] 6 MLJ 579 at paragraph 28 and *TNB Fuel Services Sdn Bhd v. China National Coal Group Corp* [2013] 4 MLJ 857 at paragraph 22. These principles have also been recognized by the High Court, in *Chin Keat Seng v. Lee Yoke Yam & Ors* [2009] 1 LNS 1799 at page 9 and *AV Asia Sdn Bhd v.*

---

1. *See* Analytical Commentary, Article 16, commentary 1.
2. *See* Analytical Commentary, Article 16, commentary 2.

Chapter 4: Jurisdiction of the Arbitral Tribunal §18.02[B]

Pengarah Kuala Lumpur Regional Centre for Arbitration & Anor [2013] 10 CLJ 115 at paragraph 17.

[B] Lean Towards Arbitration

As stated above, it is implicit in the *Kompetenz-Kompetenz* principle provided for in section 18(1) that the arbitral tribunal should rule on its own jurisdiction *first* followed by ultimate control by the courts. This implicit rule has been recognized and enforced by the courts, which have held that on questions of jurisdictions, the courts would lean towards allowing the arbitral tribunal to decide these questions first.

This position has been consistently taken by the courts, starting with the important judgment of the High Court, in *CMS Energy Sdn Bhd v. Poscon Corp* [2008] 6 MLJ 561 at paragraph 18, where it was, *inter alia*, held:

> In my view if s 10 and s 18 of the Act are read together there is [an] unmistakeable intention of the Legislature that the court should lean towards arbitration proceedings. Under s 10(1) of the Act, the court shall stay all proceedings before it in respect of a matter which is the subject of an arbitration agreement, and refer the parties to arbitration unless the court is satisfied as to any of the condition in para (a) or (b) of the section as shown above. And in this case none of the condition is applicable.

Subsequently, the Court of Appeal, in *Capping Corp supra* at paragraphs 27 and 29, *inter alia*, held:

> [27] The arbitration regime is now governed by Arbitration Act 2005 which in our view dictates that the courts take a minimal interference approach and this is reflected in s 18 of the Arbitration Act 2005 which gives the arbitrator the power to rule on his own jurisdiction.
>
> This power was not present in the 1952 Arbitration Act … .
>
> …
>
> [29] Applying that spirit of minimal interference by the courts on matters relating disputes agreed to be resolved by arbitration, we make no further rulings on any of the other issues raised by the respective counsel in this appeal or the High Court. Those issues ought to be adjudicated by an arbitrator or arbitrators.

The judgment of the High Court, in *CMS Energy supra*, was followed by the Court of Appeal, in *TNB Fuel supra* at paragraph 21, where it was, *inter alia*, held:

> … In any event, in our opinion, even if Her Ladyship entertained any doubts concerning the existence of the 'arbitration agreement', Her Ladyship ought to have leaned in favour of refusing the injunction so as to enable this jurisdictional issue to be determined by the arbitral tribunal … .

The Federal Court, in *Press Metal Sarawak Sdn Bhd v. Etiqa Takaful Bhd* [2016] 9 CLJ 1 at paragraph 40, held that a challenge as to jurisdiction should be made before the arbitral tribunal and the courts should lean towards allowing jurisdictional issues to be determined by the arbitral tribunal even when there was some doubt as to their jurisdiction:

A challenge to the jurisdiction of an arbitrator must be made during the arbitration proceedings itself, but not at the court hearing an application for a stay under s. 10(1) (see: s. 18(5)). It is the arbitrator who decides the issue of jurisdiction. Any ruling of the arbitrator that it has jurisdiction, can be appealed to the High Court which will finally decide the matter (see: s. 18(8)).

The High Court, in *Y & Y Development Sdn Bhd v. City-Lite Letrik Sdn Bhd* [2014] 1 LNS 1480 at paragraphs 36 and 37, while recognizing the principle set out in *CMS Energy supra* and *TNB Fuel supra*, appears to suggest that where the jurisdictional question was obvious, it could be determined by the courts rather than the arbitral tribunal:

> [36] I am aware that cases such as *TNB Fuel Services* and *CMS Energy Sdn. Bhd. v. Poscon Corp* [2008] 6 561 (a decision cited by His Lordship Ananthan Kasinather JCA in *TNB Fuel Services*) urge courts to lean in favour of arbitration. However, the present case is not one where an injunction is being sought to restrain an arbitral tribunal from ruling on the extent of its own jurisdiction. In *TNB Fuel Services*, the arbitral tribunal had been fully constituted and was ready to hear the respondent's jurisdictional challenge. This is not the case in the present instance.
>
> [37] I am of the view that, even if I were to remit this case to an arbitral tribunal for it to exercise the powers conferred by Section 18 of the Arbitration Act 2005 and to determine the extent of its jurisdiction in this matter, the tribunal will come to same conclusion as I have, resulting in City-Lite, as the plaintiff in the other action, having to eventually file a fresh action (as a stay granted under Section 10 would be a final stay of all current proceedings). The balance of convenience here would therefore be in favour of the respondent, City-Lite.

The High Court, in *Juaramedic Sdn Bhd v. MRCB Engineering Sdn Bhd* [2017] 11 MLJ 427 at paragraph 39, followed *TNB Fuel supra* and *Press Metal supra* and held that even if there was some doubt as to the existence of an arbitration agreement, the courts should in principle lean towards arbitration and allow the issue to be resolved by the arbitral tribunal:

> In the result, taking into account the principles of law which enjoins this court to lean in favour of arbitration and having regard to the clear statutory power and jurisdiction of the arbitrators to rule on their own jurisdiction, which will encompass the question as to whether there is in existence an arbitration agreement (as defined in s 9 of the Arbitration Act 2005) vis a vis the procurement agreement, I am of the view that even though there is some doubt as to whether the arbitration agreement namely cl 67 of the main agreement has been incorporated by reference into the procurement agreement, this court should 'lean towards arbitration' and let parties take up the challenge to jurisdiction afresh in the arbitration proceedings itself ... .

It is submitted that while the courts lean towards arbitration a balance should be struck. In this regard, where the question of jurisdiction is plain and obvious, it should perhaps be determined by the courts, especially if the arbitral tribunal has yet to be constituted. However, where there are triable issues on jurisdiction, such issues should be left to be determined by the arbitral tribunal first.

[C] Reform and Wide Powers

The courts recognize that the power given to the arbitral tribunal to determine its own jurisdiction is a wide power, which was not present in the Arbitration Act 1952. The courts also recognize that section 18 of the Arbitration Act 2005 was intended to reform the law in this context and that such reform should be given effect to by allowing the arbitral tribunal to rule on its own jurisdiction.

In this context, the High Court, in *Standard Chartered Bank Malaysia Bhd v. City Properties Sdn Bhd* [2008] 1 CLJ 496 at paragraph 14, *inter alia*, held:

> The only conclusion I can draw from the import of this entirely new provision in s. 10 when read with s. 18 of the 2005 Act, is that with this new Act, Parliament has clearly given the arbitral tribunal much wider jurisdiction and powers. And, such powers would extend to cases even when its own jurisdiction or competence or scope of its authority, or the existence or validity of the arbitration agreement is challenged. A further point to note is that even when an arbitral tribunal holds that an agreement is null and void, it 'shall not ipso jure entail the invalidity of the arbitration clause' since 'an arbitration clause which forms part of an agreement shall be treated as an agreement independent of the other terms of the agreement.' Most noteworthy is that even where its own jurisdiction or competence or its scope of authority is challenged, it may rule on such plea either as a preliminary question or in an award on the merits. And, where the tribunal rules against the challenge on such a plea as a preliminary question any party may appeal to the High Court against such ruling but while the appeal is pending the arbitral tribunal may continue with the arbitral proceedings and make an award. With the view to preventing any inordinate delay in resolution of disputes the legislature has decreed that no further appeals shall lie from the High Court against a challenge on jurisdiction of an arbitral tribunal.

Similarly, the High Court, in *CMS Energy supra* at paragraph 16, *inter alia*, held:

> In my view the language used in that section confers on the arbitration a broad and wide powers to decide on issues raised before it – not only the substantive issues but also on the point of preliminary objections as to its jurisdiction. That section also allows any party to the arbitration who is not happy with the preliminary rulings by the arbitrator to appeal to the High Court against such rulings within 30 days of its receipt.

These views have been further confirmed by the Court of Appeal, in *Capping Corp supra* at paragraphs 27 and 29.

Specifically, the High Court, in *Arul Balasingam v. Ampang Puteri Specialist Hospital Sdn Bhd (formerly known as Puteri Specialist Hospital Sdn Bhd)* [2012] 6 MLJ 104 at paragraphs 8 and 9, held that the wide powers conferred on the arbitral tribunal to determine its own jurisdiction included the power to determine whether a particular arbitration clause applies or not:

> [8] I am satisfied the plaintiff have presented facts before me that disclose bona fide serious issues to be tried without going into the merits of the same. The serious issues are justicable by way of arbitration. The defendant submit that cl 10 of the resident committee resident consultant agreement is exhaustive and preclude in

this case, reference to arbitration. Counsel for the defendant argues the relevant clause for termination is cl 10.2, ...

[9] So s 19 of the said agreement does not apply as both parties have to be bound by the agreement that they have put pen to. At this stage without making any specific finding on this argument all these are matters that the proposed arbitrator can deal with at the appropriate time ... .

Another case dealing with a specific scenario is the judgment of the High Court, in *AV Asia supra* at paragraph 17, where it was held that the wide power given to the arbitral tribunal to determine its own jurisdiction included the power to determine the number of arbitrators that would constitute the tribunal:

In my view, bearing in mind the clear terms of s. 8, the court must decline jurisdiction. In fact, as discussed earlier, the court has no jurisdiction since none have been given under s. 12. Parliament has legislated that where such matters arises, it is to be dealt with under s. 18 which provides that 'the arbitral tribunal may rule on its own jurisdiction, including any objections with respect to the existence or validity of the arbitration agreement.' Section 18(8) allows a party to appeal to the High Court when the arbitral tribunal has made a preliminary ruling on the matter. This is consistent with the principle of *kompetenz-kompetenz* – Otherwise, there will be no meaning or purpose in ss. 8 and 18.

Finally, the courts have recognized that these wide powers conferred on the arbitral tribunal, include the jurisdiction to determine questions of fraud.[3] In this context, the High Court, in *Chin Keat Seng supra* at page 10, *inter alia*, held:

It was apparent that when the facts of this instant case were applied in the context of the new law, it could not be a simple matter to be decided on the basis of an allegation of misrepresentation, fraud or general invalidity of the Shareholders' Agreement. The jurisdiction of an arbitral tribunal could not be excluded so simply, nor could resort to arbitration proceedings. On the facts, the relevant arbitration clause was very broadly worded, and it would be best if parties were held to their choice of dispute resolution. It was best if the arbitral tribunal, when appointed, to rule on its own jurisdiction.

[D] Potential Limits to These Wide Powers

Although the courts have generally given effect to sections 18(1) and (2) of the Arbitration Act 2005 and have indeed leaned in favour of arbitration, there have been decisions by the courts that have sought to limit the wide powers conferred on the arbitral tribunal by these provisions. The courts have, in these judgments, limited the application of section 18(1) by strictly construing this statutory provision. The courts have also limited section 18(1) by reading this provision together with other provisions in the Arbitration Act 2005.

For example, the High Court, in *Total Safe Sdn Bhd v. Tenaga Nasional Berhad & Anor* [2009] 1 LNS 420, interpreted the word 'may' in section 18(1) as meaning that the

---

3. *See Chut Nyak Isham Nyak Ariff v. Malaysian Technology Development Corporation Sdn Bhd & Ors* [2009] 9 CLJ 32 at paras 5-7, 12.

courts retained the power to determine jurisdictional issues. The High Court also decided that where the jurisdictional issue was raised in court rather than in the arbitral proceedings, the issue could be determined by the courts. In this context, the High Court, in *Total Safe supra* at pages 8 and 9, *inter alia*, held:

> The submission of the Second Defendant that the existence of an arbitration agreement is within the jurisdiction of the arbitration tribunal is unacceptable. For this, the court refers to the provision of section 18 (1) of the Arbitration Act 2005 which provides as follows:
>
> 'The arbitral tribunal may rule on its own jurisdiction, including any objections with respect to the existence or validity of the arbitration agreement.' (emphasis mine)
>
> The word 'may' that is present in the said provision connotes that it does not oust the jurisdiction of this court in making a ruling on the existence or the validity of the arbitration agreement. The arbitral tribunal may decide on the issue if it is raised in the arbitration proceedings. However, since the case herein has been commenced in this court, then the court can decide the same. At this stage, and considering the fact that the Second Defendant has not been able to show to this court the existence, of any arbitration agreement, it is just that the proceedings be continued in court. There is no justification for this court to stay the proceedings herein pending arbitration.

It is submitted that, while the High Court, in *Total Safe supra*, was correct in holding that the courts retained the power to determine jurisdictional issues, there does not appear to be an appreciation of the jurisprudence that the courts would lean towards allowing the arbitral tribunal to rule on its own jurisdiction first.

The High Court, in *Cyber Business Solutions Sdn Bhd v. Elsag Datamat SpA* [2012] 1 CJL 115, interpreted the word 'own' in section 18(1) of the Arbitration Act 2005 strictly. Here, there was a dispute between the parties as to which of two arbitration clauses applied. One arbitration clause provided for arbitration governed by the ICC Rules of Arbitration, while the other provided for the KLRCA Arbitration Rules. A party referred the dispute to the ICC and the International Court of Arbitration decided under Article 6(2) of the ICC Rules of Arbitration that the arbitration should proceed. Despite this, the High Court narrowly construed the word 'own' in section 18(1) to mean that an arbitral tribunal constituted under the ICC Rules of Arbitration could not determine if another set of arbitration rules applied or not. In this context, the High Court, in *Cyber Business supra* at paragraph 46, *inter alia*, held:

> Further, if the ICC can determine other arbitral tribunal's jurisdiction, then similarly the KLRCA could also determine on the jurisdiction of the ICC, which would not solve the issue at hand ie, which arbitration clause/forum of arbitration is applicable. Decision has to be made as to which forum can arbitrate on the disputes between the plaintiff and the defendant. It certainly cannot be the ICC nor the KLRCA to determine on the jurisdictional issue in view of the competing forum.

It is submitted that the judgment, in *Cyber Business supra*, does not appear to appreciate the distinction between an arbitral tribunal and institution. There is no reason in principle why an arbitral tribunal constituted under any particular set of rules cannot determine which of several competing rules of arbitration should apply to the proceeding. Indeed, this would appear to be a common jurisdictional issue that may need to be determined by an arbitral tribunal, especially where there are two competing arbitration clauses.

The High Court, in *Assar Senari Holdings Sdn Bhd v. Teratai Sanjung Holdings (M) Sdn Bhd* [2011] MLJU 834, narrowly construed the words 'arbitration agreement' used in section 18(1) to mean that the arbitral tribunal could only determine the existence of the arbitration agreement but not the substantive contract between the parties. In this context, the High Court, in *Assar Senari supra* at page 2, *inter alia*, held:

> My view of the applicability of section 18(1) in respect of this case is as follows. Although section 18(1) gives broad powers to the Arbitral Tribunal to determine the validity or existence of the arbitration agreement, it does not confer power on the Arbitral Tribunal to determine the validity of substantive agreement. In the instant case, it is common ground that the PDA and SA were not signed by the parties. Counsel for plaintiff has argued that there is a triable issue whether the substantive agreement exists even if the existence of the arbitration agreement can be decided by the Arbitral Tribunal. My reading of sections 9, 10 and 18 is that the scheme of the Arbitration Act presupposes the existence of a substantive agreement between the parties and leaves the issue of the validity and existence of the arbitration agreement to the Arbitral Tribunal. It is true that under section 8, unless otherwise provided, no court shall intervene in any of the matters governed by the Arbitration Act 2005. However, section 18(1) provides that the Arbitral Tribunal may only rule on the existence or validity of the arbitration agreement. It does not say that the Arbitral Tribunal can determine the existence of the substantive agreement. In this case, the threshold issue is whether the parties had entered into the PDA and SA. If it is found that the parties had not entered into an agreement at all, there would be nothing for the Arbitral Tribunal to 'arbitrate'. The function of the Arbitral Tribunal is to adjudicate on 'disputes' ... .

Similarly, the High Court, in *Awan Timur Palm Oil Mills Resources (Johor) Sdn Bhd v. Inno-Wangsa Oils & Fats Sdn Bhd* [2018] MLJU 622 at paragraph 79, *inter alia*, held:

> I find that the arbitrators had no business to take on jurisdiction to adjudicate whether there was a contract in the first place. It was not a clear enough case, and they certainly did not have to take it upon themselves to adjudicate on the issue of formation of contract. The civil court would be better equipped to handle such a dispute which would involve dealing with conflicting evidence.

It is submitted that the arbitral tribunal has jurisdiction to determine the existence of both the arbitration agreement and the substantive contract between the parties. This is implicit from section 18(2)(b), which expressly provides for a situation where the arbitral tribunal has determined that the 'agreement' meaning the substantive contract is null and void.

§18.03 TIME LIMITS

Sections 18(3) and (5) of the Arbitration Act 2005 provide time limits for jurisdictional challenges before the arbitral tribunal. These time limits are to prevent delay of the proceedings.

Section 18(3) provides that a plea that the arbitral tribunal does not have jurisdiction shall not be raised later than the submission of the statement of defence. Section 18(3) provides for a situation where a party alleges that the arbitral tribunal entirely lacks jurisdiction due to, for example, the absence of an arbitration agreement.

Section 18(5) provides that a plea that the arbitral tribunal is exceeding its authority should be raised as soon as the alleged act occurs. Section 18(5) provides for a situation where the arbitral tribunal, though having jurisdiction, has acted in a manner outside the scope of its jurisdiction. For example, if an arbitral tribunal directs that evidence be provided in relation to an issue that has not been referred to it, this would be in excess of its jurisdiction.[4]

The Federal Court, in *Thai-Lao Lignite Co Ltd & Anor v. Government of The Lao People's Democratic Republic* [2017] 6 AMR 219 at paragraphs 203 and 215, recognized the different time limits under sections 18(3) and (5). The Federal Court decided that if a party did not comply with these time limits and the other party did not object to this non-compliance, the other party could not subsequently complain about such non-compliance:

> [203] It was so submitted, and we agree that 'a plea that the arbitral tribunal does not have jurisdiction shall be raised not later than in the statement of defence' (Article 21(3) of the UNCITRAL Arbitration Rules 1976, which is the equivalent of Section 18(3) of AA 2005). But in relation to a plea that the arbitral tribunal is exceeding the scope of its authority, that 'shall be raised as soon as the matter alleged to be beyond the scope of its authority is raised during the arbitral proceedings' (section 18(5) of AA 2005). In other words, a plea that the arbitral tribunal is exceeding the scope of its authority could be raised during the arbitral proceedings. Hence, 'time to object' depends on whether it is a plea under section 18(3) or 18(5) of AA 2005. But that was not distinguished in the submissions before us.
>
> ...
>
> [215] *The Arbitration Act 2005* by Sundra Rajoo and WSW Davidson at 171 proposed that whether a jurisdictional issue could be later raised would depend on the nature of the jurisdictional issue; see also *A Guide to the UNCITRAL Model Law on International Commercial Arbitration* by Howard M. Holtzmann & Joseph E. Neuhaus at 482-483]. Equally, if a party raises an out of time challenge but the other party does not object to the lateness of the challenge, and the tribunal rules on the plea, the other party cannot rely on the delay to prevent the High Court from deciding the matter under art 16(3) [the equivalent of section 18(8) of AA 2005]' (*Williams & Kawharu supra* at 7.4.6). On the facts, even if the plea under section 18(3) or (5) of AA 2005 were made out of time, the Appellants could not rely on delay, which was not an issue during the arbitral proceedings, to prevent the High Court from deciding the matter under Section 37 of AA 2005. On the facts, where

---

4. *See* Analytical Commentary, Article 16, commentary 7.

there was no objection to lateness, the Appellants could not raise the 'out of time' argument. As such, we reject the 'out of time' argument.

The Federal Court, in *Thai-Lao Lignite supra*, did not draw a distinction between the derogable and non-derogable provisions of the Arbitration Act 2005. It is submitted that such a distinction should have been drawn in accordance with section 7. If such a distinction had been made, it would have been recognized that sections 18(3) and (5) are non-derogable provisions that cannot be waived.

The High Court, in *Usahasama SPNB-LTAT Sdn Bhd v. ABI Construction Sdn Bhd* [2016] 7 CLJ 275, further clarified that if a plea of lack of jurisdiction was taken prior to the Statement of Defence, there could be no question of waiver or estoppel arising prior to such a plea being taken. In this context, the High Court, in *Usahasama SPNB-LTAT supra* at paragraphs 39, 42, *inter alia*, held:

> [39] The defendant relied on various correspondences and contended that the action by the defendant to bring the disputes to arbitration had never been opposed, objected to or refuted by the plaintiff and hence constituted a waiver on the part of the plaintiff towards the precondition stipulated in cl. 54 of the contract
>
> ...
>
> ...
>
> [42] There can be no estoppel as against a statute. See the case of *JMB Silverpark Sdn Bhd v. Silverpark Sdn Bhd & Anor* [2012] 1 LNS 1082; [2013] 9 MLJ 714 at p. 726. In *United Malayan Banking Corporation Sdn Bhd v. Syarikat Perumahan Luas Sdn Bhd* [1998] 3 MLJ 352b Edgar Joseph Jr J (as he then was) at p. 356 held: 'The defence of estoppel accordingly fails since there cannot be an estoppel to evade the plain provisions of a statute.' Much earlier in *Kok Hoong v. Leong Cheong Kweng Mines Ltd* [1963] 1 LNS 61; [1964] 1 MLJ 49 Viscount Radcliffe, Privy Council, at p. 54 had affirmed that '... a party cannot set up estoppels in the face of a statute ...' Here the plaintiff had raised the jurisdictional challenge at the first preliminary meeting and in the circumstance it was timeously and promptly raised.

Sections 18(4) and (6) of the Arbitration Act 2005 provide measures to prevent the harsh application of sections 18(3) and (5).

Section 18(4) provides that a party is not precluded from raising a plea of lack of jurisdiction under section 18(3) by reason of having appointed or participated in the appointment of the arbitrator. A party who intends to challenge the jurisdiction of the arbitral tribunal may wish to still participate in the proceedings and nominate an arbitrator. In the light of section 18(4), such a party is not required to make any reservation with respect to his intended plea of lack of jurisdiction when participating in the appointment of an arbitrator.[5]

Section 18(6) allows the arbitral tribunal to admit a plea of lack of jurisdiction or excess of jurisdiction even if the time limits in sections 18(3) and (5) have not been complied with where the delay is justified. Given the intention of sections 18(3) and (5) to prevent delay, it is submitted that very strong grounds would be required to justify a delay. These grounds should be limited to situations where the party intending to

---

5. *See* Analytical Commentary, Article 16, commentary 6.

raise the plea did not have notice of the jurisdictional issue or where it was practically impossible to raise the plea earlier.

Although sections 18(3) and (5) provide time limits for raising pleas of lack of jurisdiction or excess of jurisdiction, the Arbitration Act 2005 does not provide for the consequences of failing to comply with these time limits. The Arbitration Act 2005 mirrors the 1985 Model Law in this regard, which also does not provide for the consequences of non-compliance.

It appears clear that if the time limits are not complied with and the arbitral tribunal does not admit the plea under section 18(6), the plea cannot be pursued in the arbitral proceedings.

It is, however, less clear whether the challenge on jurisdiction can still be taken in an application to set aside an award or in resisting the enforcement of the award after a plea was not taken within the time limits before the arbitral tribunal. It is submitted that generally a party should be precluded from relying on a jurisdictional issue in the setting aside or enforcement proceedings after having failed to comply with the time limits during the arbitral proceedings. Otherwise, the time limits provided for in sections 18(3) and (5) would be meaningless. Furthermore, the arbitral tribunal would not have had the first opportunity to rule on its own jurisdiction in accordance with the principles discussed in the context of sections 18(1) and (2) above.

However, there are limits to the extent to which a party that has failed to comply with the time limits in sections 18(3) and (5) should be precluded from subsequently raising jurisdictional issues in setting aside or enforcement proceedings. Where it is an issue of public policy or the arbitrability of the subject matter of the dispute, it is submitted that a party should not be precluded from subsequently raising the issue even if the time limits have not been complied with. This is because these defects cannot be corrected by submission to the arbitration proceedings.[6]

§18.04 RULINGS AND APPEALS

Sections 18(7)-(10) of the Arbitration Act 2005 set out the scheme for rulings by the arbitral tribunal on pleas with respect to jurisdiction and appeals to the High Court from such rulings.

Section 18(7) allows the arbitral tribunal the discretion to decide whether to determine a plea on jurisdiction as a preliminary question or as an award on the remits.

If the arbitral tribunal determines the plea on jurisdiction in an award on the merits, then a dissatisfied party may apply to set aside such an award under section 37 of the Arbitration Act 2005.

Alternatively, if the arbitral tribunal determines the plea on jurisdiction as a ruling on a preliminary question, then two scenarios can arise under section 18(8):

---

6. *See* Analytical Commentary, Article 16, commentary 10.

(1) where the arbitral tribunal rules that it has no jurisdiction, then that is the end of the arbitral proceedings, and the claimant can decide whether to pursue civil proceedings; or
(2) where the arbitral tribunal rules that it has jurisdiction, any party may appeal to the High Court within thirty days in accordance with section 18(8). No appeal will lie against the decision of the High Court in this regard under section 18(10).

The scheme of sections 18(7)-(10) has been lucidly explained by the High Court, in *Paramasivam Karuppannr Gounder v. PT Synergy Oil Nusantara Indonesia* [2014] AMEJ 1240 at paragraph 15:

> My interpretation of the above AA provisions is as follows:
>
> (a) any party may –
>   (i) dispute the arbitral tribunal's jurisdiction – s 18(1) and (3) AA;
>   (ii) object with respect to the existence or validity of an 'arbitration agreement' (defined in s 9 AA and will be discussed below) – s 18(1) and (3); and/or
>   (iii) raise the contention that the arbitral tribunal has exceeded its scope of authority – s 18(5) AA. (Preliminary Matter);
> (b) the arbitral tribunal has a discretion under s 18(7) AA to rule on the Preliminary Matter –
>   (i) as a preliminary question (Preliminary Question); or
>   (ii) in an 'award' [see the definition of 'award' in s 2(1) AA] on the merits;
> (c) if an arbitral tribunal has ruled as a Preliminary Question that it has no jurisdiction to decide a dispute (No Jurisdiction Ruling), s 18(8) AA does not provide for any appeal to the High Court against a No Jurisdiction Ruling. If an arbitral tribunal rules that it has no jurisdiction to hear a dispute, that dispute has to be resolved in the courts;
> (d) only when an arbitral tribunal has ruled as a Preliminary Question that it has jurisdiction to decide a dispute (Ruling) –
>   (i) any party may appeal to the High Court against the Ruling under s 18(8) AA; and
>   (ii) according to s 18(10) AA, no appeal to the Court of Appeal can be made against the High Court's decision under s 18(8) AA;
> (e) if the arbitral tribunal has ruled on the Preliminary Matter in the award on the merits, a party may apply to the High Court –
>   (i) under s 37 (1) AA to set aside the award; or
>   (ii) to refer any question of law arising out of an award in accordance with s 42(1) AA; and
> (f) any decision of the High Court under ss 37 (1) and 42 AA can be appealed to the Court of Appeal – please see s 67(1) of the Courts of Judicature Act 1964 1964 (CJA) and s 43 AA.

The High Court, in *Paramasivam Karuppannr supra* at paragraph 40, further held that an arbitral tribunal's ruling on jurisdiction need not include reasons unlike an award:

> Section 18 AA does not require the Arbitral Tribunal to provide written grounds for the Arbitral Tribunal's Ruling. Accordingly, the Arbitral Tribunal's lack of written

grounds to support the Arbitral Tribunal's Ruling is not fatal in this case. In any event, for reasons explained above, I am satisfied that the Arbitral Tribunal's Ruling has not been made erroneously as there is a written 'arbitration agreement' between the Plaintiff and Defendant in this case.

The High Court, in *Usahasama SPNB-LTAT supra* at paragraph 16, clarified that an appeal under section 18(8) will be by way of a rehearing and not merely a review of the arbitrator's ruling. The High Court would accordingly hear the issue afresh without being influenced by the arbitrator's ruling. The High Court emphasized that, unlike section 67(1) of the English Arbitration Act 1996 that uses the word 'apply', section 18(8) of the Malaysian Arbitration Act 2005 uses the word 'appeal', which clearly meant that a rehearing was required:

> This court would follow the same approach as if hearing the issue afresh and uninfluenced by the prior decision of the arbitrator either way, respecting always the cogency of reasons given by the arbitrator but unrestrained by what has undergirded his decision.

The Federal Court, in *Thai-Lao Lignite supra* at paragraph 205, decided that where an arbitral tribunal declined to rule on a plea on jurisdiction as a preliminary question, a party was entitled to participate in the proceedings and await the award:

> In the instant case, there was no immediate ruling on the plea, be it under section 18(3) or (5) of AA 2005. Without an immediate ruling by the Arbitral Tribunal that it had jurisdiction, the Respondent could not invoke section 18(8) of AA 2005 and appeal to the High Court to decide the matter. The Respondent could only await a ruling in the award, and meanwhile participate in the arbitration, which was one of the options open to the Respondent (see *Redfern and Hunter on International Arbitration* 5th Edition at 5.120 and 5126).

The High Court, in *Dceil Imex Sdn Bhd v. Pembinaan Punca Cergas Sdn Bhd* [2014] 7 CLJ 552, considered the application of section 30(5) of the Limitation Act 1953 to section 18(8) of the Arbitration Act 2005.

In this context, section 30(5) of the Limitation Act 1953 provides as follows:

> Where the High Court orders that an award be set aside or orders, after the commencement of an arbitration, that the arbitration shall cease to have effect with respect to the dispute referred, the Court may further order that the period between the commencement of the arbitration and the date of the order of the Court shall be excluded in computing the time prescribed by this Act or any such written law as aforesaid for the commencement of proceedings (including arbitration) with respect to the dispute referred.

The High Court, in *Dceil Imex supra* at paragraph 62, held that where the High Court had decided on appeal under section 18(8) of the Arbitration Act 2005 that the arbitral tribunal had no jurisdiction, then the 'arbitration shall cease to have effect' for the purposes of section 30(5) of the Limitation Act 1953, allowing for time to be excluded for the purpose of limitation.

19. *Power of Arbitral Tribunal to Order Interim Measures*

(1) Unless otherwise agreed by the parties, the arbitral tribunal may, at the request of a party, grant interim measures.
(2) An interim measure is any temporary measure, whether in the form of an award or in another form, by which, at any time prior to the issuance of the award by which the dispute is finally decided, the arbitral tribunal orders a party to –
   (a) maintain or restore the status quo pending the determination of the dispute;
   (b) take action that would prevent or refrain from taking action that is likely to cause current or imminent harm or prejudice to the arbitral process itself;
   (c) provide a means of preserving assets out of which a subsequent award may be satisfied;
   (d) preserve evidence that may be relevant and material to the resolution of the dispute; or
   (e) provide security for the costs of the dispute.

19A. *Conditions for Granting Interim Measures*

(1) The party requesting for the interim measures order under paragraphs 19(2)(a), (b) or (c) shall satisfy the arbitral tribunal that –
   (a) harm not adequately reparable by an award of damages is likely to result if the measure is not ordered, and such harm substantially outweighs the harm that is likely to result to the party against whom the measure is directed if the measure is granted; and
   (b) there is a reasonable possibility that the requesting party will succeed on the merits of the claim.
(2) The determination on the reasonable possibility referred to in paragraph (1)(b) shall not affect the discretion of the arbitral tribunal in making any subsequent determination relating to the dispute.
(3) In respect of the request for an interim measure order under paragraph 19(2)(d), the conditions in subsections (1) and (2) shall apply only to the extent the arbitral tribunal considers appropriate.

19B. **Application for Preliminary Orders and Conditions for Granting Preliminary Orders**

(1) Unless otherwise agreed by the parties, a party may, without notice to any other party, make a request for an interim measure together with an application for a preliminary order directing a party not to frustrate the purpose of the interim measure requested.

(2) The arbitral tribunal may grant a preliminary order provided that the arbitral tribunal considers that prior disclosure of the request for the interim measure to the party against whom the measure is directed risks frustrating the purpose of the interim measure.

(3) The conditions specified in section 19A shall apply to any preliminary order provided that the harm to be assessed under paragraph 19A(1)(a) is the harm that is likely to result from the order being granted or not.

19C. **Specific Regime for Preliminary Orders**

(1) Immediately after the arbitral tribunal has made a determination in respect of an application for a preliminary order, the arbitral tribunal shall –
  (a) give notice to all parties of the request for the interim measure, the application for the preliminary order, the preliminary order, if any, and all other communications, including by indicating the content of any oral communication, between any party and the arbitral tribunal in relation thereto; and
  (b) give an opportunity to any party against whom a preliminary order is directed to present its case at the earliest practicable time.

(2) The arbitral tribunal shall decide immediately on any objection to the preliminary order.

(3) A preliminary order shall expire after twenty days from the date on which the order was issued by the arbitral tribunal.

(4) Notwithstanding subsection (3), the arbitral tribunal may issue an interim measure which adopts or modifies the preliminary order, after the party against whom the preliminary order is directed has been given notice and an opportunity to present his case.

(5) A preliminary order shall be binding on the parties but shall not be subject to any enforcement by the High Court.

(6) The preliminary order referred to in subsection (5) shall not constitute an award.

19D.   Modification, suspension or termination

The arbitral tribunal may modify, suspend or terminate an interim measure it has granted, upon an application of any party or, in exceptional circumstances and upon prior notice to the parties, on the arbitral tribunal's own initiative.

19E.   Provision of Security

(1) The arbitral tribunal may require the party requesting an interim measure to provide appropriate security in connection with the measure.
(2) The arbitral tribunal shall require the party applying for a preliminary order to provide security in connection with the order unless the arbitral tribunal considers it inappropriate or unnecessary to do so.

19F.   Disclosure

(1) The arbitral tribunal may require any party to immediately disclose any material change in the circumstances on the basis of which the interim measure or preliminary order was requested or applied or granted.
(2) The party applying for a preliminary order shall disclose to the arbitral tribunal all the circumstances that are likely to be relevant to the arbitral tribunal's determination on whether to grant or maintain the order and such obligation shall continue until the party against whom the order has been requested has had an opportunity to present its case.

19G.   Costs and Damages

(1) The party requesting for an interim measure or applying for a preliminary order shall be liable for any costs and damages caused by the interim measure or the preliminary order to any party if the arbitral tribunal later determines that, in the circumstances, the interim measure or the preliminary order should not have been granted.
(2) The arbitral tribunal may award such costs and damages referred to in subsection (1) at any point during the proceedings.

19H.   Recognition and Enforcement

(1) Subject to the provisions of section 19I, an interim measure issued by an arbitral tribunal shall be recognized as binding and, unless otherwise provided by the arbitral tribunal, enforced upon application to the competent court, irrespective of the country in which it was issued.

(2) The party who is seeking or has obtained recognition or enforcement of an interim measure shall immediately inform the court of any termination, suspension or modification of that interim measure.

(3) The court where recognition or enforcement is sought may, if it considers it proper, order the requesting party to provide appropriate security if the arbitral tribunal has not already made a determination with respect to security or where such a decision is necessary to protect the rights of third parties.

19I. *Grounds for Refusing Recognition or Enforcement*

(1) Recognition or enforcement of an interim measure may be refused only –
   (a) at the request of the party against whom it is invoked if the High Court is satisfied that –
      (i) such refusal is warranted on the grounds set forth in subparagraph 39(1)(a)(i), (ii), (iii), (iv), (v) or (vi);
      (ii) the arbitral tribunal's decision with respect to the provision of security in connection with the interim measure issued by the arbitral tribunal has not been complied with; or
      (iii) the interim measure has been terminated or suspended by the arbitral tribunal or, where so empowered, by the court of the State in which the arbitration takes place or under the law of which that interim measure was granted; or
   (b) if the High Court finds that –
      (i) the interim measure is incompatible with the powers conferred upon the Court, but the Court may decide to reformulate the interim measure to the extent necessary, without modifying its substance, to adapt it to the Court's powers and procedures for the purposes of enforcing that interim measure; or
      (ii) any grounds set forth in subparagraph 39(1)(b)(i) or (ii) apply to the recognition and enforcement of the interim measure.

(2) Any determination made by the High Court on any of the grounds in subsection (1) shall be effective only for the purposes of the application to recognize or enforce the interim measure.

(3) The High Court where recognition or enforcement is sought shall not, in making any determination on any of the grounds in subsection (1), undertake a review of the substance of the interim measure.

19J. *Court-ordered Interim Measures*

(1) The High Court has the power to issue an interim measure in relation to arbitration proceedings, irrespective of whether the seat of arbitration is in Malaysia.

(2) *The High Court shall exercise the power referred to in subsection (1) in accordance with its own procedures in consideration of the specific features of international arbitration.*
(3) *Where a party applies to the High Court for any interim measure and an arbitral tribunal has already ruled on any matter which is relevant to the application, the High Court shall treat any findings of fact made in the course of such ruling by the arbitral tribunal as conclusive for the purposes of the application.*

§19.01 INTRODUCTION

Section 19 of the Arbitration Act 2005 allows the arbitral tribunal to grant interim measures and preliminary orders. The section, which is the longest in the Arbitration Act 2005, includes detailed provisions on the conditions for the grant of such measures and orders and for the enforcement of such measures.

Section 19 of the Arbitration Act 2005 closely follows Article 17 of the 2006 Model Law. The significant differences are:

(1) section 19(2)(e) expressly allows the arbitral tribunal to grant security for costs. There is no equivalent provision in the 2006 Model Law;
(2) section 19F(2) omits the words 'Thereafter, paragraph (1) of this article shall apply …' at the end of Article 17F(2);
(3) section 19H(3) omits the words 'of the State' between the words 'court' and 'where', which are found in Article 17H(3);
(4) sections 19I and 19J specify 'the High Court', which is defined in section 2, in substitution of the word 'court' used in Articles 17I and 17J; and
(5) section 19J(3) is not found in the 2006 Model Law.

Apart from these changes, there are other minor changes in drafting between section 19 and Article 17. The significance of the changes listed out above is considered below in the context of each specific provision.

Article 17 of the 2006 Model Law was subsequently reflected in Article 26 of the 2010 UNCITRAL Arbitration Rules, which provides:

1. The arbitral tribunal may, at the request of a party, grant interim measures.
2. An interim measure is any temporary measure by which, at any time prior to the issuance of the award by which the dispute is finally decided, the arbitral tribunal orders a party, for example and without limitation, to:
   (a) Maintain or restore the status quo pending determination of the dispute;
   (b) Take action that would prevent, or refrain from taking action that is likely to cause,
      (i) current or imminent harm or
      (ii) prejudice to the arbitral process itself;
   (c) Provide a means of preserving assets out of which a subsequent award may be satisfied; or

(d) Preserve evidence that may be relevant and material to the resolution of the dispute.
3. The party requesting an interim measure under paragraphs 2 (a) to (c) shall satisfy the arbitral tribunal that:
   (a) Harm not adequately reparable by an award of damages is likely to result if the measure is not ordered, and such harm substantially outweighs the harm that is likely to result to the party against whom the measure is directed if the measure is granted; and
   (b) There is a reasonable possibility that the requesting party will succeed on the merits of the claim. The determination on this possibility shall not affect the discretion of the arbitral tribunal in making any subsequent determination.
4. With regard to a request for an interim measure under paragraph 2 (d), the requirements in paragraphs 3 (a) and (b) shall apply only to the extent the arbitral tribunal considers appropriate.
5. The arbitral tribunal may modify, suspend or terminate an interim measure it has granted, upon application of any party or, in exceptional circumstances and upon prior notice to the parties, on the arbitral tribunal's own initiative.
6. The arbitral tribunal may require the party requesting an interim measure to provide appropriate security in connection with the measure.
7. The arbitral tribunal may require any party promptly to disclose any material change in the circumstances on the basis of which the interim measure was requested or granted.
8. The party requesting an interim measure may be liable for any costs and damages caused by the measure to any party if the arbitral tribunal later determines that, in the circumstances then prevailing, the measure should not have been granted. The arbitral tribunal may award such costs and damages at any point during the proceedings.
9. A request for interim measures addressed by any party to a judicial authority shall not be deemed incompatible with the agreement to arbitrate, or as a waiver of that agreement.

Article 26 of the 2010 UNCITRAL Arbitration Rules does not expressly allow for preliminary orders. However, despite this omission, it is submitted that an arbitral tribunal under the 2010 UNCITRAL Arbitration Rules would have the authority to issue preliminary orders.[7]

Article 26 of the 2010 UNCITRAL Arbitration Rules in turn form part of the 2018 AIAC Arbitration Rules. In addition, Rule 8 of the AIAC Arbitration Rules provides that a party in need of an urgent interim measure prior to the constitution of the arbitral tribunal may submit a request to appoint an emergency arbitrator to the Director of the AIAC in accordance with Schedule 3 of the 2018 AIAC Arbitration Rules.

The present section 19 was introduced by the Arbitration (Amendment) (No 2) Act 2018. Prior to the amendment, section 19 provided:

(1) Unless otherwise agreed by the parties, a party may apply to the arbitral tribunal for any of the following orders:
   (a) security for costs;
   (b) discovery of documents and interrogatories;

---

[7] *See* David D Caron and Lee M Caplan, *The UNCITRAL Arbitration Rules, A Commentary* (2nd edn, Oxford University Press 2013) at p 531.

(c) giving of evidence by affidavit;
(d) the preservation, interim custody or sale of any property which is the subject-matter of the dispute.
(2) The arbitral tribunal may require any party to provide appropriate security in connection with such measure as ordered under subsection (1).
(3) Unless otherwise agreed by the parties, sections 38 and 39 shall apply to orders made by an arbitral tribunal under this section as if a reference in those sections to an award were a reference to such an order.

The former section 19 of the Arbitration Act 2005 was based on Article 17 of the 1985 Model Law but provided for the type of interim measures that could be granted and also for the enforcement of such measures.

The current section 19, like the current Article 17 of the 2006 Model Law, is considerably more detailed. We consider the detailed provisions of the current section 19 below.

§19.02 DEFINITION OF INTERIM MEASURES

Section 19(2) of the Arbitration Act 2005 defines an interim measure as 'any temporary measure, whether in the form of an award or in another form, by which, at any time prior to the issuance of the award by which the dispute is finally decided, the arbitral tribunal orders'. An interim measure is therefore:

(1) of a temporary measure;
(2) made prior to the final award; and
(3) in the form of an award or other form.

The distinction drawn is between a temporary measure and a final award that resolves the disputes between the parties. This temporary nature of the measure is emphasized by section 19A(2) which provides that the arbitral tribunal's determination of a reasonable possibility of the applicant succeeding on the merits of the claim for the purposes of an interim measure will not affect any subsequent determination of the dispute.

Section 19(2) is intentionally neutral on the question of form, leaving it to the arbitral tribunal to grant the interim measure in the form of an award or any other form. Section 19(2) is also intended to be neutral on the question of whether an interim measure granted in the form of an award is enforceable in accordance with the 1958 New York Convention.[8]

§19.03 TWO PRECONDITIONS FOR INTERIM MEASURES

Section 19(1) of the Arbitration Act 2005 sets out two preconditions for the grant of interim measures:

---

8. *See* UNCITRAL Note by the Secretariat *'Settlement of Commercial Disputes: Interim Measures'* (39th Session 25 Apr. 2006) A/CN.9/605 at para. 5.

(1) the arbitration agreement should not preclude such measures; and
(2) a party must make a request for such measures.

These two preconditions reinforce the principle of party autonomy. The parties are entitled to agree that the arbitral tribunal shall not have the power to grant interim measures or a particular type of such measures.

Furthermore, an arbitral tribunal may only grant an interim measure at the request of a party. An arbitral tribunal may not grant such measures on their own initiative. Section 19(1) does not provide for any particular form for such a request for interim measures. In practice, such a request is likely to be made in writing with sufficient particulars to enable the other party to respond and the arbitral tribunal to consider the request. However, there is nothing to preclude such a request being made orally, and, an arbitral tribunal may permit such a request, for a particularly urgent measure.

§19.04 FIVE TYPES OF INTERIM MEASURES

Section 19(2) of the Arbitration Act 2005, after defining interim measures, proceeds to describe five types of interim measures. The five interim measures are broadly defined and overlap to an extent.

These five interim measures are identical to the five interim measures that may be granted by the High Court under section 11(1) save that the words 'whether by way of arrest of property or bail or other security pursuant to the admiralty jurisdiction of the High Court' in section 11(1)(c) have been omitted from section 19(1)(c). Therefore, reference may be made to §11.05 *supra* for an understanding of the nature of these five types of interim measures.

However, the conditions for the grant of interim measures by an arbitral tribunal are expressly set out in section 19A. This is unlike the position with respect to interim measures that may be granted by the High Court under section 11, where the conditions are not set out in the Arbitration Act 2005 but are to be determined based on judgments of the courts, as set out in §11.05 *supra*.

It is unclear whether the five interim measures described in section 19(2) are intended to be exhaustive. Article 26(2) of the 2010 UNCITRAL Arbitration Rules expressly provides that the interim measures listed are 'for example and without limitation' to the power of the arbitral tribunal to grant interim measures. However, no such express provision is found in Article 17(2) of the 2006 Model Law or section 19(2) of the Arbitration Act 2005, which adopts it. It is submitted that the five types of interim measures in section 19(2) should not be regarded as exhaustive or limiting the arbitral tribunal's powers to grant interim measures that would be appropriate in the light of the particular circumstances.

Section 19(2)(e) allows the arbitral tribunal to grant security for costs. There is no equivalent provision in Article 17 of the 2006 Model Law. There is uncertainty[9] as to whether an order for security for costs comes within Articles 17(2)(b) or (c) of the 2006 Model Law. To avoid this uncertainty, section 19(2)(e) expressly allows an arbitral tribunal to order security for costs.

§19.05 THREE CONDITIONS FOR INTERIM MEASURES

Section 19A(1) sets out the three conditions for the grant of interim measures. The three conditions are that:

(1) harm not adequately reparable by an award of damages is likely to result if the measure is not ordered;
(2) such harm substantially outweighs the harm that is likely to result to the party against whom the measure is directed if the measure is granted; and
(3) there is a reasonable possibility that the requesting party will succeed on the merits of the claim.

The applicant must satisfy all three conditions, which are mandatory, as the word 'shall' is used in section 19A(1), and conjunctive, as the word 'and' is used between section 19A(1)(a) and (b). These are conditions that need to be satisfied by the applicant and not criteria used for assessment by the arbitral tribunal, as can be seen from the express provisions of section 19A(1).

The three conditions are similar to those expressed by the Court of Appeal, in *Keet Gerald Francis Noel John v. Mohd Noor @ Harun Abdullah & Ors* [1995] 1 MLJ 193 at pages 206 and 207 in the context of interim injunctions. Although these three conditions are similar, they are not identical to the conditions in *Keet Gerald supra*. Furthermore, these are express statutory conditions, and, as such, emphasis will be placed on the precise wording and intent of the statute, as opposed to the broad principles expressed in a judgment. As such, we consider each of these three express statutory conditions below.

[A] Harm Not Adequately Reparable by an Award of Damages

The applicant must prove that they are likely to suffer harm that cannot be 'adequately reparable' by damages. The applicant is not required to prove irreparable harm, as it was felt this would be setting the bar too high, and, furthermore, almost any harm can be compensated by a monetary award.[10]

The applicant must prove that they are 'likely' to suffer such harm but does not have to prove this as a certainty. This is because, at an interlocutory stage, and prior to

---
9. *See* David A.R. Williams and Amokura Kawharu, *Williams & Kawharu on Arbitration* (2nd edn, LexisNexis 2017) at para. 9.2.6.
10. *See* David D. Caron and Lee M. Caplan, *The UNCITRAL Arbitration Rules, A Commentary* (2nd edn, Oxford University Press 2013) at p 521.

actually having suffered such harm, the applicant would only be able to prove a likelihood.

[B] Such Harm Substantially Outweighs the Harm Likely to Result to the Respondent

The applicant must also prove that the harm they are likely to suffer 'substantially outweighs' the harm likely to result to the respondent. This condition involves the familiar balance of hardship test.

The test as expressed in section 19A(1)(a) is onerous on the applicant, as the applicant must show not only that the harm they are likely to suffer will outweigh the harm likely to be suffered by the respondent but also that such harm 'substantially' outweighs the harm likely to be suffered by the respondent.[11]

[C] Reasonable Possibility That the Applicant Will Succeed on the Merits

The applicant must further prove that there is a reasonable possibility that their claim will succeed on the merits. Although not expressed, it is implicit that the applicant must, in this context, prove that the arbitral tribunal has jurisdiction over the claim, as the claim cannot succeed if the arbitral tribunal does not have jurisdiction. This implicit requirement is controversial, as an investigation as to whether an arbitral tribunal has jurisdiction may require a full hearing and may be difficult to undertake at an interlocutory stage.[12]

The applicant must prove a 'reasonable possibility' of success. The applicant must accordingly prove a prima facie case, meaning that if the facts as alleged are proved, this might possibly lead to success on the claim, or, to put it negatively, that the claim is not frivolous.[13]

Section 19A(2) expressly provides that the arbitral tribunal's determination that there is a reasonable possibility of success will not affect the arbitral tribunal's discretion in making any subsequent determination. This provision emphasizes that the arbitral tribunal's determination of a reasonable possibility of success at an interlocutory stage should not affect the final award.

The High Court, in the context of the High Court's power to grant interim measures under section 11, has explained this, in *Bumi Armada Navigation Sdn Bhd v. Mirza Marine Sdn Bhd* [2015] MLJU 953 at paragraphs 49-51 and 90(a). These principles would be equally applicable to an arbitral tribunal's determination of a reasonable possibility of success. As a matter of practice, and based on *Bumi Armada*

---

11. *See* David D. Caron and Lee M. Caplan, *The UNCITRAL Arbitration Rules, A Commentary* (2nd edn, Oxford University Press 2013) at p 522.
12. *See* David D. Caron and Lee M. Caplan, *The UNCITRAL Arbitration Rules, A Commentary* (2nd edn, Oxford University Press 2013) at p 523.
13. *See* David D. Caron and Lee M. Caplan, *The UNCITRAL Arbitration Rules, A Commentary* (2nd edn, Oxford University Press 2013) at p 523.

supra at paragraph 90(a), it may be prudent for an arbitral tribunal to expressly state in the interim award that the determination will not affect the final award.[14]

§19.06 APPLICATION OF THE THREE CONDITIONS

The applicant must satisfy all three conditions for the interim measures described in sections 19(2)(a), (b) and (c). Section 19A(3) provides that the three conditions will only apply 'only to the extent the arbitral tribunal considers appropriate' for the interim measure under section 19(2)(d), which is for the preservation of evidence.

This is because the conditions for the grant of an interim measure to preserve evidence differ from other interim measures. The conditions for the grant of an interim measure to preserve evidence are explained in §11.05[D] *supra* in the context of the grant of such a measure by the High Court and would be equally applicable here.

However, it must be emphasized that the three conditions are not inapplicable to the grant of an interim measure to preserve evidence. The arbitral tribunal must still take these three conditions into account when considering an application for an interim measure to preserve evidence. However, section 19A(3) allows the arbitral tribunal some discretion in the application of these three conditions in an application for an interim measure to preserve evidence.[15]

Section 19A(3) does not address the application of these three conditions to an application for security for costs. This is presumably because the 2006 Model Law does not provide for security for costs and the drafters of the Arbitration Act 2005 while inserting section 19(2)(e) did not amend section 19A(3) to address this additional interim measure.

The conditions for the grant of security for costs by the High Court are explained in §11.05[E] *supra*. These conditions should be applicable to a grant of security for costs by an arbitral tribunal. These conditions differ from the conditions for the grant of other interim measures. As such, it is submitted that the same position which applies to interim measures to preserve evidence should apply to security for costs. The arbitral tribunal should take the three conditions into account in an application for security for costs but should have discretion in the application of the three conditions.

§19.07 DEFINITION OF PRELIMINARY ORDERS

A preliminary order is an interim measure made by the arbitral tribunal on an ex parte basis to prevent the purpose of the interim measure being frustrated. The term 'preliminary order' is used to emphasize the temporary and extraordinary nature of such an order, as well as the distinct statutory regime which governs such orders.[16]

---

14. *See* David D. Caron and Lee M. Caplan, *The UNCITRAL Arbitration Rules, A Commentary* (2nd edn, Oxford University Press 2013) at p 523.
15. *See* David D. Caron and Lee M. Caplan, *The UNCITRAL Arbitration Rules, A Commentary* (2nd edn, Oxford University Press 2013) at p 524.
16. *See* UNCITRAL Note by the Secretariat '*Settlement of Commercial Disputes: Interim Measures*' (39th Session 25 Apr. 2006) A/CN.9/605 at para. 10.

The inclusion of provisions on preliminary orders in the 2006 Model Law was controversial. These provisions were not included in the 2010 UNCITRAL Arbitration Rules. These provisions, however, are included in the Arbitration Act 2005, as sections 19B and 19C.

The controversy arose because the proponents of such orders argued that the courts in most countries were entitled to grant temporary injunctions on an ex parte basis, where the court was satisfied that informing the other party may undermine the effectiveness of the temporary injunction sought. Furthermore, in practice, even before the 2006 Model Law, arbitral tribunals did grant interim measures on an ex parte basis. Finally, the absence of such provisions in Article 17 of the 2006 Model Law may have given the unwanted impression that an arbitral tribunal does not have jurisdiction to grant an ex parte order.[17]

On the other hand, those opposed to the adoption of the provisions on preliminary orders in the 2006 Model Law argued that such ex parte orders were contrary to the essence of arbitration, which required each party to be heard.[18]

Section 19 of the Arbitration Act 2005, and Article 17 of the 2006 Model Law, which the Act reflects, is a compromise, in the light of these arguments. Preliminary orders are permitted but there is an additional condition and several safeguards put in place.

§19.08 TWO PRECONDITIONS FOR PRELIMINARY ORDERS

Section 19B(1) of the Arbitration Act 2005 sets out two preconditions for the grant of preliminary orders:

(1) the arbitration agreement should not preclude such orders; and
(2) a party must request an interim measure and apply for such a preliminary order.

These two preconditions are the same as the preconditions for interim measures and reference may be made to §19.03 *supra*.

§19.09 ADDITIONAL CONDITIONS FOR PRELIMINARY ORDERS

Section 19B(3) provides that the applicant for a preliminary order must satisfy the three conditions for the grant of an interim measure in section 19A, which are considered in §19.05 *supra*. However, the harm to be assessed is the harm in relation to the preliminary order and not the interim measure.

In addition to satisfying these conditions, the applicant would also need to satisfy the arbitral tribunal that the disclosure of the request for an interim measure 'risks

---

17. *See* David D. Caron and Lee M. Caplan, *The UNCITRAL Arbitration Rules, A Commentary* (2nd edn, Oxford University Press 2013) at p 531.
18. *See* David D. Caron and Lee M. Caplan, *The UNCITRAL Arbitration Rules, A Commentary* (2nd edn, Oxford University Press 2013) at p 531.

frustrating the purpose of the interim measure'. This additional condition appears stricter, as it does not include words like 'likely' or 'reasonably possibility' in the three conditions in section 19A(1). This strict additional condition is in accordance with a preliminary order being extraordinary in nature.

§19.10 FIVE SAFEGUARDS FOR PRELIMINARY ORDERS

Section 19C of the Arbitration Act 2005 lays down several safeguards for preliminary orders to address the concerns raised. First, the arbitral tribunal must immediately after determining the preliminary order give notice of all documents and oral communications in relation to the preliminary order to the respondent. The arbitral tribunal must give such notice whether or not the preliminary order was allowed.[19]

Second, the arbitral tribunal must immediately after determining the preliminary order allow the respondent an opportunity to be heard. This addresses one of the concerns raised in relation to preliminary orders by ensuring that the respondent is heard at the earliest opportunity.

Third, the arbitral tribunal must decide on any objection to the preliminary order. This will be after the respondent has been given a reasonable opportunity to be heard. The arbitral tribunal's decision must be made 'immediately' after such an opportunity has been allowed to the respondent. The repeated use of the word 'immediately' in sections 19C(1) and (2) emphasizes the extremely short timeline for notice, objection and decision on a preliminary order.

Fourth, to further reinforce this immediacy, section 19C(3) provides that the preliminary order will expire within twenty days of the arbitral tribunal issuing such order. Section 19C(4) then provides that notwithstanding the expiry of the preliminary order, the arbitral tribunal may grant an interim measure that adopts or modifies such order after the arbitral tribunal has given notice to the respondent and allowed them an opportunity to be heard.

Fifth, and finally, sections 19C(5) and (6) provide that a preliminary order is binding on the parties but is not an award that can be enforced. A preliminary order is therefore in the nature of a procedural order rather than an award.[20] A preliminary order is binding on the parties and is usually respected and complied with. If a preliminary order is not complied with, an arbitral tribunal will be entitled to draw an adverse inference or take this into account when awarding costs.[21]

---

19. *See* UNCITRAL Note by the Secretariat *'Settlement of Commercial Disputes: Interim Measures'* (39th Session 25 Apr. 2006) A/CN.9/605 at para. 14.
20. *See* UNCITRAL Note by the Secretariat *'Settlement of Commercial Disputes: Interim Measures'* (39th Session 25 Apr. 2006) A/CN.9/605 at para. 11.
21. *See* David A.R. Williams and Amokura Kawharu, *Williams & Kawharu on Arbitration* (2nd edn, LexisNexis 2017) at para. 9.8.1.

§19.11 MODIFICATION, SUSPENSION OR TERMINATION

Section 19D of the Arbitration Act 2005 provides that the arbitral tribunal may modify, suspend or terminate an interim measure it has granted. An interim measure may be granted in the form of an award or any other form. An interim measure granted in the form of award is generally regarded as final. The question therefore arises as to how such an award may be modified, suspended or terminated. It is implicit in section 19D that any modification, suspension or termination will be subsequent to the interim measure being granted. As such, where the interim measure is in the form of an award, the modification, suspension or termination should be by way of a subsequent award that modifies, suspends or terminates the earlier award, rather than by way of amendment to the earlier award. The word 'amend' was deliberately not included in Article 17D, which section 19D is based on.[22]

The arbitral tribunal would generally modify, suspend or terminate an interim measure due to the emergence of new facts and circumstances. There was, indeed, a suggestion that Article 17D of the 2006 Model Law, which section 19D is based on, expressly provides that a modification, suspension or termination was to be 'in light of additional information or a change of circumstances'. However, this suggestion was rejected on the grounds that it may be superfluous and unduly restrict the discretion of the arbitral tribunal.[23]

Section 19D requires an application to be made by a party for modification, suspension or termination. However, in exceptional circumstances, the arbitral tribunal may act on its own initiative but must give prior notice to the parties. The requirement for an application by a party or prior notice by the arbitral tribunal is to ensure party autonomy.[24]

§19.12 SECURITY

Section 19E(1) of the Arbitration Act 2005 allows the arbitral tribunal to require that the applicant for interim measures provide security for such measures. The arbitral tribunal is entitled to require such security because the respondent may be subjected to substantial unnecessary costs if it is later found that an interim measure was wrongly granted. The arbitral tribunal has the discretion whether to require such security, as can be seen from the use of the word 'may' in section 19E(1).

By contrast, section 19E(2) makes it mandatory for the arbitral tribunal to require the applicant for preliminary orders unless the arbitral tribunal considers it unnecessary or inappropriate to do so. The stricter requirement for costs in relation to preliminary orders is because such orders are sought on an ex parte basis and, as such,

---

22. *See* David D. Caron and Lee M. Caplan, *The UNCITRAL Arbitration Rules, A Commentary* (2nd edn, Oxford University Press 2013) at pp 525-526.
23. *See* David D. Caron and Lee M. Caplan, *The UNCITRAL Arbitration Rules, A Commentary* (2nd edn, Oxford University Press 2013) at p 526.
24. *See* David D. Caron and Lee M. Caplan, *The UNCITRAL Arbitration Rules, A Commentary* (2nd edn, Oxford University Press 2013) at p 526.

there is an increased risk that such orders may later be found to have been wrongly granted, in the light of further information.

Although not expressly provided for in section 19E, the arbitral tribunal is entitled to require the applicant to provide security either at the time the application is made or subsequently.[25]

§19.13 DISCLOSURE

The arbitral tribunal is entitled to modify, suspend or terminate an interim measure or preliminary order, in the light of new circumstances. In order to do this, the arbitral tribunal is empowered under section 19F(1) to require any party to disclose any material change in circumstance. The arbitral tribunal is entitled to require such disclosure from either party, as the words 'any party' are used in section 19F(1). The arbitral tribunal is allowed to do this to ensure that the interim measure or preliminary order remains justified.

Section 19F(2) provides that an applicant for a preliminary order must make full and frank disclosure and that this obligation continues until the respondent has had an opportunity to present their case. As the application for a preliminary order is made ex parte, the applicant is obliged to make full and frank disclosure. This is a further safeguard that is in place in relation to such orders.

§19.14 COSTS AND DAMAGES

Section 19G(1) of the Arbitration Act 2005 provides that an applicant for an interim measure or preliminary order will be liable for any costs or damage to the respondent if the arbitral tribunal subsequently finds that such measure or order should not have been granted. Section 19G(1) should be read together with section 19E, which requires the provision of security for the costs the applicant may be liable for.

The applicant will be liable for such costs or damages if the arbitral tribunal subsequently finds that the interim measure or preliminary order should not have been granted. Therefore, the final award being against the applicant does not necessarily mean that the applicant will be liable for such costs and damages. Instead, there should be a specific determination by the arbitral tribunal that the particular measure or order should not have been granted.

Section 19G(2) provides that the arbitral tribunal may award such costs and damages at any point during the arbitral proceedings.

§19.15 RECOGNITION AND ENFORCEMENT OF INTERIM MEASURES

Sections 19H and 19I of the Arbitration Act 2005 provide for the recognition and enforcement of interim measures, as well as the grounds for refusing such recognition.

---

25. *See* David D. Caron and Lee M. Caplan, *The UNCITRAL Arbitration Rules, A Commentary* (2nd edn, Oxford University Press 2013) at p 527.

Sections 19H and 19I of the Arbitration Act 2005 are based on Articles 17H and 17I of the 2006 Model Law.

Sections 19H and 19I on the recognition and enforcement of interim measures mirror sections 38 and 39 on the recognition and enforcement of awards; in the same way Articles 17H and 17I mirror Articles 35 and 36. The intention was to have a regime tested in practice for the enforcement of interim measures.[26]

In particular, section 19H(1) is similar to section 38(1). However, section 19H(1) dispenses with the procedural requirements set out in sections 38(2)-(4). The procedural requirements in section 38 on applications to enforce awards are likely to be complied with in relation to interim measures, as the requirements are practical. This may also be formalized by way of amendments to civil procedure rules.

The enforcement provisions in section 19H(1) are also broader than section 38(1) in two material aspects:

(1) section 19H(1) applies to interim measures made in any country unlike section 38(1), which is limited to awards made in States which are a party to the 1958 New York Convention; and
(2) an application under section 19H(1) need not be made to the High Court but to any competent court, which presumably includes the subordinate courts and the High Court, unlike section 38(1) that requires an application to be made to the High Court.[27]

Section 19H(1) significantly does not provide that the interim measure will be enforced by entry as a judgment, unlike section 38(1). The interim measure not being entered as a judgment may explain the absence of procedural requirements and the broader application of these provisions. The interim measures are likely to be enforced in practice as orders of the courts.

Sections 19H(2) and (3) provide for scenarios that arise due to the temporary nature of interim measures, which is unlike an award under section 38. Section 19H(2) requires the applicant, in making the application and subsequently, if successful, to notify the courts of the termination, suspension or modification of the interim measure by the arbitral tribunal. This is to ensure that the court's assistance is only granted in relation to interim measures that remain justified and enforceable.

Section 19H(3) entitles the court to require the applicant to provide security in two scenarios:

(1) where the arbitral tribunal has not determined the need for such security; or
(2) where such security is needed to protect the rights of third parties.

---

26. *See* David A.R. Williams and Amokura Kawharu, *Williams & Kawharu on Arbitration* (2nd edn, LexisNexis 2017) at para. 9.9.
27. *See* Uba Lrus Bina Asia Sdn Bhd v. Quirk & Associates Sdn Bhd & Anor [2016] 4 CLJ 468 at para. 37, HC.

§19.16 REFUSAL OF RECOGNITION AND ENFORCEMENT OF INTERIM MEASURES

Section 19I(1) on the grounds for refusing recognition and enforcement of interim measures reflects section 39(1) on the grounds for refusing recognition and enforcement of awards.

In this context, reference may be made to §39.03 *infra* on the words 'may be refused', §39.04 *infra* on the word 'only', §39.05 *infra* on the words 'at the request of the party against whom it is invoked'. These words are used in both sections 19I(1) and 39(1).

The grounds in sections 19I(1) and 39(1) are the same save that section 19I(1):

(1) does not include the ground in section 39(1)(a)(vii); and
(2) includes three additional grounds in sections 19I(1)(a)(ii) and (iii) and 19I(1)(b)(i).

The three additional grounds have been included to provide for the temporary and extraordinary nature of interim measures. First, section 19I(1)(a)(ii) allows recognition to be refused where the applicant has not complied with the arbitral tribunal's decision on the provision of security. This gives force to any arbitral tribunal's decision on the provision of security, as failure to comply with such a decision may result in the interim measure not being recognized and enforced.

Second, section 19I(1)(a)(iii) allows recognition to be refused where the interim measure has been terminated or suspended by the arbitral tribunal that granted such measure or by the courts in the place of arbitration. Section 19I(a)(iii) is a modification of section 39(1)(a)(vii) to provide for interim measures, in particular, the temporary nature of an interim measure, which can be subsequently terminated or suspended by the arbitral tribunal under section 19D or by the courts in the place of arbitration.

Third, section 19I(1)(b)(i) gives the High Court some flexibility, where the interim measure is found to be incompatible with the High Court's powers, to reformulate the interim measure in a manner compatible with its powers without affecting such measure's substance. This provision is essential to cater for interim measures made in States other than Malaysia, where the interim measures may not have taken into account the powers of the High Court and the applicable civil procedure rules. The High Court has the power to reformulate such measures to ensure that they are compatible with the powers of the High Court.

Section 19I(2) emphasizes that any determination made by the High Court on an application to recognize and enforce an interim measure is limited to such an application and does not extend beyond that.

Section 19I(3) expressly provides, what is implicit in sections 37 and 39, that any determination of the High Court on an application to recognize and enforce an interim measure will not involve a review of the substance or merits of such measures.

§19.17 COURT-ORDERED INTERIM MEASURES

Section 19J(1) of the Arbitration Act 2005 provides that the High Court has the power to issue interim measures in relation to arbitration proceedings regardless of whether the seat is in Malaysia or not. Section 19J(1) is similar to section 11(3) of the Arbitration Act 2005 and reference may be made to §11.06 *supra*.

Section 19J(2) provides that the High Court in granting such interim measures shall have regard to 'the specific features of international arbitration'. This is not expressly provided for in section 11 but has always been an implicit requirement. The most important consideration for the High Court is that interim measures should only be granted, where such measures will aid, facilitate or support the arbitration proceedings and not where they will impede such proceedings. These general principles are considered in §11.02 *supra*, in particular §11.02[D] *supra*.

Section 19J(3) provides that, in an application for interim measures, the High Court will be bound by any finding of fact made by the arbitral tribunal. This provision is identical to section 11(2) and reference may be made to §11.02 *supra*.

CHAPTER 5
Conduct of Arbitral Proceedings

20.   Equal Treatment of Parties

The parties shall be treated with equality and each party shall be given a fair and reasonable opportunity of presenting that party's case.

§20.01   INTRODUCTION

Section 20 of the Arbitration Act 2005 provides for the equal treatment of parties and that each party shall be given a fair and reasonable opportunity to be heard.

Section 20 of the Arbitration Act 2005 is identical to Article 18 of the 1985 Model Law save that the right to a 'full' opportunity in the 1985 Model Law has been substituted with a 'fair and reasonable' opportunity to present one's case.

Article 18 of the 1985 Model Law is in turn based on Article 15 of the 1976 UNCITRAL Arbitration Rules, which provides:

> General Provisions
> Article 15
> 1. Subject to these Rules, the arbitral tribunal may conduct the arbitration in such manner as it considers appropriate, provided the parties are treated with equality and that at any stage of the proceedings each party is given a full opportunity of presenting his case.
> 2. If either party so requests at any stage of the proceedings, the arbitral tribunal shall hold hearings for the presentation of evidence by witnesses, including expert witnesses, or for oral argument. In the absence of such a request, the arbitral tribunal shall decide whether to hold such hearings or whether the proceedings shall be conducted on the basis of documents and other materials.
> 3. All documents or information supplied to the arbitral tribunal by one party shall at the same time be communicated by that party to the other party.

Elements of Article 15 of the 1976 UNCITRAL Arbitration Rules are reflected in Articles 18, 19 and 24 of the 1985 Model Law.

Article 17 of the 2013 UNCITRAL Arbitration Rules expands on Article 15 of the 1976 UNCITRAL Arbitration Rules and provides that:

General Provisions
Article 17
1. Subject to these Rules, the arbitral tribunal may conduct the arbitration in such manner as it considers appropriate, provided that the parties are treated with equality and that at an appropriate stage of the proceedings each party is given a reasonable opportunity of presenting its case. The arbitral tribunal, in exercising its discretion, shall conduct the proceedings so as to avoid unnecessary delay and expense and to provide a fair and efficient process for resolving the parties' dispute.
2. As soon as practicable after its constitution and after inviting the parties to express their views, the arbitral tribunal shall establish the provisional timetable of the arbitration. The arbitral tribunal may, at any time, after inviting the parties to express their views, extend or abridge any period of time prescribed under these Rules or agreed by the parties.
3. If at an appropriate stage of the proceedings any party so requests, the arbitral tribunal shall hold hearings for the presentation of evidence by witnesses, including expert witnesses, or for oral argument. In the absence of such a request, the arbitral tribunal shall decide whether to hold such hearings or whether the proceedings shall be conducted on the basis of documents and other materials.
4. All communications to the arbitral tribunal by one party shall be communicated by that party to all other parties. Such communications shall be made at the same time, except as otherwise permitted by the arbitral tribunal if it may do so under applicable law.
5. The arbitral tribunal may, at the request of any party, allow one or more third persons to be joined in the arbitration as a party provided such person is a party to the arbitration agreement, unless the arbitral tribunal finds, after giving all parties, including the person or persons to be joined, the opportunity to be heard, that joinder should not be permitted because of prejudice to any of those parties. The arbitral tribunal may make a single award or several awards in respect of all parties so involved in the arbitration.

The 2013 UNCITRAL Arbitration Rules form part of the 2018 AIAC Arbitration Rules.

The fifth and final draft of the 1985 Model Law had an Article 19 that combined the present Articles 18 and 19 of 1985 Model Law.[1] However, the provisions of the present Article 18 of the 1985 Model Law were separated and presented as a single article because it constituted a 'fundamental principle, which was applicable to the entire arbitral proceedings'.[2]

§20.02 FUNDAMENTAL PRINCIPLE

As stated above, section 20 of the Arbitration Act 2005 constitutes a fundamental principle. This principle is part of a duo that forms the rules of natural justice. The first

---

1. *See* Analytical Commentary, Article 19.
2. *See* UNCITRAL Report at para. 176.

principle is the right to be heard, which is reflected in section 20, and the second principle is the rule against bias, which is reflected in section 14 and has been considered in §14.01-§14.04 *supra*.

As one of the two constituent principles of the rules of natural justice, section 20 is of particular significance and has been recognized as such. The UNCITRAL deliberately placed Article 18 of the 1985 Model Law alone to reflect its fundamental importance.

§20.03 SETTING ASIDE

Section 20 has been most frequently considered by the courts in the context of an application to set aside an arbitral award under sections 37(1)(b)(ii) and (2)(b) of the Arbitration Act 2005. Section 37(1)(b)(ii) provides that an award may be set aside where it is in conflict with public policy. Section 37(2)(b) then clarifies that an award may be in conflict with public policy where there has been a breach of the rules of natural justice.

The High Court, in *Infineon Technologies (M) Sdn Bhd v. Orisoft Technology Sdn Bhd (previously known as Orisoft Technology Berhad) and another application* [2011] 7 MLJ 539, drew a distinction between a breach of the rules of natural justice in a domestic and international arbitration. While a more restrictive approach should be taken in international arbitration, a broader approach may be taken in domestic arbitration. In the context of international arbitration, what was required was a breach of the most basic notions of morality and justice. While in the context of domestic arbitration, what was required was a substantial miscarriage of justice. Notably, in adopting this test, the High Court was influenced by the KLRCA Arbitration Rules applicable at the time.

In this regard, the High Court, in *Infineon Technologies supra* at paragraphs 74 and 75, *inter alia*, held:

> [74] ... the approach is not to refuse to register on the ground of conflict of public policy unless the most basic notions of morality and justice would be offended. Thus the approach is very restrictive, being grounded in the upholding of international comity. A less rigid approach should, in principle, apply where the award is a Domestic Arbitral Award, although the comparative jurisprudence on this matter cannot as yet be said as approximating a uniform approach ... .

> [75] I find the approach taken by the New Zealand Court of Appeal [in *Downer Hill Joint Venture v. Government of Fiji* [2005] 1 NZLR 554] particularly attractive, and the test of 'substantial miscarriage of justice' is particularly apposite bearing in mind what is provided in the KLRCA Rules, namely r 13 which uses the same concept. To recapitulate, r 13 states that non-compliance 'shall not affect the validity or legality of the arbitral proceedings or the award unless such non-compliance had occasioned a substantial miscarriage of justice' ... .

The High Court, in *Sabah Medical Center Sdn Bhd v. Syarikat Neptune Enterprise Sdn Bhd* [2011] 1 LNS 849, considered an application to set aside an arbitral award due to the breach of the rules of natural justice. The High Court regarded a 'fair and reasonable' opportunity to be heard as a lesser standard than a 'full' opportunity to be heard, with this lower standard being further diluted by the arbitral tribunal's discretion under section 21(2) of the Arbitration Act 2005. The High Court held that if a decision in an arbitral award is based on grounds other than those in relation to which a breach of natural justice may have occurred, then the breach will not affect the award.

In this context, the High Court, in *Sabah Medical Center supra* at pages 18 and 19, *inter alia*, held:

> To recap, the plaintiff is relying on the contention that the arbitrator had breached the principle of natural justice. I think it can be said that the spirit of the Act is that the court should intervene only in exceptional circumstances and this is reflected in provisions contained in it. Sec 20 of the Act prescribes that the arbitral tribunal is only required to provide the parties a 'fair and reasonable opportunity' to present their case. In sec 21(2) of the Act, the arbitral tribunal is given a full discretion to determine the manner in which the proceeding is to be conducted. The court can only be seized of jurisdiction if it is the view that the Award is in conflict with the public policy of Malaysia or is tainted with fraud or corruption or the arbitral proceeding is inconsistent with the principle of natural justice. Case law is such that the courts must take a 'non interventionist' approach.

In a similar vein, the High Court,[3] in *MMC Engineering Group Bhd & Anor v. Wayss & Freytag (M) Sdn Bhd & Anor* [2015] MLJU 477, clarified that for the courts to provide a remedy, a party must show that they have suffered actual prejudice as a result of a breach of natural justice. However, the court is not to put itself in the position of the arbitrator and consider whether the court would have reached a different result if the rules of natural justice had been observed.

In this context, the High Court, in *MMC Engineering supra* at paragraphs 221 and 223, *inter alia*, held:

> [221] The Courts are not required and it is not the principle that the Court must be satisfied that it would have come to a different result before the presence of prejudice is established. The Courts are not required to assume the role of the Arbitral Tribunal ... .
>
> ...
>
> [223] Therefore, before the Plaintiffs can properly and legitimately say that that there is a breach of natural justice on the facts here, the Plaintiffs must show that the Award and the Arbitral Tribunal's conclusions and reasoning were not based on any of the parties' arguments in the arbitration. If indeed there was such a conclusion or reasoning that was the basis of the Award, the Plaintiffs must still show that that train of reasoning could not have been reasonably anticipated or foreseen from the arguments and evidence presented during the arbitration proceedings. The Plaintiffs must further show that if adequate notice of such train of reasoning had been given, the Plaintiffs could possibly have persuaded the Arbitral Tribunal to reach a result in the Plaintiffs' favour if not a result less adverse to the Plaintiffs.

---

3. The judgment of the High Court, in *MMC Engineering supra*, has since been affirmed by the Court of Appeal.

Again, similarly, the High Court, in *Tanjung Langsat Port Sdn Bhd v. Trafigura Pte Ltd & Another Case* [2016] 4 CLJ 927, in considering an application to set aside decided that:

(1) a breach of the rules of natural justice does not in itself mean that the award is in conflict with public policy;
(2) therefore, even where there has been a breach of the rules of natural justice, the courts retain the discretion as to whether to set aside the award as being in conflict with public policy; and
(3) the courts will exercise their discretion to set aside an award as being in conflict with public policy if a breach of the rules of natural justice caused actual prejudice to a party.

In this context, the High Court, in *Tanjung Langsat supra* at paragraphs 63 and 64, 71, 77, *inter alia*, held:

> [63] Hence with respect I am of the view from that not all breaches of the rules of natural justice will *ipso facto* mean that the arbitral award will be in conflict with public policy and will be liable to be set aside under s. 37(1)(b)(ii) of the AA 2005 ... .
>
> [64] Even if it can be shown that there has been a breach of natural justice, the court retains the discretion whether to set aside the arbitral award for being in conflict with public policy under s. 37(1)(b)(ii) of the AA 2005 ... .
>
> ...
>
> [71] Hence it is my respectful view in order to set [aside] the arbitral award for being in conflict with public policy, it must be shown that the alleged breach of natural justice has caused actual prejudice to the aggrieved party.
>
> ...
>
> [77] In any event in following the approach in *Soh Beng Tee*, taking it to the highest and even if it could be argued that the majority tribunal did not comply with the rules of natural justice in failing to consider TLP's defence under cl. 13.4 of the storage agreement, in my respectful view this is not a breach which has caused actual prejudice or 'shock the conscience' or offends 'fundamental principles of justice and morality' (*See MTM Millenium, PT Asuransi*).

The Court of Appeal, in *Tridant Engineering (M) Sdn Bhd v. Ssangyong Engineering and Construction Co Ltd* [2016] MLJU 599, in considering an application to set aside, decided that even if an issue was not specifically pleaded, so long as the rules of natural justice were not breached, in the sense that the parties had an opportunity to be heard with regards to the unpleaded issue, an arbitral award will not be set aside.

In this context, the Court of Appeal, in *Tridant Engineering supra* at paragraphs 30, 31 and 35, *inter alia*, held:

> [30] Further, in any arbitral proceeding, the primary concern is to ensure that the rules of natural justice are complied with. This much is made clear in section 20 of the Arbitration Act 2005 which says that the parties shall be treated with equality and each party shall be given a fair and reasonable opportunity of presenting that party's case.

> [31] Having what have been said in preceding paragraphs uppermost in our minds, we took an approach that the Appellant's failure to plead sections 26 and 27 of Limitation Act 1953 was not fatal to its claim as the Respondent was given every opportunity to submit on that issue. There was also no evidence to say that the Respondent had suffered a disadvantage or deprived of an opportunity to ventilate that issue. In fact, the learned Judge had found that the rules of natural justice had not been breached on this issue except she found that 'there is a new difference between the dispute referred and the dispute that he was finally determining.'
>
> ...
>
> [35] The principle distilled from the above is simply this. As long as there has not been any breach of the rules of natural justice and parties had been given ample opportunity to submit on the issue which was ancillary to the claim or defence, the strict rule of pleadings does not apply in the arbitral regime. In our present case, the reliance of sections 26 and 27 of the Limitation Act was a matter ancillary to the alternative defence of the Respondent.

The Court of Appeal, in *Garden Bay Sdn Bhd v. Sime Darby Property Berhad* [2018] 2 MLJ 636 at paragraph 23, decided in an application to set aside an arbitral award that if there was a breach of natural justice, the arbitral tribunal should be given an opportunity to resume the arbitral proceedings under section 37(6) to cure the breach:

> Section 37(6) of the AA 2005 is pari materia to article 34(4) of the UNCITRAL Model Law 1986. The Model Law regime does provide a procedure to save the award for breach of natural justice ... That is to say, s 37(6) does not give an option to set aside the award as of right at the trial stage or even at the apex stage. The courts must be vigilant of the jurisprudence related to s 37(6) and should not set aside the award in the first instance and create miscarriage of justice.

The High Court, in *Tan Kong Han v. QDB Ventures Sdn Bhd* [2016] MLJU 1510, in particular, decided that an arbitral tribunal was not bound to accept a position put forward by one party or the other but was entitled to take an alternative position based on the evidence before the arbitral tribunal. In this context, the High Court, in *Tan Kong Han supra* at paragraphs 31 and 33, *inter alia*, held:

> [31] More importantly, I do not find any case of any breaches or meaningful breaches of natural justice made out by the plaintiff. I do not see a case established that the learned Arbitrator's decision of affixing 1.4.2012 as the date when practical completion was achieved violates the principles of natural justice. The Arbitrator was required to deal with that very question and I agree with the defendant that she was not restricted to any date suggested by the parties.
>
> ...
>
> [33] Contrary to what the plaintiff claims, the date identified by the learned Arbitrator was based on evidence before her. It may not have been the date picked by either party but it was a date that she arrived at based on her reasons. Amongst others, she had relied on the Architect's letter of 3.4.2012 which the plaintiff claims to be erroneous as the Architect had testified that the letter had been issued by mistake. That may have been the case, but the learned Arbitrator was entitled to still examine that letter and reached the conclusion that she did.

The Court of Appeal, in *Pancaran Prima Sdn Bhd v. Iswarabena Sdn Bhd and another appeal* [2018] MLJU 968 at paragraphs 32, 33, 36 and 38, considered an arbitrator's findings on a claim for loss of profit under a construction contract based on the arbitrator's view of what a reasonable profit margin in the construction industry would be. The arbitrator did not disclose these views to the parties or give them an opportunity to respond. The profit margin used by the arbitrator was also not based on either parties' evidence or submissions. The Court of Appeal held that the arbitrator had breached the rules of natural justice by deciding on the claim for loss of profit based on his views without allowing the parties an opportunity to respond. Significantly, the Court of Appeal held that once the rules of natural justice have been breached by an arbitrator, the courts had little discretion but to set aside the award unless the breach was immaterial.

The right to be heard, being one of the two constituent principles of the rules of natural justice, has been most frequently considered by the courts in the context of applications to set aside awards. In this particular context, the courts have adopted a minimal interventionist approach, as expressed in *Sabah Medical Center supra*.

In accordance with this minimal interventionist approach, the courts have emphasized that:

(1) section 20 only requires a fair and reasonable opportunity to be heard;
(2) any breach of the rules of natural justice must be shown to have prejudiced a party; and
(3) if there is a breach of natural justice, the arbitral tribunal may be given an opportunity to resume the arbitral proceedings and cure the breach.

This can be seen from the judgments in *Sabah Medical Center, MMC Engineering, Tridant Engineering* and *Garden Bay supra*.

It is submitted that the minimal interventionist approach adopted by the courts in this context may not be wholly appropriate, given that the rules of natural justice are of fundamental importance. Specifically, although section 20 requires a fair and reasonable opportunity to be heard, as opposed to a full opportunity, this should not be regarded as a lower standard. Instead, the words 'fair and reasonable' in section 20 should be read as being intended to prevent dilatory tactics.[4]

Further, the arbitral tribunal's discretion to determine procedure under section 21(2) should be read subject to section 20 and not vice versa, as expressly provided in section 21(2).

And, finally, given the fundamental importance of the rules of natural justice, and the plain meaning of sections 37(1)(b)(ii) and 37(2)(b), any breach of the rules of natural justice should result in an award being set aside. The breach of the rules of natural justice would colour the entire arbitral proceedings and the award in an implicit manner. To require proof of actual prejudice, as in *MMC Engineering* and *Tanjung Langsat supra*, appears to be putting the threshold too high. And, to expect an arbitral

---

4. *See* Analytical Commentary, Article 19, commentary 8.

tribunal, that has breached the rules of natural justice, to resume the proceedings and cure such a breach may be unduly optimistic.

Despite the judgments of the High Court, in *Sabah Medical Center, MMC Engineering* and *Tanjung Langsat supra*, the fundamental importance of the rules of natural justice appears to have been recognized by the Court of Appeal, in *Tridant Engineering* and *Pancaran Prima supra*. The judgment of the Court of Appeal, in *Pancaran Prima supra*, recognizes that once there is a breach of the rules of natural justice, the courts have little discretion but to set aside an award unless the breach is immaterial. This is a departure from the earlier approach of the courts that was strictly minimalist.

Apart from this, there does not appear to be any basis for advancing a distinction between the test for a breach of the rules of natural justice in domestic and international arbitration, as suggested in *Infineon Technologies supra*. Instead, the test in both domestic and international arbitration should be a breach of the most basic notions of justice and morality, as explained in *Tan Kong Han supra*.

§20.04 COMPREHENSIVE

Section 20 of the Arbitration Act 2005 applies to every stage of the arbitration. The provision is not limited[5] to the conduct of the arbitral proceedings, although it appears in Chapter 5 of the Act.

This unfortunately does not appear to have been recognized by the High Court,[6] in *Sebiro Holdings Sdn Bhd v. Bhag Singh & Anor* [2014] 11 MLJ 761 at paragraph 16, where section 20 appears to have been limited in its application to the conduct of the arbitral proceedings.

---

5. *See* Analytical Commentary, Article 19, commentary 7.
6. The judgment of the High Court, in *Sebiro Holdings supra*, was affirmed by the Court of Appeal, in *Sebiro Holdings Sdn Bhd v. Bhag Singh & Anor* [2015] 4 CLJ 209.

21. Determination of Rules of Procedure

(1) Subject to the provisions of this Act, the parties are free to agree on the procedure to be followed by the arbitral tribunal in conducting the proceedings.

(2) Where the parties fail to agree under subsection (1), the arbitral tribunal may, subject to the provisions of this Act, conduct the arbitration in such manner as it considers appropriate.

(3) The power conferred upon the arbitral tribunal under subsection (2) shall include the power to –
  (a) determine the admissibility, relevance, materiality and weight of any evidence;
  (b) draw on its own knowledge and expertise;
  (c) order the provision of further particulars in a statement of claim or statement of defence;
  (d) order the giving of security for costs;
  (e) fix and amend time limits within which various steps in the arbitral proceedings must be completed;
  (f) order the discovery and production of documents or materials within the possession or power of a party;
  (g) order the interrogatories to be answered;
  (h) order that any evidence be given on oath or affirmation; and
  (i) make such other orders as the arbitral tribunal considers appropriate.

§21.01 INTRODUCTION

Section 21 of the Arbitration Act 2005 provides for the determination of the procedure to be adopted in the arbitral proceedings.

Section 21 of the Arbitration Act 2005 is based on Article 19 of the 1985 Model Law. In this regard, sections 21(1) and 21(2) of the Arbitration Act 2005 reflect Article 19(1) and the first sentence of Article 19(2) of the 1985 Model Law. Section 21(3)(a) of the Arbitration Act 2005 in turn reflects the second sentence of Article 19(2) but goes on to provide eight more examples of the powers conferred on the arbitral tribunal.

§21.02 PARTY AUTONOMY

Section 21(1) of the Arbitration Act 2005 allows the parties the freedom to agree on the rules of procedure to be adopted in the arbitration.

The parties are accordingly free to agree:

(1) on a bespoke set of rules for the conduct of the arbitration;
(2) that the arbitration be conducted as an ad hoc arbitration;

(3) to adopt any published rules of arbitration, like the ICC Rules of Arbitration or the AIAC Arbitration Rules, which is specifically allowed by section 2(c) of the Arbitration Act 2005; or
(4) to adopt the rules of civil procedure or evidence of a particular country. In this context, these rules would apply as the rules of arbitration by virtue of the agreement between the parties and not because they are the applicable rules of civil procedure in the seat of arbitration.

In practice most arbitrations in Malaysia are either ad hoc or institutional. The High Court, in *Infineon Technologies (M) Sdn Bhd v. Orisoft Technology Sdn Bhd (previously known as Orisoft Technology Bhd) and another application* [2011] 7 MLJ 539 at paragraph 61, recognized that institutional arbitration is less flexible than ad hoc arbitration, as institutional arbitration is governed by the rules of the particular arbitration institution. However, the High Court decided that such rules are facilitative and do not, generally, deprive the parties of autonomy or prevent the arbitral tribunal being the master of procedure subject to these rules.

Although the parties are free to agree on the rules of procedure, as recognized in *Infineon Technologies supra* at paragraph 62, this freedom is not absolute. The parties' freedom to agree on procedure is subject to the mandatory provisions of the Arbitration Act 2005.

The Federal Court, in *Thai-Lao Lignite Co Ltd & Anor v. Government of the Lao People's Democratic Republic* [2017] 9 CLJ 273 at paragraph 161, further explained that the parties' agreement on institutional rules would not override the mandatory provisions of the law of the seat but would override the non-mandatory provisions:

> Where the procedure chosen is different to that of the law of the seat of the arbitration then the procedure chosen will override the non-mandatory provisions of the seat of the arbitration. However, a choice of procedure by the parties cannot override the mandatory provisions of at the seat of arbitration ... .

The most important of such mandatory provisions is section 20, which has been considered above. The other mandatory provisions of the Arbitration Act 2005 include:

(1) section 25(1) on the exchange of the statement of claim and defence, which is a corollary of the right to be heard under section 20;
(2) sections 26(3)-(5) on the need for notice of hearings and communication of documents to all concerned parties, which are again related to the equal treatment of parties and the right to be heard under section 20;
(3) section 29 on the assistance of court in taking evidence, which is to ensure the rights granted under section 20 are enforceable;
(4) section 32(2) on the form and content of an award pursuant to a settlement;
(5) sections 33(1), (2), (4) and (5) on the form and content of an award;
(6) section 34 on the termination of arbitral proceedings; and
(7) sections 35(1)-(3) on the correction and interpretation of the award.

As can be seen from the above, all the mandatory provisions of the Arbitration Act 2005 that limit the freedom of the parties to agree on the rules of procedure relate to either the right to be heard or the arbitral award. The justification for the former is not hard to find as it is a fundamental principle of the rules of natural justice. The mandatory provisions with regards to the arbitral award on the other hand are to ensure the enforceability of the award in accordance with the New York Convention.

Another potential limit on the parties' freedom to agree on procedure is time. Here, it can be argued that the parties must agree on the procedure at the initial stages of the arbitration and should not be allowed to change this procedure at a later stage, as the arbitral tribunal may not have agreed to sit if they had been aware of such procedure at the outset. However, it is submitted that such an argument would be ill-conceived, as the freedom of the parties to agree on procedure is for their benefit and not for the benefit of the arbitral tribunal, who are, in any event, free to withdraw at any stage. It is therefore submitted that there should be no limitation of time on the parties' freedom to agree on procedure.[7]

§21.03 ARBITRAL TRIBUNAL'S DISCRETION

Sections 21(1) and (2) of the Arbitration Act 2005 follow the familiar 'two-level system' in the 1985 Model Law. First, section 21(1) gives the parties the freedom to agree, and, second, section 21(2) provides for what happens in the absence of agreement between the parties on procedure. Here, the default provision in section 21(2) is not specific but instead allows the arbitral tribunal a broad discretion in determining the rules of procedure.

The breadth of this discretion has been recognized by the High Court, in *Sabah Medical Center Sdn Bhd v. Syarikat Neptune Enterprise Sdn Bhd* [2011] 1 LNS 849 at page 19, where it was held that 'the arbitral tribunal is given full discretion to determine the manner in which the proceeding is to be conducted.'

This wide discretion enables the arbitral tribunal to fashion an arbitration procedure best suited to the parties. For example, where both parties are from a common law system, the arbitral tribunal may direct disclosure, witness statements and cross-examination in keeping with an adversarial system. On the other hand, if both parties are from a civil law system, the arbitral tribunal may adopt a more inquisitorial system. And, if one party is from a common law system and the other from a civil law system, the arbitral tribunal may adopt a hybrid procedure in accordance with the international setting of the arbitration.

The wide discretion given to the arbitral tribunal is, however, not without limit. The discretion is subject to the provisions of the Arbitration Act 2005. Again, the most significant limitation on the discretion would be section 20. Apart from this, the arbitral tribunal's discretion in terms of procedure may also be limited by sections 25(3), 26 and 27.

---

7. *See* UNCITRAL Report at para. 172.

§21.04 EXAMPLES OF THE ARBITRAL TRIBUNAL'S POWER

Section 21(3) of the Arbitration Act 2005 gives nine specific examples of the exercise of the arbitral tribunal's discretion pursuant to the broad discretion granted under section 21(2).

Section 21(3)(b) in particular has been considered by the Court of Appeal,[8] in *Ajwa for Food Industries Co (MIGOP), Egypt v. Pacific Inter-Link Sdn Bhd & Another Appeal* [2013] 2 CLJ 395 at paragraph 40, where it was recognized that the arbitral tribunal was entitled to draw on its own knowledge, especially in a trade arbitration, such as a palm oil commodities arbitration:

> An arbitration tribunal is empowered to draw from its own knowledge and expertise in its determination especially when the arbitration is conducted by a specialised trade body with knowledge and expertise in the palm oil trade, as in the present case. Section 21(3)(b) of the Arbitration Act 2005 states that the power conferred upon the arbitration panel includes the power to 'draw on its own knowledge and expertise' which is what the PORAM Arbitration Tribunal did in determining the measure and quantum of damages in the present case.

---

8. An appeal against this judgment was dismissed on other grounds by the Federal Court in [2013] 7 CLJ 18.

22. Seat of Arbitration

(1) The parties are free to agree on the seat of arbitration.

(2) Where the parties fail to agree under subsection (1), the seat of arbitration shall be determined by the arbitral tribunal having regard to the circumstances of the case, including the convenience of the parties.

(3) Notwithstanding subsections (1) and (2), the arbitral tribunal may, unless otherwise agreed by the parties, meet at any place it considers appropriate for consultation among its members, for hearing witnesses, experts or the parties, or for inspection of goods, other property or documents.

§22.01 INTRODUCTION

Section 22 of the Arbitration Act 2005 provides for the determination of the place of arbitration.

Section 22 of the Arbitration Act 2005 reflects Article 20 of the 1985 Model Law save that the words 'seat of arbitration' is used in the Arbitration Act 2005 as opposed to 'place of arbitration' in the 1985 Model Law.

Article 20 of the 1985 Model Law is in turn based on Article 16 of the 1976 UNCITRAL Arbitration Rules, which provides:

Place of Arbitration
Article 16
1. Unless the parties have agreed upon the place where the arbitration is to be held, such place shall be determined by the arbitral tribunal, having regard to the circumstances of the arbitration.
2. The arbitral tribunal may determine the locale of the arbitration within the country agreed by the parties. It may hear witnesses and hold meetings for consultation among its members at any place it deems appropriate, having regard to the circumstances of the arbitration.
3. The arbitral tribunal may meet at any place it deems appropriate for the inspection of goods, other property or documents. The parties shall be given sufficient notice to enable them to be present at such inspection.
4. The award shall be made at the place of arbitration.

Article 15 of the 1976 UNCITRAL Arbitration Rules has remained substantially the same in the 2013 UNCITRAL Arbitration Rules, where Article 18 provides:

Place of Arbitration
Article 18
1. If the parties have not previously agreed on the place of arbitration, the place of arbitration shall be determined by the arbitral tribunal having regard to the circumstances of the case. The award shall be deemed to have been made at the place of arbitration.
2. The arbitral tribunal may meet at any location it considers appropriate for deliberations. Unless otherwise agreed by the parties, the arbitral tribunal may also meet at any location it considers appropriate for any other purpose, including hearings.

The 2010 UNCITRAL Arbitration Rules form part of the 2018 AIAC Arbitration Rules.

§22.02 PARTY AUTONOMY

In keeping with the general framework of the 1985 Model Law, parties are given the freedom to agree on the seat of arbitration under section 22(1) of the Arbitration Act 2005.

In this context, it should be borne in mind that the 'seat of arbitration' agreed upon by the parties is in the abstract and need have no connection to the geographical location of either party, the subject matter of the agreement or the likely place of the dispute.

As the seat of arbitration is abstract and may freely be agreed upon by the parties, the question arises as to the grounds for choosing a particular seat. In this regard, a party would consider the following important consequences when deciding the seat of arbitration.

First, the seat of arbitration will determine the curial law or the procedural law applicable to the arbitration. This is expressly provided for in sections 3(2) and (3), which state which parts of the Arbitration Act 2005 will apply to domestic and international arbitration with a seat in Malaysia. Similarly, in all Model Law jurisdictions, Article 1(2) of the 1985 Model Law provides that the Model Law will apply if the place of arbitration is in the territory of the State.

Second, and as a corollary, of the first consequence above, the award will be deemed to have been made at the seat of arbitration under section 33(4) of the Arbitration Act 2005, and an application to set aside the award will have to be made at the seat of arbitration.

Third, the choice of a seat of arbitration may make an otherwise domestic arbitration an international arbitration. For example, if both Party A and Party B have their place of business in State X but agree that the seat of arbitration will be State Y then, based on the definition in section 2(1)(b)(i) of the Arbitration Act 2005, the arbitration is international.

The first and second of these consequences have been recognized by the Court of Appeal, in *Sintrans Asia Services Pte Ltd v. Inai Kiara Sdn Bhd* [2016] 5 CLJ 746 at paragraph 13:

> The Arbitration Act 2005 in particular s. 22 defines the seat of arbitration. We would hold that seat of arbitration is the juridical seat of the arbitration and it is independent of the venue where hearings or other parts of the arbitral process occurred. The seat prescribed the procedural law of the arbitration ... .
>
> ...
>
> It follows therefore that in challenges of this nature, the proper avenue for the same to be ventilated would be in the courts of Singapore.

The Federal Court, in *Thai-Lao Lignite supra* at paragraphs 173 and 174, emphasized the first of the consequences referred to above and explained that the choice of a seat meant that the laws of the seat must be observed in relation to the arbitration insofar as those laws were mandatory.

§22.03 ARBITRAL TRIBUNAL'S DISCRETION

Section 22 of the Arbitration Act 2005 follows the familiar 'two-level system' in the 1985 Model Law. If the parties do not, first, agree on the seat of arbitration, then, second, and in default, the arbitral tribunal may determine the seat of arbitration.

The arbitral tribunal is to determine the seat of arbitration based on all the circumstances of the case, with section 22(2) referring to the convenience of the parties in particular.

§22.04 ABSTRACTION

The abstract nature of the seat of arbitration is emphasized by section 22(3), which provides that the arbitral tribunal may meet and hold hearings at a place other than the seat of arbitration. Therefore even if State X is named as the seat of arbitration, all the meetings and hearings may be held in State Y with neither the arbitral tribunal nor the parties ever having set foot in State X, which nevertheless remains in abstract the seat of the arbitration. All that appears to be required to comply with maintaining the seat of arbitration is stating the seat as such in the award in accordance with section 33(4) of the Arbitration Act 2005.

23. Commencement of Arbitral Proceedings

Unless otherwise agreed by the parties, the arbitral proceedings in respect of a particular dispute shall commence on the date on which a request in writing for that dispute to be referred to arbitration is received by the respondent.

§23.01 INTRODUCTION

Section 23 of the Arbitration Act 2005 provides for the date of commencement of the arbitral proceedings.

Section 23 of the Arbitration Act 2005 is the same as Article 21 of the 1985 Model Law save that the words 'shall' and 'in writing' are not in the 1985 Model Law.

The inclusion of the word 'shall' in section 23 of the Arbitration Act 2005 does not change the meaning of the original provision in the 1985 Model Law. The word 'shall' merely seems to emphasize that the arbitration commences on the date of the request.

The inclusion of the words 'in writing' in section 23 of the Arbitration Act 2005 is a departure from Article 21 of the 1985 Model Law. In this context, it is unclear whether the 1985 Model Law requires the request for arbitration to be in writing, as neither Article 21 nor the *travaux preparatoires* makes reference to such a requirement. It appears that the requirement that the request for arbitration be writing has been included in section 23 of the Arbitration Act 2005 to avoid the uncertainty found in the 1985 Model Law in this regard.

Article 21 of the 1985 Model Law is modelled on Article 3 of the 1976 UNCITRAL Arbitration Rules, which provides:

> Notice of Arbitration
> Article 3
> 1. The party initiating recourse to arbitration (hereinafter called the 'claimant') shall give to the other party (hereinafter called the 'respondent') a notice of arbitration.
> 2. Arbitral proceedings shall be deemed to commence on the date on which the notice of arbitration is received by the respondent.
> 3. The notice of arbitration shall include the following:
>   (a) A demand that the dispute be referred to arbitration;
>   (b) The names and addresses of the parties;
>   (c) A reference to the arbitration clause or the separate arbitration agreement that is invoked;
>   (d) A reference to the contract out of or in relation to which the dispute arises;
>   (e) The general nature of the claim and an indication of the amount involved, if any;
>   (f) The relief or remedy sought;
>   (g) A proposal as to the number of arbitrators (i.e. one or three), if parties have not previously agreed thereon.
> 4. The notice of arbitration may also include:
>   (a) The proposals for the appointments of a sole arbitrator and an appointing authority referred to in article 6, paragraph 1;
>   (b) The notification of the appointment of an arbitrator referred to in article 7;
>   (c) The statement of claim referred to in article 18.

Chapter 5: Conduct of Arbitral Proceedings §23.01

Article 3 of the 1976 UNCITRAL Arbitration Rules is more detailed than Article 21 of the 1985 Model Law. This is in keeping with the purpose of the 1976 Arbitration Rules as a comprehensive set of rules to govern ad hoc arbitration, on the one hand, and the purpose of the 1985 Model Law, on the other hand, as a legal framework to be adopted by countries to achieve uniformity and preserve the autonomy of parties.

Article 3 of the present 2013 UNCITRAL Arbitration Rules provides as follows:

Notice of Arbitration
Article 3
1. The party or parties initiating recourse to arbitration (hereinafter called the 'claimant') shall communicate to the other party or parties (hereinafter called the 'respondent') a notice of arbitration.
2. Arbitral proceedings shall be deemed to commence on the date on which the notice of arbitration is received by the respondent.
3. The notice of arbitration shall include the following:
   (a) A demand that the dispute be referred to arbitration;
   (b) The names and contact details of the parties;
   (c) Identification of the arbitration agreement that is invoked;
   (d) Identification of any contract or other legal instrument out of or in relation to which the dispute arises or, in the absence of such contract or instrument, a brief description of the relevant relationship;
   (e) A brief description of the claim and an indication of the amount involved, if any;
   (f) The relief or remedy sought;
   (g) A proposal as to the number of arbitrators, language and place of arbitration, if the parties have not previously agreed thereon.
4. The notice of arbitration may also include:
   (a) A proposal for the designation of an appointing authority referred to in article 6, paragraph 1;
   (b) A proposal for the appointment of a sole arbitrator referred to in article 8, paragraph 1;
   (c) Notification of the appointment of an arbitrator referred to in article 9 or 10.
5. The constitution of the arbitral tribunal shall not be hindered by any controversy with respect to the sufficiency of the notice of arbitration, which shall be finally resolved by the arbitral tribunal.

Article 3 of the 2013 UNCITRAL Arbitration Rules forms part of the 2018 AIAC Arbitration Rules, which, in addition, provides under Rule 2:

Commencement of Arbitration
1. The Party or Parties initiating arbitration under the AIAC Arbitration Rules shall submit a request in writing to commence arbitration (the 'Commencement Request') to the Director. The Commencement Request shall be accompanied by the following:
   (a) a copy of the written arbitration clause or a separate arbitration agreement;
   (b) a copy of the contractual documentation in which the arbitration clause is contained or in respect of which the arbitration arises;
   (c) a copy of the notice of arbitration as described in Article 3 accompanied by a confirmation that it has been or is being served on all other Parties by one or more means of service to be identified in such confirmation; and

(d) a proof of payment of the non-refundable registration fee amounting to USD795.00, or its equivalent in another currency, in international arbitration and RM1,590.00 in domestic arbitration.
2. The date on which the Director has received the Commencement Request with all accompanying documentation shall be treated as the date on which the arbitration has commenced. The AIAC will notify the Parties of the date of commencement of arbitration.

§23.02 PARTY AUTONOMY

Section 23 of the Arbitration Act 2005 follows the familiar 'two-level system' found throughout the Act. The parties are first given the freedom to agree on the means for ascertaining the date of commencement of the arbitration. Second, and failing such agreement, the default provisions for ascertaining the date of commencement of the arbitration will apply.

In practice, the parties exercise their freedom to concur in this context by agreeing to the application of a set of rules published by an arbitration institute. These rules of arbitration will invariably provide for the date of commencement of the arbitration, which will usually require notice to both the other party and the arbitration institute.

For example, if the parties have agreed to the application of the 2018 AIAC Arbitration Rules, then the notice of arbitration must be served on the other party to comply with Article 3(2) of the 2013 UNCITRAL Arbitration Rules. In addition, a request to the Director of the AIAC must also be submitted in accordance with Rule 2(1) of the 2018 AIAC Arbitration Rules. In accordance with Rule 2(2) of the 2018 AIAC Arbitration Rules, the arbitration will only commence once this request to the Director and the notice of arbitration have been received by the Director.

§23.03 DEFAULT

In the event the parties do not agree on the means of ascertaining the date of commencement of the arbitration, then the default provisions of section 23 of the Arbitration Act 2005 will apply.

The default provision on the date of commencement of the arbitration is concise – it is the date a request in writing for that dispute to be referred to arbitration is received by the respondent.

Essentially, the request for arbitration must:

(1) be in writing;
(2) be received by the Respondent in accordance with section 6 of the Arbitration Act 2005; and

(3) 'identify the particular dispute and make clear that arbitration is resorted to thereby and not, for example, indicate merely the intention of later initiating arbitration proceedings'.[9]

In addition to these three requirements, the request for arbitration must also comply with section 30(3) of the Limitation Act 1953. This section provides that the request for arbitration must require the respondent to:

(1) appoint an arbitrator;
(2) agree to the appointment of an arbitrator; or
(3) submit the dispute to the arbitrator designated in the arbitration agreement if the arbitration agreement so designates an arbitrator.

§23.04   LIMITATION

Section 23 of the Arbitration Act 2005 is of particular significance because the commencement of the arbitration by the request for arbitration effectively stops time from running under the Limitation Act 1953.

In this context, section 30 of the Limitation Act 1953 provides:

30. Application of Act and other limitation enactments to arbitrations
(1) This Act and any other written law relating to the limitation of actions shall apply to arbitrations as they apply to actions.
(2) Notwithstanding any term in any submission to the effect that no cause of action shall accrue in respect of any matter required by the submission to be referred until an award is made under the submission, the cause of action shall, for the purpose of this Act and of any other such written law (whether in their application to arbitrations or to other proceedings), be deemed to have accrued in respect of any such matter at the time when it would have accrued but for that term in the submission.
(3) For the purpose of this Act and of any such written law as aforesaid, an arbitration shall be deemed to be commenced when one party to the arbitration serves on the other party or parties a notice requiring him or them to appoint an arbitrator or to agree to the appointment of an arbitrator, or, where the submission provides that the reference shall be to a person named or designated in the submission, requiring him or them to submit the dispute to the person so named or designated.
(4) Any such notice as aforesaid may be served either –
    (a) by delivering it to the person on whom it is to be served; or
    (b) by leaving it at the usual or last known place of abode in Malaysia of that person; or
    (c) by sending it by post in a registered letter addressed to that person at his usual or last known place of abode in Malaysia,
as well as in any other manner provided in the submission; and where a notice is sent by post in a manner prescribed by paragraph (c) of this subsection, service thereof shall, unless the contrary is proved, be deemed to have been

---

9. *See* Analytical Commentary, Article 21, commentary 2.

effected at the time at which the letter would have been delivered in the ordinary course of post.

(5) Where the High Court orders that an award be set aside or orders, after the commencement of an arbitration, that the arbitration shall cease to have effect with respect to the dispute referred, the Court may further order that the period between the commencement of the arbitration and the date of the order of the Court shall be excluded in computing the time prescribed by this Act or any such written law as aforesaid for the commencement of proceedings (including arbitration) with respect to the dispute referred.

(6) This section shall apply to an arbitration under any written law as well as to an arbitration pursuant to a submission, and subsections (3) and (4) thereof shall have effect, in relation to an arbitration under any written law, as if for the references to the submission there were substituted references to such of the provisions of the law or of any order, scheme, rules, regulations, or by-laws made there under as relate to the arbitration.

(7) In this section the expressions 'arbitration', 'award' and 'submission' have the same meanings as in the Arbitration Act 1952 [Act 93].

Although, section 30(7) of the Limitation Act 1953 specifically refers to the Arbitration Act 1952, the Limitation Act 1953 applies to the Arbitration Act 2005 by virtue of sections 35(1) and (2) of the Interpretation Acts 1948 and 1967, which provide:

35. References to written laws
(1) A reference to a particular written law –
   (a) is a reference to that law as amended or extended from time to time; and
   (b) includes a reference to any subsidiary legislation made thereunder.
(2) Where any written law or any provision of a written law is repealed and re-enacted (with or without modification), references in any other written law to the law or provision so repealed shall be construed as references to the re-enacted law or provision.

This was confirmed by the High Court, in *Dceil Imex Sdn Bhd v. Pembinaan Punca Cergas Sdn Bhd* [2014] 7 CLJ 552 at paragraph 58:

It follows from the foregoing that references in the Limitation Act 1953 to the Arbitration Act 1952 continue to be applicable to the Arbitration Act 2005. Accordingly it is submitted, and I would concur, that it is erroneous to conclude that s. 30(5) is redundant under the provisions of the Arbitration Act 2005.

Section 30(1) of the Limitation Act 1953 essentially makes all limitation provisions equally applicable to arbitration.

The most relevant limitation period is that applicable in contract. In this context, section 6(1)(a) of the Limitation Act 1953 provides:

6. Limitation of actions of contract and tort and certain other actions
(1) Save as hereinafter provided the following actions shall not be brought after the expiration of six years from the date on which the cause of action accrued, that is to say –
   (a) actions founded on a contract or on tort;

The Court of Appeal, in *Malaysia Steel Works (KL) Sdn Bhd v. Kamseng Machine Works Pte Ltd* [2003] 4 CLJ 526 at page 532, recognized that by virtue of sections

6(1)(a) and 30(1) of the Limitation Act 1953, the six-year limitation period applicable to a claim in contract applied in an arbitration.

Section 30(2) of the Limitation Act 1953 effectively prevents parties from altering the start date of the limitation period from the date the cause of action accrues to the date of the award. Any agreement to this effect by the parties will be ineffective and the cause of action will still accrue in accordance with the law and not in accordance with the agreement of the parties.

Therefore, the start date for the limitation period cannot be altered by the arbitration agreement. By way of contrast, however, the date to stop time from running for the purposes of limitation can be agreed upon by the parties in the arbitration agreement insofar as the parties are free to agree on the requirements for the request for arbitration.

Section 30(3) of the Limitation Act 1953 sets out certain requirements for the request for arbitration. As discussed above, these requirements must be complied with in addition to the default provisions in section 23 of the Arbitration Act 2005.

The High Court, in *Penta-Ocean Construction Co Ltd v. Penang Development Corporation* [2003] MLJU 11 at page 155, recognized the need to comply with section 30(3) to stop time from running for the purpose of limitation:

> Furthermore, the plea of limitation applies to the commencement of the action, which in the context of an arbitration, would be when one party serves on the other a notice requiring him to appoint or agree to the appointment of an Arbitrator (see Section 30(3) of the Limitation Act 1953).

Section 30(4) of the Limitation Act 1953 provides for the means for service of the request for arbitration. Section 6 of the Arbitration Act 2005 also provides for the means of service of written communications in general, which would include the request for arbitration.

Section 6 of the Arbitration Act 2005 insofar as it differs from section 30(4) of the Limitation Act 1953 should prevail because the Arbitration Act 2005 is a specific legislation, as opposed to the Limitation Act 1953, which is a general legislation.[10]

Section 30(5) of the Limitation Act 1953 provides that where the High Court orders that:

(1) an award be set aside, or
(2) the arbitration shall cease to have effect after the arbitration has commenced,

then the High Court may also order that the period between the commencement of the arbitration and the order of the High Court be excluded for the purpose of limitation.

The High Court, in *Dceil Imex supra* at paragraph 62, decided that where the High Court had decided on an appeal under section 18(8) of the Arbitration Act 2005 that the

---

10. *See House Buyer Tribunal & Anor v. Unique Creations Sdn Bhd and other appeals* [2014] 3 MLJ 850 at para. 23, CA; *Public Prosecutor v. Chew Siew Lan* [1982] CLJ (Rep) 285 at pp 286-287, FC; *Public Prosecutor v. Chu Beow Hin* [1982] 1 MLJ 135 at p 137, FC; on the general application of the principle of *generalibus specialia derogant* to the the interpretation of statutes.

arbitral tribunal does not have jurisdiction that effectively meant that the arbitration shall cease to have effect. Therefore, the High Court would be entitled to exclude time under section 30(5) of the Limitation Act 1953.

Section 30(6) of the Limitation Act 1953 clarifies that section 30 will apply to both an arbitration pursuant to an arbitration agreement and an arbitration pursuant to a written law.

24. Language

(1) The parties are free to agree on the language to be used in the arbitral proceedings.
(2) Where the parties fail to agree under subsection (1), the arbitral tribunal shall determine the language to be used in the arbitral proceedings.
(3) The agreement or the determination referred to in subsections (1) and (2) respectively shall, unless otherwise specified in the agreement or determination, apply to any written statement made by a party, any hearing and any award, decision or other communication by the arbitral tribunal.
(4) The arbitral tribunal may order that any documentary evidence shall be accompanied by a translation into the language agreed upon by the parties or determined by the arbitral tribunal.

§24.01 INTRODUCTION

Section 24 of the Arbitration Act 2005 provides for the means for determining the language of the arbitration.

Section 24 of the Arbitration Act 2005 reflects Article 22 of the 1985 Model Law save for certain minor changes in drafting. In particular, sections 24(1)-(3) of the Arbitration Act 2005 reflect Article 24(1) of the 1985 Model Law, and section 24(4) of the Arbitration Act 2005 reflects Article 24(2) of the 1985 Model Law.

§24.02 PARTY AUTONOMY

Section 24 of the Arbitration Act 2005 follows the familiar 'two-level system' of allowing the parties to agree on the language first followed by default provisions for the arbitral tribunal to determine the language.

Section 24(1) provides in clear terms that the parties are free to agree on the language of the arbitration. This is of particular significance as it dispels any doubt that parties having their seat of arbitration in Malaysia may be required to use the Malay language as the language of the arbitration.

In deciding the language or languages to be used in the arbitration, the parties would need[11] to consider:

(1) which language they would best be able to present their case in;
(2) whether more than one language should be used in the arbitration;
(3) if more than one language is to be used in the arbitration, the costs of translation related to using multiple languages;
(4) costs that may be awarded in relation to the language used. Here, where the parties have agreed to multiple languages, then the costs of translation are

---

11. *See* Analytical Commentary, Article 22, commentary 2.

likely to be regarded as the costs of the arbitration and awarded to the successful party. On the other hand if a particular language is chosen and a party requires translation, he is unlikely to entitled to recover these costs even if he is successful; and

(5) whether a suitable arbitrator may be selected in relation to the languages chosen.

§24.03 DEFAULT

In the absence of agreement between the parties, section 24(2) of the Arbitration Act 2005 provides that the arbitral tribunal may determine the language of the arbitration. Neither the Arbitration Act 2005 nor the 1985 Model Law provides for the factors to be considered by the arbitral tribunal in determining the language of arbitration.

It is submitted that the relevant factors to be considered by the arbitral tribunal in determining the language of the arbitration would include:

(1) the language of the contract, including the arbitration agreement, between the parties;
(2) the language of the correspondence and other business dealings between the parties;
(3) the languages habitually spoken by the parties;
(4) the need to ensure the equal treatment of the parties and their right to a fair and reasonable opportunity to be heard in accordance with section 20 of the Arbitration Act 2005;
(5) the translation cost of using multiple languages or a language other than the language of the documents or which the parties habitually speak; and
(6) the language the members of the arbitral tribunal are themselves able to understand.

The need to ensure the equal treatment of the parties and to allow them an opportunity to be heard is of fundamental importance being part of the rules of natural justice. However, this does not mean that the arbitral tribunal must always determine the language of the arbitration in accordance with the languages habitually spoken by the parties. Where the parties have consistently used a particular language in all their business dealings, the arbitral tribunal would be justified in determining that such language shall be the language of the arbitration, even if this is a language habitually spoken by one party but not the other. The other party would then be free to use translation and would not be deprived of an opportunity to be heard.[12]

---

12. *See* Analytical Commentary, Article 22, commentary 4.

§24.04 STATEMENTS, HEARING AND AWARD

Section 24(3) of the Arbitration Act 2005 clarifies that the language agreed upon between the parties or determined by the arbitral tribunal will apply to all statements, the hearing and the award.

§24.05 DOCUMENTS

Section 24(4) of the Arbitration Act 2005 gives the arbitral tribunal the discretion as to whether to order the translation of documentary evidence. Documentary evidence can be voluminous, and the arbitral tribunal is not obliged to order the translation of all documents. Instead, the tribunal may order the translation of certain limited documents that are relevant to the arbitration.[13]

---

13. *See* Analytical Commentary, Article 22, commentary 5.

25. *Statements of Claim and Defence*

(1) *Within the period of time agreed by the parties or, failing such agreement, as determined by the arbitral tribunal, the claimant shall state –*
 (a) *the facts supporting his claim;*
 (b) *the points at issue; and*
 (c) *the relief or remedy sought,*
 and the respondent shall state his defence in respect of the particulars set out in this subsection, unless the parties have otherwise agreed to the required elements of such statements.

(2) *The parties may –*
 (a) *submit with their statements any document the parties consider relevant; or*
 (b) *add a reference to the documents or other evidence that the parties may submit.*

(3) *Unless otherwise agreed by the parties, either party may amend or supplement the claim or defence during the course of the arbitral proceedings, unless the arbitral tribunal considers it inappropriate to allow such amendment having regard to the delay in making it.*

§25.01 INTRODUCTION

Section 25 of the Arbitration Act 2005 provides for the Statement of Claim and Defence to be delivered in the arbitration proceedings.

Section 25 of the Arbitration Act 2005 reflects Article 23 of the 1985 Model Law with changes only made in terms of drafting. In particular sections 25(1) and (2) of the Arbitration Act 2005 reflect Article 23(1) of the 1985 Model Law, and section 25(3) of the Arbitration Act 2005 reflects Article 23(2) of the 1985 Model Law.

Article 23 of the 1985 Model Law is in turn based on Articles 18-20 of the 1976 UNCITRAL Arbitration Rules, which provides:

> Statement of Claim
> Article 18
> 1. Unless the statement of claim was contained in the notice of arbitration, within a period of time to be determined by the arbitral tribunal, the claimant shall communicate his statement of claim in writing to the respondent and to each of the arbitrators. A copy of the contract, and of the arbitration agreement if not contained in the contract, shall be annexed thereto.
> 2. The statement of claim shall include the following particulars:
> (a) The names and addresses of the parties;
> (b) A statement of the facts supporting the claim;
> (c) The points at issue;
> (d) The relief or remedy sought.
> The claimant may annex to his statement of claim all documents he deems relevant or may add a reference to the documents or other evidence he will submit.

Statement of Defence
Article 19
1. Within a period of time to be determined by the arbitral tribunal, the respondent shall communicate his statement of defence in writing to the claimant and to each of the arbitrators.
2. The statement of defence shall reply to the particulars (b), (c) and (d) of the statement of claim (article 18, para. 2). The respondent may annex to his statement the documents on which he relies for his defence or may add a reference to the documents or other evidence he will submit.
3. In his statement of defence, or at a later stage in the arbitral proceedings if the arbitral tribunal decides that the delay was justified under the circumstances, the respondent may make a counter-claim arising out of the same contract or rely on a claim arising out of the same contract for the purpose of a set-off.
4. The provisions of article 18, paragraph 2, shall apply to a counter-claim and a claim relied on for the purpose of a set-off.

Amendment to the Claim or Defence
Article 20

During the course of the arbitral proceedings either party may amend or supplement his claim or defence unless the arbitral tribunal considers it inappropriate to allow such amendment having regard to the delay in making it or prejudice to the other party or any other circumstances. However, a claim may not be amended in such a manner that the amended claim falls outside the scope of the arbitration clause or separate arbitration agreement.

These provisions have since been revised in the 2013 UNCITRAL Arbitration Rules, which provide under Articles 20-22 as follows:

Statement of claim
Article 20
1. The claimant shall communicate its statement of claim in writing to the respondent and to each of the arbitrators within a period of time to be determined by the arbitral tribunal. The claimant may elect to treat its notice of arbitration referred to in article 3 as a statement of claim, provided that the notice of arbitration also complies with the requirements of paragraphs 2 to 4 of this article.
2. The statement of claim shall include the following particulars:
   (a) The names and contact details of the parties;
   (b) A statement of the facts supporting the claim;
   (c) The points at issue;
   (d) The relief or remedy sought;
   (e) The legal grounds or arguments supporting the claim.
3. A copy of any contract or other legal instrument out of or in relation to which the dispute arises and of the arbitration agreement shall be annexed to the statement of claim.
4. The statement of claim should, as far as possible, be accompanied by all documents and other evidence relied upon by the claimant, or contain references to them.

Statement of defence
Article 21
1. The respondent shall communicate its statement of defence in writing to the claimant and to each of the arbitrators within a period of time to be determined by the arbitral tribunal. The respondent may elect to treat its response to the notice of arbitration referred to in article 4 as a statement of defence, provided

that the response to the notice of arbitration also complies with the requirements of paragraph 2 of this article.
2. The statement of defence shall reply to the particulars (b) to (e) of the statement of claim (art. 20, para. 2). The statement of defence should, as far as possible, be accompanied by all documents and other evidence relied upon by the respondent, or contain references to them.
3. In its statement of defence, or at a later stage in the arbitral proceedings if the arbitral tribunal decides that the delay was justified under the circumstances, the respondent may make a counterclaim or rely on a claim for the purpose of a set-off provided that the arbitral tribunal has jurisdiction over it.
4. The provisions of article 20, paragraphs 2 to 4, shall apply to a counterclaim, a claim under article 4, paragraph 2(f), and a claim relied on for the purpose of a set-off.

Amendments to the claim or defence
Article 22

During the course of the arbitral proceedings, a party may amend or supplement its claim or defence, including a counterclaim or a claim for the purpose of a set-off, unless the arbitral tribunal considers it inappropriate to allow such amendment or supplement having regard to the delay in making it or prejudice to other parties or any other circumstances. However, a claim or defence, including a counterclaim or a claim for the purpose of a set-off, may not be amended or supplemented in such a manner that the amended or supplemented claim or defence falls outside the jurisdiction of the arbitral tribunal.

The 2013 UNCITRAL Arbitration Rules form part of the 2018 AIAC Arbitration Rules, which in addition provides under Rule 3:

Notifications

All documents served on the other Party pursuant to Articles 3, 4, 20, 21, 22, 23 and 24 shall be served on the Director at the same time or immediately thereafter.

The provisions of the Arbitration Act 2005, and the 1985 Model Law it is based on, are more general than the provisions of the UNCITRAL Arbitration Rules in this regard. In particular, the provisions in the UNCITRAL Arbitration Rules list out specifically the content to be included in the Statement of Claim in greater detail than the 1985 Model Law. This is because the two have a different role to play, with the 1985 Model Law intended to be a model for universal acceptance as an arbitration statute, while the UNCITRAL Arbitration Rules are intended as the procedural rules for an ad hoc arbitration.

The development of the UNCITRAL Arbitration Rules between 1976 and 2010 also shows a shift towards annexing documents to the pleadings that are delivered. In this context, Article 20(3) of the 2010 UNCITRAL Arbitration Rule requires the contract and the arbitration agreement to be annexed to the Statement of Claim. Article 20(4) further requires that, as far as possible, all documents are to be delivered together with the Statement of Claim or are to be referred to in such a claim.

§25.02 PARTY AUTONOMY

At first glance, section 25(1) of the Arbitration Act 2005 appears to depart from the familiar 'two-level system'. This is because, by the use of the imperative 'shall', there is the suggestion that the requirement to deliver a Statement of Claim and Defence in the manner envisaged by the Arbitration Act 2005 is mandatory.

This gives rise to concern, as the rules published by various arbitration institutes have requirements with regards to pleadings that differ from section 25(1). For example, the provisions of the 2018 AIAC Arbitration Rules, which are considered above, are considerably more detailed in this regard.

This concern is intended to be resolved by the use of the words 'unless the parties have otherwise agreed to the required elements of such statements' at the end of section 25(1).

The balance sought to be achieved is between, on the one hand, requiring the parties to deliver statements to ensure that the rules of natural justice as to equal treatment and an opportunity to be heard are complied with and, on the other hand, the need to allow the parties autonomy, especially the freedom to agree on the applicable arbitration rules.

This is recognized in the UNCITRAL Report at paragraph 196:

> The Commission was agreed that paragraph (1) expressed a basic principle of arbitral procedure from which the parties should not be able to derogate but that the specific rules of procedure in respect of the statements of claim and defence should be subject to the agreement of the parties. It was pointed out that the procedure provided in paragraph (1) was not entirely consistent with the procedure in some institutional arbitration rules. The Commission decided to express the distinction between the mandatory nature of the principle expressed in paragraph (1) and the non-mandatory nature of the procedural rules by adding to the end of the first sentence words along the lines of 'unless the parties have otherwise agreed on the contents and form of such statements'.

Therefore, it is mandatory in principle under section 25(1) that a Statement of Claim and Defence be delivered, but the procedure is not mandatory and may be agreed upon between the parties.

§25.03 WRITING

Although in practice the pleadings are always in writing, this is not expressly required by section 25(1) of the Arbitration Act 2005. The UNCITRAL has expressly stated[14] that the pleadings need not be in writing and that the 1985 Model Law was amended to reflect this.

---

14. *See* UNCITRAL Report at para. 197.

§25.04 DOCUMENTS

Section 25(2) of the Arbitration Act 2005 leaves it to the parties' discretion whether to include the documents or a reference to such documents in the pleadings.

This discretion, however, may not be an absolute one, as the arbitral tribunal would be entitled to order the parties to disclose the documents they rely on together with their pleadings in accordance with section 21(f) of the Arbitration Act 2005.

Furthermore, as discussed under §25.01 *supra*, where the 2018 AIAC Arbitration Rules have been agreed to, the claimant would be obliged to annex the contract and the arbitration agreement to the Statement of Claim and the parties will be obliged as far as possible to include all documents they rely on or at least make reference to them.

§25.05 AMENDMENTS

Section 25(3) of the Arbitration Act 2005 allows the parties to amend or supplement their pleadings unless agreed upon otherwise.

The principal factor to be considered by the arbitral tribunal is delay. In this context, it is important to note that Article 23(2) of the 1985 Model Law, on which section 25(3) of the Arbitration Act 2005 is based, intentionally does not have prejudice as a further factor to be considered, as it was thought this would unduly restrict the ability of a party to clarify his pleadings.[15]

Although not expressly stated in section 25(3), any amendment to the pleadings must not introduce issues that are outside the scope of the arbitration agreement or the initial reference to arbitration, as these issues would be outside the scope of the arbitral tribunal.

Another important feature of section 25(3) is the use of the words 'amend or supplement'. The use of these words disjunctively with the word 'supplement' used in addition to 'amend' suggests that section 25(3) may have a wider scope than amendments to pleadings in civil proceedings. In addition to merely correcting their pleadings, a party may be entitled to add to their pleadings under section 25(3) provided that such an addition is not outside the scope of the arbitration agreement or the initial reference to arbitration.

The distinction between pleadings in civil and arbitral proceedings was recognized by the Court of Appeal, in *Tridant Engineering (M) Sdn Bhd v. Ssangyong Engineering and Construction Co Ltd* [2016] MLJU 599 at paragraphs 29 and 30. The Court of Appeal emphasized the need for greater flexibility in terms of pleadings in arbitral proceedings. The principal issue was whether the rules of natural justice had been complied with insofar as the opportunity to be heard had been given to both parties. So long as this was satisfied, the fact that certain matters had not been specifically pleaded would not be fatal to an award on such matters.

---

15. *See* Peter Binder, *International Commercial Arbitration and Conciliation in UNCITRAL Model Law Jurisdictions* (3rd edn, Sweet & Maxwell 2010) at para. 5.096.

26. Hearings

(1) Unless otherwise agreed by the parties, the arbitral tribunal shall decide whether to hold oral hearings for the presentation of evidence or oral arguments, or whether the proceedings shall be conducted on the basis of documents and other materials.

(2) Unless the parties have agreed that no hearings shall be held, the arbitral tribunal shall upon the application of any party hold oral hearings at an appropriate stage of the proceedings.

(3) The parties shall be given reasonable prior notice of any hearing and of any meeting of the arbitral tribunal for the purposes of inspection of goods, other property or documents.

(4) All statements, documents or other information supplied to the arbitral tribunal by one party shall be communicated to the other party.

(5) Any expert report or evidentiary document on which the arbitral tribunal may rely in making its decision shall be communicated to the parties.

§26.01 INTRODUCTION

Section 26 of the Arbitration Act 2005 provides for the conduct of hearings and seeks to ensure the parties comply with the rules of natural justice in terms of the right to be heard and the equal treatment of parties as set out in section 20.

Section 26 of the Arbitration Act 2005 is based on Article 24 of the 1985 Model Law save for some stylistic changes, which are as follows:

(1) the words 'subject to any contrary agreement by the parties' at the start of Article 24(1) have been substituted by the words 'Unless otherwise agreed by the parties' at the beginning of section 26(1);
(2) Article 24(1) has been split into sections 26(1) and (2);
(3) the word 'However', which appears at the beginning of the second sentence of Article 24(1), has been removed from the beginning of section 26(2);
(4) the words 'sufficient advance notice' in Article 24(2) have been substituted with 'reasonable prior notice' in section 26(3);
(5) Article 24(3) has been split into sections 26(4) and (5); and
(6) the word 'Also', which appears at the beginning of the second sentence of Article 24(3), is not found in section 26(5).

These changes do not appear to be of any significance save for the change made to section 26(3), which will be considered under §26.03 *infra*.

Article 24 of the 1985 Model Law is in turn based on provisions of the 1976 UNCITRAL Arbitration Rules. In particular:

(1) Article 24(1) of the 1985 Model Law is based on Article 15(2) of the 1976 UNCITRAL Arbitration Rules;
(2) Article 24(2) of the 1985 Model Law is based on Article 25(1) of the 1976 UNCITRAL Arbitration Rules; and
(3) Article 24(3) of the 1985 Model Law is based on Articles 15(3) and 27(1) of the 1976 Arbitration Rules.

In this regard, Articles 15(2) and (3), 25(1) and 27(1) of the 1976 UNCITRAL Arbitration Rules provide:

General Provisions
Article 15

...
2. If either party so requests at any stage of the proceedings, the arbitral tribunal shall hold hearings for the presentation of evidence by witnesses, including expert witnesses, or for oral argument. In the absence of such a request, the arbitral tribunal shall decide whether to hold such hearings or whether the proceedings shall be conducted on the basis of documents and other materials.
3. All documents or information supplied to the arbitral tribunal by one party shall at the same time be communicated by that party to the other party.

...
Evidence and Hearings

...
Article 25
1. In the event of an oral hearing, the arbitral tribunal shall give the parties adequate advance notice of the date, time and place thereof.
Experts
Article 27
1. The arbitral tribunal may appoint one or more experts to report to it, in writing, on specific issues to be determined by the tribunal. A copy of the expert's terms of reference, established by the arbitral tribunal, shall be communicated to the parties.

The provisions of the 1976 UNCITRAL Arbitration Rules are now found in Articles 17(3) and (4), 28(1) and 29(1) of the 2013 UNCITRAL Arbitration Rules, which provide:

General Provisions
Article 17

...
3. If at an appropriate stage of the proceedings any party so requests, the arbitral tribunal shall hold hearings for the presentation of evidence by witnesses, including expert witnesses, or for oral argument. In the absence of such a request, the arbitral tribunal shall decide whether to hold such hearings or whether the proceedings shall be conducted on the basis of documents and other materials.
4. All communications to the arbitral tribunal by one party shall be communicated by that party to all other parties. Such communications shall be made at the same time, except as otherwise permitted by the arbitral tribunal if it may do so under applicable law.

...
Hearings
Article 28
1. In the event of an oral hearing, the arbitral tribunal shall give the parties adequate advance notice of the date, time and place thereof.

...
Experts appointed by the arbitral tribunal
Article 29
1. After consultation with the parties, the arbitral tribunal may appoint one or more independent experts to report to it, in writing, on specific issues to be determined by the arbitral tribunal. A copy of the expert's terms of reference, established by the arbitral tribunal, shall be communicated to the parties.

The 2013 UNCITRAL Arbitration Rules form part of the 2018 AIAC Arbitration Rules.

§26.02   AUTONOMY AND THE IMPORTANCE OF AN ORAL HEARING

Sections 26(1) and (2) of the Arbitration Act 2005 provide for three distinct scenarios, which are considered below. The first and second scenarios cover situations where the parties have agreed on the modalities of the hearing and have thus exercised their autonomy. The third scenario, which is far more common in practice, deals with a situation where the parties have not reached an agreement on how the hearing is to be conducted.

[A]   Where the Parties Have Agreed on an Oral Hearing

In this scenario, the arbitral tribunal will be required to hold an oral hearing in accordance with the agreement of the parties.

[B]   Where the Parties Have Agreed That No Hearing Will Be Held

In general, in this situation, the arbitral tribunal will not hold a hearing and determine the issues based on the documents that are delivered.

However, even in this situation, in exceptional cases, where not to hold an oral hearing may deprive a party of his right to a hearing under section 20 of the Arbitration Act 2005, an oral hearing may be permitted.

This view is based on the UNCITRAL Report at paragraph 205, which reads:

> As to the question whether an agreement by the parties that there would be no oral hearings was also binding, different views were expressed. Under one view, the right to oral hearings was of such fundamental importance that the parties were not bound by their agreement and a party could always request oral hearings. Under another view, the agreement of the parties that no oral hearings would be held was binding on the parties but not on the arbitral tribunal so that the arbitral tribunal, if requested by a party, had a discretion to order oral hearings. However, the prevailing view was that an agreed exclusion of oral hearings was binding on

the parties and the arbitral tribunal. Nevertheless, it was noted that article 19(3) [Article 18 of the final text of the 1985 Model Law], requiring that each party should be given a full opportunity to present his case, might in exceptional circumstances provide a compelling reason for holding an oral hearing. It was understood that parties who had earlier agreed that no hearings should be held were not precluded from later modifying their agreement, and thus to allow a party to request oral hearings.

A similar position appears to be adopted in the 2018 AIAC Fast Track Arbitration Rules, which provides for documents-only arbitration for certain disputes of a lower value but allows the arbitral tribunal to hold a hearing if necessary after consultation with the parties. In this context, Rule 16 of the 2018 AIAC Fast Track Arbitration Rules provides:

Rule 16
Documents-only Arbitration
1. Where the Parties have expressly agreed in writing to a documents-only arbitration, the arbitral tribunal shall, upon receipt of the final written submissions proceed and consider the dispute and publish the award within the period of time set out in Rule 21(1)(g).
2. Where the aggregate amount of dispute is less than USD75,000.00, or its equivalent in another currency, or is unlikely to exceed USD75,000.00, or its equivalent in another currency, in an international arbitration; or is less than RM150,000.00 or is unlikely to exceed RM150,000.00 in a domestic arbitration, the arbitration shall proceed as a documents-only arbitration, unless the arbitral tribunal deems it necessary to proceed by way of substantive oral hearings upon consultation with the Parties.

[C] Where the Parties Have Not Agreed on Whether an Oral Hearing Is to Be Held

In this scenario, the arbitral tribunal has the discretion to decide whether to hold an oral hearing or not. However, if either party insists on an oral hearing, the arbitral tribunal must hold an oral hearing. This is clear from section 26(2) of the Arbitration Act 2005 and is intended to safeguard a party's right to be heard.

Generally, sections 26(1) and (2) of the Arbitration Act 2005 are a specific expression of the general rule in section 20 that parties are to be treated equally and given an opportunity to be heard.

Apart from this, the words 'presentation of evidence or oral arguments' are used in section 26(1) to cover all forms of presentation of evidence, including oral testimony and the accompanying cross-examination, as well as oral arguments by counsel both on substantive and procedural issues.[16]

---

16. *See* Analytical Commentary, Article 24, commentary 5.

§26.03 NOTICE

Section 26(3) of the Arbitration Act 2005 requires the parties to be given reasonable prior notice of any hearing or meeting. This is again a specific expression of the general principle set out in section 20 that the parties have a right to be heard and are to be treated equally. The parties can only exercise their right to be heard if they have been given reasonable prior notice.

Section 26(3) is intended as an expression of a broad principle and does not delve into issues of procedure such as who is to notify the parties and the length of notice required. The parties are free to agree on these matters subject to the important caveat that any such agreement may be ineffective if it does not allow for reasonable prior notice. In this regard, it is unclear why the words 'sufficient advance notice' in Article 24(2) have been changed to 'reasonable prior notice' in section 26(3). However, the words appear to have the same effect, with the word 'reasonable' perhaps further emphasizing an objective standard that must comply with section 20 regardless of any agreement between the parties.[17]

§26.04 COMMUNICATION

Section 26(4) of the Arbitration Act 2005 provides that any communication by a party with the arbitral tribunal must also be communicated to the other party. Section 26(5) looks at this from the point of view of the arbitral tribunal and provides that any expert report or evidentiary document relied on by the arbitral tribunal must be communicated to both parties.

Again, these are specific expressions of the general principle of equality and the right to be heard found in section 20 of the Arbitration Act 2005. Unless a party is aware of what the other party has communicated to the arbitral tribunal, he will not be in a position to respond and exercise his right to be heard.

Similarly, unless the parties are made aware of the evidentiary material relied upon by the arbitral tribunal, they will not be in a position to respond to such material. In this regard, there is a limit though. The arbitral tribunal is only required to communicate evidentiary material relied on and not other material, for example reference to dictionaries and commentaries.[18]

---

17. *See* Analytical Commentary, Article 24, commentaries 6 and 7.
18. *See* Peter Binder, *International Commercial Arbitration and Conciliation in UNCITRAL Model Law Jurisdictions* (3rd edn, Sweet & Maxwell 2010) at para. 5.113.

27. Default of a Party

Unless otherwise agreed by the parties, if without showing sufficient cause –

(a) the claimant fails to communicate the statement of claim in accordance with subsection 25(1), the arbitral tribunal shall terminate the proceedings;

(b) the respondent fails to communicate the statement of defence in accordance with subsection 25(1), the arbitral tribunal shall continue the proceedings without treating such failure in itself as an admission of the claimant's allegations;

(c) any party fails to appear at a hearing or to produce documentary evidence, the arbitral tribunal may continue the proceedings and make the award on the evidence before it; or

(d) the claimant fails to proceed with the claim, the arbitral tribunal may make an award dismissing the claim or give directions, with or without conditions, for the speedy determination of the claim.

§27.01 INTRODUCTION

Section 27 of the Arbitration Act 2005 provides for the manner in which the arbitral tribunal is to proceed in the event of a default by the parties, such as failing to deliver their pleadings, attend hearings or prosecute the claim.

Section 27 of the Arbitration Act 2005 reflects Article 25 of the 1985 Model Law save that section 25(d) is a new provision that is not found in the 1985 Model Law.

§27.02 PARTY AUTONOMY

Section 27 of the Arbitration Act 2005 follows the familiar 'two-level system' adopted in the 1985 Model Law. The parties are, first, given the freedom to agree on the consequences of default, failing which the default provisions in section 27 apply.

In practice, the parties would agree on the consequences of default by agreeing to arbitration rules published by an institute. This is expressly permitted under section 2(c) of the Arbitration Act 2005.

If the parties have agreed to the AIAC Arbitration Rules, the consequences of default are similar to those provided for under section 27. In this regard, Article 30 of the 2013 UNCITRAL Arbitration Rules, which forms part of the 2018 AIAC Arbitration Rules, provides:

> Default
> Article 30
> 1. If, within the period of time fixed by these Rules or the arbitral tribunal, without showing sufficient cause:
>   (a) The claimant has failed to communicate its statement of claim, the arbitral tribunal shall issue an order for the termination of the arbitral proceedings,

unless there are remaining matters that may need to be decided and the arbitral tribunal considers it appropriate to do so;
(b) The respondent has failed to communicate its response to the notice of arbitration or its statement of defence, the arbitral tribunal shall order that the proceedings continue, without treating such failure in itself as an admission of the claimant's allegations; the provisions of this subparagraph also apply to a claimant's failure to submit a defence to a counter-claim or to a claim for the purpose of a set-off.
2. If a party, duly notified under these Rules, fails to appear at a hearing, without showing sufficient cause for such failure, the arbitral tribunal may proceed with the arbitration.
3. If a party, duly invited by the arbitral tribunal to produce documents, exhibits or other evidence, fails to do so within the established period of time, without showing sufficient cause for such failure, the arbitral tribunal may make the award on the evidence before it.

§27.03   DEFAULT

Section 27 of the Arbitration Act 2005 provides for the consequences of default, where the parties have not agreed on these matters. Section 27 provides for four scenarios, which are considered below.

[A]   Where the Claimant Fails to Deliver the Statement of Claim

Here, section 27 provides that the arbitral tribunal shall terminate the proceedings. The use of the imperative 'shall' in section 27(a) suggests that the arbitral tribunal does not have a discretion and must terminate the proceedings if the claimant fails to deliver the Statement of Claim.

However, the Arbitration Act 2005 does not specify the consequences of such termination. It is submitted[19] that, in general, the claimant would be entitled to recommence arbitration proceedings subject to the relevant limitation period. Further, the claimant would have to bear the costs of the arbitration proceedings that were terminated due to his failure to deliver a Statement of Claim.

[B]   Where the Respondent Fails to Deliver His Statement of Defence

Here, the arbitral tribunal shall continue with the arbitration proceedings without treating such failure as an admission.

Section 27(b) of the Arbitration Act 2005 is of significance in this regard as it departs from the rules applicable in civil proceedings, where a failure to file a Defence will generally be treated as an admission that entitles the plaintiff to enter judgment against the defendant.[20]

---

19. *See* David D. Caron and Lee M. Caplan, *The UNCITRAL Arbitration Rules, A Commentary* (2nd edn, Oxford University Press 2013) at p 675.
20. *See* Rules of Court 2012, Order 19 Rule 2 to 7.

Section 27(b) like section 27(a) uses the word 'shall' to make clear that the arbitral tribunal must proceed and not treat the failure to deliver the Statement of Defence as an admission.

Although section 27(b) is drafted in mandatory terms, it is submitted that the arbitral tribunal retains a discretion as to how to treat the failure to deliver a Statement of Defence, although this cannot be treated as an admission. The arbitral tribunal is not obliged to treat the failures to deliver a Statement of Defence as a complete denial of the claim and would be entitled to draw such inferences as the facts present.[21]

[C] Where Any Party Fails to Attend the Hearing or Provide Documentary Evidence

Here, the arbitral tribunal may continue the proceedings and make the award based on the evidence before it.

Unlike sections 27(a) and (b), section 27(c) of the Arbitration Act 2005 uses the permissive 'may' rather than the imperative 'shall'. This makes it clear that the arbitral tribunal has a discretion on how to proceed with the arbitration if any party fails to attend a hearing or to provide documentary evidence.

The arbitral tribunal's discretion includes the power not to admit or to disregard any documentary evidence presented by a party after the time limit specified for producing such documents. The arbitral tribunal also has the discretion to draw inferences from a party's failure to provide documentary evidence.[22]

[D] Where the Claimant Fails to Proceed with the Claim

Here, the arbitral tribunal may make an award dismissing the claim or give directions for the speedy determination of the claim.

Section 25(d) of the Arbitration Act 2005 also uses the word 'may', which emphasizes that the arbitral tribunal retains a discretion on how to proceed with the arbitration when the claimant fails to present a claim.

In practice, the arbitral tribunal will exercise this discretion when the respondent applies for the claim to be dismissed for want of prosecution.

§27.04 SAFEGUARDS

The default provisions in section 27 of the Arbitration Act 2005 have serious consequences as they can result in the termination of the proceedings or in the award being made ex parte.

Due to these serious consequences, and in particular, to ensure that any award made ex parte will be enforced, section 27 has certain safeguards. These safeguards are both express and implicit. Expressly, section 27 provides that all the default provisions

---

21. *See* Analytical Commentary, Article 25, commentary 4; UNCITRAL Report para. 214.
22. *See* Analytical Commentary, Article 25, commentary 5.

will apply only when the defaulting party is unable to show 'sufficient cause' for the failure. After some initial debate, it is now clear that whether or not 'sufficient cause' has been shown is a matter for the arbitral tribunal to decide rather than the courts.[23]

Implicitly, section 27 is subject to section 20 of the Arbitration Act 2005. Therefore, sufficient notice must have been given before any of the default provisions can apply.

---

23. *See* Peter Binder, *International Commercial Arbitration and Conciliation in UNCITRAL Model Law Jurisdictions* (3rd edn, Sweet & Maxwell 2010) at para. 5.120.

28. Expert Appointed by Arbitral Tribunal

(1) Unless otherwise agreed by the parties, the arbitral tribunal may –
   (a) appoint one or more experts to report to it on specific issues to be determined by the arbitral tribunal; or
   (b) require a party to give the expert any relevant information or to produce or to provide access to any relevant documents, goods or other property for the expert's inspection.

(2) Unless otherwise agreed by the parties, if a party so requests or if the arbitral tribunal considers it necessary, the expert shall, after delivery of a written or oral report, participate in a hearing where the parties have the opportunity to put questions to the expert and to present other expert witnesses in order to testify on the points at issue.

§28.01 INTRODUCTION

Section 28 of the Arbitration Act 2005 provides for the appointment of experts by the arbitral tribunal. It is important to note that section 28 does not deal with the appointment of experts by the parties.

Section 28 of the Arbitration Act 2005 reflects Article 26 of the 1985 Model Law.

§28.02 PARTY AUTONOMY

Section 28(1)(a) of the Arbitration Act 2005 is not mandatory. The parties are free to agree on whether or not the arbitral tribunal may appoint an expert. The parties are free to agree on this at any stage of the proceedings and are not obliged to agree on this either in the arbitration agreement or at the initial stages of the arbitration. Therefore, if the arbitral tribunal notifies the parties that the arbitral tribunal is considering appointing an expert, the parties are free at that stage to notify the arbitral tribunal that they do not agree to the appointment of an expert. The arbitral tribunal is then free to withdraw if they are of the view that they do not have the expertise to continue with the proceedings.[24]

Section 28(1)(a) allows for this, in the light of the importance of party autonomy in arbitration. The parties are assumed to have appointed an arbitral tribunal whom they consider have the necessary expertise to determine the dispute. The parties may also simply wish to have the dispute determined by the arbitral tribunal within their expertise rather than by using an expert. Further, the parties may not wish to incur the additional cost and delay likely to be occasioned by the appointment of an expert.[25]

---

24. *See* Analytical Commentary, Article 26, commentary 2; UNCITRAL Report para. 219.
25. *See* Analytical Commentary, Article 26, commentary 2; UNCITRAL Report para. 219.

§28.03 COOPERATION

Section 28(1)(b) of the Arbitration Act 2005 allows the arbitral tribunal to direct the parties to provide evidence or access to evidence to the expert. It is important to note that these directions are given by the arbitral tribunal and not by the expert to the parties. In the event a party fails to comply with these directions, the arbitral tribunal may continue the proceedings and make the award based on the evidence before them in accordance with section 27(c) of the Arbitration Act 2005.

§28.04 RIGHT TO BE HEARD

Section 28(2) is another specific implementation of the general right to be heard and be treated with equality set out in section 20 of the Arbitration Act 2005.

The specific implementation of this broad principle involves:

(1) the expert delivering his report to the parties;
(2) the parties being free to appoint their own experts;
(3) the tribunal-appointed expert appearing at a hearing at the request of a party; and
(4) the parties being entitled to challenge the tribunal-appointed expert at this hearing and present the testimony of party-appointed experts.

§28.05 IMPARTIALITY AND INDEPENDENCE

Section 28 of the Arbitration Act 2005 does not expressly provide for the challenge of a tribunal-appointed expert on the grounds of lack of impartiality or independence. As the expert is appointed by the arbitral tribunal, it is submitted that a challenge may be made by relying on section 14 of the Arbitration Act 2005 by way of analogy.

29. *Court Assistance in Taking Evidence*

(1) Any party may with the approval of the arbitral tribunal, apply to the High Court for assistance in taking evidence.
(2) The High Court may order the attendance of a witness to give evidence or, where applicable, produce documents on oath or affirmation before an officer of the High Court or any other person, including the arbitral tribunal.

§29.01 INTRODUCTION

Section 29 of the Arbitration Act 2005 allows a party to apply to the High Court for assistance in taking evidence and elaborates how such evidence may be obtained through the High Court.

Section 29 of the Arbitration Act 2005 differs from Article 27, which is its corresponding provision in the 1985 Model Law.

Article 27 of the 1985 Model Law provides:

Court assistance in taking evidence

The arbitral tribunal or a party with the approval of the arbitral tribunal may request from a competent court of this State assistance in taking evidence. The court may execute the request within its competence and according to its rules on taking evidence.

First, the 1985 Model Law allows either the arbitral tribunal or the parties to approach the courts for assistance. However, section 29(1) only provides for the parties to approach the courts. This is perhaps due to concerns with Article 27, which by allowing the arbitral tribunal to seek evidence appears contrary to the adversarial system familiar to parties in Malaysia.[26] Furthermore, this provision in Article 29 is intended as a compromise between those legal systems in which only the arbitral tribunal may request the court for assistance and those legal systems in which the parties may make such a request.[27] While there is a need for such a compromise in the 1985 Model Law, there is no need for such a compromise in domestic legislation.

Second, the 'competent court of this state' in Article 27 of the 1985 Model Law has been designated as the High Court in section 29(1) of the Arbitration Act 2005. This is in conformity with the practice in the Arbitration Act 2005 of designating the High Court, which is defined under section 2(1) of the Arbitration Act 2005, as the competent court.

Third, section 29(2) of the Arbitration Act 2005 provides details of how the High Court would secure evidence, which details are not found in Article 27 of the 1985 Model Law. This appears to be in accordance with the intention of Article 27 of the 1985

---

26. *See* Peter Binder, *International Commercial Arbitration and Conciliation in UNCITRAL Model Law Jurisdictions* (3rd edn, Sweet & Maxwell 2010) at para. 5.158.
27. *See* UNCITRAL Report at para. 226.

Model Law, which allows for details to be included in the adopting legislation based on the civil procedure rules applicable in the adopting State.

§29.02 APPLICATION

Section 29(1) of the Arbitration Act 2005 allows a party, with the approval of the arbitral tribunal, to apply to the High Court for assistance in taking evidence. The approval of the arbitral tribunal is required in order to prevent dilatory tactics by a party.

The need for such a provision arises from the arbitral tribunal's own lack of power to compel a person to provide evidence. Hence the need for a party to seek assistance from the courts in taking evidence.

The question arises as to whether a party may apply to the High Court for assistance in taking evidence in relation to an arbitration with a seat outside Malaysia. Due to section 3 of the Arbitration Act 2005, which limits the application of the Act to domestic and international arbitration with a seat in Malaysia, section 29 of the Arbitration Act 2005 will not apply to an arbitration with a seat outside Malaysia. This is in accordance with the view taken during the drafting of the 1985 Model Law that court assistance in relation to a foreign-seated arbitration fell within the domain of international cooperation between States, which was best achieved by conventions or bilateral treaties, rather than by domestic legislation.[28]

§29.03 ORDERS

The High Court may then order witnesses to provide evidence or produce documents in accordance with section 29(2) of the Arbitration Act 2005.

The use of the word 'may' in section 29(2) emphasizes the High Court's discretion in this matter. Therefore, the applicant would need to pass two hurdles: first, the approval of the arbitral tribunal and second, the discretion being exercised in their favour by the High Court.

---

28. *See* Peter Binder, *International Commercial Arbitration and Conciliation in UNCITRAL Model Law Jurisdictions* (3rd edn, Sweet & Maxwell 2010) at para. 5.165.

CHAPTER 6

Making of Award and Termination of Proceedings

30.   Law Applicable to Substance of Dispute

   (1) The arbitral tribunal shall decide the dispute in accordance with such rules of law as are chosen by the parties as applicable to the substance of the dispute.
   (2) [this subsection has been deleted]
   (3) Any designation of the law or legal system of a given State shall be construed, unless otherwise expressed, as directly referring to the substantive law of that State and not to its conflict of laws rules.
   (4) Failing any designation by the parties, the arbitral tribunal shall apply the law determined by the conflict of laws rules which it considers applicable.
   (4A) The arbitral tribunal shall decide according to equity and conscience only if the parties have expressly authorized it to do so.
   (5) The arbitral tribunal shall, in all cases, decide in accordance with the terms of the agreement and shall take into account the usages of the trade applicable to the transaction.

§30.01   INTRODUCTION

Section 30 of the Arbitration Act 2005 provides for the law applicable to the substance of the dispute both in situations where the parties have agreed on the law and in situations where the law has to be determined by the arbitral tribunal.

It is important to distinguish section 30 from section 21 of the Arbitration Act 2005. Section 30 provides for the determination of the substantive law, while section 21 provides for the procedural law to be applied.

Section 30 of the Arbitration Act 2005 is based on Article 28 of the 1985 Model Law. In particular:

(1) sections 30(1) and (3) are based on Article 28(1);
(2) section 30(4) is based on Article 28(2);
(3) section 30(4A) is based on Article 28(3); and
(4) section 30(5) is based on Article 28(4).

There are no significant differences between section 30 of the Arbitration Act 2005 and Article 28 of the 1985 Model Law. Section 30(4A) uses the words 'according to equity and conscience', which is a translation from Latin used in Article 28(3) of the 1985 Model Law – '*ex aequo et bono* or as *amiable compositeur*'. The words 'in all cases' have been moved from the beginning of Article 28(4) to after the words 'tribunal shall' in section 30(5), and the word 'contract' in Article 28(4) has been substituted with the word 'agreement' in section 30(5). These appear to be merely changes in drafting.

Article 28 of the 1985 Model Law is in turn based on Article 33 of the 1976 UNCITRAL Arbitration Rules, which provides:

> Applicable law, *amiable compositeur*
> Article 33
> 1. The arbitral tribunal shall apply the law designated by the parties as applicable to the substance of the dispute. Failing such designation by the parties, the arbitral tribunal shall apply the law determined by the conflict of laws rules which it considers applicable.
> 2. The arbitral tribunal shall decide as *amiable compositeur* or *ex aequo et bono* only if the parties have expressly authorized the arbitral tribunal to do so and if the law applicable to the arbitral procedure permits such arbitration.
> 3. In all cases, the arbitral tribunal shall decide in accordance with the terms of the contract and shall take into account the usages of the trade applicable to the transaction.

Article 28 of the 1985 Model Law and Article 33 of the 1976 UNCITRAL Arbitration Rules are almost identical save that Article 28(1) uses the term 'rules of law' instead of 'law' as found in Article 33(1).

Article 33 of the 1976 UNCITRAL Arbitration Rules was subsequently retained in Article 35 of the 2013 UNCITRAL Arbitration Rules, which provides:

> Applicable law, *amiable compositeur*
> Article 35
> 1. The arbitral tribunal shall apply the rules of law designated by the parties as applicable to the substance of the dispute. Failing such designation by the parties, the arbitral tribunal shall apply the law which it determines to be appropriate.
> 2. The arbitral tribunal shall decide as *amiable compositeur* or *ex aequo et bono* only if the parties have expressly authorized the arbitral tribunal to do so.
> 3. In all cases, the arbitral tribunal shall decide in accordance with the terms of the contract, if any, and shall take into account any usage of trade applicable to the transaction.

Chapter 6: Making of Award and Termination of Proceedings §30.01

Article 35(1) of the 2013 UNCITRAL Arbitration Rules and Article 28(1) of the 1985 Model Law both use the term 'rules of law'.

The 2013 UNCITRAL Arbitration Rules form part of the 2018 AIAC Arbitration Rules.

Section 30 of the Arbitration Act 2005 was amended by the Arbitration (Amendment) (No 2) Act 2018 to reflect Article 28 of the Model Law more closely. Prior to this amendment, section 30 provided as follows:

(1) Unless otherwise agreed by the parties, in respect of a domestic arbitration where the seat of arbitration is in Malaysia, the arbitral tribunal shall decide the dispute in accordance with the substantive law of Malaysia.
(2) In respect of an international arbitration, the arbitral tribunal shall decide the dispute in accordance with the law as agreed upon by the parties as applicable to the substance of the dispute.
(3) Any designation by the parties of the law of a given State shall be construed, unless otherwise expressed, as directly referring to the substantive law of that State and not to its conflict of laws rules.
(4) Failing any agreement under subsection (2), the arbitral tribunal shall apply the law determined by the conflict of laws rules.
(5) The arbitral tribunal shall, in all cases, decide in accordance with the terms of the agreement and shall take into account the usages of the trade applicable to the transaction.

There are significant differences between the old section 30, on the one hand, and the current section 30, which reflects Article 28, on the other. These differences are as follows:

(1) the old section 30(1) is not found in the current section 30 or Article 28. This is because the old section 30(1) provided for domestic arbitration, while the 1985 Model Law provides for international arbitration. The current section 30 does not make a distinction between domestic and international arbitration;
(2) the words 'in respect of an international arbitration' at the beginning of the old section 30(2) are not found in the current section 30(1) or Article 28(1). These words were included to distinguish the old section 30(2) from the old section 30(1), as the former dealt with domestic arbitration, while the latter dealt with international arbitration. As stated above, the current section 30 no longer distinguishes between domestic and international arbitration;
(3) the term 'law' was used in the old section 30(2), as opposed to the term 'rules of law' used in the current section 30(1) and Article 28(1). This is of particular significance and is considered under §30.03 *infra*;
(4) the words 'agreed upon' was used in the old section 30(2) instead of the word 'chosen' in the current section 30(1) and Article 28(1). This does not appear to be of any significance and is a stylistic change;
(5) the words 'by the parties' in the old section 30(3) are not found in the current section 30(3) or Article 28(1). This also does not appear to be of significance and is simply an alteration in drafting;

(6) the words 'or legal system' in Article 28(1) appearing after the words 'the law', which were omitted from the old section 30(3), have now been included in the new section 30(3). This appears to be merely a matter of drafting;

(7) the words 'agreement under subsection (2)' in the old section 30(4) are substituted by the words 'designation by the parties' in the current section 30(4) to reflect Article 28(2). This appears to be merely a change in drafting;

(8) the words 'which it considers applicable' at the end of Article 28(2), which were omitted from the old section 30(4), have been included in the current section 30(4). The significance of this is considered under §30.03 *infra*; and

(9) Article 28(3), which was omitted from the old section 30, has now been included in the current section 30(4A). This is considered under §30.04 *infra*.

Prior to the amendments in 2018, section 30(1) of the Arbitration Act 2005 was amended by the Arbitration (Amendment) Act 2011. The words 'unless otherwise agreed by the parties' were added at the beginning of section 30(1). This amendment was to allow parties the freedom to agree on the substantive law to be applied to a domestic arbitration with a seat in Malaysia. This amendment in 2011 has now been superseded by the amendments in 2018, which have removed the distinction between domestic and international arbitration in section 30.

§30.02 PARTY AUTONOMY

Sections 30(1) and (4) of the Arbitration Act 2005 utilize the familiar 'two-level system' in relation to the determination of the substantive law in arbitration.

First, section 30(1) of the Arbitration Act 2005 allows the parties the freedom to choose the substantive law applicable to the arbitration. This freedom is of significance as the parties will not be bound to follow the substantive law at the seat of arbitration but are instead free to agree on the substantive law to be applied.

Prior to the amendments in 2018, section 30(2) of the Arbitration Act 2005 did not go as far as Article 28(1) of the 1985 Model Law. Article 28(1) allows the parties to agree on the 'rules of law' applicable. The term 'rules of law' is wide enough to allow the parties to agree upon their own self-drafted rules of law or a mixture of several states' laws.[1]

Section 30(2) of the Arbitration Act 2005, prior to the amendments in 2018, used the term 'law' instead of 'rules of law'. The previous use of the narrower term in section 30(2) meant that the parties could only agree upon a closed body of law applicable in a particular state.[2]

This divergence between the Arbitration Act 2005 and the 1985 Model Law has been removed by the amendments in 2018. Section 30(1) now mirrors Article 28(1) and allows for the parties to agree on 'rules of law', which would embrace the parties' own

---

1. *See* Analytical Commentary, Article 28, commentary 4; UNCITRAL Report, para. 232.
2. *See* Peter Binder, *International Commercial Arbitration and Conciliation in UNCITRAL Model Law Jurisdictions* (3rd edn, Sweet & Maxwell 2010) at para. 6.008.

self-drafted rules of law or a mixture of several states' laws. This strengthens party autonomy.

Section 30(3) of the Arbitration Act 2005 provides a useful rule of interpretation.[3] The designation by the parties of a law of a given State will be interpreted as an agreement to the substantive law of that State and not to the conflict of law rules applicable in that State.

§30.03 DETERMINATION BY THE ARBITRAL TRIBUNAL

Second, if the parties have failed to agree upon the substantive law applicable, section 30(4) of the Arbitration Act 2005 provides that the arbitral tribunal shall determine the substantive law in accordance with the conflict of law rules.

The High Court, in *Innotec Asia Pacific Sdn Bhd v. Innotec GmbH* [2007] 8 CLJ 304 at paragraphs 21 and 22, explained the conflict of law rules that would be applied:

> [21] In the absence of an agreement as to the substantive law applicable to an arbitration, s. 30(4) of the Arbitration Act 2005 expressly provides the arbitral tribunal the power to determine the law applicable in an arbitration by the conflict of laws rules. Thus, it is necessary and reasonably implied that the arbitrator and/or arbitral tribunal has the jurisdiction to decide on any dispute as to the law applicable in such arbitration. (see: s. 30(4) Arbitration Act 2005; and Commentary, *The Arbitration Act 2005 UNCITRAL Model Law as applied in Malaysia*, para 30.6).
>
> [22] In determining the applicable substantive law, the arbitral tribunal will infer from the circumstances the system of law with which the transaction has its closest and most real connection. (see: *Compagnie d'Armement Maritime SA v. Compagnie Tunisiennne de Navigation SA* [1970] 3 All ER 712; and
>
> *Minousti Shipping Corp v. Trans Continental Shipping Services Pte Ltd* [1971] 1 LNS 79; [1971] 2 MLJ 5; where it was held that the law where the arbitration was to be held shall apply since the arbitration clause was silent as to what law should govern such arbitration proceedings).

The words 'which it considers applicable' at the end of Article 28(2) of the 1985 Model Law were not found in section 30(4) of the Arbitration Act 2005, prior to the amendments in 2018. This was unfortunate, as the former section 30(4) may have given the impression that there is only one set of conflict of law rules that are applicable, when there are several, of which one must be chosen as applicable by the arbitral tribunal. This unfortunate omission was addressed by the amendments in 2018. The words 'which it considers applicable' have now been included at the end of section 30(4), which mirrors Article 28(2).

Article 28(2) of the 1985 Model Law is more conservative than Article 28(1) in two respects. First, the arbitral tribunal, unlike the parties, is only entitled to determine that a closed body of law applicable in a State is the substantive law of the arbitration.[4]

---

3. *See* Analytical Commentary, Article 28, commentary 4.
4. *See* Peter Binder, *International Commercial Arbitration and Conciliation in UNCITRAL Model Law Jurisdictions* (3rd edn, Sweet & Maxwell 2010) at para. 6.010.

Second, the arbitral tribunal must determine this applicable law in accordance with conflict of law rules. This provision has been said to be too narrow and contradictory to international arbitration practice, where the applicable substantive law is determined directly by the arbitral tribunal without the tribunal first determining the applicable conflict of law rules.[5]

This has led to more than half of the adopting jurisdictions allowing the arbitral tribunal to determine the substantive law without any restriction based on the applicable conflict of law rules.[6] Article 25(1) of the 2013 UNCITRAL Arbitration Rules also allows the arbitral tribunal to apply the substantive law, which it 'determines to be appropriate' without restriction. The contrary view is that a higher degree of certainty is achieved by requiring the arbitral tribunal to first determine the applicable conflict of law rules. However, this is questionable as conflict of law rules differ between States.[7]

§30.04 EQUITY AND CONSCIENCE

Article 28(3) of the 1985 Model Law, which allows for disputes to be resolved '*ex aequo et bono*' or '*amiable compositeur*', is reflected in section 30(4A) of the Arbitration Act 2005.

The terms '*ex aequo et bono*' or '*amiable compositeur*' in Latin, or 'according to equity and conscience' in English, are not defined in the 1985 Model Law. Under these terms, essentially, an arbitral tribunal may determine a dispute according to its own understanding and not necessarily strictly in accordance with the law.[8]

§30.05 AGREEMENT AND TRADE USAGE

Section 30(5) of the Arbitration Act 2005 provides that 'in all cases', that is whether in domestic or international arbitration and whether the law has been agreed upon by the parties or determined by the arbitral tribunal, the arbitral tribunal shall determine the dispute in accordance with the terms of the agreement and trade usage.

Section 30(5) has also been relied on to contend that parties are entitled to pre-award interest. This is considered in detail under §33.09[B][2] *infra*.[9]

---

5. *See* UNCITRAL Report at para. 237.
6. *See* Peter Binder, *International Commercial Arbitration and Conciliation in UNCITRAL Model Law Jurisdictions* (3rd edn, Sweet & Maxwell 2010) at para. 6.012.
7. *See* UNCITRAL Report at para. 237.
8. *See* Peter Binder, *International Commercial Arbitration and Conciliation in UNCITRAL Model Law Jurisdictions* (3rd edn, Sweet & Maxwell 2010) at para. 6.015.
9. *See Kerajaan Malaysia (Kementerian Sumber Asli dan Alam Sekitar) v. Kumpulan Sakata Sdn Bhd* [2016] 7 CLJ 412 at paras 16, 24, HC; *Kerajaan Malaysia v. Tasja Sdn Bhd* [2016] 6 CLJ 738 at para. 52, HC.

§30.06 THIRD-PARTY DETERMINATION

Article 2(d) of the 1985 Model Law provides that the parties may allow a third party, including an institution, to determine issues the parties are entitled to determine. However, Article 28 is expressly excluded from the application of Article 2(d); this is to ensure that the parties may not agree to a third party determining the substantive law.

However, section 2(2)(b) of the Arbitration Act 2005, which is the equivalent of Article 2(d) of the 1985 Model Law, does not expressly exclude section 30. This accordingly leaves open the possibility that in an arbitration with a seat in Malaysia, the parties are free to allow a third party to determine the substantive law.

§30.07 SETTING ASIDE

Section 37(1) of the Arbitration Act 2005 does not allow for an award to be set aside on the grounds that section 30 was wrongly applied by the arbitral tribunal. To that extent, section 30 merely serves as guidance to the arbitral tribunal.[10]

This has been recognized by the High Court, in *Tanjung Langsat Port Sdn Bhd v. Trafigura Pte Ltd & Another Case* [2016] 4 CLJ 927 at paragraph 43(a):

> Sections 30(2) and (5) of the AA 2005 are not independent grounds on which the arbitral award may be set aside; the reason being the grounds for setting aside an arbitral award are limited to those found in s. 37 of the AA 2005. This is in fact apparent from a plain reading of the statute itself, ie, the opening words of s. 37 that 'An award may be set aside by the High Court only if ... .'

---

10. *See* UNCITRAL Report para. 238.

31. *Decision Making by Panel of Arbitrators*

> *(1) Unless otherwise agreed by the parties, in any arbitral proceedings with more than one arbitrator, any decision of the arbitral tribunal shall be made by a majority of all its members.*
>
> *(2) Where so authorized by the parties or by all the members of the arbitral tribunal, questions of procedure may be decided by the presiding arbitrator.*

§31.01 INTRODUCTION

Section 31 of the Arbitration Act 2005 provides for the decision-making process by the arbitral tribunal, in particular, how a decision is to be made where there is more than one member of the arbitral tribunal. This provision would have no application to a sole arbitrator, where the question of a majority decision would not arise.

Section 31 of the Arbitration Act 2005 reflects Article 29 of the 1985 Model Law save for certain stylistic changes. Section 31(1) resembles the first sentence of Article 29 and section 31(2) the second sentence of Article 29.

Article 31 of the 1985 Model Law is in turn modelled on Article 31 of the 1976 UNCITRAL Arbitration Rules, which provides:

> Decisions
> Article 31
> 1. When there are three arbitrators, any award or other decision of the arbitral tribunal shall be made by a majority of the arbitrators.
> 2. In the case of questions of procedure, when there is no majority or when the arbitral tribunal so authorizes, the presiding arbitrator may decide on his own, subject to revision, if any, by the arbitral tribunal.

Article 31 of the 1976 UNCITRAL Arbitration Rules has been retained in Article 33 of the 2013 UNCITRAL Arbitration Rules save that Article 33(1) of the 2013 Rules allows for a situation where there is more than one arbitrator that is not necessarily limited to three.

Article 33 of the 2013 UNCITRAL Arbitration Rules, which forms part of the 2018 AIAC Arbitration Rules, provides:

> Decisions
> Article 33
> 1. When there is more than one arbitrator, any award or other decision of the arbitral tribunal shall be made by a majority of the arbitrators.
> 2. In the case of questions of procedure, when there is no majority or when the arbitral tribunal so authorizes, the presiding arbitrator may decide alone, subject to revision, if any, by the arbitral tribunal.

§31.02 PARTY AUTONOMY

Section 31 of the Arbitration Act, like most other non-mandatory provisions in the Act, allows for the familiar 'two-level system'. The parties are allowed to agree on how a decision is to be made where there is more than one arbitrator, failing which, the default provisions in section 31 will apply.

The parties, will in practice, reach an agreement in this regard by the adoption of rules published by an institution, which the parties are entitled to do under section 2(2)(c) of the Arbitration Act 2005.

In this context, if the parties have agreed to the 2018 AIAC Arbitration Rules, Article 33 of the 2013 UNCITRAL Arbitration Rules, which forms part of the 2018 AIAC Arbitration Rules, effectively deals with decision-making by a majority of the arbitral tribunal in the same manner as section 31.

Alternatively, if the parties have agreed on the 2017 ICC Rules of Arbitration, Article 32(1) of these Rules will apply. Article 32(1) of the 2017 ICC Rules of Arbitration provides:

> Article 32: Making of the Award
> (1) When the arbitral tribunal is composed of more than one arbitrator, an award is made by a majority decision. If there is no majority, the award shall be made by the president of the arbitral tribunal alone.

Article 32(1) of the 2017 ICC Rules of Arbitration addresses the significant issue of how a decision is to be made when a majority cannot be reached. This can happen where the number of members of the arbitral tribunal is even or they are split. It can also happen where the number of members of the arbitral tribunal is odd but each member has a separate opinion and a majority cannot be reached. In these situations, Article 32(1) of the 2017 ICC Rules of Arbitration provides that the president of the arbitral tribunal will make a decision.

§31.03 DEFAULT

If the parties have not agreed on how more than one arbitrator will reach a decision, the default provisions of section 31 will apply. The provisions of section 31 are simple and concise and do not descend into unnecessary detail. Section 31 provides that where there is more than one arbitrator, decisions will be made by a majority.

Section 31 does not deal with a situation where a majority cannot be reached.

It had been suggested, during the drafting of the 1985 Model Law, that a presiding arbitrator be allowed to determine the matter, where there was no majority. However, this suggestion was not adopted, as it was felt that this might reduce the influence of other members of the arbitral tribunal in reaching a decision. Furthermore, if the parties desired this, they could agree to such a provision, as Article 29 of the 1985 Model Law was not mandatory.[11]

---

11. *See* UNCITRAL Report para. 244.

In this context, although section 31 of the Arbitration Act 2005, like Article 29 of the 1985 Model Law, allows a decision to be made by a majority, it still requires all members to take part in deliberations, or at least, have an opportunity to do so.[12]

It is also implicit, in this regard, that all members of the arbitral tribunal need not be present at the same place to deliberate or make decisions.[13]

Section 31(2) of the Arbitration Act 2005 allows the presiding arbitrator to determine questions of procedure, where this has been agreed by all parties or all members of the arbitral tribunal. This provision is intended to ensure the expedient resolution of procedural questions. Unfortunately, this provision in Article 29 of the 1985 Model Law is rather vague, as neither the term 'presiding arbitrator' nor 'questions of procedure' are defined.

The first of these issues is dealt with by the Arbitration Act 2005, which defines the term 'presiding arbitrator' in section 2(1). The second issue is dealt with implicitly. As the arbitral tribunal has the power to determine both questions of substance and procedure, it is implicit that the arbitral tribunal must have the power to determine what a question of procedure is and allow the presiding arbitrator to determine such questions.[14]

---

12. *See* Analytical Commentary, Article 29, commentary 2.
13. *See* UNCITRAL Report para. 246.
14. *See* Peter Binder, *International Commercial Arbitration and Conciliation in UNCITRAL Model Law Jurisdictions* (3rd edn, Sweet & Maxwell 2010) at para. 6.035.

32. Settlement

(1) If, during arbitral proceedings, the parties settle the dispute, the arbitral tribunal shall terminate the proceedings and, if requested by the parties and not objected to by the arbitral tribunal, record the settlement in the form of an award on agreed terms.

(2) An award on agreed terms shall be made in accordance with the provisions of section 33 and shall state that it is an award.

(3) An award made under subsection (1) shall have the same status and effect as an award on the merits of the case.

§32.01 INTRODUCTION

Section 32 of the Arbitration Act 2005 provides for the consequences of a settlement achieved during the arbitral proceedings. Fortunately, this is not an infrequent occurrence in arbitrations, which themselves sometimes foster a settlement by crystallizing the dispute and encouraging parties to obtain advice.

Section 32 of the Arbitration Act 2005 reflects Article 30 of the 1985 Model Law save for certain minor stylistic changes.

Article 36 of the 1985 Model Law is in turn modelled on Articles 34(1) and (3) of the 1976 UNCITRAL Arbitration Rules. These provisions are identical in all material aspects save that Article 34(1) additionally provides that 'the arbitral tribunal is not obliged to give reasons for such an award.'

Articles 34(1) and (3) of the 1976 UNCITRAL Arbitration Rules are maintained in the 2013 UNCITRAL Arbitration Rules, which form part of the 2018 AIAC Arbitration Rules, as Articles 36(1) and (3).

§32.02 TERMINATION

Section 32(1) of the Arbitration Act 2005 provides that if a settlement is achieved during the arbitral proceedings, the arbitral tribunal 'shall' terminate the proceedings.

The use of the imperative 'shall' means that, unless the alternative of an award on agreed terms is made, the arbitral tribunal must terminate the proceedings upon a settlement being achieved by the parties.

§32.03 AWARD ON AGREED TERMS

As an alternative to termination, section 32(1) allow for an award on agreed terms provided that two requirements are satisfied:

(1) there is a request by the parties for such an award; and
(2) there is no objection to such an award by the arbitral tribunal.

The first requirement appears obvious. As there has been a settlement and the parties desire an award on agreed terms, a request must come from both parties. This is also intended to avoid any potential dispute as to the existence or the terms of the settlement.[15] As a matter of practice, although both parties must desire such an award, the formal request can be made by one party.[16] This will usually be followed in practice by confirmation by the other party.

The second requirement was controversial at the time the 1985 Model Law was being drafted. It was argued that the requirement for the arbitral tribunal's consent was contrary to the principle of party autonomy, which should entitle the parties to an award on agreed terms if they desired it without the need for consent by the arbitral tribunal.

However, this argument fails to appreciate the distinction between the parties' right to have the proceedings terminated upon settlement and the right to have an award on agreed terms. The former is in accordance with the principles of party autonomy. The latter is not practical, as the arbitral tribunal should not be compelled to issue an award they did not wish to make and may simply resign to avoid this. Moreover, the arbitral tribunal may have legitimate grounds for refusing to make such an award, where, for example, if it was fraudulent, contrary to law or public policy or against fundamental notions of justice and fairness.[17]

§32.04 FORM AND EFFECT

Sections 32(2) and (3) of the Arbitration Act 2005 provide that an award on agreed terms must be in the same form as an ordinary award and will have the same effect. This is particularly important for the purpose of recognition and enforcement of an award on agreed terms in accordance with the New York Convention. An award on agreed terms is also liable to be set aside or challenged on enforcement, although this will be infrequent given the consensual nature of such an award.

---

15. *See* Analytical Commentary, Article 30, commentary 2.
16. *See* UNCITRAL Report para. 250.
17. *See* Analytical Commentary, Article 30, commentary 2; UNCITRAL Report para. 249.

33.   *Form and Contents of Award*

(1) An award shall be made in writing and subject to subsection (2) shall be signed by the arbitrator.
(2) In arbitral proceedings with more than one arbitrator, the signatures of the majority of all members of the arbitral tribunal shall be sufficient provided that the reason for any omitted signature is stated.
(3) An award shall state the reasons upon which it is based, unless—
    (a) the parties have agreed that no reasons are to be given; or
    (b) the award is an award on agreed terms under section 32.
(4) An award shall state its date and the seat of arbitration as determined in accordance with section 22 and shall be deemed to have been made at that seat.
(5) After an award is made, a copy of the award signed by the arbitrator in accordance with subsections (1) and (2) shall be delivered to each party.
(6) Subject to subsection (8), unless otherwise agreed by the parties, the arbitral tribunal may, in the arbitral proceedings before it, award simple or compound interest from such date, at such rate and with such rest as the arbitral tribunal considers appropriate, for any period ending not later than the date of payment of the whole or any part of –
    (a) any sum which is awarded by the arbitral tribunal in the arbitral proceedings;
    (b) any sum which is in issue in the arbitral proceedings but is paid before the date of the award; or
    (c) costs awarded or ordered by the arbitral tribunal in the arbitral proceedings.
(7) Nothing in subsection (6) shall affect any other power of an arbitral tribunal to award interest.
(8) Where an award directs a sum to be paid, that sum shall, unless the award otherwise directs, carry interest as from the date of the award and at the same rate as a judgment debt.

§33.01   INTRODUCTION

Section 33 of the Arbitration Act 2005 provides for the form, content and publication of an award. Essentially, an award must:

(1) be in writing;
(2) be signed;
(3) contain reasons;
(4) state its date;
(5) state its seat; and
(6) be delivered to the parties.

These requirements, together with their exceptions, are considered in this Chapter. In addition to these requirements, section 33 also provides for the arbitral tribunal's power to award interest.

Section 33 of the Arbitration Act 2005 is modelled on Article 31 of the 1985 Model Law. In particular:

(1) section 33(1) reflects the first sentence of Article 31(1);
(2) section 33(2) reflects the second sentence of Article 31(1);
(3) section 33(3) reflects Article 31(2);
(4) section 33(4) reflects Article 31(3); and
(5) section 33(5) reflects Article 31(4).

There are minor stylistic changes but these provisions are essentially the same. There is, however, no equivalent to section 33(6) of the Arbitration Act 2005 in the 1985 Model Law. Other jurisdictions that have adopted the 1985 Model Law have also made additions to Article 31 to include interest.[18]

Article 31 of the 1985 Model Law is in turn based on various provisions of the 1976 UNCITRAL Arbitration Rules. In particular:

(1) Article 31(1) of the 1985 Model Law is modeled on Article 32(4) of the 1976 UNCITRAL Arbitration Rules, which provides:

> An award shall be signed by the arbitrators and it shall contain the date on which and the place where the award was made. Where there are three arbitrators and one of them fails to sign, the award shall state the reason for the absence of the signature.

(2) Article 31(2) of the 1985 Model Law is based on Article 32(3) of the 1976 UNCITRAL Arbitration Rules, which provides:

> The arbitral tribunal shall state the reasons upon which the award is based, unless the parties have agreed that no reasons are to be given.

(3) the requirements of Article 31(3) of the 1985 Model Law are also set out in Article 32(4) of the 1976 UNCITRAL Arbitration Rules.
(4) Article 31(4) of the 1985 Model Law is similar to Article 32(6) of the 1976 UNCITRAL Arbitration Rules, which provides:

> Copies of the award signed by the arbitrators shall be communicated to the parties by the arbitral tribunal.

Articles 32(3), (4) and (6) of the 1976 UNCITRAL Arbitration Rules are preserved as Articles 34(3), (4) and (6) of the 2013 UNCITRAL Arbitration Rules, which form part of the 2018 AIAC Arbitration Rules. The only change made in this regard is the substitution of the reference to 'three arbitrators' in Article 32(4) of the 1976 UNCITRAL Arbitration Rules with the words 'more than one arbitrator' in Article 34(4) of the

---

18. *See* Peter Binder, *International Commercial Arbitration and Conciliation in UNCITRAL Model Law Jurisdictions* (3rd edn, Sweet & Maxwell 2010) at para. 6.072.

2013 UNCITRAL Arbitration Rules. This change is to allow for a scenario where there is more than a sole arbitrator but not necessarily limited to three.

In addition to Article 34 of the 2013 UNCITRAL Arbitration Rules, Rule 12 of the 2018 AIAC Arbitration Rules provides:

Technical Review and Awards
1. Following the final oral or written submissions, the arbitral tribunal shall declare the proceedings closed. The arbitral tribunal's declaration and the date on which the proceedings are closed shall be communicated in writing to the Parties and to the Director. After this date, the Parties may not submit any further evidence or make any further submission with respect to the matters to be decided in the award.
2. The arbitral tribunal shall, before signing the award, submit its draft of the final award (the 'Draft Final Award'), to the Director within three months for a technical review. The time limit shall start to run from the date when the arbitral tribunal declares the proceedings closed pursuant to Rule 12(1).
3. The time limit may be extended by the arbitral tribunal with the consent of the Parties and upon consultation with the Director. The Director may further extend the time limit in the absence of consent between the Parties if deemed necessary.
4. The Director may, as soon as practicable and without affecting the arbitral tribunal's liberty of decision, draw the arbitral tribunal's attention to any perceived irregularity as to the form of the award and any errors in the calculation of interest and costs.
5. If there are no perceived irregularities pursuant to Rule 12(4), the Director shall notify the arbitral tribunal in writing that the technical review has been completed.
6. If there are perceived irregularities pursuant to Rule 12(4), the arbitral tribunal shall resubmit the Draft Final Award to the Director within 10 days from the date on which the arbitral tribunal is notified of such irregularities. The time limit for the arbitral tribunal to consider any irregularities under Rule 12(4) may be extended by the Director. Upon completion of the technical review, the Director shall notify the arbitral tribunal in writing of the completion of the technical review.
7. The arbitral tribunal shall deliver sufficient copies of the award to the Director. The award shall only be released to the Parties by the Director upon full settlement of the costs of arbitration.
8. The Director shall notify the Parties of its receipt of the award from the arbitral tribunal. The award shall be deemed to have been received by the Parties upon collection by hand by an authorised representative or upon delivery by registered post.
9. If the Parties reach a settlement after the arbitration has commenced, the arbitral tribunal shall, if so requested by the Parties, record the settlement in the form of an award made by the consent of the Parties. If the Parties do not require a consent award, the parties shall inform the Director that a settlement has been reached. Notwithstanding the settlement reached, the arbitration shall only be deemed concluded and the arbitral tribunal discharged upon full settlement of the costs of arbitration.
10. By agreeing to arbitration under the AIAC Arbitration Rules, the Parties undertake to carry out the award immediately and without delay, and they also irrevocably waive their rights to any form of appeal, review or recourse to any court or other judicial authority insofar as such waiver may be validly

made, and the Parties further agree that an award shall be final and binding on the Parties from the date it is made.

Sections 33(6), (7) and (8) were introduced by the Arbitration (Amendment) (No 2) Act 2018. Prior to amendments in 2018, section 33(6) provided:

Unless otherwise provided in the arbitration agreement, the arbitral tribunal may-

(a) award interest on any sum of money ordered to be paid by the award from the date of the award to the date of realisation; and
(b) determine the rate of interest.

§33.02 AWARD MUST BE IN WRITING

Section 33(1) of the Arbitration Act 2005 requires the award to be in writing. This requirement, which appears obvious, is mandatory for the purpose of certainty.[19]

§33.03 AWARD MUST BE SIGNED

Sections 33(1) and (2) of the Arbitration Act 2005 require the award to be signed. Where there is more than one arbitrator, a majority is sufficient.

This approach at first glance appears consistent with section 31(1). However, section 31(1) allows parties to agree on the decision-making process. Therefore, the parties may have agreed that the decisions are to be made otherwise than by a majority, for example by the presiding arbitrator. Section 33(2) does not expressly provide for such a scenario.[20]

The question therefore arises whether the requirements for a signature in sections 33(1) and (2) are mandatory. In this regard, a distinction has to be made between sections 33(1) and (2). Insofar as section 33(1) is concerned, the requirement for a signature is mandatory, as it is necessary for the sake of certainty.[21] However, with respect to section 33(2), given that it does not appear entirely consistent with section 31(1), the requirements may not need to be strictly complied with provided that what has been agreed by the parties has been complied with. For example, if the parties have agreed that the presiding arbitrator in a three-member arbitral tribunal is entitled to decide where there is no majority, the presiding arbitrator's signature alone should suffice.[22]

Section 31(2) of the Arbitration Act 2005 provides that reasons for the omitted signature must be stated. This provision applies to situations where a member of the

---

19. *See* Peter Binder, *International Commercial Arbitration and Conciliation in UNCITRAL Model Law Jurisdictions* (3rd edn, Sweet & Maxwell 2010) at para. 6.060; Analytical Commentary, Article 31, commentary.
20. *See* Analytical Commentary, Article 31, commentary 1.
21. *See* Analytical Commentary, Article 31, commentary 1.
22. *See* Peter Binder, *International Commercial Arbitration and Conciliation in UNCITRAL Model Law Jurisdictions* (3rd edn, Sweet & Maxwell 2010) at paras 6.060 and 6.061.

arbitral tribunal has passed away, is unwell or simply cannot be reached. This provision also applies to situations where a member of the arbitral tribunal declines to sign the award. Hence, the question of whether such a member of the arbitral tribunal is entitled to give a dissenting opinion is left open by the Arbitration Act 2005, like the 1985 Model Law. The Analytical Commentary suggests that the question is one of procedure that can be determined, by the parties or, failing which, the arbitral tribunal under Articles 19(1) and (2) of the 1985 Model Law, to which sections 21(1) and (2) of the Arbitration Act 2005 correspond.[23]

Apart from this, it would appear that a member of the arbitral tribunal would be entitled to give any reason for omitting her signature. There does not appear to be any restriction in this regard.[24]

§33.04   THE AWARD MUST CONTAIN REASONS

Section 33(3) of the Arbitration Act 2005, as a general rule, requires the arbitral tribunal to give their reasons in an award. Where this general rule applies, the High Court, in *Tanjung Langsat Port Sdn Bhd v. Trafigura Pte Ltd & Another Case* [2016] 4 CLJ 927, clarified that the question is whether the award taken as a whole informs the parties of the basis on which the arbitral tribunal reached their decision. Although detailed reasons are not required, it was insufficient for the arbitral tribunal to merely refer to submissions and documents. The High Court, in *Tanjung Langsat supra* at paragraphs 81, 82, 87, *inter alia*, held:

> [81] In the Indian case of *Som Datt Builders Ltd v. State of Kerala* [2009] INSC 1600, the Supreme Court of India at 310 [25]:
> 25. The requirement of reasons in support of the award under Section 31(3) is not an empty formality. It guarantees fair and legitimate consideration of the controversy by the arbitral tribunal. It is true that arbitral tribunal is not expected to write judgment like a court nor it is expected to give elaborate and detailed reasons in support of its finding/s but mere noticing the submissions of the parties or reference to documents is no substitute for reasons which the arbitral tribunal is obliged to give. Howsoever brief these may be, reasons must be indicated in the award as that would reflect thought process leading to a particular conclusion. To satisfy the requirement of Section 31(3), the reasons must be stated by the arbitral tribunal upon which the award is based; want of reasons would make such award legally flawed.
> (emphasis added)
>
> [82] ... Whilst it is true that s. 33(3) of the AA 2005 provides that an award shall state the reasons upon which it is based, in *Som Datt* it is stated the extent of the judgment required of the arbitrator is as reflected in the statement emboldened in para. 81 above.
>
> ...

---

23. *See* Analytical Commentary, Article 31, commentary 2.
24. *See* Peter Binder, *International Commercial Arbitration and Conciliation in UNCITRAL Model Law Jurisdictions* (3rd edn, Sweet & Maxwell 2010) at paras 6.059.

[87] Applying the principles which can be gleaned from *TMM Division* which is of persuasive value, it cannot be gainsaid that when the partial award is 'taken as a whole', it more than adequately 'informs the parties of the bases on which the (majority tribunal) reached its decision' on the award of damages for Trafigura's loss of use of the facility.

There are two exceptions to this general rule. First, where the parties have agreed to dispense with reasons and, second, where there is an award on agreed terms.

With respect to the first exception, the Analytical Commentary suggests that the agreement may be express or implied. An agreement may be express where a reference is made to arbitration rules that dispense with the need for reasons. An agreement may be implied where a dispute is submitted in an established arbitral system where reasons are not required.[25]

Section 33(3) represents a compromise between the common law system and the civil law system. The common law system includes certain types of arbitration, where reasons are dispensed with for reasons of speed and to make the award more difficult to challenge. The civil law system on the other hand favours reasons for the beneficial influence it is said to have on the award and because it makes the award easier to understand. Section 33(3) represents a compromise as it requires reasons but allows the parties to agree to dispense with it.[26]

An award that does not include reasons may be liable to be set aside on the grounds that the arbitral procedure was not complied with under section 37(1)(a)(vi) of the Arbitration Act 2005.[27]

However, the absence of reasons is unlikely to amount to breach of the rules of natural justice, rendering the award liable to be set aside under sections 37(1)(b)(ii) and 37(2)(b). This was clarified by the High Court, in *Tanjung Langsat supra* at paragraph 78:

> ... *nemo judex in causa sua* (rule against bias) and *audi alteram partem* (the right to be heard) comprise the twin pillars of the rules of natural justice. Thus it is evident that since the duty to give reasons is not part of the rules of natural justice, it is my respectful view that it is not a ground on which an arbitral award may be set aside under s. 37(1)(b)(ii) read with s. 37(2)(b) of the AA 2005 ... .

§33.05 THE AWARD MUST STATE ITS DATE

Section 33(4) of the Arbitration Act 2005 requires the arbitral tribunal to date the award. Although this requirement is expressed in section 33(4) in mandatory terms, the absence of a date is unlikely to render the award invalid.[28]

---

25. *See* Analytical Commentary, Article 31, commentary 3.
26. *See* Peter Binder, *International Commercial Arbitration and Conciliation in UNCITRAL Model Law Jurisdictions* (3rd edn, Sweet & Maxwell 2010) at para. 6.063.
27. *See* Peter Binder, *International Commercial Arbitration and Conciliation in UNCITRAL Model Law Jurisdictions* (3rd edn, Sweet & Maxwell 2010) at para. 6.063.
28. *See* Peter Binder, *International Commercial Arbitration and Conciliation in UNCITRAL Model Law Jurisdictions* (3rd edn, Sweet & Maxwell 2010) at para. 6.066.

The date stated in the award may be rebutted by the parties or the arbitrators. The position may be taken that the date on the award is earlier or later than the date the award was actually rendered.[29]

It is also important to note that for the purposes of correction, interpretation or setting aside of the award under sections 35 and 37 of the Arbitration Act 2005, the date from which time starts to run is the date of receipt of the award and not the date of the award.

§33.06 THE AWARD MUST STATE ITS SEAT

Section 33(4) of the Arbitration Act 2005 also requires the arbitral tribunal to state the seat of the arbitration in the award. Section 33(4) further provides that the award shall be deemed to have been made at the seat stated therein. This is an irrebuttable presumption. This presumption recognizes that the making of an award is a legal act, which in practice is not one factual act, but deliberations at various places, as well as through telephone and correspondence.[30]

Although the requirement to state the seat is expressed in mandatory terms in section 33(4), the absence of such a statement is unlikely to render the award invalid.[31]

§33.07 THE AWARD MUST BE DELIVERED

Section 33(5) of the Arbitration Act 2005 requires the award to be delivered to each party. The delivery of the award is of significance, as the date of receipt starts time running for the purpose of an application to correct, interpret or set aside an award under sections 35 and 37 of the Arbitration Act 2005. A party is also required to produce a copy of the award for the purposes of an application for recognition and enforcement under section 38 of the Arbitration Act 2005. Apart from the delivery of the award, the Arbitration Act 2005 does not require any other administrative act, such as filing, registration or deposit of the award.[32]

The Arbitration Act 2005 does not expressly provide when the award becomes binding. During the drafting of the 1985 Model Law, the following three options were considered:

(1) an award becomes binding on the date it is made;
(2) an award becomes binding on the date it is delivered; or
(3) an award becomes binding on the date on which the period of time for making an application to set aside the award has expired.

---

29. *See* UNCITRAL Report at para. 254.
30. *See* Analytical Commentary, Article 31, commentary 5.
31. *See* Peter Binder, *International Commercial Arbitration and Conciliation in UNCITRAL Model Law Jurisdictions* (3rd edn, Sweet & Maxwell 2010) at para. 6.066.
32. *See* Analytical Commentary Article 31, commentary 6.

However, none of these options were adopted in the 1985 Model Law, or subsequently in the Arbitration Act 2005. As such, the date on which the award becomes binding remains ambiguous.

§33.08 ADDITIONAL REQUIREMENTS AGREED BY THE PARTIES

Although the requirements considered under §33.02-§33.07 are mandatory, the parties are free to agree upon additional requirements as a matter of procedure under section 21(1) of the Arbitration Act 2005. In practice, this is usually done by the parties agreeing on a particular set of arbitration rules.

For example, if the parties have agreed upon the 2018 AIAC Arbitration Rules, the additional requirements of these rules as set out in Rule 12 would need to be complied with.

The additional requirements of Rule 12 of the 2018 AIAC Arbitration Rules, which are quoted under §33.01, include:

(1) the requirement that the award be rendered in draft to the Director of the AIAC within three months of final submissions;
(2) the requirement that the Director of the AIAC may conduct a technical review of the award;
(3) the requirement that the award will only be released to the parties upon full settlement of costs; and
(4) more detailed requirements on the date the award is deemed to be received by the parties.

§33.09 INTEREST

Sections 33(6)-(8) of the Arbitration Act 2005 adopt the familiar 'two-level system' found in the 1985 Model Law. First, the parties are free to agree on the power of the arbitral tribunal to award interest, and, second, in the absence of agreement, the arbitral tribunal is given the default power to award interest.

[A] Party Autonomy

With respect to the parties' freedom to agree on the arbitral tribunal's power to award interest, this is usually done in practice by the adoption of arbitration rules in accordance with section 2(2)(c) of the Arbitration Act 2005.

[B] Default Powers

Sections 33(6)-(8) of the Arbitration Act 2005 expressly allow for the arbitral tribunal to grant pre- and post-award interest. Prior to the amendments in 2018, section 33(6)

Chapter 6: Making of Award and Termination of Proceedings §33.09[B]

expressly allowed for the grant of post-award interest, but the position on pre-award interest was unclear. §33.09[B][1] and §33.09[B][2] *infra* consider the position on pre- and post-award interest prior to the amendments in 2018.

[1] Post-award Interest

In the event the parties have not agreed on the arbitral tribunal's power to award interest, prior to the amendments in 2018, the default power under section 33(6) applied. This default power expressly included the power to grant post-award interest, as it referred to the period between the date of the award and the date of realization of the award.

This was confirmed by the High Court, in *Quality Property Development Sdn Bhd v. Xavier Francis & Anor* [2014] 1 LNS 67 at paragraph 32:

> On the issue of interest in Question (vii), the Arbitrator had allowed interest at the rate of 4% per annum from the date of the award to the date of realisation. There is nothing illegal with this as section 33 of the Arbitration Act 2005 allows the Arbitrator to award interest from date of the award to the date of realisation.

The current sections 33(6) and (8) similarly allow for the arbitral tribunal to grant post-award interest.

[2] Pre-award Interest

The question of whether section 33(6), prior to the amendments in 2018, included the default power to award pre-award interest was less clear. Section 33(6) did not previously expressly grant such a power. However, the question remained as to whether such a power was implicit.

The High Court, in *Kerajaan Malaysia (Kementerian Sumber Asli dan Alam Sekitar) v. Kumpulan Sakata Sdn Bhd* [2016] 7 CLJ 417 at paragraphs 14-18, 20-27; *Kerajaan Malaysia v. Tasja Sdn Bhd* [2016] 6 CLJ 738 at paragraphs 51-53, 56 to 58, 64, 71; and *Kejuruteraan Bintai Kindenko Sdn Bhd v. Serdang Baru Properties Sdn Bhd & Another Case (No 2)* [2018] 1 CLJ 369 at paragraphs 35 and 36, while accepting that it was bound by the judgment of the Court of Appeal, in *Far East Holdings Bhd & Anor v. Majlis Ugama Islam dan Adat Resam Melayu Pahang & Another Appeal* [2015] 8 CLJ 58 at paragraph 98, lucidly summarized the arguments in favour of allowing pre-award interest:

> (1) that, under sections 30(1) and (5) of the Arbitration Act 2005, the arbitral tribunal should decide the dispute in accordance with the substantive law of Malaysia, the terms of the agreement and the usages of the trade;
> (2) with respect to the substantive law of Malaysia, section 11 of the Civil Law Act 1956 provides that:
> Power of Courts to award interest on debts and damages
> > 11. In any proceedings tried in any Court for the recovery of any debt or damages, the Court may, if it thinks fit, order that there shall be included in the sum for which judgment is given interest at such rate as it thinks fit

on the whole or any part of the debt or damages for the whole or any part of the period between the date when the cause of action arose and the date of the judgment:
Provided that nothing in this section —
(a) shall authorize the giving of interest upon interest;
(b) shall apply in relation to any debt upon which interest is payable as of right whether by virtue of any agreement or otherwise; or
(c) shall affect the damages recoverable for the dishonour of a bill of exchange.

(3) with respect to the arbitration agreement, the arbitral tribunal had an implied power to grant pre-award interest;
(4) the courts had consistently taken the position, in the light of the foregoing, under section 21 of the Arbitration Act 1952, that the arbitral tribunal had the power to award pre-award interest;[33]
(5) that Parliament is presumed to know the law relating to an arbitral tribunal's power to grant pre-award interest at the time of enacting the Arbitration Act 2005. The Act should accordingly not be taken as effecting a fundamental alteration in the law relating to the arbitral tribunal's power to grant pre-award interest without words that unmistakably point to that conclusion;
(6) in this regard, section 33(6) merely provides for the arbitral tribunal's power to grant post award interest and is silent on pre-award interest;
(7) that the inability of an arbitrator to grant pre-award interest would be contrary to the objective of uniformity sought to be achieved by enacting the 1985 Model Law as the Arbitration Act 2005 in Malaysia; and
(8) that the inability of the arbitral tribunal to grant pre-award interest would make Malaysia less attractive as a seat of arbitration.

Despite these persuasive arguments, the Federal Court, in *Far East Holdings Bhd & Anor v. Majlis Ugama Islam dan Adat Resam Melayu Pahang (and 2 other Appeals)* [2017] 8 AMR 313 at paragraph 187, confirmed that, in the absence of agreement, the arbitral tribunal does not have the power to grant pre-award interest:

> Unless otherwise provided in the arbitration agreement, an arbitrator could only award post-award interest. The AA 2005 does not contemplate the award of pre-award interest, unless so provided in the arbitration agreement. There was no indication that pre-award interest was provided in the arbitration agreement. Pre-award interest could not be awarded. Post-award interest may be granted. But since post-award interest was not pleaded, it would not seem fair that the discretion to award interest should be exercised in favour of post-award interest.

Soon after, the Arbitration (Amendment) (No 2) Act 2018 reversed the effect of the judgment of the Federal Court, in *Far East supra*, by expressly allowing the arbitral tribunal to grant pre-award interest by the amended section 33(6).

---

33. See *Lian Hup Manufacturing Co Sdn Bhd v. Unitata Bhd* [1994] 3 CLJ 338; *Raja Lope & Tan Co v. Malayan Flour Mills Bhd* [2000] 6 CLJ 194; *Shamelin Holdings Sdn Bhd v. Mohd Anuar Ahmad* [2006] 8 CLJ 622; *Leong Kum Whay v. QBE Insurance (M) Sdn Bhd* [2006] 1 CLJ 1.

34. Termination of Proceedings

(1) The arbitral proceedings shall be terminated by a final award or by an order of the arbitral tribunal in accordance with subsection (2).

(2) The arbitral tribunal shall order the termination of the arbitral proceedings where —
   (a) the claimant withdraws the claim, unless the respondent objects to the withdrawal and the arbitral tribunal recognizes the respondent's legitimate interest in obtaining a final settlement of the dispute;
   (b) the parties agree on the termination of the proceedings; or
   (c) the arbitral tribunal finds that the continuation of the proceedings has for any other reason become unnecessary or impossible.

(3) Subject to the provisions of section 35 and subsection 37(6), the mandate of the arbitral tribunal shall terminate with the termination of the arbitral proceedings.

(4) Unless otherwise provided by any written law, the death of a party does not terminate –
   (a) the arbitral proceedings; or
   (b) the authority of the arbitral tribunal.

§34.01 INTRODUCTION

Section 34 of the Arbitration Act 2005 provides for the termination of the arbitral proceedings in five circumstances:

(1) by a final award;
(2) by withdrawal of the claim;
(3) by agreement;
(4) by lack of necessity or impossibility; and
(5) by the death of a party.

These five grounds for termination are considered in detail in §34.02-§34.06 *infra*.

There are additional grounds for the termination of arbitral proceedings that are not set out in section 34. For example, section 27(a) of the Arbitration Act 2005 provides for the termination of the arbitral proceedings if the claimant fails to communicate the statement of claim, and section 32(1) of the Arbitration Act 2005 provides for the termination of the arbitral proceedings if the dispute is settled.

Sections 34(1), (2) and (3) of the Arbitration Act 2005 are based on Articles 32(1), (2) and (3) of the 1985 Model Law respectively save for minor stylistic changes. Section 34(4) of the Arbitration Act 2005 is based on Articles 32(4) and (5) of Schedule 1 of the New Zealand Arbitration Act 1996.

The purpose of section 34 of the Arbitration Act 2005 is:

(1) to provide guidance for this last phase of the arbitral proceedings;
(2) to provide for the consequential termination of the mandate of the arbitral tribunal; and
(3) to provide for certainty with respect to the point of time of termination of the proceedings.

The High Court, in *Segamat Parking Services Sdn Bhd v. Majlis Daerah Segamat Utara & Another Case* [2009] 1 CLJ 942 at paragraph 10, clarified that the 'arbitral proceedings' referred to in section 34 are the proceedings exclusively before the arbitral tribunal and not any subsequent or related proceedings.[34]

§34.02 FINAL AWARD

Section 34(1) of the Arbitration Act 2005 provides that the arbitral proceedings shall be terminated by a final award.

The words 'final award' are not defined in the Arbitration Act 2005, although the word 'award' is defined in section 2(1) and is considered in §2.02 *supra*.

Based on the definition of 'award' in section 2(1), a final award would appear to be a decision by an arbitral tribunal on the substance of the dispute that is not an interlocutory order. To this, it can be added that the final award is the decision at the arbitral tribunal that completes and fully disposes of the substance of the dispute.[35]

§34.03 WITHDRAWAL

Section 34(2)(a) of the Arbitration Act 2005 provides that the arbitral tribunal shall order the termination of the arbitral proceedings upon the withdrawal of the claim unless the respondent objects and is found to have a legitimate interest in the final settlement of the dispute.

There was concern about this provision when the 1985 Model Law was being drafted, as it was felt that a claimant might be compelled to proceed with a claim against a respondent it did not wish to. However, the provision achieves a balance, by granting the arbitral tribunal a discretion whether to terminate or proceed with the arbitration.[36] Factors that are likely to be considered by the arbitral tribunal are:

(1) the stage at which the claim is being withdrawn;
(2) the likelihood of the claimant commencing fresh proceedings; and
(3) the existence of a counterclaim.

With respect to the first of these factors, it should be borne in mind that under section 27(a) of the Arbitration Act 2005, the arbitral tribunal mandatorily is required

---

34. *See* Analytical Commentary, Article 32, commentaries 1 and 2.
35. *See* Peter Binder, *International Commercial Arbitration and Conciliation in UNCITRAL Model Law Jurisdictions* (3rd edn, Sweet & Maxwell 2010) at para. 6.066.
36. *See* UNCITRAL Report at para. 262.

to terminate the arbitral proceeding if the Statement of Claim is not communicated. Depending on the circumstances, the later the claimant seeks to withdraw the claim; the less likely is the arbitral tribunal to allow this.

§34.04 AGREEMENT

Section 34(2)(b) of the Arbitration Act 2005 provides that the arbitral tribunal shall order the termination of the arbitral proceedings where the parties agree on the termination.

Unlike section 34(2)(a), under section 34(2)(b), the arbitral tribunal has no discretion and must terminate the arbitral proceedings upon agreement by the parties. This conforms with the principle of party autonomy in arbitration.

Section 34(2)(b) does not expressly provide for a situation where the parties have agreed in advance that the arbitration agreement will terminate, for example, within so many days after the date of the arbitration agreement. Therefore, there remains some uncertainty whether such a provision would be enforceable. It is submitted that there is no reason in principle why such an agreement should not be enforceable.

§34.05 UNNECESSARY OR IMPOSSIBLE

Section 34(2)(c) of the Arbitration Act 2005 allows the arbitral tribunal to terminate the arbitral proceedings where it finds its continuance would be unnecessary or impossible.

The words 'unnecessary' and 'impossible' are not defined in the Arbitration Act 2005. The continuation of the arbitral proceedings will be unnecessary where there has been a settlement or the dispute has been resolved by another forum, for example the courts. Insofar as settlements are concerned, this is specifically dealt with by section 32(1) of the Arbitration Act 2005. Therefore, section 34(2)(c) is probably intended to cover the latter scenario where the dispute has already been resolved by another forum and other residual situations where the continuance of the arbitral proceedings will be unnecessary.

The word 'impossible' has a specific legal meaning in Malaysia, given that it is used in section 57 of the Contracts Act 1950, which provides:

> 57. Agreement to do impossible act
> (1) An agreement to do an act impossible in itself is void.
>   Contract to do act afterwards becoming impossible or unlawful
> (2) A contract to do an act which, after the contract is made, becomes impossible, or by reason of some event which the promisor could not prevent, unlawful, becomes void when the act becomes impossible or unlawful.
>   Compensation for loss through non-performance of act known to be impossible or unlawful
> (3) Where one person has promised to do something which he knew, or, with reasonable diligence, might have known, and which the promisee did not know, to be impossible or unlawful, the promisor must make compensation to

the promisee for any loss which the promisee sustains through the non-performance of the promise.

ILLUSTRATIONS

(a) A agrees with B to discover treasure by magic. The agreement is void.
(b) A and B contract to marry each other. Before the time fixed for the marriage, A goes mad. The contract becomes void.
(c) A contracts to marry B, being already married to C, and being forbidden by the law to which he is subject to practise polygamy. A must make compensation to B for the loss caused to her by the non-performance of his promise.
(d) A contracts to take in cargo for B at a foreign port. A's Government afterwards declares war against the country in which the port is situated. The contract becomes void when war is declared.
(e) A contracts to act at a theatre for six months in consideration of a sum paid in advance by B. On several occasions A is too ill to act. The contract to act on those occasions becomes void.

The test to be applied in relation to section 57 of the Contracts Act 1950 has been set out by the Federal Court, in *Ramli bin Zakaria & Ors v. Government of Malaysia* [1982] 2 MLJ 257 at pages 261-262:

> In short it would appear that where after a contract has been entered into there is a change of circumstances but the changed circumstances do not render a fundamental or radical change in the obligation originally undertaken to make the performance of the contract something radically different from that originally undertaken, the contract does not become impossible and it is not discharged by frustration.

Similarly, the Federal Court, in *Pacific Forest Industries Sdn Bhd & Anor v. Lin Wen-Chih & Anor* [2009] 6 MLJ 293 at paragraph 22, held:

> A contract does not become frustrated merely because it becomes difficult to perform ... A contract is frustrated when subsequent to its formation, a change of circumstances renders the contract legally or physically impossible to be performed ... .

It is submitted that this test will similarly be applied to determine whether the continuance of the arbitral proceedings will be 'impossible'. The continuation of the proceedings will be impossible where the claimant does not communicate his statement of claim, does not proceed with the claim or withdraws the claim. However, all of these situations are specifically dealt with by sections 27(a), (d) and 34(2)(a) of the Arbitration Act 2005 respectively. Therefore, it is difficult to envisage the situation section 34(2)(c) is intended to cover other than residual matters that may be covered by the general test.

The High Court, in *The Government of India v. Vedanta Ltd (legal successor to Cairn India Ltd) & Anor* [2018] MLJU 630, decided that delay alone would not make the continuation of arbitral proceedings impossible. As to abandonment, this could be either expressly agreed between the parties or implied. If abandonment was to be implied, there must be clear and unequivocal conduct of the parties having abandoned the arbitral proceedings. In this context, the High Court, in *Vedanta supra* at paragraphs 162 and 164, held:

> [162] Thus an Arbitral Tribunal may not terminate an arbitral proceeding for want of prosecution on account of delay unless contractually so empowered by the agreement of the parties under the lex arbitri. I would agree with learned counsel for the Defendants that there can be no frustration, self-induced or otherwise, of a reference to Arbitration solely on account of delay.
>
> …
>
> [164] With respect to the issue of abandonment, that must certainly be facts-centric and short of a clear, unequivocal conduct of having abandoned the Arbitration proceedings, this Court must be slow to infer one when to do so would be to frustrate the parties express and original intention to resolve fully and finally the disputes between the parties which in this case had been resolved partially with the issuance of a Partial Award on liability and awaiting a Final Award on quantification if there are still disputes on it.

§34.06 DEATH

Section 34(4) of the Arbitration Act 2005 provides that the death of a party does not terminate the arbitral proceedings.

35. *Correction and Interpretation of Award or Additional Award*

(1) A party, within thirty days of the receipt of the award, unless any other period of time has been agreed upon by the parties —
  (a) upon notice to the other party, may request the arbitral tribunal to correct in the award any error in computation, any clerical or typographical error or other error of similar nature; or
  (b) upon notice to and with the agreement of the other party, may request the arbitral tribunal to give an interpretation of a specific point or part of the award.
(2) Where the arbitral tribunal considers the request made under subsection (1) to be justified, it shall make the correction or give the interpretation within thirty days of the receipt of the request and such interpretation shall form part of the award.
(3) The arbitral tribunal may correct any error of the type referred to in paragraph (1)(a) on its own initiative within thirty days of the date of the award.
(4) Unless otherwise agreed by the parties, a party may, within thirty days of the receipt of the award and upon notice to the other party, request the arbitral tribunal to make an additional award as to claims presented in the arbitral proceedings but omitted from the award.
(5) Where the arbitral tribunal considers the request under subsection (4) to be justified, it shall make the additional award within sixty days from the receipt of such request.
(6) The arbitral tribunal may, where it thinks necessary, extend the period of time within which it shall make a correction, interpretation or an additional award under this section.
(7) The provisions of section 33 shall apply to a correction or interpretation of the award or to an additional award.

§35.01 INTRODUCTION

Section 35 of the Arbitration Act 2005 allows for a correction, interpretation or addition to the award after it has been made. Section 35 is necessary because section 34 provides that the mandate of the arbitral tribunal terminates upon the final award being made.

Section 35 of the Arbitration Act 2005 is based on Article 33 of the 1985 Model Law. In particular:

(1) sections 35(1) and (2) are based on Article 33(1);
(2) section 35(3) is based on Article 33(2);
(3) sections 35(4) and (5) are based on Article 33(3);
(4) section 35(6) is based on Article 33(4); and
(5) section 35(7) is based on Article 33(5).

The only significant change is the inclusion of the words 'it thinks' in section 35(6), which are not found in Article 33(4). These words have been included to emphasize that the arbitral tribunal has the discretion to extend the time for making a correction, interpretation or addition to the award.

Article 33 of the 1985 Model Law is in turn based on Articles 36-38 of the 1976 UNCITRAL Arbitration Rules.

These provisions of the 1976 UNCITRAL Arbitration Rules have been largely retained in the 2013 UNCITRAL Arbitration Rules, which form part of the 2018 AIAC Arbitration Rules. Articles 37-39 of the 2013 UNCITRAL Arbitration Rules provide:

Interpretation of the award
Article 37
1. Within 30 days after the receipt of the award, a party, with notice to the other parties, may request that the arbitral tribunal give an interpretation of the award.
2. The interpretation shall be given in writing within 45 days after the receipt of the request. The interpretation shall form part of the award and the provisions of article 34, paragraphs 2 to 6, shall apply.

Correction of the award
Article 38
1. Within 30 days after the receipt of the award, a party, with notice to the other parties, may request the arbitral tribunal to correct in the award any error in computation, any clerical or typographical error, or any error or omission of a similar nature. If the arbitral tribunal considers that the request is justified, it shall make the correction within 45 days of receipt of the request.
2. The arbitral tribunal may within 30 days after the communication of the award make such corrections on its own initiative.
3. Such corrections shall be in writing and shall form part of the award. The provisions of article 34, paragraphs 2 to 6, shall apply.

Additional award
Article 39
1. Within 30 days after the receipt of the termination order or the award, a party, with notice to the other parties, may request the arbitral tribunal to make an award or an additional award as to claims presented in the arbitral proceedings but not decided by the arbitral tribunal.
2. If the arbitral tribunal considers the request for an award or additional award to be justified, it shall render or complete its award within 60 days after the receipt of the request. The arbitral tribunal may extend, if necessary, the period of time within which it shall make the award.
3. When such an award or additional award is made, the provisions of article 34, paragraphs 2 to 6, shall apply.

The significant alteration between the UNCITRAL Arbitration Rules and the 1985 Model Law is in the provision dealing with the interpretation of the award, which is considered in §35.03 *infra*.

The arbitral tribunal's ability to correct, interpret or make an additional award is considered separately below. Before moving to these specific issues three general matters are considered here, that is the interpretation of section 35, time and the form of the correction, interpretation or addition.

[A]   **Strictly Construed**

The courts will strictly construe section 35. The arbitral tribunal will not be construed to have any wider powers than are expressly provided for in section 35. This is confirmed by the judgment of the High Court, in *Kelana Erat Sdn Bhd v. Niche Properties Sdn Bhd & Another Case* [2013] 4 CLJ 1172 at paragraph 52:

> In any event I am of the view that the issue of 'clarifications' sought by the respondent is totally misplaced as there is no provision in the Arbitration Act 2005 or the UNCITRAL Rules which provides for 'clarifications' of an award. Sections 35(1)(a) and (b) of the Act only provides for the arbitrator to correct any error in computation, any clerical or typographical error or other error of similar nature or interpretation of a specific point of part of the award. This was not what was sought by the respondent of the arbitrator.

This strict interpretation is in accordance with the purpose of sections 34 and 35, where the mandate of the arbitral tribunal terminates with the final award being made save for specific exceptions.

[B]   **Time**

Time for the purpose of other provisions of the Arbitration Act 2005 will only start to run from the date of disposal of a request for the correction, interpretation or addition. For example, the ninety-day period for applying to set aside an award under section 37(a) expressly only runs from the disposal of such a request under section 35. Although this is not expressly provided for, in the context of a reference of questions of law under section 42(2), the High Court, in *Kluang Health Care Sdn Bhd v. Lee Yong Beng & Another Case* [2016] 1 CLJ 281 at paragraphs 43-46, confirmed that time would only start to run from the disposal of such a request.

[C]   **Form**

Any correction, interpretation or addition to the award must comply with the requirements as to form and content in section 33. This is expressly provided for in section 35(7) of the Arbitration Act 2005.

§35.02   CORRECTION

Section 35 of the Arbitration Act 2005 allows for the correction of an award. The section only allows for the correction of errors, which include computational and clerical errors. The type of error likely to be corrected under this section is an obvious error on the face of the award.

Section 35 allows for such errors to be corrected upon request either by a party or by the arbitral tribunal on its own initiative. Where an application is made by a party, the application must be made within thirty days of receipt of the award. The arbitral tribunal may then make the correction within thirty days of the request if it considers the request justified. The arbitral tribunal may extend this period where it thinks it necessary. Where the correction is made at the arbitral tribunal's initiative, such correction must be made within thirty days of the date of the award. The arbitral tribunal may extend this period, where it thinks it necessary.

These provisions are non-derogable save that the parties may agree upon a different period of time for the making of a request under section 35(1)(a) of the Arbitration Act 2005.[37]

§35.03 INTERPRETATION

Section 35 allows for the interpretation of an award after it is made. This gave rise to concern during the drafting of the 1985 Model Law that parties may attempt to revisit the merits of the award and harass the arbitral tribunal in attempting to do so. There was also concern about the finality of the award when a request was pending and the relationship between such a request and an application to set aside.

On the other hand, it was argued that in international arbitration the award might be written in a language other than an arbitrator's mother tongue and this may give rise to ambiguities that justify an interpretation.[38]

As a compromise, two restrictions are placed within section 35. First, a request may only be made of a 'specific point or part' of an award. Second, a request may only be made with the agreement of the other party.

Neither of these restrictions is found in Article 37 of the 2013 UNCITRAL Arbitration Rules, which form part of the 2018 AIAC Arbitration Rules. However, as section 35(1)(b) of the Arbitration Act 2005 is a non-derogable provision save for the time limit, it is submitted that these two restrictions would apply even if the 2018 AIAC Arbitration Rules have been agreed upon.

Section 35 allows for a request to be made with the agreement of the other party for an interpretation of the award within thirty days of the receipt of the award. The arbitral tribunal may then, if it considers the request justified, give the interpretation within thirty days of receipt of the request. The arbitral tribunal may extend this period, where the arbitral tribunal considers it necessary.

Section 35 does not allow for the arbitral tribunal to interpret the award on its own initiative, unlike corrections to the award.

§35.04 ADDITIONAL AWARD

Section 35 allows for a party to request an additional award for claims that are omitted from the award. Such a request must be made within thirty days. The arbitral tribunal then has sixty days to make an additional award if it thinks the request justified. The

---

37. *See* Peter Binder, *International Commercial Arbitration and Conciliation in UNCITRAL Model Law Jurisdictions* (3rd edn, Sweet & Maxwell 2010) at para. 6.103.
38. *See* UNCITRAL Report at paras 266, 267.

arbitral tribunal may extend this period, where it considers such an extension necessary.

A longer period is allowed for an additional award, as compared to a correction or interpretation, as it is usually a more difficult and time-consuming process.[39]

Unlike the provisions governing requests for corrections and interpretations, the provisions on additional awards are derogable. The parties are accordingly free to agree that the arbitral tribunal shall not have the power to make an additional award. However, this may result in the whole or part of the award being set aside. And, unlike the provisions on corrections, the arbitral tribunal may not on its own initiative make an additional award.

---

39. *See* Analytical Commentary, Article 33 commentary 2.

36. An Award is Final and Binding

(1) An award made by an arbitral tribunal pursuant to an arbitration agreement shall be final and binding on the parties and may be relied upon by any party by way of defence, set-off or otherwise in any proceedings in any court.

(2) The arbitral tribunal shall not vary, amend, correct, review, add to or revoke an award which has been made except as specifically provided for in section 35.

§36.01 INTRODUCTION

Section 36 of the Arbitration Act 2005 provides that an award shall be final, binding and shall not be varied except in accordance with section 35.

There is no identical provision to section 36 in the 1985 Model Law, although elements of section 36 can be seen in Articles 34(1) and 35(1).

Section 36 of the Arbitration Act 2005 is non-derogable. However, there is nothing to prevent the parties from adding to this provision. This may be done by the adoption of arbitration rules. For example, Rule 12(10) of the 2018 AIAC Arbitration Rules provides:

> By agreeing to arbitration under the AIAC Arbitration Rules, the Parties undertake to carry out the award immediately and without delay, and they also irrevocably waive their rights to any form of appeal, review or recourse to any court or other judicial authority insofar as such waiver may be validly made, and the Parties further agree that an award shall be final and binding on the Parties from the date it is made.

The extent to which such a provision may narrow or limit a party's right of recourse against an award is considered under §36.03 *infra*.

§36.02 FINAL AND BINDING

Section 36(1) of the Arbitration Act 2005 provides that an award shall be final and binding. The courts recognize that under this provision there is to be minimal interference by the courts and that there is to be no appeal against an award.

In this context, the High Court, in *Taman Bandar Baru Masai Sdn Bhd v. Dindings Corporation Sdn Bhd* [2010] 5 CLJ 83 at paragraph 33(c), held:

> Taman says the arbitrator's breach of natural justice and attitude of biasness warrants the court not to register the award as judgment on the grounds of public policy in reliance of s. 39(1)(b)(ii). And relies on pre-2005 cases which do not deal with AA 2005. I will say AA 2005 makes it compulsory for courts to respect the decision of arbitrators and only minimum intervention is allowed. In this respect, it must not be forgotten that it is the parties who selected the arbitrator and s. 36 of AA 2005 makes the award final, binding and conclusive. And real proof is

required to be shown before the court can meddle with the award. In the past, it was easily meddled. No more under AA 2005, without proof.

And, the High Court, in *Kelana Erat Sdn Bhd v. Niche Properties Sdn Bhd & Another Case* [2013] 4 CLJ 1172 at paragraphs 13 and 14, held:

> [13] An award of the arbitrator made under the Arbitration Act 2005 is for all intents and purposes final and binding. ... .
>
> [14] It is by and large immune from any interference by a court, much less to set it aside unless it is infected with the infirmities identified in s. 37(1)(a)(i) to (vi) and 37(1)(b) of the Arbitration Act 2005.

The High Court, in *Sagau Batu Bala v. Zaharah Mustapha Raja Sewa & Anor And Other Cases* [2013] 10 CLJ 683 at paragraph 23, also held:

> It is settled law that an arbitrator's award is final, binding and conclusive and can only be challenged in exceptional circumstances. Even if an arbitrator had erred by drawing wrong inferences of fact from the evidence before him be it oral or documentary, that in itself would not be sufficient to warrant the setting aside of the award. The power to set aside an award under the Act can only be exercised where the arbitrator has misconducted himself or the award has been improperly procured ... .

Further, the Court of Appeal, in *Awangku Dewa Pgn Momin & Ors v. Superintendent of Lands And Surveys, Limbang Division* [2015] 3 CLJ 1 at paragraph 12, held:

> There is a basic and important legislative policy codified in our Arbitration Act 2005, and that policy is that the award of an arbitrator is final and binding. There is no recourse to a court of law by way of an appeal. This is clearly stated by s. 36 of the Act ... .

Subsequently, the Court of Appeal, in *Antara Steel Mills Sdn Bhd v. CIMB Insurance Brokers Sdn Bhd* [2015] 5 CLJ 1018 at paragraphs 18-20, held:

> [18] ... Under the Arbitration Act, there is no right of appeal against the decision of the arbitral tribunal. The decision of the arbitral tribunal is final, binding and unappealable ...
>
> [19] Thus, there is nothing creative or innovative on the part of the parties when they entered into an agreement at the commencement of the arbitration proceedings to state that the award of the arbitral tribunal is final, binding and unappealable. The parties are just restating what is already provided for in s. 36 of the Arbitration Act ... .
>
> [20] We do, however, note that the learned Judicial Commissioner has in her grounds of judgment cited ss. 37 and 42 of the Arbitration Act as if these provisions provide for an appeal against the award of the arbitral tribunal. We do not propose to labour on these provisions. It is sufficient for us just to state here that the learned Judicial Commissioner, with respect, was mistaken in her grounds of judgment: these provisions do not provide for an appeal against the award of an arbitral tribunal. Section 37 merely provides for an application to the High Court by an aggrieved party to set aside the award of an arbitral tribunal in the limited circumstances as specified by the section. And s. 42 merely provides for referral on a question of law to the High Court. For the sake of completeness, we just wish to

add that in any event, in the present case, the defendant did not plead in its statement of defence that the plaintiff had entered into an agreement with the insurer not to invoke either s. 37 or s. 42 of the Arbitration Act; or that, based on the facts and the law (which the defendant must explain in its pleading), the plaintiff could have successfully invoked before the High Court (but failed to do so) either s. 37 or s. 42 of the Arbitration Act to impugn the arbitral award.

The High Court, in *Tanjung Langsat Port Sdn Bhd v. Trafigura Pte Ltd & Another Case* [2016] 4 CLJ 927 at paragraphs 9(a) and (b), held:

(a) Section 36 of the AA 2005 provides that 'An award made by an arbitral tribunal pursuant to an arbitration agreement shall be final and binding on the parties'. The court should be slow in interfering with an arbitral award, which award can only be set aside under the limited circumstances prescribed by s. 37 of the AA 2005 ... .

(b) That a setting aside proceeding must never be in the nature of an appeal ie, to guard against the danger of assuming the role of an appellate court ... .

Finally, the Court of Appeal, in *Pancaran Prima Sdn Bhd v. Iswarabena Sdn Bhd and another appeal* [2018] MLJU 968 at paragraph 30, *inter alia*, held:

We note that the court have had taken a minimalist intervention approach to arbitral awards under the Act by virtue of section 36(1) of the Act which provides that an arbitral award is final and binding on the parties ... .

§36.03 AGREEMENT TO EXCLUDE RECOURSE

As referred to in §36.02 *supra*, the Court of Appeal, in *Antara Steel supra*, decided that the mere repetition of the words in section 36 in an arbitration agreement would not prohibit recourse to sections 37 and 42.

Similarly, the High Court, in *Zenbay Sdn Bhd v. Yong Choo Kui Shipyard Sdn Bhd* [2015] 10 CLJ 924 at paragraphs 40 and 41, considered an arbitration agreement that provided that the award would be final and binding. The High Court decided, following *Antara Steel supra*, that such a provision in an arbitration agreement would not prevent recourse under sections 37 and 42 of the Arbitration Act 2005 for setting aside or a reference on a question of law.

In *Antara Steel* and *Zenbay supra*, the arbitration clause merely repeated the provisions of section 36(1) of the Arbitration Act 2005. However, Rule 12(10) of the 2018 AIAC Arbitration Rules appears to go further and provides that the parties will carry out the award immediately and waive their rights to any appeal, review or recourse to the courts.

Similarly, Article 35(6) of the 2017 ICC Rules of Arbitration provides:

Every award shall be binding on the parties. By submitting the dispute to arbitration under the Rules, the parties undertake to carry out any award without delay and shall be deemed to have waived their right to any form of recourse insofar as such waiver can validly be made.

Neither the Arbitration Act 2005 nor the 1985 Model Law on which it is based provides for a situation where the parties have excluded recourse against the award. The drafters of the 1985 Model Law did not contemplate such an exclusion.[40]

Section 29 of the Contracts Act 1950 provides:

> Every agreement, by which any party thereto is restricted absolutely from enforcing his rights under or in respect of any contract, by the usual legal proceedings in the ordinary tribunals, or which limits the time within which he may thus enforce his rights, is void to that extent.
>
> Saving of contract to refer to arbitration dispute that may arise
>
> Exception 1 — This section shall not render illegal a contract by which two or more persons agree that any dispute which may arise between them in respect of any subject or class of subjects shall be referred to arbitration, and that only the amount awarded in the arbitration shall be recoverable in respect of the dispute so referred.
>
> Saving of contract to refer questions that have already arisen
>
> Exception 2 — Nor shall this section render illegal any contract in writing, by which two or more persons agree to refer to arbitration any question between them which has already arisen, or affect any law as to references to arbitration.
>
> Exception 3 — Nor shall this section render illegal any contract in writing between the Government and any person with respect to an award of a scholarship by the Government wherein it is provided that the discretion exercised by the Government under that contract shall be final and conclusive and shall not be questioned by any court.
>
> In this exception, the expression 'scholarship' includes any bursary to be awarded or tuition or examination fees to be defrayed by the Government and the expression 'Government' includes the Government of a State.

In the light of exceptions 1 and 2 to section 29 of the Contracts Act 1950, an arbitration agreement restricting the parties' rights to seek recourse from the courts will not be void.

This was confirmed by the Court of Appeal, in *Dancom Telecommunication (M) Sdn Bhd v. UniAsia General Insurance Bhd* [2008] 5 CLJ 551 at paragraph 22, where it was, *inter alia*, held:

> The bringing of an action in an ordinary court of law is readily distinguishable from a reference of a dispute to arbitration. A contract which incorporates an arbitration clause, such as cl. 14, to refer the parties' dispute to arbitration within a specified period as agreed by the parties, is a contract sui generis. The hallmark of arbitration is characterised by the autonomy of the parties. By way of agreement, the parties have an unfettered choice, not only to refer their dispute to arbitration and to choose their own arbitrators or umpires, but also to prescribe the time frame for such reference. Their intention is to sustain the mechanism of alternative dispute resolution by way of arbitration and not court action. Their desire is to place arbitration under their exclusive control. They hope to achieve eg, speed in the hearing and determination of their dispute. Different considerations would

---

40. *See* Gary B. Born, *International Commercial Arbitration* (2nd edn, Kluwer Law International 2014) Vol III at §25.07[A][1].

then apply to an arbitration clause prescribing a time frame such as that expressly agreed in cl. 14. It is a product of the doctrine of freedom of contract and would attract the application of the specific provisions expressly set out in exceptions 1 and 2 to s. 29, so that the general rule embodied in s. 29 would give way to these two exceptions.

The issue is, therefore, whether such an exclusion may be interpreted by the courts as being contrary to the Arbitration Act 2005 and therefore, unenforceable. In this regard, the Arbitration Act 2005 to a limited extent allows the parties to exclude certain recourse to the courts. Section 3 of the Arbitration Act 2005 allows for the exclusion of the application of Part III of the Act. Part III includes provisions allowing recourse to the courts, such as section 42, which allows for a reference of a question of law.

Therefore, as an exclusion of recourse to the courts is in principle allowed by the Arbitration Act 2005, there is no reason why this principle should not also enable the parties to exclude recourse in terms of an application to set aside an award.

It is submitted that parties should be entitled to exclude recourse to the courts against an award. The parties are free to exclude access to the first instance court to determine the dispute and should similarly be free to exclude recourse to the courts against an award.[41] This is in line with the principle of party autonomy.

Furthermore, one of the primary reasons parties agree to arbitration is to avoid the cost, delay and risks of the courts. This reason will be defeated if parties are prohibited from excluding recourse to the courts against an award.[42] Although it is submitted that the parties should be free to exclude recourse against the award, it is acknowledged that this exclusion should not be absolute. Section 37(1)(b) of the Arbitration Act 2005 would not be excluded by an exclusion provision similar to the one in the ICC or KLRCA Arbitration Rules. This is due to two reasons. First, section 37(1)(b) allows the courts to act on their own initiative. Second, section 37(1)(b) provides for fundamental issues like arbitrability and public policy, which cannot be derogated from.

§36.04 RES JUDICATA

Section 36(1) of the Arbitration Act 2005 provides that an award is final and binding and may be relied on by the parties by way of defence, set-off or otherwise in any proceedings in any court. The words used in this provision suggest that a party may broadly rely on an award in any future proceedings.

The courts appear to be prepared to give effect to the broad meaning of the provision.

The High Court, in *Skylark Jaya Sdn Bhd & Ors v. Pengarah Tanah Dan Ukur, Jabatan Tanah Dan Ukur, Sabah & Ors* [2011] 1 LNS 578 at pages 15-17, accepted that

---

41. See Gary B. Born, *International Commercial Arbitration* (2nd edn, Kluwer Law International 2014) Vol III at §25.07[A][1].
42. See Gary B. Born, *International Commercial Arbitration* (2nd edn, Kluwer Law International 2014) Vol III at §25.07[A][1].

by virtue of section 36 an award might be used to contend that subsequent proceedings are res judicata. This position may even be taken where the subsequent proceedings are between different parties provided that the cause of action was the same.

Subsequently, the Court of Appeal, in *Tipco Asphalt Public Company Ltd & Anor v. Aras Jalinan Sdn Bhd & Other Appeals* [2013] 8 CLJ 498 at paragraphs 35-37, while declining to decide the issue on an interlocutory appeal, appeared to accept that it would at least be arguable that findings of fact made in an award would be res judicata in subsequent proceedings.

Chapter 7
Recourse Against Award

37. *Application for Setting Aside*

   (1) An award may be set aside by the High Court only if –
      (a) the party making the application provides proof that –
         (i) a party to the arbitration agreement was under any incapacity;
         (ii) the arbitration agreement is not valid under the law to which the parties have subjected it, or, failing any indication thereon, under the laws of Malaysia;
         (iii) the party making the application was not given proper notice of the appointment of an arbitrator or of the arbitral proceedings or was otherwise unable to present that party's case;
         (iv) the award deals with a dispute not contemplated by or not falling within the terms of the submission to arbitration;
         (v) subject to subsection (3), the award contains decisions on matters beyond the scope of the submission to arbitration; or
         (vi) the composition of the arbitral tribunal or the arbitral procedure was not in accordance with the agreement of the parties, unless such agreement was in conflict with a provision of this Act from which the parties cannot derogate, or, failing such agreement, was not in accordance with this Act; or
      (b) the High Court finds that –
         (i) the subject matter of the dispute is not capable of settlement by arbitration under the laws of Malaysia; or
         (ii) the award is in conflict with the public policy of Malaysia.
   (2) Without limiting the generality of subparagraph (1)(b)(ii), an award is in conflict with the public policy of Malaysia where –
      (a) the making of the award was induced or affected by fraud or corruption; or
      (b) a breach of the rules of natural justice occurred –

   (i) during the arbitral proceedings; or
   (ii) in connection with the making of the award.
(3) Where the decision on matters submitted to arbitration can be separated from those not so submitted, only that part of the award which contains decisions on matters not submitted to arbitration may be set aside.
(4) An application for setting aside may not be made after the expiry of ninety days from the date on which the party making the application had received the award or, if a request has been made under section 35, from the date on which that request had been disposed of by the arbitral tribunal.
(5) Subsection (4) does not apply to an application for setting aside on the ground that the award was induced or affected by fraud or corruption.
(6) On an application under subsection (1) the High Court may, where appropriate and so requested by a party, adjourn the proceedings for such period of time as it may determine in order to allow the arbitral tribunal an opportunity to resume the arbitral proceedings or to take such other action as in the arbitral tribunal's opinion will eliminate the grounds for setting aside.
(7) Where an application is made to set aside an award, the High Court may order that any money made payable by the award shall be brought into the High Court or otherwise secured pending the determination of the application.

§37.01 INTRODUCTION

Section 37 of the Arbitration Act 2005 provides for the grounds for setting aside an award, as well as, the time for making such an application and the security that may be required.

 Section 37 of the Arbitration Act 2005 is based on Article 34 of the 1985 Model Law with certain amendments:

(1) Article 34(1) of the 1985 Model Law is omitted from section 37 of the Arbitration Act 2005;
(2) sections 37(1) and (3) of the Arbitration Act 2005 reflect Article 34(2) of the 1985 Model Law;
(3) section 37(2) of the Arbitration Act 2005 is not found in the 1985 Model Law;
(4) section 37(4) of the Arbitration Act 2005 is based on Article 34(3) of the 1985 Model Law;
(5) section 37(5) of the Arbitration Act 2005 is an addition that is not found in the 1985 Model Law;
(6) section 37(6) is based on Article 34(4) of the 1985 Model Law; and
(7) section 37(7) of the Arbitration Act 2005 is an addition that is not found in the 1985 Model Law.

 The grounds for setting aside in section 37 reflect the grounds for refusing recognition of an award in section 39 of the Arbitration Act 2005. The grounds for refusing recognition of an award in turn reflect Article V of the 1958 New York Convention. Section 37 reflecting Article V of the New York Convention is intentional and is for the sake of harmony in interpretation.

Section 37's origins in Article 34 of the 1985 Model Law which in turn reflects Article V of the 1958 New York Convention has been recognized by the High Court, in *The Government of India v. Cairn Energy India Pty Ltd & Ors* [2014] 9 MLJ 149 at paragraphs 101-103.

Similarly, the Court of Appeal, in *Garden Bay Sdn Bhd v. Sime Darby Property Bhd* [2017] 2 MLJ 636 at paragraph 8, *inter alia*, held:

> Malaysia has adopted the Model Law (which has subsumed part of the Convention) for domestic as well as international arbitration. The Convention does not allow an arbitral award to be set aside for error of fact and/or law. The Convention only allows an award to be challenged for one of the grounds set out in article I-V and in particular V ... .

Section 37 is one of the provisions of the Arbitration Act 2005 that has been subjected to the most consideration by the courts. The provision has been considered in minute detail. These details are considered in this chapter.

§37.02 AN AWARD MAY BE SET ASIDE BY THE HIGH COURT ONLY IF ...

Section 37(1) of the Arbitration Act 2005 is of particular importance as it set outs a general precondition for the setting aside of an award. Given the importance of this provision, each of its terms will be examined below.

[A] Award

The word 'award' is defined by section 2(1) of the Arbitration Act 2005 to mean:

> 'award' means a decision of the arbitral tribunal on the substance of the dispute and includes any final, interim or partial award and any award on costs or interest but does not include interlocutory orders;

Therefore, only a final, interim or partial award on the substance of the dispute, costs or interest may be set aside. Interlocutory orders may not be set aside. This definition of an 'award' is not contained in the 1985 Model Law. The inclusion of this definition in the Arbitration Act 2005 clarifies the type of decisions by the arbitral tribunal that may be set aside.

Section 37 when referring to an award does not expressly refer to an award from a foreign state or an award from any State. In this way, section 37 differs from sections 38 and 39, which do refer to an award made in a foreign or any State.

This difference has been interpreted by the High Court, in *Twin Advance (M) Sdn Bhd v. Polar Electro Europe BV* [2013] 3 CLJ 294 at paragraphs 27 and 28 to mean that an application may only be made to the High Courts of Malaysia to set aside an award arising from an arbitration with a seat in Malaysia. This is also in accordance with

[B] May

Section 37(1) provides that the High Court 'may' set aside an award if the grounds specified in section 37(1)(a) or (b) are satisfied.

The High Court, in *The Government of India supra*, interpreted this to mean that the courts have a discretion as to whether to set aside an award even if the grounds in section 37(1)(a) or (b) are satisfied. In this regard, the High Court in *The Government of India supra* at paragraph 120, *inter alia*, held:

> From the terms of these subparas, it is evident that the court is here vested with discretion to intervene in the award. Sub-section 37(1) uses the word 'may' as opposed to the word 'shall', the latter often treated as mandatory in its dictate and application. See for example, ss 8, 10 and 41(2) in Act 646.

This was again emphasized by the High Court, in *Intraline Resources Sdn Bhd v. ExxonMobil Exploration and Production Malaysia Inc* [2017] MLJU 1299 at paragraph 26(j):

> The language of Section 37(1), specifically on the use of the word 'may' firmly confers on the Courts the discretion in the exercise of its powers to set aside arbitration awards ... .

The judgment of the High Court, in *The Government of India supra*, was followed by the High Court in *The Government of India v. Vedanta Ltd (legal successor of Cairn India Ltd) & Anor* [2018] MLJU 630 at paragraphs 66, 68 and 72. The High Court further explained that the discretion would be exercised based on the materiality of the outcome or prejudice, which would have to be proved by the applicant:

> [66] Even if the complaint is demonstrated to fall within the ambit of the specific provisions of section 37, the Court retains a discretion over whether to set aside an award or not.
>
> ...
>
> [68] Thus it has been stated that the materiality of the outcome of the violation complained of is an important factor in the Court's exercise of discretion to set aside an award ... .
>
> ...
>
> [72] The party alleging prejudice bears the burden to prove it ... .

However, the Court of Appeal, in *Sigur Ros Sdn Bhd v. Master Mulia Sdn Bhd* [2018] 3 MLJ 608 at paragraphs 63 and 64, clarified that while the court had a discretion whether to set aside an award, which involved an evaluation of the materiality of a breach, this did not mean that prejudice must be shown or that the applicant bore the burden of proving such prejudice:

[63] Because section 37 vests the Court with a wide discretion on whether to set aside an award, we agree with the learned JC that the decision to set aside an award is not an automatic outcome of a finding that there has been a breach of the rules of natural justice. The Court will still have to evaluate whether discretion should be exercised in the applicant's favour. In considering whether discretion should be exercised, there should be an evaluation of relevant factors such as those identified in *Kyburn Investments Ltd v Beca Corporate Holdings Ltd*, amongst which would be to consider the seriousness, magnitude or materiality of the breach, its nature and its impact, whether the breach would have any effect on the outcome of the arbitration; leaving room for 'casual breach or occasional error'. Costs of rehearing and delay in raising the complaint are further relevant factors to be taken into account in that evaluation. This exercise is different from undertaking an exercise to show prejudice, which may be in several respects, including monetary rights.

[64] There is however, no question of there being an onus cast on the applicant to establish these factors ... .

Significantly, the Court of Appeal, in *Pancaran Prima Sdn Bhd v. Iswarabena Sdn Bhd and another appeal* [2018] MLJU 968 at paragraph 38, decided in the context of a breach of the rules of natural justice that once a ground for setting aside is established, the courts' discretion not to set aside the award is narrow and depends on materiality:

> We note that if there is a breach of the rules of natural justice, the discretion not to set aside the Award is a very narrow one, and that too if the breaches are not material ... .

It is settled that the courts have a discretion whether to set aside an award once it is proved that a ground for setting aside exists. The courts exercise their discretion by evaluating the materiality of the ground for setting aside. The applicant does not bear the burden of proving materiality or prejudice. Once a ground is proved, the courts' discretion is limited and depends on the materiality of the ground.

[C] Set Aside

Section 37 of the Arbitration Act 2005 provides for the setting aside of an award and not an appeal against the award. This has been emphasized by the courts in the context of section 36, as discussed under §36.02 *supra*.

In addition, in relation to section 37, the High Court, in *The Government of India supra* at paragraph 171, held that:

> ... the court's powers are not invoked in the field of appellate jurisdiction. The court's powers here are specifically enacted under statute. Since the court does not sit in appellate capacity, the court does not scrutinise the merits of the parties' respective case or responses before the arbitral tribunal. The court must also resist interfering in the decisions of the arbitral tribunal save where it is prescribed under the Arbitration Act 2005.

The High Court, in *Intraline supra* at paragraphs 26(a)-(g), further elaborated that:

In my view, the following key principles, as distilled from a number of decisions here and from other common law jurisdictions applying the Model Law, presently represent the law on the setting aside of arbitration awards under Section 37 of the AA.

(a) The Courts should be slow in interfering with an arbitral award unless there is patent injustice ... .
(b) Constant judicial interference as was the case in the past will defeat the spirit of the Arbitration Act 2005 to promote one-stop adjudication in line with international practice ... .
(c) An arbitration award is final, binding and conclusive; and it can only be challenged in exceptional circumstances. Erroneous drawing of inferences of fact from the evidence in itself is not sufficient for the setting aside of the award ...
(d) It is not the function of the Court to examine the correctness of the award on merits ... .
(e) Section 37 is not an appellate provision; the Court must not sit in appeal over the view of the arbitrator by re-examining and re-assessing the materials before him ...
(f) The philosophy of party autonomy and party choice means that a challenge is not permitted to be premised on a party's change of mind by extricating from its agreement to final and binding arbitration ... .
(g) The Courts should approach arbitration awards commercially and reasonably and expect no substantial fault in the same ... .

Similarly, the High Court, in *Vedanta supra* at paragraph 64, held:

1. No Appeal/Review on the Merits

Section 37 is not an appellate provision ... .

2. No 'Hole Picking'

Secondly the Courts are to generally read the award expansively with an expectation that it is free from substantial fault.

Section 37 also does not allow the High Court to vary an award. This was recognized by the Court of Appeal, in *Petronas Penapisan (Melaka) Sdn Bhd v. Ahmani Sdn Bhd* [2016] 3 CLJ 403 at paragraph 20, where it was, *inter alia*, held:

The powers to remit or set aside is found in ss. 23 and 24 of the AA 1952 though there is no power to vary the award in those two sections. The power to do so is not restricted by any grounds as set out in ss. 37 or 42 of the AA 2005. Section 37 does not give the court the power to vary, even though it can remit or set aside the award. Section 42 gives the court power to remit, vary or set aside. One common thread in the old regime as well as ss. 37 and 42 is the requirement to remit the award. In the instant case, no attempt was made to remit the award to the arbitrator.

Further, the High Court may only set aside an award on an application by the applicant and cannot enter a judgment in on the terms prayed for. This was confirmed by the High Court, in *Konsortium Lord-Saberkat Sdn Bhd v. RP Chemicals (M) Sdn Bhd* [2018] MLJU 602 at paragraph 26:

In this respect, I am in agreement with learned counsel for the Defendant that s. 37 of the AA 2005 only provides this court with the discretionary power to set aside the Final Award in the event the statutory requirements are met. The said s. 37 does not empower this court, in the event the Final Award is set aside, to grant judgment in favour of the Plaintiff for the monetary claims it had sought in OS 8 which is the same prayers it sought in the arbitration proceedings. If the Final Award is set aside the matter would have to be re-arbitrated. In other words this court has no power to substitute the decision of the Arbitrator with a decision of this court ... .

[D] High Court

Section 37(1) specifically provides that the 'High Court' may set aside an award. The words 'High Court' are defined by section 2(1) of the Arbitration Act 2005 to mean:

> 'High Court' means the High Court in Malaya and the High Court in Sabah and Sarawak or either of them, as the case may require ...

Therefore, an application to set aside an award must be made to the High Court, as the subordinate courts do not have the power to set aside an award.[1]

[E] Only If

Section 37(1) of the Arbitration Act 2005 provides that the High Court may set aside an award 'only if' the grounds in section 37(1)(a) or (b) are satisfied.

First, this requires the applicant to specify the particular ground in section 37(1)(a) or (b) they rely on, as it is only if such a ground is established that the High Court may set aside an award. The importance of the applicant specifying the grounds relied on has been emphasized by the High Court.

For example, the High Court, in *Taman Bandar Baru Masai Sdn Bhd v. Dindings Corporations Sdn Bhd* [2010] 5 CLJ 83 at paragraphs 15 and 16, held:

> [15] In the instant case, the plaintiff is relying on ss. 37 and 42 of AA 2005 without stating the sub-section. This is fatal because ss. 37 and 42 spell out different maladies and relief in a very restrictive manner. Order 7 makes it mandatory for the originating summons to be intituled by the particulars of the rule of court and the provisions of the relevant laws the court is moved ... .
>
> [16] It is clear the plaintiff has clearly failed to state with sufficient particularity the relevant sub-section of the statute which in this case is of utmost importance. The failure results in embarrassment as adumbrated by the Court of Appeal. This is so for various reasons: (a) Section 8 of AA 2005 makes it clear that court can only intervene in any of the matters governed by the Act, thereby restricting the scope of intervention to the approved issues only. (b) The reading of s. 37 will show that in a restricted manner, there are number of instances the court can intervene and that intervention is subject to proof provided. (c) The subsection to s. 37 is not

---

1. See *Uba Urus Bina Asia Sdn Bhd v. Quirk & Associates Sdn Bhd & Anor* [2016] 4 CLJ 468 at para. 37, HC.

inter-related as a whole and almost in all cases stands independent to one another. In consequence, the plaintiff is obliged to set out the subsection it relies upon, failing which the intitulement stands as embarrassing and ought to be struck out in limine.

Similarly, the High Court, in *Perembun (M) Sdn Bhd v. Binas BMK Sdn Bhd and another case* [2015] MLJU 0283 at paragraph 38, held:

> ... I am of the opinion that Perembun should nevertheless identify the precise provision of law that affords that particular ground or basis of challenge that it relies on to set aside the Corrective Award; or how the reasons or complaints come within the particular ground in subsection 37(1) that is relied on. It is only fair and proper that the precise ground should be identified at the time of challenge; and not left for all to guess at or during the hearing of the Originating Summons. Here, the absence of such an invocation has caused some difficulties in discerning what is precisely Perembun's complaints.

In particular, the Court of Appeal, in *Sigur Ros supra* at paragraph 24, explained that the grounds in sections 37(1)(a) and (b) should be read disjunctively but may be relied on cumulatively:

> First, sections 37(1) (a) and (1) (b) are disjunctive provisions in that an award may be set aside under any of these provisions. Within sections 37(1)(a) and (1)(b) are further sub-provisions providing for the various grounds upon which an award may be set aside. These grounds may be relied on cumulatively or otherwise.

Second, in the light of the use of the words 'only if' and the provisions of section 8 of the Arbitration Act 2005, the courts will adopt a minimalist approach and strictly construe whether the grounds relied on by a party conform with section 37(1)(a) or (b).[2] The minimalist approach adopted by the courts in this regard has been considered in §8.03[F] *supra*.

However, these authorities must now be read in the light of the judgment of the Federal Court, in *Far East Holdings Sdn Bhd v. Majlis Ugama Islam dan Adat Resam Melayu Pahang* [2017] 8 AMR 313 at paragraph 66, which held that the words of section 42 should be read as they stand without additional requirements. A similar approach should, it is submitted, be adopted in relation to section 37.

§37.03 THE PARTY MAKING THE APPLICATION PROVIDES PROOF

The grounds for setting aside an award are divided into two. There are six grounds on which a party may make an application, and there are two grounds on which the court may act on its own initiative. These grounds are set out in sections 37(1)(a) and (b) respectively.

The first six grounds under section 37(1)(a) require the applicant to provide proof. As discussed under §37.02[E] *supra*, an applicant must specify the ground relied on in section 37(1)(a) and prove such ground.

---

2. See *Intraline Resources supra* at paras 26(h) and (k), HC.

Chapter 7: Recourse Against Award §37.03[A]

The standard of proof required is on a balance of probability. As discussed under §37.02[E] *supra*, only if the ground the applicant has specified and relied on is proved on a balance of probability, can the court exercise its discretion to set aside an award.

The need for proof has been repeatedly emphasized by the High Court. For example, in *Taman Bandar Baru Masai supra* at paragraph 23(b), the High Court held that 'general allegations are not sufficient as it is a mandatory requirement for need of proof.' This was subsequently followed in *Kelana Erat Sdn Bhd v. Niche Properties Sdn Bhd & Another Case* [2013] 4 CLJ 1172 at paragraphs 18-20.

The High Court, in *The Government of India supra* at paragraphs 125 and 126, dwelt on the need for proof and the standard proof required, as well as, it being a precondition for the exercise of the court's discretion:

> [125] I find further support of this view in the requirement of 'proof' as opposed to there being none called for; or a requirement on a lower evidentiary threshold when dealing with a challenge under sub-paras 37(1)(a)(iv) and (v). The choice of this word is deliberate. It is also a stringent requirement of the sufficiency of evidence that must be brought before the court. As compared to the phrase 'appear' which is used in some legislations (see for example s 360 of the Capital Markets and Services Act 2007 (Act 671) where a lower standard of proof is required, the deliberate choice of the word 'proof' indicates that there must be certainty in proof.
>
> [126] Insofar as the standard of proof is concerned, it must be on the civil balance of probabilities; and not the higher burden of beyond reasonable doubt. It is only where the court is satisfied that there is evidence certain of the matters alleged that the court has discretion to intervene for the purposes of setting aside the award. Where the court is not satisfied, it may be argued that there is no discretion at all. Again, this would be due to the presence of the clear emphatic words of 'only if'.

This was subsequently reiterated in *Kluang Health Care Sdn Bhd v. Lee Yong Beng & another Case* [2016] 1 CLJ 281 at paragraphs 33 and 34 and *Intraline Resources supra* at paragraph 26(i). The Court of Appeal, in *Sigur Ros supra* at paragraphs 25 and 39, emphasized the need to prove the grounds relied on by a party under section 37 on a balance of probabilities.

The applicants must accordingly prove the grounds they rely on on a balance of probability. The substance of the six grounds under section 37(1)(a) is considered below.

[A] Incapacity of a Party

An award may be set aside if it is proved that a party to the arbitration agreement was under an 'incapacity'.

The meaning of 'incapacity' in Malaysia will be determined based on sections 10-12 of the Contracts Act 1950, which provide:

> 10. What agreements are contracts
> (1) All agreements are contracts if they are made by the free consent of parties competent to contract, for a lawful consideration and with a lawful object, and are not hereby expressly declared to be void.

(2) Nothing herein contained shall affect any law by which any contract is required to be made in writing or in the presence of witnesses, or any law relating to the registration of documents.

11. Who are competent to contract

Every person is competent to contract who is of the age of majority according to the law to which he is subject, and who is of sound mind, and is not disqualified from contracting by any law to which he is subject.

12. What is a sound mind for the purposes of contracting

(1) A person is said to be of sound mind for the purpose of making a contract if, at the time when he makes it, he is capable of understanding it and of forming a rational judgment as to its effect upon his interests.

(2) A person who is usually of unsound mind, but occasionally of sound mind, may make a contract when he is of sound mind.

(3) A person who is usually of sound mind, but occasionally of unsound mind, may not make a contract when he is of unsound mind.

ILLUSTRATIONS

(a) A patient in a mental hospital, who is at intervals of sound mind, may contract during those intervals.
(b) A sane man, who is delirious from fever, or who is so drunk that he cannot understand the terms of a contract, or form a rational judgment as to its effect on his interests, cannot contract whilst such delirium or drunkenness lasts.

Therefore, a party will be under an incapacity if they:[3]

(1) are not acting with their free consent;
(2) have not attained the age of majority;
(3) are of unsound mind; or
(4) are disqualified from contracting.

Apart from this, the question arises under the law of which State will the incapacity of a party be determined in an international arbitration. There is no authority in Malaysia as to which State's law will be applied in this situation.

It is submitted that the capacity of an individual to enter into a contract will be governed by the law of the State with which the arbitration agreement is most closely connected or the law of his domicile and residence. If he has the capacity to contract under either the law of the State with which the arbitration agreement is most closely connected or the law of his domicile and residence, the arbitration agreement will be valid.

If he does not have the capacity to contract under either the law of the State with which the arbitration agreement is most closely connected or the law of his domicile or residence, the arbitration agreement will be invalid.[4]

---

3. *See* Tan Sri Dato' Seri Visu Sinnadurai, *Contracts Act, A Commentary* (LexisNexis 2015) at paras 10.01 to 12.03 for a detailed commentary on these four aspects of incapacity.
4. *See* generally Lord Collins, *Dicey, Morris and Collins on The Conflict of Laws* (15th edn, Sweet & Maxwell 2017) at paras 32R-168 – 32-178.

[B] Validity of the Arbitration Agreement

An award may be set aside where an arbitration agreement is proved to be invalid under the law, which governs it. If the law which governs the arbitration agreement is Malaysian law, then the question of whether there is a valid arbitration agreement will be determined in accordance with section 9 of the Arbitration Act 2005, which is considered in §9.01 to §9.03 *supra*.

The question arises as to which State's law will determine the validity of the arbitration agreement in an international arbitration. Section 37(1)(a)(ii) of the Arbitration Act 2005 addresses this question by providing that the law which will determine the validity of the arbitration agreement will be:

(1) the law the parties have subjected the arbitration agreement to;
(2) the law the parties have indicated should apply to the arbitration agreement; or
(3) the laws of Malaysia, if there is no such indication.

This follows Article 34(2)(a)(i) of the 1985 Model Law. Paragraph (1) above provides for a situation where the parties have expressly provided for the law which is to govern the arbitration agreement. Paragraph (2), it is submitted, covers a situation where the parties have implicitly agreed on the law that is to govern the arbitration agreement. Paragraph (3) covers the default situation, where there has been no express or implied agreement on the law which is to govern the arbitration agreement, in which event the laws of Malaysia apply.

The Federal Court, in *Thai-Lao Lignite Co Ltd v. Government of the Lao People's Democratic Republic* [2017] 6 AMR 219, considered a project development agreement, which expressly provided that the laws of the Lao People's Democratic Republic and New York were to govern the substantive contract. The parties did not expressly agree on the laws that were to govern the arbitration clause within the project development agreement. The arbitration clause provided for the application of the UNCITRAL Arbitration Rules, that Kuala Lumpur was to be the seat of arbitration and that the arbitral tribunal should be trained in the laws of New York.

The Federal Court held that the question of which law governed the arbitration agreement was not a choice between the law of the contract and law of the seat. Rather, the question was to be determined by conflict of law rules, that is the law which had the closest connection with the arbitration agreement was to govern it.

The Federal Court held that the laws of Malaysia had the closest connection to the arbitration agreement, as the arbitration was seated in Kuala Lumpur, with the Arbitration Act 2005 as the curial law. The Federal Court, in *Thai-Lao Lignite supra* at paragraph 187, held:

> Under the conflict of laws rules, the law that has the closest and most real connection to the arbitration agreement is the law applicable to the arbitration agreement. In the instant case, the arbitration was conducted in Malaysia at the Kuala Lumpur Regional Centre for Arbitration. Since the arbitration was conducted in Malaysia, AA 2005 (with the exception of Part III) was the lex arbitrii.

> Since the seat was Kuala Lumpur, AA 2005 was also the curial law ... AA 2005 was the lex arbitrii and the curial law. That pointed to the law of Malaysia with the closest connection to the arbitration agreement. New York law had no connection to the arbitration agreement. The PDA required the arbitral tribunal to be trained in New York law. But that was because New York law governed the substance of the dispute. The parties submitted on New York law. But that was to address the third party beneficiary issue. Only the law of Malaysia had the connection, the closest and most real at that, to the arbitration agreement. Under the conflict of laws rules, the law applicable to the arbitration agreement should be the law of Malaysia. That conclusion on the applicable law should be the same even if the three stage test espoused in *Sulamerica* were applied, as the parties' adoption of the UNCITRAL Arbitration Rules 1976 implied a choice of the law applicable to the seat. There was a tacit choice of Malaysian law to govern the arbitration agreement. Malaysian law, namely ordinary contract law principles, would govern the interpretation of the arbitration agreement ... .

[C] Lack of Notice or Inability to Present Case

An award may be set aside if a party is able to prove that they were given insufficient notice or were otherwise unable to present their case. This will amount to a breach of the statutory obligation to give each party a fair and reasonable opportunity to be heard under section 20 of the Arbitration Act 2005, which has been considered under §20.01-§20.04 *supra*.

[D] Excess of Jurisdiction

[1] General

An award may be set aside if it exceeds the scope of the submission to arbitration. Where the decisions on matters within the scope of the submission to arbitration can be separate from matters outside the scope, only that part of the award that includes matters outside the scope of the arbitration needs to be set aside.

The reason for this is party autonomy. Parties are free to agree on the matters referred to arbitration. Parties are bound by this agreement. Conversely, parties are not bound by an award that is in excess of the reference to arbitration.

This was lucidly explained by the Court of Appeal, in *Kerajaan Malaysia v. Perwira Bintang Holdings Sdn Bhd* [2015] 1 CLJ 617 at paragraph 22, where it was, *inter alia*, held:

> ... This is an area of arbitration law which allows the court to set aside an award on the ground that an arbitrator had decided on a 'new difference' which is irrelevant to the claim, the 'new difference' being understood as a new dispute not contemplated by or not falling within the terms of the arbitration submission. The underlying rationale for this rule rests on the consensual nature of arbitration. Parties are not compelled to resort to arbitration contractually, but if they provide for it and refer their dispute to arbitration, the mandate of the arbitrator must be limited to the terms defined by the parties for him to exercise his jurisdiction. If the

Chapter 7: Recourse Against Award §37.03[D]

arbitrator strays from the confines of this mandate, he will be acting in excess of his jurisdiction, even though he may have the initial and primary jurisdiction to arbitrate between the parties ... .

The High Court, in *The Government of India supra* at paragraph 129, explained that one must start with the assumption that the arbitral tribunal has substantive jurisdiction and then consider how this jurisdiction may have been exceeded:

> As discussed, a challenge under sub-paras 37(1)(a)(iv) and (v) must start with the assumption that the arbitral tribunal has substantive jurisdiction in the first place; and the complaint is that the arbitral tribunal exceeded its powers by dealing with matters that had not been submitted to the tribunal. From the submissions and the cause papers, it would appear that the plaintiff is not suggesting otherwise.

[2] The Test

The test to determine whether the award exceeds the arbitral tribunal's discretion focuses on the arbitration agreement, the terms of reference and the provisions of the Arbitration Act 2005 and assesses whether the scope thereby ascertained has been exceeded.

This was explained by the High Court, in *The Government of India supra* at paragraphs 138 and 139, and 161, 165, where it was also clarified that the law to determine jurisdiction is the law of the arbitration agreement and not the law of the substantive contract:

> [138] The areas of intense focus identified by Lord Steyn, namely the arbitration agreement, the terms of reference, the relevant Act, must necessarily be true for the determination of a challenge of excess of jurisdiction or power since the arbitral tribunal takes its mandates from such sources.
>
> [139] Further, it must be remembered that the courts tend to construe arbitration cls or agreements widely ... .
>
> [161] Although Indian law is the substantive law or proper law of the contract or PSC, and English law is the law of the arbitration agreement; that in no way means that Indian lex arbitrii applies on the determination of an application under s 37.
>
> ...
>
> [165] ... I agree with the defendants that English law which is the substantive law of the arbitration agreement answers any questions on the jurisdiction of the arbitral tribunal ... .

The test was summarized and clearly stated by the High Court, in *Intraline Resources supra* at paragraph 26(m):

> To succeed in a case under Section 37(1)(a)(iv) and (v) for excess of power or mandate, the correctness of the decision is also not relevant. The applicant must first show the matters which are within the scope of the submission to arbitration. It then must prove that the award deals with a 'new difference' which is not within the scope of reference. Thirdly, if shown, whether such 'new difference' was irrelevant to the actual issues for determination. Fourthly, if so, whether the 'new

difference' would have had a material impact on the final outcome as announced in the award. And if it would, finally, whether that part of the award inflicted by the 'new difference' may be separated from the other parts of the award to warrant only the part affected to be set aside under Section 37(3) ... .

The same test was applied by the High Court, in *Vedanta supra* at paragraph 75.

[3] **The Application of the Test**

The test set out in *The Government of India supra* can be seen in its application in several cases.

The High Court, in *Sisma Enterprise Sdn Bhd v. Solstad Offshore Asia Pacific Ltd* [2013] 1 LNS 335 at paragraphs 29-31, decided that the award was not in excess of the arbitral tribunal's discretion, as the issue that had been decided, that is the interpretation of a termination clause, was squarely within the terms of reference to arbitration.

Similarly, the High Court, in *Intraline Resources supra* at paragraphs 53 and 60, held that the fact that a particular clause of a contract was not pleaded did not mean that the arbitral tribunal acted in excess of jurisdiction by construing the whole contract:

> [53] The fact that the parties did not specifically plead this particular clause is immaterial in the context of this instant case considering the nature of the dispute, which would have required examination of the entirety of Contract at any rate, as I have emphasized earlier. Secondly, and this is especially crucial, in any event, the Arbitral Tribunal had in fact even convened a clarification meeting attended by both parties on 7 August 2015 to seek the views of the parties on the very issue, and as stated in the Final Award, 'the impact of Article 7 – Changes to the Work in the Principal Document (Contract DU3542) in the context of your respective positions as submitted in this arbitration and other factual queries that may arise.'
>
> ...
>
> [60] A party seeking to set aside an award under Section 37(1) bears the burden of providing proof which the plaintiff on the evidence in the instant case fails to establish. There is no 'new difference' let alone one which had a material impact on the final outcome of the Final Award to justify this Court exercising its discretion to set aside the Final Award. It cannot therefore be said that the Final Award dealt with a dispute not contemplated within the terms of submission to arbitration (Section 37(1)(a)(iv)) or that it contained decisions on matters beyond the scope of submissions to arbitration (Section 37(1)(a)(v)).

The High Court, in *Awan Timur Palm Oil Mills Resources (Johor) Sdn Bhd v. Inno-Wangsa Oils & Fats Sdn Bhd* [2018] MLJU 622 at paragraphs 76, 78, 79 and 81, held that an award should be set aside for want of jurisdiction, as there was no contract between the parties. The court also held that the dispute on the existence of the contract should have been determined by the courts rather than the arbitral tribunal. Further, the High Court held that there was no need for a party to comply with an appeal procedure provided by arbitration rules before applying to set aside the award:

[76] The Respondent had argued that an appeal under Section 3 of the PORAM Rules must first be exhausted as the alternative remedy before coming to the High Court ... .

...

[78] However, that argument does not gain the desired traction unless the dispute between the parties had fallen squarely within the jurisdiction of the arbitral tribunal in the first place, and that due process within their jurisdiction was then to take its course.

[79] I find that the arbitrators had no business to take on jurisdiction to adjudicate whether there was a contract in the first place. It was not a clear enough case, and they certainly did not have to take it upon themselves to adjudicate on the issue of formation of contract. The civil court would be better equipped to handle such a dispute which would involve dealing with conflicting evidence.

...

[81] In conclusion therefore, I find that the arbitrators had exceeded their jurisdiction, whereby they had failed to show sufficient and cogent basis for them to embark on the preliminary issue of whether there was a contract. It was not something that had clearly fallen within their jurisdiction, as there was nothing to indicate how the particular industry practices had come into play, or which would even make them best suited to adjudicate on the particular facts of this dispute.

[4]   Waiver

Section 18(3) of the Arbitration Act 2005 provides that a plea that an arbitral tribunal does not have jurisdiction must be raised in the defence at the latest. And, section 18(5) provides that a plea of excess of jurisdiction must be raised as soon as such a matter occurs during the arbitral proceedings. As stated in §18.02 *supra*, if such a plea is not taken in time, a party would have waived its right to object later during an application to set aside the award.

The Federal Court, in *Thai-Lao Lignite Co Ltd & Anor v. Government of the Lao People's Democratic Republic* [2017] 6 AMR 219 at paragraph 215, decided that if this timeline is not complied with but there is no objection by the other party than the other party may have waived the non-compliance:

> ... Equally, if a party raises an out of time challenge but the other party does not object to the lateness of the challenge, and the tribunal rules on the plea, the other party cannot rely on the delay to prevent the High Court from deciding the matter under art 16(3) [the equivalent of section 18(8) of AA 2005]' (*Williams & Kawharu supra* at 7.4.6). On the facts, even if the plea under section 18(3) or (5) of AA 2005 were made out of time, the Appellants could not rely on delay, which was not an issue during the arbitral proceedings, to prevent the High Court from deciding the matter under Section 37 of AA 2005. On the facts, where there was no objection to lateness, the Appellants could not raise the 'out of time' argument. As such, we reject the 'out of time' argument.

The judgment of the Court of Appeal, in *Tridant Engineering supra*, may also be seen in this light. Although an issue was not specifically pleaded, the issue was in fact raised and does not appear to have been objected to as being in excess of jurisdiction.

Due to this failure to object during the arbitral proceedings, the party was not entitled to subsequently object during the application to set aside the award.

[5] Not Bound by the Arbitral Tribunal's Award

The courts will not be bound by any findings of the arbitral tribunal on jurisdiction. Instead, in an application to set aside, the courts will rehear the dispute on jurisdiction. This was confirmed by the High Court, in *Vedanta supra* at paragraphs 77 and 78:

> [77] However where jurisdictional challenge is concerned under section 37 of the Arbitration Act 2005, the Courts have taken the approach that it is to be assessed independently by the supervising court notwithstanding any decision in relation thereto by an arbitral tribunal in the award.
>
> [78] The supervising Court is not fettered by what the Arbitral Tribunal has decided on the question of its jurisdiction with respect to its mandate or competence or that it should defer to the decision of the Tribunal on this question except that '... (depending on its cogency) that reasoning will inform and be of interest to the court.'

[E] Composition and Procedure

An award may be set aside if the composition of the arbitral tribunal or the procedure of the arbitration is not in accordance with:

(1) the arbitration agreement, which would include any rules of arbitration agreed to therein;
(2) the Arbitration Act 2005, if the arbitration agreement is in conflict with a non-derogable provision of the Act; or
(3) the Arbitration Act 2005, in the absence of provisions in the arbitration agreement dealing with these matters.

The High Court, in *Vedanta supra* at paragraphs 90-93, recognized that challenges to the composition of the arbitral tribunal are often likely to be waived, as most institutional rules allow a party to make such a challenge, which, if not exercised, will result in a waiver.

§37.04 THE HIGH COURT FINDS THAT ...

The first six grounds for setting aside an award have been considered under §37.03 *supra*. The applicant is required to provide proof of these grounds under section 37(1)(a) of the Arbitration Act 2005.

The next two grounds for setting aside an award are set out under section 37(1)(b) of the Arbitration Act 2005. The courts appear to be entitled to act of their own motion under section 37(1)(b), and the applicant accordingly does not appear to be expressly required to provide proof.

The absence of a requirement for proof in section 37(1)(b) has been recognized by the High Court. Despite the absence of such a requirement, the High Court has repeatedly emphasized that an applicant must provide sufficient basis for the High Court to 'find' one of the two grounds under section 37(1)(b).[5]

The Court of Appeal, in *Sigur Ros supra* at paragraph 25, confirmed that an applicant under section 37(1)(b) must provide evidence and that the courts will not embark on an independent exercise of their own to identify the grounds:

> Second, it is only upon proof of the presence of any of the grounds relied on that an award may be set aside. Although unlike section 37(1)(a), section 37(1)(b) does not expressly state that the appellant must prove the matters complained of, whether under section 37(1)(b)(i) or (ii), it makes sense that there must be evidence presented in order for the Court to find if either of the two grounds under section 37(1)(b), exists. The Court does not embark on any independent exercise to find if the conditions or grounds under section 37(1)(b)(i) or (ii) are met.

The two grounds under section 37(1)(b) of the Arbitration Act 2005 are considered below.

[A] Not Capable of Settlement by Arbitration

An award may be set aside if the High Court finds that the subject matter of the dispute is not capable of settlement by arbitration under section 37(1)(b)(i).

Section 37(1)(b)(i) corresponds with section 4 of the Arbitration Act 2005. Section 4 essentially provides that all disputes may be resolved by arbitration unless it is contrary to public policy. Section 4 has been considered under §4.01 and §4.02 *supra*. It is submitted that public policy will be given a restricted meaning in this context allowing most disputes to be determined by arbitration.

[B] Public Policy

An award may be set aside if the court finds that it is in conflict with the public policy of Malaysia under section 37(1)(b)(ii). The general principles used to determine if there has been a breach of public policy have evolved since the Arbitration Act 2005 came into force and are now quite settled.

First, public policy will be narrowly construed. This is in accordance with the minimal interference envisaged by section 8 of the Arbitration Act 2005 and accepted by the courts. This is also in accordance with the principle of party autonomy. As public policy is narrowly construed, the courts will not generally allow any new head of public policy. In this context, it has also been suggested in *The Government of India*

---

5. See *The Government of India supra* at para. 142, HC; followed in *Kilang Sawit Bell Sdn Bhd v. Kwantas Oil Sdn Bhd* [2015] MLJU 1985 at para. 25, HC; and *MMC Engineering Group Bhd & Anor v. Wayss & Freytag (M) Sdn Bhd & Anor* [2015] MLJU 477 at para. 159, HC.

supra at paragraph 152 that public policy must be within the genre envisaged by section 37(2) of the Arbitration Act 2005.

Second, the applicant must specify the public policy that it relies on and prove that the specified public policy has been breached. Initially, the courts required the applicant to prove that the breach had resulted in prejudice. However, the Court of Appeal, in *Sigur Ros supra* at paragraphs 48, 49, 63 and 64, has confirmed that there is no requirement to prove prejudice, as this is not provided for in sections 37(1)(b)(ii) and 37(2). However, prejudice may be considered by the courts as a factor in exercising their discretion whether to set aside the award.

These principles can be gathered from a series of judgments by the High Court culminating in a judgment of the Court of Appeal, which confirmed these judgments of the High Court. First, the High Court, in *The Government of India supra* at paragraphs 142 to 143 and 152 to 153, *inter alia*, held:

> [142] Although there appears to be no requirement of 'proof in this subpara, and whilst the question of what amounts to 'public policy' may be a difficult one, I would also venture to say that the court nevertheless requires sufficient basis for such allegation or ground in order that it may 'find' that 'the award is in conflict with the public policy of Malaysia'. This requirement extends to not only identifying the particular public policy of Malaysia which is said to be conflicted but also to providing basis of the alleged conflict; that is how it is conflicted or breached; and how the breach has prejudiced the rights of the plaintiff.
>
> [143] This makes the threshold high in that by its very nature, it should be immediately obvious or at least fairly rapidly apparent that there has been such a breach or conflict with the public policy of Malaysia court. From the reasons offered, the court must be compelled to agree or that a strong case has been made out that the award conflicts with the public policy of Malaysia. Otherwise, the contractual arrangements of the parties must be maintained ... .
>
> [152] It is clear that while sub-s 37(2) serves to provide some examples of what may be considered as conflicting with the public policy of Malaysia; and it would be those awards which were induced or affected by fraud or corruption; or where there is a breach of natural justice, as is the case with proper statutory interpretation, any other complaint of conflict with public policy must fall within this genre as set out in paras 37(2)(a) and(b). Quite undisputedly, these two areas may be said to fall within the basic and fundamental notions or principles of justice.
>
> [153] In addition, while sub-para 37(2) may contain the rider of 'Without limiting the generality of sub-para (1)(b)(ii)', a restrictive and narrow approach must be taken; and the court's curial intervention, minimum. I am fortified in my view when this provision is read together with s 8 of Act 646.

The High Court expanded on these principles in *MMC Engineering supra* at paragraphs 146-149 and 151-154.

The High Court then, in *Tan Kong Han v. QDB Ventures Sdn Bhd* [2016] 1 LNS 870 at paragraph 29, summarized these principles as a set of guidelines:

> Therefore, the guidelines or principles that may be drawn are as follow:
>
> (i) the public policy ground must be given a narrow and more restrictive construction and interpretation;

Chapter 7: Recourse Against Award §37.04[B]

(ii) the Court should be slow to find for such a ground or to expand the hitherto accepted and recognized genre of categories of public policy;
(iii) the concept of public policy cannot be vague or generalized but must be identified with clarity and particulars;
(iv) allegations must be sufficiently serious to offend or violate most basic notions and principles of morality and justice, or where upholding the award would shock the conscience or is clearly injurious to public good or wholly offend the ordinary reasonable and fully informed member of the public;
(v) Strong, compelling evidence must be established;
(vi) causative link between the alleged fraud or corrupt conduct and the award rendered must be shown;
(vii) prejudice must be proved.

And, the High Court, in *Intraline Resources supra* at paragraph 26(n), held:

> In respect of Section 37(1)(b)(ii) and Section 37(2)(b) (i) and (ii) on breaches of natural justice on grounds of conflict with public policy, the concept of 'public policy' is to be construed narrowly, such as only applicable when it is clearly injurious to the public good or where it violates the most basic notion of morality and justice ... .

The Court of Appeal, in *Sigur Ros supra*, confirmed the principles developed by the High Court, in particular in *The Government of India supra* and *MMC Engineering supra*, save that there was no requirement for the applicant to prove prejudice, which was only a factor to be considered in the exercise of the courts' discretion. The Court of Appeal also confirmed that where there has been a breach of public policy, the whole award and not part only must be set aside. The Court of Appeal, in *Sigur Ros supra* at paragraphs 27, 30-34, 48 and 49, held:

> [27] The examples or illustrations in section 37(2) to explain what circumstances or conditions may be considered as conflicting with the public policy of Malaysia, are by no means exhaustive. This is made plain by its opening terms: 'Without limiting the generality of subparagraph (1)(b)(ii)'. Any other circumstance or complaint of the presence of a conflict with public policy however, must fall within the genre set out in sections 37 (2)(a) and (b). In other words, the sui generis rule should apply. The Court should however, be slow in acceding to any suggestion to expand the recognized and established categories of conflict with public policy.
>
> ...
>
> [30] In the first place, the concept of public policy is itself a 'broad' concept ... .
>
> [31] Next, having regard to the context of the dispute, that it arises out of commercial and contractual transactions where parties may be said to have received advice including legal advice, the conflict with public policy ground that is envisaged in section 37(1)(b)(ii) ought to be read narrowly and more restrictively. The Court's curial intervention should be sparingly used; and this would be in keeping with the terms in section 8 of Act 646.
>
> [32] This then makes the threshold to be met somewhat high in that by its very nature, 'it should be immediately obvious or at least fairly rapidly apparent that there has been such a breach or conflict with the public policy of Malaysia ... The Court must be compelled to agree or that a strong case has been made out that the

award conflicts with the public policy of Malaysia. Otherwise, the contractual arrangements of the parties must be maintained.'

[33] Further, 'it must be understood that the notion or concept of public policy in arbitration is not one grounded in public law, generally understood as the Wednesbury principles. In other words, the award will not be set aside simply because it is irrational or unreasonable or one that is so irrational or unreasonable that no reasonable person could have made such an award. The concept of public policy must be one taken in the 'higher sense, where some fundamental principle of law and justice is engaged, some element of illegality, where enforcement of the award involves clear injury to public good or the 'integrity of the Court's process and powers will thereby be abused'.

[34] Fourth, where such a breach within the terms of section 37(1)(b)(ii) read with section 37(2)(b) has been established, it is the whole award that will be set aside. The terms of section 37 do not appear to allow for the operation of the principle of severance, especially in view of the terms of section 37(3) read with section 37(1)(a)(v). Subsection 37(3) provides that where the decision on matters submitted to arbitration can be separated from those not so submitted, only that part of the award which contains decisions on matters not submitted to arbitration may be set aside. The words 'matters submitted to arbitration can be separated from those not so submitted' are peculiar to the terms appearing in section 37(1)(a)(v), the only provision which makes specific reference to section 37(3), that it is read 'subject to subsection (3) ...'.

...

[48] ... his lordship rightly embarked on an examination of the duties of the arbitrator, establishing that there were these two duties which we see are core duties, and how those duties may be breached, his lordship erred when he went further to require that there must be proof of actual or real prejudice suffered by the appellant before discretion is exercised in its favour even where breach has been established. His lordship did so despite recognizing that the position under our sections 37(1) (b) (ii) and 37(2) is different from that under those two jurisdictions ... .

[49] We say, with respect, that his lordship has erred as that additional requirement is not found under section 37 of Act 646. It may be the specific requirements of the arbitration laws of Singapore or even the UK, but it is not required under section 37. To require such compliance or terms would, in our view, run contrary to the terms of section 8 of the Act. The powers of the Court to intervene in arbitration matters are as prescribed by the Act. We should refrain from importing into our arbitration or litigation regime an understanding or principle which is not provided for under our very own statute. Were the requirement for actual or real prejudice a requirement to be met under section 37(1)(b)(ii) read with section 37(2) (b), it would be for the legislation to say so, and not the Court.

Before going into the two examples of a breach of public policy provided for in section 37(2) of the Arbitration Act 2005, we will consider situations where the courts have held that there is no breach of public policy.

There are two such situations. First, the courts have emphasized that any alleged misinterpretation of a contract by the arbitral tribunal cannot amount to a breach of public policy.[6] Second, the courts have decided that a delay in the delivery of an award by the arbitral tribunal would not amount to a breach of public policy.[7]

We will now consider the two examples of a breach of public policy provided for under section 37(2)(b) of the Arbitration Act 2005.

[1] Fraud or Corruption

Fraud or corruption is an example of a breach of public policy that would render the award liable to be set aside. As fraud or corruption under section 37(2)(a) come within a breach of public policy under section 37(1)(b)(ii), the applicant is not expressly required to provide proof. Nevertheless, the applicant is required to provide a sufficient basis to enable the court to 'find' the alleged fraud or corruption. In this regard, the applicant is required to provide:

(1) strong and compelling evidence of the fraud or corruption;
(2) evidence of a causal link between the fraud or corruption and the award; and
(3) evidence that the applicant's rights were thereby prejudiced.

It appears that the words 'fraud' and 'corruption' will be given their literal meaning by the courts in applying the three-stage test above. These principles are expressed in considerable detail in the judgment of the High Court, in *MMC Engineering supra* at paragraphs 161 and 162, where it was, *inter alia*, held:

> [161] However, it is clear from the terms of subparagraph (2)(a) that the matters complained of, that is, fraud or corruption, must have induced or affected the making of the award. This indicates the requirement of a causal link between the matters complained of and the award which is sought to be set aside or remitted. I would take the same approach in cases where the allegations are premised on subparagraph (2)(b). Similarly, the procedural injustice must have affected the proceedings or the making of the Award. Otherwise, the application must be dismissed.
>
> [162] And, in this regard, I agree with the Defendant that the Plaintiffs have failed to meet all the requirements set. All that has been shown at this stage and at the most, is that Mr Holmes is a person of possibly bad character who is possibly unfit to sit as an arbitrator. On its own, that it grossly insufficient. In fact, I would say all the matters taken together would still be insufficient. As suggested by the Defendant, the focus of the Model Law and the terms of subparagraph 37(1)(b)(ii) and paragraph 37(2) is on the fairness and justice of the arbitration process; not on the character of personalities, including the arbitrators, involved in that process. Unless the Plaintiffs can show how the character ground can and has affected the rights of fairness and justice in an arbitration proceeding, it cannot possibly be the subject of a public policy category.

---

6. See *The Government of India supra* at paras 19-20, HC; *Kilang Sawit supra* at para. 32, HC.
7. See *Asean Bintulu Fertilizer Sdn Bhd v. Wekajaya Sdn Bhd and another appeal* [2017] MLJU 1530 at para. 18, CA.

[2] Natural Justice

A breach of the rules of natural justice, either in the arbitral proceedings or in the making of an award, is another example of a breach of public policy.

The rules of natural justice comprise two fundamental principles, which are the rule against bias and the right to be heard. These two principles are provided for in sections 14 and 20 of the Arbitration Act 2005, respectively, and are considered under §14.03 and §20.03 *supra*.

The applicant must identify the rule of natural justice and prove that it has been breached. However, the applicant does not need to prove that such breach caused prejudice, although such prejudice may be considered by the courts, as a factor in the exercise of the court's discretion to set aside the award. The courts initially required the applicant to prove prejudice, but this is no longer required, as the courts have recognized that sections 37(1)(b)(ii) and 37(2)(b) do not expressly include such a requirement.

The breach of the rules of natural justice may occur in the making of the award or during the arbitral proceedings, as expressly provided for in section 37(2)(b), and is not limited to the making of the award. This is again contrary to the initial position taken by the courts that limited such breach to the making of the award.

Once the rules of natural justice are shown to have been breached, the courts have little discretion but to set aside an award unless the breach was immaterial.

These principles can be seen developing in a series of judgments, starting with the judgment of the High Court in *Taman Bandar supra*, emphasized the need for the applicant to specify the particular rule of natural justice that had been breached by reference to a particular statute. The High Court also emphasized the need for an applicant to prove the prejudice suffered as a result of a breach of the specified rule of natural justice.

In this context, the High Court, in *Taman Bandar supra* at paragraph 23(6), *inter alia*, held:

> In addition the complaint of the plaintiff plainly falls within the scope and jurisdiction of the arbitrator. The AA 2005 does not permit the court to intervene in matters which does not strictly fall within any of sub-section of s. 37. In consequence general allegations are not sufficient as it is mandatory requirement for the need of proof. For example, in this case the plaintiff alleges breach of rules of natural justice without setting out the prejudice suffered and proof thereof. Further, almost all rules of natural justice are now incorporated in the Federal Constitution, relevant Acts, as well as rules of court etc. Thus, the complaint now must in almost all cases relate to one of the breaches of the Constitution, or any Act of Parliament, rules of court etc ...

The High Court, in *Intraline Resources supra*, expanded on *Taman Bandar supra* and held that four requirements must be met if an award was to be set aside on the grounds of natural justice:

(1) identify the rule of natural justice;
(2) show how such rule has been violated;

Chapter 7: Recourse Against Award §37.04[B]

(3) demonstrate how such violation was connected to the award; and
(4) show how such violation prejudiced the applicant.

The High Court, in *Intraline Resources supra*, also held that an arbitral tribunal was not bound to accept either party's position and was entitled to form their own view provided that such view could have been foreseen by a reasonably diligent party. The High Court, in *Intraline Resources supra* at paragraphs 26(o), (p) and 88, held:

[26] ...
(o) To succeed on this ground of breach of natural justice, the plaintiff must show unfairness in the limited circumstances that a reasonable litigant could not have foreseen the possibility of reasoning of the type contained in the award ... .

(p) The four elements to be established by an applicant seeking to set aside an award on account of a breach of natural justice to the satisfaction of the Court are first, to identify the rule alleged to have been violated, secondly, to show in what fashion it had been violated, thirdly, to demonstrate how the violation was connected to the making of the arbitral award, and fourthly to show in what manner the violation prejudiced the rights of the applicant ... .

...

[88] The plaintiff cannot therefore legitimately expect the Arbitral Tribunal to religiously follow the stance or any specific arguments presented by one party or the other because it is undoubtedly entitled to reformulate and refashion the way in which different arguments and concepts have been consolidated, make its own value judgements between the range of the spectrum that encompasses the multifarious contentions made available before it and exercise reasonable latitude in arriving at its own conclusions in the final award.

The Court of Appeal, in *Asean Bintulu Fertilizer Sdn Bhd v. Wekajaya Sdn Bhd and another appeal* [2017] MLJU 1530 at paragraphs 17 and 18, held that an arbitral award that was delivered four years late would not be set aside on the grounds of natural justice:

[17] In the instant case, the learned judge had taken into consideration the delay point and had censored the learned arbitrator. To save the award from being setting aside, the learned trial judge had taken a curial scrutiny of the complaint in relation to section 37 as well as section 42 to sustain the award, thereby demonstrating that the appellant did not suffer any material prejudice. The learned judge had also provided some relief by amending the interest provision. The complaint of pre-award interest on the face of record may look unjust but it being loss for use of money for the respondent at the market rate cannot be unjust or abhorrent to the notions of justice to seek court intervention in a party autonomy concept and also in the light of section 36 of AA 2005. The withholding of that money by the appellant, though no fault of its own in commercial sense, may have been advantageous to the appellant and a loss to the respondent ... .

[18] In our view, the delay issue cannot be the sole reason for appellate intervention when in the instant case the learned arbitrator had delivered a speaking award within the contemplation of the law.

The Court of Appeal, in *Sigur Ros supra* at paragraphs 48, 49 and 63, reversed the earlier requirement that an applicant must prove prejudice arising from a breach of the rules of natural justice. Prejudice would, however, remain a factor to be considered by the courts in exercising their discretion whether to set aside the award.

The Court of Appeal, in *Sigur Ros supra* at paragraph 55, also held that a breach of the rules of natural justice might occur during the making of the award or during the arbitral proceedings.

Further, the Court of Appeal, in *Sigur Ros supra* at paragraphs 71-73 and 90, emphasized that where an arbitral tribunal relied on extraneous evidence, the arbitral tribunal must give the parties an opportunity to be heard and provide rebuttal evidence, failing which there will be a breach of the rules of natural justice. This was also confirmed by the Court of Appeal, in *Pancaran Prima Sdn Bhd v. Iswarabena Sdn Bhd and another appeal* [2018] MLJU 968 at paragraphs 32, 33, 36 and 38.

§37.05 TIME LIMIT

Section 37(4) of the Arbitration Act 2005 provides that an application to set aside should be made within ninety days from:

(1) the receipt of the award; or
(2) the disposal of an application for correction, interpretation or an additional award under section 35.

Section 37(5) provides two exceptions to the general ninety-day rule. Where there is fraud or corruption, there does not appear to be any time limit for an application to set aside an award.

There is some controversy as to whether the time limit under section 37(4) is mandatory, in the sense that time cannot be extended by the courts, or discretionary in that time may be extended by the courts. This controversy has been considered under §8.03[F] *supra*.

Despite the subsequent judgments of the High Court, in *JHW Reels Sdn Bhd v. Syarikat Borcos Shipping Sdn Bhd* [2013] 7 CLJ 249 and *Kembang Semantan Sdn Bhd v. JEKS Engineering Sdn Bhd* [2016] 2 CLJ 427, the judgment of the Court of Appeal, in *Government of the Lao People's Democratic Republic v. Thai-Lao Liquite Co Ltd & Anor* [2011] 1 LNS 1903, remains binding.

The position therefore is that the time limit in section 37(4) is directory and the courts retain their discretion to extend time. The factors that will be considered are:

(1) the length of the delay;
(2) the reason for the delay;
(3) the prospect of success; and
(4) the degree of prejudice to the respondent if the extension is granted.

§37.06 REMISSION

Section 37(6) of the Arbitration Act 2005 provides that:

(1) a party may request an adjournment where an application is made to set aside an award;
(2) the High Court may then allow such an adjournment for a period of time it determines; and
(3) the arbitral tribunal may, during this adjournment, resume the arbitral proceedings or take such steps as will eliminate the grounds for setting aside.

Although the word 'remission' is not used in section 37(6), it essentially preserves the remission procedure, which is familiar to parties to arbitration in common law jurisdictions. This remission procedure is now placed within the framework of setting aside proceedings. In the event the remission before the arbitral tribunal proves futile, the High Court will resume the setting aside proceedings.[8]

Section 37(6) of the Arbitration Act 2005 reflects Article 34(4) of the 1985 Model Law. The remission procedure was found to be useful, as it would allow the arbitral tribunal to rectify a defect, which might otherwise lead to the setting aside of the award. Furthermore, the general nature of this provision allowed both the courts and the arbitral tribunal the flexibility to deal with a particular case.[9]

The Court of Appeal, in *Garden Bay Sdn Bhd v. Sime Darby Property Sdn Bhd* [2018] 2 MLJ 636 at paragraphs 23 and 24, emphasized the significance of section 37(6), which allows an arbitral tribunal to rectify a defect. The Court of Appeal suggested that it may be an abuse of process for a party to apply to set aside an award without first allowing an arbitral tribunal to correct a defect relating to natural justice. However, the Court of Appeal recognized that a party need not allow the arbitral tribunal to correct a defect where it involved public policy or incapacity of a party:

> [23] Section 37(6) of the AA 2005 is pari materia to article 34(4) of the UNCITRAL Model Law 1986. The Model Law regime does provide a procedure to save the award for breach of natural justice or allegation of related to issues such as 'not within the contemplation of parties' or issues related to pre or post award interest, etc. That is to say, s 37(6) does not give an option to set aside the award as of right at the trial stage or even at the apex stage. The courts must be vigilant of the jurisprudence related to s 37(6) and should not set aside the award in the first instance and create miscarriage of justice.

> [24] Cases in this area of law have not highlighted in detail the significance of s 37(6); a saving provision for all injustice and/or maladies complained of in relation to an award. In fact with the presence of s 37(6) regime, it will be an abuse of process of court for any applicant having submitted to an arbitration agreement and in the face of s 36 of the AA 2005, to move the court to set aside the arbitration award. In saying so, there may be instances where s 37(6) may not be applicable. For example, where the grounds relate to incapacity of parties, etc or public policy.

---

8. *See* Analytical Commentary, Article 34, commentary 14.
9. *See* Analytical Commentary, Article 34, commentary 13; UNCITRAL Report para. 30.6.

Subsequently, the Court of Appeal, in *Sigur Ros supra* at paragraph 38, emphasized that proceedings may only be adjourned under section 37(6) on the application of a party and not at the courts own motion:

> ... But, the option of sending the award back to the arbitrator to resume arbitration proceedings does not arise in this appeal as no application or request under section 37(6) was made to the High Court at the material time. Neither party applied for the proceedings before the High Court to be adjourned pending a reference back to the arbitrator for resumption of hearing of the arbitration. We are of the view that the option under section 37(6) is at either party's behest and not on the Court's own invocation.

§37.07 SECURITY

Section 37(7) of the Arbitration Act 2005 allows the High Court to order, where an application is made to set aside an award, that the applicant pay the awarded amount to the High Court or otherwise secure the amount.

The High Court has a discretion whether to order such security. The primary consideration of the High Court in exercising this discretion is whether the applicant will suffer prejudice. However, the mere fact that the applicant has been wound up or is otherwise unable to pay the security will not prevent such security being in order.

These principles were confirmed by the High Court, in *Mechanalysis Sdn Bhd (In Liquidation) v. Appraisal Property Management Sdn Bhd* [2016] 8 CLJ 81 at paragraph 59, where it was, *inter alia*, held:

> Pursuant to s. 42(8)(b) of the AA, the court clearly has the requisite discretion to determine and make an order that the award sum adjudged by the arbitral tribunal to be payable to the winning party be brought into court or otherwise secured, provided that the exercise of such discretion as empowered under the said statutory provision does not in any non-inconsequential fashion, detrimentally affect or prejudice the losing party who is now seeking to set aside the arbitration award. The *raison d'etre* of the provision is to clothe the court with the ability to exercise such powers in appropriate and deserving cases in order to ensure that the losing party who seeks to set aside the arbitral award continue to be able to meet such awards in the event its application is unsuccessful, and that the application is legitimate, and not otherwise frivolously instituted to delay and avoid making payment. In the instant case, it would be appropriate and fair that some security be provided to the defendant in connection which the arbitral award made in its favour and that in any event, as observed earlier, there is a patent lack of evidence as to the exact state of the plaintiff's financial health (apart from the fact of having been wound up) and the resources at its disposal to provide the security.

CHAPTER 8
Recognition and Enforcement of Awards

38. Recognition and Enforcement

(1) On an application in writing to the High Court, an award made in respect of an arbitration where the seat of arbitration is in Malaysia or an award from a foreign State shall, subject to this section and section 39 be recognized as binding and be enforced by entry as a judgment in terms of the award or by action.

(2) In an application under subsection (1) the applicant shall produce –
   (a) the duly authenticated original award or a duly certified copy of the award; and
   (b) the original arbitration agreement or a duly certified copy of the agreement.

(3) Where the award or arbitration agreement is in a language other than the national language or the English language, the applicant shall supply a duly certified translation of the award or agreement in the English language.

(4) For the purposes of this Act, 'foreign State' means a State which is a party to the Convention on the Recognition and Enforcement of Foreign Arbitral Awards adopted by the United Nations Conference on International Commercial Arbitration in 1958.

§38.01   INTRODUCTION

Section 38 of the Arbitration Act 2005 provides for the recognition and enforcement of arbitral awards, as well as the formal requirements that need to be satisfied for such recognition and enforcement.

Section 38 of the Arbitration Act 2005 is based on Article 35 of the 1985 Model Law. Although section 38 is based on the 1985 Model Law, there are significant differences, in particular:

(1) unlike Article 35, section 38 does not apply to arbitral awards 'irrespective of the country in which it was made'. Instead, section 38 is limited to States which are party to the New York Convention;
(2) unlike Article 35, section 38 does not draw a distinction between recognition and enforcement. Instead, an application to the High Court is required for both and recognition is accordingly not automatic; and
(3) the languages referred to as the 'official language of this State' in Article 35 is specified as the national language, which is Malay, or English in section 38.

These differences, the first two of which are of considerable significance, are considered in §38.02 and §38.04 *infra*.

Article 35 of the 1985 Model Law was amended in 2006. Essentially, the amendments in 2006 saw the removal of the need to produce the arbitration agreement or a duly certified copy of the award, with an uncertified copy of the award being sufficient. The amendments were to reflect the amendments made in 2006 to Article 7, which no longer requires an arbitration agreement in writing.

Article 35 of the 1985 Model Law is in turn based on Articles III and IV of the New York Convention, which provide:

Article III

Each Contracting State shall recognize arbitral awards as binding and enforce them in accordance with the rules of procedure of the territory where the award is relied upon, under the conditions laid down in the following articles. There shall not be imposed substantially more onerous conditions or higher fees or charges on the recognition or enforcement of arbitral awards to which this Convention applies than are imposed on the recognition or enforcement of domestic arbitral awards.

Article IV

1. To obtain the recognition and enforcement mentioned in the preceding article, the party applying for recognition and enforcement shall, at the time of the application, supply:
   (a) The duly authenticated original award or a duly certified copy thereof;
   (b) The original agreement referred to in article II or a duly certified copy thereof.
2. If the said award or agreement is not made in an official language of the country in which the award is relied upon, the party applying for recognition and enforcement of the award shall produce a translation of these documents into such language. The translation shall be certified by an official or sworn translator or by a diplomatic or consular agent.

Article 35 of the 1985 Model Law largely resembles Articles III and IV of the New York Convention. This is intentional, as the 1985 Model Law is intended to work in harmony with the New York Convention.[1]

---

1. *See* Analytical Commentary, Article 35, commentary 1.

The only significant difference between Article 35 of the 1985 Model Law and Articles III and IV of the New York Convention is the omission of the formal requirements for translation at the end of Article IV of the New York Convention in the 1985 Model Law. This omission was due to the many differences in national practice on the requirements for translation.[2]

The Federal Court, in *CTI Group Inc v. International Bulk Carriers SpA* [2017] 5 MLJ 314 at paragraphs 56 and 57, recognized the origins of section 38 in the 1985 Model Law and 1958 New York Convention:

> [56] The provisions on recognition and enforcement of arbitral awards as contained in articles 35 and 36 of the UNCITRAL Model Law on International Commercial Arbitration ('the Model Law') have been incorporated into ss 38 and 39 of our Arbitration Act.
>
> [57] Articles 35 and 36 of the Model Law are derived from articles IV and V of the New York Convention on the Recognition and Enforcement of Foreign Arbitral Awards 1958 ('the Convention').

§38.02 THE NEED FOR AN APPLICATION

Section 38 of the Arbitration Act 2005 requires an application to be made for both the recognition and enforcement of an arbitral award. This marks a significant departure from Article 35(1) of the 1985 Model Law, which only requires an application for enforcement. Under the 1985 Model Law, an award is recognized as binding automatically without the need for any application.[3]

The reason for this departure in the Arbitration Act 2005 is unclear. It also appears to be at odds with section 36 of the Arbitration Act 2005 that provides that an award is final and binding. Perhaps, sections 36 and 38 can be read together to mean that while an award is final and binding, formal recognition of this requires an application to be made.

§38.03 HIGH COURT

The application for recognition and enforcement must be made to the High Court and not the subordinate courts in accordance with section 38(1) of the Arbitration Act 2005.[4]

---

2. *See* Peter Binder, *International Commercial Arbitration and Conciliation in UNCITRAL Model Law Jurisdictions* (3rd edn, Sweet & Maxwell 2010) at para. 8-014.
3. *See* Analytical Commentary, Article 35, commentary 4.
4. *See Uba Urus Bina Asia Sdn Bhd v. Quirk & Associates Sdn Bhd & Anor* [2016] 4 CLJ 468 at para. 37.

§38.04 RECIPROCITY

Another significant departure from Article 35(1) of the 1985 Model Law is the requirement for reciprocity in section 38 of the Arbitration Act 2005. In order for an award from a foreign state to be recognized as binding and enforced, sections 38(1) and (4) require the foreign state to be a party to the New York Convention. This is the reciprocity requirement.[5]

This requirement for reciprocity marks a significant departure from Article 35(1) of the 1985 Model Law which by the use of the words 'irrespective of the country in which it was made' emphasizes that all arbitral awards are to be treated uniformly regardless of where they are made.[6]

Section 38(1) was amended by the Arbitration (Amendment) Act 2011. The words 'a domestic arbitration' were substituted with 'an arbitration where the seat of arbitration is in Malaysia'. The amendment made to section 38(1) was to address a lacuna in the section that prima facie allowed only for the enforcement of an award made in a 'domestic arbitration or an award from a foreign state' but not an international arbitration with a seat in Malaysia. It is now clear that an award made in an international arbitration with a seat in Malaysia is enforceable under section 38, which was no doubt the intention of the legislature but had previously been overlooked.

The Court of Appeal, in *Alami Vegetable Oil Products Sdn Bhd v. Hafeez Iqbal Oil & Ghee Industries (Pvt) Ltd* [2016] 7 CLJ 19 at paragraph 11, recognized that an award made in an international arbitration with a seat in Malaysia may be enforced under section 38 after the amendments in 2011 and confirmed that this was also the position prior to the amendments based on a purposive interpretation of the Arbitration Act 2005:

> A reading of the AA 2005 before 2011 amendments will show that Parliament had at least three types of award in mind which can be recognised and enforced in Malaysia. They are as follows:
>
> (a) domestic award;
> (b) domestic international award as this is borne out in s. 3 itself though the word 'domestic international' is not used but it says 'international arbitration where the seat of arbitration is in Malaysia'. That will mean and relate to the facts of the appellant's case where the respondent is a Pakistani company. If it is a domestic international award s. 3(3)(a) will apply to say that Parts I, II and IV will apply. Sections 38 and 39 come within Part II of the AA 2005. That is to say, notwithstanding a flawed definition of domestic award by the draftsman in s. 2, s. 3 makes it clear that a domestic international arbitration award is capable of recognition and enforcement under ss. 38 and 39 of the Act. This flawed

---

5. *See Lambard Commodities Ltd v. Alami Vegetable Oil Products Sdn Bhd* [2010] 1 CLJ 137 at para. 28, FC, where it was held under the old Arbitration Act 1952, section 27, and the Convention on Recognition and Enforcement of Foreign Arbitral Awards Act 1985, section 2(2), that an order in the Gazette was only one means of proving, among others, that a State was a party to the 1958 New York Convention, and, as such, an order in the Gazette was not a precondition.
6. *See* Analytical Commentary, Article 35, commentary 3.

definition was subsequently corrected by the 2011 amendment to s. 38 of the AA 2005.

The High Court, in *Twin Advance (M) Sdn Bhd v. Polar Electro Europe BV* [2013] 7 MLJ 811 at paragraph 23, confirmed that section 38 applied to an arbitration with a seat outside Malaysia, as an exception to section 3 of the Arbitration Act 2005.

§38.05 ENFORCED AS A JUDGMENT

Section 38(1) of the Arbitration Act 2005 provides that an award shall be enforced by entry as a judgment.

Therefore, once the award has been entered as a judgment, it may be executed like any other judgment of the courts in Malaysia, by way of garnishee proceedings, judgment debtor summons, writ of seizure and sale, winding-up or bankruptcy.

In terms of limitation, sections 6(1)(c) and 6(3) of the Limitation Act 1953 provide:

> 6. Limitation of actions of contract and tort and certain other actions
>
> (1) Save as hereinafter provided the following actions shall not be brought after the expiration of six years from the date on which the cause of action accrued, that is to say –
>
> ...
>
> (c) actions to enforce an award;
>
> ...
>
> (3) An action upon any judgment shall not be brought after the expiration of twelve years from the date on which the judgment became enforceable and no arrears of interest in respect of any judgment debt shall be recovered after the expiration of six years from the date on which the interest became due.

The Federal Court, in *Christopher Martin Boyd v. Deb Brata Das Gupta* [2014] 9 CLJ 887 at paragraphs 24 and 25, confirmed that an application to enforce an award must be made within six years of the award being received and the judgment entered in terms of the award may then be executed within twelve years:

> [24] It is clear to us that when parties sought to enforce an arbitration award ie, to register it under s. 27 of the Arbitration Act 1952 or s. 38(1) of the Arbitration Act 2005 the limitation period of six years pursuant to s. 6(1)(c) of the Limitation Act 1953 applies ... .
>
> [25] It is also clear to us that the limitation period for enforcement, ie, the execution of the judgment of the court, will then be 12 years as clearly prescribed under s. 6(3) of the Limitation Act 1953 ... Having said that and in applying the 12 years limitation period under s. 6(3) of the Limitation Act 1953 we find that the High Court was therefore correct in finding that the appellant's bankruptcy proceedings were not barred by limitation since it had commenced the action within 12 years from the date of the registration of the award as the judgment of the court.

§38.06 CONDITIONS AND PROCEDURE

Sections 38(2) and (3) of the Arbitration Act 2005 set out the conditions for recognition and enforcement of an award. There are two conditions. The applicant must produce the arbitration agreement and the award or a duly certified copy of these documents with a translation in English, if these documents are not in English or Malay.

Sections 38(2) and (3) only lay down these two conditions and do not provide for the procedure to be followed in making the application.[7]

[A] Procedure

The procedure is set out in Order 69 Rule 8 of the Rules of Court 2012, which provides:

8. Enforcement of awards (O. 69 r. 8)
(1) An application for permission to enforce an award in the same manner as a judgment or an order may be made without notice in an arbitration claim originating summons.
(2) The arbitration claim originating summons shall –
   (a) state the name and the usual or last known place of abode or business of the applicant, and the respondent against whom it is sought to enforce the award, respectively; and
   (b) state either that the award has not been complied with or the extent to which it has not been complied with at the date of the application.
(3) The applicant shall file by affidavit, written evidence on which he intends to rely when he files his originating summons, including exhibiting the original arbitration agreement and the duly authenticated original award or, in either case, a duly certified copy thereof and where the award or agreement is in a language other than the national language or English, a translation of it in the English language, duly certified as a correct translation by a sworn translator or by an official or by a diplomatic or consular agent of the country in which the award was made.
(4) The Court may specify parties to the arbitration on whom the arbitration claim originating summons shall be served.
(5) With the permission of the Court, the arbitration claim originating summons may be served out of the jurisdiction irrespective of where the award is, or is treated as, made.
(6) An order giving permission to enforce the award shall –
   (a) be drawn up by the applicant; and
   (b) be served on the respondent by –
      (i) delivering a copy to him personally; or
      (ii) sending a copy to him at his usual or last known place of residence or business.
(7) Within fourteen days after service of the order giving permission to enforce the award or, if the order is to be served out of the jurisdiction, within such other period as the Court may set –
   (a) the respondent may apply to set aside such order; and
   (b) the award shall not be enforced until –
      (i) after the expiration of that period; or

---

7. See Analytical Commentary, Article 38, commentary 5.

(ii) if the respondent applies within that period to set aside, until after the application made by the respondent has been finally disposed of.

(8) The order giving permission for enforcement shall contain a statement of the right to make an application to set aside the order.

(8A) Order 11, rules 5, 6, and 8 shall apply to the service out of jurisdiction of the arbitration claim originating summons, or any order made in such claim, under paragraph (5).

(9) Where a body corporate is a party, any reference in this rule to a place of residence or business shall have effect as if the reference were to the registered or principal address of the body corporate.

(10) Where the award sought to be enforced is in the nature of an interim injunction under subsection 13(6) of the 1952 Act or subsection 19(1) of the 2005 Act, the order shall be granted only if the applicant undertakes to abide by any order the Court or the arbitral tribunal may make as to damages. The order shall be enforceable immediately, and subparagraph (7)(b) shall not apply.

The Rules of Court 2012 allow for the application for recognition and enforcement to be made ex parte. Subsequently, the respondent may apply to set aside the ex parte order within fourteen days.

Generally, as there are specific conditions and procedure, an applicant should comply with this and should not attempt to seek an alternative avenue for relief. In this context, the High Court, in *David Liew Kong Ming (practicing as D Liew Architect) v. Government of the State of Sabah* [2010] MLJU 1719 at paragraphs 7 and 10, *inter alia*, held:

> [7] ... The Arbitration Act has provided a specific procedure and remedy to the Plaintiff to register and enforce the award. However, the Plaintiff in this suit is not applying to enforce the award by entry as a judgment but for the above declaratory orders. No explanation was forthcoming why the Plaintiff did not seek to enforce it by entry as a judgment since 3.5.2007, instead of filing this suit for the declaratory orders.
>
> ...
>
> [10] The Plaintiff has an alternative remedy to enforce the award. S 41 of the Specific Relief Act 1950 provides that no court shall make any such declaration where the Plaintiff, being able to seek further relief than a mere declaration or title, omits to do so ... .

Conversely, there is no need to comply with procedures that are not specifically applicable to applications for recognition and enforcement, like the Reciprocal Enforcement of Judgments Act 1958. The High Court, in *Armada (Singapore) Pte Ltd v. Ashapura Minechem Ltd* [2016] 9 CLJ 709 at paragraph 15, *inter alia*, held:

> In the light of the non-applicability of REJA in the setting aside of the 16 January 2014 order, I am of the view there is:
>
> (a) No requirement for a notice of registration and indorsement of service on the affidavit proving service as it is a requirement under O. 67 r. 10 of the ROC 2012; and

(b) No requirement for a notification that the execution of the award will not issue until the expiration of the period as it is a requirement under O. 67 r. 5(2) of the ROC 2012.

The High Court, in *Murray & Roberts Australia Pty Ltd v. Earth Support Company (SEA) Sdn Bhd* [2015] 6 CLJ 649 at paragraph 30(a), clarified that an applicant in an application to recognize and enforce an award did not need a cause of action:

> ... I am of the considered view that the purpose of s. 38 AA (which provides an avenue for a party to apply to court to recognise and enforce arbitral awards where the seat of arbitration is in Malaysia or in a foreign country) will be defeated if the OS is required in this case to disclose a reasonable cause of action. As such, O. 18 r. 19(1)(a) RC cannot apply to the OS in this case ... .

[B] The Two-Stage Test

Sections 38 and 39 of the Arbitration Act 2005 read together provide for a two-stage test for the recognition and enforcement of an award. These two stages are as follows:

(1) at the first stage, there must be evidence of a prima facie or apparently valid award and arbitration agreement; and
(2) at the second stage, if there is such evidence, the enforcement of the award may be challenged.

These two stages were recognized by the Federal Court, in *CTI Group supra* at paragraph 66, where it was, *inter alia*, held:

> Sections 38 and 39 of our Arbitration Act, read with O 69 rr 8 and 9 of the Rules of Court 2012, provide for a two-stage process:
>
> The first stage is essentially an ex parte proceeding – but subject to the power of the court as stipulated in para (4) of O 69 r 8 to require service of the arbitration claim originating summons on a party to the arbitration. An ex parte order giving permission to enforce an arbitral award is made at this stage.
>
> The second stage is an inter partes proceeding during which the court deals with the application to set aside an ex parte order giving leave to enforce an arbitral award. The application must be made within the prescribed time after that order is served on the party against whom the order is made.

We will now consider these two stages in detail.

[1] Stage 1

The Federal Court, in *CTI Group supra* at paragraphs 87-91, held that the requirements of the first stage, which would be ex parte, will be satisfied if there was evidence of a prima facie or apparently valid award and arbitration agreement. In the absence of such evidence, the courts may refuse to give leave ex parte to enforce the award and

Chapter 8: Recognition and Enforcement of Awards §38.06[B]

may instead order that the application to enforce be heard *inter partes*, which would allow the applicant to adduce fresh evidence:

> [87] In our view, the discussion on the differences in the definitions of 'agreement in writing' in the various jurisdictions does not detract from the common position taken by all the cases we have referred to above that all that the court is required to do at the first stage of the enforcement proceeding is to satisfy itself that the party seeking enforcement has produced before the court:
> (1) the arbitral award sought to be enforced, which prima facie or apparently is a valid award; and
> (2) the arbitration agreement, which is prima facie or apparently a valid agreement, between the party seeking to enforce the award and the party against whom the award is sought to be enforced, and pursuant to which the award was made.
>
> [88] If the parties are named in the arbitration agreement, or if it is obvious on the face of the arbitration agreement that they are parties to the agreement, obviously the 'apparently valid' test in *Dardana*, *Lombard-Knight* and *Dallah*, or the 'prima facie' test in *Altain*, is satisfied. There is nothing more to be done. The award creditor applying for enforcement has discharged its evidential burden. Leave must be granted, and the matter must proceed to the second stage if the award debtor seeks to challenge such leave.
>
> [89] The difficulty arises when the parties are not named in the agreement or it is not obvious from the agreement that the parties are parties to the agreement. In such circumstances, can it be said that the evidential burden on the award creditor seeking enforcement has been discharged?
>
> [90] To our minds, Lord Mance's judgments in *Dardana* and in *Dallah* do not exclude the possibility of the court refusing leave when the evidential burden on the award creditor is not discharged.
>
> [91] The inter partes hearing recommended by Hansen JA and Kyron AJA in para 140 of *Altain* in fact, in our opinion, helps the party seeking enforcement. That party gets a 'second chance', in a manner of speaking, to produce additional evidence at the first stage that would show, notwithstanding the lack of obvious reference in the arbitration agreement itself to that party or the party against whom enforcement is sought, that there is in existence an arbitration agreement between the parties.

The High Court took a similar approach, in *Kluang Health Care Sdn Bhd v. Lee Yong Beng & Another Case* [2016] 1 CLJ 281 at paragraphs 58-60, where it appears to have been recognized that the complete arbitration agreement need not be produced, where the arbitration agreement has been included by reference under section 9(5) of the Arbitration Act 2005:

> [58] The court next turns to the application by Lee Yong Beng for an order under s. 38 of the Arbitration Act. Kluang Healthcare Sdn Bhd objects to the application for recognition and enforcement on the basis that the mandatory requirements of s. 38 are not met. It contends that no original arbitration agreement or award and, certainly no certified true copy of the arbitration agreement or the award have been produced in court. Under such circumstances, the application must be dismissed.

[59] The court disagrees. The court is satisfied that it has before the court the proper arbitration agreement. By virtue of s. 9(5) of the Arbitration Act, there is an arbitration agreement by incorporation ... .

[60] There are further reasons why I am satisfied that the requirements of s. 38 have been met. The applicant had itself relied on this same arbitration agreement when it sought and was granted by the High Court, a stay of the respondent's civil action and had the subject matter referred to arbitration. That course of action has culminated in the arbitration award. I do not believe the applicant can make any credible or convincing argument that there is no arbitration agreement in this case bearing in mind the history and genesis of this arbitration award. The applicant cannot resile and deny the existence of the arbitration agreement.

The Court of Appeal, in *Agrovenus LLP v. Pacific Inter-Link Sdn Bhd & Another Appeal* [2014] 4 CLJ 525 at paragraph 13, *inter alia*, emphasized that a formalistic approach, as opposed to a substantive approach, should be taken at the first stage in relation to the production of the award and the arbitration agreement:

In our view, s. 38 reflects the obvious. An applicant for recognition or enforcement of an award must first satisfy the court that there is an award and an arbitration agreement that authorised it. That would show of the tribunal that made the award sought to be recognised and enforced is the tribunal referred to in the arbitration agreement. Although an objection as to jurisdiction of the arbitral tribunal could be argued on the basis of the terms of the arbitration agreement, we accept that a formalistic approach to compliance with s. 38, by production of the copy of the award and the sale contract of 3 April 2009 relating to the transaction in dispute and containing an arbitration agreement suffices under s. 38 as prima facie proof.

The High Court initially took the position that the procedure in the Rules of Court 2012 had to be strictly complied with. For example, the High Court, in *DML-MRP Resources (M) Sdn Bhd v. Global Minerals (Sarawak) Sdn Bhd* [2009] MLJU 688 at page 3, held that an application for the recognition and enforcement of an award was flawed, as the intitulement referred to the provision on recognition and enforcement in both the Arbitration Act 1952 and the Arbitration Act 2005.

However, subsequently, the High Court has taken the position that the rights of the parties should not be defeated merely due to a failure to comply with procedure. For example, the High Court, in *Pasukhas Constructions Sdn Bhd & Anor v. MTM Millennium Holdings Sdn Bhd* [2015] 1 LNS 591 at paragraphs 3(a) and 10(ii), *inter alia*, held:

[3] Summarily, the Defendant seeks to set aside the 10/9/2012 ex-parte Order on grounds that:-

(a) it is irregular for failure to comply with O. 69 r. 8(2)(a) of the ROC 2012 as the ex parte OS did not state the name and the usual or last known place of abode or business of the Defendant and it did not contain a statement of the right to make an application to set aside the order under O. 69 r. 8(8) of the ROC 2012;

...

[10] The Defendant's argument under this head is without merit as:-

...

> (ii) ... I am inclined to accept the Plaintiffs' argument that the consensus of the authorities suggest that the Court is more concerned 'that the rights of parties in an action are not to be defeated by technical objections' ...

Similarly, the High Court, in *Armada supra* at paragraphs 20-22, *inter alia*, held:

> [20] With respect in the circumstances of this case I am of the opinion that the omission to include the indorsement under O. 69 r. 8(8) of the ROC 2012 does not nullify the 2010 award. Firstly, I had examined the cause papers ie the OS dated 28 December 2012 (encl. 1) and the affidavit in support of the leave application to enforce the 2010 award affirmed by Andrew Grimmett on 27 December 2012 and as they were in order I granted the 16 January 2014 order.
>
> [21] Secondly, in *Pasukhas Constructions Sdn Bhd & Anor v. MTM Millenium Holdings Sdn Bhd* [2015] 1 LNS 591, one of the grounds of the defendant in setting aside the ex parte order of the court obtained by the plaintiffs pursuant to an originating summons seeking to register and enforce the final award under s. 38 of the AA 2005 was it was irregular as amongst others it did not contain a statement of the right to make an application to set aside the order under O. 69 r. 8(8) of the ROC 2012. I had dismissed the defendant's application on this issue ... .
>
> [22] Thirdly, as highlighted by the plaintiff a comparison can be drawn with penal indorsements where the penal indorsement that the respondent is liable to process of execution would sometimes be included in the drawing up of the order but sometimes omitted; however the omission is not fatal as the drawn up order could be amended to include the penal indorsement as in *Tan Bee Ang v. Siew Chee Choong* [2011] 1 LNS 121 ...

[2] Stage 2

Once the applicant has satisfied the two conditions of section 38(2) of the Arbitration Act 2005, the onus shifts to the respondent to satisfy the courts that the award should not be enforced. In this context, the High Court, in *Open Type Joint Stock Company Efirnoye ('EFKO') v. Alfa Trading Ltd* [2012] 1 CLJ 323 at paragraphs 30 and 31, *inter alia*, held:

> [30] The plaintiff here has complied with the formal requirements set out in s. 38. The Arbitration Award was made in a state which is a party to the New York Convention as the Russian Federation is one of the signatory states to the convention with effect from 29 December 1958.
>
> [31] Given the foregoing, and the express words of s. 39 of the Act, the onus of proof now shifts to the defendant who opposes the recognition and enforcement of this Arbitration Award to satisfy the court why the award should not be registered and enforced ... .

The High Court, in *Murray & Roberts supra* at paragraph 65, *inter alia*, held:

> ... The above Malaysian cases have clearly held that once the plaintiff fulfils all the formal requirements, the legal onus shifts to the defendant to prove any one of the nine grounds of refusal. If the defendant is unable to discharge such a legal burden,

the court has no discretion but to recognise and enforce the Australian Arbitral Awards under s. 38(1) AA.

The respondent opposing the recognition and enforcement of the award under section 38 is limited to challenging the applicant's compliance with the conditions and procedures referred to above. The respondent is not entitled to argue the merits of the award. The respondent also cannot raise any ground under section 39 of the Arbitration Act 2005 unless a separate application is made under this provision. These principles were outlined by the Court of Appeal, in *Alami Vegetable Oil Products Sdn Bhd v. Hafeez Igbal Oil & Ghee Industries (Pvt) Ltd* [2016] 7 CLJ 19 at paragraphs 2, 3, 7 and 8, where it was, *inter alia*, held:

> [2] What is important to note in the instant case is that it is not permissible to argue issues relating to the award or merit of the award, etc. under s. 38 of the AA 2005 as the merit of the award cannot be an issue under s. 38, whereas it is permissible to place such an argument in an application under s. 39 of the AA 2005. The respondent's application was premised under s. 38 (which has to be read with s. 39) as evidence in the intitulement to the application found at pp. 14 to 17 vol. 1 Part A of the appeal record. For s. 39 to apply, the application must be made by the respondent to the award. In this case, the respondent to the award was the appellant/defendant and no such application had been filed but only an opposing affidavit stating why the respondent/plaintiff's application should not be allowed ... .
>
> [3] The appellant had not appreciated the distinction between ss. 38 and 39 of the AA 2005. Section 38 procedure is a 'recognition procedure' to convert an arbitration award to a judgment. This can only be done by a person holding an arbitration award. If the respondent to the award wants to object to the procedure, he can file an affidavit to do so. (See *International Bulk Carriers SPA v. CTI Group Inc* [2014] 8 CLJ 854; [2014] 6 MLJ 851). If the respondent to the award wants to object to its enforcement, then an application under s. 39 setting out one of the grounds must be made by the respondent to the award. To put it in another way, the appellant in the instant case was attempting to convince the court 'to put the cart before the horse', that too without making an application under the mandatory provision to challenge the enforcement of the award.
>
> ...
>
> [7] Section 38 is a procedural provision to seek recognition of an award. As long as the procedure set out in this section is satisfied the award must be recognised. It is not at this stage for the court to hear arguments related to s. 39 of the AA 2005, unless there is a formal application by the appellant. In the instant case, there was no argument before the learned trial judge or before us that procedural requirement for s. 38 was not satisfied ... .
>
> [8] As long as there is an award and the procedure in s. 38 is satisfied, the award needs to be given recognition. Any objection to the legal validity of the award or any other complaint on the award can only be taken by s. 39 procedure ... .
>
> In the instant case, the argument of the appellant may fall within the compass of s. 39(1)(a)(ii) but it has to be taken by way of an application.

These views were echoed in the High Court, in *Armada supra* at paragraphs 33(b), where it was, *inter alia*, held:

Chapter 8: Recognition and Enforcement of Awards   §38.06[B]

Matters going into merits of the arbitration award are strictly of no relevance to the court in determining whether to allow enforcement of an arbitration award … .

The High Court, in *Armada supra* at paragraphs 25 and 26, also emphasized that the period of fourteen days to apply to set aside an ex parte order allowing recognition and enforcement of an award must be complied with, if not a satisfactory explanation with sufficient material must be provided:

> [25] Bearing in mind the existence of the specific provision wherein the first limb of O. 69 r. 8(8) of the ROC 2012 specifies that a party may within a period of 14 days 'after the service of the order giving permission to enforce the award is served', I am of the view the general provision of O. 42 r. 13 of the ROC 2012 which specifies that '[A] party intending to set aside or to vary such order or judgment shall make an application to the court and serve it on the party who has obtained the order or judgment within 30 days after the receipt of the order or judgment by him' does not apply.
>
> [26] The plaintiff argued that there is inordinate delay of approximately one year six months on the defendant's part in applying to set aside the 16 January 2014 order. In *Abdul Latif Mohamed Ibrahim v. International Factors Leasing Pte Ltd* [2001] 2 CLJ 140 at 147 [f-i], Haidar Mohd Noor JCA (as he then was) (delivering judgment on behalf of the Court of Appeal) opined:
>> This court in dealing with the delay point in *Khor Cheng Wah v. Sungai Way Leasing Sdn Bhd* [1997] 1 CLJ 396 said at p. 401:
>>> It is a cardinal principle of law, that when a litigant seeks the intervention of the court in a matter that affects his rights, he must do so timeously. The maxim vigilantibus, non dormientibus, jura subveniunt, though having its origins in the Court of Chancery, is of universal application. Even in cases where a right is exercisable ex debito justitiae, a court may refuse relief to an indolent litigant.
>>> In all cases in which delay in approaching the Court is in issue, the burden is upon the litigant who has delayed to render a satisfactory explanation for it. Whether the explanation in a given case is satisfactory or reasonable depends upon the facts and circumstances of each case. And in a matter which involves the exercise of discretion, it is for the Judge in whom the law primarily vests the discretion.
>>> The burden therefore falls on the appellant to render satisfactory explanation or to lay sufficient material for the court to consider the delay in making the application for an extension of time.

The Federal Court, in *CTI Group supra* at paragraphs 92 and 105, held that once an order is made to enforce an award, at the first stage, that award may only be set aside in the second stage upon an application under section 39:

> [92] However, once an order is made granting leave to enforce an arbitral award, the case authorities cited before us, including *Altain*, show that the order can only be set aside in the second (substantive) stage based on the exhaustive grounds available at that second stage. This, in our view, is consistent with the provisions of the Model Law and, in the context of our jurisdiction, with ss 38 and 39 of our Arbitration Act.
>
> …
>
> [105] In our view, the two-stage process for the enforcement of arbitral awards as contained in ss 38 and 39 of our Arbitration Act (read with O 69 r 8 of the Rules of

Court 2012) does not permit a party seeking to set aside an order made under s 38 to apply to set it aside under that very section on the ground that there was no arbitration agreement in existence between the parties. That party must apply to set that order aside under s 39.

39. Grounds for Refusing Recognition or Enforcement

(1) Recognition or enforcement of an award, irrespective of the State in which it was made, may be refused only at the request of the party against whom it is invoked –
  (a) where that party provides to the High Court proof that –
    (i) a party to the arbitration agreement was under any incapacity;
    (ii) the arbitration agreement is not valid under the law to which the parties have subjected it, or, failing any indication thereon, under the laws of the State where the award was made;
    (iii) the party making the application was not given proper notice of the appointment of an arbitrator or of the arbitral proceedings or was otherwise unable to present that party's case;
    (iv) the award deals with a dispute not contemplated by or not falling within the terms of the submission to arbitration;
    (v) subject to subsection (3), the award contains decisions on matters beyond the scope of the submission to arbitration;
    (vi) the composition of the arbitral tribunal or the arbitral procedure was not in accordance with the agreement of the parties, unless such agreement was in conflict with a provision of this Act from which the parties cannot derogate, or, failing such agreement, was not in accordance with this Act; or
    (vii) the award has not yet become binding on the parties or has been set aside or suspended by a court of the country in which, or under the law of which, that award was made; or
  (b) if the High Court finds that –
    (i) the subject-matter of the dispute is not capable of settlement by arbitration under the laws of Malaysia; or
    (ii) the award is in conflict with the public policy of Malaysia.
(2) If an application for setting aside or suspension of an award has been made to the High Court on the grounds referred to in subparagraph (1)(a)(vii), the High Court may, if it considers it proper, adjourn its decision and may also, on the application of the party claiming recognition or enforcement of the award, order the other party to provide appropriate security.
(3) Where the decision on matters submitted to arbitration can be separated from those not so submitted, only that part of the award which contains decisions on matters submitted to arbitration may be recognized and enforced.

§39.01 INTRODUCTION

Section 39 of the Arbitration Act 2005 provides the grounds for an application to prevent the recognition and enforcement of an award. Section 39 also provides for the adjournment of the recognition and enforcement of an award and the security that may need to be paid in that event.

Section 39 of the Arbitration Act 2005 largely reflects Article 36 of the 1985 Model Law save for the following differences:

(1) the words 'at the request of the party against whom it is invoked' have been included in section 39(1) of the Arbitration Act 2005. These words are not in Article 36(1) but in Article 36(1)(a) of the 1985 Model Law. The significance of this difference is considered in §39.05 *infra*;
(2) the words 'the party making the application' in section 36(1)(a)(iii) of the Arbitration Act 2005 substitute the words 'the party against whom the award is invoked' in Article 36(1)(a)(ii) of the 1985 Model Law;
(3) sections 39(1)(a)(iv) and (v) and 39(3) of the Arbitration Act 2005 reflect Article 36(1)(a)(iii) of the 1985 Model Law. However, only the second limb in section 39(1)(a)(v) is expressly subject to section 39(3);
(4) the words 'unless such agreement was in conflict with a provision of this Act, from which the parties cannot derogate, or, failing such agreement, was not in accordance with this Act' in section 39(1)(a)(vi) of the Arbitration Act 2005 substitute the words 'failing such agreement, was not in accordance with the law of the country where the arbitration took place'. The significance of this is considered in §39.06[E] *infra*;
(5) the words 'to the High Court on the grounds referred to in paragraphs (1)(a)(vii)' in section 39(2) of the Arbitration Act 2005 substitute 'to a court referred to in paragraph (1)(a)(v) of this article'; and
(6) the word 'only' in section 39(3) of the Arbitration Act 2005 is not found in Article 36(1)(a)(iii) of the 1985 Model Law. This appears to be merely a change in drafting.

The foregoing reflects the position under section 39 of the Arbitration Act 2005 as amended by the Arbitration (Amendment) Act 2011. Prior to the amendments in 2011, there were further significant differences between section 39 of the Arbitration Act 2005 and Article 36 of the 1985 Model Law.

The amendments brought section 39 of the Arbitration Act 2005 closer to Article 36 of the 1985 Model Law. This was achieved by:

(1) amending section 39(1)(a)(ii), of the Arbitration Act 2005, which provided for the 'laws of Malaysia' to provide now for 'laws of the State where the award was made' in accordance with Article 36(1)(a)(i) of the 1985 Model Law; and
(2) including section 39(3) of the Arbitration Act 2005, which reflects the proviso to Article 36(1)(a)(iii) of the 1985 Model Law.

Article 36 of the 1985 Model Law in turn reflects Articles V and VI of the 1958 New York Convention. This is intentional, as discussed in §38.01 *supra*.

§39.02 'RECOGNITION AND ENFORCEMENT OF AN AWARD, IRRESPECTIVE OF THE STATE IN WHICH IT WAS MADE ...'

Section 39(1) of the Arbitration Act 2005 provides for the recognition and enforcement of an award 'irrespective of the State in which it was made'. This provision is qualified by sections 38(1) and (4) of the Arbitration Act 2005, which limit recognition and enforcement to States that are a party to the New York Convention, as discussed in §38.04 *supra*.

The High Court, in *Twin Advance (M) Sdn Bhd v. Polar Electro Europe BV* [2013] 3 CLJ 294 at paragraphs 27-29, confirmed that the use of the words 'irrespective of the State in which the award was made' in section 39(1) meant that it was an exception to section 3 of the Arbitration Act 2005. Section 39 applied regardless of where the award was made and is not limited by section 3 to an arbitration with a seat in Malaysia.

The High Court, in *Lebas Technologies Sdn Bhd v. Malaysian Bio-Excell Sdn Bhd* [2018] MLJU 741 at paragraph 26, clarified that section 39(1) only allowed the courts to refuse to recognize an award and not to suspend the enforcement of an award:

> Section 39(1) of the Arbitration Act permits a refusal to recognise or enforce an arbitration award. It does not provide for any stay of an application to enforce or a suspension of the enforcement of an arbitration award. At the risk of being pedantic, the orders sought by the Defendant are therefore not within the provisions of section 39 of the Arbitration Act.

§39.03 '... MAY BE REFUSED ...'

Section 39(1) of the Arbitration Act 2005 provides that recognition and enforcement 'may be refused' on the grounds set out in sections 39(1)(a) and (b).

Even if one of the grounds set out in sections 39(1)(a) and (b) is proved, the court retains a discretion whether to refuse recognition and enforcement, as expressly provided for by the use of the word 'may' in section 39(1). This can be seen from the judgment of the Court of Appeal, in *Agrovenus LLP v. Pacific Inter-Link Sdn Bhd & Another Appeal* [2014] 4 CLJ 525 at paragraph 30.

The courts are likely to exercise this discretion against refusing recognition and enforcement, in accordance with the principle of minimal interference, which is considered in §39.04 *infra*.

§39.04 '... ONLY ...'

Section 39(1) of the Arbitration Act 2005 provides that recognition and enforcement of an award may 'only' be refused on the specified grounds listed.

The courts have repeatedly emphasized that a policy of minimal interference will be adopted in relation to section 39. This means that the courts will only intervene where one of the grounds in section 39 exists. These grounds are exhaustive. Unless the applicant proves one of these grounds, the courts will recognize and enforce an award as a matter of course.

For example, the High Court, in *Taman Bandar Baru Masai Sdn Bhd v. Dindings Corporations Sdn Bhd* [2010] 5 CLJ 83 at paragraph 33 (c), *inter alia*, held:

> I will say AA 2005 makes it compulsory for courts to respect the decision of arbitrators and only minimum intervention is allowed. In this respect, it must not be forgotten that it is the parties who selected the arbitrator and s. 36 of AA 2005 makes the award final, binding and conclusive. And real proof is required to be shown before the court can meddle with the award ... .

Subsequently, the High Court, in *Bauer (M) Sdn Bhd v. Embassy Court Sdn Bhd* [2010] MLJU 1323 at paragraph 19, *inter alia*, held:

> ... It was clearly therefore the intention of the legislature when the 2005 Act was brought into force to accord to arbitral awards a status and recognition that could only be defeated or challenged on those specific grounds or circumstances now entrenched as law. In other words, it should be as a matter of course that arbitral awards be recognized and judgments entered by the courts on those award for purposes of enforcement, unless the court is satisfied that its discretion to do so is restricted by Section 39.

Similarly, the High Court, in *Murray & Roberts Australia Pty Ltd v. Earth Support Company (SEA) Sdn Bhd* [2015] 6 CLJ 649 at paragraph 62, *inter alia*, held:

> ... Section 8 AA provides for a 'minimalist' approach by courts whereby judicial intervention in arbitral matters is only allowed if it is so provided in AA. If a ground is not provided in s. 39(1)(a) and (b) AA, the defendant cannot thus rely on such a ground ... .
>
> ... the nine grounds of refusal are exhaustive. Hence, the defendant cannot rely on any ground which is not stipulated in s. 39(1)(a) and (b) AA, to persuade this court to refuse recognition and/or enforcement of the Australian Arbitral Awards.

The High Court, in *Lebas Technologies supra* at paragraphs 39 and 45, held:

> [39] In regard to arbitral awards, there are specific grounds provided under section 39 of the Arbitration Act as to when their recognition or enforcement may be refused. This leaves no room for the Courts to admit of other grounds not provided. To do so would run counter to the legislative intent of the Arbitration Act. I would add that the legislative intent, even from the provisions of the Arbitration Act itself, is sufficiently apparent.
>
> ...
>
> [45] Regrettably, the last sentence in the Explanatory Statement could have been better worded. Nevertheless, the idea is still consistent with the view that is generally espoused and that is, in situations where there are express provisions in the Arbitration Act, there is no room for judicial intervention.

The courts have also emphasized minimal interference based on the relationship between an application to resist enforcement and an application to set aside an award. In this context, the courts regard an application to resist enforcement as the flip side of an application to set aside an award, as the grounds are similar.

Therefore, for domestic arbitrations, these two applications should be heard together. Where the applications are not heard together, the first which is heard and decided will determine the second application.

A party will not be entitled to a second bite at the cherry. For example, if an application to set aside has been dismissed, this decision will be determinative of any subsequent application to resist enforcement of the award on the same grounds.

In this context, the High Court, in *Kelana Erat Sdn Bhd v. Niche Properties Sdn Bhd & Another Case* [2013] 4 CLJ 1172 at paragraph 62, held that an application to set aside and an application to resist enforcement of an award are 'two sides of the same coin' and there was accordingly 'no need to rehash the arguments'.

Similarly, the High Court, in *JHW Reels Sdn Bhd v. Syarikat Borcos Shipping Sdn Bhd* [2012] MLJU 1790 at paragraph 25, *inter alia*, held:

> ... Given the obvious overlaps between s. 37 and s. 39, it would have made practical sense to have both applications heard before one court and before the same judge. As it now stands, the application to set aside is being heard after the other court has allowed the defendant's application to register the award. To accede to the plaintiff's application here will be to allow the plaintiff to have the proverbial second bite of the cherry.

Apart from this, in a domestic arbitration, where an application to set aside an award has not been made, it is unclear whether a party may be precluded from applying to resist enforcement on the grounds that could have been raised in an application to set aside. The High Court, in *Bauer supra*, held that a party would be precluded from resisting enforcement after having failed to apply to set aside an award. However, recently, the High Court, in *Kejuruteraan Bintai Kindenko Sdn Bhd v. Serdang Baru Properties Sdn Bhd & Another Case* [2018] 1 CLJ 369, held that a party would be entitled to resist enforcement even if an application to set aside the award had not been made. It is submitted that the approach in *Kejuruteraan Bintai Kindenko supra* should be preferred, as otherwise section 39 may be redundant.

In this context, the High Court, in *Bauer supra* at paragraph 16, *inter alia*, held:

> ... The failure of the Defendant to initiate any such application to set aside the Interim Award within the time specified, that is by the Defendant's own inaction, precludes the Defendant from now challenging the Interim Award of the learned Arbitrator of the 14.01.2010.

However, the High Court, in *Kejuruteraan Bintai Kindenko supra* at paragraph 33, held that:

> ... The reproduction in section 39 following the same grounds in a setting aside of an award under section 37 cannot be for decorative purposes but for the deliberate design of permitting the same grounds not raised because there was no previous application to set aside under section 37 to be raised in resisting or opposing an application under section 39 of the AA 2005. The repetition of the same grounds has nothing to do with it being redundant but everything to do with reiteration as in making those same grounds available in resisting an enforcement application under section 39 of the AA 2005.

In international arbitrations, with a seat of arbitration outside Malaysia, the courts are reluctant to prevent enforcement of an award on the grounds that could have been raised in an application to set aside at the seat. Similarly, if an application to set aside at the seat has been made but has been dismissed, the courts are unlikely to allow an application to resist the enforcement of the award on the grounds that have been dismissed by the court at the seat of arbitration. Generally, the courts draw a distinction between the supervisory court at the seat of arbitration and the enforcement court where the award is sought to be enforced. The courts take the position, based on the principle of minimal interference, that an objection to the award should be taken before the supervisory court and not the enforcement court.

These principles were considered in detail by the High Court, in *Murray & Roberts supra* at paragraph 69(b), where it was, *inter alia*, held:

> ... this court cannot consider the merits of the Australian Arbitral Awards. Nor can the court allow the defendant to raise any issue which the defendant could have raised before the Australian Arbitrator or the Australian supervisory courts. The issues regarding defendant's liability and extent of liability as well the plaintiff's alleged failure to mitigate loss, concern the merits of the Australian Arbitral Awards which this court cannot consider.

The Court of Appeal, in *Sintrans Asia Services Pte Ltd v. Inai Kiara Sdn Bhd* [2016] 5 CLJ 746 at paragraph 16, confirmed these principles in relation to international arbitration:

> The court in Malaysia is purely an enforcement court and must recognise a valid arbitration award save and except for the exception provided under the law. If the defendant in this case argues that the arbitration clause is not valid then they would have to establish that it is so under the Singapore law. And the matter would have to be dealt with by the courts having supervisory jurisdiction at the seat of arbitration ie, the Singapore courts or in the arbitration proceeding itself.

These principles were reiterated by the High Court, in *Armada (Singapore) Pte Ltd v. Ashapura Minechem Ltd* [2016] 9 CLJ 709 at paragraph 33(c):

> The proper place to challenge the validity of the arbitration award should be at the seat of arbitration, ie the English court who is the supervisory court rather than in this court who is merely an enforcement court ... .

§39.05 '... AT THE REQUEST OF THE PARTY AGAINST WHOM IT IS INVOKED ...'

As stated under §39.01 *supra*, the words 'at the request of the party against whom it is invoked' in Article 36(1)(a) of the 1985 Model Law were moved in the Arbitration Act 2005 from section 39(1)(a), where these words should have appeared to reflect the 1985 Model Law, to section 39(1).

Due to this change, the courts have interpreted section 39(1) as requiring, in any circumstance, an application to be made by the party against whom the award is sought to be enforced.

Furthermore, the courts have interpreted section 39(1) to mean that the courts cannot act on their own motion under even 39(1)(b).

This can be seen from the judgment of the High Court in *Murray & Roberts supra* at paragraph 65:

> ... I am not inclined to accept that the court may act of its own motion under s. 39(1)(b)(i) and (ii) AA. If the court may act suo motu under s. 39(1)(b)(i) and (ii) AA, this is contrary to the 'minimalist' approach embedded in s. 8 AA and explained by the Court of Appeal in *Capping Corp Ltd* and *SDA Architects*. The above Malaysian cases have clearly held that once the plaintiff fulfils all the formal requirements, the legal onus shifts to the defendant to prove any one of the nine grounds of refusal. If the defendant is unable to discharge such a legal burden, the court has no discretion but to recognise and enforce the Australian Arbitral Awards under s. 38(1) AA.

The need for an application under section 39 is emphasized by the Court of Appeal, in *Alami Vegetable Oil Products Sdn Bhd v. Hafeez Iqbal Oil & Ghee Industries (Pvt) Ltd* [2016] 7 CLJ 19 at paragraph 2:

> ... For s. 39 to apply, the application must be made by the respondent to the award. In this case, the respondent to the award was the appellant/defendant and no such application had been filed but only an opposing affidavit stating why the respondent/plaintiff's application should not be allowed ... .

The need for an application under section 39 has now been confirmed by the Federal Court, in *CTI Group Inc v. International Bulk Carriers SpA* [2017] 5 MLJ 314 at paragraph 105:

> In our view, the two-stage process for the enforcement of arbitral awards as contained in ss 38 and 39 of our Arbitration Act (read with O 69 r 8 of the Rules of Court 2012) does not permit a party seeking to set aside an order made under s 38 to apply to set it aside under that very section on the ground that there was no arbitration agreement in existence between the parties. That party must apply to set that order aside under s 39.

§39.06 GROUNDS FOR REFUSING RECOGNITION AND ENFORCEMENT

The grounds for refusing recognition and enforcement of an award are set out in sections 39(1)(a) and (b) of the Arbitration Act 2005. These grounds reflect the grounds for setting aside an award in sections 37(1)(a) and (b) of the Arbitration Act 2005 save for certain alterations, which are as follows:

(1) section 37(1)(a)(ii) provides that the laws of Malaysia will apply to the arbitration agreement if there is no indication which law is to apply, while section 39(1)(a)(ii) provides that the law of the State where the award was made will apply to the arbitration agreement in the absence of any other indication. This difference arises because section 37 is dealing with the setting aside of an award, which may only occur at the seat of the arbitration, that is

where the award was made. As an award may only be set aside in Malaysia, where Malaysia is the seat, section 37(1)(a)(ii) only provides for the laws of Malaysia as the default law to be applied. However, an award made in any State may be sought to be enforced in Malaysia, and that is why section 39(1)(a)(ii) has to provide for the State in which the award was made as the default law applicable to the arbitration agreement; and

(2) section 39(1)(a)(vii) does not have a corresponding provision in section 37(1)(a). This is because section 39(1)(a)(vii) provides for a scenario that cannot arise in the context of an application to set aside an award under section 37(1). That is a scenario where a party seeks enforcement of an award in Malaysia, while the award has not yet become binding or has been set aside or suspended in another State. This scenario should not arise under section 37, as the courts in Malaysia will be the supervisory courts that have the power to suspend or set aside the award and not a court in another State.

The grounds in sections 37(1) and 39(1) do, however, overlap to a large extent and this has been recognized by the courts, as discussed in §39.04 *supra*. This overlap is due to both sections reflecting Articles V and VI of the 1958 New York Convention, which was intended in the 1985 Model Law.

Like section 37(1), section 39(1) is divided between grounds the applicant is required to prove, as set out in section 39(1)(a), and ground upon which the court is entitled to act on its own motion, as set out in section 39(1)(b). However, this distinction has been somewhat blurred, by the judgment of the High Court, in *Murray & Roberts supra*, which decided that proof was required for the grounds under both sections 39(1)(a) and (b).

The courts have repeatedly emphasized the need for the applicant to prove the grounds relied on under section 39(1)(a).[8] The burden of proving these grounds is on the applicant, once the party seeking to enforce the award has satisfied the requirements under section 38.

In this context, the High Court, in *The Government of India v. Cairn Energy India Pty Ltd & Ors* [2014] 9 MLJ 149 at paragraphs 127 and 128, *inter alia*, held:

> [127] The requirement of 'proof' is also to be found in s 39 of Act 646. Although this requirement is in relation to the grounds for refusing recognition or enforcement of an award (note the earlier observations of the UNCITRAL Secretariat's explanatory note on this), the approach of other courts concerning such a requirement is of good guidance. In this respect, the House of Lords' decision in *Dallah Real Estate and Tourism Holding Co v. Ministry of Religious Affairs of the Government of Pakistan* [2011] 1 AC 763 at p 813 is of some relevance.

> [128] Lord Mance JSC opined that the respondent in that case had taken the 'correct position' on the issue of who bears the onus of proving the matters alleged of; that is was with the party objecting to the recognition of the award; that the 'objecting party has the burden of proof, which it may seek to discharge as it sees fit'. Therefore, the burden of proving the present grounds of challenge lies with the plaintiff.

---

8. *See Taman Bandar Baru supra* at para. 33(c), HC; *Bauer supra* at para. 19.

This was confirmed by the Court of Appeal, in *Agrovenus supra* at paragraph 16, where it was, *inter alia*, held:

> The respondent, in this case, is clearly the party against whom the recognition or enforcement of the award is invoked and who is requesting refusal. Section 39(1)(a) requires that it must satisfy the High Court with proof of any of the grounds set out in paras. (i) to (vii) thereof that it relied upon ... .

The need for proof of the grounds relied on was again emphasized by the High Court, in *Perembun (M) Sdn Bhd v. Binas BMK Sdn Bhd and another case* [2015] 11 MLJ 447 at paragraph 48:

> Contrary to Perembun's contentions, none of the allegations or complaints resonate in any of the grounds relied on. I do not find any of the grounds proved, be it under ss 37 or 39; and these sections do require Perembun to prove its charges. It has not.

As mentioned above, the need for proof has also been extended to the grounds under section 39(1)(b), by the High Court in *Murray & Roberts supra* at paragraph 65.

Therefore, all the grounds, regardless as to whether they are under section 39(1)(a) or (b), must be proved. We now turn to consider each of these nine individual grounds, seven under section 39(1)(a) and two under section 39(1)(b).

[A] Incapacity of Party

Section 39(1)(a)(ii) of the Arbitration Act 2005 provides that an award may not be recognized where a party to the arbitration agreement was under any incapacity. Section 39(1)(a)(i) reflects the ground for setting aside an award under section 37(1)(a)(i), and reference should be made to the commentary under §37.03 *supra*.

Section 39(1)(a)(i) does not provide under which law the incapacity of a party is to be determined. The applicable law as to the incapacity of a party will accordingly be determined in accordance with the conflicts of laws rules applicable in Malaysia.[9]

[B] Invalidity of Arbitration Agreement

Section 39(1)(a)(ii) of the Arbitration Act 2005 provides that an award may not be enforced where the arbitration agreement is invalid under the law the parties have agreed to or, in the absence of such agreement, the law where the award was made.

Section 39(1)(a)(ii) was amended by the Arbitration (Amendment) Act 2011. Prior to this amendment, in the event the parties had not agreed on the applicable law, the default law would be the laws of Malaysia. This was inconsistent with Malaysia's obligations under the New York Convention and was accordingly amended in 2011. The Court of Appeal, in *Agrovenus supra* at paragraph 217, confirmed that this amendment would not have retrospective effect.

---

9. *See* Albert Jan van den Berg, *The New York Convention of 1958* (Kluwer Law 1981) at para. III – 4.1.1.

Apart from this, section 39(1)(a)(ii) reflects the ground for setting aside in section 37(1)(a)(ii) and reference should be made to the commentary under §37.03[B] *supra*. If the parties have agreed that the laws of Malaysia should apply to the arbitration agreement, or in the absence of agreement, if the award was made in Malaysia, reference should also be made to the commentary under §9.01-§9.03 *supra*.

The courts will give effect to the law agreed by the parties to be applicable to the arbitration agreement. The courts are reluctant to consider the validity of the arbitration agreement, where the party resisting enforcement of the award had not raised this issue in the arbitral proceedings or in the proceedings to set aside the award.

This can be seen from the judgment of the Court of Appeal, in *Agrovenus supra* at paragraphs 30(b) to (d), where it was, *inter alia*, held:

> (b) the respondent, in this case, raised the objection as to the jurisdiction of the arbitral tribunal for the first time at the High Court in Malaysia when the appellant sought recognition or enforcement of the award by the arbitral tribunal. Given that arbitral tribunal proceedings are not informal proceedings, but are undertaken by parties with the clear intention of obtaining a decision that settles the dispute between the parties, parties cannot be unaware if the arbitral tribunal lacks jurisdiction because jurisdiction is conferred by the parties;
>
> (c) yet no explanation was given for the failure to object to jurisdiction before the arbitral tribunal, particularly since English law would require the respondent to have made the objections as to jurisdiction before the arbitral tribunal or lose the right to make the objection. The objection made only after having participated fully in the arbitration at all times, and even then only when the appellant sought recognition or enforcement of the award by the High Court suggests the respondent took part in the proceedings before the arbitral tribunal while keeping it up its sleeve the objection as to jurisdiction to be used to challenge the award if the award went against it. We agree with the description in *Rustall Trading Ltd v Gill & Duffus SA* [2000] 1 Lloyd's Rep 14 that this is a fundamental principle of objection. A party cannot seek to have its cake and at the same time eat it too; and
>
> (d) furthermore, the fact of failure to object at the proceedings before the arbitral tribunal and thus causing all parties to act on the basis the respondent accepted that the arbitral tribunal had jurisdiction or scope certainly does not commend itself to an exercise of discretion in favour of the respondent to refuse recognition or enforcement of the award. It calls properly for the application of the doctrine of estoppel as enunciated in *Boustead Trading (1985) Sdn Bhd v Arab-Malaysia Merchant Bank Bhd* [1995] 3 MLJ 331 (FC).

This can also be seen from the judgment of the Court of Appeal, in *Sintrans Asia Services Pte Ltd v. Inai Kiara Sdn Bhd* [2016] 5 CLJ 749 at paragraphs 15 and 16, where it was, *inter alia*, held:

> [15] The validity of the arbitration agreement which we have referred to is to be determined by the law of the country where the award was made. In our particular case since the seat of the arbitration was in Singapore, the anchor or juridical home by which the arbitration clause is to be assumed is the laws applicable in Republic of Singapore. The arbitration clause is clear in terms and parties have subjected themselves to be bound by it. Upon a careful examination of s. 39(1)(a)(ii) and

since the arbitration agreement clearly provides the law applicable to the arbitration agreement, the learned judge erred in law in subjecting the same to Malaysian law.

[16] The court in Malaysia is purely an enforcement court and must recognise a valid arbitration award save and except for the exception provided under the law. If the defendant in this case argues that the arbitration clause is not valid then they would have to establish that it is so under the Singapore law. And the matter would have to be dealt with by the courts having supervisory jurisdiction at the seat of arbitration ie, the Singapore courts or in the arbitration proceeding itself.

[C]   Notice and Inability to Present Case

Section 39(1)(a)(iii) of the Arbitration Act 2005 provides that an award may be set aside where a party has not been given proper notice of the appointment of an arbitrator or of the arbitral proceedings or was otherwise unable to present this case.

Section 39(1)(a)(iii) reflects the ground for setting aside in section 37(1)(a)(iii), and reference should be made to the commentary under §37.03[C] *supra*.

[D]   Jurisdiction

Sections 39(1)(a)(iv) and (v), as well as section 39(3), of the Arbitration Act 2005 should be read together. This is because these three sections are based on Article 36(1)(a)(iii) of the 1985 Model Law, which is in turn based on Article V(1)(c) of the New York Convention.

These sections of the Arbitration Act 2005 provide that an arbitration award may not be enforced where:

(1) the dispute is not within the 'submission to arbitration' in the sense that the dispute is outside the arbitration agreement; or
(2) the decision in the award is beyond the 'scope of the submission' meaning the mandate given by the parties to the arbitral tribunal.

In the latter situation, the parts of the decision which are within the mandate given by the parties may be enforced.

It is important to bear in mind that these sections deal with situations where the arbitral tribunal has exceeded their jurisdiction. The arbitral tribunal does have jurisdiction in these situations, but the jurisdiction they have has been exceeded. Where it is contended that the arbitral tribunal has no jurisdiction at all, section 39(1)(a)(ii) rather than (iv) and (v) would be applicable.

Sections 39(1)(a)(iii), (iv) and 39(3) reflect the grounds for setting aside an award under sections 37(1)(a)(iv), (v) and 37(3) and reference should accordingly be made to the commentary under §37.03[D] *supra*.

The courts have generally emphasized that the source of the jurisdiction of the arbitral tribunal is the arbitration agreement.[10] So long as the award is generally within the scope of the arbitration agreement, the courts are unlikely to refuse to enforce an award on the grounds of excess of jurisdiction. The courts are also reluctant to refuse to enforce an award on the ground that the decision is outside the pleadings delivered by the parties. The 'scope of the submission' does not appear to be limited by the pleadings. The outer limits of the scope would appear to be the arbitration agreement. It is unclear, however, how this would be further limited by the mandate given by the parties. This mandate does not appear to be based on the pleadings alone and may extend to the evidence led by the parties and the submissions made.

The High Court, in *Kejuruteraan Bintai Kindenko supra* at paragraphs 40 and 42, relied on section 39(3) of the Arbitration Act 2005 to 'excise' parts of the award which dealt with pre-award interest, which the arbitral tribunal had no jurisdiction to grant:

> [40] However there is no need to set aside the whole of the Award as the saving provision in section 39(3) AA 2005 allows the matter not submitted as in could not be submitted to arbitration to be excised from and separated from the matters submitted to Arbitration.
>
> ...
>
> [42] The part that is affected and infected with respect to the pre-award interest can be clearly and clinically severed or excised from the part of the Award that is intact, which integrity has not been compromised or contaminated in any way by the pre-award interest element.

[E] Composition and Procedure

Section 39(1)(a)(vi) of the Arbitration Act 2005 provides that an award may not be enforced where the composition of the arbitral tribunal or the procedure was not in accordance with:

(1) the agreement of the parties, unless such agreement was contrary to non-derogable provisions of the Act;
(2) the provisions of the Act, in the absence of such an agreement.

Section 39(1)(a)(vi) reflects the ground to set aside in section 37(1)(a)(vi). However, section 39(1)(a)(vi) should not have been identical to section 37(1)(a)(vi). This is because section 39(1)(a)(vi) needs to deal with international aspects of arbitration but section 37(1)(a)(vi) need not. This can be seen from both Article 36(1)(iv) of the 1985 Model Law and Article V(1)(d) of the New York Convention. Under these provisions, in the absence of an agreement on the composition of the arbitral tribunal or the arbitration procedure, 'the law of the country where the arbitration took

---

10. See *Taman Bandar Baru supra* at para. 33(a), HC; *Tridant Engineering (M) Sdn Bhd v. Ssangyong Engineering and Construction Co Ltd* [2016] 6 MLJ 166 at paras 35 and 36, CA; *Agrovenus supra* at para. 30(a).

place' will apply. This differs from section 39(1)(a)(vi), which imposes the provisions of the Arbitration Act 2005 on composition and procedure on an arbitration that may have taken place in another country.

This appears to be a fundamental error in the drafting of section 39(1)(a)(vi), which may result in a breach of Malaysia' obligations under the 1958 New York Convention. This error, like the error in section 39(1)(a)(ii) that has been corrected, should be corrected by an amendment to the Arbitration Act 2005.

Apart from this, the express provision in section 39(1)(a)(vi) that the agreement on composition and procedure should be subject to the non-derogable provisions of the Arbitration Act 2005 is contrary to the ethos of Article 36(1)(iv) of the 1985 Model Law and Article V(1)(d) of the New York Convention which both give supremacy to the agreement between the parties. There is no need for any qualification to this supremacy by reference to the non-derogable provisions of the Act as any such fundamental conflict will result in the award not being enforced under section 39(1)(b)(ii).[11]

Parties have rarely relied on this provision, as the composition of the arbitral tribunal usually follows the agreement of the parties. As to arbitration procedure, most published rules of arbitration allow the arbitral tribunal considerable discretion, thus making it difficult to resist the enforcement of an award on this ground.

The High Court, in *Open type Joint Stock Company Efirnoye ('EFKL') v. Altas Trading Ltd* [2012] 1 CLJ 323 at paragraph 5, considered an unusual agreement on procedure:

> Pursuant to Additional Agreement No. 6, the plaintiff and the defendant agreed that cl. 6 above would be varied to read as follows:
>
> 6. ARBITRATION
>
> 6.1 All disputes between the parties in connection with the non-fulfillment or improper fulfillment of the conditions of the contract shall be resolved by means of negotiation.
>
> 6.2 If the parties cannot come to mutual agreement, *then dispute should be passed for considering and final resolution to international Commercial Arbitration Court at the Chamber of Commerce and Industry of Ukraine* (the place for legal investigation is Kiev, Ukraine) according to its regulations with three arbitrators present in case *when the plaintiff is the Seller, and the dispute should be passed for considering and final resolution to international Commercial Arbitration Court at the Chamber of Commerce and Industry of Russian Federation* (the place of legal investigation is Moscow, the Russian Federation) according to its regulations with three arbitrators present in case *when the Plaintiff is the Buyer.*
>
> When the dispute is considered in the given courts, *the norms of the substantive and procedural laws of Ukraine when the Plaintiff is the seller is applied; the norms of the substantive and procedural laws of Russia when the Plaintiff is the Buyer is applied.* (emphasis added).

The High Court held that two arbitrations commenced by a party, one as seller and the other as buyer, in Kiev and Moscow respectively, were in accordance with the procedure agreed upon. The High Court did not accept the contention that once the

---

11. *See* Albert Jan van den Berg, *The New York Arbitration Convention of 1958 supra* at para. III 4.4.

arbitration in Kiev had been commenced a subsequent arbitration based on the same contract should not have been commenced in Moscow. In reaching this decision, the High Court emphasized that the disputes being determined in the two arbitrations differed. This decision shows that the courts will be reluctant not to enforce an award merely because the procedure agreed upon is unusual.

[F] Not Binding, Suspended or Set Aside

Sections 39(1)(a)(vii) and 39(2) of the Arbitration Act 2005 provide for three distinct but related grounds to refuse enforcement of an award:

(1) where the award has not yet become binding;
(2) where the award has been set aside or suspended; and
(3) where an application has been made to set aside or suspend an award, in which event an adjournment may be granted.

These three grounds will be considered sequentially below.

[1] Not Binding

An award may not be enforced when it has not yet become binding. This necessarily raises the question when does an award become binding. Section 36(1) of the Arbitration Act 2005 provides that an award is binding when it is made.[12] However, section 38(1) of the Arbitration Act 2005 requires that an application be made to the High Court for recognition that an award is binding.[13]

The legislative history of Article V(1)(e) of the New York Convention, on which section 39(1)(a)(vii) is based, indicates that the word 'binding' was used to avoid 'double exequatur' that would require leave to enforce to have first been obtained in the country of origin.[14]

Therefore, it is clear that leave to enforce need not be obtained before an award becomes binding. However, when exactly an award becomes binding remains unclear. Generally, this question has been determined based on the law applicable to the award or the law of the country of origin of the award. In the case of an award to which the laws of Malaysia apply, or which was made in Malaysia, it would appear that an award would be binding from the time it was made or upon an application for recognition under section 36(1) or 38(1) respectively. This may however lead to a situation where leave to enforce is required for an award to be binding, as this is a requirement of the country of origin. This would defeat the intent behind the use of the word 'binding', which is to prevent 'double exequatur'.

---

12. See §36.01 to §36.03 supra.
13. See §38.02 supra.
14. See Albert Jan van den Berg, *The New York Arbitration Convention of 1958 supra* at para. III – 4.5.2.1.

Therefore, it has been suggested that the word 'binding' should be given an autonomous meaning that is not dependent on the law applicable to the award or the country of origin.[15] The autonomous interpretation of the term 'binding' is that an award is binding when there is no longer any ordinary means of recourse against the award in the place the award was made. A distinction is drawn between ordinary and extraordinary means of recourse based on the legislative history of Article V(1)(e) of the New York Convention. Ordinary and extraordinary means of recourse are civil law concepts. An ordinary means of recourse is where a decision may be appealed on the merits. While, extraordinary means of recourse are appeals based on irregularities, particularly procedural ones. It is suggested that an award is not yet binding when it may be appealed on the merits to another arbitral tribunal or the courts. This fits into the distinction in Article V(1)(e) of the New York Convention and section 39(1)(a)(vii) of the Arbitration Act 2005 between the award not yet being binding or having been set aside or suspended. The award not being binding is where there is ordinary recourse based on the merits. The award being set aside or suspended is based on extraordinary recourse due to an irregularity.[16]

[2] Set Aside or Suspended

An award may not be enforced where it has been set aside. In this context, the award must have been set aside. An application to set aside would be insufficient. Where only an application has been made, a party would need to rely on section 39(2) of the Arbitration Act 2005 rather than section 39(1)(a)(vii).

The award must also have been set aside by the court of the country in which the award was made. This follows the universally accepted practice that an application to set aside must be made at the place of arbitration as can be seen in §39.04 *supra*.

Alternatively, the award may be set aside 'under the law of which, that, award was made'. This phrase provides for the extremely rare occurrence in practice that the award is governed upon the agreement of the parties by a law different from the law of the place of arbitration.

The use of the words '... may be refused ...' in section 39(1) of the Arbitration Act 2005 means that the courts have a discretion whether to refuse enforcement of an award even where one of the grounds in sections 39(1)(a) and (b) is established.[17]

This means that the courts may enforce an award in Malaysia even if the award has been set aside at the place of arbitration. This rather unusual situation has yet to occur in Malaysia but can be seen in judgments from France and the United States of America.[18]

---

15. *See* Albert Jan van den Berg, *The New York Arbitration Convention of 1958 supra* at para. III – 4.5.2.2.
16. *See* Albert Jan van den Berg, *The New York Arbitration Convention of 1958 supra* at para. III – 4.5.2.2.
17. *See* §39.03 *supra*.
18. *See Societe Hilmarton v. Societe Omnium de Traitment et de Valorisation* (1994) Rev Arb 327; In the matter of the Arbitration of Certain Controversies Between Chromalloy Aeroservices and the Arab Republic of Egypt 939 F Supp 907 (DDC 1996).

An award may also not be enforced where it has been suspended. The meaning of 'suspended' in section 39(1)(a)(vii) of the Arbitration Act 2005 is unclear. The word is also used in Article 36(1)(a)(v) of the 1985 Model Law and Article V(1)(e) of the New York Convention. Based on the legislative history of the New York Convention, 'suspended' appears to mean that the enforcement of the award has been suspended.[19]

[3] Application to Set Aside or Suspend

The intent of section 39(2) of the Arbitration Act 2005 is that the enforcement of an award may be adjourned by the courts of Malaysia where there is a pending application to set aside or suspend the award in the courts of the place of arbitration.

This appears to be the intent of section 39(2), as this is what is effectively provided for in Article 36(2) of the 1985 Model Law and Article VI of the New York Convention.

Unfortunately, the words 'made to the High Court on the grounds referred to in subparagraph (1)(a)(vii)' have been used in section 39(2), instead of 'made to a court referred to in paragraph (1)(a)(v)' as in Article 36(2) of the 1985 Model Law or 'made to a competent authority referred to in Article V(1)(e)' in the New York Convention.

This appears to be a drafting error. The intention cannot be that the enforcement of an award will only be adjourned if there is a pending application to set aside or suspend the award in the High Court, which is defined by section 2(1) of the Arbitration Act 2005 as the High Court of Malaya or Sabah and Sarawak. The intention must be that that an adjournment of the enforcement of the award will be allowed when there is a pending application to set aside or suspend, regardless of whether the application is pending in Malaysia or at the place of arbitration.

If there is a pending application to set aside or suspend, the courts have a discretion whether to adjourn the enforcement of the award. The discretion granted to the courts is clear from the use of the words 'may, if it considers it proper'.

The question then is how will the courts exercise this discretion. The courts will have to weigh the legitimate rights of the party applying to set aside or suspend the award against any prejudice that may be suffered by the party seeking to enforce the ward. Insofar as the party seeking to set aside or suspend the award is concerned, the courts will need to consider whether the grounds for the application are reasonable. Such a party may be required to provide some summary proof of the grounds they rely on. The courts should require such proof to prevent dilatory tactics by a party merely seeking to delay the enforcement of an award.[20]

Insofar as the party seeking enforcement is concerned, provided that such a party has applied for security, the court may consider the extent to which such security may assuage any prejudice such a party may suffer.

---

19. *See* Albert Jan van den Berg, *The New York Arbitration Convention of 1958 supra* at para. III – 4.5.3.2.
20. *See* Albert Jan van den Berg, *The New York Convention of 1958 supra* at para. III – 4.5.3.3.

[G] Arbitrability

The High Court may not enforce an award under section 39(1)(b)(i), where the subject matter of the dispute is not capable of settlement by arbitration under the laws of Malaysia.

This ground for refusing enforcement of an award reflects section 4(1) of the Arbitration Act 2005, which provides that any dispute may be resolved by arbitration unless the arbitration agreement is contrary to public policy. Reference should be made to §4.01 and §4.02 *supra* for a commentary on arbitration agreements that may be contrary to public policy.

As the arbitrability of a dispute depends on public policy, having section 39(1)(b)(i) as a separate ground from section 39(1)(b)(ii) appears superfluous. The arbitrability ground in Article V(2)(a) of the New York Convention is recognized as being superfluous and maintained as a separate ground for historic reasons.[21]

Section 39(1)(b)(i) expressly provides that the arbitrability of the dispute shall be determined in accordance with the laws of Malaysia. Nevertheless, in considering the arbitrability of the dispute, and whether it is contrary to public policy, especially where an award from a foreign state is concerned, it is submitted that the public policy the courts should consider is the international rather than the domestic public policy of Malaysia. This is considered in §39.06 [H] *infra*.

It is also submitted that the non-arbitrability should not merely be incidental to the dispute but should at least cover a category of disputes or the whole dispute if enforcement is to be refused.[22]

[H] Public Policy

The High Court may refuse to enforce an award under section 39(1)(b)(ii) of the Arbitration Act 2005, where the award is in conflict with public policy. The public policy referred to in section 39(1)(b)(ii) is expressly stated to be the public policy of Malaysia.

The courts have narrowly construed the term 'public policy' as being the most basic notions of morality. Furthermore, although the public policy is that of Malaysia, a distinction is drawn between domestic and international public policy. An act that may be contrary to the laws of Malaysia and accordingly her domestic public policy may not necessarily be contrary to her international public policy. This is because her international public policy is concerned with the most basic notions of morality.[23]

These principles are lucidly expressed by the High Court, in *Open Type Joint Stock Company Efirnoye (EFKO) v. Alfa Trading Ltd* [2012] 1 CLJ 323 at paragraphs 50, 51 and 54:

---

21. *See* Albert Jan van den Berg, *The New York Convention of 1958 supra* at para. III – 5.2.
22. *See* Albert Jan van den Berg, *The New York Convention of 1958 supra* at para. III – 5.2.
23. *See* Albert Jan van den Berg, *The New York Convention of 1958 supra* at para. III – 5.1.

[50] ... In any event applying the test set out in the *Ras Al-Khaimah* case (above) it can hardly be said that the enforcement of the Arbitration Award would be wholly offensive to the ordinary, reasonable and fully informed members of the public on whose behalf the powers of the state are exercised ...

[51] In relation to the law relating to the invoking of the public policy exception, the decision of the New Zealand Court of Appeal in the case of *Reeves v. One World Challenge LLC* [2005] NZCA 314 supports the position that a higher threshold is required to invoke this exception ... The Court of Appeal in New Zealand rejected this approach and held that the public policy exception was a narrow one that had necessarily to be confined in line with the comity of nations principle. The fact that a case would have been decided differently under New Zealand law was not sufficient to invoke the exception ...

...

[54] I also respectfully adopt the reasoning in the Malaysian High Court case of *Infineon Technologies (M) Sdn Bhd v. Orisoft Technology Sdn Bhd* [2010] 1 LNS 889 Mohamad Ariff bin Md Yusoff held, *inter alia* as follows:
> ... I now reproduce below some leading views taken on the issue of public policy in the area of arbitration law. For example in the Hong Kong Court of Final Appeal decision in *Hebei Import & Export Corp v. Polytek Engineering Co Ltd* [1999] 2 HKCFAR 111, Bokhary PJ said: '... there must be compelling reasons before enforcement of the convention award can be refused on public policy grounds. This is not to say that the reasons must be so extreme that the award falls to be cursed by bell book and candle. But the reasons must go beyond the minimum which would justify setting aside the domestic judgment award. A point to similar effect was made in a comparable context by the United States Supreme Court in *Mitsubishi Motors Corp v. Soler Chrysler Plymouth Inc* [1985] 473 US 640 ... the majority said this ... concerns of international comity, respect for the capacities of foreign and Transnational Tribunals, and sensitivity to the needs of the International commercial System for predictability in the resolution of disputes require that we enforce the parties agreement even assuming that a contrary result would be forthcoming in a domestic context ...
> ... Both leading cases in Hong Kong and Singapore relate to the enforcement of a foreign arbitral award. In both cases, the approach is not to refuse to register on the ground of conflict of public policy unless the most basic notions of morality would be offended.

The courts have considered two instances of awards said to be in conflict with the public policy of Malaysia. In neither instance did the courts accept the challenge.

In *Open Type supra* at paragraphs 41-43 and 47, the High Court accepted that if a dispute had been decided in an arbitration, it would be in accordance with the principle of res judicata and contrary to public policy to allow the same dispute to be determined by a subsequent arbitration. However, on the facts, the party resisting enforcement of the award had failed to show that the dispute decided on was the same. To the contrary, the party seeking enforcement had shown, based on the awards, that different disputes were determined by the respective awards.

The High Court, in *Tanjung Langsat Port Sdn Bhd v. Trafigura Pte Ltd & Another Case* [2016] 4 CLJ 927 at paragraphs 78, 87-89, held that the absence of reasons in an award would not render the award contrary to public policy, as the rules of natural justice did not require that reasons be given. The High Court went on to hold that, in any event, sufficient reasons had been provided to adequately notify the parties of the basis of the award.

It is submitted that where the arbitration agreement requires that reasons be given in the award, the absence of such reasons would be in conflict with public policy. The reason for this, as stated in another context in *Tanjung Langsat supra*, is that the parties are entitled to know how the arbitral tribunal has reached its decision. This must, however, be qualified by the proviso that the parties are free to dispense with such reasons either by express agreement or as a matter of practice.[24]

---

24. *See* Albert Jan van den Berg, *The New York Convention of 1958 supra* at para. III – 5.3.3.

CHAPTER 9
Additional Provisions Relating to Arbitration

40.   *Consolidation of Proceedings and Concurrent Hearings*

   (1) The parties may agree –
      (a) that the arbitration proceedings shall be consolidated with other arbitration proceedings; or
      (b) that concurrent hearings shall be held,
      on such terms as may be agreed.
   (2) Unless the parties agree to confer such power on the arbitral tribunal, the tribunal has no power to order consolidation of arbitration proceedings or concurrent hearings.

§40.01   INTRODUCTION

Section 40 of the Arbitration Act 2005 allows the parties to agree to consolidate arbitration proceedings or to hold concurrent hearings. There is no equivalent to section 40 in the 1985 Model Law. As section 40 appears in Part III of the Arbitration Act 2005, it will apply in domestic arbitrations unless the parties have opted out in accordance with section 3(2) of the Arbitration Act 2005. Section 40 will not apply in international arbitrations unless the parties have opted in under section 3(3) of the Arbitration Act 2005.

§40.02 AUTONOMY

Section 40 of the Arbitration Act 2005 expressly provides that the parties must agree before the proceedings are consolidated or concurrent hearings are held. The Arbitration Act 2005 emphasizes the need for an agreement in deference to the principle of party autonomy. To allow the courts or the arbitral tribunal to order a consolidation would be contrary to the principle of autonomy. To compel consolidation or concurrent hearings may also lead to a party being in proceedings with a third party they never intended to arbitrate a dispute with. This may also result in an unexpected loss of confidentiality.

Section 40 of the Arbitration Act 2005, however, does allow the parties to agree on consolidation or concurrent hearings, as there are advantages to this in certain circumstances. First, it avoids different findings on the same issues. Second, it may result in a saving of time and cost. Third, where a transaction involves a chain of contracts, it allows disputes arising from the same transaction and facts but different contracts to be resolved together. This can be seen, for example, in the construction industry, where a single project may result in a main building contract and a series of subcontracts, all of which involve the same or similar facts.

Parties are able to agree on consolidation expressly, or by incorporating by reference standard forms of contract or adopting institutional rules. The latter two of these are most common in practice and are considered below.

[A] PAM Contract 2018

The Malaysian Institute of Architect, or PAM by its Malay acronym, publishes the PAM suite of contracts for construction projects, which is the de facto standard form of building contract for the private sector in Malaysia.

The PAM suite of contracts expressly provides for consolidation of arbitration proceedings arising from the main contract and the nominated subcontract.

Clause 37.5 of both the PAM Contract 2018 (With Quantities) and PAM Contract 2006 (Without Quantities) provides:

> Where any dispute arises between the Employer and Contractor and the dispute relates to the works of a Nominated Sub-Contractor and arises out of or is connected with the same dispute between the Contractor and such Nominated Sub-Contractor, the Employer and Contractor shall use their best endeavour to appoint the same arbitrator to hear the dispute under Clause 31.3 of the PAM Sub-Contract 2018.

Clause 31.3 of the PAM Sub-Contract 2018 in turn provides:

> If any dispute arises in connection with the Main Contract and such dispute concerns the Sub-Contract Works, the Contractor may by written notice to the Sub-Contractor require that any such dispute under the Sub-Contract be referred to the appointed arbitrator under the Main Contract subject to the agreement of the Employer (such agreement not to be unreasonably withheld) and provided always that the arbitrator's hearing of witnesses has not commenced. Where the arbitrator

is willing to act and has no conflict of interest in so acting, and the Sub-Contractor has no valid grounds why the arbitrator should not act under the Sub-Contract, such dispute shall be referred to the same arbitrator. In such event, the arbitrator may consolidate the proceedings.

There are several conditions to consolidation under the PAM suite of contracts:

(1) a dispute must have arisen between the Employer and the Contractor (the Main Contract Dispute);
(2) a dispute must have also arisen between the Contractor and the Sub-Contractor (the Sub-Contract Dispute);
(3) the Main Contract Dispute relates to the Sub-Contract Works;
(4) the Main Contract Dispute arises out of or is related to the Sub-Contract Dispute;
(5) the Contractor requests that the Sub-Contract Dispute be referred to the appointed arbitrator under the Main Contract;
(6) the Employer agrees to this Contractor's request, with such agreement not to be unreasonably withheld;
(7) the Sub-Contractor has no valid grounds for objecting to such an arbitrator acting;
(8) such an arbitrator has not commenced hearing witnesses; and
(9) such an arbitrator is willing to act and has no conflict.

[B] AIAC Arbitration Rules 2018

Rule 10 of the AIAC Arbitration Rules 2018 allows for consolidation and concurrent hearings on the following terms:

Consolidation of Proceedings and Concurrent Hearings
1. Upon the request of any Party or, if the Director deems it appropriate, the Director may consolidate two or more arbitrations into one arbitration, if:
   (a) the Parties have agreed to consolidation;
   (b) all claims in the arbitrations are made under the same arbitration agreement; or
   (c) the claims are made under more than one arbitration agreement, the dispute arises in connection with the same legal relationships, and the Director deems the arbitration agreements to be compatible.
2. In deciding whether to consolidate, the Director shall consult all Parties and any appointed arbitrators, and shall have regard to any relevant circumstances including, but not limited to:
   (a) the stage of the pending arbitrations and whether any arbitrators have been nominated or appointed;
   (b) any prejudice that may be caused to any of the Parties; and
   (c) the efficiency and expeditiousness of the proceedings.
3. When the arbitrations are consolidated, they shall be consolidated into the arbitration that commenced first, unless otherwise agreed by the Parties.
4. Within 15 days of being notified of a decision by the Director to consolidate two or more arbitrations, all Parties may agree on the arbitrators to be

appointed, if any, to the consolidated arbitration and/or the process of such appointment. Failing such agreement, any party may request the Director to appoint the arbitral tribunal, in which case, the Director may release any arbitrators appointed prior to the consolidation decision. In these circumstances, all Parties shall be deemed to have waived their right to nominate an arbitrator.
5. The parties irrevocably waive their rights to any form of appeal, review or recourse to any court or other judicial authority, on the basis of any decision to consolidate or not to consolidate arbitrations, to the validity and/or enforcement of any award made by the arbitral tribunal, insofar as such waiver can validly be made.

Rule 10(1) allows for consolidation both at a party's request and at the Director's own initiative. Consolidation may be ordered in three circumstances as outlined in Rule 10(1) above. The first two circumstances are to be expected, as consolidation is likely where the parties have agreed to this, like in the case of the PAM Contract 2018, or where the claims all arise out of the same arbitration agreement. The third circumstance is the most likely to arise in practice and be contentious. This is a situation where claims arise out of different arbitration agreements, but the disputes arise out of the same legal relationships. It is unclear whether the words 'same legal relationships' is broad enough to capture a situation where disputes have arisen between different parties in the same chain of contracts, like disputes between an employer and a contractor on the one hand and between a contractor and a subcontractor on the other. It is submitted that Rule 10 should be given a broad purposive interpretation that allows for this.

Rule 10(2) sets out the factors to be considered when considering an application to consolidate. Clearly an application is more likely to be allowed if it is made at the initial stages of the proceedings, preferably even before the arbitral tribunal is constituted. Apart from this, the paramount consideration is likely to be whether time and cost will be saved and, in this regard, whether there are common questions of fact or of law that are of sufficient importance in proportion to the rest.

Rule 10(4) allows the parties fifteen days to agree on the arbitral tribunal once an order for consolidation is made, failing which the Director may constitute the arbitral tribunal.

41. *Determination of Preliminary Point of Law by Court*

(1) Any party may apply to the High Court to determine any question of law arising in the course of the arbitration –
  (a) with the consent of the arbitral tribunal; or
  (b) with the consent of every other party.
(2) The High Court shall not consider an application under subsection (1) unless it is satisfied that the determination –
  (a) is likely to produce substantial savings in costs; and
  (b) substantially affects the rights of one or more of the parties.
(3) The application shall identify the question of law to be determined and, except where made with the agreement of all parties to the proceedings, shall state the grounds that support the application.
(4) While an application under subsection (1) is pending, the arbitral proceedings may be continued and an award may be made.

§41.01 INTRODUCTION

Section 41 of the Arbitration Act 2005 allows for the determination of a preliminary point of law that arises in the course of the arbitration proceedings by the High Court.

There is no equivalent provision to section 41 in 1985 Model Law. Section 41 is based on clause 4 of Schedule 2 of the New Zealand Arbitration Act 1996, which provides:

> 4. Determination of preliminary point of law by court
> (1) Notwithstanding anything in article 5 of Schedule 1, on an application to the High Court by any party –
>   (a) with the consent of the arbitral tribunal; or
>   (b) with the consent of every other party,
>   the High Court shall have jurisdiction to determine any question of law arising in the course of the arbitration.
> (2) The High Court shall not entertain an application under subclause (1)(a) with respect to any question of law unless it is satisfied that the determination of the question of law concerned –
>   (a) might produce substantial savings in costs to the parties; and
>   (b) might, having regard to all the circumstances, substantially affect the rights of 1 or more of the parties.
> (3) With the leave of the High Court, any party may, within 1 month from the date of any determination of the High Court, under this clause or within such further time as that court may allow, appeal from that determination to the Court of Appeal.
> (4) If the High Court refuses to grant leave to appeal under subclause (3), the Court of Appeal may grant special leave to appeal.

The significant differences between the Malaysian and the New Zealand provision are that:

(1) section 41 applies the criteria in section 41(2) whether consent has been given by the arbitral tribunal or the other party, while clause 4 only applies these criteria where the arbitral tribunal has consented; and

(2) section 41 does not provide for leave to appeal from the decision of the High Court unlike clause 4(3). The decision of the High Court under section 41 may be appealed as of right to the Court of Appeal.

As section 41 appears in Part III of the Arbitration Act 2005, it will apply in domestic arbitrations unless the parties have opted out in accordance with section 3(2). Section 41 will not apply to international arbitrations unless the parties have opted in under section 3(3). For domestic and international arbitration with a seat in Malaysia, where the parties have agreed to adopt the AIAC Arbitration Rules 2018, section 41 will not apply in accordance with Rule 1(c).

§41.02 QUESTION OF LAW

Section 41(1) of the Arbitration Act 2005 allows for a party to apply to the High Court to determine a question of law. The question must be a pure question of law and not involve any dispute of fact. Where there is a dispute of fact, that dispute will have to be resolved by the arbitral tribunal and not the High Court. This was emphasized by the Court of Appeal, in *Bauer (M) Sdn Bhd v. Kukdong Engineering & Construction Co Ltd* [2016] MLJU 1779 at paragraphs 21 and 22:

> [21] This was a case where the jurisdiction of the High Court could not be waived by the parties including the arbitrator. The High Court's jurisdiction under section 41 of the Arbitration Act is derived only when the question framed related to a pure question of law.
>
> [22] In this case, a dispute of fact as to whether there was a waiver of rights in the arbitration proceeding by the Appellant had to be resolved first by the arbitrator who is the trier of facts before the questions framed could be asked and answered … .

§41.03 CONSENT

Section 41(1) of the Arbitration Act 2005 requires the consent of the arbitral tribunal or the other party before a party may apply to the High Court to determine a question of law arising in the course of the arbitration. In the absence of consent, the arbitral tribunal would need to determine the question itself. Section 41 does not allow for the arbitral tribunal by its own motion to refer a question to be determined by the High Court.

§41.04 COURSE OF THE ARBITRATION

Section 41(1) refers to a question that arises 'in the course of the arbitration'. This is to be contrasted with section 42(1) of the Arbitration Act 2005 which provides for a question 'arising out of an award'.

This distinction between a question arising out of the course of the arbitration and the award, with section 41 applying to the former, and section 42 to the latter, was recognized by the High Court, in *MMC Engineering Group Bhd & Anor v. Wayss Freytag Malaysia Sdn Bhd* [2015] 10 MLJ 689 at paragraph 31, where it was, *inter alia*, held:

> Hence, the questions before the Court now must necessarily be questions of law which emanate from the award and not, from the arbitration or the arbitral proceedings. For that, the jurisdiction is to be found under section 41 of the Arbitration Act 2005 which allows the Courts to examine matters arising during the arbitral proceedings.

Although section 41(1) refers to the 'course of the arbitration' it does not require the application to be made at the initial stages of the arbitration. However, an application made at a later stage may not satisfy the criteria in section 41(2), as it is less likely to produce substantial savings in costs.

§41.05 CRITERIA

Section 41(2) of the Arbitration Act 2005 provides for the criteria to be applied by the High Court once the requisite consent under section 41(1) has been obtained. The two criteria are that there must be substantial savings in costs and that the rights of the parties are substantially affected. Both criteria must be satisfied. In practice, the two criteria are likely to be entwined. For example, if the question is one of limitation, its early determination by the courts would both save costs and affect the rights of the parties. Given these two criteria, especially the first one, an application should be made at the initial stages of the arbitration.

§41.06 FORMAL REQUIREMENTS

Section 41(3) of the Arbitration Act 2005 requires the question of law to be identified in the application together with the grounds unless the application is made with the consent of all parties. These requirements are likely to be construed strictly, in the light of the authorities on the former section 42(2) of the Arbitration Act 2005, which was similarly worded and is considered in §42.02 *infra*.

§41.07 ARBITRATION MAY PROCEED

Section 41(4) of the Arbitration Act 2005 provides that the arbitration may proceed and an award made while the application is pending. This is in accordance with the general principle of minimal interference. However, where the application has been made with the consent of the arbitral tribunal and substantially affects the rights of the parties, the arbitral tribunal is unlikely to proceed until the question is finally disposed of by the courts.

Chapter 9: Additional Provisions Relating to Arbitration §41.07

41A. *Disclosure of Information Relating to Arbitral Proceedings and Awards Prohibited*

(1) Unless otherwise agreed by the parties, no party may publish, disclose or communicate any information relating to –
  (a) the arbitral proceedings under the arbitration agreement; or
  (b) an award made in those arbitral proceedings.
(2) Nothing in subsection (1) shall prevent the publication, disclosure or communication of information referred to in that subsection by a party –
  (a) if the publication, disclosure or communication is made –
    (i) to protect or pursue a legal right or interest of the party; or
    (ii) to enforce or challenge the award referred to in that subsection,
  in legal proceedings before a court or other judicial authority in or outside Malaysia;
  (b) if the publication, disclosure or communication is made to any government body, regulatory body, court or tribunal and the party is obliged by law to make the publication, disclosure or communication; or
  (c) if the publication, disclosure or communication is made to a professional or any other adviser of any of the parties.

§41A.01 Introduction

Section 41A of the Arbitration Act 2005 provides for the confidentiality of arbitral proceedings and awards, as well as, the exceptions to such confidentiality.

Section 41A was introduced by the Arbitration (Amendment) (No 2) Act 2018. Section 41A is based on section 18 of the Hong Kong Arbitration Ordinance, with which it is essentially identical.

Prior to the amendments in 2018, the Arbitration Act 2005 did not expressly provide for the confidentiality of arbitral proceedings and awards. This is because the Arbitration Act 2005 is based on the 1985 Model Law, which does not expressly provide for confidentiality. The absence of provisions in the 1985 Model Law on confidentiality was recognized by the Federal Court, in *Far East Holdings Berhad & Ors v. Majlis Ugama Islam dan Adat Resam Melayu Pahang* [2017] 8 AMR 313 at paragraph 114.

As section 41A appears in Part III of the Arbitration Act 2005, it will apply in domestic arbitrations unless the parties have opted out in accordance with section 3(2) of the Arbitration Act 2005. Section 41A will not apply in international arbitrations unless the parties have opted in in accordance with section 3(3) of the Arbitration Act 2005.

§41A.02 The Need for an Express Provision on Confidentiality

In Malaysia, the courts have always regarded arbitrations as being private and confidential. The courts have recognized that confidentiality is one of the advantages of arbitration, which is why parties opt for such proceedings rather than proceedings in court. The courts regard confidentiality as being inherent in arbitration. So, in the absence of an express term in the arbitration agreement as to the confidentiality of the arbitral proceedings, the courts will imply such a term.

In this context, the High Court, in *Malaysian Newsprint Industries Sdn Bhd v. Bechtel International, Inc & Anor* [2008] 5 MLJ 254 at page 278, held:

> The advantages of arbitration can never be listed with exactitude. Privacy of the hearing and confidentiality are two major benefits of arbitration.
>
> Coleman J in *Hassneh Insurance Co of Israel & Ors v Steuart J Mew* [1993] 2 Lloyd's Rep 243 at p 247 aptly said in regard to privacy:
>> If the parties to an English law contract refer their disputes to arbitration they are entitled to assume at the least that the hearing will be conducted in private. The assumption arises from a practice which has been universal in London for hundreds of years and, I believe, undisputed. It is a practice which represents an important advantage of arbitration over the courts as a means of dispute resolution. The informality attaching to a hearing held in private and the candour to which it may give rise is an essential ingredient of arbitration ... .
>
> On confidentiality, I need to refer to the case of *Dolling-Baker v Merrett Ors* [1991] 2 All ER 890; [1990] 1 WLR 1205 (CA) at p 1213 which held that in the absence of an express term in an arbitration clause providing for confidentiality, then the presumption of confidentiality arises as an implied term by the very nature of the arbitral process itself.
>
> It is now accepted, by all and sundry, that arbitrations are private and confidential ... It is inconceivable that with all these endearing points, the plaintiff will not want to have access to arbitration.

Although the confidentiality of arbitration is settled in Malaysia, concern arose in the Commonwealth as a result of the judgment of the High Court of Australia, in *Esso Australia Resources Ltd v. The Honourable Sidney James Plowman (the Minister for Energy and Minerals)* (1995) 128 ALR 391. The High Court of Australia, in *Esso Australia supra*, decided that arbitral proceedings are private, in the sense that such proceedings are not open to the public. However, documents or information produced in arbitral proceedings is not clothed with confidentiality, in the absence of an express term in the arbitration agreement.

The judgment of the High Court of Australia, in *Esso Petroleum supra*, which is contrary to the settled position in the Commonwealth gave rise to concern, which resulted in various countries[1] enacting legislation to expressly provide for the confidentiality of arbitration proceedings. Malaysia is the most recent country to adopt such statutory provisions by way of section 41A of the Arbitration Act 2005, which is identical to section 18 of the Hong Kong Arbitration Ordinance.

---

1. *See* the Australian International Arbitration Act 1974, sections 23C to 23G, the Hong Kong Arbitration Ordinance, sections 16 and 18; New Zealand Arbitration Act 1996, sections 14 to 14I.

§41A.03 The Confidentiality of Arbitral Proceedings and the Award

Section 41A(1) of the Arbitration Act 2005 provides that no party shall disclose any information relating to the arbitral proceedings or the award unless otherwise agreed by the parties.

Section 41A(1) of the Arbitration Act 2005 provides for confidentiality as a matter of statute and not by way of implying a term into the arbitration agreement. This is unlike section 14B(1) of the New Zealand Arbitration Act 1996, which implies an obligation of confidentiality in the arbitration agreement.

Section 41A(1) preserves party autonomy by allowing the parties to agree on the degree of confidentiality applicable to the arbitration. The parties are free to agree on a higher degree of confidentiality than that provided for in section 41A(1) or that the arbitral proceedings and the award will not be confidential.

A 'party' is bound by an obligation of confidentiality under section 41A(1). The word 'party' is defined in section 2 of the Arbitration Act 2005 as a party to the arbitration agreement, or the parties to the arbitration in the case of a multiparty arbitration agreement.

This definition has been interpreted widely by the High Court, in *Sundra Rajoo v. Mohamed Abd Majed & Anor* [2011] 6 CLJ 923 at paragraph 10(f), to include the arbitral tribunal on the basis that the arbitration agreement is trilateral. Based on this judgment, the obligation of confidentiality would extend to the arbitral tribunal. It is submitted that, for the avoidance of doubt, the obligation of confidentiality in section 41A(1) should expressly apply to the arbitral tribunal, as does section 14B(1) of the New Zealand Arbitration Act 1996.

§41A.04 The Three Exceptions to Confidentiality

Section 41A(2) of the Arbitration Act 2005 provides for the three exceptions to the confidentiality of arbitration. The three exceptions are where disclosure is to:

(1) protect a legal right, or enforce or challenge the award;
(2) the authorities; and
(3) an adviser.

We consider each of these three exceptions below.

[A] Legal Right or Interest and Enforce or Challenge the Award

Section 41A(2)(a)(i) allows a party to disclose information relating to the arbitral proceedings or the award to protect or pursue a legal right or interest of the party. A party may need to disclose such information to pursue a claim against a third party or defend a claim by a third party.

For example, an insured party may use an award against them to pursue a claim for an indemnity against their insurers. Another example, in multi-tier commercial arrangements in the construction industry, would be where a main contractor uses an award made against them in favour of a subcontractor to pursue a claim against the employer.

In these examples, disclosure is necessary for a party to pursue their claims, as unlike civil proceedings, arbitral proceedings cannot be consolidated without the consent of all parties. Therefore, a party needs to disclose information from an arbitration in subsequent unconsolidated proceedings to pursue their claims.

Section 41A(2)(a)(ii) allows a party to disclose information relating to the arbitral proceedings or the award to enforce or challenge such award. This exception is obvious, as a party would need to disclose such information in enforcement or setting aside proceedings.

However, a party may need to make applications to the High Court under the Arbitration Act 2005, which also require the disclosure of such information, but do not relate to the enforcement or challenge of the award.[2] These applications are not expressly covered by section 41A(2)(a)(ii), which is limited to applications to enforce or challenge the award. It is submitted that a party is entitled to disclose information relating to the arbitral proceedings or the award in other applications to the High Court under the Arbitration Act 2005 based on the broader exception in section 41A(2)(i) to protect or pursue a right or legal interest. For the avoidance of doubt, perhaps section 41A(2)(ii) should expressly allow for disclosure in relation to all applications to court under the Arbitration Act 2005, like section 14C(b)(i)(C) of the New Zealand Arbitration Act 1996.

[B]   The Authorities

Section 41A(2)(b) allows a party to disclose information relating to the arbitral proceedings or the award if such disclosure is made to any governmental body, regulatory body, court or tribunal and such party is obliged by law to make such disclosure.

For disclosure to be permitted under section 41A(2)(b) two conditions must be fulfilled:

(1) the party must disclose to the authorities; and
(2) the party must be 'obliged by law' to make such disclosure.

[C]   The Adviser

Section 41A(2)(c) allows a party to disclose information relating to the arbitral proceedings or the award to professional or any other adviser of the parties. This

---

2. See §2.03 *supra*.

Chapter 9: Additional Provisions Relating to Arbitration §41.07[C]

exception is regarded as being obvious.[3] The exception is not limited to advisers involved in the arbitral proceedings.

---

3. *See* Sir David AR Williams and Amokura Kawharu, *Williams & Kawharu on Arbitration* (2nd edn, LexisNexis 2017) at para. 13.6.3.

41B. Proceedings to Be Heard Otherwise Than in Open Court

(1) Subject to subsection (2), court proceedings under this Act are to be heard otherwise than in an open court.
(2) Notwithstanding subsection (1), the court may order the proceedings to be heard in an open court –
(a) on the application of any party; or
(b) if, in any particular case, the court is satisfied that those proceedings ought to be heard in an open court.
(3) An order of the court under subsection (2) is final.

§41B.01 Introduction

Section 41B of the Arbitration Act 2005 provides for the privacy of court proceedings under the Arbitration Act 2005 and exceptions to such privacy.

Section 41B was introduced by the Arbitration (Amendment) (No 2) Act 2018. Section 41A is based on section 16 of the Hong Kong Arbitration Ordinance, with which it is essentially identical, save that:

(1) section 41B(2) of the Arbitration Act 2005 begins with the words 'Notwithstanding subsection (1)', which are not found in section 16(2) of the Hong Kong Arbitration Ordinance; and
(2) section 41B(3) of the Arbitration Act 2005 uses the word 'final' instead of the words 'not subject to appeal' found in section 16(3) of the Hong Kong Arbitration Ordinance.

The changes made between section 16 of the Hong Kong Arbitration Ordinance and section 41B of the Arbitration Act 2005 do not have any material significance.

Prior to the amendments in 2018, the Arbitration Act 2005 did not expressly provide for the privacy of court proceedings arising thereunder. This is because the Arbitration Act 2005 is based on the 1985 Model Law, which does not expressly provide for the privacy of such court proceedings.

As section 41B appears in Part III of the Arbitration Act 2005, it will apply in domestic arbitrations unless the parties have opted out in accordance with section 3(2) of the Arbitration Act 2005. Section 41A will not apply in international arbitrations unless the parties have opted in in accordance with section 3(3) of the Arbitration Act 2005.

§41B.02 Enhancement of Existing Provisions on Privacy of Court Proceedings

Prior to the amendments in 2018, section 50 of the Arbitration Act 2005 provided, and still provides, that all applications to the High Court under the Arbitration Act 2005 shall be by way of originating summons. All originating summonses are to be heard in chambers.[4] To that extent, prior to the amendments in 2018, applications under the Arbitration Act 2005 were not heard in open court but in chambers. Section 41B has reinforced the existing provisions on applications under the Arbitration Act 2005 not being heard in open court.

§41B.03   *The Privacy of Court Proceedings under the Arbitration Act 2005*

Section 41B(1) provides that court proceedings under the Arbitration Act 2005 will be heard otherwise than in an open court. In practice, this means that such proceedings will be heard in chambers and to that extent will be private.

Section 41B does not provide for any judgment made pursuant to an application under the Arbitration Act 2005 to be anonymized or for the prohibition of access to the files in the registry of the court.[5] In the absence of such provisions, the privacy allowed by section 41B is of a limited nature.

§41B.04   *Order for Open Court Proceedings*

Section 41B(2) allows the courts to order that proceedings under the Arbitration Act 2005 be in open court upon the application of a party, or by the court's own motion.

Section 41B(2) does not provide for the factors to be considered by the courts in allowing open court proceedings. It is submitted that the following factors would be relevant:[6]

(1) the open justice principle, meaning that proceedings in court are generally meant to be open unless there are exceptional circumstances against this;
(2) the privacy and confidentiality of arbitral proceedings;
(3) any other public interest considerations;
(4) the terms of the arbitration agreement; and
(5) the nature of the application under the Arbitration Act 2005.

Section 41B(3) provides that any such order by the court shall be final. This is similar to other provisions in the Arbitration Act 2005, which provide for the finality of the order of the Court of First Instance, to avoid unnecessary time and cost being incurred on appeals in matters that are essentially procedural. Apart from this, the finality of such order is also practical, as any appeal is likely to be academic, if an order has been made allowing for open court proceedings.

---

4. *See* Rules of Court 2012, Order 7 Rule 2(1) and Forms 5 and 6.
5. *See* New Zealand Arbitration Act 1996, section 14I, which, by way of comparison, does provide for the anonymization of the judgment and prohibits public access to files in court.
6. *See* New Zealand Arbitration Act 1996, section 14H; *Williams & Kawharu on Arbitration supra* at para. 13.7.2.

42. *Reference on Questions of Law*

[deleted by section 12 of the Arbitration (Amendment) (No 2) Act 2018]

§42.01 INTRODUCTION

Section 42 of the Arbitration Act 2005 was deleted by section 12 of the Arbitration (Amendment) (No 2) Act 2018. Section 42, prior to its deletion, provided that:

(1) Any party may refer to the High Court any question of law arising out of an award.
(1A) The High Court shall dismiss a reference made under subsection (1) unless the question of law substantially affects the rights of one or more of the parties.
(2) A reference shall be filed within forty-two days of the publication and receipt of the award, and shall identify the question of law to be determined and state the grounds on which the reference is sought.
(3) The High Court may order the arbitral tribunal to state the reasons for its award where the award –
  (a) does not contain the arbitral tribunal's reasons; or
  (b) does not set out the arbitral tribunal's reasons in sufficient detail.
(4) The High Court may, on the determination of a reference –
  (a) confirm the award;
  (b) vary the award;
  (c) remit the award in whole or in part, together with the High Court's determination on the question of law to the arbitral tribunal for reconsideration; or
  (d) set aside the award, in whole or in part.
(5) Where the award is varied by the High Court, the variation shall have effect as part of the arbitral tribunal's award.
(6) Where the award is remitted in whole or in part for reconsideration, the arbitral tribunal shall make a fresh award in respect of the matters remitted within ninety days of the date of the order for remission or such other period as the High Court may direct.
(7) Where the High Court makes an order under subsection (3), it may make such further order as it thinks fit with respect to any additional costs of the arbitration resulting from that order.
(8) On a reference under subsection (1) the High Court may –
  (a) order the applicant to provide security for costs; or
  (b) order that any money payable under the award shall be brought into the High Court or otherwise secured pending the determination of the reference.

Section 42 of the Arbitration Act 2005 allowed a party to refer a question of law arising out of the award to the High Court. The High Court was entitled to then confirm, vary, set aside or remit the award.

Section 42 appeared in Part III of the Arbitration Act 2005. Section 42 in accordance with section 3(2)(b) applied in domestic arbitrations unless the parties had opted out. In this context, Rule 1(c) of the AIAC Arbitration Rules 2018 provides that where the seat of arbitration is Malaysia, section 42 will not apply. Section 42 in

Chapter 9: Additional Provisions Relating to Arbitration §42.01

accordance with section 3(3)(b) did not apply to international arbitrations unless the parties had opted in.

This distinction had been recognized by the High Court, in *Exceljade Sdn Bhd v. Bauer (M) Sdn Bhd* [2013] MLJU 1202 at paragraph 5:

> The Arbitration Act 2005 is modelled on UNCITRAL Model Law ('Model Law'). However section 42 is one of the few sections that has no parallel in the Model Law. As such no recourse may be made to the Model Law to ascertain or construe this section. Section 42 falls within Part III of the Act. Part III, including section 42, applies automatically to domestic arbitrations unless parties 'opt out'. International arbitrations do not fall within the scope of Part III, and thereby section 42, unless the parties specifically choose to 'opt in'.

Similarly, the High Court, in *MMC Engineering Group Bhd & Anor v. Wayss Freytag Malaysia Sdn Bhd* [2015] 10 MLJ 689 at paragraph 16, *inter alia*, held:

> Section 42 of the Arbitration Act 2005 is peculiar to the Malaysian arbitration scene. This recourse to the Courts is available in all domestic arbitrations unless the parties have specifically opted out of its operation; and unavailable to international arbitrations unless the parties have specifically opted in to its application. This is clear from the provisions of section 42 was amended in 2011 to introduce subsection 42(1A).

The Federal Court, in *Tan Sri Dato' Seri Vincent Tan Chee Yioun & Anor v. Jan De Nul (M) Sdn Bhd & Anor and another appeal* [2018] MLJU 1545 at paragraphs 50-52, confirmed that section 42 did not apply to an international arbitration, as section 42 was in Part III of the Arbitration Act 2005, which section 3(3) provided would not apply to an international arbitration unless the parties agreed otherwise. The Federal Court also emphasized that the agreement between the parties that the laws of Malaysia applied to the contract did not mean that section 42 applied to an international arbitration.

Section 42 of the Arbitration Act 2005 had no equivalent in the 1985 Model Law. Section 42 also had no equivalent in arbitration legislation in other Commonwealth jurisdictions, which generally provide for an appeal on a question of law rather than a reference. These Commonwealth jurisdictions also provide for a leave to be granted by the courts before such an appeal can be made. The Federal Court, in *Far East Holdings Bhd & Anor v. Majlis Ugama Islam dan Adat Resam Melayu Pahang and other appeals* [2018] 1 MLJ 1 at paragraph 123, emphasized that in Malaysia, unlike elsewhere in the Commonwealth, leave was not required.

The purpose of section 42 of the Arbitration Act 2005 was to allow the courts to re-examine questions of law arising out of the award. This was intended, in domestic arbitrations, to strike a balance between the complete non-interference of the courts and the courts exercising supervisory jurisdiction over the arbitral proceedings. Any risk of excessive intervention by the courts was to be limited by the threshold requirements in sections 42(1), (1A) and (2).

In this context, section 42(1A) was introduced by the Arbitration (Amendment) Act 2011. This provision was intended to serve as an additional threshold requirement or filter mechanism that prevented questions of law being referred to the courts unless they substantially affect the rights of a party.

These principles were recognized by the Court of Appeal, in *Chain Cycle Sdn Bhd v. Kerajaan Malaysia* [2016] 1 CLJ 218 at paragraphs 65 and 66:

> [65] The Arbitration Act 2005 did not provide for such a filter mechanism. We now however have s. 42(1A) of the Arbitration Act 2005 which gives the power to the courts to dismiss a reference unless the 'question of law' posed '... substantially affects the rights or one of the parties'. The scope of this provision has still to be tested but it might well allow a party opposing a reference application to seek to have, if not the whole proceedings, then at least some of the questions raised to be struck out at the preliminary stages of the proceedings itself, on that ground.
>
> [66] The pressure was definitely on the courts therefore to be ever vigilant and to resist attempts to engage the courts in a review of the arbitral award on its merits, akin to an 'appeal', often camouflaged masterly as 'questions of law'. There was no room for any dispute that the curial function of the court under s. 42 of the Arbitration Act 2005 was only intended by the legislature to be extended to questions of law per se, that too, which would affect substantially the rights of one or the other party.

Subsequently, the Court of Appeal, in *Petronas Penapisan (Melaka) Sdn Bhd v. Ahmani Sdn Bhd* [2016] 3 CLJ 403 at paragraph 38, *inter alia*, held:

> We agree with the approach of the learned judge that the court must intervene where the award is manifestly unlawful and unconscionable. Section 42 has no equivalent in the Model Law or in parallel jurisdictions. Section 42 is not a provision as to appeals but a reference on a question of law. There has been a line of authorities with regards to the limiting of juridical intervention in arbitration awards and we set out the following decisions on the point ie intervention should only be exercised in clear and exceptional circumstances (see *Chain Cycle Sdn Bhd v. Kerajaan Malaysia* [2016] 1 CLJ 218; [2015] AMEJ 1479. We are of the opinion that with the pre-requirements of s. 42, it followed there would be no danger of 'opening the floodgates' in respect of review of arbitral awards.

However, it was perceived that the judgment of the Federal Court, in *Far East Holdings supra*, shifted the balance in favour of intervention by the courts. This was because the judgment allowed for the courts to intervene whenever there was a question of law, which term was construed broadly. Furthermore, this judgment dispensed with the traditional safeguards, whereby the courts would only intervene in clear and exceptional cases, or where the award was manifestly unlawful, unconscionable or perverse. In response to this perceived shift in balance, section 42 was deleted by the Arbitration (Amendment) (No 2) Act 2018. The provisions of the deleted section 42 are considered below, as a matter of academic interest.

§42.02 THRESHOLD REQUIREMENTS

The threshold requirements for a reference on questions of law were set out in sections 42(1), (1A) and (2) of the Arbitration Act 2005.

Chapter 9: Additional Provisions Relating to Arbitration §42.02

In addition to the threshold requirements in the Arbitration Act 2005, there are certain threshold requirements set out in the Rules of Court 2012, which are more procedural in nature.

Order 69 Rule 6 of the Rules of Court 2012 provides:

6. Application to refer questions of law arising out of an award (O. 69 r. 6)
   (1) A reference of any question of law to the Court under section 42 of the 2005 Act may be made at any time within forty-two days of the publication and receipt of the award.
   (2) In every application for reference of a question of law under section 42 of the 2005 Act the originating summons shall, in addition to the matters stated in rule 4(1) –
       (a) identify the question of law arising out of the award which is sought to be determined;
       (b) state the grounds on which reference is sought; and
       (c) give particulars of each ground on which it is contended that the arbitral tribunal erred in law, with references to the paragraphs or passages of the award where each alleged error is to be found.
   (3) The applicant shall file by affidavit, written evidence on which he intends to rely when he files his originating summons, including a copy of the arbitration agreement and the award.
   (4) The originating summons and affidavit shall be served on each arbitrator and the respondents.

Based on sections 42(1), (1A) and (2) of the Arbitration Act 2005 and Order 69 Rule 6 of the Rules of Court 2012, there were eight threshold requirements for a reference on a question of law:

(1) there must be question of law;[7]
(2) the question of law must arise out of the award;[8]
(3) the question of law must substantially affect the right of the parties;[9]
(4) the reference must be filed forty-two days after the publication and receipt of the award;[10]
(5) the reference must identify the question of law to be determined;[11]
(6) the reference must state the grounds on which the reference is sought;[12]
(7) the reference must state the particulars of each ground on which the arbitral tribunal is said to have erred in law together with a reference to the award where such errors occurred;[13] and
(8) the reference must be served on the other party and the arbitral tribunal.[14]

---

7. See section 42(1) of the Arbitration Act 2005.
8. See section 42(1) of the Arbitration Act 2005.
9. See section 42(1A) of the Arbitration Act 2005.
10. See section 42(2) of the Arbitration Act 2005 and Order 69 Rule 6(1) of the Rules of Court 2012.
11. See section 42(2) of the Arbitration Act 2005 and Order 69 Rule 6(2)(a) of the Rules of Court 2012.
12. See section 42(2) of the Arbitration Act 2005 and Order 69 Rule 6(2)(b) of the Rules of Court 2012.
13. See Order 69 Rule 6(2)(c) of the Rules of Court 2012.
14. See Order 69 Rule 6(4) of the Rules of Court 2012.

These requirements were listed out and considered by the High Court, in *Zenbay Sdn Bhd v. Yong Choo Kui Shipyard Sdn Bhd* [2015] 10 CLJ 924 at paragraphs 47-49. The High Court identified potentially nine or ten requirements in *Zenbay supra*. This has been narrowed down to eight or nine, as the requirements of section 42(2) of the Arbitration Act 2005 and Order 69 Rule 6(2)(a) appear to be substantially the same. These requirements are now considered below.

[A] Question of Law

The most significant of the threshold requirements is the requirement that there is a 'question of law'. A 'question of law' is not defined in the Arbitration Act 2005. This is unlike the New Zealand Arbitration Act 1995, where a 'question of law' is defined in Schedule 2, section 5(10) as follows:

> For the purposes of this clause, question of law –
>
> (a) includes an error of law that involves an incorrect interpretation of the applicable law (whether or not the error appears on the record of the decision); but
> (b) does not include any question as to whether –
>   (i) the award or any part of the award was supported by any evidence or any sufficient or substantial evidence; and
>   (ii) the arbitral tribunal drew the correct factual inferences from the relevant primary facts.

The courts have considered the meaning of the words 'question of law' in several judgments. Two main approaches have emerged. The first, based on judgments from England, divides the reasoning process of an arbitral tribunal into these sequential stages:

(1) the arbitral tribunal ascertains the facts. Here, the arbitral tribunal determines facts that are in dispute;
(2) next, the arbitral tribunal ascertain the law. Here, the arbitral tribunal identifies:
 (a) the applicable rules of statute and common law;
 (b) the relevant parts of the contract and interprets these parts; and
 (c) facts that must be taken into account when a decision is made; and
(3) finally, the arbitral tribunal makes a decision in the light of the facts and the law so ascertained.

Stage (1) cannot give rise to a question of law. Stage (2) above will give rise to a proper question of law for determination under section 42 of the Arbitration Act 2005. Stage (3) will only give rise to a proper question of law where the decision made by the arbitral tribunal could not have been reached by applying the correct rules of law. These views were lucidly expressed by the High Court, in *Exceljade Sdn Bhd v. Bauer*

(M) Sdn Bhd [2013] MLJU 1202 at paragraphs 17 and 40. These views were subsequently affirmed by the Court of Appeal, in *Kerajaan Malaysia v. Perwira Bintang Holdings Sdn Bhd* [2015] 1 CLJ 617 at paragraphs 58-60.

The second approach is based on the definition of a 'question of law' in the New Zealand Arbitration Act 1996 and judgments from Singapore. A question of law arises here where there is a point of law in controversy that requires the determination of the courts. This would include the incorrect interpretation of the applicable law. However, questions of evidence and facts would be excluded. This approach has been developed over a series of judgments in the High Court, starting with *Magna Prima Construction Sdn Bhd v. Bina BMK Sdn Bhd and another case* [2015] MLJU 291 at paragraphs 55-57 and continuing in *MMC Engineering Group Bhd & Anor v. Wayss Freytag Malaysia Sdn Bhd* [2015] MLJU 285 at paragraph 27.

The Federal Court, in *Far East Holdings supra*, confirmed that the first approach was to be preferred to the second approach. The second approach was regarded as being too wide. The Federal Court also provided a non-exhaustive list of what would amount to a question of law. In this context, the Federal Court, in *Far East Holdings supra* at paragraphs 150 and 152, held:

> [150] 'The question of law must be one of law and not fact' (*The Arbitration Act 2005* at p 198). 'An error of fact alone is insufficient' (*Department of Education v. Azmitia* [2015] WASCA 246 per Mazza JA). But there is no universal definition of 'question of law'. Nonetheless, from our survey of the authorities, we would conclude that one of the following, which is not an exhaustive list, would meet the paradigm of 'any question of law' in s 42:
>
> (a) a question of law in relation to matters falling within (2) of Mustill J's three-stage test;
> (b) a question as to whether the decision of the tribunal was wrong (*The Chrysalis*);
> (c) a question as to whether there was an error of law, and not an error of fact (*Micoperi*): error of law in the sense of an erroneous application of law;
> (d) a question as to whether the correct application of the law inevitably leads to one answer and the tribunal has given another (*MRI Trading*);
> (e) a question as to the correctness of the law applied;
> (f) a question as to the correctness of the tests applied (*Canada v Southam*);
> (g) a question concerning the legal effect to be given to an undisputed set of facts (*Carrier Lumber*);
> (h) a question as to whether the tribunal has jurisdiction to determine a particular matter (*Premiums Brands*): this may also come under s 37 of the AA 2005; and
> (i) a question of construction of a document (*Intelek*).
>
> ...
>
> [152] Section 42 allows any question of law arising from the award. 'Any question of law' is wider than 'a question of law'. Since so, it would seem that s 42 contemplates a less narrow interpretation of 'question of law'. Unless opted in, s 42 only applies to domestic arbitration. A less narrow interpretation of 'question of law' in s 42, as we might have given it, would not widen court intervention in international arbitration. But 'a point of law in controversy which has to be resolved after opposing views and arguments have been considered' is not a 'question of law' within the meaning of s 42. There would surely be 'a point of law

in controversy' in every case. If 'a point of law in controversy' were a question of law, then there would be a 'question of law' arising in every award. And that, with respect, could not be right.

The principles set out above have been applied in practice many times. These practical applications offer some guidance as to what may and may not be considered questions of law and are explored below in categories.

[1] Facts and Evidence

The courts will not allow a reference on a question of fact under section 42 of the Arbitration Act 2005. The courts will resist any attempt to circumvent this rule by contentions that:

(1) an obvious mistake of fact made by the arbitral tribunal in an award amounts to misconduct;
(2) an obvious mistake of fact made by the arbitral tribunal in an award amounts to the arbitral tribunal acting in excess of jurisdiction;
(3) an absence of any or sufficient evidence for a finding of fact by the arbitral tribunal in the award is a question of law that allows for the court to intervene;
(4) inconsistencies in the findings of fact by the arbitral tribunal in the award;
(5) an error by the arbitral tribunal in drawing wrong inferences of fact from the evidence before them; and
(6) a misapprehension or misunderstanding of the evidence by the arbitral tribunal.

The courts have rejected all of these contentions. The courts have emphasized that most of these contentions attempt to transform questions of fact into questions of law. These principles are set out in the judgment of the High Court, in *Exceljade supra* at paragraphs 35-38 and 45-48.

The High Court, in *Exceljade supra* at paragraph 112, also emphasized, in particular, that where findings of fact are based on any practical experience in a field, the courts will be very cautious in interfering with the findings. This is of significance as a large number of commercial arbitrations are to resolve disputes arising in complex transactions, like construction or oil and gas, where the arbitral tribunal has been chosen for their experience in that field.

These principles have been consistently applied by the courts, who have declined to review findings of fact made by arbitral tribunals based on the evidence presented before such a tribunal.[15]

---

15. See *Sanlaiman Sdn Bhd v. Kerajaan Malaysia* [2013] 3 MLJ 755 at para. 47, HC; *Lembaga Kemajuan Ikan Malaysia v. WJ Construction Sdn Bhd* [2013] 8 CLJ 655 at para. 49, HC; *Quality Property Development Sdn Bhd v. Xavier Francis & Anor* [2014] 1 LNS 67 at paras 24, 30, 33, HC;

The High Court, in *Sagau Batu Bala v. Zaharah Mustapha Raja Sewa & Anor & Other Cases* [2013] 10 CLJ 683 at paragraphs 32 and 33, appears to have reviewed the findings of fact made by the arbitral tribunal. The High Court, after such a review, held that the findings of fact were based on inadmissible evidence and were not supported by evidence. This judgment does not appear to accord with the principles set out above.

The High Court, in *Telekom Malaysia Berhad v. Eastcoast Technique (M) Sdn Bhd & Another Case* [2014] 6 CLJ 1067 at paragraphs 40-42, while considering an application under section 42 of the Arbitration Act 2005 decided that the arbitral tribunal's findings of undue influence and the quantum of damages were unsupported by evidence. However, the High Court appears to have allowed the application not on these grounds but on the grounds that the law applicable to undue influence and the assessment of damages was wrongly applied by the arbitral tribunal.

The High Court, in *Sunway City Sdn Bhd v. Syarikat Pembinaan Yeoh Tiong Lay Sdn Bhd* [2018] MLJU 1086 at paragraph 67, intervened under section 42, on the basis that the arbitrator had taken an unduly restrictive view of the law on the admissibility of evidence. This decision also does not accord with the principles set out above.

[2]   Law

The purpose of section 42 is to allow a party to refer a question of law arising out of the award to the High Court for determination.

As stated above, the courts will accept such a reference where there is a 'question of law' either based on the approach that this is stage (2) of the arbitral tribunal's reasoning process.

These are the principles. In practice, a question of law that is likely to persuade the courts to intervene is where the arbitral tribunal has clearly disregarded binding precedent.

This issue arose in the judgment of the High Court, in *Sanlaiman supra* at paragraph 46, where it was held that although the issue did not need to be determined in that case, if an arbitral tribunal was so bold as not to follow judicial precedent, then that would amount to a classic instance where the courts may intervene under section 42.

The other instance where the courts will intervene is where the arbitral tribunal has misunderstood or misapplied the law. This can perhaps be best seen in the judgment of the High Court, in *Telekom Malaysia supra* at paragraph 39, where the High Court was compelled to intervene as the arbitral tribunal had misapplied the law on undue influence by deciding that parts of the contract may be void for undue influence. This was untenable, as the whole contract would be rendered void if undue influence was present.

Kilang Sawit Bell Sdn Bhd v. Kwantas Oil Sdn Bhd [2015] MLJU 1985 at para. 42, HC; *Tan Kong Han v. QDB Ventures Sdn Bhd* [2016] 1 LNS 870 at para. 56, HC; *Far East Holdings supra* at para. 155, FC.

Although the courts are prepared to intervene where the arbitral tribunal has disregarded binding judicial precedent or misapplied the law, the courts do recognize that in some instances more than one view may be held as to the application of the law to the facts and will not intervene simply because they hold a different view from the arbitral tribunal.

This can be seen from the judgment of the Court of Appeal, in *Tridant Engineering (M) Sdn Bhd v. Ssangyong Engineering & Construction Co Ltd* [2017] 2 CLJ 393 at paragraph 41, where it was, *inter alia*, held:

> ... Of course the learned arbitrator was faced with two interpretations of law and fact which we did not find them perverse and we say that for the simple reason that even we held different views among ourselves as to which interpretation should prevail. It must not be forgotten that the arbitration was convened for the simple reason to resolve the competing interpretations by their chosen arbitrator. That being the case, it would be farcical for the court to intervene when in the first place the parties had agreed to abide by the referee's decision.

This principle was confirmed by the Federal Court, in *Far East Holdings supra* at paragraphs 131 and 150(d).

[3] Construction

The courts recognize that the construction of a contract is a question of law. Therefore, questions on the construction of a contract may be referred to the court for determination under section 42 of the Arbitration Act 2005.

The Federal Court, in *Far East Holdings supra* at paragraph 155, emphasized that it was more than settled that the construction of a document is a question of law. This principle has also been applied by the High Court in *Maimunah Deraman v. Majlis Perbandaran Kemaman* [2011] 9 CLJ 689 at paragraph 28; *Lembaga Kemajuan Ikan supra* at paragraph 21; and *Sunway City supra* at paragraphs 42, 57 and 60.

Although the courts regard the construction of a contract as giving rise to a question of law, intervention under section 42 is limited, as the courts recognize that a contract may be open to more than one interpretation. The courts will not intervene simply because the arbitral tribunal has adopted one interpretation when there was another available. This can be seen from the judgment of the High Court, in *Sabah Medical Center Sdn Bhd v. Syarikat Neptune Enterprise Sdn Bhd* [2011] 1 LNS 849 at pages 31 and 32, and the judgment of the Federal Court, in *Far East Holdings supra* at paragraphs 131 and 150(d).

The courts will also not intervene, even if there is a more correct interpretation of the contract, where the arbitral tribunal has proceeded on principles of construction that are in accordance with the law.

In this context, the High Court, in *Exceljade supra* at paragraph 84, *inter alia*, held:

> Even if it is contended that the arguments put forward by the Applicant here more correctly reflect the position in law, this alone is insufficient to warrant interference from this Court under section 42 of the Arbitration Act 2005. This is because

Chapter 9: Additional Provisions Relating to Arbitration §42.02[A]

the reasoning and application of legal principles by the learned Arbitrator is not so flawed as to warrant the conclusion that the Arbitrator has proceeded on principles of construction which the law does not countenance ... .

Similarly, the High Court, in *Lembaga Kemajuan Ikan supra* at paragraph 49, recognized that there could be two possible interpretations and the arbitral tribunal was entitled to take one provided it was not abhorrent to the law:

> That conclusion or view is not one that is so abhorrent in law that it is not sustainable. There are two views, even now. The Arbitral Tribunal chose one over the other and reasons were given ... .

Recently, the High Court, in *Renoir Consulting (M) Sdn Bhd v. Alison Watson & Anor* [2018] MLJU 1352 at paragraphs 80 and 81, held that where there was a question of construction and two interpretations were possible, the courts would not intervene unless the arbitrator's decision was perverse or manifestly unlawful.

[4] Mixed Fact and Law

A question of mixed fact and law may not be referred to the court for determination under section 42 of the Arbitration Act 2005. The question referred must be a pure question of law. The Court of Appeal has repeatedly emphasised this principle which has recently been held to be trite.

In this context, the Court of Appeal, in *Awangku Dewa Pgn Momin & Ors v. Superintendent of Lands And Surveys, Limbang Division* [2015] 3 CLJ 1 at paragraph 27, *inter alia*, held:

> We wish to take the opportunity here to provide the following guidance for the benefit of High Court Judges in dealing with a s. 42 reference. A High Court in considering a s. 42 reference must not take lightly the duty to critically examine the questions posed by the applicant and to ensure that the question referred to the court is purely a question of law and not a question of mixed law and fact, and is clearly and concisely framed, before embarking to entertain the application and to answer the question posed. There should be no complication, confusion or duplicity in framing the questions. Instead, there should be simplicity and clarity. The legal burden is on the applicant to ensure that these requirements are strictly complied with.

Subsequently, the Court of Appeal, in *Tridant Engineering supra* at paragraph 42, *inter alia*, held:

> Further, in our view, the manner in which the question of law was framed was nothing more than a mixed question of law and fact 'dressed up' in a question of law. It is trite that the court has no jurisdiction to a mixed question of fact and law.

Recently, the Court of Appeal, in *Taki Engineering Sdn Bhd v. Ipoh Tower Sdn Bhd* [2019] MLJU 66 at paragraph 21, *inter alia*, held:

> ... we found that Question 9 could not be said to be purely a question of law in the first place. We were of the view that Question 9 was actually a question of fact

dressed up as a question of law. That being the case, the learned High Court Judge had erred when she found Question 9 to be purely a question of law and proceeded to rule on the issue and set aside the part of the learned Arbitrator's Award.

These principles were developed in the High Court, by judgments like *Lembaga Kemajuan Ikan supra* at paragraph 12, *Magna Prima supra* at paragraph 57 and *Tan Kong Han v. QDB Ventures Sdn Bhd* [2016] 1 LNS 860 at paragraph 56.

These principles stated by the Court of Appeal were subsequently applied by the High Court, in *Paling Construction Sdn Bhd v. The Government of Sarawak* [2015] MLJU 810 at paragraph 13; *Kluang Health Care Sdn Bhd v. Lee Yong Beng & Another Case* [2016] 1 CLJ 281 at paragraph 55; and *Renoir Consulting supra* at paragraph 76.

The High Court, in *Exceljade supra* at paragraphs 40 and 42 to 43, took a more nuanced position on this issue. The courts, when dealing with a mixed question of fact and law, should not intervene only because the courts would have decided differently from the arbitral tribunal. Instead, the courts should only intervene where the decision made by the arbitral tribunal could not have been reached by a reasonable person applying the correct legal test:

> [40] Leave to appeal on two questions of law was granted in respect of the award handed down. At the High Court Eder J relied on the principles enunciated inter alia, in *Kershaw's* case and *The Beleares* (above) in relation to the approach to be adopted by the Court in dealing with questions or errors of law arising out of an arbitration award which calls for such award to be set aside, varied or remitted. With regards to the question of mixed fact and law, it was held by the Court as follows:-
>
> ... Fourthly, when a tribunal has reached a conclusion of mixed fact and law, the court cannot interfere with that conclusion just because it would not have reached the same conclusion itself. It can interfere only when convinced that no reasonable person, applying the correct legal test, could have reached the conclusion which the tribunal did: or, to put it another way, it has to be shown that the tribunal's conclusion was necessarily inconsistent with the application of the right test: *The 'Sylvia'* [2010] 2 Lloyd's Rep 81 at 54-55. The same extremely circumscribed power of intervention applies when it is complained that a tribunal has incorrectly applied the law to the facts. It is only if the correct application of the law leads inevitably to one answer, and the tribunal has given another, that the court can interfere. Once a court has concluded that a tribunal which correctly understood the law could have arrived at the same answer as the one reached by the arbitrator, the fact that the individual judge himself would have come to a different conclusion is no ground for disturbing the Award: *The Chrysalis* [1983] 1 Lloyd's Rep 503 at 507 ... .
>
> ...
>
> [42] Eder J's decision was upheld on appeal by the English Court of Appeal (see [2013] EWCA CIV 156). Although the Court of Appeal did not articulate or prescribe the correct test to be applied in setting aside an award, it would appear that the Court of Appeal agreed with the test that no reasonable tribunal correctly applying the relevant legal principles could have reached a conclusion such as the arbitral tribunal did. At paragraph 26 of their judgment they stated:-
>
> > In the first place, given the judge's view that no reasonable tribunal correctly applying the relevant legal principles could have reached the conclusion that

the contract was unenforceable, there was no scope for remission. Only one answer is possible.

[43] Such an approach is echoed in the seminal textbook, *The Law and Practice of Commercial Arbitration in England* Second Edition by Mustill and Boyd. In essence, mistakes in factual findings will not be reviewed. The Court will also decline to intervene unless the arbitrator's conclusion stemmed from a clear misunderstanding of the true legal principles.

This more nuanced approach appears to have been confirmed by the Federal Court, in *Far East Holdings supra* at paragraphs 131 and 150(d).

[5] Damages

The Court of Appeal, in *Pancaran Prima Sdn Bhd v. Iswarabena Sdn Bhd* [2018] MLJU 968 at paragraphs 42-45, considered a situation where an arbitrator had found that a party had failed to prove loss of profits but, despite this, awarded a substantial sum based on extraneous evidence. The Court of Appeal held that this gave rise to a question of law, as based on settled principles, the arbitrator should have awarded nominal damages once the party had failed to prove their claim.

[6] Interest

The courts have taken the position that any controversy between the parties on whether interest may be awarded can give rise to a question of law.

This was decided by the Federal Court, in *Far East Holdings supra* at paragraph 187 and is also reflected in the judgments of the High Court, in *Kerajaan Malaysia (Kementerian Sumber Asli Dan Alam Sekitar) v. Kumpulan Sakata Sdn Bhd* [2016] 7 CLJ 412 at paragraph 31; *Kerajaan Malaysia v. Tasja Sdn Bhd* [2016] 6 CLJ 738 at paragraphs 71 and 72; and *Tasja Sdn Bhd v. Kementerian Kesihatan Malaysia* [2018] MLJU 536 at paragraph 31.

[7] Costs

There is uncertainty as to whether issues on costs can give rise to a question of law for the purpose of a reference under section 42 of the Arbitration Act 2005.

This uncertainty arises from the judgment delivered by the Court of Appeal, in *SDA Architects supra*, where Aziah Ali JCA at paragraph 32, *inter alia*, held:

> I am in agreement with the respondent that where it is shown on the face of the award that there has been an apparent failure by the arbitrator to exercise his discretion judicially in the award of costs, then an error of law has occurred which may give rise to a question of law that may be referred to the court under s. 42 of the Act. I find support from the case of *President of India v. Jadranska Sobodna Plovidba (supra)* which shows that a question of law may be formulated on the basis that an error of law has been occasioned when the arbitrator has failed to exercise his discretion judicially in making an award of costs ... .

Hamid Sultan Abu Backer JCA, in *SDA Architects supra* at paragraph 47(f), *inter alia*, held:

> AA 2005 specifically states that costs and expenses of the arbitration shall be at the discretion of the arbitral tribunal. And to ensure that discretion is not made illusory, s. 8 curtails the power of court to intervene in the discretionary jurisdiction of the arbitrator. As the court's role to decide on costs or quantum had been specifically taken away by virtue of ss. 8 and 44 of AA 2005 it is difficult even to fathom how the issue of costs in arbitral proceeding can be framed as a question of law for the determination of the High Court when the statute has specifically deprived the business of the High Court to deal with costs. In addition, O. 69 r. 2(1) of RC 2012 does not also reserve any right to review or decide on issue of costs which has been dealt by the arbitrator ... .

The better view appears to be that costs can give rise to a question of law where the arbitral tribunal has disregarded rules of law in awarding costs. There appears to be no reason for treating costs differently from any other issue that may need to be determined in arbitral proceedings. In determining all issues, the arbitral tribunal must act in accordance with rules of law, and, if there is any dispute on this by a party, it should give rise to a question of law that may be referred to the High Court under section 42 of the Arbitration Act 2005.

[B] Arising Out of an Award

A question of law may only be referred to the High Court for determination if it arises out of the award, as expressly provided in section 42(1) of the Arbitration Act 2005.

A question arising out of an award has been distinguished by courts from a question arising out of the arbitral proceedings. The former is permissible, while the latter cannot form the basis of a reference to the High Court under section 42.

This principle is reflected in the judgment of the Court of Appeal, in *Perwira Bintang supra* at paragraph 57(c), where it, *inter alia*, held:

> The question of law must arise from the award, not the arbitration proceeding generally ... .

This principle may also be seen in the judgments of the High Court, in *Majlis Amanah Rakyat supra* at pages 12 and 13; *Sabah Medical Centre supra* at pages 29 and 30; *Lembaga Kemajuan Ikan supra* at paragraph 17; *Sagau Batu Bala supra* at paragraph 16; and *Konsortium Lord-Saberkat supra* at paragraph 43.

Although the question must arise from the award, the arbitral tribunal need not have made an explicit ruling on the matter provided that the question can be argued based on the findings of fact made by the arbitral tribunal.

The Court of Appeal, in *Perwira Bintang supra* at paragraph 56, emphasized this in the following terms:

> The broader approach that a question of law 'arising out of an award' should not be taken to mean that the question of law must appear 'on the record' (ie, within

the four corners of an award), will be consistent with our own statutory scheme, especially when s. 42(4) is considered.

In this context, the court, though focused on the award, may also look at the documents referred to in the award. The High Court, in *MMC Engineering supra* at paragraph 41, clarified this in the following way:

> ... When determining this reference, the Court is necessarily directing its focus and attention to the four corners of the award and nothing more; although this may extend to the documents or correspondence that were referred to or mentioned in the award ... .

[C] Not the Same Question

The Federal Court, in *Far East Holdings supra* at paragraphs 116, 151 and 152, confirmed that any question of law may be referred to the courts regardless of whether or not the specific question had been decided by the arbitral tribunal:

> [116] With the common law jurisdiction of setting aside an award for 'error on the face of the award' gone, the distinction between a general reference and a specific reference, though pertinent under the AA 1952 ... is not relevant.
>
> ...
>
> [151] Given that the AA 2005 does not say so, we could not hold that a 'question of law' must be the same one which the arbitral tribunal was asked to determine ... .
>
> [152] Section 42 allows any question of law arising from the award. 'Any question of law' is wider than 'a question of law'. Since so, it would seem that s 42 contemplates a less narrow interpretation of 'question of law' ... .

Prior to the judgment of the Federal Court, in *Far East Holdings supra*, there was some concern about the requirement that a party may not refer a question for determination by the High Court that had been determined by the arbitral tribunal. This is because section 42(1) expressly allows 'any' question of law to be referred to the High Court, which should include a question that has been determined by the arbitral tribunal. These concerns were lucidly articulated by the judgment of the High Court, in *Zenbay supra* at paragraphs 48 and 49:

> [48] There is a possible tenth threshold requirement ... that a plaintiff must show that the questions of law to be determined by the court should not be the same as those decided by the arbitral tribunal ... .
>
> [49] With respect, I am not in favour of a tenth threshold requirement. My view is premised on the following reasons:
>
> (a) neither s. 42 AA nor O. 69 RC, expressly or by necessary implication, confines a court reference to a question of law which has not been decided by the arbitral tribunal;
> (b) s. 42(1) AA has expressly provided that 'any' question of law may be referred to court. The wide meaning of the word 'any' in s. 42(1) AA should be given effect ... .

(c) an arbitral tribunal may have committed a single error of law which has substantially affected the rights of a plaintiff. In such a case, if there exists a tenth threshold requirement and the plaintiff is not able to identify any question of law which has not been decided by the arbitral tribunal, there may be an injustice to the plaintiff because the plaintiff is barred from filing the court reference.

Apart from this, it is difficult to see how such a requirement can apply in the context of the principles laid down in *Exceljade supra*, which have been repeatedly affirmed by the Court of Appeal.

The judgment, in *Exceljade supra*, allows for any question of law to be referred to the High Court in accordance with section 42. If the question has already been determined by the arbitral tribunal, *Exceljade supra* suggests that the courts may still determine the question. In doing so, the courts should read the award as a whole and accord some deference to the decision of the arbitral tribunal on questions on which the arbitral tribunal has particular experience.

This is reflected in *Exceljade supra* at paragraph 33, where it was held:

> The third question considered by Justice Jackson was the degree of deference to be shown the arbitrator's decisions on questions of law ... two principles were reached, namely that:-
>
> (i) The court should read an arbitral award as a whole in a fair and reasonable way. The court should not engage in minute textual analysis.
> (ii) Where the arbitrator's experience assists him in determining a question of law, such as the interpretation of contractual documents or correspondence passing between members of his own trade or industry, the court will accord some deference to the arbitrator's decision on that question. The court will only reverse that decision if it is satisfied that the arbitrator, despite the benefit of his relevant experience, has come to the wrong answer.

These concerns have now been addressed by the Federal Court, in *Far East Holdings supra*.

The earlier requirement that a party may not refer a question for determination by the High Court under section 42 of the Arbitration Act 2005, that is, the same question referred to the arbitral tribunal for determination, is reflected in the judgment of the Court of Appeal, in *Chain Cycle Sdn Bhd v. Kerajaan Malaysia* [2016] 1 CLJ 218 at paragraphs 27 and 31, where it was, *inter alia*, held:

> [27] The respondent relied on the principle that has come to be known as the Absalom exception and referred to the decision of the Federal Court in *The Government of India v. Cairn Energy India Pty Ltd & Anor* [2012] 3 CLJ 423; [2011] 6 MLJ 441, affirming the same particularly the following passage:
> ...
> [30] With respect we are not persuaded that we should depart from the long line of authorities holding such a distinction. Thus, where a specific matter is referred to arbitration for consideration, it ought to be respected in that 'no such interference is possible upon the ground that the decision upon the question of law is an erroneous one'. However, if the matter is a general reference,

interference may be possible 'if and when any error appears on the face of the award' ... .

...

[31] On our part having given consideration to the submission of respective counsel we were not convinced that that Absalom exception was confined to situations where the court was called upon to deal with 'error of law on the face of the award' only. There was no valid reason why, in a situation under s 42 of the AA, where '... any question of law arising out of an award' was before the court, such an exception or limitation ought not to also apply.

A similar position was taken by the Court of Appeal, in *Tridant Engineering supra* at paragraphs 41 and 43. There is also a series of judgments by the High Court[16] that have applied this principle based on the judgment of the Federal Court, in *The Government of India v. Cairn Energy India Pty Ltd & Anor* [2012] 3 CLJ 423 at paragraph 30. Despite the judgment of the Federal Court, in *Far East Holdings supra*, the Court of Appeal, in *Taki Engineering supra* at paragraphs 19 and 23, continued to apply the Absalom exception.

[D] Substantially Affects the Rights of One or More of the Parties

Section 42(1A) of the Arbitration Act 2005 provides that the High Court shall dismiss a reference unless the question of the law substantially affects the rights of the parties. This requirement in section 42(1A) is mandatory, given the use of the word 'shall'.[17]

To satisfy this mandatory requirement, the applicant must affirm an affidavit asserting that one or more parties' rights have been affected. The applicant will also have to provide an explanation as to whose rights have been affected and the extent to which they have been affected. As the rights affected most often are of a financial nature, the applicant should provide particulars in terms of figures. The extent to which a party's rights are affected should be particularized, as the question of whether a party's rights have been substantially affected is relative and will depend on the facts of a particular case.[18]

The rights of a party that are substantially affected include rights arising from the award.[19]

In the event this requirement is not satisfied, a reference shall be dismissed by the High Court. It may also be open to the respondent to apply to strike out a reference, or certain questions in a reference, where this requirement is not satisfied.[20]

---

16. See *Sabah Medical Centre supra* at para. 31; *Sanlaiman supra* at para. 5; *Sagau Batu Bala supra* at para. 24; *MMC Engineering supra* at para. 32.
17. See *Perwira Bintang supra* at para. 52, CA; *Magna Prima supra* at para. 77, HC; *MMC Engineering supra* at para. 40, HC.
18. See *Magna Prima supra* at paras 78-79, HC; *MMC Engineering supra* at para. 39, HC; *Konsortium Lord-Sebarkat supra* at para. 32, HC; *Renoir Consulting supra* at paras 71-72, 94, HC.
19. See *SDA Architects supra* at para. 33, CA.
20. See *Chain Cycle supra* at para. 65, CA.

[E] Mandatory Time Period

Section 42(2) of the Arbitration Act 2005 provides that a reference shall be filed within forty-two days of the publication and receipt of the award. The time period provided for is mandatory.[21]

Further, and in the light of section 8 of the Arbitration Act 2005, the High Court does not appear to have the jurisdiction to extend the time provided for in section 42.[22]

The High Court will also not allow an application to amend a reference under section 42 after the timeline has expired, even if the original reference was made within the timeline.[23]

[F] Identify the Question of Law

Section 42(2) of the Arbitration Act 2005 requires the applicant to identify the question of law in the reference.

Based on this provision, the High Court, in *Taman Bandar Baru supra* at paragraph 23(d), held that the applicant was obliged to 'state the question of law arising from the award in a concise manner'. This was confirmed by the Court of Appeal, in *Perwira Bintang supra* at paragraph 57(a), where it was held that the question of law must be identified with sufficient precision. The judgment in *Taman Bandar Baru supra* has also been followed by several judgments of the High Court.[24]

The Court of Appeal, in *Awangku Dewa supra* at paragraph 27, further emphasized that the question of law should be clearly and concisely framed. There should be no complication, confusion or duplicity in framing the questions. Instead, there should be simplicity and clarity.[25]

Therefore, the applicant must identify a question of law that is clear, concise, precise and simple. The High Court, in *Zenbay supra* at paragraph 47(5), has held that if these requirements are not met, an applicant may apply to amend the questions:

> ... the question of law should be clearly and sufficiently identified ... If the questions of law are not clearly and sufficiently identified ... I am of the respectful view that a plaintiff may apply to court to amend ... so as to identify clearly and sufficiently the questions of law to be determined by the court (amendment application) ...
>
> Needless to say, an amendment application should be dismissed if there is prejudice to a defendant which cannot be compensated in costs ... .

---

21. See *Chip Lam Seng Berhad v. R1 International Pte Ltd* [2010] MLJU 104 at p 1, HC; *Pacific & Orient Insurance Co Berhad v. Tetuan Kumar Jaspal Quah & Aishah* [2015] 1 LNS 501 at para. 15, HC; *Kluang Healthcare supra* at para. 47, HC.
22. See *Kluang Healthcare supra* at para. 47, HC.
23. See *Pacific & Orient supra* at paras 15-17, HC.
24. See *Maimunah Deraman supra* at para. 21, HC; *Sanlaiman supra* at para. 3, HC; *Sagau Batu Bala supra* at para. 6, HC; *Tan Kong Han supra* at para. 35, HC.
25. See also *SDA Architects supra* at paras 12, 15, CA.

[G] Grounds on Which the Reference Is Sought

Section 42(2) of the Arbitration Act 2005 provides that the applicant shall identify the grounds on which the reference is sought. This requirement has been emphasized in several judgments.[26]

The High Court, in *MMC Engineering supra* at paragraph 30, elaborated on this requirement by explaining that the applicant would need to set out the findings of fact and law from which the questions arise:

> The Plaintiffs must furthermore explain the grounds for their grievance, the basis for their claims. Here, the relevant factual findings and legal analysis that form the grounds must be pointed out as the questions of law could not possibly exist on their own, but necessarily emanate from some findings of fact or analysis of the applicable legal principles.

The High Court, in *Zenbay supra* at paragraph 47(7), again held that if this requirement was not complied with, the applicant could apply to amend the grounds in the application:

> ... the grounds for the court reference (grounds) should be stated ... If the grounds are not stated ... in my view, an amendment application should be filed to specify the grounds ... .

[H] Particulars of Each Ground

Order 69 Rule 6(2)(c) of the Rules of Court 2012 requires the applicant to give particulars of each ground on which the arbitral tribunal erred in law, with references to the paragraphs or passages in the award where the alleged error was made.

There is no equivalent express provision in section 42 of the Arbitration Act 2005. However, this may be implicit in section 42(2), which requires the applicant to state the grounds on which the reference is sought.

The need for particulars of the grounds can be seen from the judgment of the High Court, in *Taman Bandar Baru supra* at paragraph 23(d), where it was emphasized that the applicant must state the 'facts leading to the grounds'. The judgment of the High Court, in *Taman Bandar Baru supra*, has subsequently been followed in several judgments of the High Court.[27]

The Court of Appeal, in *Awangku Dewa supra* at paragraph 25, also emphasized the need for the applicant to 'set out the complete facts of the case, facts that are necessary or relevant for the purposes of the questions posed'.

The High Court, in *Zenbay supra* at paragraph 47(8), recognized the need to state the particulars of each ground as a threshold requirement. The High Court also

---

26. See *Taman Bandar Baru supra* para. 23(d), HC; confirmed in *Perwira Bintang supra* at para. 57(b), CA; followed in *Maimunah Deraman supra* para. 21, HC; *Sanlaiman supra* para. 3, HC; *Sagau Batu Bala supra* para. 16, HC; *Tan Kong Han supra* para. 35, HC.
27. See *Maimunah Deraman supra* at para. 21, HC; *Sanlaiman supra* at para. 3, HC; *Sagau Batu Bala supra* at para. 16, HC.

suggested that if this requirement was not complied with, the applicant might apply to amend the application.

[I] Service of the Application

Order 69 Rule 6(4) of the Rules of Court 2012 requires the applicant to serve the application and the affidavit on each arbitrator and the respondent.

The High Court, in *Zenbay supra* at paragraph 47(9), recognized the need for service as an additional threshold requirement. The High Court also suggested that if the application had not been served on the arbitral tribunal, the applicant could undertake to do so. In any event, the High Court opined that such non-compliance may be cured.

§42.03 DETERMINATION STAGE

The High Court may, once the threshold requirements in sections 42(1), (1A) and (2) of the Arbitration Act 2005 are met, determine the reference on a question of law.

[A] The Correct Approach

In determining the reference, the approach the court should take is that if there is indeed a question of law, as considered in §42.02[A] *supra*, then the court should proceed to determine it.

This can be seen from the judgment of High Court, in *Exceljade supra* at paragraphs 52 and 53, where it was, *inter alia*, held:

> [52]... the question that a court needs to ask itself is whether the question framed before it is indeed a question of law.
>
> [53] If it is, the Court should then proceed to decide it ... It is pertinent that no restrictive language is used, and the Court is given express power to set aside the award in whole or in part as a result of the reference on 'any question of law arising out of an award'.

This approach was subsequently endorsed by the Court of Appeal, in *Perwira Bintang supra* at paragraphs 53-57.

Subsequently, the Court of Appeal, in *Chain Cycle supra* at paragraph 20, noted that the parties accepted that the approach to be taken by the courts during the determination stage was settled, in the light of *Exceljade supra* and *Perwira Bintang supra*. This approach was also confirmed by the Federal Court, in *Far East Holdings supra* at paragraph 156.

This approach has been termed the 'process of reasoning' approach, by the High Court in *Zenbay supra* at paragraph 52 based on *Exceljade supra*, where the High Court emphasized the need to consider the three-stage reasoning of an arbitral tribunal, as explained in §42.02[A] *supra*, with the second stage being the most likely to yield a question of law.

There is an alternative approach, which has been termed the 'patent error of law' approach by the High Court in *Zenbay supra* at paragraph 51. This approach requires an erroneous legal proposition that forms the basis of the arbitral tribunal's decision and that appears on the face of the award or in a document incorporated in the award. This approach is stricter than the 'process of reasoning' approach that allows for questions of law that arise from the award, even if they do not appear on the face of the award, and are not the subject of an explicit ruling by the arbitral tribunal, so long as they can be argued as the basis of the findings of fact made by the arbitral tribunal.[28]

The stricter 'patent error of law' approach was first adopted by the High Court, in *Majlis Amanah Rakyat supra* at page 13. This approach was subsequently followed by the High Court, in *Maimunah Deraman supra* at paragraphs 22 and 23, *Rmarine Engineering supra* at paragraph 16 and *Lembaga Kemajuan Ikan supra* at paragraphs 18-21.

All these judgments by the High Court were prior to *Exceljade supra*. This is significant because Ariff JCA, who had adopted the 'patent error of law approach' in *Majlis Amanah Rakyat supra*, accepted in *Perwira Bintang supra*, after *Exceljade supra*, that the 'process of reasoning' approach was the better approach.

Despite this, there has been subsequent reliance by the courts on the 'patent error of law approach'. The Court of Appeal, in *SDA Architects supra* at paragraph 32, and the High Court, in *Jamilah Abdul Hamid supra* at pages 9 and 10, appear to adopt this approach without any consideration of the judgment in *Exceljade supra*. The High Court, in *MMC Engineering supra* at paragraph 52, and the minority judgment of Hamid Sultan JCA, in *Petronas Penapisan supra* at paragraphs 25-27, appear to support the continued application of the 'patent error of law' approach, despite the judgments in *Exceljade supra* and *Perwira Bintang supra*. However, the majority judgment of Abraham JCA, in *Petronas Penapisan supra* at paragraph 38, appears to endorse the 'process of reasoning' approach by reference to *Chain Cycle supra*.

It is submitted that, in the light of the judgment of the High Court, in *Exceljade supra*, that was endorsed by the Court of Appeal, in *Perwira Bintang supra*, regarded as settled by the Court of Appeal, in *Chain Cycle supra*, and confirmed by the Federal Court, in *Far East Holdings supra*, that the 'process of reasoning' approach is the correct approach to be adopted by the courts at the determination stage.

[B]   Not an Appeal

A reference under section 42 of the Arbitration Act 2005 is not an appeal to the High Court. The High Court does not have the broad appellate jurisdiction it has over subordinate courts when considering a reference under section 42. Instead, the High Court has a supervisory jurisdiction that is confined to the express provisions of section 42.

These principles have been repeatedly emphasized by the Court of Appeal. For example, in *Chain Cycle supra* at paragraph 66:

---

28. See *Perwira Bintang supra* at paragraphs 55 to 56, CA.

The pressure was definitely on the courts therefore to be ever vigilant and to resist attempts to engage the courts in a review of the arbitral award on its merits, akin to an 'appeal', often camouflaged masterly as 'questions of law'. There was no room for any dispute that the curial function of the court under s. 42 of the Arbitration Act 2005 was only intended by the legislature to be extended to questions of law per se, that too, which would affect substantially the rights of one or the other party.

Similarly, in *Petronas Penapisan supra* at paragraph 38, it was held that 'section 42 is not a provision as to appeals but a reference on questions of law.' Subsequently, in *Tridant Engineering supra* at paragraph 43, it was held 'Further, the courts do not sit in an appellate function when hearing references from arbitral proceeding. Their function is only one of very limited supervisory nature.'[29]

[C] Minimal Intervention

Section 42 of the Arbitration Act 2005 expressly allows the High Court to determine a question of law arising from an award. To that extent, the High Court is entitled to intervene in accordance with section 8 of the Arbitration Act 2005. The High Court may only intervene if all the threshold requirements specified in §42.02 *supra* are satisfied. However, once these threshold requirements are met, the High Court should proceed to determine the question of law referred. The High Court should not, at the determination stage, hesitate to determine the question posed on any overriding principle of non-intervention.

These principles were lucidly set out in the judgment of the High Court, in *Exceljade supra* at paragraphs 31 and 32, where it was, *inter alia*, held:

[31] Under our Arbitration Act 2005, section 42 expressly allows for a question of law to be referred to the Court without the need for any preliminary filter or leave application, the only qualification being that such question of law must affect substantially the rights of the parties in order to warrant interference or intervention by the High Court. To this end therefore the reasoning adopted by Justice Jackson in *Kershaw's* case may well be similarly applicable to our present case under section 42.

[32] In other words, while there may well be a spirit and philosophy of non-interference underlying the promulgation of the Arbitration Act 2005, such a philosophy must give way to the express provisions of the Act, such as section 42. It articulates an entitlement to refer a question of law to the High Court where such a question of law substantially affects the rights of the parties. Therefore effect must be accorded as legislatively pronounced.

The jurisprudence behind these principles and the attempt to find a middle path through section 42 between total non-intervention by the courts and the courts continuing to exercise supervisory or appellate oversight over arbitral proceedings was

---

29. *See also Lembaga Kemajuan Ikan supra* at para. 6, HC; *Jamilah Abdul Hamid supra* at p. 10, HC; *Awangku Dewa supra* at paras 22, 28, CA; *Zenbay supra* para. 44, HC.

Chapter 9: Additional Provisions Relating to Arbitration   §42.03[C]

elaborated by the Court of Appeal, in *Chain Cycle supra* at paragraphs 63 and 64, where it was, *inter alia*, held:

> [63] ... We have on the one side those who advocate a stance that there should be absolute judicial restraint and deference to the finality of an arbitral award. They say that the parties agreeing to arbitration were agreeing to the arbitrator getting it wrong and there should be total non-intervention by the civil courts. On the other end of the swing of the pendulum were those who argue that national courts, particularly in domestic arbitration, should not abdicate their sovereignty to have complete supervisory and appellate oversight over subordinate tribunals, which they equate the arbitral process to be one. Hence, the views expressed yet by some that the checks on arbitral awards should be structured and tested more in the nature of 'judicial review' proceedings that is currently on the rule book.
>
> [64] The legislative intent behind allowing reference to be brought on questions of law (s. 42 of the Arbitration Act 2005) to the court appear to be to cut a middle path between those divergent positions, namely, to allow the courts a limited role to re-examine issues or questions of law arising out of an award ... .

This was subsequently endorsed by the Court of Appeal, in *Petronas Penapisan supra* at paragraph 38, where it was also emphasized that once the threshold requirements were met the court should proceed to determine the question as there was no risk of opening the floodgates:

> We agree with the approach of the learned judge that the court must intervene where the award is manifestly unlawful and unconscionable. Section 42 has no equivalent in the Model Law or in parallel jurisdictions. Section 42 is not a provision as to appeals but a reference on a question of law ... We are of the opinion that with the pre-requirements of s. 42, it followed there would be no danger of 'opening the floodgates' in respect of review of arbitral awards.

General statements about the non-intervention of the courts should be read in the light of these specific principles. The Federal Court, in *Far East Holdings supra* at paragraph 118, emphasized that there were no additional requirements to the effect that the courts would only intervene in clear and exceptional cases, where the award was manifestly perverse, unconscionable or unlawful, as such additional requirements were not expressly stated in section 42:

> An award might or might not be perverse, unconscionable, unreasonable, and the like. But it only matters whether there is a question of law arising out of the award that substantially affects the rights of one or more of the parties. Under s 42, that is the only ground for the court to intervene. Perverse, unconscionable, unreasonable, and the like are not tests for the setting aside of an award. The so-called guidelines (g) 'This jurisdiction under s 42 is not to be lightly exercised, and should be exercised only in clear and exceptional cases'; (h) 'Nevertheless, the court should intervene if the award is manifestly unlawful and unconscionable'; and (j) 'While the findings of facts and the application of legal principles by the arbitral tribunal may be wrong (in instances of findings of mixed fact and law), the court should not intervene unless the decision is perverse', stated in *Perwira Bintang* are not in line with s 42 and should not be followed.

The judgment of the Federal Court, in *Far East Holdings supra*, and its effect, was later summarized by the High Court, in *Tidalmarine Engineering Sdn Bhd v. Kerajaan Malaysia (Jabatan Kerja Raya Malaysia)* [2018] MLJU at paragraph 45:

> However, subsequently the Federal Court in the case of *Far East Holdings Bhd & Anor v. Majlis Ugama Islam dan Adat Resam Melayu Pahang & Other Appeals* [2018] 1 CLJ 693 held that the guidelines (g), (h) and (j) stated in *Perwira Bintang* are not in line with section 42 and should not be followed. The Federal Court held that under s. 42, the only ground for the court to intervene is whether there is a question of law arising out of the award that substantially affects the rights of the parties.

[D]   Relationship with an Application to Set Aside

Section 37 of the Arbitration Act 2005 provides for applications to set aside an award due to errors of process. Section 42 allows for an award to be confirmed, varied, remitted or set aside due to errors of substantive law.

As the two sections deal with separate matters, there is no need for the grounds in section 37 to be satisfied before a reference may be made under section 42. This was confirmed by the High Court, in *Lembaga Kemajuan Ikan supra* at paragraph 10, where it was, *inter alia*, held:

> While the courts generally take a limited jurisdiction approach in matters concerning arbitration and arbitral awards, it is quite different to say that s. 42 is not engaged unless and until the applicant proves that its questions of law are founded on the grounds set out in s. 37. If s. 37 is examined, it can be seen that the grounds there are not necessarily those relating to only questions of law but instead are more of mixed fact and law. For example, grounds such as incapacity or sufficiency of notice (sub-ss. 37(a) and (c)).

Although section 37 deals with errors of process and section 42 deals with errors of substantive law, the two provisions are not mutually exclusive. This was explained by the Court of Appeal, in *Petronas Penapisan supra* at paragraph 36:

> ... the approach of the learned judge was to treat applications under both sections as not being mutually exclusive ... .

> We are therefore in agreement with the views of the learned judge expressed on this point.

A similar position was taken by the Court of Appeal, in *Perwira Bintang supra* at paragraph 62, where it was, *inter alia*, held that the same grounds could form the basis of an application under sections 37 and 42 provided that the threshold requirements of section 42 were met:

> Counsel for the appellant has, in the course of her submission, questioned whether it was right to duplicate the grounds under s. 37 as grounds under s. 42 of the Act. We are not persuaded why similar grounds cannot be raised under s. 42, if all the requirements under the section can be fulfilled.

§42.04 RELIEF STAGE

Section 42(2) of the Arbitration Act 2005 provides that the High Court 'may', on determination of the reference, confirm, vary, remit or set aside the award. The use of the word 'may' in section 42(4) means that the High Court has the discretion on the type of relief to be granted even if the threshold requirements are met and the question has been determined in the applicant's favour.[30] The High Court will exercise this discretion in accordance with the principles in §42.03 *supra*.

§42.05 ORDER TO STATE REASONS

Section 42(3) of the Arbitration Act 2005 allows the High Court to order the arbitral tribunal to state the reasons for the award, where the award does not have reason or has insufficient reasons.

The power granted to the High Court is discretionary, as can be seen from the use of the word 'may' in section 42(3).

The High Court is likely to exercise its discretion in favour of an applicant where the arbitration agreement expressly requires reasons. Where the arbitration agreement is silent as to whether reasons are to be provided for an award, the presumption under section 33(3) of the Arbitration Act 2005 is that reasons are to be given. This presumption will only be displaced if there is an agreement that reasons need not be given for the award. Such an agreement may be express or implicit, where it is the practice in an industry that reasons are not given for an award, as explained in §33.04 *supra*. Where there is an agreement, express or implied, that reasons will not be given, the High Court is unlikely to exercise their discretion, under section 42(3) by ordering reasons. In any event, it is submitted that the High Court may not be entitled to order reasons where there is an agreement to dispense with reasons for the award.

The ability of the High Court to order that reasons be given may be viewed as an attempt to overcome the High Court's inability otherwise to determine a question of law arising from the award. By ordering reasons, the High Court can determine, from these reasons, if there has been an error.

This view was expressed by the High Court, in *Exceljade supra* at paragraph 62:

> ... Section 42(3) overcomes this problem by allowing the Court to order the arbitrator to give reasons supporting the award so that it can determine whether or not to set aside or vary or confirm the award premised on the question of law posed ... .

Section 42(7) of the Arbitration Act 2005 provides that the High Court may make an order as to costs, where an order is made for reasons to the award to be stated.

---

30. *See SDA Architects supra* at para. 49, CA; *Zenbay supra* para. 57, HC.

§42.06 ORDER FOR SECURITY

Section 42(8) of the Arbitration Act 2005 provides that the High Court may, pending the determination of the reference, order the applicant to provide security for costs and that any money payable under the award be brought into court or otherwise secure.

Hamid Sultan JCA, in *Petronas Penapisan supra* at paragraph 22, held that the need for security should be the first consideration when a reference is made under section 42:

> The first step is to consider the provision of s. 42(8) which relates to security. That was not done in this case. Though I take note on the facts of the case and financial strength of the parties, it was not necessary.

However, this judgment, which was in the minority in the Court of Appeal, in *Petronas Penapisan supra*, does not appear to have been subsequently applied.

The High Court has the discretion whether to order security for costs, as can be seen from the use of the word 'may'. The High Court is likely to exercise this discretion against the applicant, where there is credible evidence that the applicant is unable to pay costs and the applicant does not provide any grounds against security being ordered.

This can be seen from the judgment of the High Court, in *Mechanalysis Sdn Bhd (in liquidation) v. Appraisal Property Management Sdn Bhd* [2016] 8 CLJ 81 at paragraphs 48-55. The High Court also held that where the applicant was in liquidation, this would be a sufficient basis for an order for security. Further, where the arbitral tribunal had found that the applicant was unable to pay costs, in a similar application during the arbitral proceedings, and the applicant had not provided any evidence of a change in circumstances, the High Court would treat the findings of the arbitral tribunal as conclusive.

The High Court similarly has the discretion whether to order the applicant to bring the amount awarded into court or otherwise secure such sum. The High Court will exercise this discretion by considering the following factors:

(1) whether an order for security will detrimentally affect or prejudice the applicant;
(2) whether the applicant continues to be able to meet the award;
(3) whether the reference is legitimate and is not otherwise frivolously instituted to delay the proceedings.

This again can be seen from the judgment of the High Court, in *Mechanalysis supra* at paragraphs 59-61.

43. Appeal

[deleted by section 13 of the Arbitration (Amendment) (No 2) Act 2018]

§43.01 INTRODUCTION

Section 43 of the Arbitration Act 2005, prior to its deletion by the Arbitration (Amendment) (No 2) Act 2018, provided that:

> A decision of the High Court under section 42 shall be deemed to be a judgment of the High Court within the meaning of section 67 of the Courts of Judicature Act 1964 [Act 91].

Section 43 of the Arbitration Act 2005 equated a decision of the High Court under section 42 with a judgment of the High Court under section 67 of the Courts of Judicature Act 1964.

Section 67 of the Courts of Judicature Act 1964 provides:

> Jurisdiction to hear and determine civil appeals
>
> 67. (1) The Court of Appeal shall have jurisdiction to hear and determine appeals from any judgment or order of any High Court in any civil cause or matter, whether made in the exercise of its original or of its appellate jurisdiction, subject nevertheless to this or any other written law regulating the terms and conditions upon which such appeals shall be brought.
>
> (2) The Court of Appeal shall have all the powers conferred by section 24A on the High Court under the provisions relating to references under order of the High Court.

Section 43 effectively provided, therefore, that a decision of the High Court under section 42 may be appealed to the Court of Appeal.

This can be contrasted with other provisions of the Arbitration Act 2005, which provide that no appeal shall lie against a decision of the High Court under these provisions.[31]

Section 43, which is consequential to section 42, was also deleted by the Arbitration (Amendment) (No 2) Act 2018 for the same reasons as set out under §42.01 *supra*.

---

31. *See* Arbitration Act 2005, sections 15(5) and 18(10).

44. *Costs and Expense of an Arbitration*

(1) *Unless otherwise agreed by the parties –*
   (a) *the costs and expenses of an arbitration shall be in the discretion of the arbitral tribunal who may –*
      (i) *direct to and by whom and in what manner those costs or any part thereof shall be paid;*
      (ii) *tax or settle the amount of such costs and expenses; and*
      (iii) *award such costs and expenses to be paid as between solicitor and client;*
   (b) *any party may apply to the High Court for the costs to be taxed where an arbitral tribunal has in its award directed that costs and expenses be paid by any party, but fails to specify the amount of such costs and expenses within thirty days of having being requested to do so; or*
   (c) *each party shall be responsible for its own legal and other expenses and for an equal share of the fees and expenses of the arbitral tribunal and any other expenses relating to the arbitration in the absence of an award or additional award fixing and allocating the costs and expenses of the arbitration.*
(2) *Unless otherwise agreed by the parties, where a party makes an offer to the other party to settle the dispute or part of the dispute and the offer is not accepted and the award of the arbitral tribunal is no more favourable to the other party than was the offer, the arbitral tribunal, in fixing and allocating the costs and expenses of the arbitration, may take the fact of the offer into account in awarding costs and expenses in respect of the period from the making of the offer to the making of the award.*
(3) *An offer to settle made under subsection (2) shall not be communicated to the arbitral tribunal until it has made a final determination of all aspects of the dispute other than the fixing and allocation of costs and expenses.*
(4) *Where an arbitral tribunal refuses to deliver its award before the payment of its fees and expenses, the High Court may order the arbitral tribunal to deliver the award on such conditions as the High Court thinks fit.*
(5) *A taxation of costs, fees and expenses under this section may be reviewed in the same manner as a taxation of costs.*

§44.01 INTRODUCTION

Section 44 of the Arbitration Act 2005 provides for the manner in which the costs and expenses in an arbitration may be determined. In particular, section 44 also provides for the determination of costs in the face of an offer to settle, and for a situation where the arbitral tribunal refuses to deliver their award until their fees and expenses are settled.

Section 44 of the Arbitration Act 2005 is not based on the 1985 Model Law. The 1985 Model Law does not provide for costs. This was left to each State to legislate on.

Section 44 of the Arbitration Act 2005 is based on clause 6 of Schedule 2 of the New Zealand Arbitration Act 1996. In particular:

(1) section 44(1)(a) is similar to clause 6(1)(a) but does not include the definition of costs found in clause 6(1)(a). Sections 44(1)(a)(i) to (iii) provide for the authority the arbitral tribunal has in awarding costs in detail, which details are not found in clause 6;
(2) section 44(1)(b) is not found in the New Zealand Arbitration Act 1996. Section 44(1)(b) provides for a particular situation where the arbitral tribunal has specified which party is to pay costs but has not fixed the amount of such costs;
(3) section 44(1)(c) is effectively the same as clause 6(1)(b);
(4) section 44(2) is effectively the same as clause 6(2)(a);
(5) section 44(3) is effectively the same as clause 6(2(b);
(6) section 44(4) is effectively the same as clause 6(4)(a);
(7) section 44(5) is not found in the New Zealand Arbitration Act 1996; and
(8) clauses 6(3), (5) and (6) are not found in the Arbitration Act 2005. The omission of clause 6(3) is particularly significant. The High Courts in Malaysia do not have the express authority to review the allocation and amount of costs fixed by the arbitral tribunal on the grounds that such allocation or amount is unreasonable unlike the position in New Zealand.

Section 44 appears in Part III of the Arbitration Act 2005. Therefore, it applies to domestic arbitrations unless the parties agree to exclude this section. Section 44 will not apply in an international arbitration unless the parties agree to include it.

§44.02 DETERMINATION OF COSTS

Section 44(1) of the Arbitration Act 2005, like the 1985 Model Law, allows the parties to agree on how costs are to be determined. In the absence of such agreement:

(1) section 44(1)(a) provides that the arbitral tribunal shall determine costs;
(2) section 44(1)(b) provides that the High Court may determine the amount of costs where the arbitral tribunal has only determined who is to pay costs; and
(3) section 44(1)(c) provides that the parties shall bear their own costs and an equal portion of the arbitral tribunal's fees and expenses where the arbitral tribunal has not made any award on costs.

These four scenarios are considered below, namely:

(1) where there is an agreement on how costs are to be determined;
(2) where the arbitral tribunal determines costs;

(3) where the arbitral tribunal determines who will bear the costs and the High Court determines the amount of such costs; and
(4) where the arbitral tribunal does not determine costs.

[A] Agreement on How Costs Will Be Determined

In practice, the parties, if they agree on how costs are to be determined, will do so by agreeing to the rules published by an arbitration institution.

For example, the parties may agree to the adoption of the 2018 AIAC Arbitration Rules. Rule 13 of the 2018 AIAC Arbitration Rules provides:

> Costs
> 1. The term 'costs' as specified in Article 40 shall also include the expenses reasonably incurred by the AIAC in connection with the arbitration, the administrative fees of the AIAC as well as the costs of the facilities made available by the AIAC under Rule 11.
> 2. Unless otherwise agreed by the Parties and the arbitral tribunal pursuant to Rule 13(4), the fees of the arbitral tribunal shall be fixed by the Director in accordance with Schedule 1.
> 3. Unless otherwise agreed upon by Parties in writing, Schedule 1(A) shall apply to international arbitrations (USD scale) and Schedule 1(B) shall apply to domestic arbitrations (RM scale).
> 4. Notwithstanding the above, all Parties and arbitral tribunal are at liberty to agree on the fees and expenses of the arbitral tribunal within the period of time of 30 days from the appointment of the arbitral tribunal (the 'Fee Agreement'). The arbitral tribunal shall inform the Director that the Fee Agreement has been executed. If the Fee Agreement is executed after the 30 day period has expired, the Fee Agreement shall be subject to approval by the Director.
> 5. The AIAC administrative fees shall be fixed by the Director in accordance with Schedule 1. Unless otherwise agreed by the Parties, Schedule 1(A) shall apply to international arbitrations and Schedule 1(B) shall apply to domestic arbitrations.
> 6. The costs of arbitration may, in exceptional, unusual or unforeseen circumstances, be adjusted from time to time at the discretion of the Director.
> 7. The arbitrator's fees and the AIAC administrative fees under Schedule 1 are determined based on the amount in dispute. For the purpose of calculating the amount in dispute, the value of any counterclaim and/or set-off will be taken into account.
> 8. Where a claim or counterclaim does not state a monetary amount, an appropriate value for the claim or counterclaim shall be settled by the Director in consultation with the arbitral tribunal and the Parties for the purpose of computing the arbitrator's fees and the administrative fees.
> 9. The arbitral tribunal may determine the proportion of costs to be borne by the Parties.

Articles 40-42 of the 2013 UNCITRAL Arbitration Rules, which form part of the 2018 AIAC Arbitration Rules, provide:

Chapter 9: Additional Provisions Relating to Arbitration §44.02[A]

Definition of costs
Article 40
1. The arbitral tribunal shall fix the costs of arbitration in the final award and, if it deems appropriate, in another decision.
2. The term 'costs' includes only:
   (a) The fees of the arbitral tribunal to be stated separately as to each arbitrator and to be fixed by the tribunal itself in accordance with article 41;
   (b) The reasonable travel and other expenses incurred by the arbitrators;
   (c) The reasonable costs of expert advice and of other assistance required by the arbitral tribunal;
   (d) The reasonable travel and other expenses of witnesses to the extent such expenses are approved by the arbitral tribunal;
   (e) The legal and other costs incurred by the parties in relation to the arbitration to the extent that the arbitral tribunal determines that the amount of such costs is reasonable;
   (f) Any fees and expenses of the appointing authority as well as the fees and expenses of the Secretary-General of the PCA.
3. In relation to interpretation, correction or completion of any award under articles 37 to 39, the arbitral tribunal may charge the costs referred to in paragraphs 2 (b) to (f), but no additional fees.

Fees and expenses of arbitrators
Article 41
1. The fees and expenses of the arbitrators shall be reasonable in amount, taking into account the amount in dispute, the complexity of the subject matter, the time spent by the arbitrators and any other relevant circumstances of the case.
2. If there is an appointing authority and it applies or has stated that it will apply a schedule or particular method for determining the fees for arbitrators in international cases, the arbitral tribunal in fixing its fees shall take that schedule or method into account to the extent that it considers appropriate in the circumstances of the case.
3. Promptly after its constitution, the arbitral tribunal shall inform the parties as to how it proposes to determine its fees and expenses, including any rates it intends to apply. Within 15 days of receiving that proposal, any party may refer the proposal to the appointing authority for review. If, within 45 days of receipt of such a referral, the appointing authority finds that the proposal of the arbitral tribunal is inconsistent with paragraph 1, it shall make any necessary adjustments thereto, which shall be binding upon the arbitral tribunal.
4. (a) When informing the parties of the arbitrators' fees and expenses that have been fixed pursuant to article 40, paragraphs 2 (a) and (b), the arbitral tribunal shall also explain the manner in which the corresponding amounts have been calculated;
   (b) Within 15 days of receiving the arbitral tribunal's determination of fees and expenses, any party may refer for review such determination to the appointing authority. If no appointing authority has been agreed upon or designated, or if the appointing authority fails to act within the time specified in these Rules, then the review shall be made by the Secretary-General of the PCA;
   (c) If the appointing authority or the Secretary-General of the PCA finds that the arbitral tribunal's determination is inconsistent with the arbitral tribunal's proposal (and any adjustment thereto) under paragraph 3 or is otherwise manifestly excessive, it shall, within 45 days of receiving such a referral, make any adjustments to the arbitral tribunal's determination that

are necessary to satisfy the criteria in paragraph 1. Any such adjustments shall be binding upon the arbitral tribunal;
   (d) Any such adjustments shall either be included by the arbitral tribunal in its award or, if the award has already been issued, be implemented in a correction to the award, to which the procedure of article 38, paragraph 3, shall apply.
5. Throughout the procedure under paragraphs 3 and 4, the arbitral tribunal shall proceed with the arbitration, in accordance with article 17, paragraph 1.
6. A referral under paragraph 4 shall not affect any determination in the award other than the arbitral tribunal's fees and expenses; nor shall it delay the recognition and enforcement of all parts of the award other than those relating to the determination of the arbitral tribunal's fees and expenses.

Allocation of costs
Article 42
1. The costs of the arbitration shall in principle be borne by the unsuccessful party or parties. However, the arbitral tribunal may apportion each of such costs between the parties if it determines that apportionment is reasonable, taking into account the circumstances of the case.
2. The arbitral tribunal shall in the final award or, if it deems appropriate, in any other award, determine any amount that a party may have to pay to another party as a result of the decision on allocation of costs.

The benefits of incorporating the rules of an arbitration institution can be seen from these provisions on costs, particularly:

(1) the detailed definition of 'costs' provided in Article 40(2) of the 2013 UNCITRAL Arbitration Rules and Rule 13(1) of the 2018 AIAC Arbitration Rules;
(2) the arbitrator's scale of fees in Schedule I of the 2018 AIAC Arbitration Rules; and
(3) the principles for the allocation of costs set out in Article 42 of the 2013 UNCITRAL Arbitration Rules.

[B]   Arbitral Tribunal Determines Costs

Section 44(1)(a) of the Arbitration Act 2005 gives the arbitral tribunal the discretion to decide:

(1) who shall pay costs;
(2) the amounts of such costs; and
(3) that such amount may be on a solicitor-client basis.

Generally, costs will follow the event, and the arbitral tribunal will order the unsuccessful party to pay the costs of the successful party. If this rule is departed from, it would be prudent for the arbitral tribunal to give reasons for the departure.

The amount of costs awarded, in terms of legal fees, will depend on the complexity of the dispute and the length of time spent. Other costs, such as the arbitral tribunal's fees and expenses, the arbitral institution's fees and venue rentals will reflect the actual cost incurred by a party which may be readily proved.

The courts will not generally interfere with an arbitral tribunal's discretion in determining costs. This is because section 44(1)(a) expressly grants the discretion to award costs to the arbitral tribunal. This section, taken together with section 8 of the Arbitration Act 2005, suggests that the courts should not intervene in the exercise of this discretion by the arbitral tribunal.[32]

However, where the arbitral tribunal fails to exercise this discretion judicially, it may give rise to a question of law that can be referred to the High Court under section 42 of the Arbitration Act 2005.[33]

[C] Where the Arbitral Tribunal Determines Who Pays Costs and the High Court Taxes the Amount of Costs

Section 44(1)(b) of the Arbitration Act 2005 provides that:

(1) where the arbitral tribunal specifies who is to pay costs but does not fix the amount of costs in the award;
(2) and, the arbitral tribunal does not fix the amount of such costs thirty days after having been requested to do so;
(3) then, either party may apply to the High Court to fix the amount of such costs.

The High Court, in fixing such costs, will apply similar principles as those outlined in §44.02[B] *supra*.

[D] Where Costs Are Not Determined

Section 44(1)(c) of the Arbitration Act 2005 provides for a situation where the arbitral tribunal has not made any determination of costs. In this circumstance, a distinction is made between:

(1) the parties, legal and other expense; and
(2) the arbitral tribunal's fees and expenses.

The former is to be borne by each party, while the latter is to be equally shared.

---

32. See *Magnificient Diagraph Sdn Bhd v. JWC Ariatektura Sdn Bhd* [2009] MLJU 583 at para. 4(b), HC; and *SDA Architects supra* at paras 47(f), (h) and (j), CA.
33. See *SDA Architect supra* at para. 32.

§44.03 OFFER TO SETTLE

Sections 44(2) and (3) of the Arbitration Act 2005 provide that where:

(1) Party A makes a settlement offer to Party B;
(2) Party B does not accept Party A's settlement offer;
(3) the award is no more favourable to Party B than Party A's settlement offer;
(4) Party A has communicated their settlement offer to the arbitral tribunal after the determination of all aspects of the dispute other than costs;
(5) then the arbitral tribunal may take Party A's settlement offer into account when determining costs between the date of the settlement offer and the award.

Generally, in these circumstances, the arbitral tribunal will order Party B to pay the costs between the date of Party A's settlement offer and the award. If the arbitral tribunal departs from this general rule, it would be prudent to provide reasons. It is important to bear in mind, however, that the arbitral tribunal retains their general discretion under section 44(1)(a), as section 44(2) expressly provides that the arbitral tribunal 'may take the fact of the offer into account'.

It should also be emphasized that sections 44(2) and (3) may be excluded by express agreement of the parties.

§44.04 ORDER FOR DELIVERY

Section 44(4) of the Arbitration Act 2005 provides that where the arbitral tribunal refuses to deliver its award until the payment of its fees and expenses, the High Court may order the arbitral tribunal to deliver the award on such conditions as it thinks fit. It is unclear what conditions the High Court may order under this provision. Perhaps, the High Court may order that the fees and expenses of the arbitral tribunal be deposited with the relevant arbitral institution or the High Court pending the resolution of any genuine dispute on such fees and expenses.

§44.05 REVIEW

Section 44(5) of the Arbitration Act 2005 provides that a taxation of costs, fees and expenses may be reviewed in the same way as a taxation of costs. The meaning and purpose of this provision are unclear. It is unclear whether the High Court has the authority pursuant to this section to review the arbitral tribunal's taxation of costs, fees and expenses.

The judgment of the Court of Appeal, in *SDA Architect supra*, and the High Court, in *Magnificient Diagraph supra*, suggest that the High Court does not have the authority to conduct such a review, as costs are at the discretion of the arbitral tribunal.

Therefore, it is submitted that section 44(5) is intended to cover a limited situation, where the High Court has taxed costs, expenses or fees under section

44(1)(b) because the arbitral tribunal has not taxed such costs. In this situation, where the High Court has taxed costs, such taxation may be reviewed by an appellate court, under section 44(5). This interpretation also accords with the principle of minimal intervention by the courts.

45. Extension of Time for Commencing Arbitration Proceedings

Where an arbitration agreement provides that arbitral proceedings are to be commenced within the time specified in the agreement, the High Court may, notwithstanding that the specified time has expired, extend the time for such period and on such terms as it thinks fit, if it is of the opinion that in the circumstances of the case undue hardship would otherwise be caused.

§45.01 INTRODUCTION

Section 45 of the Arbitration Act 2005 allows the High Court to extend the time for the commencement of an arbitration, where the arbitration agreement specifies the time within which the arbitration is to be commenced.

Section 45 has no equivalent provision in the 1985 Model Law. Section 45 is based on clause 7 of Schedule 2 of the New Zealand Arbitration Act 1996. Section 45 has also been recognized as the re-enactment of section 28 of the Arbitration Act 1952, by the Court of Appeal, in *Dancom Telecommunication (M) Sdn Bhd v. UniAsia General Insurance Bhd* [2008] 5 CLJ 551 at paragraph 32.

Section 28 of the Arbitration Act 1952 provides:

> Power of High Court to extend time for commencing arbitration proceedings
>
> 28. Where the terms of an agreement to refer future disputes to arbitration provide that any claims to which the agreement applies shall be barred unless notice to appoint an arbitrator is given, or an arbitrator is appointed, or some other step to commence arbitration proceedings is taken, within a time fixed by the agreement and a dispute arises to which the agreement applies, the High Court, if it is of opinion that in the circumstances of the case undue hardship would otherwise be caused, and notwithstanding that the time so fixed has expired, may, on such terms, if any, as the justice of the case may require, but without prejudice to any written law limiting the time for the commencement of arbitration proceedings, extend the time for such period as it thinks proper.

Section 45 appears in Part III of the Arbitration Act 2005. Therefore, based on section 3(2), section 45 applies in domestic arbitration unless the parties have agreed to exclude it and does not apply in international arbitration unless the parties have agreed to include it.

§45.02 UNDUE HARDSHIP

The test under both section 45 of the Arbitration Act 2005 and section 28 of the Arbitration Act 1952 is whether 'undue hardship' would be caused. The authorities on section 28 therefore continue to be applicable to section 45.

The factors to be considered by the courts in assessing 'undue hardship' have been summarized as follows by the High Court, in *Penta-Ocean Construction v. Penang Development Corporation* [2003] 2 AMR 311 at pages 326 and 327:

> (1) The words 'undue hardship' ... should not be construed too narrowly.

(2) 'Undue hardship' means excessive hardship and, where the hardship is due to the fault of the claimant, it means hardship of the consequences of which are out of proportion to such fault.
(3) In deciding whether to extend time or not, the court should look at all the relevant circumstances of the particular case.
(4) In particular, the following matters should be considered:
   (a) the length of the delay;
   (b) the amount at stake;
   (c) whether the delay was due to the fault of the claimant or to circumstances outside his control;
   (d) if it was due to the fault of the claimant, the degree of such fault;
   (e) whether the claimant was misled by the other party;
   (f) whether the other party has been prejudices by the delay, and, if so, the degree of such prejudice.

These principles appear to be quite settled, in the light of the earlier judgment of the Federal Court, in *Safety Insurance Company Sdn Bhd v. Chow Soon Tat* [1975] 1 MLJ 193 at page 200, and the subsequent judgment of the Court of Appeal, in *Mascom (M) Sdn Bhd & Ors v. Ken Grouting System Specialist Sdn Bhd* [2004] 2 MLJ 163 at paragraphs 33-35.

§45.03 RESTRAINT OF LEGAL PROCEEDINGS

The question arises whether an arbitration agreement which limits the time within which a party may enforce his rights is void, as being contrary to section 29 of the Contract Act 1950.

Section 29 of the Contract Act 1950 provides:

Agreements in restraint of legal proceedings void

29. Every agreement, by which any party thereto is restricted absolutely from enforcing his rights under or in respect of any contract, by the usual legal proceedings in the ordinary tribunals, or which limits the time within which he may thus enforce his rights, is void to that extent.

Saving of contract to refer to arbitration dispute that may arise

Exception 1 – This section shall not render illegal a contract by which two or more persons agree that any dispute which may arise between them in respect of any subject or class of subjects shall be referred to arbitration, and that only the amount awarded in the arbitration shall be recoverable in respect of the dispute so referred.

Saving of contract to refer questions that have already arisen

Exception 2 – Nor shall this section render illegal any contract in writing, by which two or more persons agree to refer to arbitration any question between them which has already arisen, or affect any law as to references to arbitration.

Exception 3 – Nor shall this section render illegal any contract in writing between the Government and any person with respect to an award of a scholarship by the Government wherein it is provided that the discretion exercised by the Government under that contract shall be final and conclusive and shall not be questioned by any court.

In this exception, the expression 'scholarship' includes any bursary to be awarded or tuition or examination fees to be defrayed by the Government and the expression 'Government' includes the Government of a State.

The Court of Appeal, in *Dancom supra* at paragraphs 22 and 29, confirmed that arbitration agreement that limited the time for the commencement of proceedings was not void under section 29, as arbitral tribunals were not 'ordinary tribunals' under section 29, and in the light of the principle of party autonomy, which applied to arbitration, as well as the express recognition of the right of the parties, to limit time by section 45:

> [22] ... A contract which incorporates an arbitration clause, such as cl. 14, to refer the parties' dispute to arbitration within a specified period as agreed by the parties, is a contract sui generis. The hallmark of arbitration is characterised by the autonomy of the parties. By way of agreement, the parties have an unfettered choice, not only to refer their dispute to arbitration and to choose their own arbitrators or umpires, but also to prescribe the time frame for such reference. Their intention is to sustain the mechanism of alternative dispute resolution by way of arbitration and not court action. Their desire is to place arbitration under their exclusive control. They hope to achieve eg, speed in the hearing and determination of their dispute. Different considerations would then apply to an arbitration clause prescribing a time frame such as that expressly agreed in cl. 14. It is a product of the doctrine of freedom of contract and would attract the application of the specific provisions expressly set out in exceptions 1 and 2 to s. 29, so that the general rule embodied in s. 29 would give way to these two exceptions.
>
> ...
>
> [29] The validity of cl. 14 is given statutory recognition in s. 28 of the Arbitration Act 1952 ('s. 28') which vests the High Court with the power to extend the time for the purpose of referring a dispute to arbitration after the expiry of the prescribed 12 month time frame ... .

§45.04 UNAMBIGUOUS

The High Court, in *Mun Seng Fook v. AIG Malaysia Insurance Bhd* [2018] MLJU 310 at paragraphs 24 and 36, decided that despite provisions in the agreement limiting the time to commence arbitral proceedings, clear and unambiguous terms were also required to bar a party from commencing civil proceedings:

> [24] The other relevant clauses of the policy are as follows:
>
> Clause 15
>
> 'Legal Proceedings
>
> No action in law or equity shall be brought to recover on this policy prior to the expiration of sixty (60) days after written proof of loss has been filed in accordance with the requirements of this policy, nor shall such action be brought at all unless brought within one (1) year from the expiration of the time within which the written proof or loss is required by the policy.'
>
> Clause 20

'Limitation of Time of Bringing Arbitration

If a claim is made under the policy and is rejected by the CMI, the Insured or his/her legal personal representatives shall commence arbitration proceedings in accordance with Clause 19 of Section 7 hereof within six (6) months of such rejection, failing which CMI shall be discharged from all liability whatsoever for that claim.'

...

[36] This Court finds that in the policy herein, the Respondent has not made it clear to the Appellant that in the event there is no referral to arbitration, the Appellant will lose his rights under Clause 15 of the policy to refer the matter to the courts. As such, the contra proferentum rule applied in favour of the Appellant in view of the conflict between Clause 15 and Clause 19 of the policy and the Appellant is entitled to maintain his action in court. Clause 19 being the arbitration clause referred to by the Respondent cannot be viewed in isolation to defeat the Appellant's claim under the policy.

46. *Extension of Time for Making Award*

(1) Where the time for making an award is limited by the arbitration agreement, the High Court may, unless otherwise agreed by the parties, extend that time.
(2) An application under subsection (1) may be made –
 (a) upon notice to the parties, by the arbitral tribunal; or
 (b) upon notice to the arbitral tribunal and the other parties, by any party to the proceedings.
(3) The High Court shall not make an order unless –
 (a) all available tribunal processes for obtaining an extension of time have been exhausted; and
 (b) the High Court is satisfied that substantial injustice would otherwise be done.
(4) The High Court may exercise its powers under subsection (1) notwithstanding that the time previously fixed by or under the arbitration agreement or by a previous order has expired.

§46.01 INTRODUCTION

Section 46 of the Arbitration Act 2005 allows the High Court to extend the time to make an award, where such time is limited by the arbitration agreement.

Section 46 has no equivalent in the 1985 Model Law. Section 46 is based on section 50 of the English Arbitration Act 1996. Section 50 of the English Arbitration Act 1996 is also the basis for section 36 of the Singapore Arbitration Act 2001.

Section 46 appears in Part III of the Arbitration Act 2005. Therefore, section 46 applies in domestic arbitration unless the parties have agreed to exclude it. And, section 46 does not apply in international arbitration unless the parties have agreed to include it.

§46.02 PARTY AUTONOMY

Section 46(1) of the Arbitration Act 2005 provides that the High Court may extend the time for the making of the award 'unless otherwise agreed by the parties'. Therefore, the parties may agree to exclude the right of the High Court to allow such an extension. Such an agreement may, in a domestic arbitration, be to exclude Part III of the Arbitration Act 2005 in general or section 46 in particular.

Alternatively, the parties may exclude section 46 by adopting a set of arbitration rules. For example, Rule 1(1)(c) of the 2018 AIAC Arbitration Rules excludes the application of section 46 of the Arbitration Act 2005 to an arbitration seated in Malaysia.

The High Court of Singapore, in *Ting Kang Cheng John v. Teo Hee Lai Building Constructions Pte Ltd* [2010] 2 SLR 625 at paragraph 43, when commenting on section

36 of the Singapore Arbitration Act 2001, suggest that it may be prudent to expressly exclude this right if the parties so intend.

Section 46(1) preserves the principles of party autonomy insofar as the parties are free to exclude the power of the High Court to extend time should they so wish.[34]

§46.03 PROCEDURE

Section 46(2) of the Arbitration Act 2005 sets out the procedure for applying for an extension of time. Either the arbitral tribunal or a party may make the application, with notice to the other parties. Section 46(4) of the Arbitration Act 2005 clarifies that the High Court may extend time even if time has expired under the arbitration agreement or a previous order.

§46.04 DISCRETION AND PRECONDITIONS

Section 46(3) of the Arbitration Act 2005 sets out the two preconditions for an application. These preconditions are mandatory given the use of the word 'shall' in section 46(3). Even if these mandatory preconditions are satisfied, the High Court retains a discretion whether to grant the extension, in the light of the word 'may' used in section 46(1).

The two mandatory preconditions are that all available tribunal processes for obtaining an extension have been exhausted and that substantial injustice would otherwise occur.

[A] Tribunal Processes Exhausted

Section 46(3)(a) of the Arbitration Act 2005 provides that all available tribunal processes for obtaining an extension of time must have been exhausted before an application can be made to the High Court.

Where the parties have adopted a particular set of arbitration rules, the arbitral tribunal should exhaust the procedure for an extension under those rules before applying to court for an extension.

For example, Article 31 of the 2017 ICC Arbitration Rules provides:

Article 31: Time Limit for the Final Award
1) The time limit within which the arbitral tribunal must render its final award is six months. Such time limit shall start to run from the date of the last signature by the arbitral tribunal or by the parties of the Terms of Reference or, in the case of application of Article 23(3), the date of the notification to the arbitral tribunal by the Secretariat of the approval of the Terms of Reference by the Court. The Court may fix a different time limit based upon the procedural timetable established pursuant to Article 24(2).

---

34. See *Ting Kang Chung supra* at para. 43, HC (Singapore).

2) The Court may extend the time limit pursuant to a reasoned request from the arbitral tribunal or on its own initiative if it decides it is necessary to do so.

Based on these rules, the arbitral tribunal should make a reasoned request to the ICC International Court of Arbitration for an extension, failing which, an application may be made to the High Court.

In the absence of any arbitration rules, the arbitral tribunal may still be obliged to seek the consent of the parties to an extension before applying to the High Court. This was indicated by the High Court of Singapore, in *Ting Kang Chung supra* at paragraph 43, when considering section 36 of the Singapore Arbitration Act 2001.

[B]   Substantial Injustice

Section 46(3)(b) of the Arbitration Act 2005 provides that the applicant must satisfy the High Court that 'substantial injustice' will be caused if the extension was not granted.

The High Court of Singapore, in *Ting Kang Chung supra* at paragraph 43, emphasized that the applicant must prove on a balance of probabilities that substantial injustice would be done if time was not extended. This includes balancing any prejudice that the other party may suffer if time is extended. The court will be entitled to weigh all relevant facts and, in particular, would consider:

(1) the relative fault of the parties;
(2) the sum at stake; and
(3) the consequences of failure to act.

CHAPTER 10
Miscellaneous

47.   Liability of Arbitrator

An arbitrator shall not be liable for any act or omission in respect of anything done or omitted to be done in the discharge of his functions as an arbitrator unless the act or omission is shown to have been in bad faith.

§47.01   INTRODUCTION

Section 47 of the Arbitration Act 2005 provides for an arbitrator tribunal's immunity. Section 47 has no equivalent in the 1985 Model Law. Section 47 is based on section 29 of the English Arbitration Act 1996.

The Court of Appeal, in *Asean Bintulu Fertilizer Sdn Bhd v. Wekajaya Sdn Bhd and another appeal* [2017] MLJU 1530, at paragraphs 14 and 16, while recognizing the immunity granted by section 47, which is not found in the 1985 Model Law, expressed concern that arbitrators were not regulated like other professionals in Malaysia:

> [14] Basically, section 47 to some extent gives immunity to the arbitrator for misconduct. The Model Law does not have a similar provision. Thus, the arbitrator in Malaysia is a protected species and his conduct in arbitration proceedings in a limited sense cannot be challenged unless bad faith can be established ... .
>
> ...
>
> [16] The Model Law concept leans in favour of the arbitrator without provision for disciplinary tribunal and any form of misconduct during the arbitral process or failure of the arbitrator to disclose information which may be material consideration for appointment, etc. may not be strictly within the purview of the court once the award has been made. Malaysian law also does not have a disciplinary mechanism for arbitrators coming from the panel of institutional bodies like KLRCA to check the integrity of arbitration process, the arbitrator as well as the award. Many professional bodies in Malaysia where there is some form of statutory recognition such as for the lawyers or medical practitioners, comes with

a disciplinary body to keep in check with the conduct and professionalism of their members to sustain rule of law as well as administration of justice ... Misconduct of arbitrators will generally undermine the growing arbitration industry as it will compromise administration of justice and rule of law. Our constitutional framework requires it to be checked by legislative measures, to uphold the rule of law.

§47.02 PURPOSE OF IMMUNITY

Immunity is granted to an arbitrator:

(1) to ensure the independence of the arbitral tribunal;
(2) to avoid threats to decision-making by the arbitral tribunal; and
(3) to prevent a rehearing which would inevitably follow if the arbitral tribunal were subject to claims of negligence.[1]

The High Court, in *MMC Engineering Group Bhd & Anor v. Wayss & Freytag (M) Sdn Bhd & Anor* [2015 MLJU 477 at paragraph 55, emphasized that an arbitral tribunal's immunity arises from their acting in a quasi-judicial capacity:

> This general rule stems from the fundamental principle that arbitrators or arbitral tribunals act in a quasi-judicial capacity to deliberate and determine the dispute referred. This principle is not altered even though arbitral tribunals assume mandates and jurisdiction from reference and decisions of the contracting parties. Insofar as their role in the arbitration is concerned, they are appointed by the disputing parties to resolve their differences. The parties have further agreed to be bound by the decision of the arbitrator, regardless how the decision may pan out to be; in their favour or otherwise.

§47.03 LIMITS OF IMMUNITY

Although the arbitral tribunal has immunity, there are limits to this immunity. There are two limits on the arbitral tribunal's immunity, one express and the other implicit. The express qualification is where the arbitral tribunal has acted in bad faith. Implicitly, the immunity only applies where the arbitral tribunal has acted or omitted to act in discharge of their function. These two limitations on the arbitral tribunal's immunity are considered below.

[A] Bad Faith

Section 47 of the Arbitration Act 2005 provides that an arbitral tribunal will be liable where they have acted or omitted to act in bad faith.

There are no judgments on the meaning of 'bad faith' in this particular context. However, in the context of administrative law, the Federal Court, in *Karam Singh v.*

---

1. *See* Robert Merkin and Louis Flannery, *Arbitration Act 1996* (4th edn, Informa 2008) at p 75.

Chapter 10: Miscellaneous §47.04

Minister of Home Affairs, Malaysia [1969] 2 MLJ 129 at pages 138, 141, 144, 157, held that a power was exercised *mala fide* or in bad faith where it was exercised for a collateral or ulterior purpose, that is a purpose other than that provided for in the statute. A power was also exercised *mala fide*, where it was exercised in a casual or cavalier fashion, without care, caution and a proper sense of responsibility, although personal animosity was not required. The question of whether the power had been exercised in bad faith was essentially one of fact.

[B] Not in Discharge of Functions

Section 47 of the Arbitration Act 2005 will only provide immunity where the arbitral tribunal has acted or omitted to act in discharge of their function. There will be no immunity where the arbitral tribunal is not acting in discharge of their functions but in another capacity.

There will also be no immunity where the arbitral tribunal has not acted at all. In this circumstance, the arbitral tribunal may be liable under their contract with the parties, depending on the terms of such contract.[2]

§47.04 NON-DEROGABLE

Section 47 is a non-derogable provision of the Arbitration Act 2005. Nevertheless, the parties may be entitled to exclude the exceptions on immunity considered in §47.03 *supra*. The parties may do this by adopting the rules published by an arbitration centre. For example, Rule 17 of the 2018 AIAC Arbitration Rules provides:

> No Liability
>
> Neither the AIAC nor the arbitral tribunal shall be liable for any act or omission related to the conduct of the arbitral proceedings.

This rule appears to provide for the unqualified immunity of the arbitral tribunal without the bad faith exception considered in §47.03[A] *supra*.

---

2. See *Arbitration Act 1996 supra* at p 75.

48. Immunity of Arbitral Institution

The Director of the Asian International Arbitration Centre (Malaysia) or any other person or institution designated or requested by the parties to appoint or nominate an arbitrator, shall not be liable for anything done or omitted in the discharge of the function unless the act or omission is shown to have been in bad faith.

§48.01 INTRODUCTION

Section 48 of the Arbitration Act 2005 provides for the immunity of arbitral institutions.

Section 48 has no equivalent in the 1985 Model Law. Section 48 is based on section 74(1) of the English Arbitration Act 1996. The Arbitration Act 2005 did not adopt section 74(2) and (3) of the English Arbitration Act 1996, which provides:

(1) immunity for the arbitral institution against anything done by an arbitrator appointed by such institution; and
(2) that the employees and agents of the arbitral institution will also be similarly immune.

The reasons for the Arbitration Act 2005 not adopting sections 74(2) and (3) of the English Arbitration Act 1996 are unclear. Perhaps, section 48 was considered to be sufficiently general to cover the particulars provided for in sections 74(2) and (3) of the English Arbitration Act 1996. There appears to be no reason in principle for the omission of these provisions.

§48.02 PURPOSE OF THE IMMUNITY

The purpose of granting this immunity to arbitral institutions is:

(1) arbitral institutions are unlikely to have the funds to meet claims against them;
(2) arbitral institutions are also unlikely to have the funds to take out the necessary insurance; and
(3) therefore, the absence of immunity may hamper the beneficial work of arbitral institutions.[3]

§48.03 LIMITS OF IMMUNITY

The immunity provided for in section 48 of the Arbitration Act 2005 is limited in two ways, which are considered below.

---

3. *See* Robert Merkin and Louis Flannery, *Arbitration Act 1996* (4th edn, Informa 2008) at p 179.

[A] Bad Faith

Section 48 of the Arbitration Act 2005 will not grant immunity to the arbitral institution where they have acted in bad faith.

There are no judgments that define 'bad faith' in this context. Reference should be made to §47.03[A] *supra* on the meaning of 'bad faith'.

[B] Discharge of the Function

Section 48 of the Arbitration Act 2005 does not give an arbitral institution immunity except where they have acted in discharge of their function to appoint or nominate an arbitrator. The arbitral institution will be liable for all the other functions they perform. The arbitral institution may also be liable in contract, where they have entirely failed to discharge their function to appoint or nominate an arbitrator rather than having discharged this function negligently.[4]

§48.04 NON-DEROGABLE

Although section 48 of the Arbitration Act 2005 appears non-derogable, it is submitted that the parties would be entitled to extend the immunity granted under this provision.

For example, Rule 17 of the 2018 AIAC Arbitration Rules appears to extend the immunity by removing the bad faith exception considered under §48.03[A] *supra*.

---

4. See *Arbitration Act 1996 supra* at p 179.

49. *Bankruptcy*

(1) Where a party to an arbitration agreement is a bankrupt and the person having jurisdiction to administer the property of the bankrupt adopts the agreement, the arbitration agreement shall be enforceable by or against the person.

(2) The High Court may direct any matter in connection with or for the purpose of bankruptcy proceedings to be referred to arbitration if –
   (a) the matter is one to which the arbitration agreement applies;
   (b) the arbitration agreement was made by a person who has been adjudged a bankrupt before the commencement of the bankruptcy proceedings; and
   (c) the person having jurisdiction to administer the property does not adopt the agreement.

(3) An application under subsection (2) may be made by –
   (a) any other party to the arbitration agreement; or
   (b) any person having jurisdiction to administer the property of the bankrupt.

§49.01 INTRODUCTION

Section 49 of the Arbitration Act 2005 provides for a situation where one of the parties to the arbitration agreement becomes bankrupt.

There is no equivalent to section 49 in the 1985 Model Law. There is also no equivalent to this provision in the English Arbitration Act 1996 and the New Zealand Arbitration Act 1996, on which certain other provisions of the Arbitration Act 2005 are based.

Section 49 of the Arbitration Act 2005 is a re-enactment of section 5 of the Arbitration Act 1952.

§49.02 ADOPTION OF THE ARBITRATION AGREEMENT

Where the person having jurisdiction to administer the property of the bankrupt adopts an arbitration agreement the bankrupt is party to, the arbitration agreement may be enforced by or against that person. Therefore, where the arbitration agreement is adopted, things will continue as usual between the parties.

§49.03 NON-ADOPTION OF THE ARBITRATION AGREEMENT

On the other hand, where the person having jurisdiction to administer the property of the bankrupt does not adopt the arbitration agreement, the other party to the arbitration agreement may apply to the High Court for the matter to be referred to arbitration.

The High Court may refer the matter to arbitration where two preconditions are satisfied:

(1) the dispute is one to which the arbitration agreement applies; and
(2) the person made the arbitration agreement before he was adjudged bankrupt.

The High Court has discretion whether to refer the dispute to arbitration, in the light of the use of the permissive 'may' in section 49(2), even if these two preconditions are satisfied.

Section 49(3) of the Arbitration Act 2005 also allows the party who has jurisdiction to administer the property of the bankrupt to apply to the High Court under section 49(2) to refer the dispute to arbitration. However, it is unclear why a person would make the application after declining to adopt the arbitration agreement in the first instance.

50. *Mode of Application*

Any application to the High Court under this Act shall be by an originating summons as provided in the Rules of the High Court 1980 [P.U.[A]50/1980].

§50.01 INTRODUCTION

Section 50 of the Arbitration Act 2005 provides that any application to the High Court under the Act shall be by way of originating summons.

There is no equivalent to section 50 in the 1985 Model Law, which generally leaves matters of procedure to be dealt with by domestic legislation.

Section 31 of the Arbitration Act 1952 provides that:

> Rules of court may be made for giving effect to this Act and may confer on the Registrar of the High Court or any other officer of that Court all or any of the jurisdiction conferred by this Act on the High Court.

The High Court, in *Kembang Serantau Sdn Bhd v. JEKS Engineering Sdn Bhd* [2016] 2 CLJ 427 at paragraphs 39 and 40, emphasized that section 50 of the Arbitration Act 2005 is not the equivalent of section 31 of the Arbitration Act 1952 and that the extent of court intervention is now more limited:

> [39] ... That was actually a decision under the old law relating to arbitration, the Arbitration Act of 1952; a regime quite different from that under the new Arbitration Act of 2005. The role of the court and the recourse to court intervention is substantially different. Under s. 31 of the 1952 Act, rules of court may be made to deal with the matters governed by the Act. Hence, the provision of O. 69 of the Rules of the High Court 1980 which deals with arbitration and arbitration related matters.
>
> [40] Under Act 646, there is no equivalent to s. 31. There is only s. 50 which provides for the mode of originating motions when seeking any court intervention. I am conscious of O. 69 of the new Rules of Court 2012; the presence of which does not make any difference to this reading.

Section 50 of the Arbitration Act 2005 refers to the Rules of the High Court 1980. The Rules of Court 2012 have since replaced the Rules of the High Court 1980. Section 50 should now be read as referring to the Rules of Court 2012, in the light of section 76 of the Interpretation Acts 1948 and 1967.

§50.02 SCOPE

Section 50 of the Arbitration Act 2005 only applies to applications made under and pursuant to the Act. The provision does not extend to any other actions.

The High Court, in *MMC Engineering Group Bhd & Anor v. Wayss & Freytag (M) Sdn Bhd & Anor* [2015 MLJU 477 at paragraph 63, held to this effect and decided that an applicant could not combine a civil action against a member of the arbitral tribunal together with an application to set aside:

Section 50 provides for matters which fall within or under the Act. It does not extend to or include personal actions, be it under civil law of contract, tort or trusts. The Plaintiffs have moved this court under section 37. That section is clear in that its single purpose is the setting aside of the award. There is no other remedy or relief that may be sought or granted by the court; unlike for instance, section 42. Hence, there is simply no right of action under section 37 against any member of the arbitral tribunal, including the 2nd Defendant. That being the case, the Plaintiffs' concerns under section 50 are unfounded.

§50.03 HIGH COURT

Section 50 of the Arbitration Act 2005 expressly refers to 'any application to the High Court'. However, the Arbitration Act 2005 allows certain applications to be made to the subordinate courts. For example, an application for stay of proceedings in court under section 10 may be made to the court in which those proceedings were commenced regardless of whether such court is a High Court or a subordinate court.

This has been recognized by the High Court, in *Uba Urus Bina Asia Sdn Bhd v. Quirk & Associates Sdn Bhd* [2016] 4 CLJ 468 at paragraphs 37-39, where it is suggested that section 50 may be redundant:

> [37] Unlike ss. 11, 15, 18, 29, 37, 38, 39, 41, 42, 43, 44, 45, 46 and 50 of the Arbitration Act 2005, where the word 'court' is specifically identified as the 'High Court', the words used in s. 10 is 'a court'. Arguably, this will include the Magistrates and Sessions courts as the term 'court' is not defined in s. 2 of the Arbitration Act 2005; but the term 'High Court' is. With the amendments to the financial limits of the subordinate courts, applications for orders under s. 10 can properly come within the jurisdiction of the subordinate courts.
>
> [38] However, s. 50 of the Arbitration Act which provides that applications to the High Court under the Act shall be by way of an originating summons; and the Rules of Court 2012 may need to be relooked at. Given that there is now a common set of Rules of Court governing procedures in both the High Court and the subordinate courts, s. 50 may have become redundant while O. 69 of the new Rules of Court 2012 may need some tweaking.
>
> [39] Order 69 of the old Rules of the High Court 1980 dealt specifically with arbitration and arbitration related matters. When the new Rules of Court were enacted in 2012, O. 69 was retained with updates. However, O. 69 envisages arbitration and matters under the Arbitration Act 2005 to be heard and disposed of by the High Court – see O. 69 sub-r. 1(2). There is nothing mentioned of the role of the subordinate courts even though there is a specific provision on stay at O. 69 r. 10. There is, therefore, a need to also relook at O. 69 to deal with this slight variance.

It is submitted that section 50 of the Arbitration Act 2005 may need to be amended to refer more generally to the courts rather than specifically to the High Court.

§50.04 RELATIONSHIP BETWEEN ARBITRATION ACT 2005 AND RULES OF COURT 2012

The relationship between the Arbitration Act 2005 and Order 69 of the Rules of Court 2012, which provides for the procedure for applications to the courts pursuant to the Act, has been considered by the courts in several judgments since the Act came into force.

Essentially, three principles have emerged:

(1) the Arbitration Act 2005 will take precedence over Order 69 of the Rules of Court 2012, which is subsidiary legislation. This was emphasised by the Federal Court, in *Press Metal Sarawak Sdn Bhd v. Etiqa Takaful Bhd* [2016] 9 CLJ 1 at paragraph 110:

> It must be noted that O. 69 r. 10(3) of the ROC 2012 is a procedural subsidiary legislation while s. 10(1) of the 2005 Act is a substantive provision in an Act of Parliament. Therefore O. 69 r. 10(3) of the ROC 2012 can only be interpreted in a manner which is not inconsistent with the mandatory provisions of s. 10(1) of the 2005 Act. In any event, O. 69 r. 10(1) of the ROC 2012 provides an option for the court either to 'decide that question'; or 'give direction to enable it to be decided'; and 'may order the proceedings to be stayed pending its decision'. The mandatory provisions of s. 10(1) of the 2005 Act, must prevail. The matter ought to be stayed pending arbitration if all the necessary requirements under the section are fulfilled. Again, we find that the plaintiff's submission on this point does not hold water and ought to be disregarded.

(2) a particular interpretation of a provision of the Arbitration Act 2005 may be reinforced by a rule in Order 69 of the Rules of Court 2012;[5] and
(3) any non-compliance with Order 69 of the Rules of Court 2012 will not be fatal to an application if it is merely a technicality and has not caused a substantial miscarriage of justice. If the non-compliance can be covered by an amendment, this is likely to be allowed.[6]

---

5. See *CTI Group Inc v. International Bulk Carriers SpA* [2017] MLJU 1194 at para. 66, FC; *Zenbay Sdn Bhd v. Yong Choo Kui Shipyard Sdn Bhd* [2015[10 CLJ 924 at para. 47, HC; *Pacific & Orient Insurance Co Berhad v. Tetuan Jaspal Quah & Aishah* [2015] 1 LNS 501 at para. 16; *Magna Prima Construction Sdn Bhd v. Bina MBK Sdn Bhd and another case* [2015] MLJU 291 at paras 81-82, HC; *SDA Architects v. Metro Millennium Sdn Bhd* [2014] 3 CLJ 632 at para. 47(f), CA.
6. See *Armada (Singapore) Pte Ltd v. Ashapura Minechem Ltd* [2016] 9 CLJ 709 at para. 21, HC; *Zenbay supra* at para 47, HC.

51. Repeal and Savings

(1) The Arbitration Act 1952 [Act 93] and the Convention on the Recognition and Enforcement of Foreign Arbitral Awards Act 1985 [Act 320] are repealed.

(2) Where the arbitral proceedings were commenced before the coming into operation of this Act, the law governing the arbitration agreement and the arbitral proceedings shall be the law which would have applied as if this Act had not been enacted.

(3) Nothing in this Act shall affect any proceedings relating to arbitration which have been commenced in any court before the coming into operation of this Act.

(4) Any court proceedings relating to arbitration commenced after the commencement of this Act shall be governed by this Act notwithstanding that such proceedings arose out of arbitral proceedings commenced before the commencement of this Act.

§51.01 INTRODUCTION

Section 51 of the Arbitration Act 2005 provides for the repeal of the old legislation and transition to the current Act. There is no equivalent to section 51 in the 1985 Model Law, which leaves matters of repeal and transition to the domestic legislature.

Section 51 of the Arbitration Act 2005 was amended by the Arbitration (Amendment) Act 2011. Section 51(2) of the Malay text was amended to remove a discrepancy and section 51(4) was inserted. The reasons for these amendments and their effect are considered in §51.04 *infra*.

§51.02 REPEAL

Section 51(1) repeals the Arbitration Act 1952 and the Convention on the Recognition and Enforcement of Foreign Arbitration Awards Act 1985.

The repeal of the Arbitration Act 1952 and the enactment of the Arbitration Act 2005 has fundamentally changed the ethos of arbitration in Malaysia. The courts recognize this and have repeatedly emphasized the significant shift that has been made by 2005 Act.[7]

Although the Convention on the Recognition and Enforcement of Foreign Arbitral Awards Act 1985, which gave effect to the 1958 New York Convention, is repealed by the Arbitration Act 2005, this is a matter of form rather than substance.

The 1958 New York Convention continues to apply in Malaysia through provisions within the Arbitration Act 2005 itself, like sections 9, 10, 38 and 39 of the Arbitration Act 2005, which reflect Articles II-VI of the 1958 New York Convention.

---

7. See *Far East Holdings Berhad & Ors v. Majlis Ugama Islam dan Adat Resam Melayu Pahang* [2017] 8 AMR 313 at paras 93, 100, 108 and 109, FC.

§51.03 ARBITRAL PROCEEDINGS

Section 51(2) of the Arbitration Act 2005 provides for two scenarios:

(1) where arbitral proceedings were commenced before the Arbitration Act 2005 came into force on 15 March 2006, the Arbitration Act 1952 will apply;
(2) where arbitral proceedings were commenced after the Arbitration Act 2005 came into effect on 15 March 2006, the Arbitration Act 2005 will apply.

The words 'arbitral proceedings' are not defined in the Arbitration Act 2005. However, by reading sections 23 and 34 of the Arbitration Act 2005, together, it would appear that the arbitral proceedings commence with the request for arbitration and conclude with the final award or an order for termination by the arbitral tribunal.[8]

Therefore, if the request for arbitration was issued prior to 15 March 2006, the Arbitration Act 1952 will apply. And, if the request for arbitration is issued after 15 March 2006, the Arbitration Act 2005 will apply.[9]

The key event is the commencement of the arbitration, which is marked by the date of the request for arbitration. The date of the arbitration agreement is irrelevant to determining whether the Arbitration Act 1952 or 2005 applies.

Unfortunately, the original Malay text of section 51(2) had a discrepancy as it provided that where the arbitration agreement was entered into or the arbitral proceedings were commenced prior to 15 March 2006, the Arbitration Act 1952 will apply.

A notification in the Gazette dated 21 February 2006 (PU(B)61) pursuant to section 6 of the National Language Act 1963/67 provides that the authoritative text of the Arbitration Act 2005 is the English text.

Despite this, due to the discrepancy in the Malay text, the High Court, in *Putrajaya Holdings Sdn Bhd v. Digital Green Sdn Bhd* [2008] 10 CLJ 437 at paragraphs 46-58, held that because the arbitration agreement was entered into prior to 15 March 2006, the Arbitration Act 1952 applied.

Fortunately, this judgment was not followed by subsequent judgments of the High Court, in *Total Safe Sdn Bhd v. Tenaga Nasional Berhad & Anor* [2009] 1 LNS 420 at page 4 and *Taman Bandar Baru Masai Sdn Bhd v. Dindings Corporations Sdn Bhd* [2010] 5 CLJ 83 at paragraphs 8, 11 and 12, which recognize that the English text of the Arbitration Act 2005 is authoritative and, as a result, the Arbitration Act 2005 will apply if the arbitration was commenced after 15 March 2006 regardless of when the arbitration agreement was entered.

The discrepancy in the Malay text of section 51(2) of the Arbitration Act 2005 was removed by the Arbitration (Amendment) Act 2011. The English and Malay text both

---

8. See *Segamat Parking Services Sdn Bhd v. Majlis Daerah Segamat Utama & Another Case* [2009] 1 CLJ 942 at para. 10, HC.
9. See *Renault SA v. Inokom Corporation Sdn Bhd & Anor and Other Applications* [2010] 5 CLJ 32 at para. 21, CA; *Majlis Ugama Islam dan Adat Resam Melayu Pahang v. Far East Holdings Bhd & Anor* [2007] 10 CLJ 318 at paras 20-21, HC.

now provide that the key event is the date of commencement of the arbitral proceedings.

§51.04 COURT PROCEEDINGS

Sections 51(3) and 51(4) of the Arbitration Act 2005 provide for two scenarios:

(1) where court proceedings were commenced prior to 15 March 2006, the Arbitration Act 1952 will apply; and
(2) where court proceedings are commenced after 15 March 2006, the Arbitration Act 2005 will apply.

Section 51(4) of the Arbitration Act 2005, which provides for the second scenario above, was introduced by the Arbitration (Amendment) Act 2011.

Prior to the Arbitration (Amendment) Act 2011, there was uncertainty whether the Arbitration Act 2005 would apply to court proceedings commenced after 15 March 2006 arising from arbitral proceedings that had been commenced prior to 15 March 2006.

The High Court, in *Hiap-Taih Welding & Construction Sdn Bhd v. Boustead Pelita Tinjar Sdn Bhd (formerly known as Loagan Bunut Plantations Sdn Bhd)* [2008] MLJU 375 at pages 2-4, held that the Arbitration Act 1952 would apply to court proceedings commenced after 15 March 2006 arising from arbitral proceeding commenced prior to 15 March 2006.

However, the High Court, in *Segamat Parking Services Sdn Bhd v. Majlis Daerah Segamat Utama & Another Case* [2009] 1 CLJ 942 at paragraphs 10 and 11, held that, where court proceedings were commenced after 15 March 2006, the Arbitration Act 2005 would apply even if the arbitral proceedings were commenced prior to 15 March 2006. This is because the savings provisions in section 51(2) are limited to arbitral proceedings and do not extend to subsequent court proceedings after the conclusion of the arbitral proceedings.

> [10] It is thus very clear from the section that an arbitral proceedings is confined to proceedings exclusively before the arbitrator or arbitral tribunal only. Any other related proceedings not before the arbitrator or arbitral tribunal are not arbitral proceedings. It goes without saying that any other proceedings taking place after a final award is handed down or after the termination of the proceeding under any one of the circumstances envisaged under s. 34(2) of the 2005 Act is no longer part of the arbitral proceedings.
>
> [11] That being said, the saving clause offered by s. 51 of the 2005 Act operates only in respect of arbitral proceedings couched in terms as above. Other related proceedings upon termination of arbitral proceedings are proceedings relating to arbitration. Such proceedings, including the one presently before me, shall be governed by the new Act (2005 Act), provided in Part III, under the headings 'Additional Provisions Relating to Arbitration'.

Subsequently, the judgment in *Segamat Parking supra* was given statutory recognition by the introduction of section 51(4) by the Arbitration (Amendment) Act 2011.

The effect of section 51(4) was recognized by the High Court, in *M-10 Builders Sdn Bhd v. Tunas Selatan Consortium Sdn Bhd* [2014] 1 LNS 1564 at paragraphs 5 and 8, where it was held:

> [5] Defendant contends otherwise and says section 51(4) applies such that 2005 Act is the applicable law. The court finds this to be the correct interpretation. This is evident from the clear provisions in section 51(4) that 2005 applies to 'any court proceedings' 'notwithstanding that such proceedings' (ie, court proceedings) 'arose out of arbitral proceedings commenced before the commencement of this Act'. This would apply to a court proceeding to set aside an award in arbitration proceedings commenced under 1952 Act as in this instant case.
>
> ...
>
> [8] It is therefore clear section 51(2) deals with arbitral proceedings and not court proceedings. All that it provides is where arbitral proceedings were commenced before the coming into operation of 2005 Act the law applicable to the arbitration agreement and the arbitral proceedings would be the 1952 Act. It is section 51(4) that deals specifically with court proceedings relating to arbitration and where it is a court proceeding arising out of arbitral proceedings commencing before Act 2005, Act 2005 is to apply.

Therefore, it is now clear that any court proceedings commenced will be governed by the Arbitration Act 2005 regardless of when the arbitral proceedings commenced.

Appendix

ARBITRATION ACT 2005

An Act to reform the law relating to domestic arbitration, provide for international arbitration, the recognition and enforcement of awards and for related matters.

ENACTED by the Parliament of Malaysia as follows:

Part I

PRELIMINARY

1. Short title and commencement

    (1) This Act may be cited as the Arbitration Act 2005.
    (2) This Act comes into operation on a date to be appointed by the Minister by notification in the Gazette.

2. Interpretation

    (1) In this Act, unless the context otherwise requires –
    'award' means a decision of the arbitral tribunal on the substance of the dispute and includes any final, interim or partial award and any award on costs or interest but does not include interlocutory orders;
    'High Court' means the High Court in Malaya and the High Court in Sabah and Sarawak or either of them, as the case may require;
    'Minister' means the Minister charged with the responsibility for arbitration;
    'State' means a sovereign State and not a component state of Malaysia, unless otherwise specified;
    'presiding arbitrator' means the arbitrator designated in the arbitration agreement as the presiding arbitrator or chairman of the arbitral tribunal, a single arbitrator or the third arbitrator appointed under subsection 13(3);
    'arbitration agreement' means an arbitration agreement as defined in section 9;

'party' means a party to an arbitration agreement or, in any case where an arbitration does not involve all the parties to the arbitration agreement, means a party to the arbitration;

'seat of arbitration' means the place where the arbitration is based as determined in accordance with section 22;

'international arbitration' means an arbitration where –

(a) one of the parties to an arbitration agreement, at the time of the conclusion of that agreement, has its place of business in any State other than Malaysia;

(b) one of the following is situated in any State other than Malaysia in which the parties have their places of business:
   (i) the seat of arbitration if determined in, or pursuant to, the arbitration agreement;
   (ii) any place where a substantial part of the obligations of any commercial or other relationship is to be performed or the place with which the subject-matter of the dispute is most closely connected; or

(c) the parties have expressly agreed that the subject matter of the arbitration agreement relates to more than one State;

'domestic arbitration' means any arbitration which is not an international arbitration;

'arbitral tribunal' means an emergency arbitrator, a sole arbitrator or a panel of arbitrators.

(2) For the purposes of this Act –
   (a) in the definition of 'international arbitration' –
      (i) where a party has more than one place of business, reference to the place of business is that which has the closest relationship to the arbitration agreement; or
      (ii) where a party does not have a place of business, reference to the place of business is that party's habitual residence;
   (b) where a provision of this Act, except section 3, leaves the parties free to determine a certain issue, such freedom shall include the right of the parties to authorize a third party, including an institution, to determine that issue;
   (c) where a provision of this Act refers to the fact that the parties have agreed or that they may agree or in any other way refers to an agreement of the parties, that agreement shall include any arbitration rules referred to in that agreement;
   (d) where a provision of this Act refers to a claim, other than in paragraphs 27(a) and 34(2)(a), it shall also apply to a counterclaim, and where it refers to a defence, it shall also apply to a defence to that counterclaim.

Appendix

3. Application to arbitrations and awards in Malaysia

   (1) This Act shall apply throughout Malaysia.
   (2) In respect of a domestic arbitration, where the seat of arbitration is in Malaysia –
       (a) Parts I, II and IV of this Act shall apply; and
       (b) Part III of this Act shall apply unless the parties agree otherwise in writing.
   (3) In respect of an international arbitration, where the seat of arbitration is in Malaysia –
       (a) Parts I, II and IV of this Act shall apply; and
       (b) Part III of this Act shall not apply unless the parties agree otherwise in writing.
   (4) For the purposes of paragraphs (2)(b) and (3)(b), the parties to a domestic arbitration may agree to exclude the application of Part III of this Act and the parties to an international arbitration may agree to apply Part III of this Act, in whole or in part.

3A. Representation

Unless otherwise agreed by the parties, a party to arbitral proceedings may be represented in the proceedings by any representative appointed by the party.

4. Arbitrability of subject matter

   (1) Any dispute which the parties have agreed to submit to arbitration under an arbitration agreement may be determined by arbitration unless the arbitration agreement is contrary to public policy or the subject matter of the dispute is not capable of settlement by arbitration under the laws of Malaysia.
   (2) The fact that any written law confers jurisdiction in respect of any matter on any court of law but does not refer to the determination of that matter by arbitration shall not, by itself, indicate that a dispute about that matter is not capable of determination by arbitration.

5. Government to be bound

This Act shall apply to any arbitration to which the Federal Government or the Government of any component state of Malaysia is a party.

Appendix

Part II

ARBITRATION

Chapter 1 General Provisions

6. Receipt of written communications

    (1) Unless otherwise agreed by the parties –
        (a) a written communication is deemed to have been received if it is delivered to the addressee personally or if it is delivered at his place of business, habitual residence or mailing address; and
        (b) where the places referred to in paragraph (a) cannot be found after making a reasonable inquiry, a written communication is deemed to have been received if it is sent to the addressee's last known place of business, habitual residence or mailing address by registered post or any other means which provides a record of the attempt to deliver it.
    (2) Unless otherwise agreed by the parties, a written communication sent electronically is deemed to have been received if it is sent to the electronic mailing address of the addressee.
    (3) The communication is deemed to have been received on the day it is so delivered.
    (4) This section shall not apply to any communications in respect of court proceedings.

7. Waiver of right to object

    A party who knows –

    (a) of any provision of this Act from which the parties may derogate; or
    (b) that any requirement under the arbitration agreement has not been complied with,

and yet proceeds with the arbitration without stating its objection to such non-compliance without undue delay or, if a time limit is provided for stating that objection, within that period of time, shall be deemed to have waived its right to object.

8. Extent of court intervention

No court shall intervene in matters governed by this Act, except where so provided in this Act.

Appendix

Chapter 2: Arbitration Agreement

9. Definition and form of arbitration agreement

> (1) In this Act, 'arbitration agreement' means an agreement by the parties to submit to arbitration all or certain disputes which have arisen or which may arise between them in respect of a defined legal relationship, whether contractual or not.
> (2) An arbitration agreement may be in the form of an arbitration clause in an agreement or in the form of a separate agreement.
> (3) An arbitration agreement shall be in writing.
> (4) An arbitration agreement is in writing -
>> (a) if its content is recorded in any form, whether or not the arbitration agreement or contract has been concluded orally, by conduct, or by other means; or
>> (b) if it is contained in an exchange of statement of claim and defence in which the existence of an agreement is alleged by one party and not denied by the other.
>
> (4A) The requirement that an arbitration agreement be in writing is met by any electronic communication that the parties make by means of data message if the information contained therein is accessible so as to be useable for subsequent reference.
> (5) A reference in an agreement to a document containing an arbitration clause shall constitute an arbitration agreement, provided that the agreement is in writing and the reference is such as to make that clause part of the agreement.
> (6) For the purpose of this section, 'data message' means information generated, sent, received or stored by electronic, magnetic, optical or similar means, including, but not limited to, electronic data interchange, electronic mail, telegram, telex or telecopy.

10. Arbitration agreement and substantive claim before court

> (1) A court before which proceedings are brought in respect of a matter which is the subject of an arbitration agreement shall, where a party makes an application before taking any other steps in the proceedings, stay those proceedings and refer the parties to arbitration unless it finds that the agreement is null and void, inoperative or incapable of being performed.
> (2) The court, in granting a stay of proceedings pursuant to subsection (1), may impose any conditions as it deems fit.
> (2A) Where admiralty proceedings are stayed pursuant to subsection (1), the court granting the stay may, if in those proceedings property has been arrested or bail or other security has been given to prevent or obtain release from arrest—

(a) order that the property arrested be retained as security for the satisfaction of any award given in the arbitration in respect of that dispute; or
　　　(b) order that the stay of those proceedings be conditional on the provision of equivalent security for the satisfaction of any such award.
　(2B) Subject to any rules of court and to any necessary modifications, the same law and practice shall apply in relation to property retained in pursuance of an order under subsection (2A) as would apply if it were held for the purpose of proceedings in the court making the order.
　(2C) For the purpose of this section, admiralty proceedings refer to admiralty proceedings under Order 70 of the Rules of the High Court 1980 [P.U. (A) 50/1980] and proceedings commenced pursuant to paragraph 24(b) of the Courts of Judicature Act 1964.
　(3) Where the proceedings referred to in subsection (1) have been brought, arbitral proceedings may be commenced or continued, and an award may be made, while the issue is pending before the court.
　(4) This section shall also apply in respect of an international arbitration, where the seat of arbitration is not in Malaysia.

11. Arbitration agreement and interim measures by High Court

　(1) A party may, before or during arbitral proceedings, apply to a High Court for any interim measure and the High Court may make the following orders for the party to –
　　　(a) maintain or restore the status quo pending the determination of the dispute;
　　　(b) take action that would prevent or refrain from taking action that is likely to cause current or imminent harm or prejudice to the arbitral process;
　　　(c) provide a means of preserving assets out of which a subsequent award may be satisfied, whether by way of arrest of property or bail or other security pursuant to the admiralty jurisdiction of the High Court;
　　　(d) preserve evidence that may be relevant and material to the resolution of the dispute; or
　　　(e) provide security for the costs of the dispute.
　(2) Where a party applies to the High Court for any interim measure and an arbitral tribunal has already ruled on any matter which is relevant to the application, the High Court shall treat any findings of fact made in the course of such ruling by the arbitral tribunal as conclusive for the purposes of the application.
　(3) This section shall also apply in respect of an international arbitration, where the seat of arbitration is not in Malaysia.

Appendix

Chapter 3: Composition of Arbitrators

12. Number of arbitrators

   (1) The parties are free to determine the number of arbitrators.
   (2) Where the parties fail to determine the number of arbitrators, the arbitral tribunal shall –
      (a) in the case of an international arbitration, consist of three arbitrators; and
      (b) in the case of a domestic arbitration, consist of a single arbitrator.

13. Appointment of arbitrators

   (1) Unless otherwise agreed by the parties, no person shall be precluded by reason of nationality from acting as an arbitrator.
   (2) The parties are free to agree on a procedure for appointing the arbitrator or the presiding arbitrator.
   (3) Where the parties fail to agree on the procedure referred to in subsection (2), and the arbitration consists of three arbitrators, each party shall appoint one arbitrator, and the two appointed arbitrators shall appoint the third arbitrator as the presiding arbitrator.
   (4) Where subsection (3) applies and –
      (a) a party fails to appoint an arbitrator within thirty days of receipt of a request in writing to do so from the other party; or
      (b) the two arbitrators fail to agree on the third arbitrator within thirty days of their appointment or such extended period as the parties may agree,
      either party may apply to the Director of the Asian International Arbitration Centre (Malaysia) for such appointment.
   (5) Where in an arbitration with a single arbitrator –
      (a) the parties fail to agree on the procedure referred to in subsection (2); and
      (b) the parties fail to agree on the arbitrator,
      either party may apply to the Director of the Asian International Arbitration Centre (Malaysia) for the appointment of an arbitrator.
   (6) Where, the parties have agreed on the procedure for appointment of the arbitrator –
      (a) a party fails to act as required under such procedure;
      (b) the parties, or two arbitrators, are unable to reach an agreement under such procedure; or
      (c) a third party, including an institution, fails to perform any function entrusted to it under such procedure,
      any party may request the Director of the Asian International Arbitration Centre (Malaysia) to take the necessary measures, unless the agreement on the appointment procedure provides other means for securing the appointment.
   (7) Where the Director of the Asian International Arbitration Centre (Malaysia) is unable to act or fails to act under subsections (4), (5) and (6) within thirty

days from the request, any party may apply to the High Court for such appointment.

(8) In appointing an arbitrator the Director of the Asian International Arbitration Centre (Malaysia) or the High Court, as the case may be, shall have due regard to –
  (a) any qualifications required of the arbitrator by the agreement of the parties;
  (b) other considerations that are likely to secure the appointment of an independent and impartial arbitrator; and
  (c) in the case of an international arbitration, the advisability of appointing an arbitrator of a nationality other than those of the parties.

(9) No appeal shall lie against any decision of the Director of the Asian International Arbitration Centre (Malaysia) or the High Court under this section.

14. Grounds for challenge

(1) A person who is approached in connection with that person's possible appointment as an arbitrator shall disclose any circumstances likely to give rise to justifiable doubts as to that person's impartiality or independence.

(2) An arbitrator shall, without delay, from the time of appointment and throughout the arbitral proceedings, disclose any circumstances referred to in subsection (1) to the parties unless the parties have already been informed of such circumstances by the arbitrator.

(3) An arbitrator may be challenged only if –
  (a) the circumstances give rise to justifiable doubts as to that arbitrator's impartiality or independence; or
  (b) that arbitrator does not possess qualifications agreed to by the parties.

(4) A party may challenge an arbitrator appointed by that party, or in whose appointment that party has participated, only for reasons which that party becomes aware of after the appointment has been made.

15. Challenge procedure

(1) Unless otherwise agreed by the parties, any party who intends to challenge an arbitrator shall, within fifteen days after becoming aware of the constitution of the arbitral tribunal or of any reasons referred to in subsection 14(3), send a written statement of the reasons for the challenge to the arbitral tribunal.

(2) Unless the challenged arbitrator withdraws from office or the other party agrees to the challenge, the arbitral tribunal shall make a decision on the challenge.

(3) Where a challenge is not successful, the challenging party may, within thirty days after having received notice of the decision rejecting the challenge, apply to the High Court to make a decision on the challenge.

(4) While such an application is pending, the arbitral tribunal, including the challenged arbitrator, may continue the arbitral proceedings and make an award.

(5) No appeal shall lie against the decision of the High Court under subsection (3).

16. Failure or impossibility to act

(1) Where an arbitrator becomes in law or in fact unable to perform the functions of that office, or for other reasons fails to act without undue delay, that arbitrator's mandate terminates on withdrawal from office or if the parties agree on the termination.

(2) Where any party disagrees on the termination of the mandate of the arbitrator, any party may apply to the High Court to decide on such termination and no appeal shall lie against the decision of the High Court.

(3) Where, under this section or subsection 15(2), an arbitrator withdraws from office or a party agrees to the termination of the mandate of an arbitrator, it shall not imply acceptance of the validity of any ground referred to in this section or subsection 14(3).

17. Appointment of substitute arbitrator

(1) A substitute arbitrator shall be appointed in accordance with the provisions of this Act where –
   (a) the mandate of an arbitrator terminates under section 15 or 16;
   (b) an arbitrator withdraws from office for any other reason;
   (c) the mandate of the arbitrator is revoked by agreement of the parties; or
   (d) in any other case of termination of mandate.

(2) Unless otherwise agreed by the parties –
   (a) where a single or the presiding arbitrator is replaced, any hearings previously held shall be repeated before the substitute arbitrator; or
   (b) where an arbitrator other than a single or the presiding arbitrator is replaced, any hearings previously held may be repeated at the discretion of the arbitral tribunal.

(3) Unless otherwise agreed by the parties, any order or ruling of the arbitral tribunal made prior to the replacement of an arbitrator under this section shall not be invalid solely on the ground there has been a change in the composition of the arbitral tribunal.

Appendix

Chapter 4: Jurisdiction of the Arbitral Tribunal

18. Competence of arbitral tribunal to rule on its jurisdiction

    (1) The arbitral tribunal may rule on its own jurisdiction, including any objections with respect to the existence or validity of the arbitration agreement.
    (2) For the purposes of subsection (1)—
        (a) an arbitration clause which forms part of an agreement shall be treated as an agreement independent of the other terms of the agreement; and
        (b) a decision by the arbitral tribunal that the agreement is null and void shall not ipso jure entail the invalidity of the arbitration clause.
    (3) A plea that the arbitral tribunal does not have jurisdiction shall be raised not later than the submission of the statement of defence.
    (4) A party is not precluded from raising a plea under subsection (3) by reason of that party having appointed or participated in the appointment of the arbitrator.
    (5) A plea that the arbitral tribunal is exceeding the scope of its authority shall be raised as soon as the matter alleged to be beyond the scope of its authority is raised during the arbitral proceedings.
    (6) Notwithstanding subsections (3) and (5), the arbitral tribunal may admit such plea if it considers the delay justified.
    (7) The arbitral tribunal may rule on a plea referred to in subsection (3) or (5), either as a preliminary question or in an award on the merits.
    (8) Where the arbitral tribunal rules on such a plea as a preliminary question that it has jurisdiction, any party may, within thirty days after having received notice of that ruling appeal to the High Court to decide the matter.
    (9) While an appeal is pending, the arbitral tribunal may continue the arbitral proceedings and make an award.
    (10) No appeal shall lie against the decision of the High Court under subsection (8).

19. Power of arbitral tribunal to order interim measures

    (1) Unless otherwise agreed by the parties, the arbitral tribunal may, at the request of a party, grant interim measures.
    (2) An interim measure is any temporary measure, whether in the form of an award or in another form, by which, at any time prior to the issuance of the award by which the dispute is finally decided, the arbitral tribunal orders a party to –
        (a) maintain or restore the status quo pending the determination of the dispute;
        (b) take action that would prevent or refrain from taking action that is likely to cause current or imminent harm or prejudice to the arbitral process itself;

Appendix

(c) provide a means of preserving assets out of which a subsequent award may be satisfied;
(d) preserve evidence that may be relevant and material to the resolution of the dispute; or
(e) provide security for the costs of the dispute.

19A. Conditions for granting interim measures

(1) The party requesting for the interim measures order under paragraphs 19(2)(a), (b) or (c) shall satisfy the arbitral tribunal that –
   (a) harm not adequately reparable by an award of damages is likely to result if the measure is not ordered, and such harm substantially outweighs the harm that is likely to result to the party against whom the measure is directed if the measure is granted; and
   (b) there is a reasonable possibility that the requesting party will succeed on the merits of the claim.
(2) The determination on the reasonable possibility referred to in paragraph (1)(b) shall not affect the discretion of the arbitral tribunal in making any subsequent determination relating to the dispute.
(3) In respect of the request for an interim measure order under paragraph 19(2)(d), the conditions in subsections (1) and (2) shall apply only to the extent the arbitral tribunal considers appropriate.

19B. Application for preliminary orders and conditions for granting preliminary orders

(1) Unless otherwise agreed by the parties, a party may, without notice to any other party, make a request for an interim measure together with an application for a preliminary order directing a party not to frustrate the purpose of the interim measure requested.
(2) The arbitral tribunal may grant a preliminary order provided that the arbitral tribunal considers that prior disclosure of the request for the interim measure to the party against whom the measure is directed risks frustrating the purpose of the interim measure.
(3) The conditions specified in section 19A shall apply to any preliminary order provided that the harm to be assessed under paragraph 19A(1)(a) is the harm that is likely to result from the order being granted or not.

19C. Specific regime for preliminary orders

(1) Immediately after the arbitral tribunal has made a determination in respect of an application for a preliminary order, the arbitral tribunal shall –
   (a) give notice to all parties of the request for the interim measure, the application for the preliminary order, the preliminary order, if any, and all

other communications, including by indicating the content of any oral communication, between any party and the arbitral tribunal in relation thereto; and

(b) give an opportunity to any party against whom a preliminary order is directed to present its case at the earliest practicable time.

(2) The arbitral tribunal shall decide immediately on any objection to the preliminary order.

(3) A preliminary order shall expire after twenty days from the date on which the order was issued by the arbitral tribunal.

(4) Notwithstanding subsection (3), the arbitral tribunal may issue an interim measure which adopts or modifies the preliminary order, after the party against whom the preliminary order is directed has been given notice and an opportunity to present his case.

(5) A preliminary order shall be binding on the parties but shall not be subject to any enforcement by the High Court.

(6) The preliminary order referred to in subsection (5) shall not constitute an award.

19D. Modification, suspension or termination

The arbitral tribunal may modify, suspend or terminate an interim measure it has granted, upon an application of any party or, in exceptional circumstances and upon prior notice to the parties, on the arbitral tribunal's own initiative.

19E. Provision of security

(1) The arbitral tribunal may require the party requesting an interim measure to provide appropriate security in connection with the measure.

(2) The arbitral tribunal shall require the party applying for a preliminary order to provide security in connection with the order unless the arbitral tribunal considers it inappropriate or unnecessary to do so.

19F. Disclosure

(1) The arbitral tribunal may require any party to immediately disclose any material change in the circumstances on the basis of which the interim measure or preliminary order was requested or applied or granted.

(2) The party applying for a preliminary order shall disclose to the arbitral tribunal all the circumstances that are likely to be relevant to the arbitral tribunal's determination on whether to grant or maintain the order and such obligation shall continue until the party against whom the order has been requested has had an opportunity to present its case.

Appendix

19G. Costs and damages

(1) The party requesting for an interim measure or applying for a preliminary order shall be liable for any costs and damages caused by the interim measure or the preliminary order to any party if the arbitral tribunal later determines that, in the circumstances, the interim measure or the preliminary order should not have been granted.
(2) The arbitral tribunal may award such costs and damages referred to in subsection (1) at any point during the proceedings.

19H. Recognition and enforcement

(1) Subject to the provisions of section 19I, an interim measure issued by an arbitral tribunal shall be recognized as binding and, unless otherwise provided by the arbitral tribunal, enforced upon application to the competent court, irrespective of the country in which it was issued.
(2) The party who is seeking or has obtained recognition or enforcement of an interim measure shall immediately inform the court of any termination, suspension or modification of that interim measure.
(3) The court where recognition or enforcement is sought may, if it considers it proper, order the requesting party to provide appropriate security if the arbitral tribunal has not already made a determination with respect to security or where such a decision is necessary to protect the rights of third parties.

19I. Grounds for refusing recognition or enforcement

(1) Recognition or enforcement of an interim measure may be refused only –
   (a) at the request of the party against whom it is invoked if the High Court is satisfied that –
      (i) such refusal is warranted on the grounds set forth in subparagraph 39(1)(a)(i), (ii), (iii), (iv), (v) or (vi);
      (ii) the arbitral tribunal's decision with respect to the provision of security in connection with the interim measure issued by the arbitral tribunal has not been complied with; or
      (iii) the interim measure has been terminated or suspended by the arbitral tribunal or, where so empowered, by the court of the State in which the arbitration takes place or under the law of which that interim measure was granted; or
   (b) if the High Court finds that –
      (i) the interim measure is incompatible with the powers conferred upon the Court, but the Court may decide to reformulate the interim measure to the extent necessary, without modifying its substance, to adapt it to the Court's powers and procedures for the purposes of enforcing that interim measure; or

Appendix

        (ii) any grounds set forth in subparagraph 39(1)(b)(i) or (ii) apply to the recognition and enforcement of the interim measure.

(2) Any determination made by the High Court on any of the grounds in subsection (1) shall be effective only for the purposes of the application to recognize or enforce the interim measure.

(3) The High Court where recognition or enforcement is sought shall not, in making any determination on any of the grounds in subsection (1), undertake a review of the substance of the interim measure.

19J. Court-ordered interim measures

(1) The High Court has the power to issue an interim measure in relation to arbitration proceedings, irrespective of whether the seat of arbitration is in Malaysia.

(2) The High Court shall exercise the power referred to in subsection (1) in accordance with its own procedures in consideration of the specific features of international arbitration.

(3) Where a party applies to the High Court for any interim measure and an arbitral tribunal has already ruled on any matter which is relevant to the application, the High Court shall treat any findings of fact made in the course of such ruling by the arbitral tribunal as conclusive for the purposes of the application.

Chapter 5: Conduct of Arbitral Proceedings

20. Equal treatment of parties

The parties shall be treated with equality and each party shall be given a fair and reasonable opportunity of presenting that party's case.

21. Determination of rules of procedure

(1) Subject to the provisions of this Act, the parties are free to agree on the procedure to be followed by the arbitral tribunal in conducting the proceedings.

(2) Where the parties fail to agree under subsection (1), the arbitral tribunal may, subject to the provisions of this Act, conduct the arbitration in such manner as it considers appropriate.

(3) The power conferred upon the arbitral tribunal under subsection (2) shall include the power to –
    (a) determine the admissibility, relevance, materiality and weight of any evidence;
    (b) draw on its own knowledge and expertise;
    (c) order the provision of further particulars in a statement of claim or statement of defence;

(d) order the giving of security for costs;
(e) fix and amend time limits within which various steps in the arbitral proceedings must be completed;
(f) order the discovery and production of documents or materials within the possession or power of a party;
(g) order the interrogatories to be answered;
(h) order that any evidence be given on oath or affirmation; and
(i) make such other orders as the arbitral tribunal considers appropriate.

22. Seat of arbitration

    (1) The parties are free to agree on the seat of arbitration.
    (2) Where the parties fail to agree under subsection (1), the seat of arbitration shall be determined by the arbitral tribunal having regard to the circumstances of the case, including the convenience of the parties.
    (3) Notwithstanding subsections (1) and (2), the arbitral tribunal may, unless otherwise agreed by the parties, meet at any place it considers appropriate for consultation among its members, for hearing witnesses, experts or the parties, or for inspection of goods, other property or documents.

23. Commencement of arbitral proceedings

Unless otherwise agreed by the parties, the arbitral proceedings in respect of a particular dispute shall commence on the date on which a request in writing for that dispute to be referred to arbitration is received by the respondent.

24. Language

    (1) The parties are free to agree on the language to be used in the arbitral proceedings.
    (2) Where the parties fail to agree under subsection (1), the arbitral tribunal shall determine the language to be used in the arbitral proceedings.
    (3) The agreement or the determination referred to in subsections (1) and (2) respectively shall, unless otherwise specified in the agreement or determination, apply to any written statement made by a party, any hearing and any award, decision or other communication by the arbitral tribunal.
    (4) The arbitral tribunal may order that any documentary evidence shall be accompanied by a translation into the language agreed upon by the parties or determined by the arbitral tribunal.

25. Statements of claim and defence

    (1) Within the period of time agreed by the parties or, failing such agreement, as determined by the arbitral tribunal, the claimant shall state –

(a) the facts supporting his claim;
(b) the points at issue; and
(c) the relief or remedy sought,
and the respondent shall state his defence in respect of the particulars set out in this subsection, unless the parties have otherwise agreed to the required elements of such statements.
(2) The parties may –
   (a) submit with their statements any document the parties consider relevant; or
   (b) add a reference to the documents or other evidence that the parties may submit.
(3) Unless otherwise agreed by the parties, either party may amend or supplement the claim or defence during the course of the arbitral proceedings, unless the arbitral tribunal considers it inappropriate to allow such amendment having regard to the delay in making it.

26. Hearings

(1) Unless otherwise agreed by the parties, the arbitral tribunal shall decide whether to hold oral hearings for the presentation of evidence or oral arguments, or whether the proceedings shall be conducted on the basis of documents and other materials.
(2) Unless the parties have agreed that no hearings shall be held, the arbitral tribunal shall upon the application of any party hold oral hearings at an appropriate stage of the proceedings.
(3) The parties shall be given reasonable prior notice of any hearing and of any meeting of the arbitral tribunal for the purposes of inspection of goods, other property or documents.
(4) All statements, documents or other information supplied to the arbitral tribunal by one party shall be communicated to the other party.
(5) Any expert report or evidentiary document on which the arbitral tribunal may rely in making its decision shall be communicated to the parties.

27. Default of a party

Unless otherwise agreed by the parties, if without showing sufficient cause –

(a) the claimant fails to communicate the statement of claim in accordance with subsection 25(1), the arbitral tribunal shall terminate the proceedings;
(b) the respondent fails to communicate the statement of defence in accordance with subsection 25(1), the arbitral tribunal shall continue the proceedings without treating such failure in itself as an admission of the claimant's allegations;

(c) any party fails to appear at a hearing or to produce documentary evidence, the arbitral tribunal may continue the proceedings and make the award on the evidence before it; or
(d) the claimant fails to proceed with the claim, the arbitral tribunal may make an award dismissing the claim or give directions, with or without conditions, for the speedy determination of the claim.

28. Expert appointed by arbitral tribunal

    (1) Unless otherwise agreed by the parties, the arbitral tribunal may –
        (a) appoint one or more experts to report to it on specific issues to be determined by the arbitral tribunal; or
        (b) require a party to give the expert any relevant information or to produce or to provide access to any relevant documents, goods or other property for the expert's inspection.
    (2) Unless otherwise agreed by the parties, if a party so requests or if the arbitral tribunal considers it necessary, the expert shall, after delivery of a written or oral report, participate in a hearing where the parties have the opportunity to put questions to the expert and to present other expert witnesses in order to testify on the points at issue.

29. Court assistance in taking evidence

    (1) Any party may with the approval of the arbitral tribunal, apply to the High Court for assistance in taking evidence.
    (2) The High Court may order the attendance of a witness to give evidence or, where applicable, produce documents on oath or affirmation before an officer of the High Court or any other person, including the arbitral tribunal.

Chapter 6: Making of Award and Termination of Proceedings

30. Law applicable to substance of dispute

    (1) The arbitral tribunal shall decide the dispute in accordance with such rules of law as are chosen by the parties as applicable to the substance of the dispute.
    (2) [this subsection has been deleted]
    (3) Any designation of the law or legal system of a given State shall be construed, unless otherwise expressed, as directly referring to the substantive law of that State and not to its conflict of laws rules.
    (4) Failing any designation by the parties, the arbitral tribunal shall apply the law determined by the conflict of laws rules which it considers applicable.
    (4A) The arbitral tribunal shall decide according to equity and conscience only if the parties have expressly authorized it to do so.

(5) The arbitral tribunal shall, in all cases, decide in accordance with the terms of the agreement and shall take into account the usages of the trade applicable to the transaction.

31. Decision making by panel of arbitrators

(1) Unless otherwise agreed by the parties, in any arbitral proceedings with more than one arbitrator, any decision of the arbitral tribunal shall be made by a majority of all its members.
(2) Where so authorized by the parties or by all the members of the arbitral tribunal, questions of procedure may be decided by the presiding arbitrator.

32. Settlement

(1) If, during arbitral proceedings, the parties settle the dispute, the arbitral tribunal shall terminate the proceedings and, if requested by the parties and not objected to by the arbitral tribunal, record the settlement in the form of an award on agreed terms.
(2) An award on agreed terms shall be made in accordance with the provisions of section 33 and shall state that it is an award.
(3) An award made under subsection (1) shall have the same status and effect as an award on the merits of the case.

33. Form and contents of award

(1) An award shall be made in writing and subject to subsection (2) shall be signed by the arbitrator.
(2) In arbitral proceedings with more than one arbitrator, the signatures of the majority of all members of the arbitral tribunal shall be sufficient provided that the reason for any omitted signature is stated.
(3) An award shall state the reasons upon which it is based, unless—
    (a) the parties have agreed that no reasons are to be given; or
    (b) the award is an award on agreed terms under section 32.
(4) An award shall state its date and the seat of arbitration as determined in accordance with section 22 and shall be deemed to have been made at that seat.
(5) After an award is made, a copy of the award signed by the arbitrator in accordance with subsections (1) and (2) shall be delivered to each party.
(6) Subject to subsection (8), unless otherwise agreed by the parties, the arbitral tribunal may, in the arbitral proceedings before it, award simple or compound interest from such date, at such rate and with such rest as the arbitral tribunal considers appropriate, for any period ending not later than the date of payment of the whole or any part of –

(a) any sum which is awarded by the arbitral tribunal in the arbitral proceedings;
(b) any sum which is in issue in the arbitral proceedings but is paid before the date of the award; or
(c) costs awarded or ordered by the arbitral tribunal in the arbitral proceedings.
(7) Nothing in subsection (6) shall affect any other power of an arbitral tribunal to award interest.
(8) Where an award directs a sum to be paid, that sum shall, unless the award otherwise directs, carry interest as from the date of the award and at the same rate as a judgment debt.

34. Termination of proceedings

(1) The arbitral proceedings shall be terminated by a final award or by an order of the arbitral tribunal in accordance with subsection (2).
(2) The arbitral tribunal shall order the termination of the arbitral proceedings where —
    (a) the claimant withdraws the claim, unless the respondent objects to the withdrawal and the arbitral tribunal recognizes the respondent's legitimate interest in obtaining a final settlement of the dispute;
    (b) the parties agree on the termination of the proceedings; or
    (c) the arbitral tribunal finds that the continuation of the proceedings has for any other reason become unnecessary or impossible.
(3) Subject to the provisions of section 35 and subsection 37(6), the mandate of the arbitral tribunal shall terminate with the termination of the arbitral proceedings.
(4) Unless otherwise provided by any written law, the death of a party does not terminate –
    (a) the arbitral proceedings; or
    (b) the authority of the arbitral tribunal.

35. Correction and interpretation of award or additional award

(1) A party, within thirty days of the receipt of the award, unless any other period of time has been agreed upon by the parties —
    (a) upon notice to the other party, may request the arbitral tribunal to correct in the award any error in computation, any clerical or typographical error or other error of similar nature; or
    (b) upon notice to and with the agreement of the other party, may request the arbitral tribunal to give an interpretation of a specific point or part of the award.
(2) Where the arbitral tribunal considers the request made under subsection (1) to be justified, it shall make the correction or give the interpretation within

Appendix

thirty days of the receipt of the request and such interpretation shall form part of the award.
(3) The arbitral tribunal may correct any error of the type referred to in paragraph (1)(a) on its own initiative within thirty days of the date of the award.
(4) Unless otherwise agreed by the parties, a party may, within thirty days of the receipt of the award and upon notice to the other party, request the arbitral tribunal to make an additional award as to claims presented in the arbitral proceedings but omitted from the award.
(5) Where the arbitral tribunal considers the request under subsection (4) to be justified, it shall make the additional award within sixty days from the receipt of such request.
(6) The arbitral tribunal may, where it thinks necessary, extend the period of time within which it shall make a correction, interpretation or an additional award under this section.
(7) The provisions of section 33 shall apply to a correction or interpretation of the award or to an additional award.

36. An award is final and binding

(1) An award made by an arbitral tribunal pursuant to an arbitration agreement shall be final and binding on the parties and may be relied upon by any party by way of defence, set-off or otherwise in any proceedings in any court.
(2) The arbitral tribunal shall not vary, amend, correct, review, add to or revoke an award which has been made except as specifically provided for in section 35.

Chapter 7: Recourse Against Award

37. Application for setting aside

(1) An award may be set aside by the High Court only if –
    (a) the party making the application provides proof that –
        (i) a party to the arbitration agreement was under any incapacity;
        (ii) the arbitration agreement is not valid under the law to which the parties have subjected it, or, failing any indication thereon, under the laws of Malaysia;
        (iii) the party making the application was not given proper notice of the appointment of an arbitrator or of the arbitral proceedings or was otherwise unable to present that party's case;
        (iv) the award deals with a dispute not contemplated by or not falling within the terms of the submission to arbitration;
        (v) subject to subsection (3), the award contains decisions on matters beyond the scope of the submission to arbitration; or

(vi) the composition of the arbitral tribunal or the arbitral procedure was not in accordance with the agreement of the parties, unless such agreement was in conflict with a provision of this Act from which the parties cannot derogate, or, failing such agreement, was not in accordance with this Act; or
   (b) the High Court finds that –
      (i) the subject matter of the dispute is not capable of settlement by arbitration under the laws of Malaysia; or
      (ii) the award is in conflict with the public policy of Malaysia.
(2) Without limiting the generality of subparagraph (1)(b)(ii), an award is in conflict with the public policy of Malaysia where –
   (a) the making of the award was induced or affected by fraud or corruption; or
   (b) a breach of the rules of natural justice occurred –
      (i) during the arbitral proceedings; or
      (ii) in connection with the making of the award.
(3) Where the decision on matters submitted to arbitration can be separated from those not so submitted, only that part of the award which contains decisions on matters not submitted to arbitration may be set aside.
(4) An application for setting aside may not be made after the expiry of ninety days from the date on which the party making the application had received the award or, if a request has been made under section 35, from the date on which that request had been disposed of by the arbitral tribunal.
(5) Subsection (4) does not apply to an application for setting aside on the ground that the award was induced or affected by fraud or corruption.
(6) On an application under subsection (1) the High Court may, where appropriate and so requested by a party, adjourn the proceedings for such period of time as it may determine in order to allow the arbitral tribunal an opportunity to resume the arbitral proceedings or to take such other action as in the arbitral tribunal's opinion will eliminate the grounds for setting aside.
(7) Where an application is made to set aside an award, the High Court may order that any money made payable by the award shall be brought into the High Court or otherwise secured pending the determination of the application.

Chapter 8: Recognition and Enforcement of Awards

38. Recognition and enforcement

   (1) On an application in writing to the High Court, an award made in respect of an arbitration where the seat of arbitration is in Malaysia or an award from a foreign State shall, subject to this section and section 39 be recognized as binding and be enforced by entry as a judgment in terms of the award or by action.
   (2) In an application under subsection (1) the applicant shall produce –

(a) the duly authenticated original award or a duly certified copy of the award; and

(b) the original arbitration agreement or a duly certified copy of the agreement.

(3) Where the award or arbitration agreement is in a language other than the national language or the English language, the applicant shall supply a duly certified translation of the award or agreement in the English language.

(4) For the purposes of this Act, 'foreign State' means a State which is a party to the Convention on the Recognition and Enforcement of Foreign Arbitral Awards adopted by the United Nations Conference on International Commercial Arbitration in 1958.

39. Grounds for refusing recognition or enforcement

(1) Recognition or enforcement of an award, irrespective of the State in which it was made, may be refused only at the request of the party against whom it is invoked –

(a) where that party provides to the High Court proof that –

(i) a party to the arbitration agreement was under any incapacity;

(ii) the arbitration agreement is not valid under the law to which the parties have subjected it, or, failing any indication thereon, under the laws of the State where the award was made;

(iii) the party making the application was not given proper notice of the appointment of an arbitrator or of the arbitral proceedings or was otherwise unable to present that party's case;

(iv) the award deals with a dispute not contemplated by or not falling within the terms of the submission to arbitration;

(v) subject to subsection (3), the award contains decisions on matters beyond the scope of the submission to arbitration;

(vi) the composition of the arbitral tribunal or the arbitral procedure was not in accordance with the agreement of the parties, unless such agreement was in conflict with a provision of this Act from which the parties cannot derogate, or, failing such agreement, was not in accordance with this Act; or

(vii) the award has not yet become binding on the parties or has been set aside or suspended by a court of the country in which, or under the law of which, that award was made; or

(b) if the High Court finds that –

(i) the subject-matter of the dispute is not capable of settlement by arbitration under the laws of Malaysia; or

(ii) the award is in conflict with the public policy of Malaysia.

(2) If an application for setting aside or suspension of an award has been made to the High Court on the grounds referred to in subparagraph (1)(a)(vii), the High Court may, if it considers it proper, adjourn its decision and may also, on

the application of the party claiming recognition or enforcement of the award, order the other party to provide appropriate security.
(3) Where the decision on matters submitted to arbitration can be separated from those not so submitted, only that part of the award which contains decisions on matters submitted to arbitration may be recognized and enforced.

Part III

ADDITIONAL PROVISIONS RELATING TO ARBITRATION

40. Consolidation of proceedings and concurrent hearings

(1) The parties may agree –
    (a) that the arbitration proceedings shall be consolidated with other arbitration proceedings; or
    (b) that concurrent hearings shall be held,
    on such terms as may be agreed.
(2) Unless the parties agree to confer such power on the arbitral tribunal, the tribunal has no power to order consolidation of arbitration proceedings or concurrent hearings.

41. Determination of preliminary point of law by court

(1) Any party may apply to the High Court to determine any question of law arising in the course of the arbitration –
    (a) with the consent of the arbitral tribunal; or
    (b) with the consent of every other party.
(2) The High Court shall not consider an application under subsection (1) unless it is satisfied that the determination –
    (a) is likely to produce substantial savings in costs; and
    (b) substantially affects the rights of one or more of the parties.
(3) The application shall identify the question of law to be determined and, except where made with the agreement of all parties to the proceedings, shall state the grounds that support the application.
(4) While an application under subsection (1) is pending, the arbitral proceedings may be continued and an award may be made.

41A. Disclosure of information relating to arbitral proceedings and awards prohibited

(1) Unless otherwise agreed by the parties, no party may publish, disclose or communicate any information relating to –
    (a) the arbitral proceedings under the arbitration agreement; or
    (b) an award made in those arbitral proceedings.

(2) Nothing in subsection (1) shall prevent the publication, disclosure or communication of information referred to in that subsection by a party –
   (a) if the publication, disclosure or communication is made –
      (i) to protect or pursue a legal right or interest of the party; or
      (ii) to enforce or challenge the award referred to in that subsection,
   in legal proceedings before a court or other judicial authority in or outside Malaysia;
   (b) if the publication, disclosure or communication is made to any government body, regulatory body, court or tribunal and the party is obliged by law to make the publication, disclosure or communication; or
   (c) if the publication, disclosure or communication is made to a professional or any other adviser of any of the parties.

41B. Proceedings to be heard otherwise than in open court

(1) Subject to subsection (2), court proceedings under this Act are to be heard otherwise than in an open court.
(2) Notwithstanding subsection (1), the court may order the proceedings to be heard in an open court –
   (a) on the application of any party; or
   (b) if, in any particular case, the court is satisfied that those proceedings ought to be heard in an open court.
(3) An order of the court under subsection (2) is final.

42. Reference on questions of law

[deleted by section 12 of the Arbitration (Amendment) (No 2) Act 2018]

43. Appeal

[deleted by section 13 of the Arbitration (Amendment) (No 2) Act 2018]

44. Costs and expense of an arbitration

(1) Unless otherwise agreed by the parties –
   (a) the costs and expenses of an arbitration shall be in the discretion of the arbitral tribunal who may –
      (i) direct to and by whom and in what manner those costs or any part thereof shall be paid;
      (ii) tax or settle the amount of such costs and expenses; and
      (iii) award such costs and expenses to be paid as between solicitor and client;
   (b) any party may apply to the High Court for the costs to be taxed where an arbitral tribunal has in its award directed that costs and expenses be paid

by any party, but fails to specify the amount of such costs and expenses within thirty days of having being requested to do so; or
  (c) each party shall be responsible for its own legal and other expenses and for an equal share of the fees and expenses of the arbitral tribunal and any other expenses relating to the arbitration in the absence of an award or additional award fixing and allocating the costs and expenses of the arbitration.
(2) Unless otherwise agreed by the parties, where a party makes an offer to the other party to settle the dispute or part of the dispute and the offer is not accepted and the award of the arbitral tribunal is no more favourable to the other party than was the offer, the arbitral tribunal, in fixing and allocating the costs and expenses of the arbitration, may take the fact of the offer into account in awarding costs and expenses in respect of the period from the making of the offer to the making of the award.
(3) An offer to settle made under subsection (2) shall not be communicated to the arbitral tribunal until it has made a final determination of all aspects of the dispute other than the fixing and allocation of costs and expenses.
(4) Where an arbitral tribunal refuses to deliver its award before the payment of its fees and expenses, the High Court may order the arbitral tribunal to deliver the award on such conditions as the High Court thinks fit.
(5) A taxation of costs, fees and expenses under this section may be reviewed in the same manner as a taxation of costs.

45. Extension of time for commencing arbitration proceedings

Where an arbitration agreement provides that arbitral proceedings are to be commenced within the time specified in the agreement, the High Court may, notwithstanding that the specified time has expired, extend the time for such period and on such terms as it thinks fit, if it is of the opinion that in the circumstances of the case undue hardship would otherwise be caused.

46. Extension of time for making award

  (1) Where the time for making an award is limited by the arbitration agreement, the High Court may, unless otherwise agreed by the parties, extend that time.
  (2) An application under subsection (1) may be made –
    (a) upon notice to the parties, by the arbitral tribunal; or
    (b) upon notice to the arbitral tribunal and the other parties, by any party to the proceedings.
  (3) The High Court shall not make an order unless –
    (a) all available tribunal processes for obtaining an extension of time have been exhausted; and
    (b) the High Court is satisfied that substantial injustice would otherwise be done.

Appendix

(4) The High Court may exercise its powers under subsection (1) notwithstanding that the time previously fixed by or under the arbitration agreement or by a previous order has expired.

PART IV

MISCELLANEOUS

47. Liability of arbitrator

An arbitrator shall not be liable for any act or omission in respect of anything done or omitted to be done in the discharge of his functions as an arbitrator unless the act or omission is shown to have been in bad faith.

48. Immunity of arbitral institution

The Director of the Asian International Arbitration Centre (Malaysia) or any other person or institution designated or requested by the parties to appoint or nominate an arbitrator, shall not be liable for anything done or omitted in the discharge of the function unless the act or omission is shown to have been in bad faith.

49. Bankruptcy

(1) Where a party to an arbitration agreement is a bankrupt and the person having jurisdiction to administer the property of the bankrupt adopts the agreement, the arbitration agreement shall be enforceable by or against the person.
(2) The High Court may direct any matter in connection with or for the purpose of bankruptcy proceedings to be referred to arbitration if –
   (a) the matter is one to which the arbitration agreement applies;
   (b) the arbitration agreement was made by a person who has been adjudged a bankrupt before the commencement of the bankruptcy proceedings; and
   (c) the person having jurisdiction to administer the property does not adopt the agreement.
(3) An application under subsection (2) may be made by –
   (a) any other party to the arbitration agreement; or
   (b) any person having jurisdiction to administer the property of the bankrupt.

50. Mode of application

Any application to the High Court under this Act shall be by an originating summons as provided in the Rules of the High Court 1980 [P.U.[A]50/1980].

51. Repeal and savings

   (1) The Arbitration Act 1952 [Act 93] and the Convention on the Recognition and Enforcement of Foreign Arbitral Awards Act 1985 [Act 320] are repealed.
   (2) Where the arbitral proceedings were commenced before the coming into operation of this Act, the law governing the arbitration agreement and the arbitral proceedings shall be the law which would have applied as if this Act had not been enacted.
   (3) Nothing in this Act shall affect any proceedings relating to arbitration which have been commenced in any court before the coming into operation of this Act.
   (4) Any court proceedings relating to arbitration commenced after the commencement of this Act shall be governed by this Act notwithstanding that such proceedings arose out of arbitral proceedings commenced before the commencement of this Act.

Glossary

Analytical Commentary: United Nations Commission on International Trade Law, 18th session, Vienna, 3 to 21 June 1985, International Commercial Arbitration, Analytical Commentary on draft text of a model law on international commercial arbitration (A/CN.9/264).

CISG: United Nations Convention on Contracts for the International Sale of Goods (Vienna, 1980).

Secretariat's Report: United Nations Commission on International Trade Law, 12th session, Vienna, 18 to 29 June 1979, Report of the Secretary-General: study on the application and interpretation of the Convention on the Recognition and Enforcement of Foreign Arbitral Awards (New York, 1958) (A/CN.9/168).

travaux preparatoires: all the documents, such as memoranda, minutes of conferences, and drafts of the treaty under negotiation, for the purpose of interpreting the treaty.

UNCITRAL Report A/40/17: United Nations Commission on International Trade Law, 18th session, Vienna, 3 to 21 June 1985, Report of the United Nations Commission on International Trade Law on the work of its 18th session (A/40/17).

Warsaw Convention: Convention for the Unification of certain rules relating to international carriage by air (Warsaw, 1929).

1958 New York Contention: Convention on the Recognition and Enforcement of Foreign Arbitral Awards (New York, 1958).

1965 Washington Convention: Convention on the Settlement of Investment Disputes between States and Nationals of other States (Washington, 1965).

1985 Model Law: United Nations Commission on International Trade Law Model Law on International Commercial Arbitration, as adopted on 21 June 1985 (A/40/17, annex I).

2006 Model Law: United Nations Commission on International Trade Law Model Law on International Commercial Arbitration, as adopted on 21 June 1985, and as amended on 7 July 2006 (A/40/17, annex I and A/61/17, annex I).

Index

A

AIAC Arbitration Rules 2018, 303–304, 306, 316
Appeal, 341
Application to arbitrations and awards in Malaysia
  commercial arbitration, 15
  domestic and international arbitration, 14
  opt-in or opt-out, 17–18
  seat of arbitration in Malaysia, 15–17
Arbitrability
  not capable of settlement by arbitration, 22
  public policy, contrary to, 22
  recognition and enforcement of awards, 297
  of subject matter, 21
Arbitral proceedings, 368–369
  conduct of (*see* Conduct of arbitral proceedings)
  consolidation and concurrent hearings (*see* Consolidation, subhead: proceedings and concurrent hearings, of)
  court proceedings, 369–370
  extension of time for commencing, 350
    restraint of legal proceedings, 351–352
    unambiguous terms, 352–353
    undue hardship, 350–351

  restraint of legal proceedings
    Section 29 of the Contract Act 1950, 351–352
  time limitation for commencement of proceedings, 352
  unambiguous terms
    legal proceedings, 352
    limitation of time of bringing arbitration, 353
  undue hardship, 350–351
Arbitral tribunal
  competence to rule on its jurisdiction
    Kompetenz-Kompetenz and separability (*see* Kompetenz-Kompetenz and separability principles)
    rulings and appeals, 137–139
    time limits, 135–137
  conditions for granting interim measures
    claim succeed on merits, 149–150
    harm not adequately reparable by award of damages, 148–149
    harm substantially outweighs, 149
  costs
    determination, 346–347
    whom to pay cost, determination of, 347
  defined, 10–11
  interim measures, 144–146
    conditions for granting, 140, 148–150
    costs and damages, 142, 154

Index

court-ordered, 143–144, 157
definition of, 146
disclosure, 142, 154
modification, suspension or termination of, 142, 153
power to order, 140
preconditions for, 146–147
recognition and enforcement, 142–143, 154–155
refusal of recognition and enforcement, 143, 156
security, 153–154
three conditions, application of, 150
jurisdiction
competence to rule on (*see* subhead: competence to rule on its jurisdiction)
costs and damages, 142, 154
disclosure, 142, 154
grounds for refusing recognition or enforcement, 143
modification, suspension or termination of interim measure, 142
power to order interim measures (*see* subhead: power to order)
preliminary orders (*see* subhead: preliminary orders)
provision of security, 142
recognition and enforcement of interim measure, 142–143
time limits for challenges (*see* subhead: time limits for jurisdictional challenges)
modification, suspension or termination, 142
power to order
interim measures (*see* subhead: interim measures)
preliminary orders (*see* subhead: preliminary orders)
preliminary orders
additional conditions, 151–152
application for, 141
conditions for granting, 141
definition of, 150–151
safeguards for, 152
specific regime for, 141
two preconditions, 151
time limits for jurisdictional challenges
derogable *v.* non-derogable provisions, 136
non-compliance, 135–136
plea of lack of jurisdiction, 136–137
Arbitration Agreement
adoption of, 362
defined, 6, 46
form of, 50–51
agreement in writing, 51
electronic communications, 51
exchange of letters, 51–52
exchange of pleadings, 52
recorded in any form, 51–52
reference in agreement, 52–56
interim measures by High Court, and (*see* Interim measures, subhead: High Court, by)
non-adoption of, 362–363
reference in agreement
contract for sale and purchase of latex, 56
letter of acceptance, 53
letter of award for subcontract works, 54, 55
main contract, 53–54
subscription agreement, 56
unsigned contracts, 54–55
steps in proceedings, 67–68
appearance, 68–69
application for stay before taking any step in proceeding, 73
defence, 73
discovery, process of, 71–72
qualified position, 69–71
resisting injunction, 71
resisting winding-up, 72
substance of, 46–47
defined legal relationship, 47–49
existing disputes, 47

Index

future disputes, 47
subject matter capable of settlement by arbitration, 50
substantive claim before court, and, 57–59
absence of dispute, 79–80
arbitration and exclusive jurisdiction clauses, 63–65
'court,' 60
effect of stay, 84–85
fraud and mistake, 78
general scheme, 59–60
'impose any conditions' when granting a stay, 83
incapable of being performed, 78–79
incomplete agreement, 79
international arbitration seated outside Malaysia, 83
jurisdictional issues, 65
lean towards arbitration, 76
linking words in arbitration clause, 65
multiplicity, 78–79
no dispute between parties, 80–82
parties, 73–76
prior to amendments, 80
'proceedings,' 61–62
Section 29 of Contracts Act 1950, 77
'shall' in section 10(1) of Arbitration Act 2005, 66–67
steps in proceedings, 67–73
Arbitrators
  appointment, 105–106
    assistance with agreed procedure, 108–109
    default procedure, 107–108
    Director's failure to act, 109
    guidelines, 109–110
    no appeal, 110
    no restriction on nationality, 106
    party autonomy, 106
  challenge procedure, 116
    application to High Court, 117

default procedure, 117
dilatory tactics, preventing, 117–118
composition
  appointment of arbitrators (*see* subhead: appointment)
  challenge procedure (*see* subhead: challenge procedure)
  failure or impossibility to act (*see* subhead: failure or impossibility to act)
  grounds for challenging an arbitrator (*see* subhead: grounds for challenge)
  number of arbitrators (*see* subhead: number of)
  substitute arbitrator, appointment of (*see* subhead: substitute arbitrator, appointment of)
decision making by panel of arbitrators, 210
  default, 211–212
  party autonomy, 211
estoppel, 114–115
failure or impossibility to act
  application to High Court, 120
  inability and delay, 119–120
  replacement of arbitrators, 121
  withdrawal does not imply acceptance, 120–121
fees and expenses, 345–346
grounds for challenge
  bribery, 113–114
  disclosure, 111–112
  estoppel, 114–115
  impartiality or independence, 112–114
  qualifications agreed to by the parties, 114
liability (*see* Liability)
number of
  described, 101–102
  party autonomy, 102–103
  single arbitrator, 103
  three arbitrators, 103

Index

two-level system, 102
substitute arbitrator, appointment of,
    122–123
  effect of substitution, 124–125
  substitution, 124
  termination of mandate of
    arbitrator, additional grounds for,
    123–124
  two-level system, 102
Awards
  additional award, 233–234
  agreed terms, on, 213–214
  agreement to exclude recourse,
    237–239
    Article 35(6) of the 2017 ICC Rules
      of Arbitration, 237
    Section 29 of the Contracts Act
      1950, 238–239
  application to arbitrations and awards
    in Malaysia (*see* Application to
    arbitrations and awards in
    Malaysia)
  confidentiality of arbitral proceedings
    and awards (*see* Confidentiality
    of arbitral proceedings and
    awards)
  correction, 232–233
  date, 220–221
  delivered, to be, 221–222
  extension of time for making award
    discretion and preconditions,
      355–356
    party autonomy, 354–355
    procedure, 355
    substantial injustice, 356
    tribunal processes exhausted,
      355–356
  final and binding, 235–237
    agreement to exclude recourse,
      237–239
    res judicata, 239–240
  final award, 226
  form and contents of, 215–218
    additional requirements agreed by
      parties, 222
    date the award, 220–221
    delivered, award to be, 221–222
    interest, 222–224
    reasons in an award, 219–220
    signed, award in, 218–219
    state the seat of the arbitration in
      the award, 221
    writing, award in, 218
  grounds for refusing recognition and
    enforcement, 281–282
    application to set aside or suspend,
      296
    arbitrability, 297
    arbitration agreement, invalidity of,
      289–291
    'at the request of the party against
      whom it is invoked,' 286–287
    composition and procedure,
      292–294
    incapacity of party, 289
    invalidity of arbitration agreement,
      289–291
    'irrespective of the State in which it
      was made,' 283
    jurisdiction, 291–292
    'may be refused,' 283
    need for proof, 288–289
    not binding, 294–295
    notice and inability to present case,
      291
    'only' be refused on the specified
      grounds, 283–286
    public policy, 297–299
    setting aside an award and,
      287–288, 295–296
    suspension of an award, 296
  interpretation, 233
  recognition and enforcement, 267–269
    application, need for, 269
    conditions, 272
    enforced as a judgment, 271
    grounds for refusing (*see* subhead:
      grounds for refusing recognition
      and enforcement)
    High Court, 269

404

Index

judgment, enforced as a, 271
procedure, 272-274
reciprocity, 270-271
two-stage test, 274-280
recourse against award (*see* Setting aside of an award)
setting aside of an award (*see* Setting aside of an award)
signed, in, 218-219
state the seat of the arbitration, 221
time limit for the final award, 355-356
writing, in, 218

B

Bad faith
arbitral institution, 361
arbitral tribunal, 358-359
Bankruptcy
arbitration agreement
adoption of, 362
non-adoption of, 362-363
Bias, 112

C

Claim, 13
Commencement
arbitral proceedings, of, 174-176
default, 176-177
limitation, 177-180
party autonomy, 176
time limitation for commencement of proceedings, 352
time limitation of proceedings, 352
Commercial arbitration, 15
Communication
hearings, 193
written (*see* Written communications)
Concurrent hearing. *See* Consolidation, subhead: proceedings and concurrent hearings, of
Conduct of arbitral proceedings
commencement of arbitral proceedings, 174-176
default, 176-177
limitation, 177-180
party autonomy, 176
court assistance in taking evidence, 200-201
application, 201
orders, 201
default of party
claimant fails to deliver statement of claim, 195
claimant fails to proceed with claim, 196
default, 195-196
party autonomy, 194-195
party fails to attend hearing or provide documentary evidence, 196
respondent fails to deliver his statement of defence, 195-196
safeguards, 196-197
determination of rules of procedure
arbitral tribunal's discretion, 169
examples of arbitral tribunal's power, 170
party autonomy, 167-169
equal treatment of parties, 159-160
comprehensive, 166
fundamental principle, 160-161
setting aside, 161-166
expert appointed by arbitral tribunal
cooperation, 199
impartiality and independence, 199
party autonomy, 198
right to be heard, 199
hearings, 189-191
communication, 193
notice, 193
oral hearing (*see* Oral hearing)
language
default, 182
documents, 183
party autonomy, 181-182
statements, hearing and award, 183
seat of arbitration, 171-172
abstraction, 173

Index

arbitral tribunal's discretion, 173
party autonomy, 172–173
statements of claim and defence,
  184–186
  amendments, 188
  documents, 188
  party autonomy, 187
  writing, 187
Confidentiality of arbitral proceedings
  and awards, 309, 311
  exceptions to confidentiality
    adviser of parties, 312–313
    authorities, 312
    legal right or interest and enforce or
      challenge the award, 311–312
    need for an express provision,
      309–310
Consolidation
  AIAC Arbitration Rules 2018, 303–304
  PAM Contract 2018, 302–303
  party autonomy, 302–304
  proceedings and concurrent hearings,
    of, 301
Contract Act 1950
  Section 29
    agreements in restraint of legal
      proceedings void, 351
    saving of contract to refer questions
      that have already arisen, 351–352
    saving of contract to refer to
      arbitration dispute that may
      arise, 351
Correction
  awards, 232–233
Corruption, 261
Costs
  allocation of, 346
  definition of, 345
  described, 344
  determination of, 343–344
    agreement on how costs will be
      determined, 344–346

arbitral tribunal determination of
  whom to pay cost and High Court
  taxing the amount of costs, 347
arbitral tribunal determines costs,
  346–347
situation where costs are not
  determined, 347
fees and expenses of arbitrators,
  345–346
question of law, 327–328
Costs and expense of an arbitration,
  342–343
determination of costs (*see* Costs,
  subhead: determination of)
offer to settle, 348
order for delivery, 348
review of taxation of costs, fees and
  expenses, 348–349
Counterclaim, 13
Court intervention, 32–33
express and implied provision, 33–35
Court-ordered interim measures,
  143–144, 157

D

Damages
  costs and, 142, 154
  question of law, 327
Death, 229
Default
  conduct of arbitral proceedings
    commencement of arbitral
      proceedings, 176–177
    language, 182
    party, default of (*see* Conduct of
      arbitral proceedings, subhead:
      default of party)
  decision making by panel of
    arbitrators, 211–212
  interest (*see* Interest, subhead: default
    powers)
  procedure, 107–108, 117

Index

Defence
    arbitration agreement, 73
    respondent fails to deliver his statement of defence, 195–196
    statements of claim and defence (*see* Conduct of arbitral proceedings, subhead: statements of claim and defence)
Disclosure, 111–112, 142, 154
    information relating to arbitral proceedings and awards prohibited (*see* Confidentiality of arbitral proceedings and awards)
Domestic arbitration, 7–10, 14, 270
    seat of arbitration, 172

E

Enforcement
    grounds for refusing recognition and enforcement (*see* Awards, subhead: grounds for refusing recognition and enforcement)
English Arbitration Act 1996
    section 29, 357
Estoppel, 114–115
Evidence
    court assistance in taking evidence, 200–201
        application, 201
        orders, 201
    interim measures, 97–98
    question of law, 322–323
Expert. *See* Conduct of arbitral proceedings, subhead: expert appointed by arbitral tribunal
Extension of Time
    commencing arbitral proceedings, for (*see* Arbitral proceedings, subhead: extension of time for commencing)
    making an award, for (*see* Awards, subhead: extension of time for making award)

F

Fees
    and expenses of arbitrators, 345–346
Final award
    defined, 226
Fraud, 261

G

Government, 23

H

Hearing
    conduct of arbitral proceedings (*see* Conduct of arbitral proceedings, subhead: hearings)
    consolidation of proceedings and concurrent hearings (*see* Consolidation, subhead: proceedings and concurrent hearings, of)
    oral (*see* Oral hearing)
High Court
    arbitral tribunal determination of whom to pay cost and High Court taxing the amount of costs, 347
    definition, 4–6
    interim measures by (*see* Interim measures, subhead: High Court, by)
    mode of application, 364, 365
        Arbitration Act 2005 and Order 69 of Rules of Court 2012, 366
    scope, 364–365
Hong Kong Arbitration Ordinance, 309

Index

I

ICC Rules of Arbitration, 133,
  Article 15 of the 2017, 121
  Article 32(1) of the 2017, 211
  Article 35(6) of the 2017, 237
Immunity
  arbitral institution
    limits of immunity, 360–361
    purpose of immunity, 360
  arbitral tribunals
    limits of immunity, 258–259
    purpose of immunity, 358
  bad faith
    arbitral institution, 361
    arbitral tribunals, 358–359
  not in discharge of functions
    arbitral institution, 361
    arbitral tribunals, 359
Impartiality, 112–114, 199
Independence, 112–114, 199
Interest
  default powers, 222–223
  party autonomy, 222
  post-award, 223
  pre-award, 223–224
  question of law, 327
Interim measures
  High Court, by
    application for interim measures made before or during arbitral proceedings, 94
    assets, preserve, 96–97
    evidence, preserve, 97–98
    general principles, 88
    aid the arbitration, 90–93
    arbitral proceedings commenced within reasonable time, 93
    arbitration agreement, 89
    cause of action, 89
    interim in nature, 89
    international arbitration with seat outside Malaysia, application to, 98–99
    maintain the Status Quo, 94–96
    merits, 93
    prevent harm to arbitral process, 96
    security for costs, 98
    specific principles, 94–98
    assets, preserve, 96–97
    evidence, preserve, 97–98
    general principles applicable in court for grant of an interim injunction, 94–95
    general principles applicable to mandatory injunctions to section 11, 95
    maintain the Status Quo, 94–96
    prevent harm to arbitral process, 96
    security for costs, 98
International arbitration, 3–4, 7–10, 14, 103
Interpretation
  arbitral tribunal, 10–11
  arbitration, 11–12
  arbitration agreement, 6
  arbitration rules, 13
  award, of an, 4, 233
  claim and counterclaim, 13
  High Court
    applications, 5
    definition, 4–6
  international arbitration and domestic arbitration, 7–10
  minister, 6
  party, 7
  presiding arbitrator, 6
  seat of arbitration, 7
  State, 6
  third party, 12
  written communications, of, 26–27

J

Jurisdiction
  arbitral tribunal (*see* Arbitral tribunal, subhead: jurisdiction)

Index

grounds for refusing recognition and enforcement of awards, 291–292
setting aside of an award (*see* Setting aside of an award, subhead: excess of jurisdiction)

K

Kompetenz-Kompetenz and separability principles
Kompetenz-Kompetenz meaning, 128
lean towards arbitration, 129–130
potential limits to wide powers, 132–134
reform and wide powers, 131–132
separability meaning, 128

L

Language
default, 182
documents, 183
party autonomy, 181–182
statements, hearing and award, 183
Law applicable to substance of dispute
agreement and trade usage, 208
determination by arbitral tribunal, 207–208
equity and conscience, 208
party autonomy, 206–207
rules of law, 206–207
setting aside, 209
third-party determination, 209
Liability, 357–358
immunity
limits of, 358–359
purpose of, 358
limits of immunity
bad faith, 358–359
not in discharge of functions, 359
non-derogable provision, 359

M

Minister
defined, 6

N

Natural justice
breach of the rules, 263–264
fundamental principles, 262
prejudice, 262
requirements, 262–263
New York Convention, 46, 50–52, 59, 146, 169, 214, 243, 268–269, 288, 292–295, 296, 367
New Zealand Arbitration Act 1996, 310, 311, 312, 315, 320, 321, 343, 362
clause 4 of Schedule 2, 305
clause 7 of Schedule 2, 350

O

Open Court
order for open court proceedings, 315
Oral hearing
parties agreed on, 191
parties agreed that no hearing will be held, 191–192
parties not agreed on whether an oral hearing is to be held, 192
Order
open court proceedings, for, 315
reference on questions of law
order for security, 339
order to state reasons, 339

P

PAM Contract 2018, 302–303
Party
defined, 7

Index

Preliminary orders
  application for, 141
  conditions for granting, 141
  specific regime for, 141
Preliminary point of law by court, determination of, 305-306
  arbitration may proceed, 307-308
  consent, 306
  course of the arbitration, 307
  criteria, 307
  formal requirements, 307
  question of law, 306
Presiding arbitrator
  defined, 6
Privacy of court proceedings, 314
  Arbitration Act 2005, under, 315
  enhancement of existing provisions on, 314-315
Public policy
  grounds for refusing recognition and enforcement, 297-299
  setting aside of an award (see Setting aside of an award, subhead: public policy)

Q

Question of law
  any question of law and, 321-322
  construction of contract, 324-325
  costs, 327-328
  damages, 327
  definition, 320
    judgments from England, based on, 320-321
    New Zealand Arbitration Act 1996 and judgments from Singapore, 321
  facts and evidence, 322-323
  law, 323-324
  mixed fact and law, 325-327
  non-exhaustive list, 321
  preliminary point of law by court, determination of, 306

R

Reference on questions of law, 316-318
  determination stage
    application to set aside, relationship with, 338
    correct approach, 334-335
    minimal intervention, 336-338
    not an appeal to High Court, 335-336
    patent error of law approach, 335
    process of reasoning approach, 334
  order for security, 339
  order to state reasons, 339
  relief stage, 339
  threshold requirements, 318
    arising out of an award, 328-329
    grounds on which the reference is sought, 333
    identifying question of law, 332
    mandatory time period, 332
    not the same question, 329-331
    Order 69 Rule 6 of the Rules of Court 2012, 319
    particulars of each ground, 333-334
    question of law (see Question of law)
    service of application, 334
    substantially affecting the rights of the parties, 331
Repeal, 367
Representation, 19-20
Res judicata, 239-240

S

Savings, 351-352
Seat of arbitration
  conduct of arbitral proceedings (see Conduct of arbitral proceedings, subhead: seat of arbitration)
  defined, 7

international arbitration with seat
outside Malaysia, application
to, 98–99
Security
interim measures, 153–154
setting aside of an award, 266
Setting aside of an award
award defined, 243–244
excess of jurisdiction, 252–253
application of test, 254–255
composition of arbitral tribunal, 256
not bound by arbitral tribunal's
award, 256
procedure of arbitration, 256
test, 253–254
waiver, 255–256
grounds for, 242–243
High Court, by, 243–248, 256–257
not capable of settlement by
arbitration, 257
public policy (see subhead: public
policy)
party making the application provides
proof, 248–249
inability to present case, 252
incapacity of party, 249–250
lack of notice, 252
validity of arbitration agreement,
251–252
public policy
breach of, 258–261
corruption, 261
fraud, 261
guidelines or principles, 258–259
narrowly construed, 257
rules of natural justice (see
subhead: rules of natural justice)
remission, 265–266
rules of natural justice
breach of the rules, 263–264
fundamental principles, 262
prejudice, 262

requirements, 262–263
security, 266
time limit, 264
Settlement, 213
award on agreed terms, 213–214
form and effect, 214
termination, 213
Statement of claim
claimant fails to deliver, 195
Stay
effect of granting, 84–85
Substantial injustice
extension of time for making award,
356

T

Termination
arbitral proceedings, 213, 225–226
agreement, 227
death, 229
final award, 226
grounds for, 213, 225–226
unnecessary or impossible
continuance, 227–229
withdrawal of claim, 226–227
final award, 226
Third party, 12
Two-level system, 102
Two-stage test
recognition and enforcement of an
award, 274–280

W

Waiver
effect of, 31
requirements
derogable provision, 28–30
failure to state objection, 30
non-compliance, 30
proceeding with arbitration, 31
right to object. of, 28–31

Index

setting aside of an award, 255–256
Written communications, 25
  court proceedings, 27
  interpretation of, 26–27
  notice and calculation of periods of time, 26
  receipt of, 25–27